W9-CDF-746

We recognize that certain terms in this book are trademarks, and we have made every effort to print these throughout the text with the capitalization and punctuation used by the holder of the trademark.

The previous edition of this book was published under the title of *Introduction to Information Systems in Business Management.*

Cover illustration by Valerie Sinclair

Senior sponsoring editor: *Rick Williamson*
Developmental editor: *Lena Buonanno*
Project editor: *Rita McMullen*
Production manager: *Bob Lange*
Designer: *Heidi J. Baughman*
Art coordinator: *Mark Malloy*
Art studio: *Rolin Graphics*
Photo research coordinator: *Patricia A. Seefelt*
Photo researcher: *Sarah Evertson/Photosynthesis*
Compositor: *Better Graphics, Inc.*
Typeface: *10/12 Berkeley Old Style*
Printer: *Von Hoffmann Press*

Library of Congress Cataloging-in-Publication Data

O'Brien, James A.,
Introduction to information systems / James A. O'Brien.—7th ed.
p. cm.
Rev. ed. of : Introduction to information systems in business management. 6th ed. © 1991.
Includes index.
ISBN 0-256-11884-1 ISBN 0-256-15610-7 (International ed.)
1. Business—Data processing. 2. Management—Data processing. I. O'Brien, James A., 1936- Introduction to information systems in business management., II. Title.
HF5548.2.023 1994
658'.05—dc20 93-24018

Printed in the United States of America
1 2 3 4 5 6 7 8 9 0 VH 0 9 8 7 6 5 4 3

SEVENTH EDITION

Introduction to Information Systems

James A. O'Brien
College of Business Administration
Northern Arizona University

IRWIN

Burr Ridge, Illinois
Boston, Massachusetts
Sydney, Australia

To those who learn and those who teach
about the use and management of information systems
and to Erika
The lightness of my being

About the Author

James A. O'Brien is a professor of computer Information Systems in the College of Business Administration at Northern Arizona University. He did his undergraduate studies at the University of Hawaii and Gonzaga University and earned an M.S. and Ph.D. in Business Administration from the University of Oregon. He has been coordinator of the CIS area at Northern Arizona University, professor of Finance and Management Information Systems and chairman of the Department of Management at Eastern Washington University, and a visiting professor at the University of Alberta and the University of Hawaii.

Dr. O'Brien's business experience includes the Marketing Management Program of the IBM Corporation, as well as serving as a financial analyst for the General Electric Company. He is a graduate of General Electric's Financial Management Program. He has also served as an information systems consultant to several banks and computer services firms.

Jim's research interests lie in developing and testing basic conceptual frameworks used in information systems development and management. He has written eight books, including several that have been published in Dutch, French, or Japanese translations. He has also contributed to the field of information systems through the publication of numerous articles in business and academic journals, as well as through his active participation in academic and industry associations in the field of information systems.

Preface

Introducing Information Systems to Business Students

This text is written as an introduction to information systems for business students. Thus, it has a business end user focus, which has been the primary reason for its success over six editions. So, this text continues to provide the following unique features:

- Loading the text with real world cases and problems about real people and companies in the business world.
- Organizing the text around a simple five level framework that emphasizes the IS knowledge a managerial end user needs to know.
- Distributing and integrating IS foundation theory throughout the text instead of concentrating it in several early chapters.
- Placing a major emphasis on the strategic role of information systems in providing competitive advantage, as well as on the operational and decision support roles of information technology.

This new seventh edition is a major revision that retains these important features, while significantly updating coverage of IS technology and theory. In addition, it adds new chapter sections on international and ethical issues in information systems and provides all new Real World Cases and Problems, including a new continuing case at the end of each module. Major revisions have been made to the organization of topics in many chapters, and several new pedagogical components have been added to the end-of-chapter materials. And the seventh edition now features full color art and photos to increase its attractiveness and visual appeal to students.

This text is designed for use in undergraduate courses that introduce information systems in a business management context. Such courses are required in many business administration or management programs as part of the *common body of knowledge* required of all business majors. Thus, this text treats the subject area known as information systems (IS), management information systems (MIS), or computer information systems (CIS) as a major functional area of business that is as important to management education as the areas of accounting, finance, operations management, marketing, and human resources management.

Like my other text, *Management Information Systems: A Managerial End User Perspective*, this text is designed to support **information system literacy** by students. That is, its objective is to build a basic understanding of the value and uses of information systems for business operations, management decision making, and strategic advantage. In addition, this text can also be used to help support student **computer literacy**. For example, Module II, entitled "Technology," contains four chapters on computer concepts and hardware, software, telecommunications, and database management, which review the technological foundations of computer literacy.

An Information Systems Framework

This text provides a teaching-learning resource that reduces the complexity of an introductory course in information systems by using a conceptual framework that organizes the knowledge needed by business students into five major areas:

- **Foundation concepts**. Basic information systems concepts and the operations, decision making, and strategic roles of information systems (Chapters 1 and 6). Other behavioral, managerial, and technical concepts are presented where appropriate in other chapters.
- **Technology**. Major concepts, developments, and managerial implications involved in computer hardware, software, telecommunications, and database management technologies (Chapters 2, 3, 4, and 5). Other technologies used in computer-based information systems are discussed where appropriate in selected chapters.
- **Applications**. How information systems support end user activities, business operations, managerial decision making, and strategic advantage (introduced in Chapter 6 and discussed in detail in Chapters 7, 8, and 9).
- **Development**. Developing information system solutions to business problems using a variety of systems development tools and methodologies (presented in Chapter 10 and in other chapters when discussing development issues for major types of information systems).
- **Management**. The challenges and methods of managing information systems technologies, activities, and resources (emphasized in each chapter, but discussed specifically in Chapters 11 and 12).

Real World Cases, Problems and Exercises

This text makes extensive use of up-to-date, real world case studies and problems. These are not fictional stories, but actual situations faced by business firms and other organizations as reported in current business and IS periodicals. Included is a continuing case at the end of each module, two short real world case studies in each chapter that apply specifically to that chapter's contents, and four real world problems at the end of every chapter. In addition, each chapter contains several Application Exercises, including two hands-on spreadsheet or database assignments in Chapters 2 through 11. The purpose of this variety of assignment options is to give instructors and students many opportunities to apply each chapter's material to real world situations.

Strategic, International and Ethical Dimensions

This text covers the strategic, international, and ethical dimensions of information systems with both text material and case studies on such topics. For example, the use of information technology for competitive advantage is covered in Chapter 6, the necessity of telecommunications networks for competition in global markets is mentioned in Chapter 4, while their potential for causing violations of international law is discussed in Chapter 12. Computer crime and ethics are also discussed in Chapter 12 with an emphasis on what it takes to be a *responsible* end user. Finally, the text contains many cases and problems illustrating the strategic, international, and ethical dimensions of IS. Examples include Royal Bank of Canada, WalMart Stores, BASF Corporation, United Parcel Service, RE/Max Mexico, ABB Power

Generation and the Hypo Bank, Atlantic Richfield and Siemens Corporations, Virgin Atlantic and British Airways, and many, many others. These examples repeatedly demonstrate the strategic and ethical challenges of managing information technology for competitive advantage in global business markets and in the global information society in which we all live and work.

Modular Structure of the Text

The text is organized according to the five major areas of the framework for information systems knowledge mentioned earlier. Figure 1 illustrates how the chapters of the text are organized into four modules. Also, each chapter is organized into two or three distinct sections. This is done to avoid proliferation of chapters, as well as to provide better conceptual organization of the text and each chapter. This organization increases instructor flexibility in assigning course material, since it structures the text into modular levels (i.e., modules, chapters, and sections) while reducing the number of chapters that need to be covered.

Each chapter starts with a Chapter Outline and Learning Objectives and ends with a Summary, Key Terms and Concepts, a Review Quiz tied directly to the Key Terms and Concepts, Discussion Questions, Real World Problems, Applications Exercises, Review Quiz Answers, and Selected References. Real World Cases are also provided at the end of each section and module of the book.

Module I: Introduction

The first chapter of this text is designed as an introductory core module of foundation IS concepts. Once instructors have covered Chapter 1 of Module I, they can assign any other module, depending on their pedagogical preferences. Chapter 1 introduces students to the importance of information systems, a framework of information systems knowledge, and the generic components and properties of information systems. It then briefly introduces the major roles and types of information systems.

Module II: Technology

Module II contains four chapters on computer concepts, hardware, software, telecommunications, and database management. Its purpose is to give students an introduction to the technology used in modern computer-based information sys-

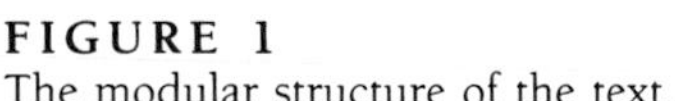

FIGURE 1
The modular structure of the text.

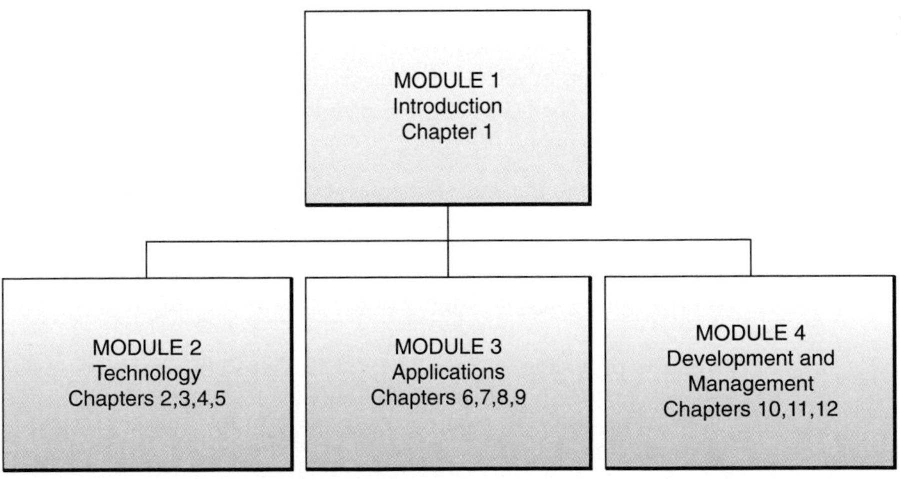

tems and its implications for end users. This material is consolidated in an independent module so instructors can selectively use the chapters and sections of this module, depending on the preparation of their students. This is especially useful in the case of the important topics of telecommunications and database management, in which many students have typically had only brief exposure.

Module III: Applications

Module III contains four chapters that discuss the basic types and major applications of computer-based information systems. It emphasizes how information systems support end user activities and the operations, management, and strategic advantage of business firms and other organizations. Thus, it includes an overview of IS classifications and the use of information systems to gain competitive advantages (Chapter 6); coverage of end user computing and office automation (Chapter 7); transaction processing and business information systems (Chapter 8); and decision support and executive information systems, and expert systems (Chapter 9).

Module IV: Development and Management

It is important that end users learn that although information systems can help them develop solutions to business problems, they also pose major managerial challenges. That is the focus of the three chapters of Module IV. Chapter 10 introduces the systems development and prototyping processes, IS planning, and implementation issues and includes an introduction to the use of system development tools. The impact of information technology, the importance of information resource management, and the managerial implications of the global use of information technology are covered in Chapter 11. Chapter 12 discusses the controls needed for information systems performance and security, as well as the legal and ethical implications of the control of computer crime and other societal impacts of information systems.

New Features

Four Part Continuing Case: Omaha Vision Center

This continuous case appears at the end of each module and contains case study questions for students to answer. The purpose of the case is to integrate student understanding of the concepts discussed in each module. The continuing case gives students an opportunity to apply such concepts to the solution of the problems facing a computer-using organization.

Omaha Vision Center is based on real-life events at an actual medical clinic in Omaha, Nebraska. The case traces how this center initiated and implemented a computer-based information system.

Software Application Exercises

There are two hands-on application exercises at the end of Chapters 2 to 11 that give students an opportunity to use spreadsheet and database management packages to solve business problems. These exercises are identified by a disk icon in the margin of the page. The Data/Solutions disk for these exercises is located in the Instructor's Resource Manual.

Review Quiz Answers

The answers to the end-of-chapter review quizzes are provided so that students can check their understanding of chapter key terms and concepts.

Discussion Questions

Ten discussion questions are provided at the end of each chapter. They provide an opportunity for open-ended class discussion of important chapter topics.

Summary of Changes

Besides providing all new Real World Cases and Problems, the 7th edition represents a major revision of chapter contents. Highlights of the changes made in the 6th edition material are found in the following 7th edition chapters:

Chapter 1: Analysis of a Real World Case in Section I to demonstrate the importance of information systems, a revision of the model of information system components in Section II to stress the vital role of data resources, and the addition of an overview of the roles and types of IS.

Chapters 2, 3: Updated and reorganized coverage of computer hardware and software formerly in Chapters 3 and 4.

Chapter 4: Updated coverage of the operational and strategic impact and managerial issues of telecommunications in Section I, and technical telecommunications network developments in Section II (formerly in Chapter 5).

Chapter 5: Updated and simplified coverage of the role of database management in managing organizational and end user data resources in Section I, and technical topics in database management in Section II (formerly Chapter 6).

Chapter 6: Increased coverage of information systems for operations and management in Section I with conceptual material on management and decision making, and increased coverage in Section II to the use of information technology for competitive advantage (formerly Chapter 2).

Chapter 7: Revisions that emphasize the importance of end user computing and office automation applications to managerial end users, including substantial new material on work group computing and computer graphics and multimedia.

Chapter 8: Increased coverage of the strategic role of transaction processing systems and EDI in Section I, with extensive material on information systems for the functional areas of business formerly in Chapter 12.

Chapter 9: Increased coverage of executive information systems in Section I and new material on artificial intelligence and expert systems in Section II.

Chapter 10: Simplified coverage of IS development and planning in Section I, revised coverage of IS implementation issues in Section II, and revised material on systems development tools (formerly in Chapters 11 and 12).

Chapter 11: A revised Section I covering managerial issues in IT formerly found in Chapter 13, and a new Section II on global IT management, emphasizing the managerial and international impacts of IT and information resource management, especially planning its use for competitive advantage.

Chapter 12: Substantial new material on ethical and societal issues in IT in Section II, augmenting revised material on IS security and controls in Section I (formerly Chapter 14).

Support Materials

The IRWIN Advantage Series is a collection of laboratory tutorials for the most popular microcomputer software packages available. There are over 30 lab manuals available, so you can choose any combination to accommodate your individual class needs.

A new **software case book**, *Application Cases in MIS: Using Spreadsheet and Database Software*, by James N. Morgan of Northern Arizona University is available to supplement the hands-on exercises in this edition. This optional case book contains an extensive number of hands-on cases, many of which include a suggested approach for solving each case with a spreadsheet or database management package. This software case book should be a valuable supplement that gives students many opportunities to learn to use spreadsheet and database management software packages to develop solutions for realistic business problems.

A **Student Study Guide** that supplements the text has been improved for this edition by Albert Kagan of Arizona State University. It contains detailed chapter outlines, chapter learning objectives, chapter overviews, definitions of key terms and concepts, chapter test-yourself questions (true-false, multiple-choice, fill-in-the-blanks, matching), answers to test-yourself questions, and short chapter assignments. The study guide should thus be a valuable supplement to the main text.

An **Instructor's Resource Manual**, revised by Linda Behrens of the University of Central Oklahoma is available to instructors upon adoption of the text. It contains instructional aids and suggestions, detailed annotated chapter outlines with instructional suggestions for use in lectures, answers to chapter questions, and problems and case study questions. A data/solutions disk is included for use with the spreadsheet and database exercises in the text.

A set of 100 **color overhead transparencies** of line art from the book is available to adopters. In addition, there is a set of 28 color overhead transparencies created by Albert Kagan of Arizona State University. These images support class discussion of each real world case and the continuous case. Each transparency is accompanied by a teaching note.

A **Test Bank**, which contains over 1,000 true-false, multiple choice, and fill-in-the-blank questions, has been revised by William Burrows of the University of Washington. It is available as a separate test manual and in computerized form on floppy disk for use with the Irwin Test Generator Program.

Acknowledgments

The author wishes to acknowledge the assistance of the following reviewers whose constructive criticism and suggestions helped invaluably in shaping the form and content of this text:

Johannes Aarsen, The Wichita State University

Kevin Brennan, University of Rochester

Gerald Bucher, University of Wyoming

Mark Gruskin, University of Michigan - Dearborn

Diana Kao, University of Windsor

John N. Landon, University of LaVerne

Diane M. Larson, Purdue University - Calumet

Douglas Lund, University of Minnesota

Kuang-Wei Wen, University of Connecticut

My thanks also go to James N. Morgan of Northern Arizona University, who authored the software casebook that can be used with this text and developed most of the hands-on Application Exercises in the text, as well as the Data/Solutions disk in the Instructor's Resource Manual. Additional acknowledgments are owed to Linda Behrens of the University of Central Oklahoma, who revised the Instructor's Resource Manual; William Burrows of the University of Washington, who revised the Test Bank, and to Albert Kagan of Arizona State University who revised the Study Guide and provided additional transparencies for use with this text. I am indebted to Bill Macmillan of Madonna University, Tom Pollack of Duquesne University, and Ed Roche of Seton Hall University for research material they provided on international or ethical issues in information systems.

Much credit should go to several individuals who played significant roles in this project. My thanks go to the editorial and production team at Irwin, especially Rick Williamson, senior sponsoring editor; Lena Buonanno, developmental editor; Rita McMullen, project editor; and Heidi Baughman, design manager. Their ideas and hard work were invaluable contributions to the successful completion of the project. Thanks also to Michele Allen and Jory Gerken, whose word processing skills helped me meet several manuscript deadlines. The contributions of many authors, periodicals, and firms in the computer industry who contributed case material, ideas, illustrations, and photographs used in this text are also thankfully acknowledged.

Acknowledging the Real World of Business

The unique contribution of over 100 business firms and other computer-using organizations that are the subject of the real world cases, problems, exercises, and case studies in each chapter is also gratefully acknowledged. The real-life situations faced by these firms and organizations provide the readers of this text with a valuable demonstration of the benefits and limitations of using information technology to support business operations, managerial decision making, and strategic advantage.

James A. O'Brien

Contents in Brief

Contents

M O D U L E I

Introduction

What are information systems and what is their role in business firms and other organizations? What do business end users need to know about the use and management of information systems? The introductory chapter in Module I is designed to answer these fundamental questions.

Chapter 1, "Introduction to Information Systems," introduces you to the importance of information systems in business, the framework of information systems knowledge needed by business end users, careers in the information systems field, and the conceptual system components and basic types of information systems.

Introduction to Information Systems

CHAPTER OUTLINE

CHAPTER 1

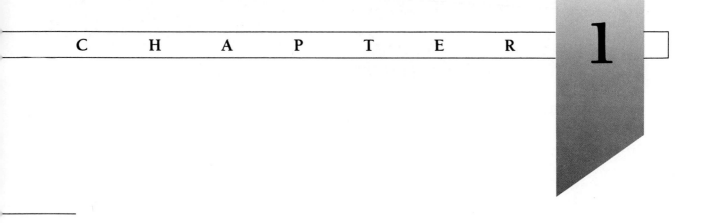

LEARNING OBJECTIVES

The purpose of this chapter is to give you an understanding of information systems by analyzing (1) the field of information systems as it relates to business end users, and (2) fundamental concepts used in the study of information systems.

Section I of this chapter introduces the field of information systems. It discusses the importance of the information systems field to individuals, organizations, and society, and it provides a framework for organizing an end user's knowledge of information systems.

Section II introduces basic concepts about the components and types of information systems that are important for business end users.

After reading and studying this chapter, you should be able to:

1. Explain why knowledge of information systems is important for business end users and identify five areas of information systems knowledge they need.
2. Identify and give examples of the components and functions of the generic concept of a system introduced in this chapter.
3. Identify and give examples of the components of real world information systems. Emphasize the concept that an information system uses people (end users and IS specialists), hardware (machines and media), and software (programs and procedures) as resources to perform input, processing, output, storage, and control activities that transform data resources into information products.
4. Identify several types of jobs available in the information systems field.
5. Identify and give examples of several major types of information systems used in business organizations.

SECTION I
The Importance of Information Systems

Why Information Systems Are Important

Why study **information systems?** That's the same as asking why anyone should study accounting, finance, operations management, marketing, human resource management, or any other major business function. Information systems have become a vital component of successful business firms and other organizations. They thus constitute an essential field of study in business administration and management. That's why most business majors must take a course in information systems. Since you probably intend to be a manager, entrepreneur, or business professional, it is just as important to have a basic understanding of information systems as it is to understand any other functional area in business.

An End User Perspective

An **information system** is a set of people, procedures, and resources that collects, transforms, and disseminates information in an organization. Today's end users rely on many types of information systems (IS). They might include simple *manual* (paper-and-pencil) information systems and *informal* (word-of-mouth) information systems. However, in this text, we will concentrate on *computer-based information systems* that use hardware, software, telecommunications, and other forms of *information technology* (IT) to transform data resources into a variety of information products. In particular, we will discuss several types of *management information systems* (MIS) that provide information for decision making by managers.

Anyone who uses an information system or the information it produces is an **end user**. This term usually applies to most people in an organization, as distinguished from the smaller number of people who are *information system specialists*, such as systems analysts or professional computer programmers. A *managerial end user* is a manager, entrepreneur, or managerial-level professional who personally uses information systems. Most managers are managerial end users. This book is written for potential managerial end users like you and other students of business administration and management.

Whatever your career will be, you can increase your opportunities for success by becoming a knowledgeable end user of computers and information systems. Businesses and other organizations need people who can use computers to enhance their own personal productivity and the productivity of their work groups, departments, and organizations. For example, you should be able to use word processing and electronic mail to communicate more effectively, spreadsheet packages to more effectively analyze decision situations, and database management packages to provide better reports on organizational performance. You should also be aware of the management problems and opportunities presented by the use of computers, and how you can effectively confront such challenges. Then you can play a major role in seeing that information system resources are used efficiently and effectively to benefit your career goals and the goals of the business firms or other organizations you may work for in the future.

Information systems play a vital role in business success. They can provide the information a business needs for efficient operations, effective management, and competitive advantage. However, information systems can fail. If information systems do not properly support the strategic objectives, business operations, or management needs of an organization, they can seriously damage its prospects for survival and success. So, the proper management of information systems is a major challenge for managers. Thus, the information systems function represents:

- A major functional area of business that is as important to business success as the functions of accounting, finance, operations management, marketing, and human resource management.
- A major part of the resources of an organization and its cost of doing business, thus posing a major resource management challenge.
- An important factor affecting operational efficiency, employee productivity and morale, and customer service and satisfaction.
- A major source of information and support needed to promote effective decision making by managers.
- An important ingredient in developing competitive products and services that give an organization a strategic advantage in the global marketplace.
- A vital, dynamic, and challenging career opportunity for millions of men and women.

The Real World of Information Systems

Let's take a moment to bring the real world into our discussion of the importance of information systems. Read the Real World Case of Waldenbooks on page 6. Then let's analyze it together.

Analyzing Waldenbooks

We can learn a lot about the importance of computers and information systems from the Real World Case of Waldenbooks. Waldenbooks relies on a network consisting of PCs in each of their stores, microcomputer servers, and a mainframe computer at company headquarters. The network provides updates and access to store management software and a book titles database, and processes special order requests and confirmations. These computer-based information systems have significantly improved the flow of information, the level of customer service, and the amount of special-order sales at Waldenbooks.

Store personnel can quickly and easily process special order requests and provide confirmation information to customers. Store managers can also track sales from their in-store inventory, as well as special orders, to make better decisions on which books to stock. So the use of computer-based information systems improves the efficiency of business operations and the quality of information provided to the managers of Waldenbooks bookstores. This also helps improve their prospects for competing successfully with the threat of superstore bookstores.

International and Ethical Dimensions of IS

Information is a basic resource in today's society. We are living in a global **information society**, with a global economy which is increasingly dependent on the creation, management, and distribution of information resources. People in many nations no longer live in agricultural societies, composed primarily of farmers, or even industrial societies, where a majority of the work force consists of factory workers. Instead, the work force in many nations consists primarily of workers in service occupations or **knowledge workers**, that is, people who spend most of their workday creating, using, and distributing information. See Figure 1.1.

Knowledge workers include executives, managers, and supervisors; professionals such as accountants, engineers, scientists, stockbrokers, and teachers; and staff personnel such as secretaries and clerical office personnel. Most of them are end users who make their living using information systems to create, distribute, manage, and use information resources. Thus, information systems help them manage the human, financial, material, energy, and other resources involved in their work responsibilities.

REAL WORLD CASE

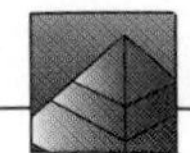

Waldenbooks: Competing with Information Systems

Waldenbooks Company faced a fast growing threat to its business in the last few years: Superstore bookstores. These superstores have at least three times the space and three times the inventory of books of a typical Waldenbooks Bookstore. Waldenbooks' 1,250 retail stores are locked into small sites at shopping malls across the United States and Canada.

So how could Waldenbooks compete against the giant stores? By using computer-based information systems which allow Waldenbooks store clerks to let customers know within 36 hours whether Waldenbooks can deliver a requested book to them. "A superstore may have 18,000 to 30,000 square feet, and our stores are a lot smaller," said Jeff Kish, project manager of store systems for the Stamford, Connecticut, company. "With our special-order system, within 36 hours I can be confident I can ship the same book that a superstore has the room to carry."

Waldenbooks' computerized system is being used at over 1,000 of its stores. It has cut the delivery time for special orders from 14 days to between 2 to 10 days, reports Ed Berndt, director of in-store systems and technical services. The use of computers to automate the special-order process has resulted in large gains in business, more than doubling special order sales.

The new special-order system uses a telecommunications network that links the microcomputers at each bookstore to two microcomputer servers that access a large mainframe computer at Waldenbooks' Stamford, Connecticut, headquarters. The original purpose of this network was to provide updates to store management software and to make updates to each store's titles database. This database is stored on bookstore PC magnetic disk drives and provides store manager and employees with the titles and other information on over 500,000 books. "The whole thing revolves around our titles database, which tells us what's in print and what is available from us," says Berndt.

Each day, special orders by customers for books found in the database are entered by store personnel assisted by data entry displays on their PCs. Each evening, the bookstore's PC is programmed to dial an IBM PS/2 microcomputer server using special software that helps store employees enter special orders and control data communications actively. A second PS/2 server then collects all special orders and transmits them to an IBM ES 9000 mainframe computer. After the special-order information is processed, detailed confirmation information on the availability of one special order is passed from one server to another for transmittal back to individual store PCs. The next day, store employees can access this information on their PCs and notify customers by phone or mail of the status of their special orders.

Waldenbooks has not been able to measure exactly how much the new special order system has helped them compete with superstores. But Waldenbooks' management is happy about how much the new system has improved customer service information availability and special-order sales. Says Ed Berndt, "We can now be more proactive with our customers." In the future, Waldenbooks plans to provide instantaneous responses to customer requests and employee queries at each store's PC.

CASE STUDY QUESTIONS

1. How important are computer-based information systems to the success of Waldenbooks? Explain.
2. How important is the computerized special-order information system to the manager of a Waldenbooks bookstore? Explain.

Source: Adapted from Paula Musich, "Waldenbooks System Helps Special Orders, *PC Week*, March 15, 1993, pp. 41, 44.

This brings up the question of what your responsibilities are in the ethical use of information technology. As a prospective managerial end user and knowledge worker, you should begin to think about the **ethical responsibilities** that are generated by the use of information systems. For example, what uses of information systems might be considered improper or irresponsible to other individuals or to society? What is the proper use of an organization's information resources? What does it take to be a *responsible end user* of information technology? These are some of the questions that outline the ethical dimensions of information systems which we will discuss in this text.

FIGURE 1.1
Business end users are knowledge workers who are part of a global information society.

Greg Pease/Tony Stone Worldwide.

Information and information systems, then, are valuable resources for knowledge workers, their organizations, and society. A major challenge for our global information society is to manage its information resources to benefit all members of society while meeting the strategic goals of organizations and nations. This means, for example, using information systems to find more efficient, profitable, and socially responsible ways of using the world's limited supplies of material, energy, and other resources. Since the information systems of so many organizations are interconnected by local, regional, and global telecommunications networks, knowledge workers can now access and distribute information and manage resources all over the world. For these reasons, information systems play an increasingly vital role in our global economy, as many real world cases and problems in the text will demonstrate.

Technological and Behavioral Dimensions of IS

Computer science, engineering, and mathematics are disciplines that contribute to the *technological* aspects of information systems in business. It is these disciplines, along with the information systems discipline, whose research drives developments in computer hardware, software, telecommunications, database management, and other information technologies. Areas such as psychology, sociology, and political science, on the other hand, contribute to the *behavioral* aspects of information systems in organizations. The research findings of these behavioral disciplines and the discipline of information systems shed light on how individuals and organizations can effectively use and manage information technology. The behavioral side of MIS focuses on adjusting information technology to support individual and group communications, decision making, and cooperative work, as well as helping individuals and organizations learn to take advantage of the benefits of information technology.

Both of these aspects, the technological and the behavioral, are important for business end users. That's because computer-based information systems, though heavily dependent on information processing technologies, are designed, operated, and used by people in a variety of organizational settings. Thus, the success of an information system should be measured, not only by its *efficiency* in the use of information technologies, but also by its *effectiveness* in meeting the goals of end users and their work groups and organizations. So both of these dimensions, the technological and the behavioral, are found in the text material and case studies in each chapter.

Careers in Information Systems

Computers and their use in information systems have created interesting, highly paid, and challenging career opportunities for millions of men and women. Employment opportunities in the field of computers and information systems are excellent, as organizations continue to expand their use of computers. National employment surveys continually forecast shortages of qualified information systems personnel in many job categories. For these reasons, learning more about computers may help you decide if you want to pursue a computer-related career. Job opportunities in computers and information systems are continually changing due to dynamic developments in information technology, including computer hardware, software, telecommunications, and other technologies. One major source of jobs is the computer industry itself. Thousands of companies develop, manufacture, market, and service computer hardware and software, or provide related services such as computer training or data communications networks.

Academic Programs in IS

Many of the more technical jobs in the computer industry are held by graduates of computer science programs. Their education helps prepare them for careers in the research and development of computer hardware, systems software, and application software packages. Millions of other jobs are held by graduates of college and university programs in information systems (IS), management information systems (MIS) or computer information systems (CIS). The focus of these programs is training students to be information systems specialists. That's because the biggest source of jobs is the hundreds of thousands of businesses, government agencies, and other organizations that use computers. They need many types of IS managers and specialists to help them support the work activities and supply the information needs of their end users.

IS Specialists

Information systems specialists are IS professionals who develop, implement, and operate computer-based information systems. Typical examples include systems analysts, programmers, and computer operators. Basically, systems analysts design information systems based on the information requirements of end users, programmers prepare computer programs based on the specifications of systems analysts, and computer operators operate large computer systems.

Many other managerial, technical, and clerical IS personnel are also needed. For example, the top IS management job in many organizations belongs to the *chief information officer* (CIO). This executive oversees the use of information technology throughout an organization, concentrating especially on IS planning and strategy. Examples of more technical job categories include database analysts and administrators who help develop and oversee the use of the common databases of an organization, telecommunications analysts and network managers who develop and supervise the use of the telecommunications network resources, and EDP (electronic data processing) auditors who audit the security and performance of computer-based systems. Examples of jobs in end user services include positions as user consultants, user trainers, and user liaisons. These IS specialists support efforts by employees to use computers to accomplish their work activities more easily and productively.

	IS Budget		
	Under $20 Mil	**$20 Mil–$100 Mil**	**Over $100 Mil**
Chief Information Officer	$126,667	$174,107	$239,773
Senior/VP of IS	120,519	163,068	196,033
Director of IS	94,017	113,750	128,500
Manager of IS	75,192	93,269	147,500
	20th Percentile	**Median**	**80th Percentile**
Operating Management			
Data Center Operations Manager	$37,000	$45,000	$61,000
Programming Development Manager	48,000	61,000	72,000
Systems Development Manager	48,000	58,000	69,000
Technical Services Manager	45,000	59,000	74,000
Systems Development			
Systems Consultant	37,000	45,000	58,000
Project Leader/Systems Analyst	37,000	45,000	54,000
Business Applications Programmer	28,000	40,000	49,000
Engineering/Scientific Programmer	30,000	43,000	53,000
Systems Software Programmer	32,000	49,000	60,000
Technical Specialists			
Technical Data Center Analyst	28,000	46,000	58,000
Database Management Analyst	33,000	49,000	61,000
Telecommunications Planner	30,000	45,000	55,000
Information Center Analyst	25,000	43,000	51,000
EDP Auditor	29,000	45,000	55,000

Source: Adapted from Society for Information Management, "1991 SIM Member Profile Survey," *Special Report,* November 1991, p. 5; and Source-EDP, *Computer Salary Survey and Planning Guide,* 1992, p. 9.

FIGURE 1.2
Examples of annual salaries for a variety of job categories in IS.

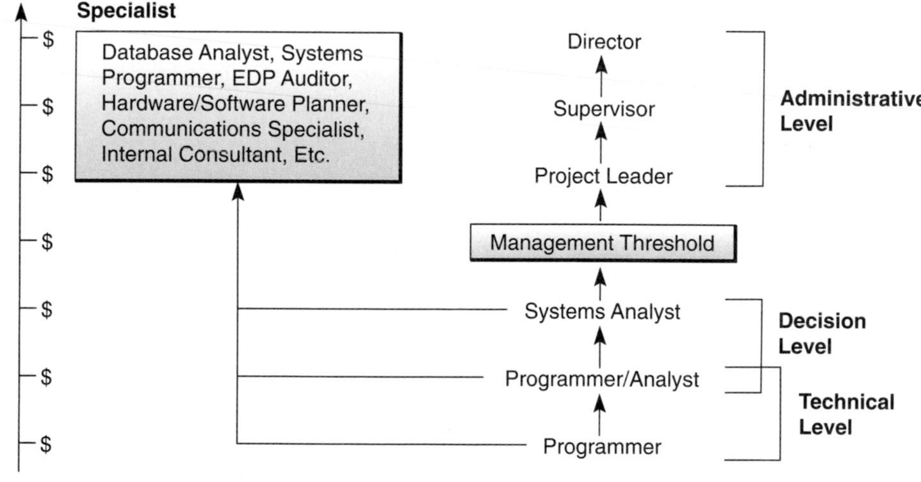

Source: Courtesy Source-EDP.

FIGURE 1.3
Career paths for systems development personnel. Note the traditional upward path into management and the new path into various specialist positions.

Figures 1.2 and 1.3 give valuable insight into the variety of job types and salaries commanded by many IS managers and specialists. Actual salaries range higher and lower than the average shown, depending on such factors as the size and geographic location of an organization. Also shown are the career paths for IS professionals, showing how they can move upward into management or specialist positions.

What Business End Users Need to Know

The real world example of Waldenbooks should convince you that business end users need to know how information systems can be employed successfully in a global business environment. That's why this text contains over 75 Real World Cases and Problems describing actual situations (not fictional stories) occurring in real companies and organizations throughout the world. Business firms and other organizations need people who can help them manage their information resources. Knowledgeable managerial end users can play a major role in *information resource management* (IRM). That is, they can learn to manage information system hardware, software, data, and information resources so they are used for the efficient operation, effective management, and strategic success of their organizations.

However, what exactly does a business end user need to know about information systems? The answers are as diverse and dynamic as the area itself. As just mentioned, the field of information systems, like other areas in management and business administration, is based on a variety of academic disciplines and encompasses a great amount of technological and behavioral knowledge. The IS field is constantly changing and expanding as dramatic technological developments and behavioral research findings push back the frontiers of this dynamic discipline.

A Framework for End Users

> Most of our top management team really don't have a clue what to do about IT. They are at the mercy of the techies. They just nod their heads and hope they don't show their ignorance [6].

That's a comment from a senior manager of a large bank that is a leader in the use of information technology! Even top executives can feel overwhelmed by the complex technologies, abstract behavioral concepts, and specialized applications involved in the field of information systems. However, most managers and other end users do not have to absorb all of this knowledge. Figure 1.4 illustrates a useful conceptual framework that outlines what end users need to know about information systems. It emphasizes that you should concentrate your efforts in five areas of

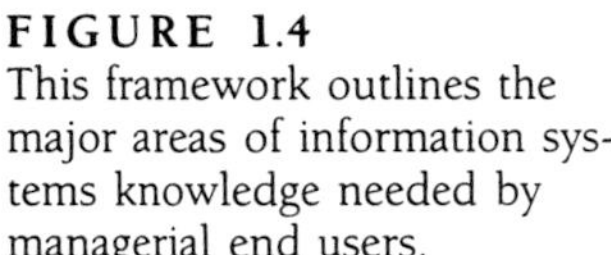
FIGURE 1.4
This framework outlines the major areas of information systems knowledge needed by managerial end users.

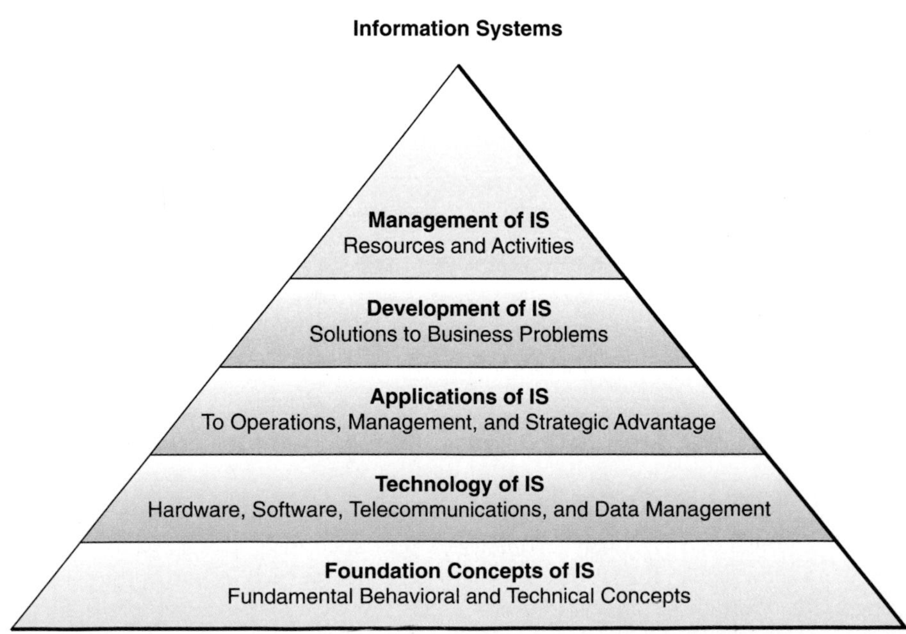

knowledge: foundation concepts, technology, applications, development, and management.

Foundation Concepts

What are information systems? Why are they important to end users and their organizations? In order to answer these questions, you need to understand what the basic components and types of information systems are. This requires an understanding of some fundamental concepts in *general systems theory* and information processing. However, you should also appreciate the vital roles played by information systems in businesses and other organizations. For example, you should learn some fundamental behavioral and technical concepts that will help you understand how information systems can support the business operations, managerial decision making, and strategic advantage of business firms and other organizations. Chapters 1 and 6 and other chapters of the text support this area of knowledge.

Technology

What should end users know about the technologies used in computer-based information systems? The answer to this question is that they should have an understanding of major concepts, developments, and management issues in **information technology**, that is, hardware, software, telecommunications, database management, and other information processing technologies. Technology is so dynamic in this field that a factual knowledge that concentrates on detailed characteristics and capabilities would soon be outdated. Instead, you should focus on generic capabilities, major developmental trends, and management challenges in the use of information systems technology. Chapters 2 through 5 of Module II along with other chapters of the text support this area of information systems knowledge.

Applications

In what ways can information systems assist end users and organizations in accomplishing their work activities and meeting their strategic objectives? Answering this question requires a knowledge of the major applications of information systems for end user activities and the operations, management, and strategic advantage of organizations. You should gain a basic understanding of information systems concepts and applications in areas such as end user computing, office automation, transaction processing, the functional areas of business, management reporting, decision support, executive support, and artificial intelligence. Chapters 6 to 9 of Module III support this learning objective.

Development

How should end users or information specialists develop information systems solutions to business problems? To answer this question, you should learn some fundamental problem-solving and developmental concepts. You should understand how methodologies such as the *systems approach*, the *systems development life cycle*, and *prototyping* can be used by end users and IS specialists to construct information systems applications that successfully meet end user and organizational needs. Chapter 10 of Module IV helps you gain such knowledge and begin applying it to simple business problems. The goals of this chapter are to help you propose information systems solutions to business problems found in the case studies in each chapter, and to introduce you to important systems development tools and considerations.

Management

How should business end users meet the major challenges they face in managing the information systems of their organizations? Answering this question requires understanding what methods you can use to manage the resources, technologies, and activities of information systems. Developing and using information technology can be as difficult and costly as it is beneficial to a firm. Thus, you should understand concepts such as *information resource management* and *information systems planning, implementation*, and *control* as well as important international and ethical issues in information systems. Chapters 11 and 12 of Module IV specifically cover these topics, but all of the chapters in the text emphasize the managerial challenges of information systems. Their goal is to help you develop solutions with a managerial outlook when you face information systems problems encountered by organizations in real world situations.

SECTION

Fundamentals of Information Systems

System concepts underlie the field of information systems. That's why this section introduces you to generic system concepts as they apply to business firms and the components and activities of information systems. Understanding system concepts will help you understand many other concepts in the development, technology, applications, and management of information systems that we will cover in this text.

System Concepts

What is a system? A **system** can be simply defined as *a group of interrelated or interacting elements forming a unified whole*. Many examples of systems can be found in the physical and biological sciences, in modern technology, and in human society. Thus, we can talk of the physical system of the sun and its planets, the biological system of the human body, the technological system of an oil refinery, and the socioeconomic system of a business organization. However, the following generic system concept provides a more appropriate framework for describing information systems:

A **system** is a group of interrelated components working together toward a common goal by accepting inputs and producing outputs in an organized transformation process.

Such a system (sometimes called a *dynamic system*) has three basic interacting components or functions:

- **Input** involves capturing and assembling elements that enter the system to be processed. For example, raw materials, energy, data, and human effort must be secured and organized for processing.
- **Processing** involves transformation processes that convert input into output. Examples are a manufacturing process, the human breathing process, or mathematical calculations.
- **Output** involves transferring elements that have been produced by a transformation process to their ultimate destination. For example, finished products, human services, and management information must be transmitted to their human users.

EXAMPLE

A manufacturing system accepts raw materials as input and produces finished goods as output. An information system can be viewed as a system that accepts data resources as input and processes them into information products as output. See Figure 1.5.

Feedback and Control

The systems concept can be made even more useful by including two additional components: feedback and control. A system with feedback and control components is sometimes called a *cybernetic* system, that is, a self-monitoring, self-regulating system.

- **Feedback** is data about the performance of a system. For example, data about sales performance is feedback to a sales manager.
- **Control** involves monitoring and evaluating feedback to determine whether a system is moving toward the achievement of its goal. The control function

FIGURE 1.5
This manufacturing system illustrates the generic components of many types of systems.

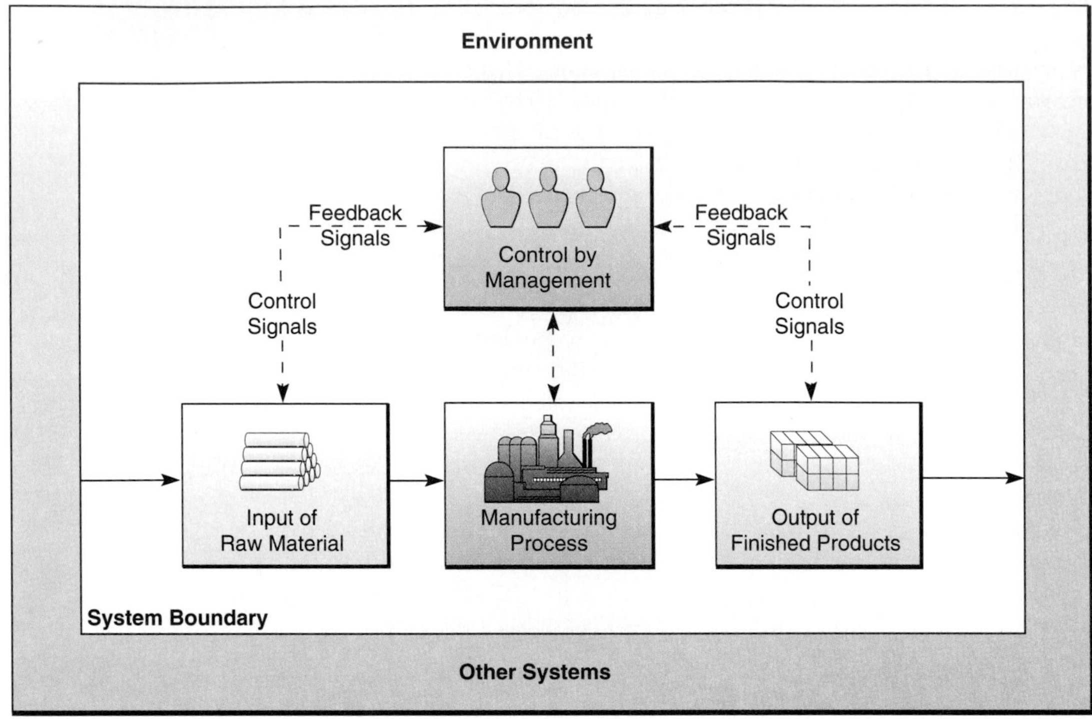

then makes necessary adjustments to a system's input and processing components to ensure that it produces proper output. For example, a sales manager exercises control when he or she reassigns salespersons to new sales territories after evaluating feedback about their sales performance.

Feedback is frequently included as part of the concept of the control function because it is such a necessary part of its operation. Figure 1.5 shows the relationship of feedback and control to the other components of a system. The flow of feedback data to the managerial control component and the resulting control signals to the other components are shown as dashed arrows. This emphasizes that the role of feedback and control is to ensure that other system components properly transform inputs into outputs so a system can achieve its goal.

EXAMPLE

A familiar example of a self-monitoring, self-regulating system is the thermostat-controlled heating system found in many homes, which automatically monitors and regulates itself to maintain a desired temperature. Another example is the human body, which can be regarded as a cybernetic system that automatically monitors and adjusts many of its functions, such as temperature, heartbeat, and breathing. A business also has many control activities. For example, computers may monitor and control manufacturing processes, accounting procedures help control financial systems, data entry displays provide control of data entry activities, and sales quotas and sales bonuses attempt to control sales performance.

Other System Characteristics

Figure 1.5 points out several other system characteristics that are important to a proper understanding of information systems. Note that a system does not exist in a vacuum; rather, it exists and functions in an **environment** containing other systems. If a system is one of the components of a larger system, it is called a **subsystem**, and the larger system is its environment. Also, a system is separated from its environment and other systems by its system *boundary*.

Several systems may share the same environment. Some of these systems may be connected to one another by means of a shared boundary, or **interface**. Figure 1.5 also illustrates the concept of an *open system*, which is a system that interacts with other systems in its environment. In this diagram, the system exchanges inputs and outputs with its environment. Thus, we could say that it is connected to its environment by input and output interfaces. Finally, if a system has the ability to change itself or its environment in order to survive, it is known as an *adaptive system*.

EXAMPLE

Organizations such as businesses and government agencies are good examples of the systems in society, which is their environment. Society contains a multitude of such systems, including individuals and their social, political, and economic institutions. Organizations themselves consist of many subsystems, such as departments, divisions, and other work groups. Organizations are examples of open systems, since they interface and interact with other systems in their environment. Finally, organizations are examples of adaptive systems, since they can modify themselves to meet the demands of a changing environment. Figure 1.6 shows the roles played by business processes, information systems, and management when a business firm in viewed as an organizational system.

Components of an Information System

We are now ready to apply the systems concepts we have learned to help us better understand how an information system works. For example, we have said that an information system is a system that accepts data resources as input and processes them into information products as output. How does an information system accomplish this? What system components and activities are involved?

Figure 1.7 illustrates an **information system model** that expresses a fundamental conceptual framework for the major components and activities of information systems:

An information system uses the resources of people (end users and IS specialists), hardware (machines and media), and software (programs and procedures), to perform input, processing, output, storage, and control activities that convert data resources into information products.

This information system model highlights the relationships among the components and activities of information systems. It provides a framework that emphasizes four major concepts that can be applied to all types of information systems:

- People, hardware, software, and data are the four basic resources of information systems.
- People resources include end users and IS specialists, hardware resources consist of machines and media, software resources include both programs and procedures, and data resources can include data, model, and knowledge bases.
- Data resources are transformed by information processing activities into a variety of information products for end users.

FIGURE 1.6
A business is an organizational system where *economic resources* (input) are transformed by various *organizational processes* (processing) into *goods and services* (output). *Information systems* provide information (feedback) on the operations of the system to *management* for the direction and maintenance of the system (control), as it exchanges inputs and outputs with its environment.

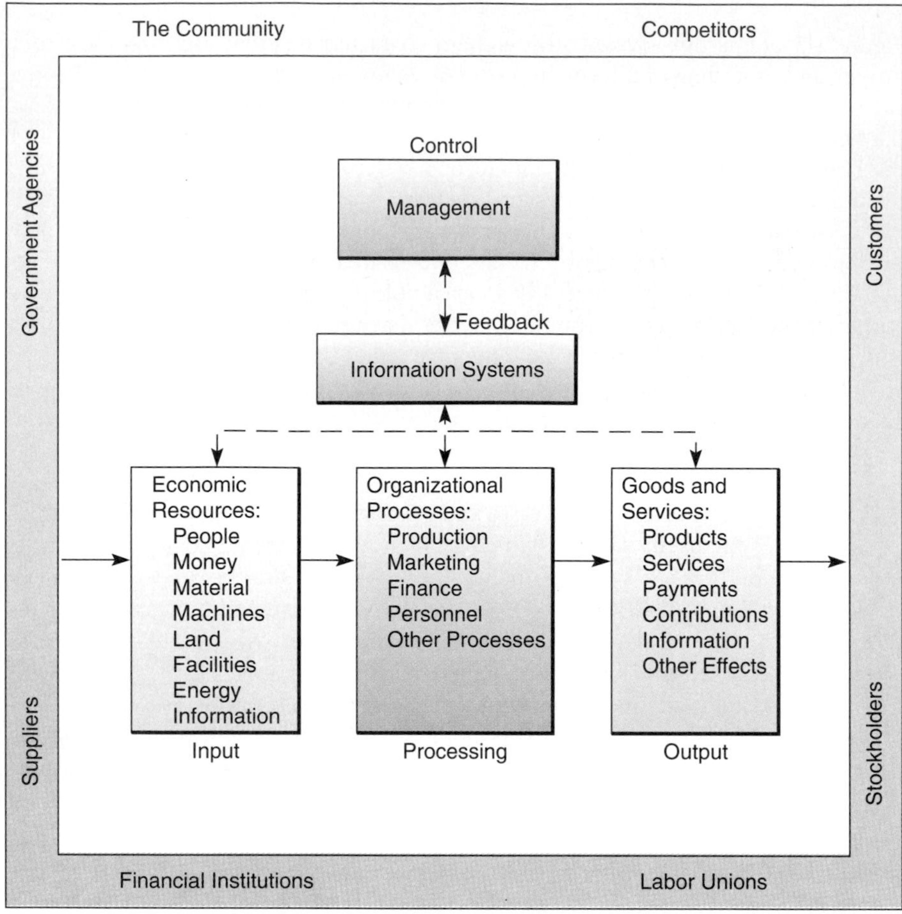

FIGURE 1.7
The components of an information system. All information systems use people, hardware, and software resources to perform input, processing, output, storage, and control activities that transform data resources into information products.

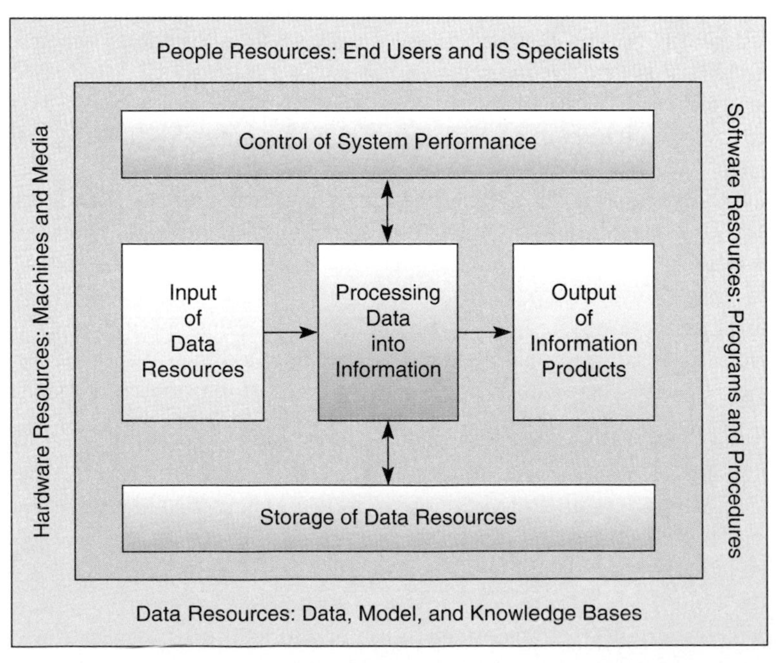

- Information processing consists of input, processing, output, storage, and control activities.

Information System Resources

Our basic IS model shows that an information system consists of four major resources: people, hardware, software, and data. Let's briefly discuss several basic concepts and examples of the roles these resources play as the fundamental components of information systems. You should be able to recognize these four components at work in any type of information system you encounter in the real world. Figure 1.8 outlines several examples of typical information system resources and products.

People Resources

People are required for the operation of all information systems. These people resources include *end users* and *IS specialists*.

- **End users** (also called *users* or *clients*) are people who use an information system or the information it produces. They can be accountants, salespersons, engineers, clerks, customers, or managers. Most of us are information system end users.
- **IS specialists** are people who develop and operate information systems. They include systems analysts, programmers, computer operators, and other managerial, technical, and clerical IS personnel. Basically, systems analysts design information systems based on the information requirements of end users; programmers prepare computer programs based on the specifications of systems analysts; and computer operators operate computer systems.

Hardware Resources

The concept of **hardware resources** includes all physical devices and materials used in information processing. Specifically, it includes not only **machines**, such as computers and calculators, but also all data **media**, that is, all tangible objects on which data is recorded, from sheets of paper to magnetic disks. Examples of hardware in computer-based information systems are:

- *Computer systems*, which consist of central processing units (CPUs) and a variety of interconnected peripheral devices. Examples are large mainframe computer systems, minicomputers, and microcomputer systems.

People Resources
Specialists—systems analysts, programmers, and computer operators.
End users—anyone else who uses information systems.
Hardware Resources
Machines—computers, video monitors, magnetic disk drives, printers, and optical scanners.
Media—floppy disks, magnetic tape, optical disks, plastic cards, and paper forms.
Software Resources
Programs—operating system programs, spreadsheet programs, word processing programs, and payroll programs.
Procedures—data entry procedures, error correction procedures, and paycheck distribution procedures.
Data Resources
Product descriptions, customer records, employee files, and inventory databases.
Information Products
Management reports and business documents using text and graphics displays, audio responses, and paper forms.

FIGURE 1.8
Examples of Information System Resources and Products

- *Computer peripherals*, which are devices such as a keyboard or electronic mouse for input of data and commands, a video screen or printer for output of information, and magnetic or optical disks for storage of data resources.
- Telecommunications networks, which consist of computers, communications processors, and other devices interconnected by a variety of telecommunications media to provide computing power throughout an organization.

Software Resources

The concept of **software resources** includes all sets of information processing instructions. This generic concept of software includes not only the sets of operating instructions called **programs**, which direct and control computer hardware, but also the sets of information processing instructions needed by people, called **procedures**. So even information systems that don't use computers have a software resource component. The following are examples of software resources:

- *System software*, such as an *operating system* program, which controls and supports the operations of a computer system.
- *Application software*, which is the programs that direct processing for a particular use of computers by end users. Examples are a sales analysis program, a payroll program, and a word processing program.
- *Procedures*, which are operating instructions for the people who will use an information system. Examples are instructions for filling out a paper form or using a software package.

Data Resources

Data is more than the raw material of information systems. The concept of data resources has been broadened by managers and information systems professionals. They realize that data constitute a valuable organizational resource. Thus, you should view data as **data resources** which must be managed effectively to benefit all end users in an organization.

Data can take many forms, including traditional *alphanumeric data*, composed of numbers and alphabetical and other characters that describe business transactions and other events and entities. *Text data*, consisting of sentences and paragraphs used in written communications, *image data*, such as graphic shapes and figures, and *audio data*, the human voice and other sounds, are also important forms of data.

The data resources of information systems are typically organized into:

- **Databases**, which hold processed and organized data.
- **Model bases**, which hold conceptual, mathematical, and logical models that express business relationships, computational routines, or analytical techniques.
- **Knowledge bases**, which hold knowledge in a variety of forms such as facts and rules of inference about various subjects.

For example, data about sales transactions may be accumulated and stored in a sales database for subsequent processing, which yields daily, weekly, and monthly sales analysis reports for management. *Decision support systems*, on the other hand, are information systems that rely on model bases to help managers explore and evaluate decision alternatives. Knowledge bases are used by information systems called *expert systems* to give end users expert advice on specific subjects. We will explore these concepts further in later chapters.

Data versus Information

The word *data* is the plural of *datum*, though data is commonly used to represent both singular and plural forms. Data are raw facts or observations, typically about

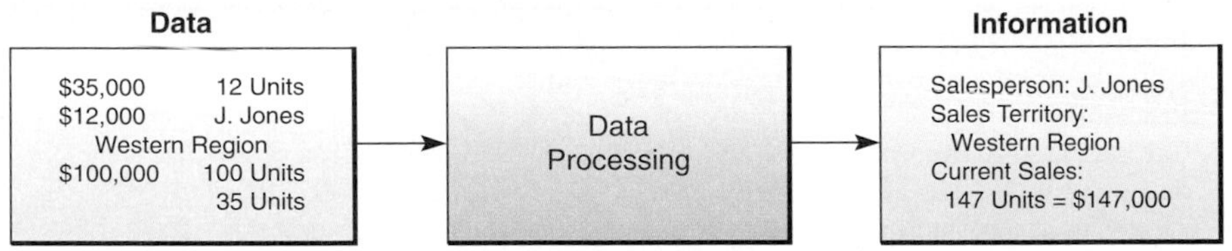

FIGURE 1.9
Data versus information. Note that information is processed data placed in its proper context to give it value for specific end users.

physical phenomena or business transactions. For example, a spacecraft launch or the sale of an automobile would generate a lot of data describing those events. More specifically, data are objective measurements of the *attributes* (the characteristics) of *entities* (such as people, places, things, and events).

EXAMPLE

A spacecraft launch generates vast amounts of data. Electronic transmissions of data (*telemetry*) from thousands of sensors are converted to numeric and text data by computers. Voice and image data are also captured through video and radio monitoring of the launch by mission controllers. Of course, buying a car or an airline ticket also produces a lot of data. Just think of the hundreds of facts needed to describe the characteristics of the car you want and its financing, or the details for even the simplest airline reservation.

The terms *data* and *information* are often used interchangeably. However, it is better to view data as raw material *resources* that are processed into finished information *products*. **Information** can then be defined as data that has been converted into a meaningful and useful context for specific end users. Thus, data is usually subjected to a "value-added process" (we call *data processing* or *information processing*) where (1) its form is aggregated, manipulated, and organized; (2) its content is analyzed and evaluated; and (3) it is placed in a proper context for a human user. So, you should view information as *processed data* placed in a context that gives it value for specific end users. See Figure 1.9.

EXAMPLE

Names, quantities, and dollar amounts recorded on sales forms represent data about sales transactions. However, a sales manager may not regard these as information. Only after such facts are properly organized and manipulated can meaningful sales information be furnished, specifying, for example, the amount of sales by product type, sales territory, or salesperson.

Information System Activities

Let's take a closer look now at each of the basic **information processing** (or **data processing**) activities that occur in information systems. You should be able to recognize input, processing, output, storage, and control activities taking place in any information system you are studying. Figure 1.10 lists business examples that illustrate each of these information system activities.

Input of Data Resources

Data about business transactions and other events must be captured and prepared for processing by *data entry* activities such as recording and editing. End users typically *record* data about transactions on some type of physical medium, such as a

FIGURE 1.10
Business Examples of the Basic Activities of Information Systems

Input
Optical scanning of bar-coded tags on merchandise.
Processing
Calculating employee pay, taxes, and other payroll deductions.
Output
Producing reports and displays about sales performance.
Storage
Maintaining records on customers, employees, and products.
Control
Generating audible signals to indicate proper entry of sales data.

paper form, or enter it directly into a computer system. This usually includes a variety of *editing* activities to ensure that they have recorded data correctly. Once entered, data may be transferred onto a *machine-readable* medium, such as magnetic disk or tape, until needed for processing.

For example, data about sales transactions can be recorded on *source documents* such as paper sales order forms. (A **source document** is the original formal record of a transaction.) Alternatively, sales data could be captured by salespersons using computer keyboards or optical scanning devices who are visually prompted to enter data correctly by video displays. This provides them with a more convenient and efficient **user interface**, that is, methods of end user input and output with a computer system. Methods such as optical scanning and displays of menus, prompts, and fill-in-the-blanks formats make it easier for end users to enter data correctly into an information system.

Processing of Data into Information

Data is typically manipulated by such activities as calculating, comparing, sorting, classifying, and summarizing. These activities organize, analyze, and manipulate data, thus converting it into information for end users. The quality of any data stored in an information system must also be *maintained* by a continual process of correcting and updating activities.

For example, data received about a purchase can be (1) *added* to a running total of sales results, (2) *compared* to a standard to determine eligibility for a sales discount, (3) *sorted* in numerical order based on product identification numbers, (4) *classified* into product categories (such as food and nonfood items), (5) *summarized* to provide a sales manager with information about various product categories, and, finally, (6) used to *update* sales records.

Output of Information Products

Information in various forms is transmitted to end users and made available to them in the output activity. The goal of information systems is the production of appropriate **information products** for end users. Common information products are *video displays*, *paper documents*, and *audio responses* that provide us with *messages, forms, reports, listings, graphics displays,* and so on. We routinely use the information provided by these products as we work in organizations and live in society. For example, a sales manager may view a video display to check on the performance of a salesperson, accept a computer-produced voice message by telephone, and receive a printout of monthly sales results.

Storage of Data Resources

Storage is a basic system component of information systems. Storage is the information system activity in which data and information are retained in an organized manner for later use. For example, just as written text material is organized into

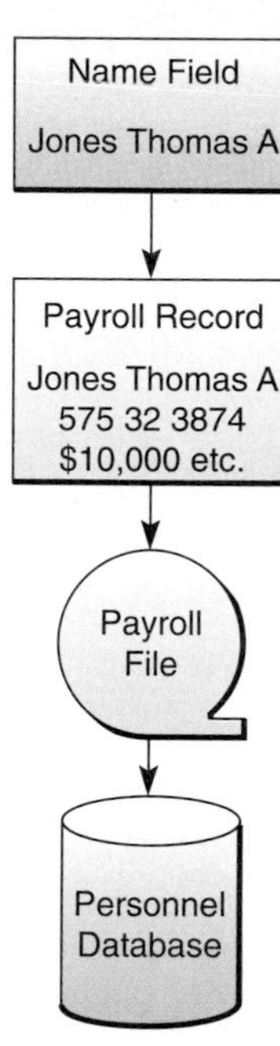

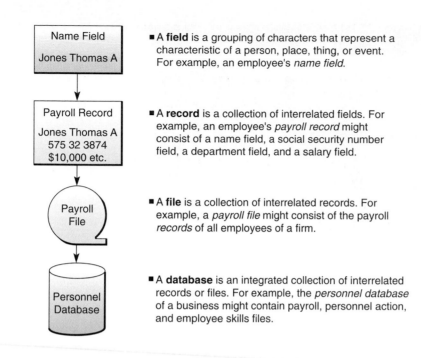

- A **field** is a grouping of characters that represent a characteristic of a person, place, thing, or event. For example, an employee's *name field.*
- A **record** is a collection of interrelated fields. For example, an employee's *payroll record* might consist of a name field, a social security number field, a department field, and a salary field.
- A **file** is a collection of interrelated records. For example, a *payroll file* might consist of the payroll *records* of all employees of a firm.
- A **database** is an integrated collection of interrelated records or files. For example, the *personnel database* of a business might contain payroll, personnel action, and employee skills files.

FIGURE 1.11
Common data elements. This is a common method of organizing stored data in information systems.

words, sentences, paragraphs, and documents, stored data is commonly organized into *fields, records, files,* and *databases.* This facilitates its later use in processing or its retrieval as output when needed by users of a system. These common *data elements* are shown in Figure 1.11.

Control of System Performance

An information system should produce feedback about its input, processing, output, and storage activities. This feedback must be monitored and evaluated to determine if the system is meeting established performance standards. Then appropriate system activities must be adjusted so that proper information products are produced for end users. For example, a manager may discover that subtotals of sales amounts in a sales report do not add up to total sales. This might mean that data entry or processing procedures need to be corrected. Then changes would have to be made to ensure that all sales transactions would be properly captured and processed by a sales information system.

Recognizing Information Systems

As a managerial end user, you should be able to recognize the fundamental components of information systems you encounter in the real world. This means that you should be able to identify:

- The people, hardware, software, and data resources they use.
- The types of information products they produce.
- The way they perform input, processing, output, storage, and control activities.

This kind of understanding will help you be a better user, developer, and manager of information systems. And that, as we have pointed out in this chapter, is important to your future success as a manager, entrepreneur, or professional in business. See Figure 1.12.

FIGURE 1.12
You should be able to recognize the basic components of any information systems you encounter in the real world.

Frank Siteman/Stock Boston

Analyzing Waldenbooks' Information Systems

Earlier in the chapter (Section I, page 5), we analyzed the importance of computer-based information systems to the success of Waldenbooks. Now let's analyze the resources used, activities performed, and information products produced by their information systems to help you recognize the components of information systems you encounter in the real world.

Figure 1.13 illustrates some of the components you might see in Waldenbooks information systems. People resources include bookstore managements and employees who use the system. Hardware resources include machines such as the bookstore PCs, microcomputer servers, and mainframe computer, as well as media such as magnetic disks. Software resources include order processing, titles management and store management programs, and the procedures followed by bookstore employees and managers. Data resources are contained in titles, customer, and special orders databases. Information products include video displays for order entry support, confirmation information, and store management reports.

Special-order requests and the inquiries of bookstore employees and managers are entered into the system as input through the keyboards of the bookstore PCs. Processing is accomplished by PCs, microcomputer servers, and a mainframe computer executing programs to accomplish special order processing, titles management, and store management. Output of information products produces video displays for order entry support, confirmation information, and store management reporting. Storage of data and software resources is provided by magnetic disk drives, on which are stored the titles, customer, and special orders databases and order processing, titles and sales management programs. Control is accomplished by special-order processing programs and procedures which ensure quick and accurate order entry and customer service.

So you see, analyzing an information system to identify its basic components is not a difficult task. Just identify the resources that the information system uses, the information processing activities it performs, and the information products it produces. Then you will be better able to identify ways to improve these components, and thus the performance of the information system itself. That's a goal that every business end user should strive to attain.

FIGURE 1.13
Information system components in Waldenbooks' computer-based information systems.

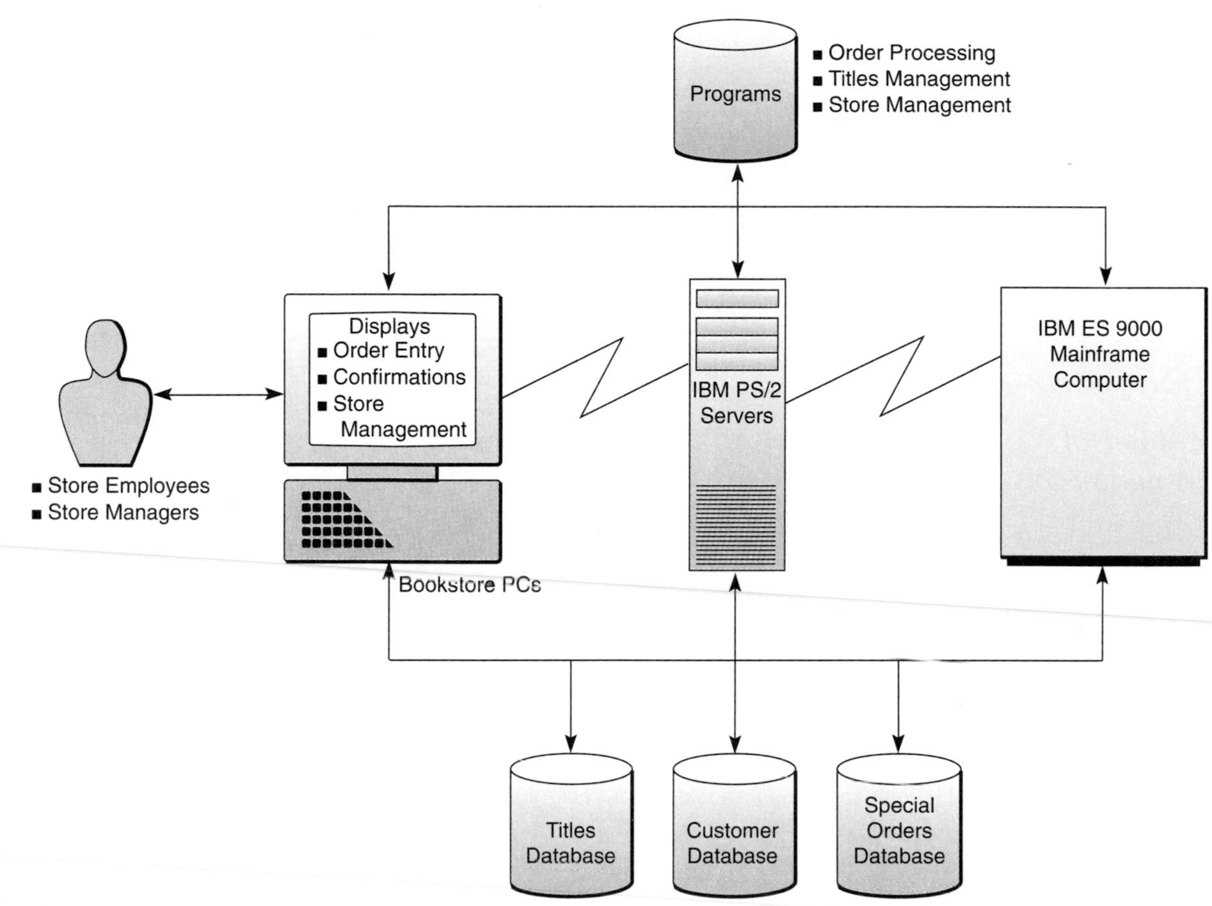

Overview of Information Systems

There are many kinds of information systems in the real world. All of them use hardware, software, and people resources to transform data resources into information products. Some are simple *manual* information systems, where people use simple tools such as pencils and paper, or machines such as calculators and typewriters. Others are **computer-based information systems** that rely on a variety of computer systems to accomplish their information processing activities.

It is important not to confuse our discussion of *information systems* with the concept of *computer systems*. As we will see in Chapter 2, a computer system is a group of interconnected hardware components that may take the form of a *microcomputer, minicomputer,* or large *mainframe* computer system. However, whether it sits on a desk or is one of many computers in a telecommunications network, a computer system still represents only the *hardware resources* component of a computer-based information system. As we have just seen, an information system also consists of people, software, and data resources.

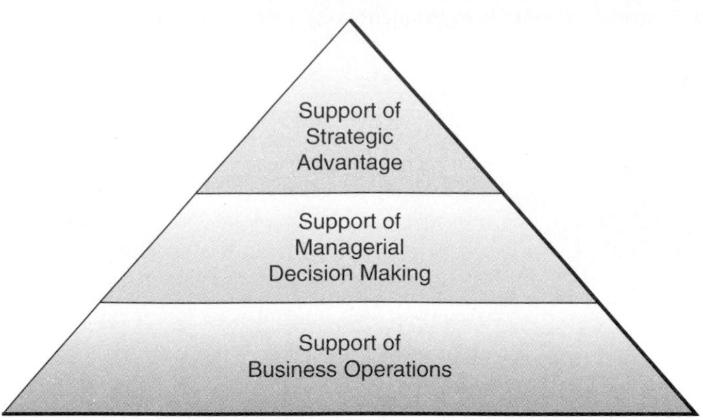

FIGURE 1.14
The three major roles of information systems. Information systems provide an organization with support for business operations, managerial decision making, and strategic advantage.

The Roles of Information Systems

Another important fact about information systems is shown in Figure 1.14. No matter how they may be classified, information systems perform only three basic roles in an organization:

- Support of business operations.
- Support of managerial decision making.
- Support of strategic competitive advantage.

Let's take a retail store as an example to illustrate this important point. As a consumer, you have to deal regularly with information systems used to support business operations at the many retail stores where you shop. For example, most department stores use computer-based information systems to help them record customer purchases, keep track of inventory, pay employees, buy new merchandise, and evaluate sales trends. Store operations would grind to a halt without the support of such information systems.

Information systems also help store managers make better decisions and attempt to gain a strategic competitive advantage. For example, decisions on what lines of clothing or appliances need to be added or discontinued, or what kind of investments they require, are typically made after an analysis provided by computer-based information systems. This not only supports the decision making of store managers but also helps them look for ways to gain an advantage over other retailers in the competition for customers. For example, store managers might make a decision to invest in a computerized touch-screen catalog ordering system as a strategic information system. This might lure customers away from other stores, based on the ease of ordering merchandise provided by such a computer-based information system. Thus, strategic information helps provide strategic products and services that give an organization a comparative advantage over its competitors.

Types of Information Systems

Conceptually, information systems in the real world can be classified in many ways. For example, some information systems process data resulting from business transactions such as sales to customers, purchases from suppliers, wages paid to employees, and so on. These information systems are commonly called *transaction processing systems*. Other information systems provide reports and displays that help managers make more informed decisions. These are typically called *information reporting systems*.

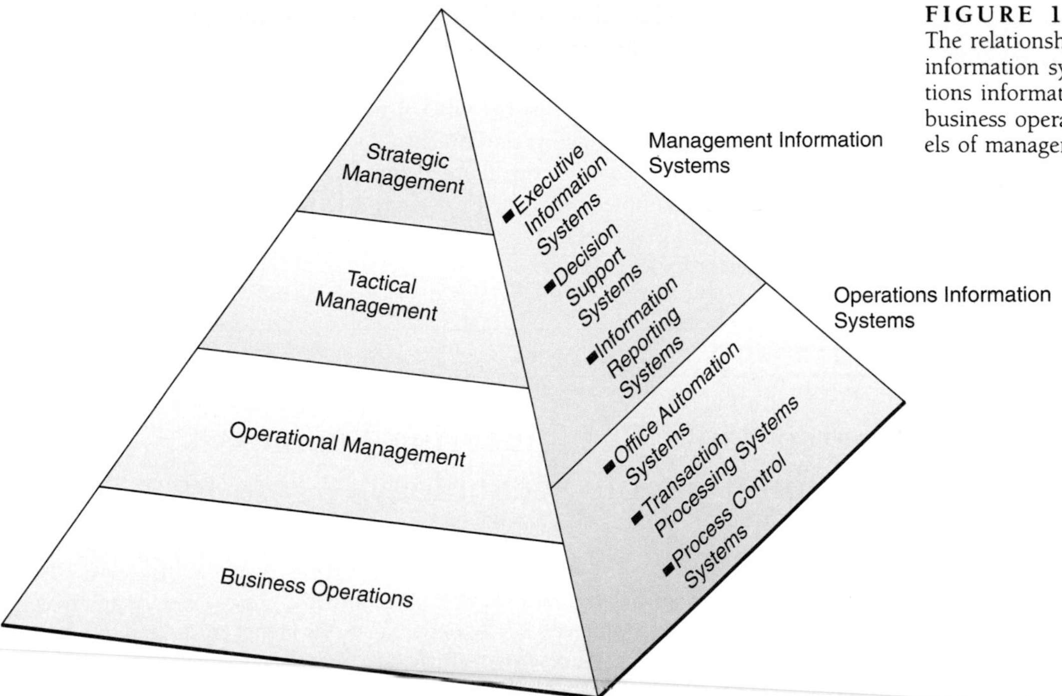

FIGURE 1.15
The relationship of management information systems and operations information systems to business operations and the levels of management.

Figure 1.15 illustrates the relationship of *management information systems* and *operations information systems* to business operations and management. **Management information systems** support the decision-making needs of strategic (top) management, tactical (middle) management, and operating (supervisory) management. **Operations information systems** support the information processing requirements of the day-to-day operations of a business, as well as some lower-level operations management functions. Let's look briefly at some examples of how information systems exist in the business world.

Transaction processing systems record and process data resulting from business transactions. They process transactions in two basic ways. In *batch processing*, transactions data is accumulated over a period of time and processed periodically. In *realtime* (or *online*) *processing*, data is processed immediately after a transaction occurs. For example, point-of-sale (POS) systems at many retail stores use electronic cash register terminals to electronically capture and transmit sales data over telecommunications links to regional computer centers for immediate (realtime) or nightly (batch) processing.

Process control systems monitor and control physical processes. For example, a petroleum refinery uses electronic sensors linked to computers to continually monitor chemical processes and make instant (realtime) adjustments that control the refining process. **Office automation systems** enhance office communications and productivity. For example, a corporation may use word processing for office correspondence, electronic mail to send and receive electronic messages, and teleconferencing to hold electronic meetings.

Information reporting systems provide information in the form of reports and displays to managers. For example, sales managers may use their computer workstations to get instantaneous displays about the sales record of their products and also receive weekly sales analysis reports that evaluate sales made by each salesperson. **Decision support systems** give direct computer support to managers during the decision-making process. For example, advertising managers may use an electronic spreadsheet package to do what-if analysis as they test the impact of alternative advertising budgets on the forecasted sales of new products. **Executive information systems** provide critical information in easy-to-use displays to top management. For example, top executives may use touchscreen terminals to instantly view text and graphics displays that highlight key areas of organizational and competitive performance.

REAL WORLD CASE

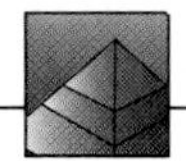

Texas Commerce Bank: Reengineering Business Processes with Information Technology

Changes in the legal environment of business can frequently provide opportunities for new uses of information technology. Take Texas Commerce Bank, for instance. They have made a major leap into personal computing to capitalize on changes in state banking regulations in Texas. "We're basically in the process of [data center] consolidation as we move from a unit bank environment to a branch banking one," says Allen L. Cournyer, senior vice president and manager of the bank's computer center.

Cournyer says that as recently as 10 years ago, banking laws restricting branch banking made it even difficult to receive approval to install automated teller machines. But as soon as Texas legalized branch banking, Texas Commerce Bank began to decentralize its computer operations and reduce duplication in data processing functions. The shift in laws "handed us an opportunity to use new technology, so we've done a lot of reengineering," Cournyer said.

For example, Texas Commerce decided to dramatically speed up its loan making process. It originally planned to have its loan officers access seven mainframe-based information systems, including loan-processing and credit card–processing systems, and credit checks with various credit bureaus. However, the bank soon found that it would require as many as five terminals on a loan officer's desk to access such systems.

Instead, Texas Commerce installed PCs on every loan officer's desk. Then it designed front-end software that integrated displays of documents produced by each of the separate mainframe systems. This imaging software retrieves images of documents stored on optical disks, thus allowing loan officers to quickly display documents they need on their PC video screens.

Texas Commerce also replaced a system that relied on a central optical scanner to make copies of documents received by courier from its 96 branches. Instead, fax machines were installed at each branch which transmitted images of documents to Compaq microcomputer servers. These fax servers converted the electronic documents into the format needed to store them as document images on optical disks for use by bank loan officers.

Texas Commerce Bank's use of information technology has resulted in several major benefits. "We have doubled our volume of business without increasing staff," Cournyer noted. "We've also been able to offer new products as we've gotten better at figuring out how to automate things." One example is the bank's new loan-by-phone program.

In addition, error rates in loan processing have dropped and service has improved. For example, a request for a personal loan that used to take up to two days to process is now decided within three hours. Virtually no paper is now produced by the new loan approval process. In the future, the bank plans to enable loan officers to generate copies of reports they need when they need them, instead of waiting for mainframe produced reports.

CASE STUDY QUESTIONS

1. What people, hardware, software, and data resources and information products do you recognize at Texas Commerce Bank?
2. What IS input, processing, output, storage, and control activities do you recognize in the bank's personal loan-processing system?
3. How has the use of information technology benefitted Texas Commerce Bank?

Source: Adapted from Michael Fitzgerald, "PCs Are Money in the Bank," *Computerworld,* March 15, 1993, p.39.

Summary

- **The Importance of Information Systems.** An understanding of the effective and responsible use and management of information systems is important for business end users in today's global information society. Information systems play a vital role in the operations, management, and strategic success of businesses and other organizations and have become a major functional area of business administration.
- **Careers in Information Systems.** Computers and their use in information systems have created career opportunities for millions of men and women in the computer industry and in computer-using organizations. Examples include information systems specialists like systems analysts, programmers, and end user consultants.
- **System Concepts.** A system is a group of interrelated components working toward the attainment of a common goal by accepting inputs and producing outputs in an organized transformation process. Feedback is data about the performance of a system. Control is the component that monitors and evaluates feedback and makes any necessary adjustments to the input and processing components to ensure that proper output is produced.
- **Information System Concepts.** An information system uses the resources of hardware (machines and media), software (programs and procedures), and people (specialists and users) to perform input, processing, output, storage, and control activities that convert data resources into information products. Data is first collected and converted to a form that is suitable for processing (input). Then the data is manipulated and converted into information (processing), stored for future use (storage), or communicated to its ultimate user (output) according to correct processing procedures (control).
- **IS Resources and Products.** Hardware resources include machines and media used in information processing. Software resources include computerized instructions (programs) and instructions for people (procedures). People resources include information systems specialists and users. Data resources include alphanumeric, text, image, video, audio, tactile, and sensor data. Information products produced by an information system can take a variety of forms, including paper reports, visual displays, documents, messages, graphics, and audio responses.
- **Overview of Information Systems.** Information systems perform three basic roles in an organization. That is, they support an organization's business operations, managerial decision making, and strategic advantage. Conceptually, information systems can be classified in many ways. Examples include transaction processing systems, office automation systems, management information systems, decision support systems, and so on. However, it is important to realize that information systems in the real world are typically combinations of these conceptual classifications.

Key Terms and Concepts

These are the key terms and concepts of this chapter. The page number of their first explanation is in parentheses.

1. Careers in information systems (8)
2. Computer-based information system (23)
3. Control (13)
4. Data (18)
5. Data or information processing (19)
6. Data resources (18)
7. Environment (15)
8. Feedback (13)
9. Hardware resources (17)
   a. Machines (17)
   b. Media (17)
10. Information (19)
11. Information society (5)
12. Information system (4)
13. Information system activities (19)
    a. Input (19)
    b. Processing (20)
    c. Output (20)
    d. Storage (20)
    e. Control (21)
14. Information system resources (17)
15. Information technology (11)
16. Interface (15)
17. Knowledge needed about information systems (10)
18. Knowledge workers (5)
19. Management information system (25)
20. People resources (17)
    a. IS specialists
    b. End users
21. Roles of information systems (24)
22. Software resources (18)
    a. Programs (18)
    b. Procedures (18)
23. Subsystem (15)
24. System (13)
25. Types of information systems (24)

Review Quiz

Match one of the key terms and concepts listed above with one of the brief examples or definitions listed below. Look for the best fit for answers that seem to fit more than one key term or concept. Defend your choices.

____ 1. A system that uses hardware, software, and people resources to perform information processing activities that transform data resources into information products for end users.

____ 2. An information system that uses computers and their hardware and software.

____ 3. An information system that provides information and support for decision making by managers.

____ 4. Anyone who uses an information system or the information it produces.

____ 5. Examples include jobs such as computer operators, programmers, and systems analysts.

____ 6. People who spend most of their workday creating, using, and distributing information.

____ 7. You should know some fundamental concepts about information systems and their technology, development, applications, and management.

____ 8. A group of interrelated components working together toward the attainment of a common goal.

____ 9. Data about a system's performance.

____ 10. Making adjustments to a system's components so that it operates properly.

____ 11. A shared boundary between systems.

____ 12. Information systems support the operations, decision making, and competitive advantage of a business.

____ 13. Examples include management information systems, transaction processing systems, and executive information systems.

____ 14. Facts or observations.

____ 15. Data that has been placed into a meaningful context for an end user.

____ 16. The act of converting data into information.

____ 17. Programs and procedures.

____ 18. A set of instructions for a computer.

____ 19. A set of instructions for people.

____ 20. Machines and media.

____ 21. Computers, disk drives, video monitors, and printers are examples.

____ 22. Magnetic disks, magnetic tape, and paper forms are examples.

____ 23. End users work with these information systems professionals.

____ 24. Using the keyboard of a computer to enter data.

____ 25. Computing loan payments.

____ 26. Printing a letter you wrote using a computer.

____ 27. Saving a copy of the letter on a magnetic disk.

____ 28. Having a sales receipt as proof of a purchase.

Discussion Questions

1. Who is an end user? Is a business end user also a knowledge worker? Explain.
2. What are five major areas of information systems knowledge? How could a knowledge of these areas help a business end user?
3. Refer to the Real World Case of Waldenbooks in the chapter. Would their computerized special-order system entice you to shop at Waldenbooks? Why or why not?
4. What software resources are required in a manual or mechanical (noncomputerized) information system? Give several examples to illustrate your answer.
5. Identify several uses of the term *system* in the chapter. Why is this term so useful in the study of computers and information systems?
6. Refer to the Real World Case of Texas Commerce Bank in the chapter. What other ways do banks use information technology? Give several examples.
7. Identify several types of data resources and information products mentioned in the chapter. What other examples can you think of?
8. How can a manager demonstrate that he or she is a responsible end user of information systems? Give several examples.
9. What is the difference between a computer system and a computer-based information system? Give an example to illustrate your answer.
10. What are several major types of information systems? Give three examples, and explain how they might support the operations, managerial decision making, and competitive advantage of a business.

Real World Problems

1. Jordan's Furniture: Succeeding with Information Systems

While over 1,500 furniture retailers went out of business in the United States in 1992 alone, Jordan's Furniture has continued to grow. Why does Jordan's succeed where others fail? Information technology may be the answer. "Our computer system has allowed us to expand and grow in a controlled way. It has given us a real competitive advantage over other furniture stores," said Eliot Jordan, co-owner of the $70 million company. Jordan relies on a retail furniture software package and a Data General (DG) minicomputer and over 200 terminals in its main store and warehouse in Avon, Massachusetts, and two other stores in Waltham, Massachusetts, and Nashua, New Hampshire.

Jordan's premier application is a computerized receiving system which allows their store to make inventory available to customers just 20 minutes after it has been unloaded from delivery trucks. Since over 14 trucks and 1,500 pieces of furniture arrive each day, Jordan uses a bar-coding system where bar coded stickers are placed on furniture as soon as it arrives. When the furniture is stored in the warehouse, the bar coding is scanned and transmitted to the DG mini, which updates their inventory database. Salespeople can then use their video terminals to check the availability of stock. The system has reduced inventory errors by 90 percent, and gives Jordan instant access to up to five years of customer data, giving it a vital edge in customer service.

a. How have computer-based information systems benefitted Jordan's Furniture?

b. What people, hardware, software, and data resources and information products do you see at Jordan's Furniture? What input processing, output, storage, and control activities do you recognize?

Source: Adapted from David Kelley, "From Truck to Customer in 20 Minutes," *Computerworld*, January 11, 1993, p. 48.

2. First Interstate Bancorporation: IS Careers Are Changing

"To anyone who says, 'We're a leading-edge, technology-driven bank, and we have a competitive advantage from that,' I say, 'That's bunk,' " says Webb Edwards, executive vice president and manager of information services at Los Angeles-based First Interstate Bancorp. Competitors can quickly duplicate technology, he continues, but they cannot as easily match carefully trained and integrated teams of IS people and users. First Interstate recently consolidated 13 data centers into 2, reduced its IS staff from 2,100 to 700 people, and lopped $93 million off its annual IS budget. This required a major overhaul of its IS training, recruiting, and management development.

First Interstate's IS downsizing resulted from losses from bad real estate loans and the bank's decision to standardize applications, processes, and banking products across all of its affiliated, semiautonomous banks. IS was told to become "a catalyst for a change in culture" for the entire organization, Edwards says. This required IS practitioners to break out of their specialty molds. "For example, we might have had a guy whose sole job was to oversee the writing of code," Edwards says. "Today, we'd expect him to be involved with the user group, to be involved in planning where that business is going, to be conversant in business concepts."

a. How are the jobs of IS personnel changing at First Interstate?

b. Would you like to be one of these new breed of IS professionals? Why or why not?

Source: Adapted from Gary Anthes, "Say Goodbye to the Lone Worker," *Computerworld*, January 4, 1993, p. 13–14.

3. Mobil Oil Corporation: Using Global Information Systems

If Mobil Oil Corp. wanted to determine whether a sandstone deposit off the coast of Nigeria merited drilling oil wells, it just might call on some of its engineers in Canada, Australia, Dallas, or Singapore. Mobil has installed a series of minicomputer-based networks that permit its staff in one corner of the world to share research and analysis with regions that may not have available personnel or resources to do the job. "We can't always afford to move people to a problem," noted Eric Dion, technical team leader at Mobil's exploration operations. "We need to be able to bring technical expertise to solve a problem irrespective of where people and problems are located."

Mobil is installing Hewlett-Packard (HP) HP9000 minicomputers at 11 sites around the globe. Tied to these minicomputers are over 1,000 personal computers and technical computer workstations doing everything from word processing and spreadsheet accounting, to seismic and chemical analysis. With the HP system, a Mobil scientist drawing a diagram or performing an analysis in say, Indonesia, can send realtime renderings to his or her counterpart in Norway, Dion said.

a. How dependent on computer-based information systems are the knowledge workers at Mobil Oil?

b. How has information technology affected the international operations of Mobil Oil?

Source: Adapted from Mark Halper, "Mobil Nets Unite staff," *Computerworld*, January 11, 1993, pp. 51, 54.

4. **Neiman Marcus: Working Smarter with Information Systems**

Neiman Marcus is converting its nationwide chain of 27 department stores and two warehouses from point-of-sale (POS) terminals to IBM microcomputers that act as cash registers and data entry terminals. These PCs are connected to an IBM RS/6000 workstation-computer in each store and one at company headquarters in Dallas. The new system will change the daily work routines of over 15,000 salespeople. Most sales associates used to record all commission sales in ink in their own "clientele books." The new sales system automates the record-keeping and updates a personal database for each sales associate that is stored in the RS/6000 servers in each store.

Because sales information is also stored centrally in an IBM mainframe database, Neiman Marcus will gain new insights into customer spending patterns, said Keiffer Buggs, the firm's manager of credit, finance, and administrative systems. "Each time a sale is made, one update is made in the sales associate's database and another is made to the IBM mainframe," Buggs said. The mainframe runs a centrally managed commission systems and sales audit system. Sales personnel will have less paperwork, and they will be able to alert customers when favored brands of merchandise arrive at the store, said Buggs. "I used to be bogged down in recording all of my customers' purchases in my clientele book," said Greg Lim, a senior sales associate at the North Park store in Dallas. "Now, we build our customer list daily and we always have that information available. The software makes it easier for us to carry out the transactions, and it prompts us to do things that used to be written in manuals." For example, Lim said, the new system supports on-line credit authorization and lists out-of-state sales taxes.

a. How will the new sales processing information system at Neiman Marcus improve the jobs of their 15,000 sales associates?

b. What people, hardware, software, and data resources and information products do you recognize in the Neiman Marcus sales information system? What input, processing, output, storage, and control activities do you recognize?

Source: Adapted from Jean Bozeman, "Retailer Has Client/Server Makeover," *Computerworld*, February 22, 1993, p. 47.

Application Exercises

1. **ABC Department Stores**

The president of ABC Department Stores asked the following questions at a recent meeting of store managers and the vice president of information systems. Match each question with one of the major areas of information systems knowledge illustrated in Figure 1.4. Explain your choices.

a. How can we use information systems to support sales floor activities and store manager decision making and outhustle the competition?

b. How can we involve store managers in building such applications?

c. How can we use information technology to motivate our employees, please our customers, and build a close-knit organization?

d. What hardware, software, telecommunications, and database management resources do we need to support our goals?

e. How are we going to manage the hardware, software, people, and data resources of our information systems at the store and corporate level?

2. **Jefferson State University**

Students in the College of Business Administration of Jefferson State University use its microcomputer lab for a variety of assignments. For example, a student may load a word processing program from a microcomputer's hard disk drive into main memory and then proceed to type a case study analysis. When the analysis is typed, edited, and properly formatted to an instructor's specifications, the student will save it on a floppy disk and print a copy on the microcomputer's printer. If the student tries to save the case study analysis using a file name he or she has already used for saving another document, the program will display a warning message and wait until it receives an additional command.

Make an outline that uses the framework of the information systems model discussed in the chapter (illustrated in Figure 1.7) to identify the information system components in the preceding example.

a. Identify the people, hardware, software, and data resources and the information products of this information system.

b. Identify the input, processing, output, storage, and control activities that occurred.

3. **Analyzing an Information System**

Make an outline that identifies the system activities, resources, and products of a manual or computerized information system with which you are familiar, using the framework of the information system model illustrated in

Figure 1.7. For example, you could analyze your use of an information system such as a department store POS system, a supermarket checkout system, a university registration system, or a bank ATM system. Refer to the example of the analysis of information systems for Waldenbooks illustrated in Figure 1.13 to help you in your analysis of:

a. The people, hardware, software, and data resources and the information products of this information system.

b. The input, processing, output, storage, and control activities of the information system.

Review Quiz Answers

1. *12*
2. *2*
3. *19*
4. *20b*
5. *1*
6. *18*
7. *17*
8. *24*
9. *8*
10. *3*
11. *16*
12. *21*
13. *25*
14. *4*
15. *10*
16. *5*
17. *22*
18. *22a*
19. *22b*
20. *9*
21. *9a*
22. *9b*
23. *20a*
24. *13a*
25. *13b*
26. *13c*
27. *13d*
28. *13e*

Selected References

1. Beniger, James. *The Control Revolution: Technological and Economic Origins of the Information Society*. Cambridge, Mass.: Harvard Business School Press, 1986.
2. Checkland, Peter. *Systems Thinking, Systems Practice*. New York: John Wiley & Sons, 1981.
3. Davis, Gordon, and Margarethe Olson. *Management Information Systems: Conceptual Foundations, Structure, and Development*. New York: McGraw-Hill, 1985.
4. Galliers, Robert, ed. *Information Analysis: Selected Readings*. Sidney, Australia: Addison-Wesley Publishing, 1987.
5. "Information Technology." *The Economist*, June 16, 1990.
6. Keen, Peter. *Shaping the Future: Business Design through Information Technology*. Cambridge, Mass.: Harvard Business School Press, 1991.
7. Naisbitt, John, and Patricia Aburdene. *Megatrends 2000*. New York: William Morrow & Co., 1990.
8. Nass, Clifford. "Following the Money Trail: Twenty-Five Years of Measuring the Information Economy." *Communication Research*, December 1987.
9. Roach, Stephen. "The Information Economy Comes of Age."*Information Management Review*, Summer 1986.
10. Wand, Yair, and Ron Weber. "An Ontological Analysis of Some Information Systems Concepts." *Proceedings of the Ninth International Conference on Information Systems*, 1988.

Continuing Real World Case

Omaha Vision Center—Part 1: The Importance of Information Systems

Introduction

Dr. Jerry Creighton walked down the hallway of the Vision Center, passing within earshot of the center administrator's office. ". . . and that computer was a waste of $20,000. It doesn't do anything," he remarked to one of the technicians. The center administrator, Carl Weber, obviously overhearing the comment, was not surprised by the doctor's complaints. "What a wonderful year this is going to be," he thought.

Weber joined the practice in May 1991 to handle the business affairs of the center; he saw immediately the need to upgrade the office system. From the beginning, he had argued with the doctor, pushing for computerization.

Weber felt that, with time, Dr. Creighton could be talked out of his negative feelings about computers. In the meantime, the information systems would be upgraded. The questions were:

1. How could this be done with the least disturbance to an ongoing enterprise?
2. What hardware systems should be used?
3. What software capabilities should be introduced and in which order?

Company Background

The Omaha Vision Center was formed in 1979 as the private practice of Dr. Jerry Creighton. Creighton was a graduate of the University of Nebraska Medical School, had spent a tour of duty in the military, and then embarked on his private career. The practice developed a fine reputation, based largely on the doctor's skills as an excellent cataract surgeon.

In 1988, the practice staff included the doctor, two ophthalmologic technicians, and two clerical employees. As this point, the decision was made to create an outpatient surgical center. The surgical center would provide the surgeon with greater control over patient pre-op and post-op care and would be a potential source of increased revenue. By 1991, the Outpatient Surgical Center (OSC) was completed and with that came a substantial increase in personnel and administrative requirements (see Figure 1).

Source: This case was originally prepared by Timothy L. Cross and is based on real-life events at an actual medical clinic in Omaha, Nebraska. Adapted from the text by Richard J. Lorette of RJL Associates and H. Charles Walton of Gettysburg College, *Cases in the Management of Information Systems and Information Technology* (Homewood, Ill.: Richard D. Irwin, Inc., 1990). Reprinted with permission.

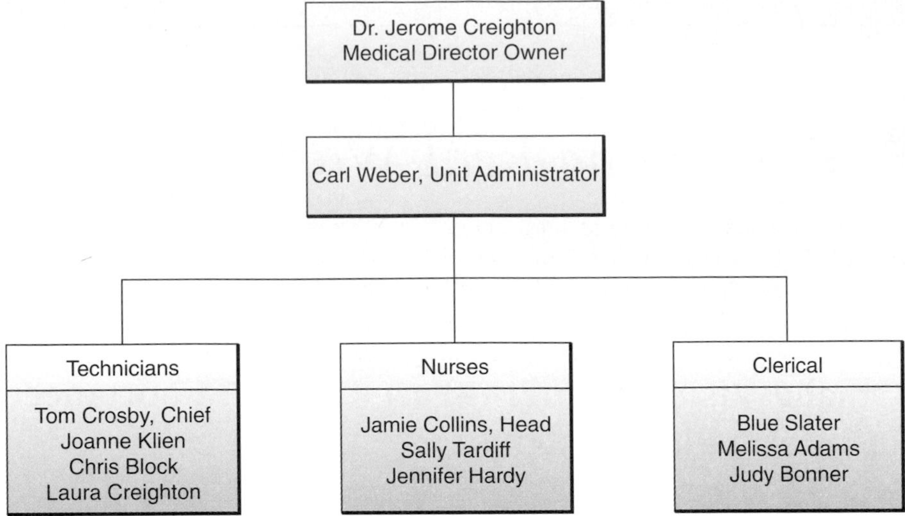

FIGURE 1
Organization Chart of the Omaha Vision Center.

Carl Weber was brought on board soon after completion of the OSC. As center administrator, he was responsible for managing all business functions including personnel, accounting systems, and operations of both the clinic and surgical units. It was not long before he recognized the potential for computers in the practice. To date, only manual systems had been used for accounting (accounts receivable, billing, payroll, etc.) and for clerical work (correspondence, patient scheduling, and medical charts). Weber believed that development of automated information systems would greatly improve efficiency and provide more information for management.

Business Requirements

As of July 1991, the practice had over 8,000 patient charts and handled more than 4,500 patient visits annually. All patients were scheduled in a logbook, up to one year in advance. Scheduling was determined by the type of examination, and preference was given to potential surgical patients. Patients were reminded of their appointments by telephone on the day before they were scheduled. A medical secretary spent a large part of her day maintaining the schedule, calling patients, and searching the book for openings. Weber believed simple computer applications could reduce her scheduling workload significantly.

A more urgent need involved a severe cash flow problem. The practice, due largely to the administrative morass in the local Medicare carrier's operation, had developed a serious accounts receivable problem. (Note: *Accounts Receivable* refers to the amounts owed to a business by its customers for goods sold or services rendered.) In the past year receivables had increased significantly because the time it took for customers to pay their bills had risen from under 35 days payment time to an average of 62 days. This increase in repayment time had created a cash shortage that forced the doctor to defer his own salary on occasion.

Identifying and correcting the problems was difficult because of the manual system. It was evident that Medicare was the prime culprit, but statistical breakdowns of accounts receivable and other support data were nearly impossible to acquire. Without such data, communication with Medicare was an exercise in futility. Weber looked to computerized billing and accounting as the solution to what caused the center's receivables problem.

Medical charts and recordkeeping presented another data headache and was an obvious target for Weber's investigation. With over 8,000 of these charts, all handwritten and filed in large vertical file cabinets, the potential for lost or illegible records mounted with each patient.

Finally, there were no general lists of patients from which to cull mailing lists or to use for quality assurance studies. Again, it seemed a computer would provide the solution. Having identified some areas for immediate remedy, Weber decided to approach the doctor at the practice's strategic planning meeting to be held in December. He intended to present his recommendations for a computer-based system and inform the doctor of the expected value of this addition to the office. In the meantime, Weber began the search for the computer hardware and software that would be required.

Case Study Questions

1. What business problems and opportunities do you recognize at the Omaha Vision Center.
2. Does the Omaha Vision Center need computer-based information systems? Why or why not?
3. How could computer-based information systems benefit the Omaha Vision Center? Give several specific examples.

M O D U L E II

Technology

What challenges do information systems technologies pose for business end users? What basic knowledge should business end users possess about information technology? The four chapters of this module give you an overview of the major technologies used in modern computer-based information systems and their implications for end users and managers.

Chapter 2, Introduction to Computer Hardware, reviews micro, mini, mainframe, and networked computer systems, and the major types of peripheral devices used for computer input, output, and storage by end users.

Chapter 3, Introduction to Computer Software, reviews the basic features and functions of major types of system and application software packages used to support traditional and end user computing.

Chapter 4, Introduction to Telecommunications, presents you with an overview of major trends, concepts, applications, and technical alternatives in telecommunications. The implications of telecommunications for managerial end users and the strategic success of organizations are emphasized.

Chapter 5, Introduction to Database Management, emphasizes management of the data resources of computer-using organizations. It outlines the managerial implications of basic concepts and applications of database management in organizational information systems.

Introduction to Computer Hardware

CHAPTER OUTLINE

CHAPTER 2

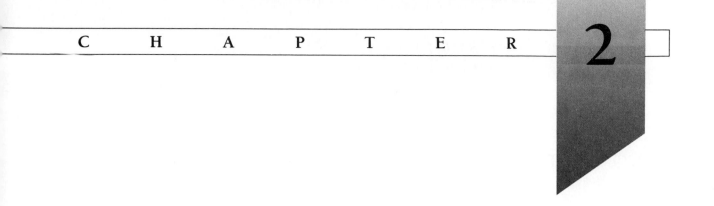

LEARNING OBJECTIVES

The purpose of this chapter is to provide a managerial overview of computer hardware by reviewing the basic types of computer systems and the major types of computer peripheral devices used for input, output, and storage.

Section I of this chapter analyzes the basic functions, components, and major trends in computer systems. It then presents an overview of microcomputer, minicomputer, mainframe, and networked computer systems.

Section II surveys the major characteristics and functions of computer peripheral devices, including support of the user interface through visual and voice input/output methods, and the use of semiconductor memory, magnetic disks and tape, and optical disks to provide storage capabilities for computer systems.

After reading and studying this chapter, you should be able to:

1. Identify the components and functions of a computer system.
2. Outline the major differences and uses of microcomputers, minicomputers, mainframes, and networked computers.
3. Identify the major types and uses of computer peripherals for input, output, and storage.
4. Explain the benefits, limitations, and trends in major types of computer systems and peripheral devices.

SECTION I

Computer Systems: Micros, Minis, Mainframes, and Networked Computers

The Computer System Concept

Before we examine the major types of computers in use today, we should review what the term *computer system* means. A computer is more than a processing box or a collection of electronic devices performing a variety of information processing chores. A computer is a **system**, an interrelated combination of components that performs the basic system functions of *input, processing, output, storage,* and *control*, thus providing end users with a powerful information processing tool. Understanding the computer as a **computer system** is vital to the effective use and management of computers. You should be able to visualize any computer this way, from a microcomputer like that shown in Figure 2.1 to a large computer system whose components are interconnected by a telecommunications network and spread throughout a building or geographic area.

Figure 2.2 illustrates that a computer is a system of hardware devices organized according to the following system functions:

- **Input.** The input devices of a computer system include keyboards, touch screens, pens, electronic mice, optical scanners, and so on. They convert data into electronic *machine-readable* form for direct entry or through telecommunications links into a computer system.
- **Processing.** The *central processing unit* (CPU) is the main processing component of a computer system. (In microcomputers, it is the *main microprocessor.*) In particular, the *arithmetic-logic unit*, one of the CPU's major components, performs the arithmetic and logic functions required in computer processing.
- **Output.** The output devices of a computer system include video display units, printers, audio response units, and so on. They convert electronic information produced by the computer system into *human-intelligible* form for presentation to end users.

Jim Cambon/Tony Stone Worldwide.

FIGURE 2.1
A microcomputer is a system of computing components. This microcomputer system includes (1) a keyboard, mouse, and optical scanner for input, (2) microprocessors and other circuitry in its main system unit for processing and controls, (3) a video monitor and laser printer for output, and (4) memory chips and a built-in floppy disk drive and hard disk unit for storage.

- **Storage.** The storage function of a computer system takes place in the computer's *primary storage unit*, or *memory*, and in *secondary storage* devices such as magnetic disk and tape units. These devices store data and program instructions needed for processing.
- **Control.** The *control unit* of the CPU is the control component of a computer system. It interprets computer program instructions and transmits directions to the other components of the computer system.

Computer System Components

Let's take a closer look now at how each of these vital system functions is accomplished by the components of computer systems. Then we will discuss the major types of computer systems in use today.

The Central Processing Unit

The **central processing unit** is the most important hardware component of a computer system. It is also known as the CPU, the *central processor* or *instruction processor,* and the *main microprocessor* in a **microcomputer**. Conceptually, the CPU can be subdivided into two major subunits: the arithmetic-logic unit ALU and the control unit. The CPU also includes specialized circuitry and devices such as *registers* for high-speed, temporary storage of instruction and data elements, and various subsidiary processors such as those for arithmetic operations, input/output, and telecommunications support. (Conceptually, a computer's primary storage unit or memory is sometimes shown as part of a CPU.)

The **control unit** obtains instructions from those stored in the primary storage unit and interprets them. Then it transmits directions to the other components of the computer system, ordering them to perform required operations. The **arithmetic-logic unit** performs required arithmetic and comparison operations. A computer

FIGURE 2.2
The computer system concept. A computer is a system of hardware components and functions.

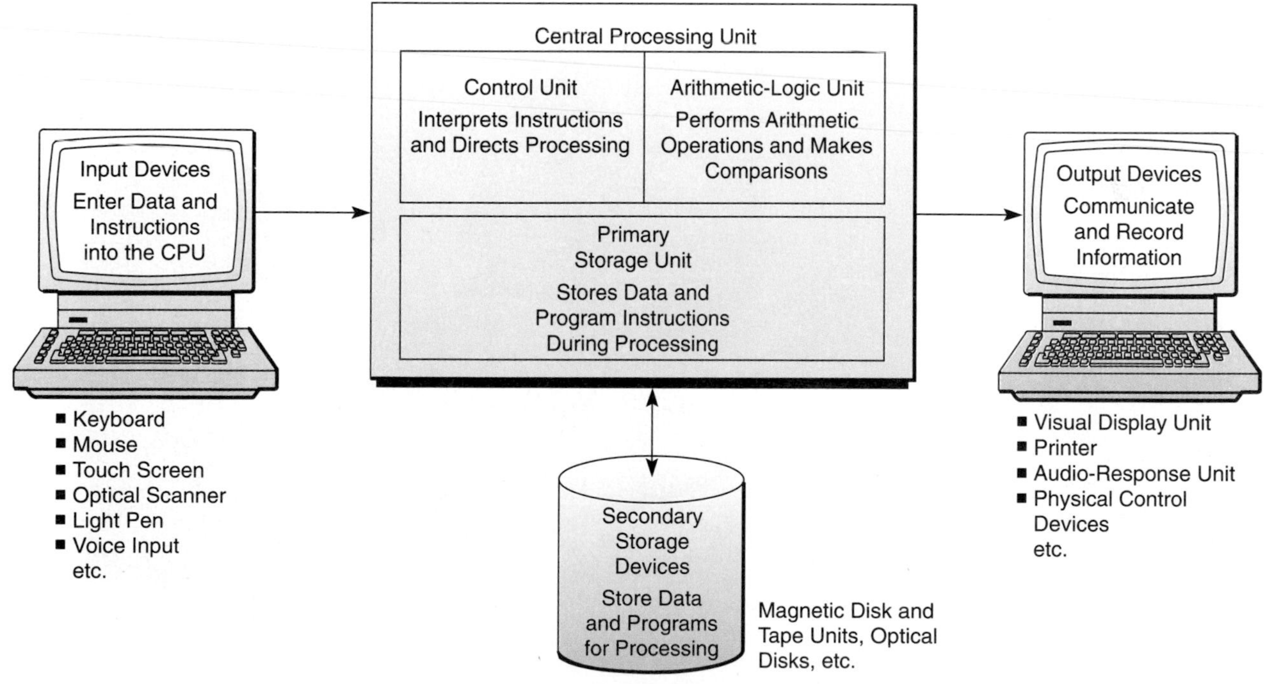

can make *logical* changes from one set of program instructions to another (e.g., overtime pay versus regular pay calculations) based on the results of comparisons made in the ALU during processing.

Multiple Processors

Many current computers, from microcomputers to large mainframes, use multiple processors for their processing functions. Instead of having one CPU with a single control unit and arithmetic-logic unit, the CPUs of these computers contain several types of processing units. Let's briefly look at the major types of such **multiprocessor** designs.

A **support processor** design relies on specialized microprocessors to help the main CPU perform a variety of functions. These microprocessors may be used for input/output, memory management, arithmetic computations, and telecommunications, thus freeing the main processor to do the primary job of executing program instructions. For example, many microcomputers rely on support microprocessors, such as arithmetic coprocessors, video display controllers, and magnetic disk controllers, to reduce the processing on their main microprocessors. A large computer may use support microprocessors called *channels* to control the movement of data between the CPU and input/output devices. Advanced microprocessor designs integrate the functions of several support processors on a single main microprocessor. See Figure 2.3.

A **coupled processor** design uses multiple CPUs or main microprocessors to do *multiprocessing*, that is, execute more than one instruction at the same time. Some configurations provide a *fault-tolerant* capability, since multiple CPUs provide a built-in backup to each other should one of them fail.

Courtesy Intel Corporation.

FIGURE 2.3
The Intel Pentium microprocessor contains over three million transistors and features dual-execution units and high-speed memory caches that give it a top processing speed of over 100 million instructions per second.

A **parallel processor** design can use several instruction processors, or even hundreds or thousands, organized in clusters or networks. For example, some massively parallel designs containing thousands of processors are based on simple models of the human brain called *neural networks*. These systems can therefore execute many instructions at a time in *parallel*. This is a major departure from the traditional design of current computers, called the *Von Neumann design*, which executes instructions *serially* (one at a time). Though difficult to program, many experts consider parallel processor systems the key to providing artificial intelligence capabilities to fifth-generation computers.

RISC Processors

Many advanced technical workstations and other computers rely on a processor design called RISC (reduced instruction set computer). This contrasts with most current computers, which use CISC (complex instruction set computer) processors. RISC processor designs optimize a CPU's processing speed by using a smaller *instruction set*. That is, they use a smaller number of the basic *machine instructions* that a processor is capable of executing. By keeping the instruction set simpler than CISC processors and using more complex software, a RISC processor can reduce the time needed to execute program instructions. Thus, computers that use RISC processors have become popular for computational-intensive applications in engineering and the physical sciences and are moving into general use.

Computer Processing Speeds

How fast are computer systems? Computer operating speeds that were formerly measured in **milliseconds** (thousandths of a second) are now being measured in the **microsecond** (millionth of a second) and **nanosecond** (billionth of a second) range, with **picosecond** (trillionth of a second) speed being attained by some computers. Such speeds seem almost incomprehensible. For example, an average person taking one step each nanosecond would circle the earth about 20 times in one second! See Figure 2.4.

Many microcomputers and minicomputers, and most mainframe computers, operate at nanosecond speeds and can thus process several *million instructions per second* (MIPS). Another measure of processing speed is *megahertz* (MHz), or millions of cycles per second. It is commonly used to rate microprocessors by the speed of their timing circuits. However, megahertz ratings can be misleading indicators of the effective processing speed of microprocessors as measured in MIPS and other measures. That's because processing speed depends on factors such as the size of circuitry paths, or *busses*, that interconnect microprocessor components, the use of high-speed memory *caches*, and the use of specialized microprocessors such as a *math coprocessor* to do arithmetic calculations faster. For example, Intel's 80486 microprocessor, which has a cache memory and math coprocessor built into the chip, is rated at 15 to 40 MIPS, about twice the processing speed of the 80386

FIGURE 2.4
Computer Speed and Storage Capacity Elements

Computer Time Elements	Storage Elements (Approximate Capacities)
Millisecond = One thousandth of a second	Kilobyte = One thousand bytes
Microsecond = One millionth of a second	Megabyte = One million bytes
Nanosecond = One billionth of a second	Gigabyte = One billion bytes
Picosecond = One trillionth of a second	Terabyte = One trillion bytes

microprocessor even when running at similar megahertz speeds. Just for comparison, some technical workstations are rated at over 100 MIPS, while supercomputers have been clocked at more than 1,000 MIPS and perform arithmetic computations in billions of floating point operations per second, or *gigaflops*.

Primary and Secondary Storage

The **primary storage unit** (also called *main memory*) holds data and instructions between processing steps and supplies them to the control unit and arithmetic-logic unit during processing. All data and programs must be placed in memory before they can be used in processing.

The primary storage unit is also used to hold data and program instructions between processing steps and after processing is completed but before output. In modern computers, the primary storage unit consists of microelectronic *semiconductor memory* chips. Most of memory is known as RAM (random access memory). The contents of these memory chips can be instantly changed to store new data. Other, more permanent memory chips are called ROM (read only memory).

Data and programs are also stored in secondary storage devices, such as magnetic disk and tape units, which greatly enlarge the storage capacities of computer systems. Also, since memory circuits typically lose their contents when electric power is turned off, most secondary storage media provide a more permanent type of storage. However, the contents of secondary storage devices cannot be processed without first being brought into the primary storage unit. Thus, external secondary storage devices play a supporting role to the primary storage unit of a computer system. For example, programs and files are typically stored until needed on magnetic floppy disks and hard disks on microcomputer systems, and on large magnetic tape disk and tape units on larger computer systems.

Computer Storage Capacities

Data is processed and stored in a computer system through the presence or absence of electronic or magnetic signals in the computer's circuitry or in the media it uses. This is called a *two-state* or **binary representation** of data, since the computer and the media can exhibit only two possible states or conditions. For example, transistors and other semiconductor circuits are either in a conducting or nonconducting state. Thus, for electronic circuits, the conducting (ON) state could represent the number one, while the nonconducting (OFF) state could represent the number zero.

The smallest element of data is called a **bit**, or binary digit, which can have a value of either zero or one. The capacity of memory chips is usually expressed in terms of bits. A **byte** is a basic grouping of bits that the computer operates as a single unit. It typically consists of eight bits and is used to represent one character of data in most computer coding schemes. Thus, the capacity of a computer's memory and secondary storage devices is usually expressed in terms of bytes.

Storage capacities are frequently measured in **kilobytes** (abbreviated as KB or K) or **megabytes** (abbreviated as MB or M). Although *kilo* means "one thousand" in the metric system, the computer industry uses *K* to represent 1,024 (or 2^{10}) storage positions. Therefore, a memory size of 640K, for example, is really 655,360 storage positions, rather than 640,000 positions. However, such differences are frequently disregarded in order to simplify descriptions of storage capacity. Thus, a megabyte is roughly 1 million bytes of storage, while a **gigabyte** is roughly 1 billion bytes and a **terabyte** represents about 1 trillion bytes. Typically, computer primary storage capacities range from 640 kilobytes to 16 megabytes for microcomputer memories to several gigabytes of memory for large mainframe computer systems. Magnetic disk capacities generally range from 360K bytes to several megabytes for floppy disks, over 200 megabytes for hard disk drives, and over 500 megabytes for an optical disk. Mainframe magnetic disk units supply many gigabytes of online storage. Figure 2.4 summarizes these important storage capacity elements.

Types and Trends in Computers

As an informed business end user, it is important that you recognize several major trends in computer systems. These trends have developed in the past during each major stage, or **generation**, of computers, and they are expected to continue into the future. The first generation of computers began in the early 1950s; the second generation in the late 1950s; the third generation in the mid-1960s; and the fourth generation began in the 1970s and continues to the present. A fifth generation of computers is expected to arrive in the 1990s. Figure 2.5 highlights trends in the characteristics and capabilities of computers. Notice that computers continue to become smaller, faster, more reliable, and less costly to purchase and maintain.

Computer Origins

The modern computer has many origins, some well known, others lost in antiquity. However, the use of machinery to perform arithmetic operations is frequently attributed to Blaise Pascal of France and Gottfried von Leibnitz of Germany for their

FIGURE 2.5
Major trends in computer characteristics and capabilities.

	First Generation	Second Generation	Third Generation	Fourth Generation	Fifth Generation
SIZE (Typical computers)	Room Size Mainframe	Closet Size Mainframe	Desk-Size Minicomputer	Desktop and Laptop Microcomputers	Credit Card-Size Micro?
CIRCUITRY	Vacuum tubes	Transistors	Integrated Semi-conductor Circuits	Large-Scale Integrated (LSI) Semi-Conductor Circuits	Very Large-Scale Integrated (VSLI) Superconductor Circuits?
DENSITY (Circuits per component)	One	Hundreds	Thousands	Hundreds of Thousands	Millions?
SPEED (Instructions/second)	Hundreds	Thousands	Millions	Tens of Millions	Billions?
RELIABILITY (Failure of circuits)	Hours	Days	Weeks	Months	Years?
MEMORY (Capacity in characters)	Thousands	Tens of Thousands	Hundreds of Thousands	Millions	Billions?
COST (Per million instructions)	$10	$1.00	$.10	$.001	$.0001?

Trends in computer characterisitics and capabilities

development of the adding machine and the calculating machine, respectively, in the 17th century. (The programming language **Pascal** is named in honor of Blaise Pascal.) Electromechanical punched card machines for data processing were first developed by Dr. Herman Hollerith of the U.S. Bureau of the Census in the 1880s.

Charles Babbage is generally recognized as the first person to propose the concept of the modern computer. In 1833, this English mathematician outlined in detail his plans for an "analytical engine," a mechanical steam-driven computing machine. However, his ideas were too advanced for the steam-driven technology of his time, and they had to await the development of electronic components over 100 years later. Many of Babbage's ideas were recorded and analyzed by Lady Augusta Ada Byron, Countess of Lovelace, the daughter of Lord Byron, the famous English poet. She is considered by some to be the world's first computer programmer. The programming language **Ada** is named in her honor.

The first working model of an electronic digital computer was built by John Atanasoff of Iowa State University in 1942. The ABC (Atanasoff-Berry Computer) used vacuum tubes instead of electrical relays to carry out its computations. The first operational electronic digital computer, the ENIAC (Electronic Numerical Integrator and Calculator), was developed by John Mauchly and J. P. Eckert of the University of Pennsylvania in 1946. The ENIAC weighed over 30 tons and utilized over 18,000 vacuum tubes. See Figure 2.6.

Computer Generations

First-generation computers (1951–1958) used hundreds or thousands of **vacuum tubes** for their processing and memory circuitry. These computers were quite large and generated enormous amounts of heat; vacuum tubes had to be replaced frequently. Thus, they had large electrical-power, air-conditioning, and maintenance requirements. First-generation computers had main memories of only a few thousand characters and millisecond processing speeds. They used magnetic drums or tape for secondary storage and punched cards or paper tape as input and output media.

Second-generation computers (1959–1963) used **transistors** and other *solid-state, semiconductor* devices which were wired to circuit boards. Transistorized circuits were much smaller and much more reliable, generated little heat, were less expensive, and required less power than vacuum tubes. Tiny *magnetic cores* were used for the computer's memory, or internal storage. Many second-generation computers had main-memory capacities of less than a hundred kilobytes and microsecond processing speeds. Removable *magnetic disk packs* were introduced, and magnetic tape emerged as the major input, output, and secondary storage medium for large computer installations.

Third-generation computers (1964–1979) began using **integrated circuits**, in which thousands of transistors and other circuit elements are etched on tiny chips of silicon. Main memory capacities of several megabytes and processing speeds of millions of instructions per second were achieved, and telecommunications capabilities became common. This made possible the widespread use of *operating system* programs that automated and supervised the activities of many types of peripheral devices and the processing of several programs at the same time, sometimes from networks of users at remote terminals. Integrated circuit technology also made possible the development and widespread use of small computers called **minicomputers** in the third computer generation.

Fourth-generation computers (1979 to the present) use LSI (large-scale integration) and VSLI (very large-scale integration) technologies which cram hun-

FIGURE 2.6
Computer pioneers.

Charles Babbage: He first proposed the concept of a computer.

Augusta Ada Byron: Considered to be the first computer programmer.

Blaise Pascal: Developer of the first adding machine.

The ENIAC computer. The first operational general-purpose electronic digital computer. Also shown is one of its inventors, J. P. Eckert.

dreds of thousands or millions of transistors and other circuit elements on each chip. Main memory capacities ranging from a few megabytes to several gigabytes can be achieved by the memory chips that replaced magnetic core memories. LSI and VLSI technologies also allowed the development of **microprocessors**, in which all of the circuits of a CPU are contained on a single chip with processing speeds of millions of instructions per second. **Microcomputers**, which use microprocessor CPU's and a variety of peripheral devices and easy-to-use software packages to form small personal computer systems (PCs) or networks of linked PCs, are a hallmark of the fourth generation of computing.

Computer Categories

Today's computer systems display striking differences as well as basic similarities. Differing end user needs and technological discoveries have resulted in the development of several major categories of computer systems with a variety of characteristics and capabilities. Thus, computer systems are typically classified as *microcomputers*, *minicomputers*, and *mainframe computers*. However, as Figure 2.7 illustrates, these are not precise classifications. For example, variations of these categories include *superminicomputers*; small, medium, and large mainframe computers; and *supercomputers*. Also, a variety of application categories, which describe major uses for various types of computers, are common. Examples are host computers, network servers, and technical workstations.

Such categories are attempts to describe the relative computing power provided by different *computing platforms*, or types of computers. Computers may differ in their processing speed and memory capacity, as well as in the number and capabilities of peripheral devices for input, output, and secondary storage they can support. However, you will find microcomputers that are more powerful than some minicomputers, and minicomputers that are more powerful than some mainframe computers. Thus, these computer classifications do overlap each other, as Figure 2.7 illustrates. In addition, experts continue to predict the merging or disappearance of several computer categories. For example, they argue that minicomputers and many mainframe computers are being made obsolete by the power and versatility of networks of microcomputer systems.

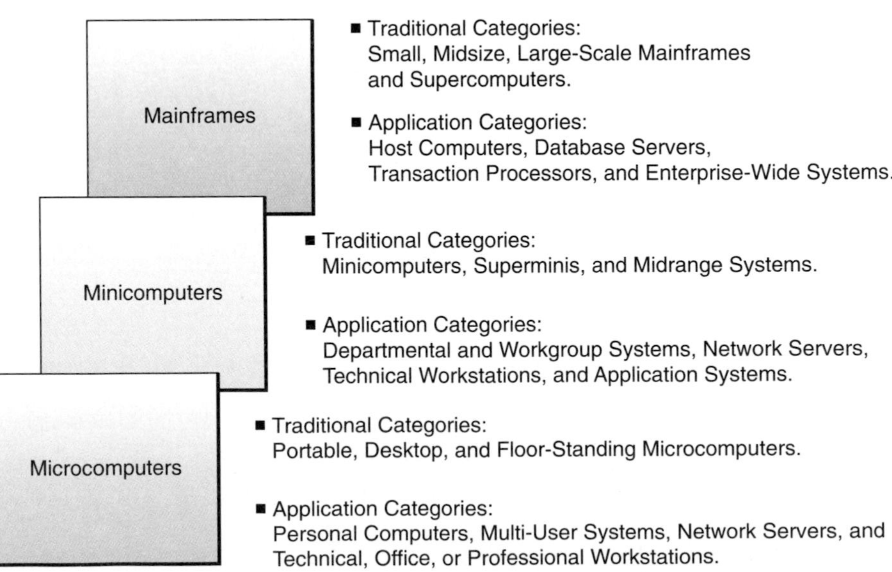

Mainframes
■ Traditional Categories:
Small, Midsize, Large-Scale Mainframes and Supercomputers.
■ Application Categories:
Host Computers, Database Servers, Transaction Processors, and Enterprise-Wide Systems.
Minicomputers
■ Traditional Categories:
Minicomputers, Superminis, and Midrange Systems.
■ Application Categories:
Departmental and Workgroup Systems, Network Servers, Technical Workstations, and Application Systems.
Microcomputers
■ Traditional Categories:
Portable, Desktop, and Floor-Standing Microcomputers.
■ Application Categories:
Personal Computers, Multi-User Systems, Network Servers, and Technical, Office, or Professional Workstations.

FIGURE 2.7
Computer system classifications. Note the overlap among the traditional and application categories of the three major classifications of computers.

Computer manufacturers typically produce *families*, or product lines, of computers. So computer systems can have a variety of models with different processing speeds, memory capacities, and other capabilities. This allows manufacturers to provide a range of choices to customers to accommodate their information processing needs. Most models in a family are compatible; that is, programs written for one model can usually be run on other models of the same family with little or no change. This allows customers to move up (*migrate*) to larger models of the same computer product line as their needs grow.

Microcomputer Systems

Microcomputers are the smallest but most important category of computer systems for end users. A microcomputer is typically referred to as a *personal computer*, or PC. However, microcomputers have become much more than small computers used by individual persons. Their computing power now exceeds that of the mainframes of previous computer generations at a fraction of their cost. For this reason, they have become powerful *professional workstations* for use by end users in businesses and other organizations.

Microcomputers come in a variety of sizes and shapes for a variety of purposes, as Figure 2.8 illustrates. Microcomputers categorized by size include *handheld, notebook, laptop, portable, desktop*, and *floor-standing* microcomputers. Or, based on their use, they include *home, personal, professional, workstation*, and *multiuser* computers and special-purpose categories such as telecommunications *network servers*. However, the classifications of *desktop* versus *portable* and *single-user* versus *multiuser* are the most widely used distinctions. That is because most microcomputers are designed either to fit on top of an office desk, transforming it into an end user workstation, or to be conveniently carried by end users, such as by salespersons or consultants who do a lot of traveling.

Most microcomputers are single-user computers designed to support the work activities of a variety of end users. However, also available are powerful **workstation computers** (*technical workstations*) that support applications with heavy mathematical computing and graphics display demands such as computer-aided design (CAD) in engineering, or investment and portfolio analysis in the securities industry. *Multiuser* models, which support computing by several end users at multiple terminals, are also available, as are *network servers* that coordinate processing in the local area networks (LANs) of microcomputers and other devices.

A Microcomputer System

Remember that a microcomputer is a computer system which uses a variety of devices to perform the systems function of input, processing, output, storage, and control. Typically, a microcomputer consists of a main microprocessor (a CPU on a chip); several support microprocessors and associated control, primary storage, and input/output circuitry located on one or more circuit boards; and a variety of input/output and secondary storage devices. Figure 2.9 shows the microprocessors and storage devices inside a microcomputer's main system unit.

Input and Output

A keyboard is the most widely used input device, followed by the electronic mouse and other devices such as touch screens, pens, optical scanners, and voice input devices. Video display monitors and printers are the most widely used output devices in microcomputer systems. Other devices, such as audio speakers and graphics plotters, are also used.

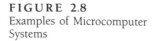

FIGURE 2.8
Examples of Microcomputer Systems

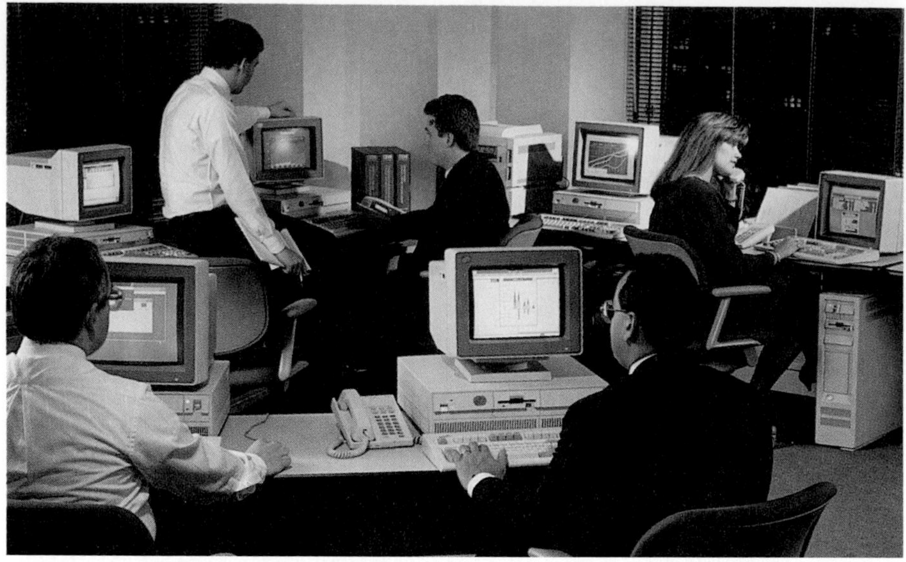

a A local area network of microcomputer systems.
Courtesy of IBM Corporation.

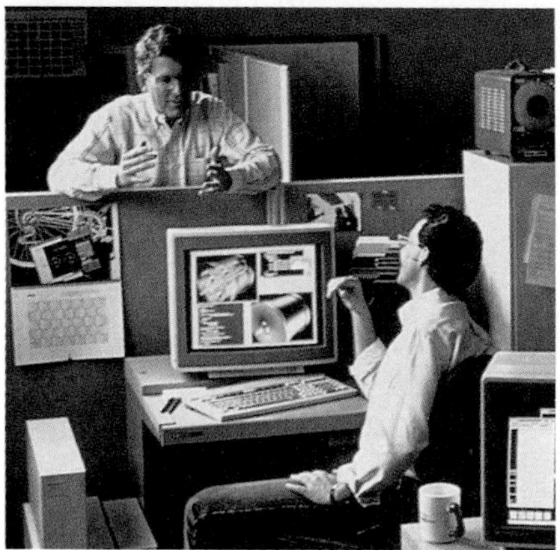

b The microcomputer as a technical workstation.
Courtesy of Hewlett Packard.

c The microcomputer as a professional workstation.
Courtesy of IBM Corporation.

Processing and Control

In most microcomputers, a main system unit contains the main microprocessor, subsidiary processors, and other devices located on circuit boards. These serve as the central processing unit and as support processors and control devices for the microcomputer system. The most popular main microprocessors for microcomputers are the Intel 8088, 80286, 80386, and 80486, used by IBM and IBM-compatible microcomputers, and the Motorola 68000, 68020, 68030, and 68040, used by Apple Macintosh microcomputers.

Storage

Primary storage is provided by semiconductor memory chips on the circuit boards in the main system unit. Primary storage capacities typically range from 256 kilobytes to 16 megabytes of semiconductor storage, though larger capacities are possible. Secondary storage is provided by floppy disk drives, hard disk drives, and

Courtesy of IBM Corporation.

FIGURE 2.9
The main system unit of a microcomputer with its major components identified.

other devices, all of which can be either part of the main system unit or externally connected. They provide from several hundred kilobytes to several hundred megabytes of online storage.

Microcomputer Applications

Microcomputers are used for many information processing jobs by end users. These end user computing applications are directly related to the wide variety of software packages available for microcomputers. (We will discuss such software in Chapter 3.) The most popular types of microcomputer applications include the following:

- **Word processing.** Automated, electronic typing and editing. Microcomputers are used as word processors to prepare memos, letters, reports, and other documents with the help of word processing and other writing support software. Professional-looking publications can also be produced with the use of *desktop publishing* software.
- **Decision support.** Computerized worksheet analysis and modeling. Electronic spreadsheet software allows end users to build spreadsheet models of business situations. This computerizes business planning, budgeting, and analysis of business performance, and provides interactive support for decision making.
- **Database management.** Electronic record-keeping, interrogation, and report generation. File and database management software allow end users to build and maintain files and databases of business records. End users can then display information they need electronically or produce a variety of analytical reports from the data in the database.
- **Graphics.** Generation of charts and other graphic images. Graphics software packages, with laser printers, optical scanners, and other devices, allow end users to produce a variety of charts and graphics images. These visually enhance both the analysis and the presentation of information in reports and group presentations.
- **Communications.** Telecommunications with other end users, computers, and data banks. Telecommunications networks, software packages, and hardware allow end users to access the databases of their organization and the data banks of external information services and to communicate with other end users. Microcomputer workstations can be connected to corporate mainframes and databases or be interconnected in *local area networks* which support end user work group activities.

- **Application development.** Computer-supported systems and software development. A variety of programming languages and computer-aided software engineering (CASE) tools enhance and automate many parts of the development process for information systems.
- **Engineering.** Computer-aided design and analysis. Supermicrocomputers are being used as powerful *technical workstations* for computer-aided design. This supports the analysis and design processes of computer-aided engineering (CAE) and other applications that require significant computational power and graphics capabilities.
- **Personal and home use.** Entertainment, home management, personal finance, education, and so on. Microcomputers use a variety of video game, educational, and home management software packages to entertain, educate, and support personal and family financial management.

Minicomputer Systems

Minicomputers are *midrange systems* that are larger and more powerful than most microcomputers but are smaller and less powerful than most large mainframe computer systems. However, this is not a precise distinction. High-end models of microcomputer systems (supermicros) are more powerful than some minicomputers, while high-end models of minicomputers (superminis) are more powerful than some smaller models of mainframe computers. Consequently, a controversy exists on the prospects of minicomputers remaining as a separate computer category, since microcomputers and mainframes provide a wide range of computer models with similar capabilities.

Minicomputers cost less to buy and maintain than mainframe computers. Most minicomputers can function in ordinary operating environments, as they do not need special air conditioning or electrical wiring. In addition, since they are comparatively easy to operate, the smaller models of minicomputers do not need a staff of data processing professionals, but can rely on properly trained regular employees. Therefore, many organizations continue to use minicomputer systems. See Figure 2.10.

FIGURE 2.10
In the foreground is one of the smaller models of the AS/400 series of minicomputers or midrange computers from IBM.

Sygma Photo News

Applications

Minicomputers are being used for a large number of business and scientific applications. They first became popular in scientific research, instrumentation systems, engineering analysis, and industrial process monitoring and control. Minicomputers can easily handle such uses because these applications are narrow in scope and do not demand the processing versatility of mainframe systems. Thus, minicomputers serve as industrial process-control and manufacturing plant computers, and they play a major role in computer-aided manufacturing (CAM). They can also take the form of powerful *technical workstations* for computer-aided design applications. Minicomputers are being used as *front-end* computers to help mainframe computers control data communications networks and large numbers of data entry terminals.

Minicomputers have also become popular as departmental or office computers. They are being used for departmental computing assignments in distributed processing networks. They can also act as *network servers* to help control local area networks that tie together the microcomputer workstations, data entry terminals, and other computer devices in departments, offices, and other work groups. In addition, some larger minicomputers are used because they can provide more processing power and online storage, and support more users at the same time than networked microcomputers.

Mainframe Computer Systems

Mainframe computers are large, powerful computers that are physically larger than micros and minis and usually have one or more central processors with faster instruction processing speeds. For example, they may be able to process over 200 million instructions per second. Mainframes have large primary storage capacities. For example, their main memory capacity can range from about 32 megabytes to several gigabytes of storage. Many mainframe models have the ability to service hundreds of users at once. For example, a large mainframe can process hundreds of different programs and handle hundreds of different peripheral devices (terminals, disk and tape drives, printers, etc.) for hundreds of different users at the same time. See Figure 2.11.

Applications

Mainframe computers are designed to handle the information processing needs of organizations with many employees and customers or with complex computational problems. Small and medium sizes of mainframe computers can handle the process-

FIGURE 2.11
An IBM ES/9000 large mainframe computer system.

ing chores of smaller organizations or of the regional divisions of larger organizations. They can handle the processing of thousands of customer inquiries, employee paychecks, student registrations, sales transactions, and inventory changes, to give a few examples. Mainframe computers can also handle large numbers of users needing simultaneous access to the centralized databases and libraries of application programs of *time-sharing* networks.

Large mainframe computer systems are used by major corporations and government agencies, which have enormous and complex data processing assignments. For example, large computers are necessary for organizations processing millions of transactions each day, such as major national banks and the national stock exchanges. Large mainframes can handle the great volume of complex calculations involved in scientific and engineering analyses and simulations of complex design projects, such as the designing of aircraft and spacecraft. A large computer can also act as a host computer for distributed processing networks that include many smaller computers. For these reasons, large mainframe computers are used in the national and international computing networks of such major corporations as airlines, banks, and oil companies.

Supercomputer Systems

The term **supercomputer** has been coined to describe a category of extremely powerful mainframe computer systems specifically designed for high-speed numeric computation. A small number of large supercomputers are built each year for government research agencies, military defense systems, national weather forecasting agencies, large time-sharing networks, and major corporations.

The leading maker of supercomputers is Cray Research, followed by NEC, Fugitsu, and a few others. These models can process hundreds of millions of instructions per second. Expressed another way, they can perform arithmetic calculations at a speed of billions of floating-point operations per second (gigaflops). *Teraflop* (one trillion floating point operations per second) supercomputers using a *massively parallel* design are expected to appear in the 1990s.

Purchase prices for large supercomputers are in the $5 million to $50 million range. However, the use of parallel processing designs of interconnected microprocessors has spawned a breed of *minisupercomputers* with prices below $1 million. Thus, supercomputers continue to advance the state of the art for the entire computer industry.

Networked Computer Systems

Solitary computer systems are becoming a rarity in corporate computing. From the smallest microcomputer to the largest mainframe, computers are being *networked*, or interconnected by telecommunications links with other computer systems. This distribution of computer power throughout an organization is called *distributed processing*. It frequently takes the form of a *client/server* approach, with networks of end user microcomputers (*clients*) and network servers tied together, sometimes with minicomputers or mainframes acting as *superservers*. Networked computer systems allow end users to communicate electronically and share the use of hardware, software, and data resources. For example, end users in an office *local area network* of microcomputers can share the use of software packages, laser printers, and work group databases.

So, many computer systems consist of peripheral devices interconnected by communications links to one or more central processing units. Thus, networked computing depends on telecommunications. **Telecommunications**, or, more narrowly, *data communications*, is the use of networks of interconnected computers and peripheral devices to process and exchange data and information. Telecommunications networks use a variety of telecommunications media, hardware, and software to accomplish and control communications among computers and peripheral devices. For example, microcomputers rely on *modems* to convert data from digital to analog form and back, while *network operating system* programs control resource sharing and communications flow among computers and peripherals in a local area network. We will discuss telecommunications further in Chapter 4.

Networks of small computers have become a major alternative to the use of larger computer systems, as many organizations *downsize* their computing platforms. For example, a network of several minicomputers may replace a large mainframe computer system. More commonly, networks of microcomputers are replacing both minicomputers and mainframes in many organizations. Networked microcomputers have proven to be easier to install, use, and maintain, and they provide a more efficient, flexible, lower-cost alternative to large computer systems for many applications. See Figure 2.12.

Applications

Networked microcomputer systems are being used for jobs formerly given to large minicomputer or mainframe systems. For example, a local area network of microcomputers can replace the use of groups of end user terminals connected to a minicomputer or mainframe. Many LANs can easily handle the sharing of computing power, software, and databases that is required in such *time-sharing* and resource-sharing applications. Networked computers also support *work group computing*. For example, end users in a work group can use their networked computers to communicate electronically and share data as they work together on joint projects. Finally, networked microcomputers are even being used for *transaction processing* applications. For example, some organizations are using networks of microcomputers to process thousands of daily credit card purchases, money transfers, credit checks, customer account inquiries, and other business transactions.

Courtesy of IBM Corporation.

FIGURE 2.12
Networked microcomputers are replacing minicomputers and mainframes in many organizations.

REAL WORLD CASE

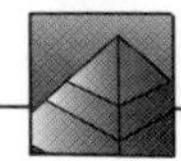

Associated Grocers: Downsizing Computers Keeps Costs Down

Associated Grocers, Inc., is a $1.2 billion supermarket supply cooperative. In an industry known for its paper-thin profit margins, the drive to keep information systems costs down has led to downsizing the computer systems used by the Seattle, Washington-based cooperative. Associated Grocers supplies over 350 supermarkets in Oregon, Washington, Alaska, and Hawaii. The firm is in the middle of a five-year effort to downsize its computing platforms, says Richard Lester, vice president of information services. "Cost is a big part of it," Lester said. "But more than anything else, it's the flexibility. Downsizing systems changes the cost structure dramatically. We've got to find ways to make better use of computing to take costs out of the pipeline."

The cost of information systems services at Associated Grocers is just under 1 percent of its total annual revenue, but Lester would like to halve that percentage. He plans to re-engineer many of the firm's transaction processing systems, eventually removing the mainframes that power them. Lower upfront hardware costs, combined with much lower monthly software maintenance costs for small microcomputer servers than for large mainframes, will have a big impact on the bottom line. At the same time, Associated Grocers expects to gain more productivity in its business by adding new functions to the servers, such as electronic exchange of data with suppliers to reduce warehousing of goods.

Associated Grocers has stopped using one of its two Hitachi Data Systems mainframe computers. "It is there in a standby situation," IS project manager David Okimura said. "It will be fired up if our production system goes down." So mainframe applications are being rewritten for smaller systems, which will act as network application servers. So far, these include nine IBM RISC System/6000 workstation computers, and two Hewlett-Packard 9000 minicomputers, most of them stored under desks or in computer room cabinets.

A multilevel telecommunication network links the mainframes, application servers, and hundreds of PCs in the stores served by Associated Grocers. Lester sketched out a three-tier architecture based on a *presentation layer* of microcomputer applications, a *functional layer* of applications running on network servers, and a *data layer* of databases stored in servers and in the mainframe. The built-in flexibility of this "plug and play" network will prove itself as Associated Grocers' business changes, Lester said. Plug-and-play systems and quick application development will allow the firm to adapt to changing business conditions. A new cross-dock application, for example, will allow groceries to be handed across the loading dock—going directly from the supplier's truck to the store's truck, bypassing Associated Grocers' warehouses. That will help the company reduce costs as it competes with larger national rivals such as Minneapolis-based Super Valu Stores, Inc.

Some of Associated Grocers' open systems applications are ready to go into production. For example, a new post-billing system, which will separate the billing process from grocery-handling online transaction systems, is set to roll out to the chain's stores this spring. A new warehouse inventory system went into production one year ago, and a number of packaged accounting applications were purchased to handle the cooperative's need for accounting systems.

CASE STUDY QUESTIONS

1. How did Associated Grocers downsize its computing systems?
2. Why would their three-tier network of computers provide a built-in flexibility?
3. What are the benefits and limitations to Associated Grocers of moving to a three-tier computing platform?

Source: Adapted from Jean S. Bozeman, "Grocer Buys into Open System." *Computerworld*, March 22, 1993, pp. 57, 59. Used with permission.

SECTION II

Computer Peripherals: Input, Output, and Storage Devices

Peripherals is the generic name given to all input/output equipment and secondary storage devices that depend on direct connections or telecommunications links to the central processing unit of a computer system. Thus, all peripherals are **online** devices; that is, they are separate from, but can be electronically connected to and controlled by, a CPU. (This is the opposite of **offline** devices, which are separate from and not under the control of the CPU.) The major types of peripherals and media that can be part of a computer system are discussed in this section.

Input/Output Hardware Trends

There are many hardware devices for input and output at the *user interface* between computer systems and end users. Figure 2.13 shows you the major trends in input/output media and methods that have developed over four generations of computers and are expected to continue into a future fifth generation.

Figure 2.13 emphasizes that there is a major trend toward the increased use of a variety of **direct input/output devices** to provide a more natural user interface. More and more, data and instructions are entered into a computer system directly, through input devices such as keyboards, electronic mice, pens, touch screens, and optical scanning wands. These direct input/output devices drastically reduce the need for paper source documents and their conversion to machine-readable media. Direct output of information through video displays of text and graphics and voice response devices is increasingly becoming the dominant form of output for end users.

Computer Terminal Trends

The most common user interface method still involves a keyboard for entry of data and a video display screen for output to users. **Computer terminals** of various types are widely used for such input and output. Technically, any input/output device connected by telecommunications links to a computer is called a terminal. However, most terminals use a keyboard for input and a TV-like screen for visual output, and are called **visual** (or video) **display terminals** (VDTs) or, more popularly, CRT

FIGURE 2.13
Input/output hardware trends. Note the trend toward direct input and output media and methods to provide a more natural user interface.

	First Generation	Second Generation	Third Generation	Fourth Generation	Fifth Generation?
INPUT MEDIA/ METHOD	Punched Cards Paper Tape	Punched Cards	Key to Tape/Disk	Keyboard Data Entry Direct Input Devices Optical Scanning	Speech Input Tactile Input
TREND: Towards Direct Input Devices that Are Easy to Use.					
OUTPUT MEDIA/ METHOD	Punched Cards Printed Reports	Punched Cards Printed Reports	Printed Reports Video Displays	Video Displays Audio Responses Printed Reports	Graphics Displays Voice Responses
TREND: Towards Direct Output Devices that Communicate Quickly and Clearly.					

(cathode ray tube) terminals. They allow keyed-in data to be displayed and edited before entry into a computer system.

There is a trend away from *dumb terminals*, which have no processing capabilities themselves, toward **intelligent terminals**, which have their own microprocessors and memory circuits. Many intelligent terminals are really microcomputers used as telecommunications terminals to larger computers. Therefore, they can perform data entry and other information processing tasks independently. Another trend is the widespread use of **transaction terminals** in banks, retail stores, factories, and other work sites. Examples are automated teller machines (ATMs), factory transaction recorders, and retail point-of-sale (POS) terminals. These terminals use a variety of input/output methods to capture data from end users during a transaction and transmit it over telecommunications networks to a computer system for processing.

Pointing Devices

Keyboards are the most widely used devices for entering data and text into computer systems. However, **pointing devices** are a better alternative for issuing commands, making choices, and responding to prompts displayed on your video screen. For example, pointing devices such as electronic mice and trackballs allow you to easily choose from menu selections and icon displays using *point-and-click* or *point-and-drag* methods. **Icons** are small figures that look like familiar devices, such as a file folder (for accessing a file), a wastebasket (for deleting a file), a calculator (for switching to a calculator mode), and so on. Using icons helps simplify computer use since they are easier to use with pointing devices than menus and other text-based displays. See Figure 2.14.

The **electronic mouse** is a device used to move the cursor on the screen, as well as to issue commands and make icon and menu selections. Some mice contain a roller ball, which moves the cursor in the direction the ball is rolled. Others use an optical sensing technology that recognizes points on a special pad. By moving the mouse on a desktop or pad, an end user can move the cursor onto an icon displayed on the screen. Pressing a button on the mouse begins the activity represented by the icon selected.

The **joystick** and the **trackball** are other devices used to move the cursor on the display screen. A joystick looks like a small gear shift level set in a box. Joysticks are widely used for computer-assisted design and are popular control devices for

FIGURE 2.14
The keyboard and the mouse are the most widely used computer input devices.

Courtesy of Digital Equipment Corporation.

video games. A trackball is a stationary device related to the mouse. An end user turns a roller ball with only its top exposed outside its case to move the cursor on the screen. Trackballs are thus easier to use than a mouse for many end users and are built in to some portable microcomputer keyboards.

Touch-sensitive screens are devices that allow you to use a computer by touching the surface of its video display screen. Such screens emit a grid of infrared beams, sound waves, or a slight electric current, which is broken when the screen is touched. The computer senses the point in the grid where the break occurs and responds with an appropriate action. For example, you could indicate your selection on a menu display by just touching the screen next to that menu item.

Pen-based Computing

End users can write or draw directly on a video screen or on other surfaces using a variety of penlike devices. One example is the **light pen**. This pen-shaped device uses photoelectric circuitry to enter data into the computer through a video screen. A user can write on the video display because the light-sensitive pen enables the computer to calculate the coordinates of the points on the screen touched by the light pen. A **graphics tablet** is a form of *digitizer* which allows you to draw or write on its pressure-sensitive surface with a pen-shaped *stylus*. Your handwriting or drawing is digitized by the computer, accepted as input, and displayed on its video screen.

Light pen and graphics pad technologies are being used in a new generation of **pen-based computers** that recognize handwriting. These *notebook* PCs are portable, tablet-style microcomputers that contain software that recognizes and digitizes handwriting, handprinting, and hand drawing. They have a pressure-sensitive layer like a graphics pad under their slatelike liquid crystal display (LCD) screen. So instead of writing on a paper form fastened to a clipboard, inspectors, field engineers, and other mobile workers can use a pen to enter handwritten data directly into a computer. See Figure 2.15.

Courtesy of NCR Corporation.

FIGURE 2.15
This pen-based notebook PC recognizes handwriting on its display screen.

Video Input/Output

Video images can serve as input as well as output. For example, input from a TV receiver, camcorder, or VCR can be digitized and compressed for storage on magnetic or optical disks. Digitizing *snapshot* images is not expensive, but capture of *full motion* video images using technologies like *digital video interactive* (DVI) can be costly. DVI usually requires a high-powered PC with additional software, circuit boards, memory, and magnetic or optical disk capacity. Also expensive is a *multimedia development* capability which allows you to merge text, graphics, sound, and TV images for computer-generated video presentations.

Video Output

Video displays are the most common type of computer output. Most video displays use a **cathode ray tube** technology similar to the picture tubes used in home TV sets. Usually, the clarity of the display and the support of monochrome or color displays depend on the type of video monitor used and the graphics circuit board, or *video adapter*, installed in the microcomputer. These can provide a variety of graphics modes of increasing capability. A high level of clarity is especially important to support the more complex graphical displays of many current software packages. These packages provide a *graphical user interface* (GUI), which uses icons and a variety of screen images and typically splits the screen into multiple *window* displays.

Liquid crystal displays, such as those used in electronic calculators and watches, are also being used to display computer output. Their biggest use is to provide a visual display capability for portable microcomputers and terminals. Advances in technology have improved the clarity of such displays, which were formerly hard to see in bright sunlight and artificial light. LCD displays need significantly less electric current and provide a thin, flat display. Full-color LCD displays are now available. See Figure 2.16.

Plasma display devices have replaced CRT devices in a limited number of applications where a flat display is needed. Plasma displays are generated by electrically charged particles of gas (plasma) trapped between glass plates. Plasma display units are significantly more expensive than CRT and LCD units. However, they use less power, provide faster display speeds, and produce clearer displays that are easier to see from any angle and in any lighting conditions.

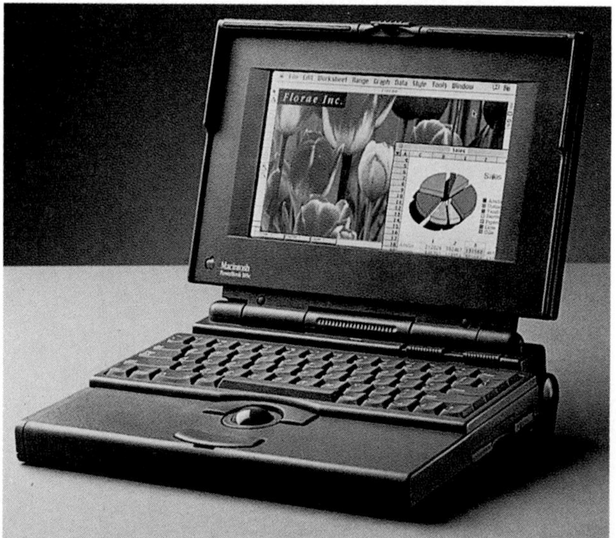

FIGURE 2.16
This laptop microcomputer features a color LCD display and built-in trackball.

John Greenleigh/Courtesy of Apple Computer, Inc.

Printed Output

After video displays, printed output is the most common form of visual output for the user interface. Most computer systems use **printers** to produce permanent (hard copy) output in human-readable form. End users need printed output if they want copies of output to take away from the computer and to share with others. Hard copy output is also frequently needed for legal documentation. Thus, computers can usually produce printed reports and documents, such as sales invoices, payroll checks, and bank statements, as well as hard copy of graphics displays. **Plotters**, which draw graphics displays on paper, also produce printed paper output.

Many printers are **impact printers**. They form characters and other images on paper through the impact of a printing mechanism that presses a printing element (such as a print wheel or cylinder) and an inked ribbon or roller against the face of a sheet of paper. Multiple copies can be produced because the impact of the printing mechanism can transmit an image onto several layers of multiple copy forms. Popular impact printers for microcomputer systems use a **dot matrix** printing element, which consists of short print wires that form a character as a grouping or matrix of dots. Speeds of several hundred characters per second are attainable. Mainframe computer systems typically use high-speed line printers, which can print up to several thousand lines per minute. A moving metal chain or cylinder of characters is used as the printing element.

Nonimpact printers are quieter than impact printers, since the sound of a printing element being struck is eliminated. However, they do not produce multiple copies like impact printers. **Laser printers** and **ink jet printers** are examples of popular nonimpact printing methods for producing high-quality printed output. Laser printers allow companies to produce their own business forms, as well as formal reports and manuals. Such *desktop publishing* applications are discussed in Chapter 7. Laser printers for microcomputer systems have speeds from less than 5 to over 200 pages per minute. See Figure 2.17.

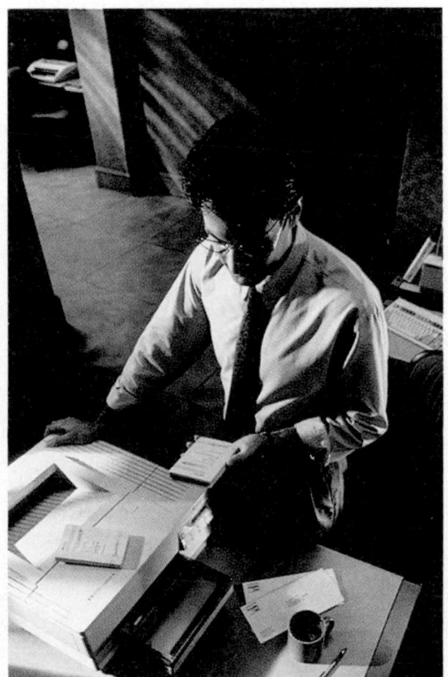

Courtesy of Hewlett Packard.

FIGURE 2.17
A laser printer produces high-quality printed output.

Voice Recognition and Response

Voice recognition and *voice response* promise to be the easiest method of providing a user interface for data entry and conversational computing, since speech is the easiest, most natural means of human communication. Voice input and output of data has now become technologically and economically feasible for a variety of applications. For example, a voice recognition capability can be added to a microcomputer by acquiring a voice recognition circuit board and software for several thousand dollars. The circuit board contains voice recognition microprocessors and other circuitry, including a vocabulary in ROM ranging from 1,000 to 10,000 words.

Voice recognition systems analyze and classify speech or vocal tract patterns and convert them into digital codes for entry into a computer system. Most voice recognition systems require "training" the computer to recognize a limited vocabulary of standard words for each user. Operators train the system to recognize their voices by repeating each word in the vocabulary about 10 times. Trained systems regularly achieve a 99 percent plus word recognition rate. Speaker-independent voice recognition systems, which allow a computer to understand a voice it has never heard before, are used in a limited number of applications.

Voice recognition devices are used in work situations where operators need to perform data entry without using their hands to key in data or instructions, or where it would provide faster and more accurate input. For example, voice recognition systems are being used by manufacturers for the inspection, inventory, and quality control of a variety of products, and by airlines and parcel delivery companies for voice-directed sorting of baggage and parcels. Voice recognition is also available for some microcomputer software packages for voice input of data and commands. However, voice input is still too slow and error prone for most word processing applications. See Figure 2.18.

Voice response devices range from mainframe *audio-response* units to *voice-messaging* minicomputers to *speech synthesizer* microprocessors. Speech microprocessors can be found in toys, calculators, appliances, automobiles, and a variety of other consumer, commercial, and industrial products.

Fredrik D. Bodin/Offshoot.

FIGURE 2.18
Using voice recognition for inventory control.

Voice-messaging minicomputer and mainframe audio response units use voice-response software to verbally guide an operator through the steps of a task in many kinds of activities. They may also allow computers to respond to verbal and touch-tone input over the telephone. Examples of applications include computerized telephone call switching, telemarketing surveys, bank pay-by-phone bill-paying services, stock quotations services, university registration systems, and customer credit and account balance inquiries.

Optical and Magnetic Recognition

Optical Scanning

Optical scanning devices read text or graphics and convert them into digital input for a computer. They include **optical character recognition** (OCR) equipment that can read special-purpose characters and codes. Optical scanning of pages of text and graphics is especially popular in desktop publishing applications. Thus, optical scanning provides a method of direct input of data from source documents into a computer system.

There are many types of optical readers, but they all employ photoelectric devices to scan the characters being read. Reflected light patterns of the data are converted into electronic impulses, which are then accepted as input into the computer system. Devices can currently read many types of printing and graphics. Progress is continually being made in improving the reading ability of scanning equipment. See Figure 2.19.

OCR-based optical scanning systems are used extensively in the credit card billing operations of credit card companies, banks, and oil companies. They are also used to process utility bills, insurance premiums, airline tickets, and cash register machine tapes. OCR scanners are used to automatically sort mail, score tests, and process a wide variety of forms in business and government.

Optical scanning devices such as hand-held **wands** are used to read data on merchandise tags and other media. This frequently involves reading *bar coding*, a

Lee F. Snyder/Photo Researchers, Inc.

FIGURE 2.19
Using an optical scanning wand to read bar coding of product data on merchandise.

code that utilizes bars to represent characters. Thus, Universal Product Code (UPC) bar coding on packages of food items and other products has become commonplace. For example, UPC bar coding is read by the automated checkout scanners found in many supermarkets. Supermarket scanners emit laser beams, which are reflected off a UPC bar code. The reflected image is converted to electronic impulses, which are sent to the in-store minicomputer, where they are matched with pricing information. Pricing information is returned to the terminal, visually displayed, and printed on a receipt.

Magnetic Data Entry

The computer systems of the banking industry can magnetically read checks and deposit slips using **magnetic ink character recognition** (MICR) technology. Computers can thus sort, tabulate, and post checks to the proper checking accounts. Such processing is possible because the identification numbers of the bank and the customer's account are preprinted on the bottom of the checks with an iron oxide–based ink. The first bank receiving a check after it has been written must encode the amount of the check in magnetic ink on the check's lower right-hand corner. The MICR system uses 14 characters (the 10 decimal digits and 4 special symbols) of a standardized design.

MICR characters can be either preprinted on documents or encoded on documents using a keyboard-operated machine called a *proof-inscriber*. Equipment known as an MICR *reader-sorter* reads a check by first magnetizing the magnetic ink characters and then sensing the signal induced by each character as it passes a reading head. In this way, data are electronically captured by the computer system. The check is then sorted by directing it into one of the pockets of the reader-sorter. Reader-sorters can read over 2,400 checks per minute, with a data transfer rate of over 3,000 characters per second. A few large banks have begun replacing MICR technology with optical scanning systems.

Another familiar form of magnetic data entry is the **magnetic stripe** technology that helps computers read credit cards. The dark magnetic stripe on the back of credit and debit cards is the same iron oxide coating as on magnetic tape. Customer account numbers can be recorded on the stripe so it can be read by bank ATMs, credit card authorization terminals, and other *magnetic stripe readers*.

Storage Trends and Trade-Offs

Data and information need to be stored after input, during processing, and before output. Even today, many organizations still rely on paper documents stored in filing cabinets as a major form of storage media. However, computer-based information systems rely primarily on the memory circuits and secondary storage devices of computer systems to accomplish the storage function. Figure 2.20 illustrates major trends in primary and secondary storage methods. Continued developments in very large scale integration, which packs millions of electronic circuit elements on tiny semiconductor memory chips, are responsible for a significant increase in the main-memory capacity of computers. Secondary storage capacities are also expected to escalate into the billions and trillions of characters, due primarily to use of optical media.

There are many types of storage media and devices. Figure 2.21 illustrates the speed, capacity, and cost relationships of several alternative primary and secondary storage media. Note the cost/speed/capacity trade-offs as one moves from semiconductor memories to magnetic media, such as magnetic disks and tapes, to optical disks. High-speed storage media cost more per byte and provide lower capacities.

FIGURE 2.20
Major trends in primary and secondary storage methods.

	First Generation	Second Generation	Third Generation	Fourth Generation	Fifth Generation?
PRIMARY STORAGE	Magnetic Drum	Magnetic Core	Magnetic Core	LSI Semiconductor Memory	VLSI Semiconductor Memory
TREND: Towards Large Capacities Using Smaller Microelectronic Circuits.					
SECONDARY STORAGE	Magnetic Tape Magnetic Drum	Magnetic Tape Magnetic Disk	Magnetic Disk Magnetic Tape	Magnetic Disk Optical Disk	Optical Disk Magnetic Disk
TREND: Towards Massive Capacities Using Magnetic and Optical Media.					

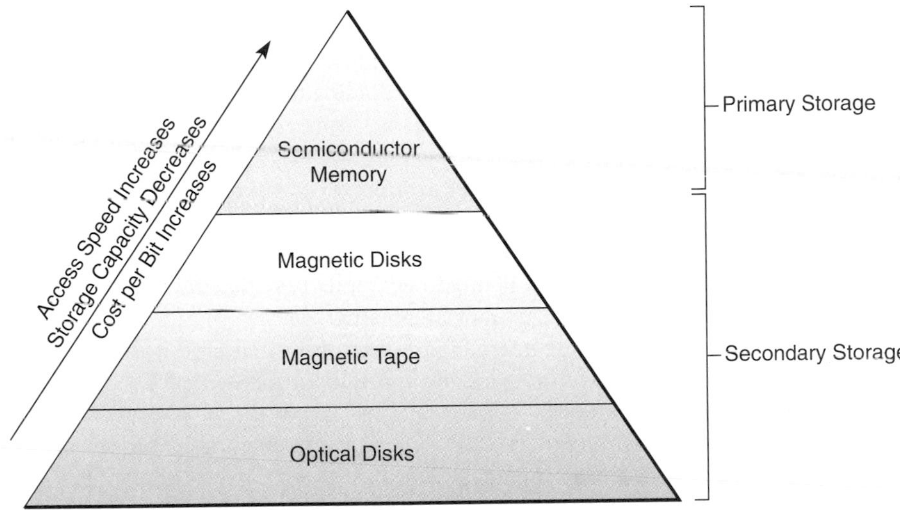

FIGURE 2.21
Storage media cost, speed, and capacity trade-offs. Note how cost increases with faster access speeds but decreases with increased capacity.

Large-capacity storage media cost less per byte but are slower. This is why we have different kinds of storage media.

Note in Figure 2.21 that semiconductor memories are used mainly for primary storage, though they are finding increasing use as high-speed secondary storage devices. Magnetic disk and tape and optical disk devices, on the other hand, are used as secondary storage devices to greatly enlarge the storage capacity of computer systems. Also, since most primary storage circuits use random access memory chips, which lose their contents when electrical power is interrupted, secondary storage devices provide a more permanent type of storage media for storage of data and programs.

Direct and Sequential Access

Primary storage media such as semiconductor memory chips are called **direct access** or *random access memory* (RAM). Magnetic disk devices are frequently called *direct access storage devices* (DASD). On the other hand, media such as magnetic tapes are known as **sequential access** devices.

The terms *direct access* and *random access* describe the same concept. They mean that an element of data or instructions (such as a byte or word) can be directly stored and retrieved by selecting and using any of the locations on the storage media. They also mean that each storage position (1) has a unique address and (2) can be individually accessed in approximately the same length of time without having to search through other storage positions. For example, each memory cell on a microelectronic semiconductor RAM chip can be individually sensed or changed in the same length of time. Also any data record stored on a magnetic or optical disk can be accessed directly in approximately the same time period. See Figure 2.22.

Sequential access storage media such as magnetic tape do not have unique storage addresses that can be directly addressed. Instead, data must be stored and retrieved using a sequential or serial process. Data are recorded one after another in a predetermined sequence (such as in numeric order) on a storage medium. Locating an individual item of data requires searching much of the recorded data on the tape until the desired item is located.

Semiconductor Memory

The primary storage (main memory) of most modern computers consists of microelectronic **semiconductor memory** circuits. Millions of storage circuits can be etched on tiny chips of silicon or other semiconducting materials. *Memory chips* with capacities of 256K bits, 1 million bits (1 megabit), 4 megabits, and 16 megabits are now used in many computers.

Some of the major attractions of semiconductor memory are small size, great speed, shock and temperature resistance, and low cost due to mass production capabilities. One major disadvantage of most semiconductor memory is its **volatility**. Uninterrupted electric power must be supplied or the contents of memory will be lost. Therefore, emergency transfer to other devices or standby electrical power (through battery packs or emergency generators) is required if data are to be saved. Another alternative is to permanently "burn in" the contents of semiconductor devices so that they cannot be erased by a loss of power.

Thus, there are two basic types of semiconductor memory: **random access memory** (RAM) and **read only memory** (ROM).

- **RAM: random access memory.** These memory chips are the most widely used primary storage medium. Each memory position can be both sensed

FIGURE 2.22
Sequential versus direct access storage. A magnetic tape is a typical sequential access medium. A magnetic disk is a typical direct access storage device.

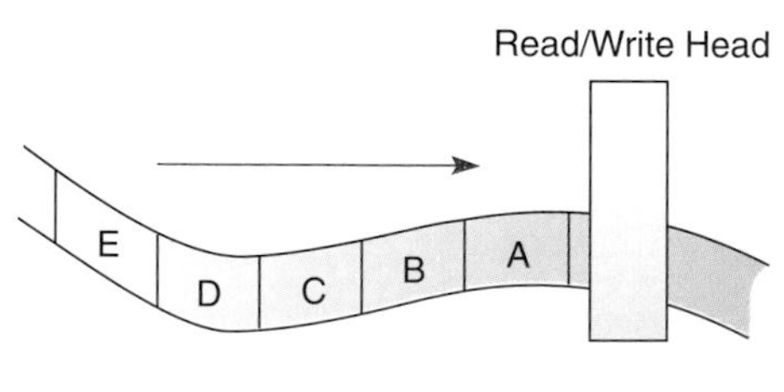

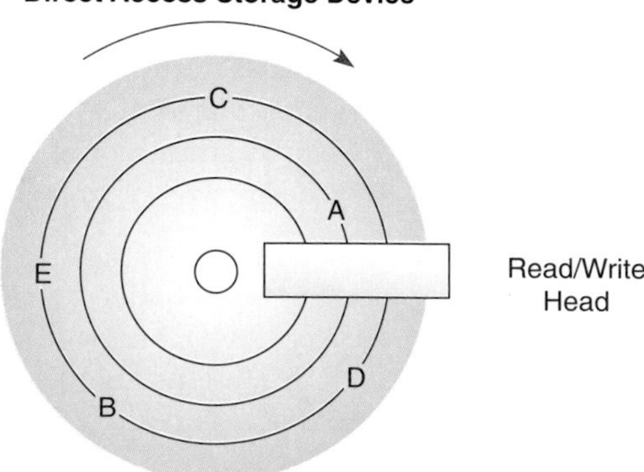

(read) and changed (written), so it is also called read/write memory. This is volatile memory.

- **ROM: read only memory.** Nonvolatile read only memory chips are used for permanent storage. ROM can be read but not erased or overwritten. Frequently used control instructions in the control unit and programs in primary storage (such as parts of the operating system) can be permanently "burned in" to the storage cells during manufacture. This is sometimes called *firmware*. Variations include PROM (programmable read only memory) and EPROM (erasable programmable read only memory), which can be permanently or temporarily programmed after manufacture.

Semiconductory Secondary Storage

Semiconductor memory chips are being used as direct access primary and secondary storage media for both large and small computers. Plug-in memory circuit boards containing up to several megabytes of semiconductor memory chips (RAM cards) can be added to a microcomputer to increase its memory capacity. These provide additional primary storage, but they can also be used for secondary storage. A computer's operating system program can be instructed to treat part of RAM as if another disk drive has been added to the system. This provides a very high speed semiconductor secondary storage capability, sometimes called a RAM *disk*. Semiconductor secondary storage devices also include removable credit-card-size "flash memory" RAM *cards*. They provide up to 40 megabytes of erasable direct access storage for some notebook or hand-held PCs. Peripheral devices consisting of semiconductor memory chips are also marketed as high-speed alternatives to magnetic disk units for mainframe computers.

Magnetic Disk Storage

Magnetic disks are the most common form of secondary storage for modern computer systems. They provide fast access and high storage capacities at a reasonable cost. The two basic types of magnetic disk media are conventional (hard) metal disks and flexible (floppy) diskettes. Several types of magnetic disk peripherals are used as DASDs in both small and large computer systems.

Magnetic disks are thin metal or plastic disks that are coated on both sides with an iron oxide recording material. Several disks may be mounted together on a vertical shaft, which typically rotates the disks at speeds of 2,400 to 3,600 revolutions per minute (rpm). Electromagnetic read/write heads are positioned by access arms between the slightly separated disks to read and write data on concentric, circular **tracks**. Data is recorded on tracks in the form of tiny magnetized spots to form binary digits arranged in serial order in common computer codes. Thousands of bytes can be recorded on each track, and there are several hundred data tracks on each disk surface, each of which is subdivided into a number of **sectors**. See Figure 2.23.

Types of Magnetic Disks

There are several types of magnetic disk arrangements, including removable disk packs and cartridges as well as fixed disk units. The removable disk devices are popular because they can be used interchangeably in magnetic disk units and stored offline for convenience and security when not in use. See Figure 2.24.

- **Floppy disks**, or magnetic *diskettes*, are disks that consist of polyester film covered with an iron oxide compound. A single disk is mounted and rotates freely inside a protective flexible or hard plastic jacket, which has access openings to accommodate the read/write head of a disk drive unit. The

FIGURE 2.23
Characteristics of magnetic disks. Note especially the concepts of cylinders, tracks, and sectors.

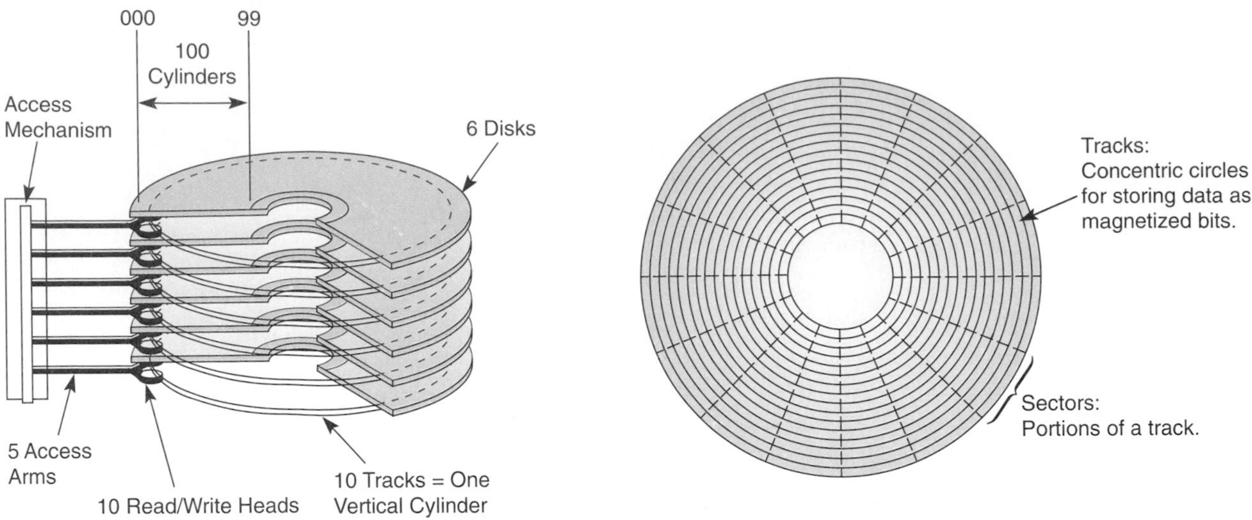

FIGURE 2.24
Magnetic disk media: A 3½-inch floppy disk and hard magnetic disk drives.

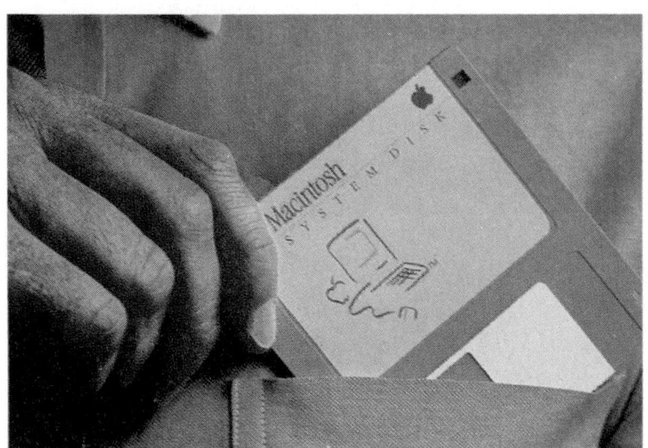

Courtesy of Apple Computer, Inc.

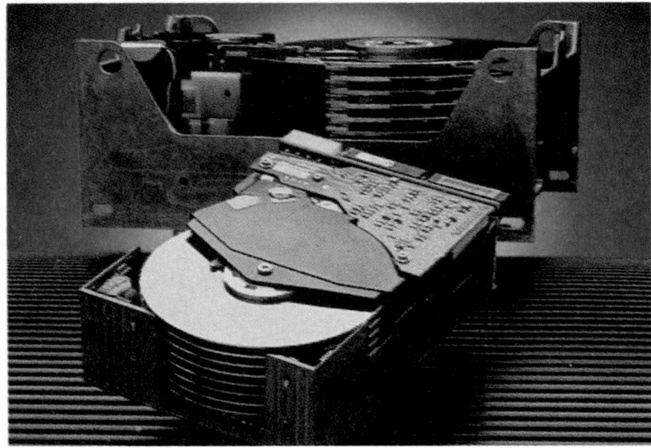

Courtesy of IBM Corporation.

3½-inch floppy disk, with capacities of 720 kilobytes and 1.44 or 2.8 megabytes, is rapidly replacing the older 5¼-inch size.

- **Hard disk drives** combine magnetic disks, access arms, and read/write heads into a sealed module. These nonremovable devices allow higher speeds, greater data-recording densities, and closer tolerances within a sealed, more stable environment. Removable *disk cartridge* versions are also available. Capacities of hard drives typically range from 40 megabytes to several gigabytes of storage. Large-capacity mainframe disk drives are being challenged by *disk arrays* of interconnected microcomputer hard disk drives to provide many gigabytes of online storage.

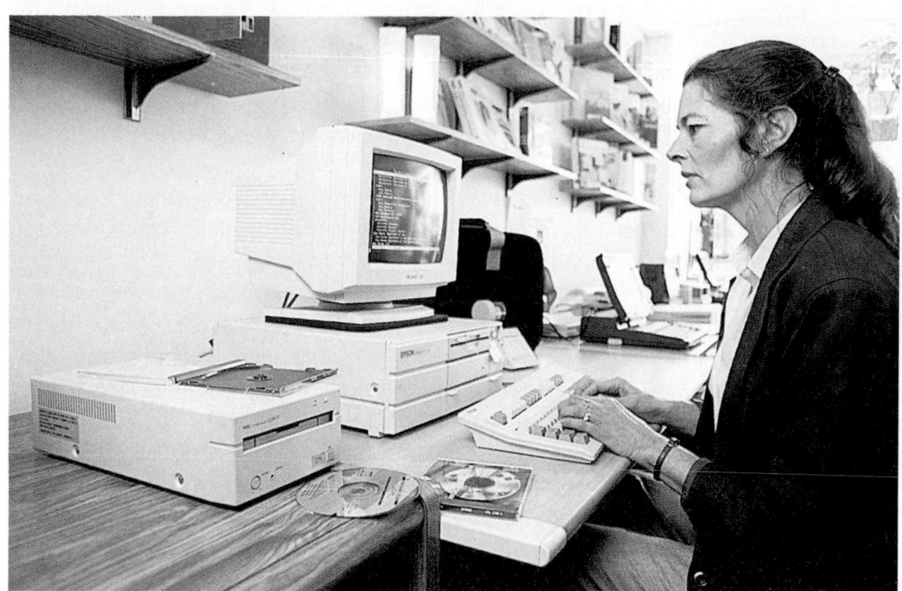

Frederick D. Bodin/Offshoot.

FIGURE 2.25
CD-ROM disks can hold over 500 million characters of information.

Magnetic Tape Storage

Magnetic tape is another widely used secondary storage medium. Data is recorded in the form of magnetized spots on the iron oxide coating of the plastic tape by the read/write heads of magnetic tape drives. Magnetic tape is usually subdivided into horizontal tracks to accommodate recording bits into common computer codes. Blank spaces, known as *gaps*, are used to separate individual data records and blocks of grouped records. These gaps are required to allow for such mechanical operations as the start/stop time of a magnetic tape unit. Most devices group records into blocks to conserve storage space instead of leaving gaps between each record.

Magnetic tape comes in the form of tape reels and cartridges for mainframes and minicomputers, and small cassettes or cartridges for microcomputers. Mainframe magnetic cartridges are replacing tape reels and can hold over 200 megabytes. Small cartridges can store over 100 megabytes and are a popular means of providing backup capabilities for microcomputer hard disk drives.

Optical Disk Storage

Optical disks are a relatively new storage medium. Mainframe versions use 8- and 12-inch plastic disks with capacities of several gigabytes of information. The version for use with microcomputers is called CD-ROM (compact disk–read only memory). It uses 12-centimeter (4.7-inch) compact disks (CDs) similar to those used in stereo music systems. Each disk can store over 500 megabytes. Data are recorded by using a laser to burn permanent microscopic pits in a spiral track on a master disk from which compact disks can be mass produced. Then CD-ROM disk drives use a laser device to read the binary codes formed by those pits. See Figure 2.25.

Another optical disk technology produces *write once, read many* (WORM) disks. This allows microcomputers with the proper optical disk drive units to record their own data once on an optical disk, and then to be able to read it indefinitely. The major limitation of CD-ROM and WORM disks is that recorded data cannot be erased. However, **erasable optical disk** systems have now become available. This technology records and erases data by using a laser to heat a microscopic point of the disk's surface. In some versions, a magnetic coil changes the spot's reflective properties from one direction to another, thus recording a binary one or zero. A laser device can then read the binary codes on the disk by sensing the direction of reflected light.

One of the major uses of optical disks is in *image processing*, where long-term *archival storage* of historical files of document images must be maintained. Financial institutions, among others, are using optical scanners to capture digitized document images and store them on WORM optical disks as an alternative to microfilm media. The major use of CD-ROM disks is to provide organizations and end users with fast access to reference materials and data banks in a convenient, compact form. This includes encyclopedias, directories, manuals, periodical abstracts, part listings, and statistical databases of business and economic activity. Interactive educational and industrial training applications have also been developed for CD-ROM disks.

Thus, optical disks have emerged as a popular storage medium for image processing, and they appear to be a promising alternative to magnetic disks and tape for very large (mass) storage capabilities for end user computing systems. However, erasable optical technologies are still being perfected. Also, optical disk devices are significantly slower and more expensive than magnetic disk devices. So optical disk systems are not expected to displace magnetic disk technology in the near future.

REAL WORLD CASE

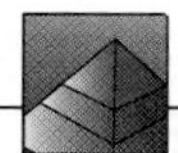

Boston College: A User-Friendly Interface

Bernard W. Gleason Jr., Boston College's executive director of information technology, was in line at an automated teller machine (ATM) in San Francisco back in 1984, when he was struck with an idea. "Hell, if I can access money from my bank in Boston 3,000 miles away, I should be able to do the same thing from systems on campus," he thought.

Four years later, Gleason's idea materialized in the user information system (UIS). UIS is a key part of Project Glasnost, Boston College's long-term strategy initiated in the late 1970s for furnishing users with direct access to administrative computing systems. UIS is a campuswide network that enables 15,000 students, 8,500 faculty members, and thousands of full- and part-time staff members to use ATM cards to do things such as check out library materials or pay dining hall tabs. Other applications accessible from six on-campus ATM kiosks enable users to register for courses, check on grades, and receive printed bills for housing and long-distance telephone service.

Users off-campus or in dormitory rooms can also reach UIS, accessing mainframe-based student accounts, student records, and other systems from desktop PCs and Apple MacIntoshes via a single graphical user interface (GUI) for all applications. For some applications, notably course registration, even a Touch-Tone telephone will do the job.

"At the beginning of each semester, the lines of students at our counter used to be four and five deep," says Louise Lonabocker, registrar at the Chestnut Hill, Massachusetts, college. "But with UIS, students register themselves from the device that is most convenient to them." The result: Lonabocker's office has cut back staffing as well as taken on new work, including the design and production of all student catalogs. Last year, the registration counter that was once thronged with students was removed.

Gleason says laying the groundwork for UIS actually began some 15 years ago, with the adoption of what he describes as very basic yet very critical computing concepts. Topping the list was the notion that all of the college's systems should be part of one secure system and that the system should be accessible to all through a consistent GUI.

ATM security is furnished on two levels. One way is through identifying information embedded in the magnetic stripe on each ATM card, which allows users to enter the network. The other is through the applications, which contain expert systems-based rules, technology developed and implemented by the college's 12-person IS applications staff. "One of our specifications for the system was that it had to be low management," Gleason says. "We didn't want a lot of security managers in IS. We didn't want to spend time and money doing routine tasks."

Gleason says calculating the overall cost of the ATM project and Project Glasnost as a whole is impossible "because you can't put a price tag on a vision. Glasnost isn't a project with a defined start and finish date but a philosophy of opening up all systems to end users," he says.

CASE STUDY QUESTIONS

1. What specific input/output devices are used in Boston College's ATM-based user interface system?
2. What are the benefits and limitations of UIS to students? To faculty and staff?
3. Could Boston College's UIS be used at your school? Why or why not?

Source: Adapted from Julia King, "The Secret of Their Success," *Computerworld*, March 29, 1993, p. 101. Used with permission.

SECTION III
How Computers Work

How Computers Execute Instructions

Computers work by executing the instructions in a program. The specific form of a computer instruction depends on the type of programming language and computer being used. However, in its simplest form, an instruction consists of:

- An **operation code** that specifies what is to be done (add, compare, read, etc).
- One or more **operands**, which specify the primary storage addresses of data or instructions and/or indicate which input/output and secondary storage devices will be used.

The operation code and operands of the instruction being executed, as well as data elements affected by the instruction, are moved through the special-purpose circuitry of the CPU or microprocessor during the execution of an instruction. A fixed number of electrical pulses emitted by a CPU's timing circuitry, or *internal clock*, determines the timing of such basic CPU operations as fetching and interpreting instructions. The time period to accomplish each basic operation is called a **machine cycle**. We will see examples of such basic operations shortly. The number of machine cycles required to execute an instruction varies with the complexity of the central processor's design and the instruction being executed.

During each machine cycle, electrical pulses generated by the internal clock energize special-purpose circuitry elements that sense and interpret specific instructions and data and move them (in the form of electrical pulses) between various specialized circuitry components of the CPU. One of the most important of these are **registers**, which are small, high-speed storage circuit areas used for the temporary storage of an individual program instruction or an element of data during the operation of the control and arithmetic-logic units.

Executing an Instruction

The executing of an instruction can be divided into two segments, the instruction cycle and the execution cycle. Simply stated, the **instruction cycle** consists of processes in which an instruction is fetched from primary storage and interpreted by the control unit. The **execution cycle** consists of performing the operations specified by the instruction that was interpreted. Let's look at a simplified illustration and explanation of what happens in a CPU during the instruction and execution cycles.

Figure 2.26 illustrates and explains the execution of a typical instruction by a computer. Let's state the instruction first in conversational English, then in a form more like the machine language instruction executed by computers. Then you should follow the steps used by the computer to execute this instruction as shown in Figure 2.26.

English Instruction: Add the amount of hours worked today by an employee to his or her total hours worked this week.

Computer Instruction: Add the amount stored in primary storage at address 006 to the amount contained in the accumulator register and store the result in primary storage location 008.

The Order of Execution

The computer automatically repeats instruction and execution cycles until the final instruction of a program is executed. Usually, instructions are sequentially executed in the order in which they are stored in primary storage. An instruction counter,

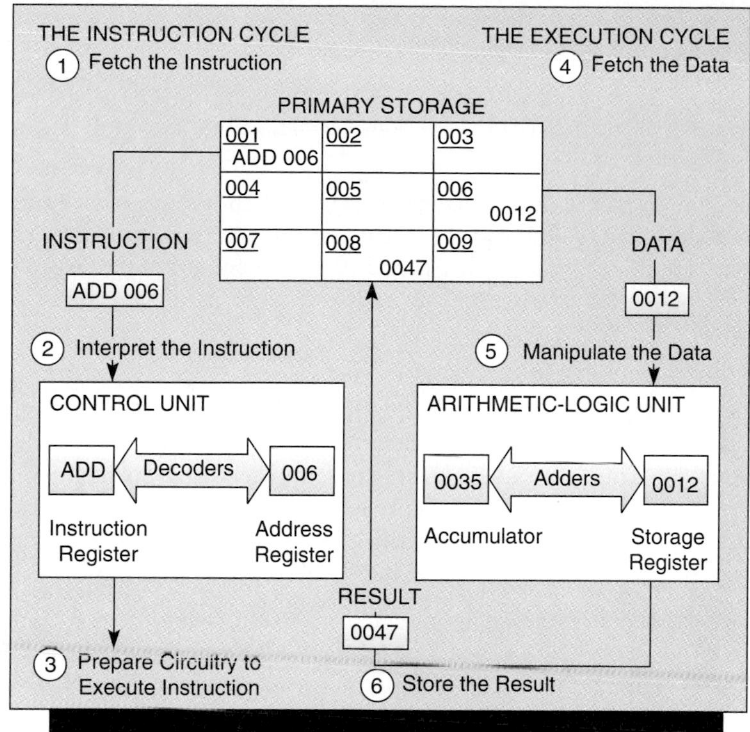

FIGURE 2.26
How computers execute an instruction. Notice the steps involved in this example.

THE INSTRUCTION CYCLE

1. First, an instruction is *fetched* from its location in primary storage and temporarily stored in the registers of the control unit. In this example, the instruction had been stored in primary storage location 001. The operation code part of the instruction (ADD) is moved to an instruction register, and its operand portion (006) is moved to an address register.

2. Next, the instruction is *interpreted* by the circuitry of the control unit. This involves decoding the operation code and operands of the instruction using specialized decoder circuits.

3. Finally, the control unit prepares electronic circuitry "paths" within the CPU to carry out the required operations. For example, this may involve activating the circuits that will "read" the data stored in the memory location (006) described in the instruction.

THE EXECUTION CYCLE

4. First, the data to be processed is fetched from its locations in primary storage and temporarily stored in a storage register of the arithmetic-logic unit. In this example, storage location 006 contained a value of 0012 (12 hours).

5. Next, the operations specified by the instruction are performed (addition, subtraction, comparisons, etc.). In this example, the contents of the storage register (0012) are added to the contents of an important register known as the accumulator by the use of specialized circuitry called adders. For this example, let's assume that the amount of hours worked this week (0035) was stored in the accumulator by a previous instruction.

6. Finally, the result arising from the manipulation of the data is stored in primary storage. In this example, the contents of weekly hours worked will be 0047. This amount will be transferred to primary storage at address 006 when an operand specifying this address is executed.

which automatically advances in sequential order to the address of the next instruction stored in memory, is used to indicate what instruction is to be executed next.

Sometimes, a *branch* instruction is brought from storage. It tells the control unit that it may have to execute an instruction in another part of the program, instead of the next sequential instruction. This change in the sequence of instructions can be unconditional or conditional. A *conditional branch* is usually the result of a test or comparison instruction, which can cause a change in the sequential order of processing if a specified condition occurs. For example, in a payroll program, a different sequence of instructions is typically used for employees whose hours worked exceeded 40 hours per week. These employees have earned overtime pay (typically one and one-half times the regular pay rate). Thus, the payroll program could contain the following instruction:

> If the total of hours worked this week is greater than 40, then execute the instruction at storage address 020 next.

Since the employee in our example in Figure 2.26 has worked 47 hours this week, the control unit would reset the instruction counter to address 020. The CPU would then *branch*, or jump, to that part of the program and begin executing the instructions for computing overtime pay, rather than the instructions for computing regular pay.

How Computers Represent Data

The letters of the alphabet in this book are symbols that when properly organized, or coded, into the English language will represent data that you, the reader, can process into information. Thus, we can say that words, numbers, and punctuation are the *human-sensible* code by which data is represented in this book. Similarly, data must be represented in a *machine-sensible* code before it can be processed and stored in a computer system.

The Binary Number System

As we said in Section I, data is represented in a computer system by either the presence or the absence of electronic or magnetic signals in its circuitry or in the media it uses. This is called a *binary*, or two-state, representation of data since the computer is indicating only two possible states or conditions. For example, transistors and other semiconductor circuits are either in a conducting or nonconducting state.

Media such as magnetic disks and tapes indicate these two states by having magnetized spots whose magnetic fields can have two different directions or *polarities*. These binary characteristics of computer circuitry and media are the primary reason why the **binary number system** is the basis for various coding schemes used to represent data in computers. Thus, for electronic circuits, the conducting (ON) state represents a one and the nonconducting (OFF) state represents a zero. For magnetic media, the magnetic field of a spot magnetized in one direction represents a one, while magnetism in the other direction represents a zero.

Therefore, the binary number system has only two symbols, 0 and 1. Thus, it is said to have a *base* of two. The familiar decimal system has a base of 10 since it uses 10 symbols (0 through 9). The binary symbol 0 or 1 is commonly called a **bit**, which is a contraction of the term *binary digit*. In the binary number system, all numbers are expressed as groups of binary digits (bits), that is, as groups of zeros and ones.

Just as in any other number system, the value of a binary number depends on the position or place of each digit in a grouping of binary digits. Values are based on the right-to-left position of digits in a binary number, using powers of 2 as position values, for example (2^3, 2^2, 2^1, 2^0). Therefore, the rightmost position has a value of 1 (2^0); the next position to the left has a value of 2 (2^1); the next position a value of 4 (2^2); the next, 8 (2^3); the next, 16 (2^4); and so forth. Thus, the value of any binary number consists of adding together the values of each position in which there is a binary one digit and ignoring those positions that contain a binary zero digit. Figure 2.27 gives you a simple illustration of how the binary number system can represent decimal values.

Binary Position Values							
2^6	2^5	2^4	2^3	2^2	2^1	2^0	
64	32	16	8	4	2	1	
Binary Numbers							**Examples of Equivalent Decimal Numbers**
0	0	0	0	0	0	0	0
0	0	0	0	0	0	1	1
0	0	0	0	0	1	0	2
0	0	0	0	0	1	1	3
0	0	0	0	1	0	0	4
0	0	0	0	1	0	1	5
0	0	0	0	1	1	0	6
0	0	0	0	1	1	1	7
0	0	0	1	0	0	0	8
0	0	0	1	0	0	1	9
0	0	0	1	0	1	0	10
0	0	0	1	1	1	1	15
0	0	1	0	0	0	0	16
0	0	1	0	0	0	1	17
0	0	1	1	1	1	1	31
0	1	0	0	0	0	0	32
0	1	0	0	0	0	1	33
0	1	1	1	1	1	1	63
1	0	0	0	0	0	0	64
1	0	0	0	0	0	1	65

FIGURE 2.27
Examples of how the binary number system represents decimal values. Can you determine that the decimal number 34 is equivalent to 0100010 in binary?

The Hexadecimal Number Systems

The binary number system has the disadvantage of requiring a larger number of bits to express a given number value. The hexadecimal number system, which is proportionately related to the binary number system, provides a shorthand method of reducing the long *string* of ones and zeros that make up a binary number. This is also helpful in simplifying computer codes based on the binary number system, as we will see shortly. For example, several popular computer codes use eight bit positions to represent a character. The hexadecimal equivalent would need only two positions to represent the same character. This makes it easier for professional programmers to decipher displays or printouts (memory dumps) of the data or instruction contents of primary storage.

Figure 2.28 shows examples of the binary and hexadecimal equivalents of the decimal numbers 0 through 20. Using the relationships in Figures 2.28, you should be able to determine that the decimal number 21 would be expressed by the binary number 10101 and the hexadecimal number 15, and so on. Several methods can be used to convert decimal numbers to a binary or hexadecimal form, or vice versa, or to use them in arithmetic operations, but they are beyond the scope of this text.

The ASCII and EBCDIC Codes

The internal circuitry of a computer needs to represent only binary ones and zeros in its operations. However, several binary-based coding systems have been devised to

FIGURE 2.28
Examples of the equivalents of decimal numbers in the binary and hexadecimal number systems. Can you tell that the decimal number 21 would be equivalent to 10101 in binary and 15 in hexadecimal?

Decimal	Binary	Hexadecimal
0	0	0
1	1	1
2	10	2
3	11	3
4	100	4
5	101	5
6	110	6
7	111	7
8	1000	8
9	1001	9
10	1010	A
11	1011	B
12	1100	C
13	1101	D
14	1110	E
15	1111	F
16	10000	10
17	10001	11
18	10010	12
19	10011	13
20	10100	14

express the machine language instruction codes executed by the CPU and to represent the characters of data processed by the computer. These computer codes make the job of communicating with a computer easier and more efficient. They should be considered as shorthand methods of expressing the binary patterns within a computer.

The most widely used computer code is the American Standard Code for Information Interchange (ASCII) (pronounced *as-key*). This was originally a seven-bit code which represented 128 (2^7) different characters. However, eight-bit versions (sometimes called *ASCII-8*) which can represent 256 characters are now widely used. ASCII is a standardized code first developed for data communications between computers and input/output devices. However, it is used by most microcomputers and minicomputers, as well as by many larger computers. ASCII has been adopted as a standard code by national and international standards organizations. The Extended BCD Interchange Code (EBCDIC) (pronounced *eb-si-dick*) is used by IBM and some other mainframe computers and can provide 256 (2^8) different coding arrangements. See Figure 2.29.

Bits, Bytes, and Words

A **byte** is a basic grouping of **bits** (binary digits) that the computer operates on as a single unit. It typically consists of eight bits and is used to represent a character by the ASCII and EBCDIC coding systems. For example, each storage location of computers using EBCDIC or eight-bit ASCII codes consists of electronic circuit elements or magnetic or optical media positions that can represent at least eight binary digits. Thus, each storage location can hold one character. The capacity of a computer's primary storage and its secondary storage devices is usually expressed in terms of bytes.

A **word** is a grouping of binary digits (usually larger than a byte) that is transferred as a unit between primary storage and the registers of the arithmetic-

Character	ASCII Code	Character	ASCII Code
0	00110000	I	01001001
1	00110001	J	01001010
2	00110010	K	01001011
3	00110011	L	01001100
4	00110100	M	01001101
5	00110101	N	01001110
6	00110110	O	01001111
7	00110111	P	01010000
8	00111000	Q	01010001
9	00111001	R	01010010
A	01000001	S	01010011
B	01000010	T	01010100
C	01000011	U	01010101
D	01000100	V	01010110
E	01000101	W	01010111
F	01000110	X	01011000
G	01000111	Y	01011001
H	01001000	Z	01011010

FIGURE 2.29
Examples of the ASCII computer code.

logic unit and control unit. Thus, a computer with a 32-bit word length might have registers with a capacity of 32 bits. It should process data faster than computers with a 16-bit or 8-bit word length. However, processing speed also depends on the size of a CPU's *data path*, or *data bus*, which is the circuits that interconnect various CPU components. For example, a microprocessor like the Intel 80386 SX has 32-bit registers but only a 16-bit data bus. It thus only moves data and instructions 16 bits at a time. Thus, it is slower than the Intel 80386 SX microprocessor, which has 32-bit registers and data paths.

Representing Data

Figure 2.30 illustrates how data is physically represented in many modern computers. It uses the eight-bit ASCII code to show how each character in the word *computer* can be represented by an eight-bit code. The circles represent semiconductor circuit elements or other forms of storage media. The shaded circles represent an electronic or magnetic ON state, while the nonshaded circles represent the OFF state of binary devices. Also notice that a ninth, or **check bit**, is ON to make odd parity; that is, an odd number of bits are turned on for each letter. If the check bit were OFF, this would result in even parity; that is, an even number of bits would be turned on.

Most computer codes include this additional check bit. The check bit is also known as a *parity bit* and is used for verifying the accuracy or validity of coded data. Many computers have a built-in checking capacity to detect the loss or addition of bits during the transfer of data between components of a computer system. For example, the computer may be designed to continuously check for an odd parity, that is, an odd number of binary ones (electronically ON bit positions) in each character of data that is transferred. In such cases, a check bit is turned on when needed to ensure that an odd number of electronically ON bit positions is present in each character of data in storage. Thus, the check bit allows the computer to automatically determine whether the correct number of bit positions representing a character of data have been transferred.

FIGURE 2.30
An example of how computers represent data. Note how the word *computer* is represented using the ASCII computer code.

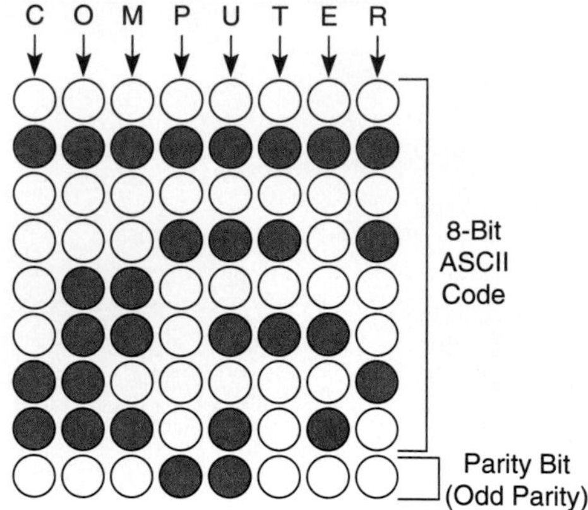

FIGURE 2.31
A summary of important input/output methods. Note especially the advantages and disadvantages of each method in providing hardware support of the user interface.

Peripheral Equipment	Media	Primary Functions	Typical I/O Speed Range	Major Advantages and/or Disadvantages
Video display terminals	None	Keyboard input and video output	250–50,000 characters per second output	Conventional and inexpensive, but limited display capacity and no hard copy
Printers	Paper	Printed output of paper reports and documents	Character printer: 20–600 characters per second; line printer: 200–3,000 lines per minute; page printer: 4–200 pages per minute.	Hard copy, but inconvenient and bulky; many printers are relatively slow
Pointing devices	None	Input by mouse, track-ball, joy-stick, pen, touch screen, and graphics pad. Video output.	Not applicable	Input devices are easy to use and inexpensive, but may have limited applications and software support
Voice input/output devices	None	Voice input and output	Not applicable	Easiest I/O but is slow, has limited vocabulary, and accuracy problems
Optical scanners	Paper documents	Direct input from written or printed documents	100–3,600 characters per second for Optical Character Recognition (OCR) readers	Direct input from paper documents, but some limitations on input format
Magnetic ink character recognition (MICR) readers	MICR paper documents	Direct input of MICR documents	700–3,200 characters per second. 180–2,400 documents per minute.	Fast, high-reliability reading, but documents must be preprinted and the character set is limited

Summary

- **Computer Systems.** A computer is a system of information processing components that perform input, processing, output, storage, and control functions. Its hardware components include input and output devices, a central processing unit, and primary and secondary storage devices. The major functions and hardware in a computer system are summarized in Figure 2.2. Major types and trends in computer systems are summarized in Figures 2.5 and 2.7.
- **Microcomputer Systems.** Microcomputers are used as personal computers, professional workstations, and multiuser computer systems. Microcomputers typically use a keyboard for input, a system unit containing the main microprocessor for processing and control, semiconductor RAM and ROM circuits for primary storage, floppy disk and hard disk drives for secondary storage, and a video display monitor and printer for output. A wide variety of other hardware devices are available, as are thousands of application software packages. Popular applications include word processing, electronic spreadsheets, graphics, telecommunications, business accounting, personal finance, and home management.
- **Other Computer Systems.** Minicomputers are small, general-purpose computers that are larger and more powerful than most microcomputers. They are used by small groups of users for many business data processing and scientific applications. Mainframe computers are larger and more powerful than most minicomputers. They are usually faster, have more memory capacity, and can support more input/output and secondary storage devices. They are designed to handle the information processing needs of organizations with many customers and employees, or with complex computational problems. Supercomputers are a special category of extremely powerful mainframe computer systems designed for massive computational assignments.
- **Peripheral Devices.** Refer to Figures 2.31 and 2.32 for summaries of the functions, characteristics, advantages, and disadvantages of peripheral devices for input, output, and storage discussed in this chapter.

FIGURE 2.32
A summary of important computer storage methods. Note the advantages and disadvantages of each method.

Peripheral Equipment	Media	Primary Functions	Typical Speed and Capacity Ranges	Major Advantages and/or Disadvantages
Magnetic disk drive	Hard disk Disk pack Disk cartridge	Secondary storage (direct access) and input/output	Access time: 10–100 milliseconds Capacity: From 10 megabytes to 15 gigabytes per disk drive	Large capacity, fast, direct access storage device (DASD), but relatively expensive
Floppy disk drive	Magnetic diskette: 3½- and 5¼-inch diameters	Secondary storage (direct access) and input/output	Access time: 100–600 milliseconds Capacity: From 360 kilobytes to several gigabytes per disk	Small, inexpensive, and convenient, but slower and smaller capacity than other DASDs
Magnetic tape drive	Magnetic tape reel and cartridge	Secondary storage (sequential access), input/output, and disk backup	Data transfer: 15,000 to 2 million bytes per second Capacity: Up to one gigabyte per tape reel or cartridge	Inexpensive, with a fast transfer rate, but only sequential access
Optical disk drive	Optical disk: CD-ROM, WORM, and erasable	Secondary storage (direct access) and archival storage	Access time: 350–800 milliseconds Capacity: CD-ROM: up to 700 megabytes; WORM: up to 3 gigabytes; erasable: up to one gigabyte	Large capacity, high-quality storage of data, text, and images. Primarily a read-only medium

Key Terms and Concepts

These are the key terms and concepts of this chapter. The page number of their first explanation is given in parentheses.

1. Arithmetic-logic unit (41)
2. Binary representation (44)
3. Cathode ray tube (60)
4. Central processing unit (41)
5. Computer system (40)
6. Computer terminals (57)
7. Control unit (41)
8. Direct access (65)
9. Direct input/output devices (57)
10. Electronic mouse (58)
11. Generations of computing (45)
12. Graphics tablet (59)
13. Icon (58)
14. Joystick (58)
15. Light pen (59)
16. Liquid crystal displays (60)
17. Magnetic disk storage (67)
    a. Disk pack (68)
    b. Floppy disk (67)
    c. Hard disk (68)
18. Magnetic ink character recognition (64)
19. Magnetic tape (69)
20. Mainframe computer (53)
21. Microcomputer (49)
22. Microprocessor (48)
23. Minicomputer (52)
24. Multiple processors (42)
25. Networked computer systems (54)
26. Offline (57)
27. Online (57)
28. Optical character recognition (63)
29. Optical disk storage (69)
    a. CD-ROM (69)
    b. Erasable disks (70)
    c. WORM disks (69)
30. Optical scanning (63)
31. Pen-based computing (59)
32. Peripheral devices (57)
33. Plasma displays (60)
34. Plotters (61)
35. Pointing devices (58)
36. Primary storage unit (44)
37. Printers (61)
38. Secondary storage device (44)
39. Semiconductor memory (66)
    a. RAM (66)
    b. ROM (67)
40. Sequential access (65)
41. Storage capacity elements (44)
    a. Bit
    b. Byte
    c. Kilobyte
    d. Megabyte
    e. Gigabyte
    f. Terabyte
42. Storage media trade-offs (64)
43. Supercomputer (54)
44. Time elements (43)
    a. Millisecond
    b. Microsecond
    c. Nanosecond
    d. Picosecond
45. Touch-sensitive screen (59)
46. Trackball (58)
47. Trends in computers (45)
48. User interface hardware (57)
49. Video input/output (60)
50. Voice recognition (62)
51. Voice response (62)
52. Volatility (66)
53. Wand (63)
54. Workstation (49)

Review Quiz

Match one of the key terms and concepts listed above with one of the brief examples or definitions listed below. Try to find the best fit for answers that seem to fit more than one term or concept. Defend your choices.

____ 1. Computers will become smaller, faster, more reliable, easier to use, and less costly.

____ 2. Major stages in the development of computers.

____ 3. A computer is a combination of components that perform input, processing, output, storage, and control functions.

____ 4. Contains the arithmetic-logic unit and control unit.

____ 5. Performs computations and comparisons.

____ 6. Interprets instructions and directs processing.

____ 7. The memory of a computer.

____ 8. Magnetic disks and tape and optical disks perform this function.

____ 9. Capture data or communicate information without media.

____ 10. Input/output and secondary storage devices for a computer system.

____ 11. Connected to and controlled by a CPU.

____ 12. Separate from and not controlled by a CPU.

____ 13. Results from the presence or absence or change in direction of electric current, magnetic fields, or light rays in computer circuits and media.

____ 14. The central processing unit of a microcomputer.

____ 15. Can be a desktop or portable computer and a single- or multiuser unit.

____ 16. A computer category between microcomputers and mainframes.

____ 17. Can handle the information processing needs of large organizations.

____ 18. Using telecommunications networks to interconnect computer systems.

____ 19. A computer with several CPUs is an example.

____ 20. The most powerful type of computer.

____ 21. One billionth of a second.

____ 22. Roughly one billion characters of storage.

____ 23. Input/output methods and devices for end users.

____ 24. You can write on the pressure-sensitive LCD screen of notebook-size microcomputers with a pen.

____ 25. Helps you write on a video screen with a light-sensitive pen.

____ 26. Moving this along your desktop moves the cursor on the screen.

____ 27. You can communicate with a computer by touching its display.

____ 28. A peripheral device that digitizes data drawn on its pressure-sensitive surface.

____ 29. Produces hard copy output such as paper documents and reports.

____ 30. May use a mechanical arm with several pens to draw hard copy graphics output.

____ 31. Promises to be the easiest, most natural way to communicate with computers.

____ 32. Capturing data by processing light reflected from images.

____ 33. Optical scanning of bar codes and other characters.

____ 34. Bank check processing uses this technology.

____ 35. Small figures are displayed to help you indicate activities to be performed.

____ 36. A device with a keyboard and a video display connected to a computer is a typical example.

____ 37. The most common video display technology.

____ 38. Computer voice output.

____ 39. Includes electronic mice, trackballs, and joysticks.

____ 40. A hand-held device that reads bar coding.

____ 41. Storage media cost, speed, and capacity differences.

____ 42. You cannot erase the contents of these storage circuits.

____ 43. You can read and write data on these storage circuits.

____ 44. The property that determines whether data is lost or retained when power fails.

____ 45. Each position of storage can be accessed in approximately the same time.

____ 46. Each position of storage can be accessed according to a predetermined order.

____ 47. Microelectronic storage circuits on silicon chips.

____ 48. Uses magnetic spots on metal or plastic disks.

____ 49. Uses magnetic spots on plastic tape.

____ 50. Uses a laser to read microscopic points on plastic disks.

Discussion Questions

1. Why is it important to think of a computer as a system instead of an information processing box?
2. What trends are occurring in the development and use of the major types of computer systems?
3. What is the difference between microcomputers used as professional or end user workstations and those used as workstation computers or technical workstations?
4. Refer to the Real World Case of Associated Grocers. Why are such firms hanging on to their mainframe computers?
5. Are networked computers making minicomputers and mainframe computers obsolete? Explain.
6. What are the benefits and limitations of parallel processors? RISC processors?
7. Refer to the Real World Case of Boston College. What input/output devices do you think will be used in the universities of the future?
8. Why are there so many types of peripheral devices for input and output? For secondary storage?
9. How does the way computers execute instructions and represent data affect the capabilities needed by hardware and software?
10. What trends are occurring in the development and use of peripheral devices? Why are these trends occurring?

Real World Problems

1. **McKesson Drug: Wearing PCs in the Warehouse**

   At McKesson Drug Co. in San Francisco, a new technology has all but eliminated what was once an annoying and costly source of errors for the $10 billion pharmaceuticals distributors: mispicks. At any complex distribution center, the job of tracking millions of individual items as they shuffle from forklift to tote box is extremely complicated and vulnerable to human error. Douglas Thompson, senior vice president of distribution services, estimates that each warehouse mispick was costing the company about $80 in lost time and shipping costs—seven times more than the cost of filling an order correctly the first time. McKesson tried to rely on pistol-shaped bar-code readers. But because these portable scanners require two hands to operate, they never really caught on in a warehouse where workers need both hands to do their job.

But now, McKesson warehouse workers are using in-house-built "wearable PCs" to track deliveries, increase the accuracy of customer shipments, and generally improve service. Weighing less than 13 ounces, the AcuMax fits over the worker's hand and forearm like a glove. When the employee picks up an order form, he activates a scanner in the glove by pointing an index finger at the customer's bar-coded shipping label. The scanner then tells the picker the exact location of the item to be picked. The picker goes to the case lot and confirms the order by using laser beams from the AcuMax to read data on bar codes up to 20 feet above the warehouse floor.

a. What input/output devices are integrated in the AcuMax wearable PCs?

b. Why is the AcuMax better than other devices used by McKesson?

Source: Adapted from James Daly, "What Happens When Close Enough Isn't Close Enough Anymore?" *Computerworld*, January 4, 1993, p. 38. Used with permission.

2. Michigan Department of Transportation: Doing Pen Computing

The Michigan Department of Transportation (MDOT) is planning to outfit its highway inspectors with pen computers. This should make life easier for the MDOT's 300 highway inspectors and save money. Currently, inspectors file daily reports on the progress, material needs, and other factors involved in highway construction. In the past, these reports have been reentered by hand. The use of pen computers and standard floppy disks to transfer data should greatly reduce the cost of processing these reports, the agency said.

The pen computers are also expected to relieve pressure on the MDOT's staff. Michigan has the same budget constraints that most states have these days, and the MDOT cannot replace people who leave the staff. "Our staff has been going down, so this is one way to save work," said Kevin Fox, senior systems analyst at MDOT. Fox said the department plans to purchase 275 Grid Convertibles from the Grid Systems Corp. in Westlake, Texas. The department estimates that its investment will be paid back in 11 months. "We'll begin statewide implementation in April, in time for the summer building season," Fox said.

a. Why does the Michigan Department of Transportation need pen computers?

b. What other occupations could benefit from the use of pen computers?

Source: Adapted from Michael Fitzgerald, "Automation to Save Time for Highway Inspectors," *Computerworld*, January 18, 1993, p. 37. Used with permission.

3. Circuitest, Inc.: Voice Recognition on the Factory Floor.

Circuitest, Inc. in Nashua, New Hampshire, is using a voice recognition product called Verbex to free the hands of printed circuit board testers, who typically must use both of their hands to inspect boards using a pair of electronic probes. The Verbex product, with an introductory price of $695, consists of Listen for Windows software and a digital signal processing (DSP) board that converts continuous human speech into keystrokes that a Microsoft Windows application software package can understand. "Voice recognition applications require lots of floating-point calculations that are provided by fast RAM in DSP boards. The price of fast RAM has come down to the point where we can now offer a Windows product on PCs," said Verbex President Larry Dooling.

Verbex is capable of recognizing up to 300 words out of a palette of 420 words supplied by Verbex. The Verbex software allows circuit board testers to display and manipulate a schematic of the board while they test it. "It makes an incredible difference. The testers are about 30 percent more productive." said Mike Gowing, a software engineer at Circuitest.

a. What makes circuit board testing a good application for voice recognition?

b. What other applications would be good candidates for voice recognition technology?

Source: Adapted from Michael Vizard, "Verbex Delivers Continuous Speech Interface for Windows," *Computerworld*, April 5, 1993, p. 42. Used with permission.

4. New York Clearinghouse Association: Optical Disk Imaging

The New York Clearinghouse, founded in 1853 and supported by 11 New York banks, is the nation's largest bank clearinghouse. Clearinghouse Interbank Payments Systems (Chips) is an online, real-time electronic payment system that transfers funds and settles international transactions for 122 banks in U.S. dollars. It handles $1 trillion each day. Their other main application, the New York Automated Clearinghouse (AC), acts as a network for domestic consumer and commercial payments by 650 depository financial institutions in New York, northern New Jersey, Puerto Rico, and the U.S. Virgin Islands. AC is a batch-oriented system that handles nearly $170 billion—or 18 million transactions—each month for commercial banks, savings and loans, savings banks, and credit unions.

Until recently the Clearinghouse downloaded Chips and AC transactions from magnetic disks and a microfiche system. However, the microfiche system has been expensive to maintain and cannot conduct text searches as can the optical disk-based system, according to George F. Thomas, senior vice president and director of data processing at the Clearinghouse. "We wanted multiple indexes for things like system sequence numbers," said Thomas, who noted that these tasks can now be performed using their new image software system. Clearinghouse wrote a program designed to download data from the magnetic disks on its Unisys A-15 mainframe systems to its local-area network environment. From there, the information is downloaded to 12-inch optical disks, which are housed in a Rapid Changer jukebox. Speed is a key benefit from the new system. According to Thomas, daily Chips data can be downloaded in $2^1/_2$ hours on optical disks. Using microfiche, that process took 14 hours. Clearinghouse expects to save $50,000 annually in microfiche maintenance for both the Chips and AC systems and $60,000 each year on microfiche costs alone, Thomas said.

a. What are the advantages of an optical disk imaging system compared to microfiche?
b. What other business uses could benefit from optical disk imaging technology?

Source: Adapted from Thomas Hoffman, "Optical Disc Yields Far Speedier Storage System," *Computerworld*, January 25, 1993, p. 47. Used with permission.

Application Exercises

1. Input Alternatives
Which method of input would you recommend for the following activities? Explain your choices. Refer to Figure 2.31 to help you.
a. Entering data from printed questionnaires.
b. Entering data from telephone surveys.
c. Entering data from bank checks.
d. Entering data from merchandise tags.
e. Entering data from engineering drawings.

2. Output Alternatives
Which method of output would you recommend for the following information products? Explain your choices. Refer to Figure 2.31 to help you.
a. Visual displays for portable microcomputers.
b. Legal documents.
c. Engineering drawings.
d. Financial results for top executives.
e. Responses for telephone transactions.

3. Storage Alternatives
Indicate which secondary storage medium you would use for each of the following storage tasks. Select from the choices on the right, using Figure 2.32 to help you.

a. Primary storage.	1. Magnetic hard disk
b. Large capacity, permanent storage.	2. Floppy disk 3. Magnetic tape
c. Large capacity, fast direct access.	4. Semiconductor memory 5. Optical disk
d. Large files for occasional processing.	
e. Inexpensive, portable direct access.	

4. Selecting a Computer Hardware Supplier
Your department is in the process of acquiring a number of microcomputer systems. A purchase of seven PC systems and two laser printers is planned. All seven PCs are to have SVGA color monitors. Four of the PCs should have 125 megabyte hard disks, while the other three will require 250 megabyte hard disks. You have been assigned the task of getting bids from three local suppliers of computer equipment and developing estimates of the cost of acquiring the needed equipment from each supplier. All items are to be purchased from a single supplier; no splitting of the order is allowed. Assume that the prices quoted by each supplier are as shown below, where the price shown is for a single unit of the component indicated.

Unit Price of System Components from Alternative Suppliers

	Supplier		
Component	**ACME Systems**	**ACE Computers**	**Orange PC Palace**
PC systems unit with keyboard	$ 785	$ 760	$ 810
SVGA color monitor	260	265	250
Hard disk upgrade to:			
125 megabytes	60	65	70
250 megabytes	145	155	160
Laser printer	1,190	1,210	1,185

a. Prepare a spreadsheet comparing the costs of acquiring this equipment from each of the three alternative suppliers.
b. (1) Based on cost alone, which supplier would you recommend?
(2) If you were actually making a recommendation about this type of purchase, what factors, in addition to cost, would you want to consider?
c. Suppose your boss decided to modify the order by purchasing five laser printer units rather than the two origi-

nally planned. Modify your spreadsheet to reflect this change. Would this affect your recommendation?

5. **Microcomputers at ABC Company**

ABC Company has many microcomputers assigned to employees in various departments. You have been assigned the task of keeping track of your department's inventory of microcomputers. You need to keep records identifying each microcomputer system by its ID number, which employee the system is assigned to, the manufacturer's name, and the type of processor chip it uses. Data for the systems currently in use are shown in the figure below.

Lists of Microcomputers Assigned to Department Members

Identification Number	Manufacturer's Name	Processor Type	Employee Name
V673829	Vale	386	Barnes, V.
PX289476	Honeydale	486	Smith, W.
RT87931	Fast Systems	8088	Evan, D.
V510293	Vale	486	Powers, B.
LV692013	PC Powers	386	Morris, H.
V938124	Vale	286	Owens, M.
PX347923	Honeydale	486	Adams, A.
RV30129	Fast Systems	386	Jarvis, J.

a. Using a database management software package, create a database file to store this information. Then enter the appropriate data for the microcomputer systems listed in the figure below.

b. Create and print a simple report showing all of the information for each system, sorted in alphabetical order by the name of the employee to whom the system is assigned.

c. Using the data retrieval capabilities of your database software, perform the following retrievals:

(1) Retrieve the ID# and EMP_Name for all systems manufactured by Vale.

(2) Retrieve a count of the number of systems with a 486 processor.

(3) Retrieve all information recorded for the system assigned to Smith, W.

Review Quiz Answers

1. *47*
2. *11*
3. *5*
4. *4*
5. *1*
6. *7*
7. *36*
8. *38*
9. *9*
10. *32*
11. *27*
12. *26*
13. *2*
14. *22*
15. *21*
16. *23*
17. *20*
18. *25*
19. *24*
20. *43*
21. *44c*
22. *41e*
23. *48*
24. *31*
25. *15*
26. *10*
27. *45*
28. *12*
29. *37*
30. *34*
31. *50*
32. *30*
33. *28*
34. *18*
35. *13*
36. *6*
37. *3*
38. *51*
39. *35*
40. *53*
41. *42*
42. *39b*
43. *39a*
44. *52*
45. *8*
46. *40*
47. *39*
48. *17*
49. *19*
50. *29*

Selected References

1. *Computerworld, Datamation, PC Week, PC Magazine,* and *PC World.* (Examples of good sources for current information on computer systems hardware and other developments in information systems technology.)
2. Datapro Corporation. *Datapro Reports.* (Series of regular, detailed reports on selected computer systems hardware.)

Introduction to Computer Software

CHAPTER OUTLINE

CHAPTER 3

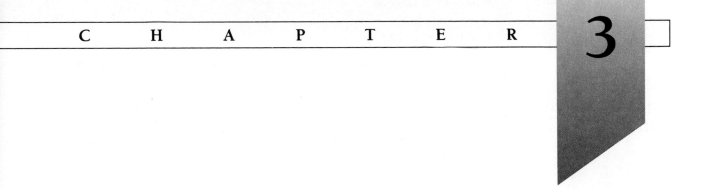

LEARNING OBJECTIVES

The purpose of this chapter is to give you an overview of computer software by analyzing the functions, benefits, and limitations of major types of system and application software packages.

Section I of this chapter presents an overview of software types and trends and summarizes the major features and functions of operating systems and other system software, including programming languages.

Section II surveys the major types of software available for end user computing applications, with an emphasis on microcomputer productivity software. Included are word processing, electronic spreadsheet, database management, telecommunications, graphics, and integrated packages.

After reading and studying this chapter, you should be able to:

1. Describe two major trends occurring in computer software.
2. Identify several major types of system and application software.
3. Outline the functions of operating systems and operating environments.
4. Describe the role of database management systems, telecommunications monitors, and programming language translator programs.
5. Explain the difference between machine, assembler, high-level, and fourth-generation languages.
6. Identify and explain the purpose of several popular microcomputer software packages for end user computing.

SECTION I

System Software: Computer System Management

Introduction to Software

This chapter presents an overview of the major types of software you will depend on as you work with computers. It discusses their characteristics and purposes and gives examples of their uses. Information systems depend on software resources to help end users use computer hardware to transform data resources into a variety of information products. Software is needed to accomplish the input, processing, output, storage, and control activities of information systems. As we said in Chapter 1, computer software is typically classified into two major types of programs:

System software. Programs that manage and support the resources and operations of a computer system as it performs various information processing tasks.

Application software. Programs that direct the performance of a particular use, or *application,* of computers to meet the information processing needs of end users.

Let's begin our analysis of software by looking at an overview of the major types and functions of software available to computer users, shown in Figure 3.1. This figure summarizes the major categories of system and application software we will discuss in this chapter. Of course, this is a conceptual illustration. The types of software you will encounter depend primarily on the manufacturer and the model of

FIGURE 3.1
An overview of computer software. Note the major types and examples of system and application software.

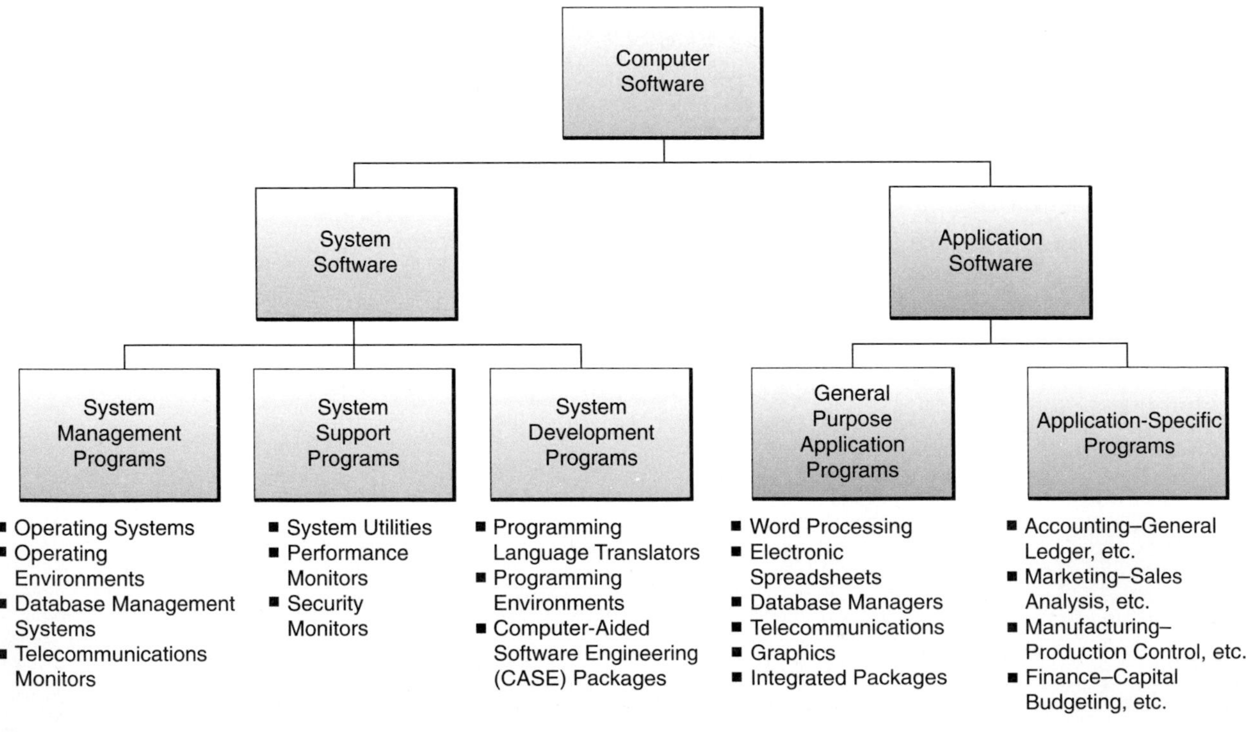

the computer you use and, second, on what additional software is acquired to increase your computer's performance or to accomplish specific tasks for you and other end users.

Software Trends

Figure 3.2 emphasizes two major software trends important to managerial end users. First, there is a trend away from custom-designed one-of-a-kind programs developed by the professional programmers or end users of an organization. Instead, the trend is toward the use of off-the-shelf software packages acquired by end users from software vendors. This trend accelerated with the development of relatively inexpensive and easy-to-use productivity software packages for microcomputers, and it continues to grow, even for minicomputer and mainframe users.

Second, there is a major trend away from (1) technical, machine-specific programming languages using binary-based or symbolic codes and (2) *procedural languages*, which use brief statements and mathematical expressions to specify the sequence of instructions a computer must perform. Instead, the trend is toward *nonprocedural, natural languages* that are closer to human conversation. This trend has accelerated with the creation of easy-to-use, nonprocedural *fourth-generation languages* (4GL). It continues to grow as developments in graphics and artificial intelligence produce natural language and *graphical user interfaces* that make software packages easier to use. In addition, expert system modules and other artificial intelligence features are being built into a new generation of expert-assisted software packages.

These two major trends seem to be converging to produce a fifth generation of powerful, multipurpose, expert-assisted software packages with natural language and graphical interfaces for end users.

System Software Overview

System software consists of programs that manage and support a computer system and its information processing activities. These programs serve as a vital *software interface* between computer system hardware and the application programs of end users. See Figure 3.3 Note that such progams can be grouped into three major functional categories:

FIGURE 3.2
Trends in computer software. The trend in software is toward multipurpose, expert-assisted packages with natural language and graphical user interfaces.

	FIRST GENERATION	SECOND GENERATION	THIRD GENERATION	FOURTH GENERATION	FIFTH GENERATION?
Trend: Toward Conversational Natural Programming Languages.					
Software Trends	User-Written Programs Machine Languages	Packaged Programs Symbolic Languages	Operating Systems High-Level Languages	Database Management Systems Fourth-Generation Languages Microcomputer Packages	Natural Languages Multipurpose Graphic-Interface Expert-Assisted Packages
Trend: Toward Easy-to-Use Multipurpose Application Packages.					

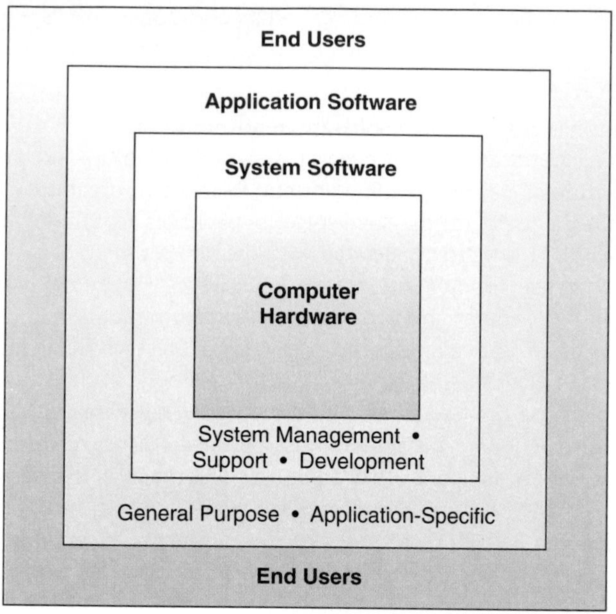

FIGURE 3.3
The system and application software interface between end users and computer hardware.

- **System management programs.** Programs that manage the hardware, software, and data resources of the computer system during its execution of the various information processing jobs of users. The most important system management programs are operating systems and operating environments, followed by telecommunications monitors and database management systems.
- **System support programs.** Programs that support the operations and management of a computer system by providing a variety of support services. Major support programs are system utilities, performance monitors, and security monitors.
- **System development programs.** Programs that help users develop information system programs and procedures and prepare user programs for computer processing. Examples include language translators, programming tools, and CASE (computer-aided software engineering) packages.

Operating Systems

The most important system software package for any computer is its **operating system.** An operating system is an integrated system of programs that manages the operations of the CPU, controls the input/output and storage resources and activities of the computer system, and provides various support services as the computer executes the application programs of users.

The primary purpose of an operating system is to maximize the productivity of a computer system by operating it in the most efficient manner. An operating system minimizes the amount of human intervention required during processing. It helps your application programs perform common operations such as entering data, saving and retrieving files, and printing or displaying output. If you have any hands-on experience on a computer, you know that the operating system must be loaded and activated before you can accomplish other tasks. This emphasizes the fact that operating systems are the most indispensable component of the software interface between users and the hardware of their computer systems.

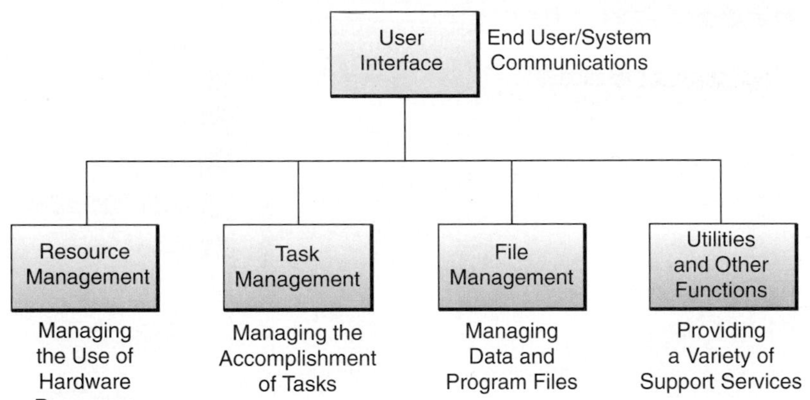

FIGURE 3.4
The basic functions of an operating system include a user interface, resource management, task management, file management, and utilities and other functions.

Operating System Functions

An operating system performs five basic functions in the operation of a computer system: providing a user interface, resource management, task management, file management, and utilities and support services. See Figure 3.4.

The User Interface

The **user interface** is the part of the operating system that allows you to communicate with it so you can load programs, access files, and accomplish other tasks. Three main types of user interfaces are the *command-driven, menu-driven,* and *graphical-user interfaces*. The trend in user interfaces for operating systems, operating environments, and other software is moving away from the entry of brief end user commands, or even the selection of choices from menus of options. Instead, the trend is toward an easy-to-use **graphical-user interface** (GUI) which uses icons, bars, buttons, boxes, and other images. GUIs rely on pointing devices like the electronic mouse to make selections that help you get things done. See Figure 3.5.

The user interface of operating systems can be enhanced by the use of **operating environments**, such as OS/2's Workplace Shell, or add-on packages such as Microsoft Windows and Desqview. Operating environments enhance the user interface between computers and end users by adding a graphical-user interface between end users, the operating system, and their application programs. These packages serve as a *shell* to interconnect several separate application packages so that they can communicate and work together and share common data files. Operating environment packages provide icon displays and support the use of electronic mouse or other pointing devices. They also allow the output of several programs to be displayed at the same time in multiple windows. Finally, several of these packages support some type of *multitasking*, where several programs or tasks can be processed at the same time.

Resource Management

An operating system uses a variety of programs to manage the hardware resources of a computer system, including its CPU, memory, secondary storage devices, and input/output peripherals. For example, memory management programs keep track of where data and programs are stored. They may also subdivide memory into a number of sections and swap parts of programs and data between memory and magnetic disks or other secondary storage devices. This can provide a computer system with a **virtual memory** capability which is significantly larger than the real memory capacity of its primary storage unit. So, a computer with a virtual memory capability can process larger programs and greater amounts of data than the capacity of its memory circuits would normally allow.

FIGURE 3.5
The graphical user interface of the Workplace Shell of the OS/2 operating system and the Microsoft Windows operating environment package. Notice how OS/2 can run DOS and Windows and its applications programs.

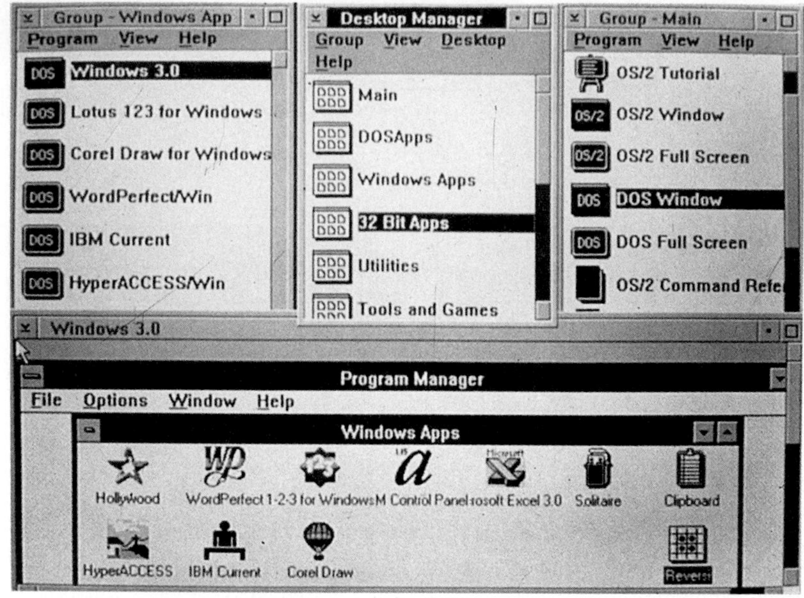

Courtesy of IBM Corporation.

File Management

An operating system contains file management programs that control the creation, deletion, and access of files of data and programs. File management also involves keeping track of the physical location of files on magnetic disks and other secondary storage devices. Thus, operating systems maintain directories of information about the location and characteristics of files stored on a computer system's secondary storage devices.

Task Management

The task management programs of an operating system manage the accomplishment of the computing tasks of end users. They give each task a slice of a CPU's time and interrupt the CPU operations to substitute other tasks. Task management may involve a **multitasking** capability where several computing tasks can occur at the same time. Multitasking may take the form of *multiprogramming,* where the CPU can process the tasks of several programs at the same time, or *time-sharing,* where the computing tasks of several users can be processed at the same time. The efficiency of multitasking operations depends on the processing power of a CPU and the virtual memory and multitasking capabilities of the operating system it uses.

Operating environment packages, some microcomputer operating systems, and most minicomputer and mainframe operating systems provide a multitasking capability. With multitasking, end users can do two or more operations (for example, keyboarding and printing) or applications (for example, word processing and financial analysis) *concurrently,* that is, at the same time. Multitasking on microcomputers has also been made possible by the development of more powerful microprocessors and their ability to directly address much larger memory capacities. This allows an operating system to subdivide primary storage into several large partitions, each of which can be used by a different application program.

In effect, a single computer can act as if it were several computers, or *virtual machines,* since each application program is running independently at the same time. The number of programs that can be run concurrently depends on the amount of memory that is available and the amount of processing each job demands. That's

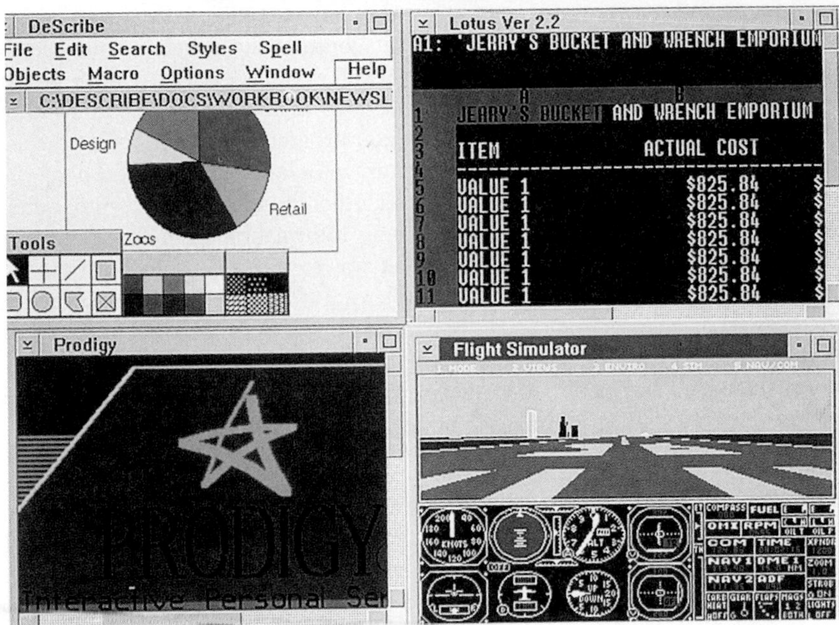

Courtesy of IBM Corporation.

FIGURE 3.6
Multitasking with OS/2. Note how the OS/2 operating system enables this end user to run graphics, spreadsheet, and flight simulator programs while using the Prodigy online information service.

because a microprocessor (or CPU) can become overloaded with too many jobs and provide unacceptably slow response times. However, if memory and processing capacities are adequate, multitasking allows end users to easily switch from one application to another, share data files among applications, and process some applications in a background mode. Typically, background tasks include large printing jobs, extensive mathematical computation, or unattended telecommunications sessions. See Figure 3.6.

Popular Operating Systems

The most popular microcomputer operating systems are MS-DOS, OS/2, and Macintosh System 7. UNIX is a popular operating system that is available for microcomputers, minicomputers, and mainframe computer systems. Examples of other popular mainframe and minicomputer operating systems are VM or MVS for IBM mainframes and VMS for Digital VAX minicomputers. Several versions of popular microcomputer operating systems may be available. Which version you should use depends primarily on your computing needs and on the main microprocessor and memory capacity of your microcomputer.

MS-DOS (Microsoft Disk Operating System) is the most widely used microcomputer system. It is a single-user, single-tasking operating system, but can be given a graphical-user interface and multitasking capabilities by adding an operating environment package like Microsoft Windows. OS/2 (Operating System/2) is a multitasking operating system for advanced IBM and compatible microcomputers that provides a graphical-user interface and a virtual memory capability. UNIX was originally developed by AT&T and is a multitasking, multiuser operating system whose *portability* allows it to run on mainframes, minicomputers, and microcomputers. The Macintosh System 7 is an operating system for Macintosh microcomputers that has a popular graphical-user interface, as well as multitasking and virtual memory capabilities.

Database Management Systems

In mainframe and minicomputer systems, a **database management system** (DBMS) is viewed as a system software package that controls the development, use, and maintenance of the databases of computer-using organizations. A DBMS program helps organizations use their integrated collections of data records and files known as *databases*. It allows different user application programs to easily access the same database. For example, a DBMS makes it easy for an employee database to be accessed by payroll, employee benefits, and other human resource programs. A DBMS also simplifies the process of retrieving information from databases in the form of displays and reports. Instead of having to write computer programs to extract information, end users can ask simple questions in a *query language*. Thus, many DBMS packages provide *fourth-generation languages* (4GLs) and other application development features. Examples of popular mainframe packages are DB2 by IBM and Oracle by Oracle Corporation. We will explore the use of database management packages in information systems in Chapter 5.

Telecommunications Monitors

Modern information systems rely heavily on telecommunications networks to provide electronic communication links between end user workstations, other computer systems, and an organization's databases. This requires system software called **telecommunications monitors.** These programs are used by the main computer in a network (called the *host*), or in telecommunications control computers such as *front-end processors* and *network servers*.

Telecommunications monitors and similar programs perform such functions as connecting or disconnecting communication links between computers and terminals, automatically checking terminals for input/output activity, assigning priorities to data communications requests from terminals, and detecting and correcting transmission errors. Thus, they control and support the data communications activities occurring in a telecommunications network. We will discuss communications software in more detail in Chapter 4.

System Support Programs

System support programs are a category of software that performs routine support functions for the users of a computer system. **Utility programs,** or *utilities,* are an important example. These programs perform miscellaneous *housekeeping* and file conversion functions. For example, *sort programs* are important utility programs that perform the sorting operations on data required in many information processing applications. Utility programs also clear primary storage, load programs, record the contents of primary storage, and convert files of data from one storage medium to another, such as from tape to disk. Many of the operating system commands used with microcomputers and other computer systems provide users with utility programs and routines for a variety of chores.

Other system support programs include *performance monitors* and *security monitors*. Performance monitors are programs that monitor the performance and usage of computer systems to help its efficient use. Security monitors are packages that monitor and control the use of computer systems and provide warning messages and record evidence of unauthorized use of computer resources. These packages will be discussed further in Chapters 11 and 12.

Programming Languages

A proper understanding of computer software requires a basic knowledge of **programming languages.** A programming language allows a programmer or end user to develop the sets of instructions that constitute a computer program. To be a knowledgeable end user, you should know the basic categories of programming languages. Many different programming languages have been developed, each with its own unique vocabulary, grammar, and uses. Programming languages can be grouped into the four major categories shown in Figure 3.7.

Machine Languages

Machine languages (or *first-generation languages*) are the most basic level of programming languages. In the early stages of computer development, all program instructions had to be written using binary codes unique to each computer. This type of programming involves the difficult task of writing instructions in the form of strings of binary digits (ones and zeros) or other number systems. Programmers must have a detailed knowledge of the internal operations of the specific type of CPU they are using. They must write long series of detailed instructions to accomplish even simple processing tasks. Programming in machine language requires specifying the storage locations for every instruction and item of data used. Instructions must be included for every switch and indicator used by the program. These requirements make machine language programming a difficult and error-prone task. A machine language program to add two numbers together in the CPU of a specific computer and store the result might take the form shown in Figure 3.8.

Assembler Languages

Assembler languages (or *second-generation languages*) are the next level of programming languages. They were developed to reduce the difficulties in writing machine language programs. The use of assembler languages requires language translator programs called *assemblers,* which allow a computer to convert the instructions of such languages into machine instructions. Assembler languages are frequently called *symbolic languages,* because symbols are used to represent operation codes and storage locations. Convenient alphabetic abbreviations called *mnemonics* (memory aids) and other symbols are used to represent operation codes, storage locations, and data elements. For example, the computation X = Y + Z in an assembler language might take the form shown in Figure 3.8.

Advantages and Disadvantages

In an assembler language, alphabetic abbreviations that are easier to remember are used in place of the actual numeric addresses of the data. This greatly simplifies programming, since the programmer does not need to know the exact storage locations of data and instructions. However, assembler language is still *machine-oriented,* because assembler language instructions correspond closely to the machine language instructions of the particular computer model being used. Also, note that each assembler instruction corresponds to a single machine instruction, and that the same number of instructions are required in both illustrations.

Assembler languages are still widely used as a method of programming a computer in a machine-oriented language. Most computer manufacturers provide an assembler language that reflects the unique machine language instruction set of a particular line of computers. This feature is particularly desirable to *system programmers,* who program systems software (as opposed to *applications programmers,* who

Fourth-Generation Languages: Use natural and nonprocedural statements
High-Level Languages: Use brief statements or arithmetic notation
Assembler Languages: Use symbolic coded instructions
Machine Languages: Use binary coded instructions

FIGURE 3.7
The four major levels of programming languages. They range from conversational, fourth-generation languages to the binary codes of machine languages.

FIGURE 3.8
Examples of four levels of programming languages. These programming language instructions might be used to compute the sum of two numbers, as expressed by the formula X = Y + Z.

Machine Language	High-Level Languages
1010 11001 1011 11010 1100 11011	BASIC: X = Y + Z COBOL: COMPUTE X = Y + Z
Assembler Language	**Fourth-Generation Language**
LOD Y ADD Z STR X	SUM THE FOLLOWING NUMBERS

program applications software), since it provides them with greater control and flexibility in designing a program for a particular computer. They can then produce more *efficient* software—that is, programs that require a minimum of instructions, storage, and CPU time to perform a specific processing assignment.

High-Level Languages

High-level languages (or *third-generation languages*) use instructions, called *statements,* that closely resemble human language or the standard notation of mathematics. Individual high-level language statements are actually *macroinstructions;* that is, each individual statement generates several machine instructions when translated into machine language by high-level language translator programs called *compilers* or *interpreters*. The use of macroinstructions is also common in fourth-generation languages and software packages such as spreadsheet and database management programs. High-level language statements resemble the phrases or mathematical expressions required to express the problem or procedure being programmed. The *syntax* (vocabulary, punctuation, and grammatical rules) and the *semantics* (meanings) of such statements do not reflect the internal code of any particular computer. For example, the computation X = Y + Z would be programmed in the high-level languages of BASIC and COBOL as shown in Figure 3.8.

Advantages and Disadvantages

A high-level language is obviously easier to learn and understand than an assembler language. Also, high-level languages have less-rigid rules, forms, and syntaxes, so the potential for error is reduced. However, high-level language programs are usually less efficient than assembler language programs and require a greater amount of computer time for translation into machine instructions. Since most high-level languages are machine independent, programs written in a high-level language do not have to be reprogrammed when a new computer is installed, and computer programmers do not have to learn a new language for each computer they program. Figure 3.9 highlights some of the major high-level languages in use today. Note that the most widely used languages include COBOL for business application programs, BASIC for microcomputer end users, and FORTRAN for scientific and engineering applications.

Fourth-Generation Languages

The term **fourth-generation language** is used to describe a variety of programming languages that are more nonprocedural and conversational than prior languages. These languages are called *fourth-generation languages* to differentiate them from

Ada: Named after Augusta Ada Byron, considered the world's first computer programmer. Developed for the U.S. Department of Defense as a standard "high-order language" to replace COBOL and FORTRAN.

ALGOL: (ALGOrithmic Language). An international algebraic language designed primarily for scientific and mathematical applications. It is widely used in Europe in place of FORTRAN.

APL: (A Programming Language). A mathematically oriented interactive language. It utilizes a very concise symbolic notation designed for efficient interactive programming of analytical business and scientific applications.

BASIC: (Beginner's All-Purpose Symbolic Instruction Code). A simple procedure-oriented language widely used for end user programming.

C: A mid-level structured language developed as part of the UNIX operating system. It resembles a machine-independent assembler language and is presently popular for system software programming and development of application software packages.

COBOL: (COmmon Business Oriented Language). Designed as an English-like language specifically for business data processing. It is the most widely used programming language for business applications.

FORTRAN: (FORmula TRANslation). The oldest of the popular high-level languages. It is still the most widely used programming language for scientific and engineering applications.

Pascal: Named after Blaise Pascal. Developed as a powerful successor to ALGOL, and designed specifically to incorporate structured programming concepts

PL/1: (Programming Language/1). A general-purpose language developed to combine some of the features of COBOL, FORTRAN, ALGOL, and other languages. It is a flexible language used for business and scientific applications.

RPG: (Report Program Generator). A problem-oriented language that generates programs that produce reports and perform other data processing tasks. It is a popular language with many business minicomputer users.

FIGURE 3.9
Highlights of high-level languages. Note the differences in the characteristics and purposes of each language.

machine languages (first generation), assembler languages (second generation), and high-level languages (third generation). It should be noted that some industry observers have begun to use the term *fifth-generation language* to describe languages using artificial intelligence techniques to accomplish results for users.

Most fourth-generation languages are **nonprocedural languages** that encourage users and programmers to specify the results they want, while the computer determines the *sequence of instructions* that will accomplish those results. Users and programmers no longer have to spend a lot of time developing the sequence of instructions the computer must follow to achieve a result. Thus, fourth-generation languages have helped simplify the programming process. **Natural languages** are 4GLs that are very close to English or other human languages. Research and development activity in artificial intelligence (AI) is developing programming languages that are as easy to use as ordinary conversation in one's native tongue. In Figure 3.10, INTELLECT, a natural language 4GL, is compared to using 3GLs BASIC, Pascal, and COBOL to program a simple average exam score task.

Advantages and Disadvantages

There are major differences in the ease of use and technical sophistication of 4GL products. For instance, INTELLECT and CLOUT are natural query languages that impose no rigid grammatical rules, while SQL and FOCUS require concise structured statements. However, the ease of use of 4GLs is gained at the expense of some loss in flexibility. It is frequently difficult for an end user to override some of the prespecified formats or procedures of a 4GL. Also, the machine language code

FIGURE 3.10
Comparing a natural 4GL with third-generation languages. Note how brief, nonprocedural, and conversational INTELLECT is compared to BASIC, Pascal, and COBAL to accomplish the same task.

INTELLECT 4GL

```
WHAT ARE THE AVERAGE EXAM SCORES FOR STUDENTS
IN MIS 200?
```

COBOL (Procedure Division)

```
PROCEDURE DIVISION.
MAIN.
    PERFORM INITIALIZATION.
    PERFORM PROCESS-RECORDS UNTIL END-OF-FILE.
    PERFORM END-OF-JOB.
INITIALIZATION.
    OPEN INPUT IN-FILE.
    OPEN OUTPUT OUT-FILE.
    PERFORM READ-RECORD.
PROCESS-RECORDS.
    ADD SCORES TO STORE-SCORE.
    ADD 1 TO STORE-NUMBER.
    MOVE NAME-IN TO NAME-OUT.
    MOVE SCORE TO SCORE-OUT.
    WRITE OUT-REC FROM PRINTER-LINE
        AFTER ADVANCING 1.
    PERFORM READ-RECORD.
END-OF-JOB.
    DIVIDE STORE-NUMBER INTO STORE-SCORE GIVING
      AVERAGE.
    WRITE OUT-REC FROM AVERAGE-LINE
        AFTER ADVANCING 2 LINES.
    CLOSE IN-FILE.
    CLOSE OUT-FILE.
    STOP RUN.
READ-RECORD.
    READ IN-FILE
        AT END MOVE "Y" TO EOF-FLAG.
```

BASIC

```
10 REM AVERAGE EXAM SCORE PROGRAM
20 LET COUNTER = 0
30 LET TOTAL = 0
40 OPEN "STUDDATA" FOR INPUT AS #1
50 INPUT #1, SCORE
60 WHILE SCORE <> 9999
70     LET COUNTER = COUNTER + 1
80     LET TOTAL = TOTAL + SCORE
90     INPUT #1, SCORE
100 WEND
110 LET AVERAGE = TOTAL/COUNTER
120 PRINT "AVERAGE SCORE IS", AVERAGE
130 END
```

Pascal

```
PROGRAM averagescore {infile, outfile}
VAR score, sum, average, count:   real;
    infile, outfile:  text;
BEGIN
    sum. = 0.0, count. 0.0;
    REPEAT
      read{infile,score};
      sum: = sum + score;
      count: = count + 1.0
    UNTIL eof{infile};
    average: = sum/count;
    write{outfile. 'Average score is', average}
END.
```

generated by a program developed by a 4GL is frequently much less efficient (in terms of processing speed and amount of storage capacity needed) than a program written in a language like COBOL. Major failures have been reported in some large transaction processing applications programmed in a 4GL. These applications were unable to provide reasonable response times when faced with a large amount of realtime transaction processing and end user inquiries. However, 4GLs have shown great success in end user and departmental applications which do not have a high volume of transaction processing.

Object-Oriented Languages

Object-oriented programming (OOP) languages have been around since Xerox developed Smalltalk in the 1960s. However, object-oriented languages have become a major consideration in software development. Briefly, while most other programming languages separate data elements from the procedures or actions that will be performed upon them, OOP languages tie them together into *objects*. Thus, an object consists of data and the actions that can be performed on the data. For example, an

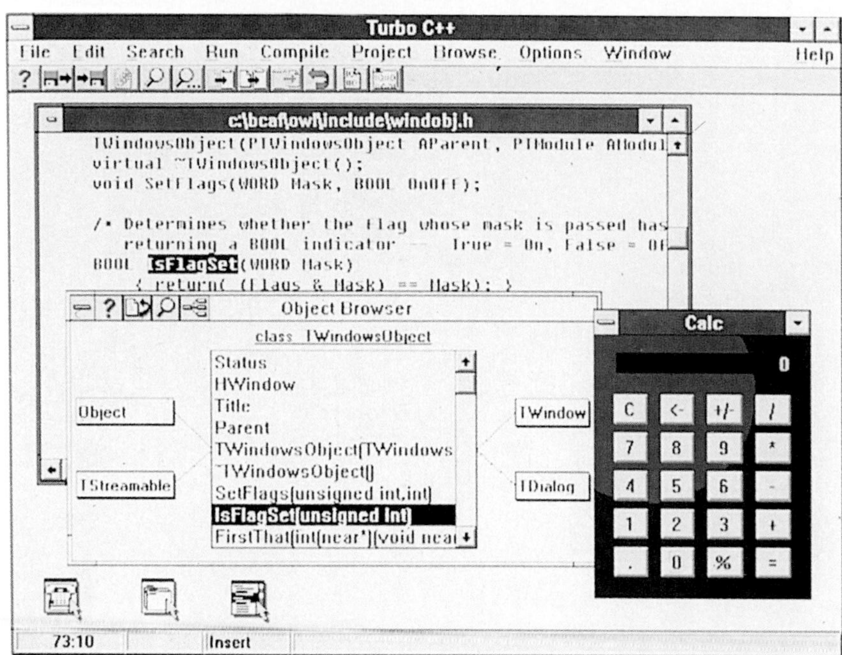

Courtesy of Borland International Inc.

FIGURE 3.11
Using the Turbo C++ object-oriented programming package.

object could be data about an employee and all the operations (such as payroll calculations) that might be performed upon the data. Or an object could be data in graphic form such as a video display window, plus the display actions that might be used upon it.

In procedural languages, a program consists of procedures to perform actions on each data element. However, in object-oriented systems, programs tell objects to perform actions on themselves. For example, a video display window does not need to be drawn upon the screen by a series of instructions. Instead, a window object could be sent a message to open and it will appear on the screen. That's because the window object contains the program code for opening itself.

Object-oriented languages like Objective C and C++ are easier to use and more efficient for programming the graphics-oriented user interfaces required by many applications. Once objects are programmed, they are reusable. For example, programmers can construct a user interface for a new program by assembling standard objects such as windows, bars, buttons, and icons. Thus, the use of object-oriented languages for such *visual programming* is expected to continue to increase. Figure 3.11 shows a display of the Turbo C++ object-oriented programming environment.

Language translators (or *language processors*) are programs that translate other programs into machine language instruction codes the computer can execute. They also allow you to write your own programs by providing program creation and editing facilities. Computer programs consist of sets of instructions written in programming languages, such as BASIC, COBOL, or Pascal, which must be translated by a *compilation* process into the computer's own machine language before they can be processed, or *executed*, by the CPU.

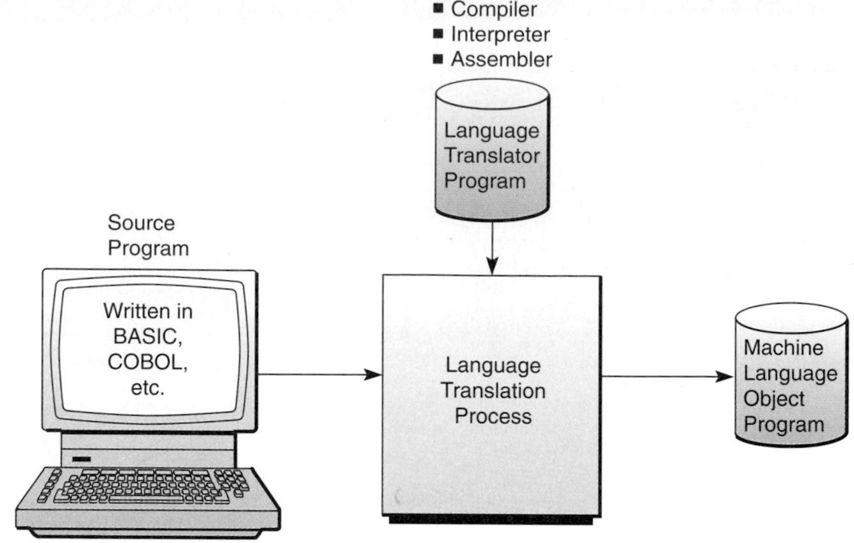

FIGURE 3.12
The language translation process. A program must be translated into machine language before it can be executed by a computer.

Programming language translator programs are known by a variety of names. An **assembler** translates the symbolic instruction codes of programs written in an assembler language into machine language instructions, while a **compiler** translates high-level language statements. An **interpreter** is a special type of compiler that translates and executes each program statement one at a time, instead of first producing a complete machine language program, like compilers and assemblers do. Figure 3.12 illustrates the typical language translation process. A program written in a language such as BASIC or COBOL is called a *source program.* When the source program is translated into machine language, it is called the *object program,* which can then be executed by a computer.

Programming Tools

The *programmer interface* of many language translator programs is being enhanced by a variety of built-in capabilities or add-on packages. Language translators have always provided some editing and diagnostic capabilities to identify programming errors or bugs. However, many language translator programs now include powerful graphics-oriented *editors* and *debuggers.* These programs help programmers identify and avoid errors while they are programming. Such **programming tools** provide a computer-aided programming *environment* or *workbench.* Their goal is to decrease the drudgery of programming while increasing the efficiency and productivity of programmers. Other programming tools include diagramming packages, code generators, libraries of reusable program code, and prototyping tools. Many of these same tools are part of the *toolkit* provided by Computer-Aided Software Engineering (CASE) packages.

REAL WORLD CASE

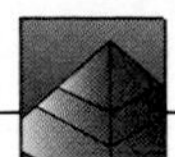

Operating Systems: What Business Users Want

What do end users want from their microcomputer operating systems? Which operating systems are they using now and plan to use in the future? Let's take a look at what four business end users have to say.

Carol Meadows is manager, Great Western Bank, Chatsworth, California. She currently uses DOS/Windows. She says: "I'd like faster print spooling and disconnected printing capabilities so that I can work on other things while something is printing. As it stands now, I have to wait for it to happen. We work in DOS 5/0 and Windows and will go forward with Windows NT. I'm generally in about five or six applications at a time, and Windows makes it easy to switch between applications, check E-mail, and cross around."

Wayne Dunn is manager, end-user support, Massachusetts Bay Transit Authority, Boston. He currently is migrating to OS/2. He says: "People here are transforming the way they do business, and I'm getting demand for high-end graphics and sharing information across platforms. I needed a 32-bit operating system that was fully graphical object-oriented and truly multitasking. OS/2 2.0 gives me the flexibility to migrate to new applications when I want to and continue to use the ones I own already. Because of all those factors, OS/2 was the only one. Unix is powerful, but it wasn't a fit, given that users in this particular department were doing a lot on PCs. Unix didn't have a graphical environment at the same cost."

Bill Westenberg is systems supervisor, technical support, health care department, Southern California Edison, Rosemead, California. He currently uses Macintosh, DOS/Windows, and OS/2. He says: "I would like to see a graphical user interface and user-friendly comprehensive help facilities. Some of the common utilities that people use day in and day out—such as file compressions, backup to file, and tape—should be built in. Ideally, the operating system should make it easy to locate data that resides anywhere on your disk. In this day and age, there should be some built-in, peer-to-peer networking. We see it in the Mac but don't see it in DOS, Windows, and OS/2. I see our direction going more toward OS/2 because we are downsizing applications to a client/server architecture in a LAN environment, and OS/2 is a better operating system to support client/server relationships."

Sally Atkins is a consultant of a large financial company in Boston. She currently uses DOS/Windows. She says: "We're using DOS and Windows, which will lead us in an NT [New Technology] direction because Microsoft has positioned NT as a growth path for Windows. We need scalability, which means I can use it on my portable up to my supercomputer and be able to use any of my programs. If we start with a new line of business and write code for five customers, that code can be sealed up if a product of ours takes off."

CASE STUDY QUESTIONS

1. Why is the choice of an operating system an important software decision for business end users?
2. Why do some of these users prefer OS/2 or Windows NT?
3. What are the benefits of the operating system capabilities that these end users want?

Source: Adapted from Alice Bredin, "What Users Want on Their Desks." *Computerworld*, February 22, 1993, p. 74. Used with permission.

SECTION II

Applications Software: End User Applications

Application Software for End Users

Application software consists of programs that direct computers to perform specific information processing activities for end users. These programs are called *application* packages because they direct the processing required for a particular use, or *application*, that end users want accomplished. Thousands of application packages are available because there are thousands of different jobs end users want computers to do. The use of personal computers has multiplied the growth of such programs.

General-Purpose Programs

Figure 3.1 showed that application software includes a variety of programs that can be subdivided into *general-purpose* and *application-specific* categories. **General-purpose application programs** are programs that perform common information processing jobs for end users. For example, word processing programs, spreadsheet programs, database management programs, integrated packages, and graphics programs are popular with microcomputer users for home, education, business, scientific, and many other purposes. Because they significantly increase the productivity of end users, they are also known as *productivity packages*. We will briefly explain some of the most popular types of such packages in this section.

Application-Specific Programs

Thousands of application software packages are available to support specific applications of end users. Major categories of such application-specific programs are:

- **Business application programs.** Programs that accomplish the information processing tasks of important business functions or industry requirements. Examples of such business functions and their corresponding applications are accounting (general ledger), marketing (sales analysis), finance (capital budgeting), manufacturing (material requirements planning), operations management (inventory control), and human resource management (employee benefits analysis).
- **Scientific application programs.** Programs that perform information processing tasks for the natural, physical, social, and behavioral sciences; and for mathematics, engineering, and all other areas involved in scientific research, experimentation, and development. Some broad application categories include scientific analysis, engineering design, and monitoring of experiments.
- **Other application programs.** There are so many other application areas of computers that we lump them all into this category. Thus, we can talk of computer applications in education, entertainment, music, art, law enforcement, medicine, and so on. Some specific examples are computer-assisted instruction programs in education, video game programs in entertainment, and computer-generated music and art programs.

Word Processing Packages

Word processing packages are programs that computerize the creation, editing, and printing of *documents* (such as letters, memos, and reports) by electronically processing *text data* (words, phrases, sentences, and paragraphs). Thus, word processing is an important application of *office automation,* which we will discuss in Chapter 7. Figure 3.13 illustrates the use of a popular word processing package.

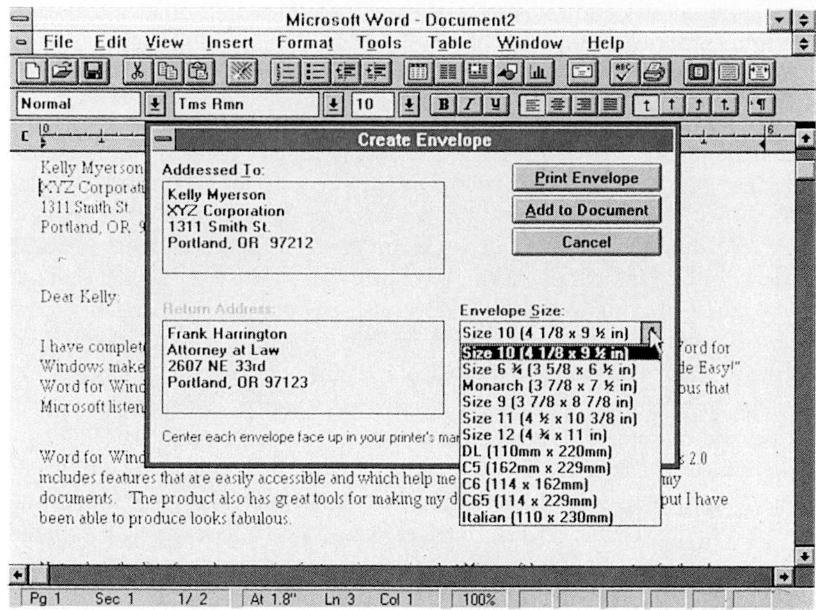

FIGURE 3.13
Using the Microsoft Word for Windows processing package.

Courtesy of Microsoft Corporation.

Word processing packages such as WordPerfect and Microsoft Word allow end users to do the following:

- Use a computer to create and edit a document and have each line of text automatically adjusted to fit prespecified margins.
- Move to any point in a document, and add, delete, or change, words, sentences, or paragraphs.
- Move a block of text from one part of a document to another and insert standard text from another document file.
- Check a document for spelling or grammatical errors and selectively change all occurrences of a particular word or phrase.
- Store a document as a document file on a magnetic disk, retrieve it any time, and print it according to a variety of predesigned formats.

Many word processing packages provide advanced features or can be upgraded with supplementary packages. One example is a *spelling checker* program, which uses built-in dictionaries to identify and correct spelling errors in a document. Another is a *thesaurus* program, which helps you find a better choice of words to express ideas. *Grammar* and *style checker* programs can be used to identify and correct grammar and punctuation errors, as well as to suggest possible improvements in your writing style. Another text productivity tool is an *idea processor* or *outliner* program. It helps you organize and outline your thoughts before you prepare a document or develop a presentation. Also popular is a *mail-merge* program, which can automatically merge the names and addresses in a mailing list file with letters and other documents. Finally, many word processing programs are able to support a limited amount of *desktop publishing* activity. As we will discuss in

Chapter 7, this allows end users to merge text, graphics, and other illustrations on each page to produce documents that look professionally published.

Electronic Spreadsheet Packages

Electronic spreadsheet packages are application programs used for analysis, planning, and modeling. They provide an electronic replacement for more traditional tools such as paper worksheets, pencils, and calculators. They generate an electronic *spreadsheet,* which is a worksheet of rows and columns stored in the computer's memory and displayed on its video screen. You use the computer's keyboard to enter data and relationships (formulas) into the worksheet. This results in an *electronic model* of your problem. In response to your commands, the computer performs necessary calculations based on the relationships you defined in the spreadsheet. Results are immediately displayed for you to see. See Figure 3.14.

Once an electronic spreadsheet has been developed, it can be stored for later use or printed out as a report. Popular electronic spreadsheet packages for microcomputers include Lotus 1-2-3, Excel, and Quattro Pro. Mainframe and minicomputer users can also use the electronic spreadsheet modules of products such as Lotus 1-2-3 M and Focus. Special-purpose spreadsheet models called *templates* are available for most spreadsheet packages. These worksheets are developed for specific applications such as tax accounting or real estate investment.

What-If-Analysis

The worksheet created by an electronic spreadsheet package is a *visual model* of the mathematical and other relationships within a particular business activity. It can thus be used to record and analyze past and present activity. It can also be used as a decision-support tool to answer *what-if questions.* For example, "**What** would happen to net profit **if** advertising expense increased by 10 percent?" To answer this question, you would simply change the advertising expense formula on an income

FIGURE 3.14
Using an electronic spreadsheet. The Lotus 1-2-3 for Windows spreadsheet allows you to work with multiple related spreadsheets and graphics.

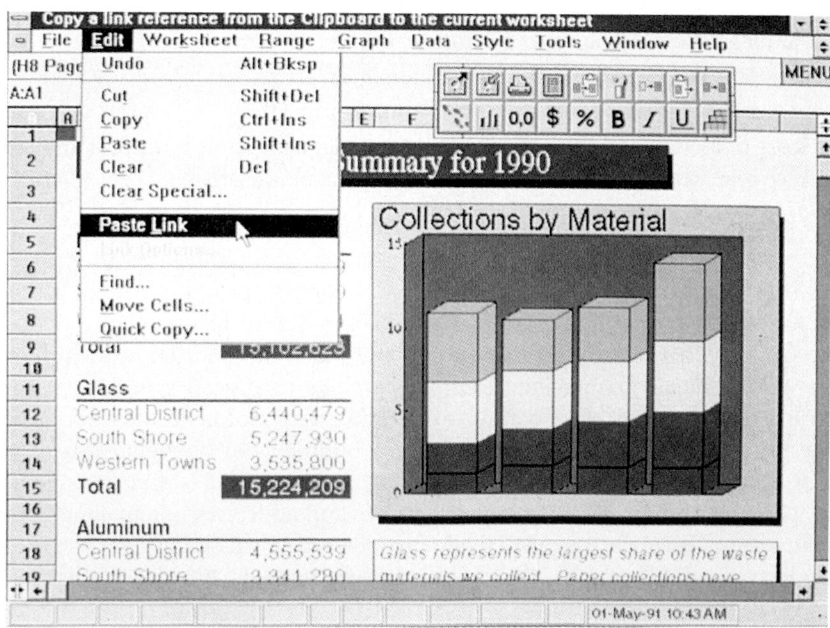

Courtesy of Lotus Development Corporation.

statement worksheet. The affected figures would be recalculated, producing a new net profit figure. You would then have a better insight into whether advertising expense should be increased. The use of electronic spreadsheets for such decision support will be discussed further in Chapter 9.

Database Management Packages

Microcomputer versions of file management and database management programs have become so popular that they are now viewed as general-purpose *application software* packages like word processing and spreadsheet packages. Packages such as dBASE IV and Paradox by Borland International allow end users to set up databases of files and records on their personal computer systems and quickly store data and retrieve information. As Figure 3.15 illustrates, most DBMS packages can perform four primary tasks:

- **Database development.** Define and organize the content, relationships, and structure of the data needed to build a database.
- **Database interrogation.** Access the data in a database for information retrieval and report generation. End users can selectively retrieve and display information and produce printed reports and documents.
- **Database maintenance.** Add, delete, update, correct, and protect the data in a database.
- **Application development.** Develop prototypes of data entry screens, queries, forms, reports, and labels for a proposed application. Or use a 4GL or application generator to develop program codes.

Telecommunications Packages

Telecommunications software packages for microcomputers are also viewed as general-purpose application packages for end users. These packages can connect a microcomputer equipped with a modem to public and private networks. Communications control packages such as Procomm Plus, Crosstalk, and Kermit provide microcomputer users with several major telecommunications capabilities:

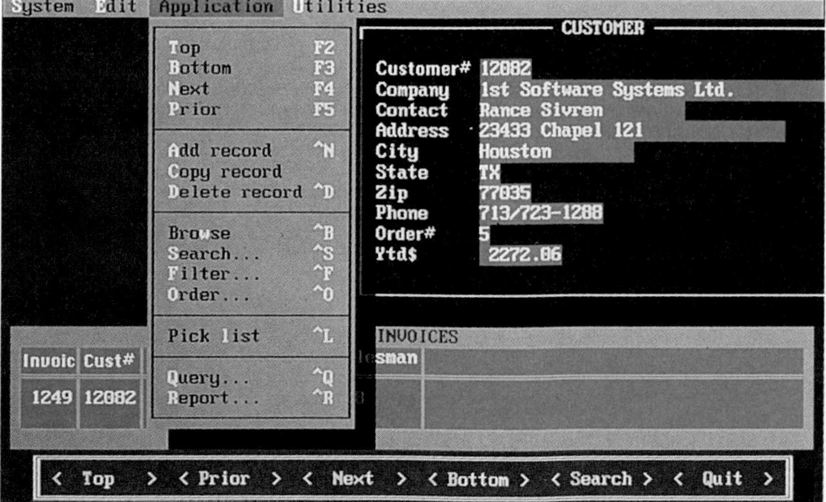

Courtesy of Microsoft Corporation.

FIGURE 3.15
Using a DBMS package. Note how the Fox Pro database management package lets you perform a variety of operations to a customer database.

- **Terminal emulation.** The microcomputer can act as a generic *dumb terminal* that can only send, receive, and display data one line at a time. It can also act as a generic *intelligent terminal* and transmit, receive, and store entire files of data and programs. Finally, some packages allow a microcomputer to *emulate* (act like) a specific type of smart terminal, especially those used with large computer systems.
- **File transfer.** Files of data and programs can be *downloaded* from a host computer to a microcomputer and stored on a disk. Or files can be *uploaded* from the microcomputer to a host computer. Some programs allow files to be transferred automatically between unattended computer systems.

Telecommunication packages for microcomputers are fairly easy to use. Once you load the program, you are usually provided with a display that asks you to set communications *parameters* (transmission speed and mode, type of parity, etc.). Then you dial the computer system or network you want or have it done automatically for you. Most networks will provide you with a series of prompts or menus to guide you in sending or receiving messages, information, and files. See Figure 3.16.

Graphics Packages

Graphics packages convert numeric data into graphics displays such as line charts, bar graphs, and pie charts. Many other types of *presentation graphics* displays are possible. *Draw* and *paint* graphics packages support freehand drawing, while desktop publishing programs provide predrawn *clip art* graphics for insertion into documents. Images are displayed on your video monitor or copies can be made on your system printer or plotter. Not only are such graphic displays easier to comprehend and communicate than numeric data, but multiple-color displays can more easily emphasize strategic differences and trends in the data. Presentation graphics have proved to be much more effective than tabular presentations of numeric data

FIGURE 3.16
Using the Crosstalk telecommunications package for file transfer between computers.

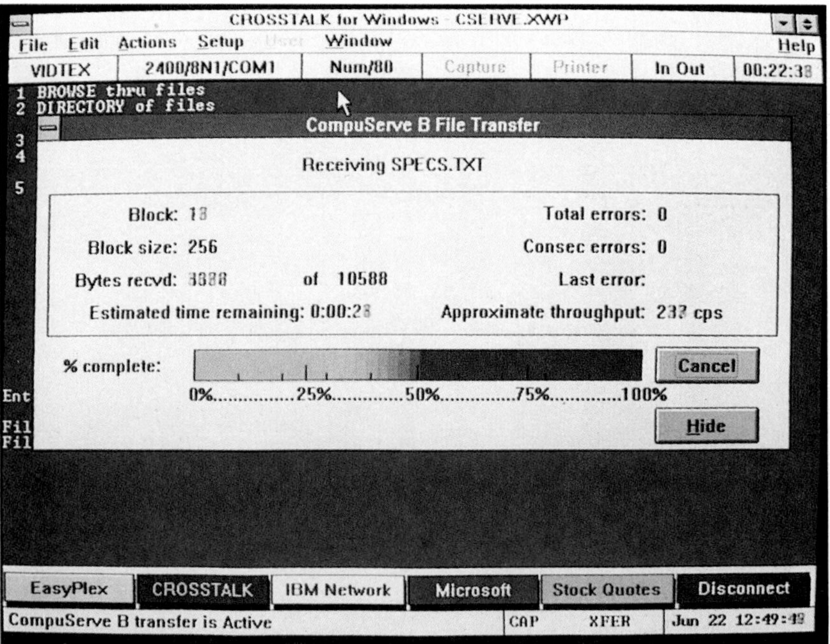

Courtesy of Digital Communications Associates, Inc.

for reporting and communicating in management reports or in presentations to groups of people.

Presentation graphics can be produced by graphics packages, such as Harvard Graphics and Lotus Freelance for microcomputers, and SAS Graph and Tell-A-Graph for minicomputers and mainframes, or by the graphics modules of electronic spreadsheets or integrated packages. To use such packages, you typically select the type of graph you want and enter the categories of data you want plotted. This is done in response to prompts displayed on your screen, or you can highlight the data you want graphed. The graphics program then analyzes the file of data you specify and generates the requested graphics. See Figure 3.17.

Integrated Packages

Integrated packages combine the abilities of several general-purpose applications in one program. Integrated packages were developed to solve the problems caused by the inability of individual programs to communicate and work together with common files of data. However, some integrated packages require significant amounts of memory and may compromise on the speed, power, and flexibility of some of their functions in order to achieve integration. Therefore, users may prefer single-function packages for applications they use heavily.

Examples of popular integrated packages are Microsoft Works, Symphony, Framework IV, PFS First Choice, and Enable. Such packages combine many of the functions of general-purpose application software such as electronic spreadsheets, word processing, graphics, database management, and data communications. Thus, you can process the same file of data with one package, moving from one function to the other by pressing a few keys on your keyboard. You can view displays from each function separately, or together in multiple windows on your video screen. See Figure 3.18.

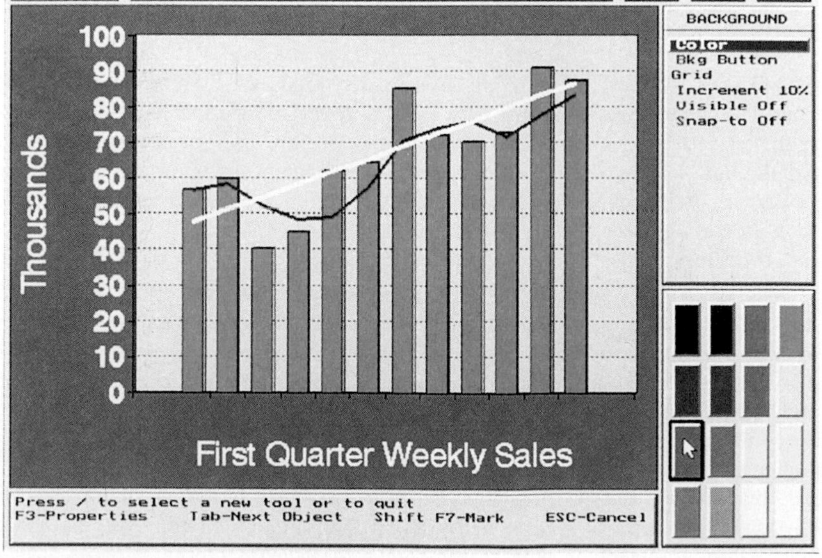

Courtesy of Lotus Development Corporation.

FIGURE 3.17
Using the Lotus Freelance graphics package.

FIGURE 3.18
Using the Microsoft Works integrated package. It provides word processing, spreadsheet, file management, telecommunications, and graphics capabilities in one package.

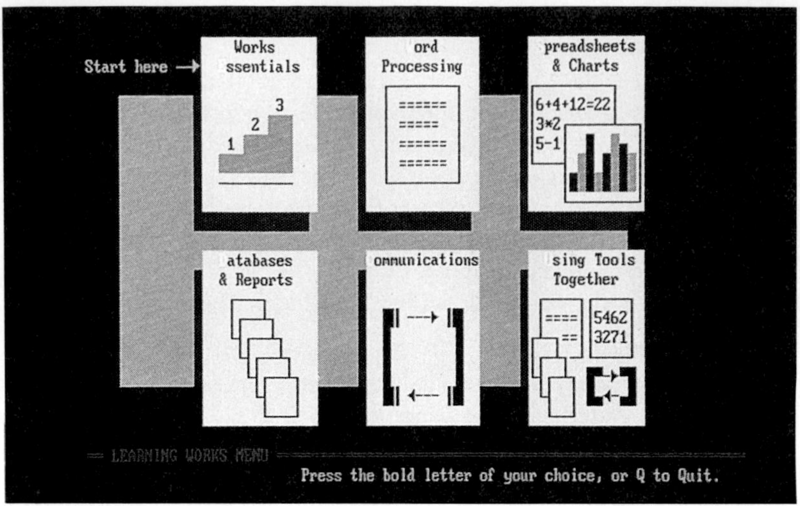

Courtesy of Microsoft Corporation.

Other End User Packages

We could spend a lot more time discussing the many application packages available to end users for use on mainframes, minicomputers, and microcomputers. As we have already noted, microcomputer application packages support managerial, professional, and business uses such as decision support, accounting, project management, investment analysis, and desktop publishing. Still other packages support end users by helping them organize random pieces of information and accomplish routine tasks, or support applications such as personal finance, home management, entertainment, education, and information services. These and other software packages are discussed in upcoming chapters on telecommunications, database management, end user computing, office automation, decision support, expert systems, and other information systems.

Summary

- **Software.** Computer software consists of two major types of programs: (1) system software, which controls and supports the operations of a computer system as it performs various information processing tasks, and (2) application software, which directs the performance of a particular use, or application, of computers to meet the information processing needs of users. Refer to Figure 3.1 for an overview of the major types of software.
- **System Software.** System software can be subdivided into system management programs, system support programs, and system development programs. System management programs manage the hardware, software, and data resources of a computer system during its execution of information processing jobs. Major system management programs are operating systems, operating environments, database management systems, and communications monitors. System support programs support the operations, management, and users of computer systems by providing a variety of support services. Major support programs are system utilities, performance monitors, and security monitors. System development programs help users develop information processing programs and procedures and prepare user programs for computer processing. Major development programs are language translators, programming editors and debuggers, code generators, and CASE tools.
- **Operating Systems.** An operating system is an integrated system of programs that supervises the operation of the CPU, controls the input/output storage functions of the computer system, and provides various support services. An operating system performs five basic functions: (1) a user interface for communication with users and operators, (2) resource management for managing the hardware resources of a computer system, (3) file management for managing files of data and programs, (4) task management for managing the tasks a computer must accomplish, and (5) utilities and other functions that provide miscellaneous support services.
- **Other System Software.** Operating environment programs add a graphical user interface to an operating system and may

REAL WORLD CASE

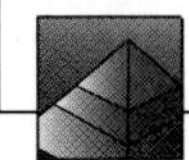

Chase Manhattan Bank: Windows-Based Application Software

Committing to a technology such as Microsoft Windows would have been a risky step for any organization, but especially so for a multibillion-dollar global bank like Chase Manhattan Bank NA, which measures those risks in millions of dollars. Nevertheless, an insightful Chase charged forward and is now reaping the profitable results, with more expected to come.

"Our challenge, as we go into the future, is to simplify the presentation and to provide the ease of one interface to all users," Chief Information Officer Craig Goldman said. To do so meant applying the interface to a wide variety of systems that run on everything from PCs to mainframes—hardly a task for the fainthearted. Undaunted, Chase's information systems staff turned to a variety of Windows-based software tools and applications to aid in this massive undertaking. The company eventually settled on Easel Graphics presentation software from Easel Corporation, Visual Basic, and the Excel spreadsheet package from Microsoft, the Lightship executive information system package from Pilot Executive Software, and Lotus Notes and 1-2-3 for Windows for electronic mail, workgroup computing, and spreadsheets from Lotus Development Corporation.

In addition, Chase's IS staff needed to find a way to make their existing systems comply with the "common interface" goal at Chase. For example, the Easel package was important in giving the company control of graphical interfaces attached to older business systems. These included applications such as the cone that allowed customer service representatives to view customer information in real time. The graphics screens that Easel provides ensure that the updated applications can be used quite easily, allowing customer service representatives to retrieve and view documents submitted by the customer—all while talking to them on the phone.

"The [key] issue for us has been how to help provide better customer service by giving the people who are on the phone with customers something that is more user-friendly and easier," thereby allowing them to worry about the customer, not the application Fiedman said.

Key to the development of the new Windows applications and their acceptance is the fact that business users were involved early on in the design process, according to Goldman. Even the chairman of the company was consulted on his needs, and today he has Windows on his desktop computer. Thus, the bank's staple of Windows-based application software packages has allowed it to take advantage of this user involvement in a timely manner.

CASE STUDY QUESTIONS

1. Why did Chase Manhattan Bank select Windows-based application software packages for their end users?
2. How can Windows-based software packages support end user involvement in developing business applications?
3. Should other companies imitate Chase's application software strategy? Explain.

Source: Adapted from Christopher Lindquist, "Chase Manhattan Bets the Bank on Windows Strategy." *Computerworld,* April 6, 1992, p. 101. Used with permission.

provide multitasking capabilities. Database management systems control the development, integration, and maintenance of databases. Telecommunications monitors control and support the telecommunication activities among the computers and terminals in a telecommunications network. Utilities are programs that perform routine computing functions, such as sorting data or copying files, as part of an operating system or as a separate package.

- **Programming Languages.** Programming languages are a major category of system software. They require the use of language translator programs to convert programming language instructions into machine language instruction codes. The four major levels of programming languages are machine languages, assembler languages, high-level languages, and fourth-generation languages. High-level languages such as BASIC and COBOL are the most widely used programming languages for business applications. However, natural, nonprocedural fourth-generation languages, including object-oriented languages, are also widely used.
- **Application Software.** Application software includes a variety of programs that can be segregated into general-purpose, business, scientific, and other application-specific categories. General-purpose application programs perform common information processing jobs for end users. Examples are word processing, electronic spreadsheet, database management, telecommunications, and graphics programs. Business application programs accomplish information processing tasks that support specific business functions or industry requirements.

Key Terms and Concepts

These are the key terms and concepts of this chapter. The page number of their first explanation is given in parentheses.

1. Application software (102)
2. Application-specific programs (102)
3. Assembler language (95)
4. Database management package (94, 105)
5. Electronic spreadsheet package (104)
6. File management (92)
7. Fourth-generation language (96)
8. General-purpose application programs (102)
9. Graphical user interface (91)
10. Graphics package (106)
11. High-level language (96)
12. Integrated package (107)
13. Language translator program (99)
14. Machine language (95)
15. Multitasking (92)
16. Natural language (97)
17. Nonprocedural language (97)
18. Object-oriented language (98)
19. Operating environment package (91)
20. Operating system (90)
21. Programming tools (100)
22. Resource management (91)
23. System management programs (90)
24. System software (89)
25. System support programs (94)
26. Task management (92)
27. Telecommunications package (105)
28. Trends in software (89)
29. User interface (91)
30. Utility programs (94)
31. Virtual memory (91)
32. Word processing package (102)

Review Quiz

Match one of the **key terms and concepts** listed above with one of the brief examples or definitions listed below. Try to find the best fit for answers that seem to fit more than one term or concept. Defend your choices.

____ 1. Programs that manage and support the operations of computers.

____ 2. Programs that direct the performance of a specific use of computers.

____ 3. An integrated system of programs that manages the operations of a computer system.

____ 4. Managing the processing of tasks in a computer system.

____ 5. Managing the use of CPU time, primary and secondary storage, and input/output devices.

____ 6. Managing the input/output, storage, and retrieval of files.

____ 7. Provides a means of communication between end users and an operating system.

____ 8. The use of icons, bars, buttons, and other image displays to help you get things done.

____ 9. Provides a greater memory capability than a computer's actual memory capacity.

____ 10. Serves as an end user graphics-based interface that integrates the use of the operating system and application programs.

____ 11. Manages and supports the maintenance and retrieval of data stored in databases.

____ 12. Manages and supports telecommunications in a network.

____ 13. Translates high-level instructions into machine language instructions.

____ 14. Performs housekeeping chores for a computer system.

____ 15. A category of application software that performs common information processing tasks for end users.

____ 16. Allows you to create and edit documents.

____ 17. Software available for the specific applications of end users in business, science, and other fields.

____ 18. Creates and displays a worksheet for analysis.

____ 19. Produces line, bar, and pie charts and other displays.

____ 20. A program that performs several general-purpose applications in one package.

____ 21. Uses instructions in the form of coded strings of ones and zeros.

____ 22. Uses instructions consisting of symbols representing operation codes and storage locations.

____ 23. Uses instructions called statements that resemble human language or the standard notation of mathematics.

____ 24. Might take the form of query languages and report generators.

____ 25. Languages that tie together data and the actions that will be performed upon the data.

____ 26. You don't have to tell the computer how to do something, just what result you want.

____ 27. As easy to use as one's native tongue.

____ 28. Performing two or more operations or applications at the same time.

____ 29. Includes programming editors, debuggers, and code generators.

____ 30. Toward powerful general-purpose integrated packages with easy to use natural language interfaces.

Discussion Questions

1. What major trends are occurring in software? What capabilities do you expect to see in future software packages?
2. How do the differences between system software and application software affect you as an end user?
3. Refer to the Real World Case on Operating Systems: What Business End Users Want. What operating system feature do you find most useful? Most inconvenient? Most needed?
4. Why is an operating system necessary? That is, why can't an end user just load an application program in a computer and start computing?
5. Which type of user interface do you prefer: command-driven, menu-driven, or graphical user interface? Explain why.
6. Refer to the Real World Case on Chase Manhattan in the chapter. What are the benefits and limitations of a common user interface for all software?
7. What capabilities does a multitasking virtual memory operating system give to a business end user?
8. Should a managerial end user know how to use a programming language to develop custom programs? Explain.
9. How important are programming tools to today's computer programmers? Today's end users?
10. Which application software packages are the most important for a business end user to know how to use? Explain the reasons for your choices.

Real World Problems

1. Royal Bank of Canada: Onward with OS/2

Royal Bank of Canada is rolling out an OS/2-based, private banking application to help account managers provide better service to its wealthiest customers. Using the latest version of the OS/2 operating system will give account managers at the Toronto-based bank (assets $100 billion) faster access to mainframe data. The intent, says Rob Brodie, manager of technology planning for Royal Bank's Private Banking Group, which uses the application, is to give end users "greater access to more information sources than ever before." The first phase of the migration has already begun; Royal Bank, for example, has already begun converting hundreds of DOS servers to OS/2. "The quantum leap in productivity we're looking for is not to be had on mainframes or PCs. It's on OS/2-based networks," says George Oliver, manager of information delivery technology.

Long frustrated by the limited memory of their DOS-based systems, account managers must wait up to two minutes for something as simple as a customer balance inquiry. The new application, expects Brodie, will shave that response time down to a few seconds. Known as the Private Banking OS/2 Workbench, the application is actually a pilot for a much bolder plan to migrate bank PC users from DOS to the more advanced OS/2. Within three or four years, 15,000 to 20,000 desktops at the Royal Bank of Canada will be running OS/2, says Oliver. The bank has several OS/2 2.0-based applications that are scheduled for a "very, very early deployment," he says. Applications expected to run under OS/2 2.0 include credit management for chief inspectors and a rewrite of its 8,000-user bank teller system. "We are deploying as fast as we can find the money to do it," Oliver says.

a. Why is the Royal Bank switching from DOS to OS/2?

b. What capabilities do operating systems like OS/2 provide to end users?

Source: Adapted from John McMullen, "OS/2 Gets the Royal Treatment," *Information Week*, February 24, 1992, p. 44; and Christopher Lindquest and Rosemary Cafasso, "What's Hot, What's Not," *Computerworld*, January 4, 1993, p. 24. Used with permission.

2. PED Manufacturing: Using Windows Software

PED Manufacturing in Oregon City, Oregon, is typical of a company facing a new crop of Windows challenges. In 1987, the 100-employee firm, which manufactures casings for the aerospace and medical industries, had strong business motivations for spending nearly $100,000 to switch its 45 computer users to Windows-based applications package. "We were bringing in lots of new employees, and we wanted them to get up to speed quickly on several applications," says Information Systems Manager Dave Howell. "But we didn't want to do a lot of development. And we wanted applications to talk to each other so we could ensure optimum productivity."

Prior to Windows' arrival, most users at PED were Johnny-one-notes who used a single DOS application—either 1-2-3 or WordPerfect—and didn't experiment with other programs. Today, PED feels the investment has largely paid off. Training time has been cut by 40 percent, and almost everyone now uses five applications—Word for Windows for word processing, Excel for spreadsheet analysis, Mail for telecommunications, PackRat for contact information, and Superbase for data management. "By cross-training on several programs, people can easily move among departments and contribute more to the entire organization," says President Richard Day. Now PED has a new hurdle ahead—its integrating the company's bread-and-butter applications into the Windows front end. "We have all our accounting, order-entry, job-costing, and quality-assurance applications running under UNIX, and all our touchy-feely tools under Windows," says Day. "Now we want our back-office applications to run under Windows on the network, but we're not sure where to start."

a. What benefits did PED Manufacturing gain from using Windows-based application packages?

b. What challenges are they facing? What do you think they should do?

Source: Adapted from Bronwyn Fryer, "Is Windows Worth It?" *PC World*, March 1992, pp. 224–25. Reprinted with permission of *PC World*.

3. Consumer Health Service, Inc.: Changing Spreadsheets

Electronic spreadsheets have undergone quite a transformation since the first spreadsheet software, VisiCalc, was unveiled at the West Coast Computer Faire in 1979. Users were thrilled that an electronic spreadsheet made extinct the painstaking manual calculation of ledger sheets; today, much more is expected of spreadsheets. Now many corporate buyers use spreadsheets as development platforms, crafting customized business units. The current leader of the Windows spreadsheet market is Microsoft Excel for Windows. But Lotus 1-2-3 still commands a 90 percent share of the DOS spreadsheet market and is pursuing a dual Windows spreadsheet strategy: getting 1-2-3 diehards to upgrade to a much improved version of 1-2-3 for Windows or adopt a new analytical spreadsheet add-on package using Improv for Windows.

To Frank Gregg, senior data analyst at Consumer Health Services Inc., a physicians' information and referral service in Boulder, Colorado, the ability to make changes on the fly and immediately see the results displayed is the most important feature of a spreadsheet. "In Lotus 1-2-3, that's enhanced even further by being able to see changes on a graph right on the spot," Gregg said. "We bought Lotus 1-2-3 as a spreadsheet, though we've taken it beyond the capabilities of a simple spreadsheet," he added. "Via macros, I've been able to do things that the folks at Lotus had no idea their product would be used to do. To me, Lotus is a language. The physician-tracking system I developed on 1-2-3 runs from menu selections, which access files [of macro instructions] that automate everything."

a. What changes have occurred in how electronic spreadsheets are used in business?

b. What does Frank Gregg mean when he says: "To me Lotus is a language"?

Source: Adapted from Sara Humphrey, "DOS Spreadsheet Buyers Target Macro Muscle," *PC Week*, June 24, 1992, p. 143; and Michael Vizard, "Dueling for Windows," *Computerworld*, April 12, 1993, p. 39. Used with permission.

4. Consolidated Edison: Using Object-Oriented Programming Tools

"If automation does anything, it should make workers more productive," says Israel Littman, manager of management analysis at Consolidated Edison's Central Engineering Division in New York. "If a company can reduce the amount of time its people spend on routine administration, they will have extra hours to spend on activities that more immediately affect the bottom line." Littman's automation philosophy led Con Edison to build an executive information system (EIS) for the engineering management staff. Above all, he wanted to provide EIS applications that were easy to use and learn. His idea? Build a common graphical front end to all business applications using an object-oriented software development tool.

Littman chose ObjectView, which accomplishes two phases of the application development cycle: screen design and program logic creation. Developers use an editor to design the way application windows look. A compiler provides a text-editing area for coding the actions triggered by the objects. For more complex logic functions, programmers must integrate subroutines written in Basic, C, or C++. "Simple GUI applications are very easy to do with Object-View," Littman says. "But we had very complicated systems to develop with extensive calculations, tables, lookups, and links to other programs." But Object-View made a tough programming job a lot easier and faster to accomplish.

a. How does object-oriented programming compare to traditional programming?

b. What are the benefits of object-oriented programming tools like Object-View?

Source: Adapted from David Braun, "Client Server Tools," *Computerworld*, February 1, 1993, p. 86. Used with permission.

Application Exercises

1. ABC Department Stores

ABC Department Stores would like to acquire software to do the following tasks. Identify what software packages they need.

a. Support telecommunications among their end users.

b. Control access and use of the hardware, software, and data resources of the system.

c. Monitor and record how the system resources are being used.

d. Make it easier to update and integrate their databases.

e. Add a graphical user interface and multitasking capabilities to their microcomputer operating systems.
f. Type correspondence and reports.
g. Analyze rows and columns of figures.
h. Develop line, bar, and pie charts.

2. Evaluating Software Packages

Have you used one of the software packages mentioned in this chapter?

a. Briefly describe the advantages and disadvantages of one of the packages you have used so far.
b. How would such a package help you in a present or future job situation?
c. How would you improve the package you used?

3. Morris Manufacturing Company: Spreadsheet Analysis

Susan Sanders is the assistant manager of the personnel department of Morris Manufacturing Company. She has been given the responsibility of selecting a copy machine for her office. After some preliminary research, she determines that there are three copiers available that will serve the needs of her office: the Canica 12000, the Duplicon plus, and the Repro 882. Each of these copiers is available on an annual lease basis. For each copier there is a fixed lease fee, plus some additional expenses which are proportional to the number of copies produced. The expected costs of each copier are as follows:

Canica 12000—This copier leases for $2,500 for the year. There is a charge of 1/2 cent per copy for service and maintenance of this copier. Paper and expendable copier supplies are expected to cost 2.5 cents per copy. This copier will handle all types of jobs automatically.

Duplicon Plus—This copier leases for $3,200 per year. Service and maintenance are included in the lease cost. Paper and expendable copier supplies are expected to cost 2.3 cents per copy. This copier will handle all types of jobs automatically.

Repro 882—This copier leases for $1,900 for the year. Service and maintenance cost $50 per hour, and it is expected that one hour of maintenance will be needed for each 7,500 copies made. Paper and expendable copier supplies are expected to cost 2.8 cents per copy. This copier has limited sorting features. The need for manual sorting is expected to require one hour of additional labor for each 3,000 copies made, at an average rate of $9.50 per hour.

Last year Susan's office made 68,000 copies. The number of copies needed this year is unknown and could range from the same level as last year to as much as 50 percent higher. Susan wants to be able to see how the costs of the copiers will compare if the number of copies is the same as last year, and if the number of copies is 25 percent or 50 percent higher than last year.

a. Create a spreadsheet that will let Susan compare the costs of the three alternative copiers and will let her see how changes in the number of copies affect these costs. Make a printout of your spreadsheet showing the costs for each copier if the number of copies is the same as last year.
b. Do what-if analysis. That is, analyze what would happen if the number of copies were 25 percent or 50 percent higher than last year. Print out the spreadsheets that result from these changes.
c. After discussions with several users, Susan finds that they have needed an hour of service for every 5,000 copies made. Make this adjustment on your spreadsheet and get a printout showing how this affects the relative cost of the copiers.
d. Based on the information in this case, which copier would you recommend? Why?

4. Software Training at ABC Company

ABC Company has recently purchased microcomputers for use by all office staff. All employees in your department are to be trained in the use of various software packages. Training is available for: DOS, word processing, spreadsheet, and database management software. Each employee must complete a total of at least 16 hours of training but is free to choose the type of training to meet his or her own needs. Training is offered by your organization's information center. Employees are responsible for scheduling their own training.

You have been assigned the task of keeping track of the training records of employees in your department. Each time an employee in your department attends a training session, you are notified of the employee's name, the type of training, and the number of hours. The training received by your department's employee to date is shown below. Assume that you have been maintaining this data in hand-written form but now wish to create a spreadsheet to maintain this information and record all future changes.

ABC Company Software Training History

	Hours of Training Completed by Type			
Employee Name	**DOS**	**Word Processing**	**Spreadsheet**	**Database**
Allen, D.	2	0	4	0
Barnett, S.	0	4	0	0
Davis, J.	4	0	0	4
Evans, W.	2	4	0	0
Forbes, M.	2	0	4	4
Grant, V.	0	0	0	0
Jenkins, J.	3	6	0	0
Milton, J.	0	4	4	0
Price, T.	2	0	4	4
Travis, B.	0	4	4	0

a. Using spreadsheet software, create an application to store the information shown below. Your spreadsheet should also indicate the total hours of training for each employee and the total amount of training (across all employees in your department) in each type of software. Print a copy of this spreadsheet.

b. You receive word from the information center that the following additional training has been completed: Davis, J., spreadsheet, 4 hours; Evans, W., DOS, 2 hours; and Forbes, M., word processing, 6 hours. Post the information to your spreadsheet and then print an updated copy of your spreadsheet.

Review Quiz Answers

1. *24*
2. *1*
3. *20*
4. *26*
5. *22*
6. *6*
7. *29*
8. *9*
9. *31*
10. *19*
11. *4*
12. *27*
13. *13*
14. *30*
15. *8*
16. *32*
17. *2*
18. *5*
19. *10*
20. *12*
21. *14*
22. *3*
23. *11*
24. *7*
25. *18*
26. *17*
27. *16*
28. *15*
29. *21*
30. *28*

Selected References

1. *Business Software Review, Computerworld, PC Magazine, PC Week,* and *Software Digest.* (Examples of good sources of current information on computer software packages.)
2. Datapro Corporation. *Datapro Reports.* (Series of regular detailed reports on selected software packages).
3. Brandt, Richard. "Can the U.S. Stay Ahead in Software?," *Business Week,* March 11, 1991.
4. McClure, Steve. "Object Technology: A Key Software Technology for the '90s." Supplement to *Computerworld,* May 11, 1992.
5. Souza, Eileen. "CASE and Traditional Software Development." In *Handbook of IS Management.* 3rd ed. Boston: Auerbach Publishers, 1991.

Introduction to Telecommunications

CHAPTER OUTLINE

C H A P T E R 4

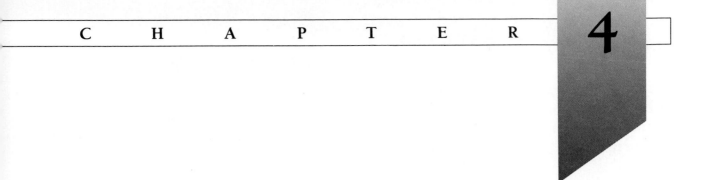

LEARNING OBJECTIVES

The purpose of this chapter is to give you an understanding of telecommunications networks, the role they play in organizations and information systems, and the challenges posed by telecommunications to managerial end users.

Section I discusses basic trends and concepts of telecommunications networks, provides examples of major applications of telecommunications in businesses and other organizations, and emphasizes the implications of such telecommunications uses to managerial end users.

Section II reviews some of the major technical characteristics of telecommunications networks needed for a basic understanding of this technology by managerial end users.

After reading and studying this chapter, you should be able to:

1. Identify several major trends and managerial challenges in the use and management of telecommunications networks.
2. Use examples to illustrate how businesses and end users benefit from using telecommunications networks.
3. Identify the basic components, functions, and types of telecommunications networks.
4. Explain the functions of major types of telecommunications network hardware, software, and media.

SECTION I

A Manager's View of Telecommunications

Why Telecommunications Is Important

Think about it—telecommunications can enable anyone in the world to communicate with anyone else in the world, almost at the speed of light. "Anyone in the world" could be your customer. "Anyone else" could be you or your competitor. Or vice versa. Think about it again [1].

Clearly, the direction of the computer field today is toward "increased connectivity"—where any computer in an organization, from mainframe to micro, can communicate with any other one. There are a lot of technical hurdles to overcome before reaching this goal. But there are also some key management decisions and policies that can help ease the task [3].

End users need to communicate electronically to succeed in today's global information society. Managers, end users, and their organizations need to electronically exchange data and information with other end users, customers, suppliers, and other organizations. Only through the use of telecommunications can they perform their work activities, manage organizational resources, and compete successfully in today's fast-changing global economy. Thus, many organizations today could not survive without interconnected *networks* of computers to service the information processing and communications needs of their end users. As a managerial end user, you will thus be expected to make or participate in decisions regarding a great variety of telecommunications options. That's why we need to study the applications, technology, and managerial implications of telecommunications. See Figure 4.1.

Telecommunications is the sending of information in any form (e.g., voice, data, text, and images) from one place to another using electronic or light-emitting media. *Data communications* is a more specific term that describes the transmitting and receiving of data over communication links between one or more computer systems and a variety of input/output terminals. The terms *teleprocessing* and *telematics* may also be used since they reflect the integration of telecommunications and computer-based information processing technologies. However, all forms of telecommunications now rely heavily on computers and computerized devices. For this reason, the broader term *telecommunications* is used as a synonym for data communications activities. Therefore, in this text, we will use these terms interchangeably.

A Telecommunications Network Model

Before we discuss the use and management of telecommunications, we should understand the basic concept of a *telecommunications network*. Generically, a *communications network* is any arrangement where a *sender* transmits a *message* to a *receiver* over a *channel* consisting of some type of *medium*. Figure 4.2 illustrates a simple conceptual model of **telecommunications network**, which shows that it consists of five basic categories of components:

- **Terminals**, such as video display terminals and other end user workstations. Of course, any input/output device that uses telecommunications networks to transmit or receive data is a terminal, including microcomputers, telephones, office equipment, and the *transaction terminals* discussed in Chapter 2.
- **Telecommunications processors**, which support data transmission and reception between terminals and computers. These devices, such as *modems, multiplexers,* and *front-end processors,* perform a variety of control and support

Sepp Seitz/Woodfin Camp & Associates.

FIGURE 4.1
Telecommunications networks are a vital part of today's businesses.

FIGURE 4.2
The five basic categories of components in a telecommunications network: (1) terminals, (2) telecommunications processors, (3) telecommunications channels and media, (4) computers, and (5) telecommunications software.

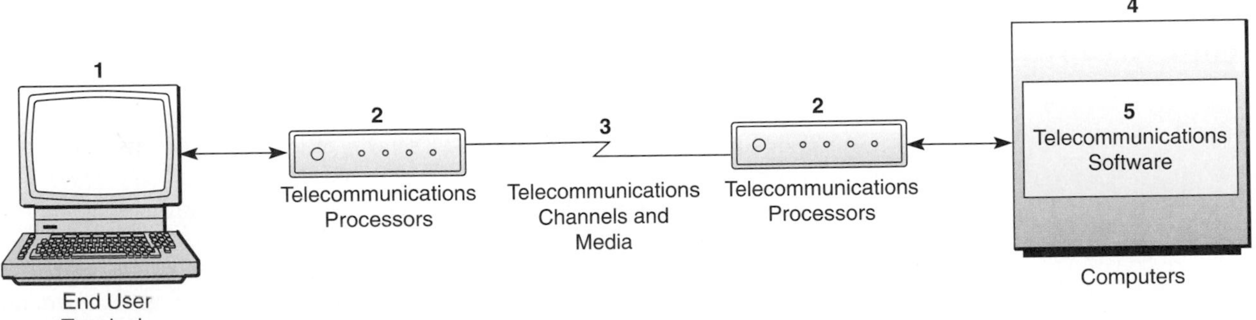

functions in a telecommunications network. For example, they convert data from digital to analog and back, code and decode data, and control the accuracy and efficiency of the communications flow between computers and terminals in a telecommunications network.

- **Telecommunications channels and media** over which data are transmitted and received. Telecommunications *channels* use combinations of *media,* such as copper wires, coaxial cables, fiber optic cables, microwave systems, and communications satellites, to interconnect the other components of a telecommunications network.
- **Computers** of all sizes and types are interconnected by telecommunications networks so that they can carry out their information processing assignments. For example, a mainframe computer may serve as a *host computer* for a large network, assisted by a minicomputer serving as a *front-end processor,* while a microcomputer may act as a *network server* for a small network of microcomputer workstations.
- **Telecommunications control software** consists of programs that control telecommunications activities and manage the functions of telecommunications networks. Examples include *telecommunications monitors* for mainframe host computers, *network operating systems* for microcomputer network servers, and *communications packages* for microcomputers.

No matter how large and complex real world telecommunications networks may appear to be, these five basic categories of components must be at work to support an organization's telecommunications activities. This framework can thus be used to help you understand the various types of telecommunications networks in use today.

Types of Telecommunications Networks

There are many different types of telecommunications networks. However, from an end user's point of view, there are two basic types: *wide area* and *local area* networks. Telecommunications networks covering a large geographic area are called *remote networks, long distance networks*, or, more popularly, **wide area networks** (WANs). Networks that cover a large city or metropolitan area (*metropolitan area networks*) can also be included in this category. Such large networks have become a necessity for carrying out the day-to-day activities of many business and government organizations and their end users. Thus, WANs are used by manufacturing firms, banks, retailers, distributors, transportation companies, and government agencies to transmit and receive information among their employees, customers, suppliers, and other organizations across cities, regions, countries, or the world. Figure 4.3 illustrates an example of a global wide area network for a major multinational corporation [8].

Local Area Networks

Local area networks (LANs) connect information processing devices within a limited physical area, such as an office, building, manufacturing plant, or other work site. LANs have become commonplace in many organizations for providing telecommunications network capabilities to end users in offices, departments, and other work groups.

LANs use a variety of telecommunications media, such as ordinary telephone wiring, coaxial cable, or even wireless radio systems to interconnect microcomputer workstations and computer peripherals. Most LANs use a powerful microcomputer having a large hard disk capacity called a *file server* or **network server** that contains a *network operating system* program that controls telecommunications and the use of

FIGURE 4.3
The wide area network (WAN) of a major multinational corporation.

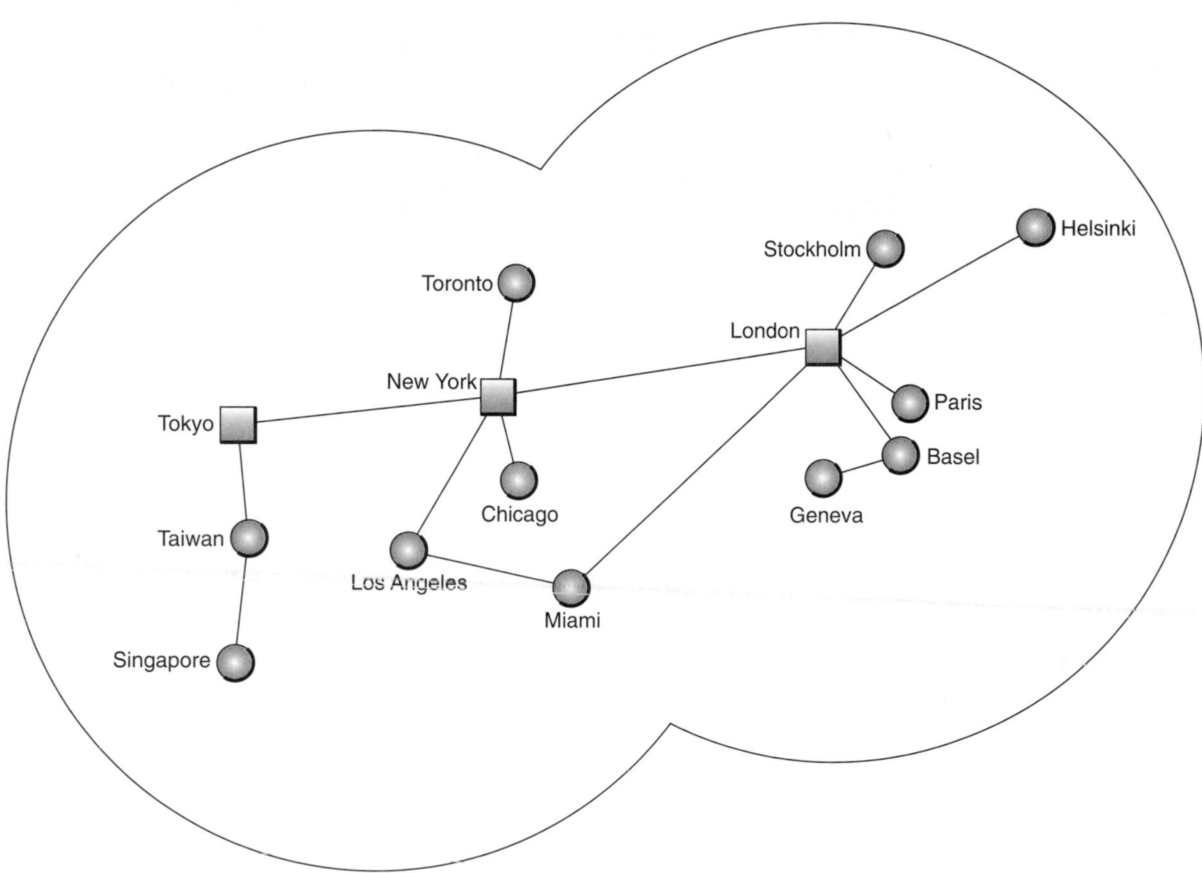

network resources. For example, it distributes copies of common data files and software packages to the other microcomputers in the network and controls access to laser printers and other network peripherals. Local area networks are connected to the computing resources and databases of wide area networks by communications processors forming a common interface called a *gateway*. See Figure 4.4.

LANs allow end users in a work group to communicate electronically; share hardware, software, and data resources; and pool their efforts when working on group projects. For example, a project team of end users whose microcomputer workstations are part of a LAN can send each other *electronic mail* messages and share the use of laser printers and hard magnetic disk units, copies of electronic spreadsheet or word processing packages, and project databases. LANs have thus become a more popular alternative to the use of terminals connected to minicomputers or smaller mainframes for end user computing in many organizations.

Applications of Telecommunications

Telecommunications applications provide invaluable capabilities and benefits to organizations and their end users. For example, local area networks enable end users to communicate electronically and share hardware, software, and data resources. Wide area networks let a company process sales transactions immediately from

FIGURE 4.4
A local area network (LAN). Note how this LAN allows users to share hardware, software, and data resources.

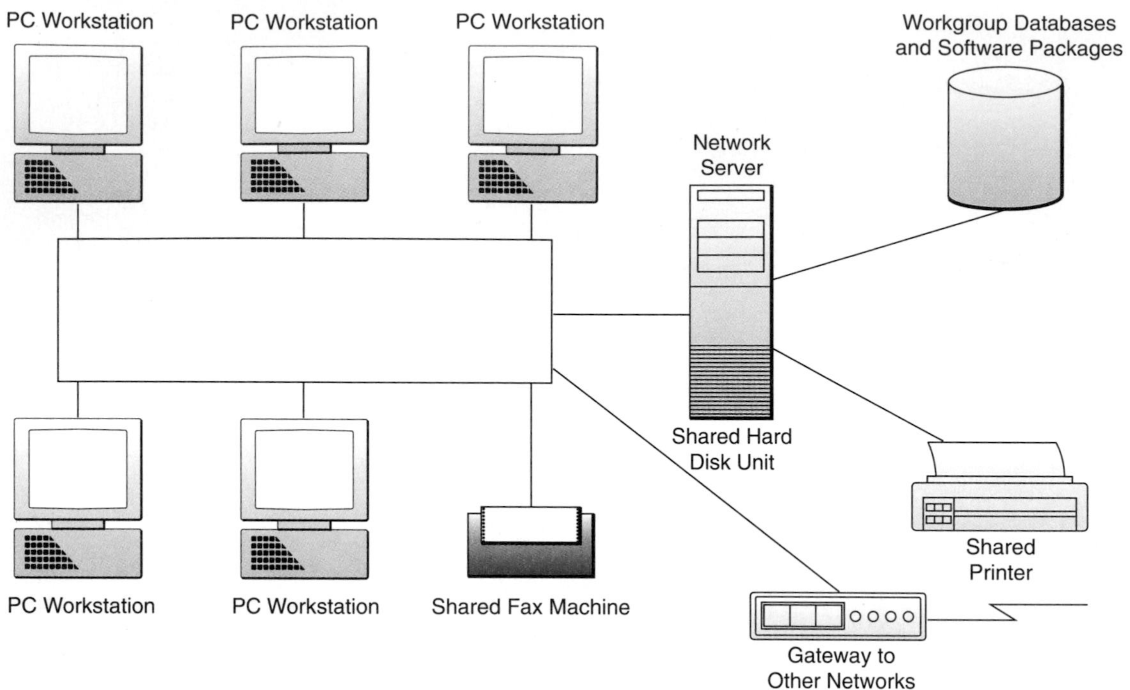

many remote locations, exchange business documents electronically with its customers and suppliers, or remotely monitor and control production processes. Distributed processing networks interconnect the computer systems of a business so their computing power can be shared by end users throughout the organization. And, of course, telecommunications networks enhance many types of communications among individuals both inside and outside an organization.

Figure 4.5 emphasizes the many possible applications of telecommunications. It groups a large number of telecommunications applications into the major categories of data communications, voice communications, text and messaging communications, information retrieval, image transmission, and monitoring and control. Now look at Figure 4.6. It outlines several basic objectives of telecommunications applications with examples of possible methods and benefits. Figure 4.6 emphasizes that telecommunications can help a firm capture and provide information quickly to end users at remote geographic locations at reduced costs, as well as supporting its strategic organizational objectives.

Let's take a brief look now at several major categories of telecommunications applications. We will discuss many of them further in later chapters. For example, electronic mail and message systems, and teleconferencing and electronic meeting systems are discussed in the context of office automation in Chapter 7. Likewise, online transaction processing and electronic data interchange (EDI) are discussed as major forms of transaction processing systems in Chapter 8.

Transaction Processing and Inquiry/Response

Telecommunications networks allow data generated by business transactions to be captured immediately by online terminals and transmitted from many remote sites to computer systems for processing. For example, many *online transaction processing* (OLTP) systems rely on wide area networks of *point-of-sale* (POS) terminals and

FIGURE 4.5
Applications of telecommunications. Note the major categories and types of applications supported by telecommunications networks.

Voice Communications	Data Communications
Standard telephone service Voice response systems Audio conferencing systems Voice mail Voice recognition Public address systems Intercom systems	Online transaction processing Inquiry/response systems Hardware and software sharing File and database transfers Cooperative processing Electronic funds transfer systems Point-of-sale systems Electronic document interchange
Text and Messaging Communications	**Information Retrieval**
Electronic mail Computer conferencing systems Electronic bulletin boards	Bibliographic search services News and economic database services Videotex
Image Transmission	**Monitoring and Control**
Image processing Facsimile Closed circuit television Video teleconferencing Electronic meeting systems	Process control systems Equipment monitoring Security surveillance Hospital patient monitoring Energy management

Source: Adapted from Ralph Sprague and Barbara McNurlin, ed., *Information Systems Management in Practice* (Englewood Cliffs, N.J.: Prentice Hall, 1986), pp. 142, 144.

FIGURE 4.6
Business objectives of telecommunications applications, with examples and benefits.

Application Objectives	Application Examples	Application Benefits
Geographic: Capture information about business transactions from remote locations	Transmission of customer orders from traveling salespeople and regional sales offices to a corporate data center for order processing, billing, and inventory control	Provides better customer service by reducing delay in filling orders; improves cash flow by speeding up the billing cycle; allows inventory records to be kept current
Speed: Provide information to remote locations within a relatively short time after it is requested	Credit authorization at the point of sale by inquiry/response of corporate databases	Credit inquiries can be made and answered in seconds, allowing credit authorizations to be made without customer irritation
Cost: Reduce the cost of more traditional means of communication	Audio and/or video teleconferencing	Reduces expensive business trips; allows more people to participate in a meeting, thus improving the quality of decisions reached
Strategic: Support linkages for competitive advantage	Electronic data interchange (EDI) of transaction data to and from suppliers and customers	Fast, convenient service locks in customers and suppliers

Source: Adapted from George W. Reynolds, *Introduction to Business Telecommunications* (Columbus, Ohio: Charles E. Merrill, 1984), p. 6.

computers to instantly capture sales transactions and update corporate databases. Transactions data can also be accumulated into batches, stored on magnetic disk or tape devices, and transmitted periodically to a central computer for processing from remote locations, which is called *remote job entry* (RJE). Telecommunications networks allow business offices, banks, retail stores, and distribution centers to minimize manual data entry and expedite transaction processing, thus cutting costs, reducing errors, and improving service. In particular, **electronic data interchange** (EDI) networks support direct electronic exchanges of business transaction documents among businesses and their customers and suppliers. Thus, EDI replaces the exchange of paper transaction documents such as purchase orders and sales invoices. EDI and other aspects of transaction processing systems are discussed in Chapter 8.

Electronic funds transfer (EFT) systems in banking and retailing industries specialize in the capture and processing of money and credit transfers between businesses and customers. Bank telecommunications systems support teller terminals in all branch offices and automated teller machines (ATMs) at locations throughout a city or region. Also supported are pay-by-phone services, which allow bank customers to use their telephones as computer terminals to electronically pay bills. Wide area networks also connect POS terminals in retail stores to bank EFT systems. See Figure 4.7.

Inquiry/response systems allow managers and other end users to make inquiries about information stored in personal, departmental, corporate, and external databases and receive immediate responses through telecommunications networks. This provides up-to-date information for business operations and managerial decision making. End users can also use telecommunications networks to access external data bank services providing economic, demographic, and financial data to individual and corporate users.

Distributed and Cooperative Processing

Distributed processing and *cooperative processing* are major applications of telecommunications. In **distributed processing**, information processing activities in an organization are accomplished by using a network of computers interconnected by telecommunications links instead of relying on one large *centralized* computer facility or on the *decentralized* operation of several independent computers. For example, a distributed processing network may consist of mainframes, minicompu-

Charles Gupton/Tony Stone Worldwide

FIGURE 4.7
Banks use networks of ATM terminals to provide 24-hour electronic funds transfer services.

ters, and microcomputers, dispersed over a wide geographic area and interconnected by wide area networks, or they may be distributed within user departments in local area networks.

Cooperative processing takes this concept one step further. It allows the various types of computers in a distributed processing network to share the processing of parts of an end user's application. Application software packages are available which have common user interfaces and functions so they can operate consistently on networks of micro, mini, and mainframe computer systems. For example, an end user could use a spreadsheet package provided to his or her microcomputer workstation by a local area network server to perform financial analysis on databases managed by a mainframe computer system. This is also called **client/server computing**, since application processing is shared by end user workstations (clients) connected to LAN servers and possibly to mainframe *superservers*. See Figure 4.8.

With distributed and cooperative processing, local users can handle a broad range of information processing tasks. This includes data entry, database inquiry, transaction processing, updating databases, generating reports, and providing decision support. Thus, data can be completely processed locally, where most input and output (and errors and problems) must be handled anyway, while still providing access to the resources of other computers in the network. This provides computer processing more tailored to the needs of end users and increases information processing efficiency and effectiveness as users become more responsible for their own application systems.

Distributed and cooperative processing lets large central-site computers handle those jobs they can do best, such as high-volume transaction processing, communications network control, and maintenance of large corporate databases. Users at local sites can access central computers to receive corporatewide management information or transmit summary transaction data reflecting local site activities to corporate mainframes.

Office Automation and End User Computing

Telecommunications plays a vital role in office automation and end user computing. Office workstations are typically tied together in local area networks with other office devices such as intelligent copiers, laser printers, and facsimile machines and may be linked to department and corporate networks. Software packages and common databases are typically shared in such networks. Services such as electronic mail, voice mail, facsimile, and teleconferencing allow end users to send and receive

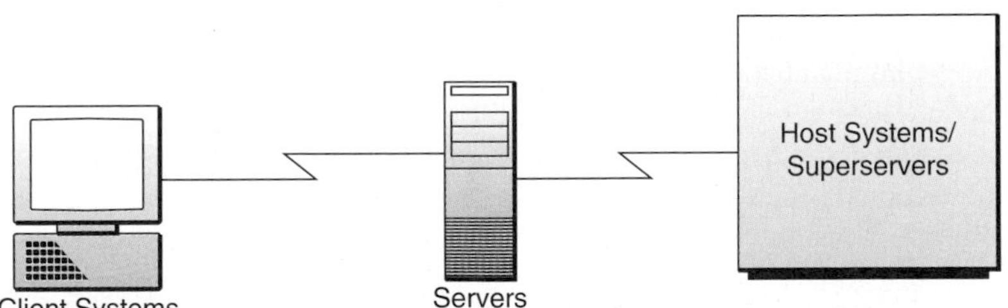

- Types: Workstations, PC's, Macintoshes.
- Functions: Provide user interface, perform some/most processing on an application.

- Types: Supermicros, workstations, or midrange systems.
- Functions: Shared computation, application control, distributed databases.

- Types: Mainframes, superminicomputers.
- Functions: Central database control, security, directory management, heavy-duty processing.

FIGURE 4.8
A client/server model for distributed and cooperative processing. Note the functions performed by different types of computers acting as clients, servers, and superservers.

messages electronically in text, voice, image, or video form. Telecommunications networks also support work group computing, where end users in a network work together on joint projects. Networks allow them to share data, perform joint analysis, and integrate the results of individual efforts by members of the work group. We will discuss such office automation and end user computing applications in Chapter 7.

Public Information Services

Public information services are another major category of telecommunications applications. For example, companies such as CompuServe, Genie, and Prodigy offer a variety of information services for a fee to anyone with an appropriately equipped personal computer. They offer such services as electronic mail, financial market information, airline reservations, use of software packages for personal computing, electronic games, home banking and shopping, news/sports/weather information, and a variety of specialized data banks. Gaining access to these services is easy if you have a personal computer equipped with a modem and a communications software package.

Videotex

Another way end users can get information using an information services network is **videotex**. In its simplest form (teletext), videotex is a one-way, repetitive broadcast of pages of text and graphics information to your TV set. This method uses cable, telephone lines, or standard TV transmission. A control device allows you to select the page you want to display and examine. Videotex, however, is meant to be an interactive information service provided over phone lines or cable TV channels. End users can select specific video displays of data and information, such as electronic Yellow Pages and personal bank checking account registers. Thus, you can use a special terminal or personal computer to do banking and shopping electronically. Videotex is widely used in Europe. Many companies tried pilot programs of videotex services in the 1980s, but most efforts failed to generate sufficient consumer interest. Videotex services are currently available from several sources, including personal computer networks such as Prodigy, a joint venture of IBM and Sears, and the CompuServe Bank-at-Home and Shop-at-Home services.

Bulletin Board Systems

Bulletin board systems (BBSs) are a popular telecommunications service provided by public information services, and thousands of business firms, organizations, and user groups. An electronic bulletin board system allows you to post public or private messages that other end users can read by accessing the BBS with their computers. Establishing a small BBS is not that difficult. Minimum requirements are a microcomputer with a hard disk drive, custom or packaged BBS software, and a modem and telephone line for as many simultaneous users as the BBS computer can handle. Bulletin board systems serve as a central location to post and pick up messages or upload and download data files or programs 24 hours a day. A BBS helps end users ask questions, get advice, locate and share information, and get in touch with other end users. Thus, bulletin board systems are being used by many business firms as a convenient, low-cost way to enhance the flow of information among their employees and customers.

Interorganizational Networks

Many of the applications of telecommunications we have just mentioned can be classified as **interorganizational networks**. As Figure 4.9 illustrates, such networks link a company's wide area and local area networks to the networks of its customers, suppliers, information service providers, and other organizations. For example, you can think of a computerized account inquiry system for access by customers as an

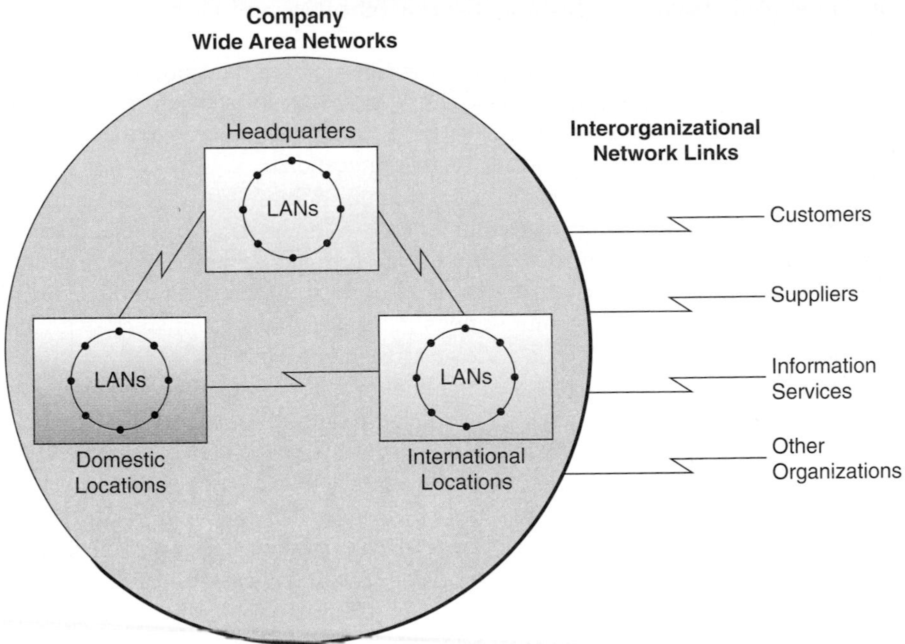

FIGURE 4.9
Interorganizational systems rely on network links between an organization and its customers, suppliers, and other organizations.

example of an interorganizational network. So is the use of electronic document interchange, which links the computers of a company with its suppliers and customers. Accessing information services such as Dow Jones News Retrieval or the data banks of government agencies for information about market and economic conditions is another example. Electronic funds transfer applications also depend on interorganizational networks established among banks, businesses, employees, customers, and suppliers.

Thus, the business use of telecommunications has moved beyond the boundaries of work groups and the organization. Now many business firms have extended their telecommunications networks to their customers and suppliers, both domestically and internationally. As we will see in Chapter 6, such *interorganizational systems* build new strategic business relationships and alliances with those *stakeholders* in an attempt to increase and lock in their business, while locking out competitors. Also, transaction processing costs are frequently reduced, and the quality of service increases. In addition, the availability of external information about industry, market, economic, and political developments provides better information for managerial decision making. Because of these benefits, the trend toward increased connectivity between the networks of an organization and its external stakeholders is expected to continue.

Telecommunications Carriers

Common Carriers

Telecommunications channels for wide area networks can be owned by an organization or provided by other companies. In the United States, several companies have traditionally used a variety of communications media to create networks that can provide a broad range of communications services. These **common carriers** provide the wide area communications networks used by most computer-using firms and individuals. They have traditionally been authorized by government agencies to provide a selected number of communication services to the public. Examples are the former Bell operating companies, General Telephone and Electronics, Western Union, and many independent telephone companies. Some common carriers specialize in selling long-distance voice and digital data communications services in high-density areas of the country and the world. Examples of such specialized carriers are AT&T Long Distance, ITT World Communications, Southern Pacific Communications, U.S. Sprint, and MCI Communications.

Common carriers can provide an organization needing the data communications capabilities of a wide area telecommunications network with several options. For example, an organization could use regular, voice-grade, direct distance dialing (DDD), which is more expensive, slower, and less reliable than other options due to delays caused by excessive communications traffic and the noise of voice-switching circuits. Or it could sign up for a wide area telephone service (WATS) and pay a monthly fee for unlimited use of a set amount of telephone line capacity. This would be cheaper for an organization with a lot of communications activity, but it would have the same reliability problem as DDD. Or it could lease its own communications lines (called *leased lines*) from telephone companies and be guaranteed exclusive use of a low-noise, fast communications channel. However, this is an expensive alternative that is economically feasible only for large corporations and government agencies with massive data communications needs. Another expensive option is the use of a company that provides communications satellite services. Or an organization could build a *bypass* system, in which it installs its own dish antennas and bypasses the common carrier networks and transmits directly to communications satellites. Once again, this is a more expensive alternative, attractive only to organizations with a high volume of data communications.

Value-Added Carriers

Other major communications carriers are companies called **value-added carriers**. These are third-party vendors who lease communications lines from common carriers and offer communications services to customers. Typically, messages from customers are transmitted in groupings called packets, via *packet-switching* networks. However, the networks of such carriers are known as *value-added networks* (VANs), because they add value to their leased communications lines by using communications hardware and software and their expertise to provide not only packet switching but other data communication services. Value-added networks also take over the responsibility for the management of the network, thus relieving their customers of the technical problems inherent in long-distance communications.

Value-added carriers offer their customers or *subscribers* high-quality, relatively low cost service in return for a membership fee and usage charges based on the amount of communications activity accomplished. By spreading the cost of leasing the lines among many subscribers and using the capacity of the lines intensively, they are able to sell their services at attractive prices and still make a profit. Examples of value-added companies are GTE Telenet, General Electric's Mark Net, and Compunet by CompuServ. These VANs have become so popular that common carriers such as the Bell operating companies, AT&T, MCI, and Western Union, and large corporations such as IBM and RCA now offer VAN services.

A Managerial Perspective on Telecommunications

Investing in telecommunications is inherently a business gamble. The technology is expensive, rapidly changing, and complex. The stakes increase as traditional marketplaces are changed by electronic delivery, as new markets open up, as some firms use communications successfully to reposition their business, and as others succeed only in creating expensive write-offs on the income statement [12].

Statements such as this and the ones at the beginning of this chapter emphasize the importance of telecommunications from a managerial perspective. Thus, you should view telecommunications not only as a method of electronic communications, but as a competitive weapon, as a means of organizational connectivity, and as a vital investment in technology. Given this managerial perspective on the importance of communications, you should develop an appreciation for (1) the potential benefits and problems of telecommunications and (2) how to plan and implement a proper role for telecommunications in an organization.

Trends in Telecommunications

Major trends occurring in the field of telecommunications have a significant impact on management decisions in this area. Informed managerial end users should thus be aware of major trends in telecommunications industries, technologies, and applications that significantly increase the decision alternatives confronting their organizations. See Figure 4.10.

Industry Trends

The competitive arena for telecommunications service has changed dramatically in the United States, from a few government-regulated monopolies to many fiercely competitive suppliers of telecommunications services. With the breakup of AT&T and the Bell System in 1984, global telecommunications services became available from a variety of telecommunications companies offering long-distance telephone service, communications satellites, and many other services, as well as from smaller companies specializing in selected telecommunications equipment and services, such as cellular radio and electronic mail. Thus, the telecommunications services and vendor options available to meet an organization's needs have increased significantly.

Technology Trends

Telecommunications is being revolutionized by a change from analog to digital network technologies. Telecommunications has always depended on voice-oriented analog transmission systems designed to transmit the variable electrical frequencies generated by the sound waves of the human voice. However, telecommunications technology is rapidly converting to digital transmission networks, which transmit information in the form of discrete pulses, as computers do, rather than waves. Digital transmission systems greatly enhance the use of computer-based communications control devices and communications media. This provides (1) significantly higher transmission speeds, (2) the movement of larger amounts of information, (3) greater economy, and (4) much lower error rates than analog systems. In addition, a digital technology, ISDN (Integrated Services Digital Network), which will allow telecommunications networks to carry multiple types of communications (data, voice, video) on the same circuits, is now being implemented.

Another major trend in telecommunications technology is a change in communications media. Many telecommunications networks are switching from copper wire–based media (such as coaxial cable) and land-based microwave relay systems

Industry trends	Toward a greater number of competitive vendors, carriers, and telecommunications services.
Technology trends	Toward integrated digital global networks for voice, data, and video with heavy use of fiber optic lines and satellite channels.
Application trends	Toward the pervasive use of telecommunications networks in support of business operations, managerial decision making, and strategic advantage in global markets.

FIGURE 4.10
Major trends in telecommunications.

to fiber optic lines and communications satellite transmissions. Fiber optic transmission, which uses pulses of laser-generated light, offers significant advantages in terms of reduced size and installation effort, vastly greater communication capacity, and freedom from electrical interference. Satellite transmission offers significant advantages in speed and capacity for organizations that need to transmit massive quantities of data over global networks. These trends in technology give organizations more alternatives to use in overcoming the limitations of their present telecommunications systems.

Application Trends

The changes in telecommunications industries and technologies just mentioned are causing a significant change in the business use of telecommunications. The trend toward more vendors, services, and advanced technologies dramatically increases the number of feasible applications. Thus, telecommunications is playing a more important role in support of the operations, management, and strategic objectives of both large and small companies. An organization's telecommunications function is no longer relegated to office telephone systems, long-distance calling arrangements, and a limited amount of data communications with corporate mainframes. Instead, it is becoming an integral part of computer-based information systems used to cut costs, improve operational processes, share resources, lock in customers and suppliers, and develop new products and services. This makes telecommunications a more complex and important decision area for businesses which must increasingly compete in both domestic and global markets.

Adding Value with Telecommunications

Figure 4.11 outlines a framework for understanding how telecommunications can add value to a business. It emphasizes that telecommunications can have three basic effects on the operation of a business:

- Compress the time taken to accomplish business activities.
- Reduce the limits placed on a firm's business activities by geographic distances.
- Restructure traditional business relationships with a firm's customers and suppliers and with other organizations.

These impacts of telecommunications can add value to a business in three major dimensions. Figure 4.11 shows how managers can use telecommunications to improve the efficiency of business operations, the effectiveness of business functions, and the extent of business innovation. For example, the use of telecommunications networks could result in the following benefits for a chain of retail stores:

- **Operational efficiency.** Telecommunications can provide immediate, online processing of sales transactions, centralized purchasing in large quantities by online connections from remote stores, and direct sales by telephone.
- **Business effectiveness.** Telecommunications can provide electronic mail and facsimile services for instant transmission of interstore messages, teleconferencing facilities to conduct online video meetings with store managers, and customer hotlines for remote diagnosis and assistance of customer service problems.
- **Organizational innovation.** Telecommunications can provide instant credit authorization for major purchases by customers, in-store banking through the installation of ATMs, and electronic shopping by customers from in-home terminals.

FIGURE 4.11
Adding value through telecommunications. Note how telecommunications can add value to a business by improving operational efficiency, business effectiveness, and organizational innovation.

	Value		
Impact	**Operational Efficiency**	**Business Effectiveness**	**Organizational Innovation**
Compress time	Accelerate business operations and processes	Reduce information float	Create superior service
Examples:	*Online transaction processing*	*Electronic mail*	*Instant credit checks*
Reduce geographic limits	Generate economies of scale	Ensure control of dispersed operations	Penetrate new markets
Examples:	*Online, centralized purchasing*	*Teleconferencing*	*Remote ATM banking*
Restructure relationships	Bypass intermediaries in the distribution chain	Provide expertise to remote sites	Lock in customers and suppliers
Examples:	*Direct sales by phone*	*Remote diagnostics and maintenance*	*Electronic in-home shopping*

Source: Adapted from Michael Hammer and Glen Mangurian, "The Changing Value of Telecommunications Technology," *Sloan Management Review*, Winter 1987, p. 66.

Developing a Telecommunications Strategy

Using telecommunications to increase the value of a business will not happen without careful planning by management. First, a **telecommunications strategy** must be created. That is, top management must decide how much of the organization's strategic business goals depend on the use of telecommunications technology. For example, a business that chooses to remain a small, neighborhood enterprise has less need of telecommunications technology than a business that wants to service world markets.

Let's assume a firm finds that its long-term survival and success depend on the effective use of telecommunications. Its management must then identify how this technology can be integrated into its long-range business plans. This requires the identification of improvements in operational efficiency, business effectiveness, and organizational innovation that could be gained by the use of telecommunications technology. Figure 4.11 could be used as a framework for this analysis. Then the present role of telecommunications must be identified. For example, what telecommunications hardware, software, personnel, and networks exist? What are their purposes and capabilities? Answering these questions will help managers identify telecommunications problems and opportunities that must be addressed in the organization's telecommunications strategy.

Finally, a **telecommunications architecture** must be developed. This is a master plan for building an integrated telecommunications capability that supports business operations, managerial decision making, and strategic organizational objectives. The telecommunications architecture is therefore a technical blueprint that outlines the design of an integrated telecommunications capability for attaining the business objectives of an organization.

Figure 4.12 illustrates a useful concept for determining how to position the telecommunications architecture and other IT capabilities of an organization [8]. **Reach** refers to the types of business stakeholders and locations that can be connected by telecommunications network links to a firm's IS resources, that is, its IT *platform* or base. **Range** refers to the types of information and information processing which can be shared automatically through telecommunications net-

FIGURE 4.12
Telecommunications can help a business develop open integrated systems to build strategic relationships among its internal locations and external stakeholders.

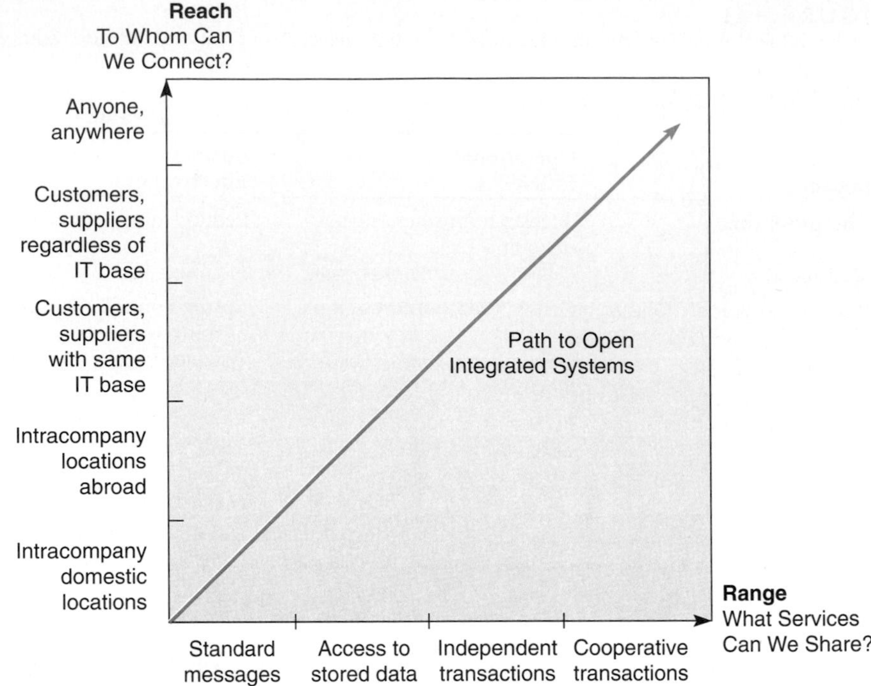

Source: Adapted from Peter Keen, *Shaping the Future: Business Design through Information Technology* (Boston: Harvard Business School Press, 1991).

works. Figure 4.12 emphasizes that one of the strategic objectives of many organizations is to use telecommunications and other information technologies to develop *open integrated* interorganizational information systems. That is, these organizations are committed to developing an open telecommunications network architecture that allows them to provide an integrated selection of applications to service their internal needs and those of their present and future stakeholders.

REAL WORLD CASE

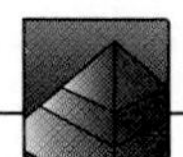

Fisher-Price, Inc.: Using Global and Local Networks

Fisher-Price, Inc. is in the midst of installing a global network that could hardly be called child's play. The $700 million toy maker expects the new network to help the firm better coordinate its manufacturing and distribution requirements while providing long-term cost savings. Earlier this month, Fisher-Price installed LAN-to-LAN connections between its manufacturing and distribution sites in Peterlee, UK, and Hong Kong, and its East Aurora, New York, headquarters, according to Jim Carrier, director of computer technical services.

Prior to the networking overhaul, Fisher-Price used remote intelligent processors to link video terminals and printers in the field to a Unisys mainframe computer over leased lines. Fisher-Price is now installing LANs using Novell Netware network operating systems in eight North American manufacturing and distribution sites, with plans to connect all of those over a wide-area network by year's end.

The WAN was designed to provide Fisher-Price employees worldwide with improved access to the processing power and databases of the company's Unisys A17 mainframe, which handles the bulk of the firm's processing, Carrier said. However, Carrier added that Fisher-Price's move to more open systems will eventually make the Unisys mainframe obsolete. The company is replacing its proprietary Unisys equipment with Hewlett-Packard Unix-based machines, with an eye toward improved processing and increased interoperability, Carrier said. Thus, Fisher-Price has installed six HP I486-based 50 MHz network servers at its headquarters. The company uses DTK Computer PCs for its employees, Carrier said. However, he added that the toy maker will use Intel 486-based PCs with the best value, as long as replacement parts are interchangeable.

Although Fisher-Price recently added electronic data interchange, master planning, and market research applications to two HP Unix, it will make the switch to more open systems a gradual move. "We intend to do that very slowly over a long period of time," said Carrier, who added that Fisher-Price intends to replace its A17 mainframe with a smaller model within the next three years.

CASE STUDY QUESTIONS

1. What telecommunications network components do you recognize at Fisher-Price? Use Figure 4.2 to help you organize your answer.
2. What is Fisher-Price's telecommunications strategy? Why did it choose this strategy?
3. How is Fisher-Price adding business value with telecommunications?

Source: Adapted from Thomas Hoffman, "Fisher-Price Fields Grown-Up Network," *Computerworld*, March 15, 1993, p. 57. Used with permission.

SECTION II
Technical Telecommunications Alternatives

Telecommunications is a highly technical, rapidly changing field of information systems technology. Most end users do not need a detailed knowledge of its technical characteristics. However, it is important that you understand some of the important characteristics of the basic components of telecommunications networks. This understanding will help you participate effectively in decision making regarding telecommunications alternatives. Figure 4.13 outlines key telecommunications network components and alternatives. Remember, a basic understanding and appreciation, not a detailed knowledge, is sufficient for most business end users.

Telecommunications Media

Telecommunications channels (also called communications *lines* or *links*) are the means by which data and other forms of communications are transmitted between the sending and receiving devices in a telecommunications network. A telecommunications channel makes use of a variety of **telecommunications media**. These include twisted-pair wire, coaxial cables, and fiber optic cables, all of which physically link the devices in a network. Also included are terrestrial microwave, communications satellites, cellular and LAN radio, all of which use microwave and other radio waves, and infrared systems, which use infrared light to transmit and receive data. Figure 4.14 illustrates some of the major types of media used in modern telecommunications networks.

Twisted-Pair Wire

Ordinary telephone wire, consisting of copper wire twisted into pairs (*twisted-pair wire*), is the most widely used media for telecommunications. These lines are used in established communications networks throughout the world for both voice and data transmission. Thus, twisted-pair wiring is used extensively in home and office telephone systems and many local area networks and wide area networks. See Figure 4.15.

Coaxial Cable

Coaxial cable consists of a sturdy copper or aluminum wire wrapped with spacers to insulate and protect it. This insulation minimizes interference and distortion of the signals the cable carries. Groups of coaxial cables may be bundled together in a big cable for ease of installation. These high-quality lines can be placed underground and laid on the floors of lakes and oceans. They allow high-speed data transmission

FIGURE 4.13
Key telecommunications network components and alternatives.

Network Component	Examples of Alternatives
Media	Twisted-pair wire, coaxial cable, fiber optics, microwave, communications satellites, cellular and LAN radio, infrared
Processors	Modems, multiplexers, concentrators, controllers, front-end processors, private branch exchanges
Software	Telecommunications monitors, telecommunications access programs, network operating systems, end user communications packages
Channels	Analog/digital, switched/nonswitched, transmission speed, circuit/message/packet switching, simplex/duplex, asynchronous/synchronous
Topology/architecture	Point-to-point, multidrop, star/ring/bus, OSI, ISDN

FIGURE 4.14
An example of the telecommunications media in a telecommunications channel. Note the use of a communications satellite, earth stations with dish antennas, microwave links, fiber optic and coaxial cable, and a wireless LAN.

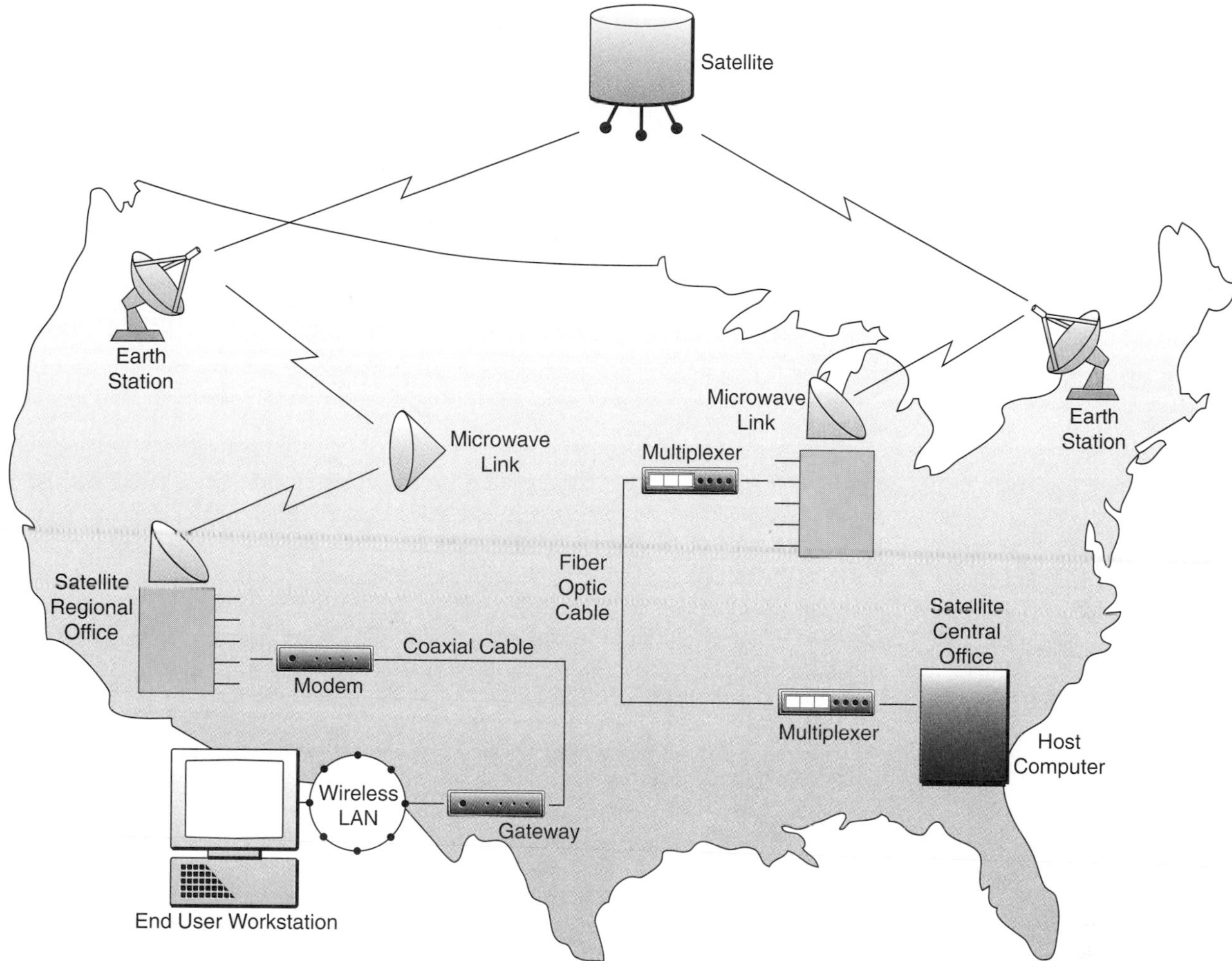

and are used instead of twisted-pair wire lines in high-service metropolitan areas, for cable TV systems, and for short-distance connection of computers and peripheral devices. Coaxial cables are also used extensively in office buildings and other work sites for local area networks.

Fiber Optics

Fiber optics uses cables consisting of one or more hair-thin filaments of glass fiber wrapped in a protective jacket. They can conduct light pulses generated by lasers at transmission rates as high as two billion bits per second. This is about 10 times greater than coaxial cable and 200 times better than twisted-pair wire lines. Fiber optic cables provide substantial size and weight reductions as well as increased speed and greater carrying capacity. A half-inch-diameter fiber optic cable can carry up to 50,000 channels, compared to about 5,500 channels for a standard coaxial cable.

Fiber optic cables are not affected by and do not generate electromagnetic radiation; therefore, multiple fibers can be placed in the same cable. Fiber optic

FIGURE 4.15
Telecommunications wire and cable alternatives.

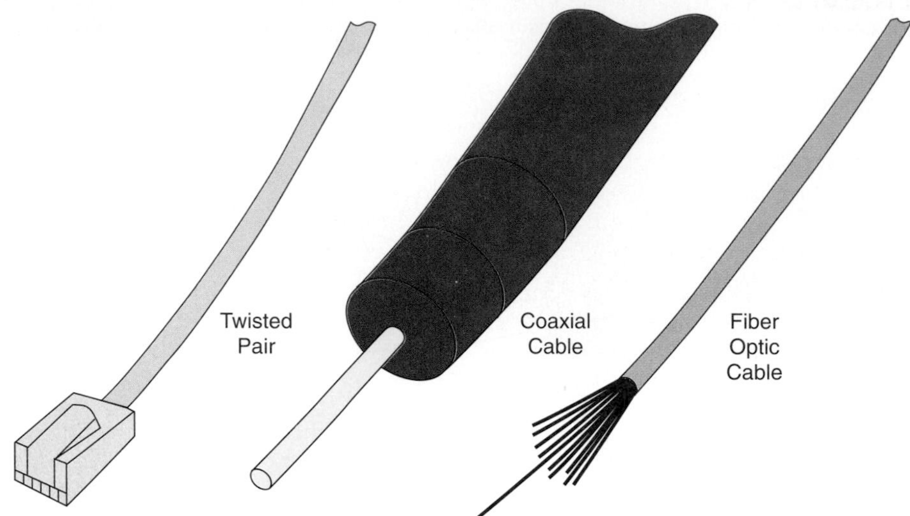

cables have a minimal need for repeaters for signal retransmissions, unlike electrical wire media. Fiber optics also has a much lower data error rate than other media and is harder to tap than electrical wire and cable. The biggest disadvantage of fiber optics is the difficulty of splicing the cable to make connections, though this is also a security advantage that limits line tapping. Fiber optic cables have already been installed in many parts of the United States, and they are expected to replace other communications media in many applications in the near future.

Terrestrial Microwave

Terrestrial microwave involves earthbound microwave systems which transmit high-speed radio signals in a line-of-sight path between relay stations spaced approximately 30 miles apart. Microwave antennas are usually placed on top of buildings, towers, hills, and mountain peaks, and they are a familiar sight in many sections of the country. They are still a popular medium for both long-distance and metropolitan area networks.

Communications Satellites

An important telecommunications medium is the use of **communications satellites** for microwave transmission. There are several dozen communications satellites from several nations placed into stationary "parking orbits" approximately 22,000 miles above the equator. Satellites are powered by solar panels and can transmit microwave signals at a rate of several hundred million bits per second. They serve as relay stations for communication signals transmitted from *earth stations*. Earth stations use *dish antennas* to beam microwave signals to the satellites, which amplify and retransmit the signals to other earth stations thousands of miles away.

While communications satellites were used initially for voice and video transmission, they are now also used for high-speed transmission of large volumes of data. Because of time delays caused by the great distances involved, they are not suitable for interactive, realtime processing. Communications satellite systems are operated by several firms, including AT&T, Western Union, American Satellite Company, and Intellsat, an international consortium of over 100 nations. Many large corporations and other users have developed networks of small satellite dish antennas known as VSAT (very small aperture terminal) to connect their distant work areas. These satellite networks are also called *bypass networks* because firms are bypassing the regular communications networks provided by communications carriers.

Cellular Radio

Cellular radio is a radio communications technology that divides a metropolitan area into a honeycomb of cells. This greatly increases the number of frequencies and users that can take advantage of mobile phone service. Each cell has its own low-power transmitter, rather than having one high-powered radio transmitter to serve an entire city. This significantly increases the number of radio frequencies available for mobile phone service. However, this technology requires a central computer and other communications equipment to coordinate and control the transmissions of thousands of mobile phone users as they drive from one cell to another. Cellular radio has become an important communications medium for mobile voice and data communications. For example, Federal Express uses cellular radio for data communications with terminals in each of its thousands of delivery vans as part of its competitive edge.

Wireless LANs

Wiring an office or a building for a local area network is often a difficult and costly task. Older buildings frequently do not have conduits for coaxial cables or additional twisted-pair wire, and the conduits in newer buildings may not have enough room to pull additional wiring through. Repairing mistakes and damages to wiring is often difficult and costly, as are major relocations of LAN workstations and other components.

One increasingly popular solution to such problems is installing a **wireless LAN**, using one of several wireless technologies. One example is **LAN radio**, which uses radio transmissions to interconnect LAN components. LAN radio may involve a high-frequency radio technology similar to cellular radio, or a low-frequency radio technology called *spread spectrum*. The other wireless LAN technology is called **infrared**, because it uses beams of infrared light to establish network links between LAN components. See Figure 4.16.

Obviously, a wireless LAN eliminates or greatly reduces the need for wires and cables, thus making a LAN easier to set up, relocate, and maintain. However, current wireless technologies have higher initial costs and other limitations. For example, an infrared LAN transmits faster than radio LANs but is limited to line-of-sight arrangements to a maximum of about 80 feet between components. High-frequency radio LANs do not need line-of-sight links, but are limited to 40 to 70 feet between components in enclosed areas. Spread spectrum radio LANs can penetrate masonry walls and link components from 100 to 200 feet away in enclosed areas, but are more subject to receiving or generating radio interference. However, even with these limitations, the use of wireless LAN technologies is expected to increase significantly [2].

Telecommunications Processors

Telecommunications processors such as modems, multiplexers, concentrators, front-end processors, and other devices perform a variety of support functions between the terminals and computers in a telecommunications network. Let's take a look at some of these devices and their functions.

Modems

Modems are the most common type of communications processor. They convert the *digital* signals from a computer or transmission terminal at one end of a communications link into analog frequencies, which can be transmitted over ordinary telephone lines. A modem at the other end of the communications line converts the transmitted data back into digital form at a receiving terminal. This process is known as *modulation* and *demodulation*, and the word *modem* is a combined abbreviation of those two words. Modems come in several forms, including small stand-alone units, plug-in circuit boards, and microelectric modem chips.

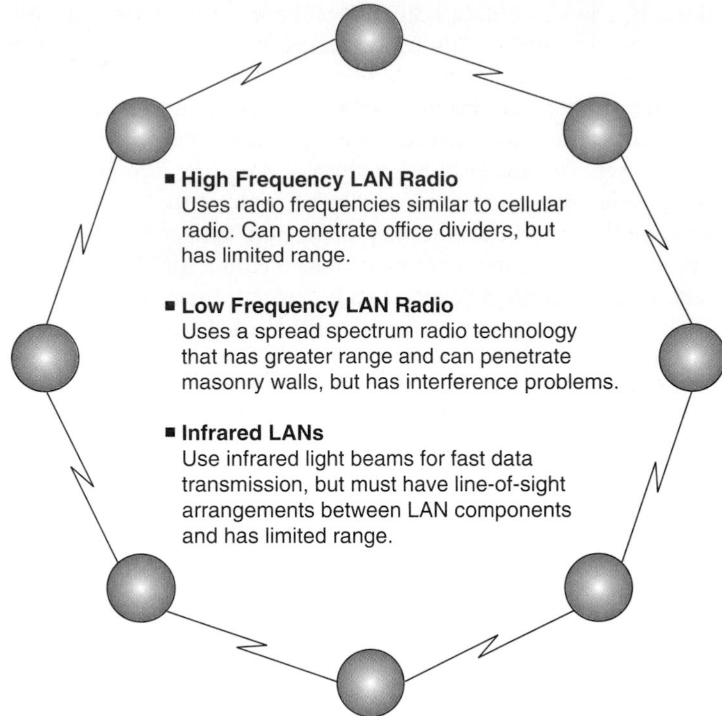

■ High Frequency LAN Radio
Uses radio frequencies similar to cellular radio. Can penetrate office dividers, but has limited range.
■ Low Frequency LAN Radio
Uses a spread spectrum radio technology that has greater range and can penetrate masonry walls, but has interference problems.
■ Infrared LANs
Use infrared light beams for fast data transmission, but must have line-of-sight arrangements between LAN components and has limited range.

FIGURE 4.16
Three competing wireless LAN technologies. Note the benefits and limitations of each.

Modems are necessary because ordinary telephone lines were primarily designed to handle continuous analog signals (electromagnetic frequencies), such as those generated by the human voice over the telephone. Since data from computers are in digital form (voltage pulses), devices are necessary to convert digital signals into appropriate analog transmission frequencies and vice versa. However, *digital communications networks* that transmit only digital signals are rapidly being developed. Modems that perform only the digital/analog conversion function are not required for such networks. See Figure 4.17.

Multiplexers, Concentrators, and Controllers

A **multiplexer** is a communications processor that allows a single communications channel to carry simultaneous data transmissions from many terminals. Thus, a single communications line can be shared by several terminals. Typically, a multiplexer merges the transmissions of several terminals at one end of a communications channel, while a similar unit separates the individual transmissions at the receiving end.

This is accomplished in two basic ways. In *frequency division multiplexing* (FDM), a multiplexer effectively divides a high-speed channel into multiple slow-speed channels. In *time division multiplexing* (TDM), the multiplexer divides the time each terminal can use a high-speed line into very short time slots, or time frames. The most advanced and popular type of multiplexer is the *statistical time division multiplexer*, most commonly referred to as a *statistical multiplexer*. Instead of giving all terminals equal time slots, it dynamically allocates time slots only to active terminals according to priorities assigned by a telecommunications manager.

Devices known as concentrators and controllers have microprocessor intelligence, stored communications programs, and buffer storage. *Concentrators* concentrate many slow-speed lines into a high-speed line through the use of buffer storage,

FIGURE 4.17
Modems perform a modulation-demodulation process that converts digital signals to analog and back.

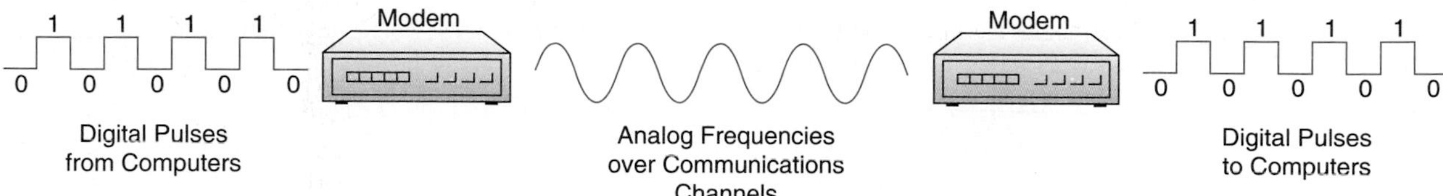

and they also route data to its proper destination. *Controllers*, or *cluster controllers*, link groups of terminals or other devices to a communications channel. The controller polls the status of each terminal connected to it and transfers data from a terminal to the host computer when necessary.

Front-End Processors

A **front-end processor** is typically a minicomputer dedicated to handling the data communications control functions for large mainframe **host** computers. For example, a front-end processor uses telecommunications control programs to provide temporary buffer storage, data coding and decoding, error detection, recovery, and the recording, interpreting, and processing of control information (such as characters that indicate the beginning and end of a message). It can also poll remote terminals to determine if they have a message to send or if they are ready to receive a message.

However, a front-end computer has more advanced responsibilities. It controls access to a network and allows only authorized users to use the system, assigns priorities to messages, logs all data communications activity, computes statistics on network activity, and routes and reroutes messages among alternative communication links. Thus, the front-end processor can relieve the host computer of its data communications control functions so it can concentrate on its other information processing chores.

Private Branch Exchange

The **private branch exchange** (PBX) is a communications processor that serves as a switching device between the telephone lines within a work area and the local telephone company's main telephone lines, or *trunks*. PBXs can be as small as a telephone or as large as a minicomputer. They not only route telephone calls within an office but also provide other services, such as automatic forwarding of calls, conference calling, and least-cost routing of long-distance calls. Some PBX models can control communications among the terminals, computers, and other information processing devices in local area networks in offices and other work areas. This gives a PBX a big advantage over other LAN technologies since a PBX-based LAN can use ordinary office telephone wiring instead of the special wiring needed by other types of LANs. Other PBXs can integrate the switching of voice, data, and images in *integrated digital services networks*, which we will be discussing shortly. See Figure 4.18.

Telecommunications Software

Software is a vital component of all telecommunications networks. Communications control software includes programs stored in the host computer as well as programs in front-end computers and other communications processors. Such software controls and supports the communications occurring in a telecommunications network. For example, telecommunications software packages for mainframe-based wide area

FIGURE 4.18
The role of a PBX as a telecommunications processor for voice, data, and image transmission in a local area network.

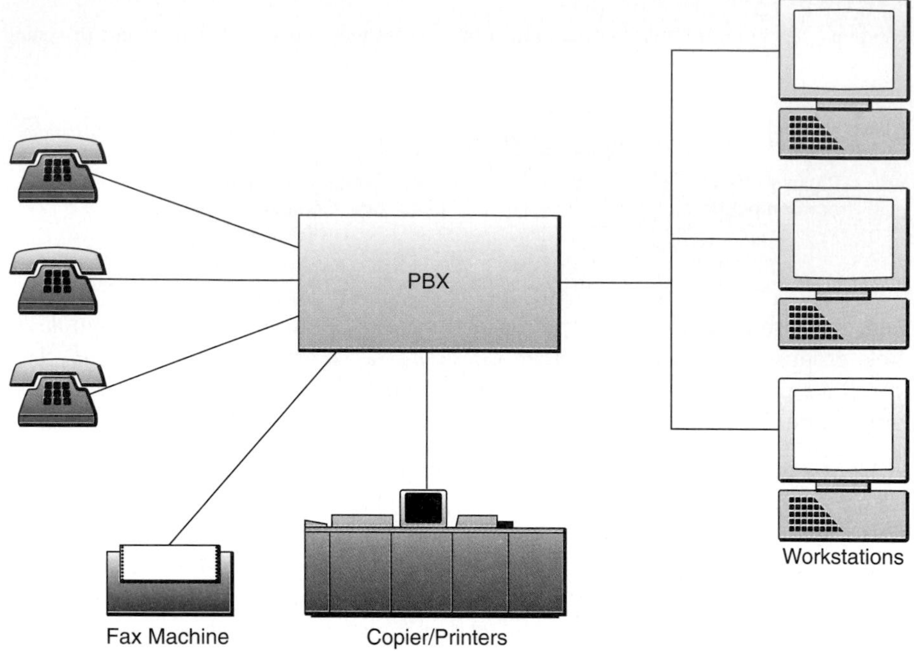

networks are frequently called *telecommunication monitors* or *teleprocessing* (TP) *monitors*. CICS (Customer Identification Control System) for IBM mainframes is a typical example. Local area networks rely on software called *network operating systems*, such as Novell NetWare or Microsoft LAN Manager. Many communications software packages are also available for microcomputers, as we discussed in the last chapter. See Figure 4.19.

Common Software Functions

Telecommunications software packages provide a variety of communications support services. The number and type of terminals, computers, communications processors, and communications activities involved determine the capabilities of the programs required. However, several major functions are commonly provided by telecommunications packages.

Access Control

This function establishes the connections between terminals and computers in a network. The software works with a communications processor (such as a modem) to connect and disconnect communications links and establish communications parameters such as transmission speed, mode, and direction. Access control may also involve automatic telephone dialing and redialing, logging on and off with appropriate account numbers and security codes, and automatic answering of telephone calls from another computer. Many communications packages include a *script language* which allows you to develop programs to customize access control, such as accessing other computers at night or while you are away.

Transmission Control

This function allows computers and terminals to send and receive commands, messages, data, and programs. Some error checking and correction of data transmissions may also be provided. Data and programs are usually transmitted in the form of files, so this activity is frequently called *file transfer*.

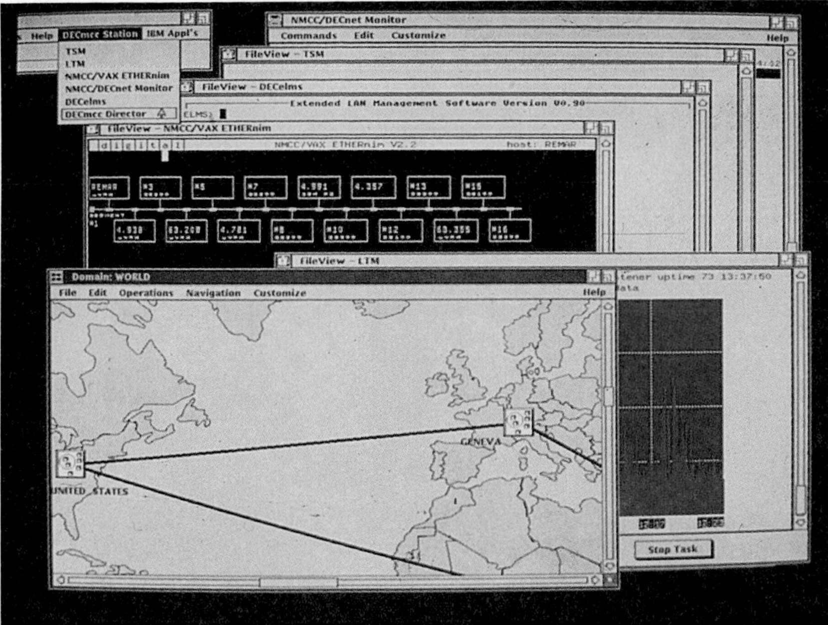

Courtesy Digital Equipment Corporation.

FIGURE 4.19
This display of the DECnet telecommunications monitor shows the status of local area and international networks.

Network Management

This function manages communications in a telecommunications network. Software such as LAN network operating systems and WAN telecommunications monitors determines transmission priorities, routes (switches) messages, polls, and terminals in the network, and forms waiting lines (*queues*) of transmission requests. It also logs statistics of network activity and the use of network resources by end user workstations.

Error Control

This function involves detection and correction of transmission errors. Errors are usually caused by distortions in the communications channel, such as line noise and power surges. Communications software and processors control errors in transmission by several methods, including *parity checking*. Parity checking involves determining whether there is an odd or even number of *binary one digits* in a character being transmitted or received. Besides parity bits, additional *control codes* are usually added to the message itself. These specify such information as the destination of the data, their priority, and the beginning and end of the message, plus additional error-detecting and correcting information. Most error correction methods involve retransmissions. A signal is sent back to the computer or terminal to retransmit the previous message.

Security Management

This function protects a communications network from unauthorized access. Network operating systems or other security programs restrict access to data files and other computing resources in LANs and other types of networks. This restriction usually involves control procedures that limit access to all or parts of a network by various categories of users, as determined by the *network manager* or *administrator* of the network. Automatic disconnection and callback procedures may also be used. Data transmissions can also be protected by coding techniques called **encryption**. Data is scrambled into a coded form before transmission and decoded upon arrival.

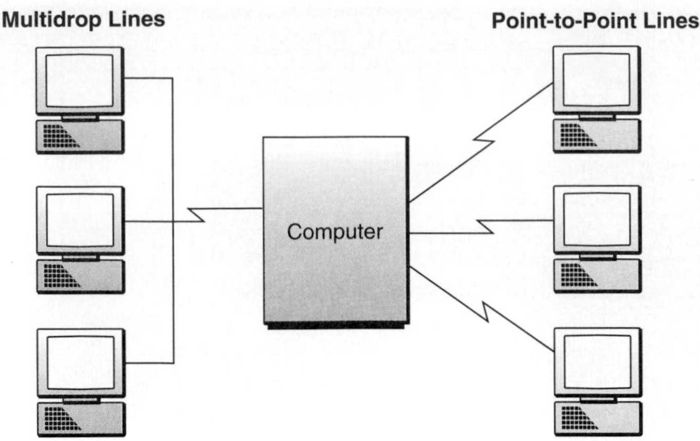

FIGURE 4.20
Multidrop lines allow terminals to share a communications line. Point-to-point lines provide a separate communications line for each terminal.

Telecommunications Network Topologies

There are several basic types of network *topologies*, or structures, in telecommunications networks. The two simplest are *point-to-point* lines and *multidrop* lines. When point-to-point lines are used, each terminal is connected by its own line to a computer system. When multidrop lines are used, several terminals share each data communications line to a computer. Obviously, point-to-point lines are more expensive than multidrop lines: All of the communications capacity and equipment of a communications line is being used by a single terminal. Therefore, point-to-point lines are used only if there will be continuous communications between a computer and a terminal or other computer system. A multidrop line decreases communications costs, because each line is shared by many terminals. Communications processors such as multiplexers and concentrators help many terminals share the same line. See Figure 4.20.

Star, Ring, and Bus Networks

Figure 4.21 illustrates three basic topologies used in wide area and local area telecommunications networks. A **star network** ties end user computers to a central computer. In a **ring network** local computer processors are tied together in a ring on a more equal basis. A **bus network** is a network in which local processors share the same bus, or communications channel. In many cases, star networks take the form of hierarchical networks. In hierarchical networks, a large headquarters computer at the top of the company's hierarchy is connected to medium-size computers at the divisional level, which are connected to small computers at the departmental or work group level. A variation of the ring network is the *mesh* network. This uses direct communications lines to connect some or all of the computers in the ring to each other. Another variation is the *tree* network, which joins several bus networks together.

In most cases, distributed processing systems use a combination of star, ring, and bus approaches. Obviously, the star network is more centralized, while ring and bus networks have a more decentralized approach. However, this is not always the case. For example, the central computer in a star configuration may be acting only as a **switch**, or message-switching computer, that handles the data communications between autonomous local computers.

Star, ring, and bus networks differ in their performances, reliabilities, and costs. A pure star network is considered less reliable than a ring network, since the other computers in the star are heavily dependent on the central host computer. If it fails, there is no backup processing and communications capability, and the local

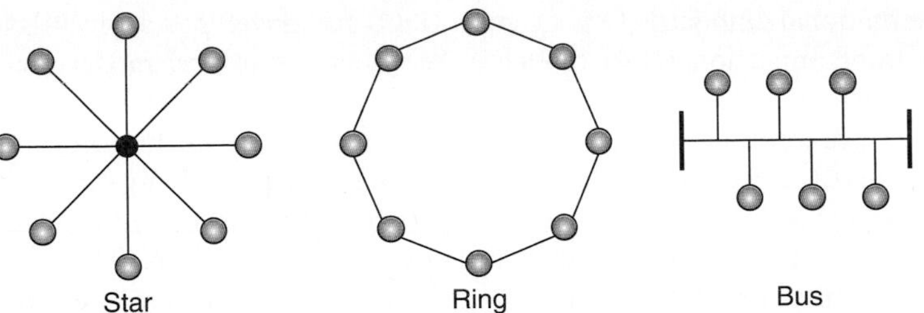

FIGURE 4.21
The star, ring, and bus network topologies.

computers will be cut off from the corporate headquarters and from each other. Therefore, it is essential that the host computer be highly reliable. Having some type of *multiprocessor architecture* to provide a *fault tolerant* capability is a common solution.

Star network variations are common because they can support the *chain-of-command* and hierarchical structures of most organizations. Ring and bus networks are most common in local area networks. Ring networks are considered more reliable and less costly for the type of communications in such networks. If one computer in the ring goes down, the other computers can continue to process their own work as well as to communicate with each other.

Network Architectures and Protocols

Until quite recently, there was a lack of sufficient standards for the interfaces between the hardware, software, and communications channels of data communication networks. For this reason, it is quite common to find a lack of compatibility between the data communications hardware and software of different manufacturers. This situation has hampered the use of data communications, increased its costs, and reduced its efficiency and effectiveness. In response, computer manufacturers and national and international organizations have developed standards, called *protocols*, and master plans, called *network architectures*, to support the development of advanced data communications networks.

Protocols

A **protocol** is a standard set of rules and procedures for the control of communications in a network. However, these standards may be limited to just one manufacturer's equipment, or to just one type of data communications. Consequently, there are many competing and incompatible protocols in use today. Part of the goal of communications network architectures is to create more standardization and compatibility among communications protocols. One example of a protocol is a standard for the physical characteristics of the cables and connectors between terminals, computers, modems, and communications lines. Other examples are the protocols that establish the communications control information needed for *handshaking*, which is the process of exchanging predetermined signals and characters to establish a telecommunications session between terminals and computers. Other protocols deal with control of data transmission/reception in a network, switching techniques, internetwork connections, and so on.

Network Architectures

The goal of **network architectures** is to promote an open, simple, flexible, and efficient telecommunications environment. This is accomplished by the use of standard protocols, standard communications hardware and software interfaces, and the design of a standard multilevel interface between end users and computer systems.

The OSI Model and Other Architectures

The International Standards Organization (ISO) has developed a seven-layer Open System Interconnection (OSI) model to serve as a standard model for network architectures. By dividing data communications functions into seven distinct layers, the ISO hopes to promote the development of modular network architectures. This would assist the development, operation, and maintenance of large data communications networks. Network architectures currently being implemented by computer manufacturers include IBM's System Network Architecture (SNA) and the Digital Network Architecture (DNA) of the Digital Equipment Corporation. Another important example is the Manufacturing Automation Protocol (MAP), a local area network architecture for automated factories, sponsored by General Motors and other manufacturers. Figure 4.22 illustrates the functions of the seven levels of the OSI model architecture.

Integrated Services Digital Network

Related to the development of network architectures is the development of a set of standards for ISDN, the Integrated Services Digital Network. This is a set of international standards needed to establish public and private digital telecommunications networks capable of handling voice, data, image, and video communications throughout the world. ISDN will replace the many types of networks in use today with a single type of digital network incorporating a standard set of communications processors to provide voice, data, image, and video services to any terminal in the network. Many communications carriers and corporations are developing,

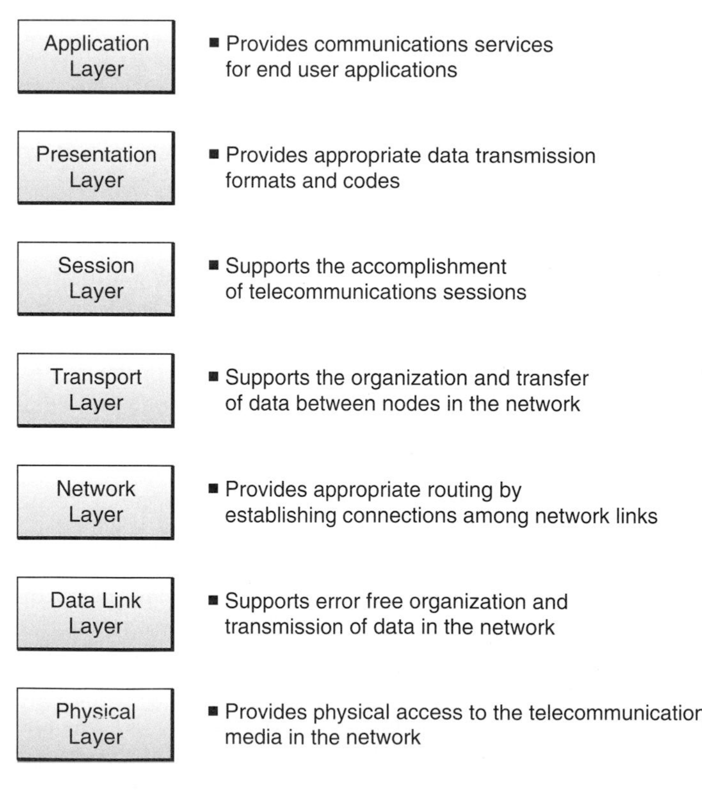

Application Layer
■ Provides communications services for end user applications
Presentation Layer
■ Provides appropriate data transmission formats and codes
Session Layer
■ Supports the accomplishment of telecommunications sessions
Transport Layer
■ Supports the organization and transfer of data between nodes in the network
Network Layer
■ Provides appropriate routing by establishing connections among network links
Data Link Layer
■ Supports error free organization and transmission of data in the network
Physical Layer
■ Provides physical access to the telecommunications media in the network

FIGURE 4.22
The seven layers of the OSI communications network architecture. The OSI model is recognized as an international standard for telecommunications networks.

testing, and installing ISDN networks. ISDN is scheduled to be implemented in most major U.S. cities by the mid-1990s and in all U.S. and major international locations by 2010 [1].

ISDN promises to revolutionize telecommunications and networking. Voice, video, and data transmissions will be available through your telephone company and the normal twisted-pair telephone wiring of your office or home just by plugging your computer or *videophone* into a telephone wall socket. So ISDN will enable end users to enjoy multimedia computing and communications. However, much more development work remains to be done by communications carriers, computer manufacturers, and end user organizations. ISDN's technology must still be perfected, costs must become competitive, and organizations must learn how to use this new communications service. Only then will the promise of ISDN become a reality.

Communications Channel Characteristics

Transmission Speed

The communication capabilities of telecommunication channels can be classified by *band width*. This is the frequency range of the channel, which determines the channel's maximum transmission rate. Data transmission rates are typically measured in bits per second (BPS). This is sometimes referred to as the *baud* rate, though baud is more correctly a measure of signal changes in a transmission line.

Voiceband, or low-speed analog, channels allow transmission rates from 300 to 9,600 BPS. They are "voice grade" analog communication lines commonly used for voice communications, but are also used for data communications by microcomputers, video terminals, and fax machines. *Medium-band*, or medium-speed, channels use specially conditioned leased lines so they can handle transmission speeds from 9,600 to 256,000 BPS.

Broadband, or high-speed digital, channels allow transmission rates at specific intervals from 256,000 BPS to several billion BPS. They typically use microwave, fiber optics, or satellite transmission. Examples are 64,000 BPS for digital telephone service and 1.54 million BPS for T1 communications channels developed by AT&T and used by many large private communications networks. See Figure 4.23.

Transmission Mode

The two modes of transmitting data are called *asynchronous* and *synchronous* transmission. Asynchronous transmission transmits one character at a time, with each character preceded by a *start bit* and followed by a *stop bit*. Asynchronous transmission is normally used for low-speed transmission at rates below 2,400 BPS. Synchronous transmission transmits groups of characters at a time, with the beginning and end of a character determined by the timing circuitry of a communications processor. Synchronous transmission is normally used for high-speed transmission exceeding 2,400 BPS.

Transmission Direction

Communications channels can provide three types of data transmission directions. A *simplex* channel allows data to be transmitted in one direction only. A *half-duplex* channel allows transmission in either direction, but in only one direction at a time. This is usually sufficient for low-speed terminals (such as transaction terminals). Alternating sending and receiving is a typical characteristic of their normal communications activities. The *full duplex* channel allows data to be transmitted in both directions at the same time. It is used for high-speed communications between computer systems.

FIGURE 4.23
Telecommunications transmission speeds. Note the wide range of transmission speeds possible with each of these media.

Media	Speed
Twisted pair—voice telephone	300–9,600 BPS
Twisted pair—conditioned	96–256 KBPS
Coaxial cable—baseband	10–264 MBPS
Coaxial cable—broadband	10–550 MBPS
Terrestrial microwave	56 KBPS–50 MBPS
Satellite microwave	56 KBPS–50 MBPS
LAN radio	2–3.3 MBPS
Infrared LAN	230 KBPS–4 MBPS
Fiber optic cable	500 KBPS–30 GBPS

BPS = bits per second
KBPS = thousand BPS, or kilobits per second
MBPS = million BPS or megabits per second
GBPS = billion BPS, or gigabits per second

Switching Alternatives

Regular telephone service relies on *circuit switching*, in which a circuit is opened to establish a link between a sender and receiver that remains open until the communication session is completed. In *message switching*, a message is transmitted a block at a time from one switching device to another. This method is sometimes called *store-and-forward transmission* because messages may be temporarily stored by the switching device before being retransmitted.

Packet switching involves subdividing communications messages into groups called *packets*, typically 128 characters long. The packet switching network carrier uses computers and other communications processors to control the packet switching process and transmit the packets of various users over its leased lines. Packet switching networks are also known as X.25 networks, which is the international protocol governing the operations of public packet switching networks. Packet switching is most widely used by value-added networks.

Access Methods

How can terminals and other devices access and share a network to transmit and receive data? As Figure 4.24 indicates, a variety of *access methods* are used to provide this capacity. In the *polling* approach, a host computer or communications processor polls (contacts) each terminal in sequence to determine which terminals have messages to send. The sequence in which the terminals are polled is based on the communications traffic expected from each terminal. Thus, the transmission of each terminal is based on a "roll call" of each terminal on the line. Polling can be an effective method because the speed of mainframe and communications processors computers allow them to poll and control transmissions by many terminals sharing the same line, especially if the typical communications consist of brief messages and inquiries.

In the *contention* approach, line use is on a first-come, first-served basis, where a terminal can transmit data if the line is not in use, but it must wait if it is busy. One way to make contention work is a widely used method called *carrier-sense multiple access with collision detection* (CSMA/CD). This requires a terminal or other device to continually monitor the network and send a message only if it senses the network is not in use. If a collision is detected, the terminal must stop transmission, wait until the network is clear, and try again. This access method is used by Ethernet and some other local area networks.

Another widely used method in local area networks is *token passing*. A token is a special signal code sent around the network. If a terminal or other device wants to

- **Polling.** A communications processor conducts a roll call of the terminals in a network to determine if they have messages to send.
- **Contention.** Terminals send messages on the network on a first-come, first-served basis.
- **Token passing.** Terminals use an electronic signal code or *token* to send messages which are passed on to the appropriate terminal in the network.

FIGURE 4.24
Common telecommunications access methods.

transmit a message, it must wait for the token to come by, examine it to see if it is in use and pass it on, or use the token to help route its message to its destination on the network. After transmission is completed, the token is returned to the network by the receiving terminal if it is not needed. This access method is used in IBM *token ring* networks and other widely used LANs, including the Datapoint and MAP *token bus* networks.

REAL WORLD CASE

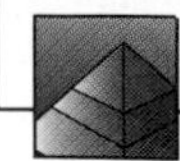

Wal-Mart Stores, Inc.: Competing with LANs and Satellites

Wal-Mart Stores is installing high-speed local area networks that can be directly connected to very small aperture terminal (VSAT) satellite antennas at each of their stores and warehouses and at company headquarters in Bentonville, Arkansas. These networks will increase LAN-to-satellite transmission speeds from 19.2 kilobits per second (KBS) to hundreds of thousands of KBS, according to Michael Fitzgerel, special project manager of the retailer's network.

The faster connections are crucial, given that "we have a number of applications coming along, each of which has the need to move multiple gigabytes of data per day to and from the stores," Fitzgerel said. Among the more strategic of these applications are Wal-Mart's multiyear push toward direct store-to-supplier ordering as well as recent experiments with multimedia PCs as training vehicles. The new direct LAN-to-satellite links will make file transfers go five to seven times faster and will speed up server-to-host interactions by as much as 50 percent—all without the need to replace Wal-Mart's basic satellite infrastructure, Fitzgerel added.

Like most major retailers, Wal-Mart needs satellite links to reach its more remote sites, which are still inaccessible to high-speed carrier services such as frame relay, he added. For some time now, Wal-Mart has been in the vanguard of an industry trend toward tracking products in greater and greater detail, for purposes of market analysis and faster inventory turnover. "It used to be we just tracked, say, sweaters, by the number sold," Fitzgerel said. "Now we track by size and color—much finer detail. And with that comes additional data" to be sent back to the data center for analysis.

In addition, Wal-Mart is four or five years ahead of its competitors when it comes to implementing "a continuous replenishment system," in which stores send orders for new merchandise directly to the suppliers as soon as the consumer takes it out the door, Fitzgerel said. At Wal-Mart, stores order replacement items directly from the supplier daily, Fitzgerel said. Point-of-sale (POS) terminals that record the transactions send the data to a Unix server via a Token Ring LAN; the server then sends the orders, via satellite link, to the home office IBM Enterprise System/9000s mainframes. There they are batched together with other store orders, he said.

Store purchasing can also be done through hand-held bar-code terminals connected into the LAN via radio-frequency modem. The bar-code terminals are used to ensure accuracy of pricing and shelf-level data. The advantage of direct store-to-supplier ordering is the ability to keep the right products in stock while maintaining extremely low inventory costs. For example, Wal-Mart's inventory-to-sales ratio in 1991 was 1 to 5.94, compared to Kmart Corp.'s ration of 1 to 4.58.

Several other strategic applications of the new network are now in the works at Wal-Mart. One that came out about a month ago involves downloading to store department managers images that depict how a given item can best be displayed. The retail chain is also experimenting with replacing "thousands of trees worth" of training manuals with online training support delivered via multimedia PCs installed at stores. The LAN-to-VSAT link also promises to boost customer satisfaction and get customers out the door faster by speeding up POS transactions, such as credit-card verification, Fitzgerel said.

CASE STUDY QUESTIONS

1. What telecommunications network changes are being made at Wal-Mart? Why are they being implemented?
2. How is Wal-Mart using telecommunications to add business value and compete with their rivals?
3. How important to their success is the use of telecommunications by major retailers?

Source: Adapted from Elisabeth Hoswitt, "Wal-Mart Spotlights Fast LANs," *Computerworld*, January 25, 1993, pp. 1, 16. Used with permission.

Summary

- **Telecommunications Trends.** The information systems of many organizations depend on telecommunications networks to service the communications and information processing needs of their end users. Telecommunications has entered a competitive environment with many vendors, carriers, and services. It is moving toward integrated digital networks for voice, data, and video, and the pervasive use of this technology to support business operations, managerial decision making, and strategic advantage in a global economy.

- **Networks and Applications.** There are two basic types of telecommunications networks: wide area networks (WANs) and local area networks (LANs). WANs cover a wide geographic area, while LANs interconnect end user workstations and other devices at local work sites. Telecommunications networks support a variety of applications, as outlined in Figure 4.6. This includes applications in transaction processing, inquiry/response, distributed and cooperative processing, office automation, end user computing, public information services, and interorganizational systems. Such applications can help a firm capture and provide information quickly to end users at remote locations at reduced costs while supporting its strategic organizational objectives.
- **A Managerial Perspective.** Telecommunications can help a firm compress the time taken by business activities, reduce geographic limits on business markets, and restructure business relationships. This can lead to significant improvements in operational efficiency, business effectiveness, and organizational innovation. These results can occur only through strategic telecommunications planning, which develops a telecommunications strategy for an organization. Many companies are pursuing a strategy that leads to open, integrated IS applications based on telecommunications networks.
- **Network Components.** The major components of a telecommunications network are (1) terminals, (2) telecommunications processors, (3) communications channels and media, (4) computers, and (5) telecommunications control software. Telecommunications processors include modems, multiplexers, and various devices to help enhance the capacity and efficiency of telecommunications channels. Telecommunications channels include such media as twisted-pair wire, coaxial cables, fiber optic cables, terrestrial microwave, communications satellites, cellular and LAN radio, and infrared systems. Use of public communications channels is provided by companies known as carriers and value-added carriers that offer a variety of telecommunication services. Telecommunications software consists of a variety of programs that control and support the communications occurring in a telecommunications network.
- **Network Alternatives.** Key telecommunications network alternatives and components are summarized in Figure 4.13 for telecommunications media, processors, software, channels, and network architectures. A basic understanding of these major alternatives will help managerial end users participate effectively in decisions involving telecommunications issues.

Key Terms and Concepts

These are the key terms and concepts of this chapter. The page number of their first explanation is in parentheses.

1. Bulletin board system (126)
2. Cellular radio (137)
3. Client/server computing (125)
4. Coaxial cable (134)
5. Common carriers (127)
6. Communications satellites (136)
7. Cooperative processing (125)
8. Distributed processing (124)
9. Electronic data interchange (124)
10. Electronic funds transfer (124)
11. Fiber optic cables (135)
12. Front-end processors (139)
13. Host computer (139)
14. Interorganizational networks (126)
15. Local area networks (120)
16. Modems (137)
17. Multiplexers (138)
18. Private branch exchange (139)
19. Protocol (143)
20. Public information services (126)
21. Telecommunications applications (121)
    a. Business value (130)
22. Telecommunications architecture (131)
23. Telecommunications channels and media (120)
24. Telecommunications control software (139)
25. Telecommunications network
    a. Architecture (143)
    b. Components (118)
    c. Topology (142)
26. Telecommunications processors (137)
27. Telecommunications strategy (131)
28. Trends in telecommunications (129)
29. Value-added carriers (128)
30. Videotex (126)
31. Wide area networks (120)
32. Wireless LANs (137)

Review Quiz

Match one of the key terms and concepts listed above with one of the brief examples or definitions listed below. Try to find the best fit for answers that seem to fit more than one term or concept. Defend your choices.

____ 1. Fundamental changes have occurred in the competitive environment, the technology, and the applications of telecommunications.

____ 2. Includes terminals, telecommunications processors, channels and media, computers, and control software.

____ 3. A communications network covering a large geographic area.

____ 4. A communications network in an office, a building, or other work site.

____ 5. Provide a variety of communications networks and services.

____ 6. They lease lines from common carriers and offer telecommunications services.

____ 7. Specialize in providing telecommunications network services to microcomputer users.

____ 8. An interactive information service for home computers.

____ 9. Systems for the capture and processing of money and credit transactions.

____ 10. Computers at central and local sites interconnected by a network.

____ 11. Networked computers sharing the processing of parts of an end user's application.

____ 12. End users can post public or private messages for other computer users.

____ 13. Telecommunications can improve operational efficiency, business effectiveness, and organizational innovation.

____ 14. A master plan for building an integrated telecommunications capability to support business objectives.

____ 15. The electronic exchange of documents between the computers of a business and its customers and suppliers.

____ 16. Includes coaxial cable, microwave, fiber optics, and satellites.

____ 17. A communications media that uses pulses of laser light in glass fibers.

____ 18. Supports mobile data communications in urban areas.

____ 19. Includes modems, multiplexers, and front-end processors.

____ 20. Includes programs for control of communications access, transmission, networks, errors, and security.

____ 21. A common communications processor for microcomputers.

____ 22. Helps a communications channel carry simultaneous data transmissions from many terminals.

____ 23. The main computer in a data communications network.

____ 24. A minicomputer dedicated to handling communications functions.

____ 25. Handles the switching of both voice and data in a local area network.

____ 26. A standard, multilevel interface to promote compatibility among telecommunications networks.

____ 27. A standard set of rules and procedures for control of communications in a network.

____ 28. End user workstations are tied to LAN servers to share application processing.

____ 29. Telecommunications networks interconnect an organization with its customers and suppliers.

Discussion Questions

1. Some people argue that one can no longer separate telecommunications from computing in business. What do you think?
2. Why have local area networks become so popular? What management problems are posed by the use of LANs?
3. "Telecommunications is much too technical an area for managerial end users, and should be left to telecommunications specialists." Do you agree? Why or why not?
4. What examples can you give that trends in telecommunications include (1) more telecommunications providers, (2) a greater variety of telecommunications services, and (3) an increased use of telecommunications applications in business?
5. Do you agree with MIS author Peter Keen that a business could have a strategic objective where telecommunications would be used to provide a variety of integrated IS applications "to anybody, anywhere"?
6. "Telecommunications doesn't add value to a business it just speeds up communications with remote locations." Do you agree with this statement? Why or why not?
7. What do online transaction processing, electronic data interchange, and electronic data funds transfer systems have in common?
8. What are the benefits and limitations of the following telecommunications technologies: (1) fiber optics, (2) communications satellites, (3) wireless LANs, and (4) ISDN?
9. Refer to the Real World Case on Fisher-Price in the chapter. What is "open systems"? What role does telecommunications play in an open systems environment?
10. Refer to the Real World Case on Wal-Mart in the chapter. What lessons could a small retailer or other small business learn from Wal-Mart's use of telecommunications?

Real World Problems

1. SRI International and Tadpole Technology: Using the Internet

What is made up of more than 8,000 connected networks, has more than 1.3 million connected computers, and has users numbering about 8 million? Answer: the Internet. The Intenet, which is the world's largest computer network, has been doubling in size (number of hosts and networks) every year since 1988. Once the exclusive domain of research and education groups whose interest, among other things, was access to supercomputer power, the Internet is gaining stature among business users. Companies are being enticed by the Internet's speedy, low-cost global communications, its appropriateness for collaborative work, its online software, and its unique databases. Many organizations see the meganetwork as a complement to their existing networks. With the low connection cost—often a flat monthly fee for leased line or dial-up access—users can access commercial and noncommercial services in the United States and 40 other countries.

Tom Mandel, senior management consultant at SRI International, a research and consulting firm in Menlo Park, California, says the Internet's electronic mail function enables more efficient, frequent, and inexpensive message exchanges than was possible before between SRI's California and London offices. Previously, Mandel's department exchanged mail with its foreign office by having a machine in Menlo Park call a modem on a local-area network in London. Because of the cost of a trans-Atlantic phone call, messaging British staffers occurred only sporadically.

Notebook computer vendor Tadpole Technology, Inc., with headquarters in Cambridge, England, and offices in Austin, Texas, San Jose, California, Dallas, New York, Washington, D.C., and France, keeps everyone together through the Internet. "Even when the salespeople are traveling, they carry notebooks and connect to us through the Internet from the customer premises, their hotel room, or even from the airport lounge," says Jim Thompson, portability scientist.

a. What are the advantages of Internet to business users?

b. How could you benefit from using Internet at your university?

Source: Adapted from John Quarterman, "In Depth: The Internet," *Computerworld*, February 22, 1993. Used with permission.

2. BASF Corporation: Integrating a Global Network

It is not uncommon for organizations to find themselves saddled with multiple, incompatible systems and protocols after years of ad hoc, incremental systems development. And that's exactly what had happened at BASF, where individual departments built systems and local-area networks for specific tasks such as manufacturing, engineering, and administration—around one or another proprietary technology. What company management wanted and what the business demanded was a network that connected these various islands across 40 U.S. sites. Even more than that, BASF needed a running start toward an even more ambitious vision—distributed, integrated networks running client/server applications across the entire far-flung organization. Clearly, getting to that ideal level of sharing was not going to be easy. In fact, it turned into a two-year, multimillion-dollar project involving not only the U.S. operations but also BASF's German headquarters and worldwide operations.

Today, the BASF integrated worldwide network is up and running. The company has established anywhere-to-anywhere connectivity, integrating its various LANs into a network able to support open systems and client/server, Windows-based applications. In the United States alone, the BASF network currently embraces 40 sites, 600 servers, and more than 6,600 workstations. A worldwide E-mail application on a X.25 network now supports 30,000 mail users. But now the hard part really begins: re-engineering business applications to take advantage of the network. "We believe in the model of one integrated system where, say, a salesperson or manager anywhere in the world can get on the network and see what is being produced, what's been shipped, or what's going on with a particular customer," says Ameet Patel, manager of BASF's emerging technologies group. Reworking applications to permit that is no snap, Patel says. "It's a steep learning curve and a process that can take years."

a. Why do companies need to integrate their telecommunications networks?

b. Why do business applications have to be reengineered to take advantage of an integrated network?

Source: Adapted from Alan Radding, "Two Years, Millions Later," *Computerworld*, February 1, 1993, p. 76. Used with permission.

3. Commodity Exchange, Inc.: Using Wireless Networks

Thanks to wireless networking, the Commodity Exchange, Inc., (ComEx) has expanded the number of goods it trades without adding staff and is saving about $200,000 a year in data entry clerk salaries, according to ComEx information systems officials. Sixteen trading floor "price reporters" using handheld, touch-screen computers communicating commodity price changes over a spread-spectrum, local-area network are eliminating a couple of costly time-consuming steps in the reporting process, said Arthur Markowitz, senior vice president of operations and systems. This also gives customers faster market information as they buy and sell gold, silver, other metals, and European options, he said. Changed prices are now reported in one or two seconds, down from three to five seconds.

Previously, price reporters would listen for a price change and use hand signals to alert a trading floor supervisor, who would call the price change through a headset to a data entry operator off the trading floor. The operator would then enter the price into ComEx's price reporting system—a fault-tolerant IBM System/88—that would transfer the information across a high-speed ticker network to wall boards, CRTs, and securities quote services. Now, the PC server communicates directly with the System/88. Besides being faster, "this frees trading floor supervisors from being involved in price reporting, so they can focus on ensuring orderly trades," Markowitz said.

a. How did the Commodity Exchange benefit from the use of handheld computers and a wireless network?

b. How could other types of business benefit from this technology?

Source: Adapted from Joanie Wexler, "Exchange to Save $200,000 Annually," *Computerworld*, January 18, 1993, pp. 45–46.

4. **Mobil Oil Corporation**

Mobil Oil Corporation is making a companywide transition to a standards-based network capable of supporting a truly open exchange of information on a worldwide basis. The giant oil company has functioning global networks supporting its technical activities and commercial side. But there were gaps and breaks in the communications structure that prevented some kinds of information exchange. For example, while the company had a proprietary electronic-mail system, users around the world could not easily access graphical applications or transparently exchange and share documents. Regional local-area networks had sprung up in great number and variety, separate from each other and the corporatewide networks.

But now Mobil is installing telecommunications technology that will integrate these networks. This has caused an increase in the capabilities needed by employees and their PCs. "The networking initiative has caused us to accelerate our PC upgrading," Ted Lumley, chief of Technical Computing of Mobil's Exploration and Production Division, notes. "We've scrapped some Intel 286 machines and brought in more 486s that can support the kind of networking applications we're doing. Along with the new Unix servers and desktop tools, our people have a big job getting up to speed." So Mobil is spending several million dollars retraining employees so they will benefit from the business capabilities of the new network.

a. Why is Mobil redoing its telecommunications networks?

b. Why does this increase the capabilities needed by Mobil employees and their PCs?

Source: Adapted from Mark Mehler, "Mobil Net Exec Preaches Patience," *Computerworld*, February 1, 1993, p. 72–73. Used with permission.

Application Exercises

1. **Analyzing Telecommunications Networks**

Apply the telecommunications network model illustrated in Figure 4.2 to the telecommunications networks of the preceding Real World Problems. That is, make an outline that identifies as many of the five basic components of a telecommunications network as you can find in the Southeast Manufacturing Network, Maryland National Bank, General Electric Company, Dana-Farber Cancer Institute, St. Paul Company, and Intel Corporation examples.

2. **Identifying Telecommunications Components and Media**

Apply the telecommunications network model illustrated in Figure 4.2 to the telecommunications network of a business, university, or other organization you know that uses telecommunications. Do a short report which outlines the following:

a. Identifies as many of the five basic components of a telecommunications network that might exist in this particular network. Make assumptions about the network if necessary.

b. Describe how almost all of the communication media illustrated in Figure 4.15 could be used in this network.

3. **Morris Manufacturing Examines Communications Costs**

Until recently, the volume of long distance communication at Morris Manufacturing Company has been quite small. For this reason, Morris has always used traditional direct distance dialing service for all of its long distance communication. However, the cost of long distance service at Morris Manufacturing has increased sharply in recent years. There are several likely reasons for this. Morris has recently opened up a second plant in another state, and there is a substantial and expanding volume of both voice and data communications between the two plants. Also Morris has begun to market its products aggressively through the sales staff making on-site visits to potential customers. The sales staff members use telephone credit cards to call the home office with orders and inquiries while in the field. Also, customers who have service agreements with Morris Manufacturing can call the company collect when they need repair or servicing.

You have been asked to take a look at Morris Manufacturing's long distance communications expenses over the past three years. You are to prepare materials to present to an executive committee that will highlight recent trends in Morris's long distance communications costs. You are also to recommend any needed changes in the way Morris Manufacturing purchases its long distance communication services.

By examining records you have been able to obtain the estimates shown below. These figures indicate long distance communication expenses by category for the past three years.

Morris Manufacturing Long Distance Expenses by Category of Call

Type of Call	Year 1991	1992	1993
Outgoing Calls			
Plant-to-Plant Voice	$13,275	$17,650	$26,840
Plant-to-Plant Data	$8,625	$18,430	$33,715
Other Outgoing Calls	$17,235	$16,430	$14,270
Incoming Calls Charged to Morris			
Credit Card Calls from Employees	$5,320	$9,840	$14,280
Collect Calls from Customers	$7,260	$7,415	$7,300

a. Using spreadsheet software, create a spreadsheet application that will allow you to print reports and graphs highlighting trends in Morris's long distance communications costs.

b. What changes in their long distance communications services would you recommend that Morris Manufacturing consider?

4. ABC Products Buys a LAN

ABC Products Company has decided to purchase a small network of microcomputers for the use of its office staff. ABC buys all of its computing equipment from local suppliers who have agreed to give ABC a substantial discount on its purchases. You have been asked to determine the minimum configuration of the network and then develop estimates of the cost of acquiring this network. Your estimate is to include the costs of installation and two years of service by the vendor. You determine that the proposed network will need one high-capacity PC to act as the file server for the network and five additional PCs to serve as network stations. In addition, one laser printer will be attached to the file server unit and will serve the printing needs of all of the network's users. Each of the six PCs will need to be equipped with a network communications card.

You have been asked to solicit pricing information from the two local firms and to prepare a spreadsheet comparing their costs. Since installation and servicing are included, this order cannot be split between the two vendors. The prices quoted by the two vendors are as shown below. The prices of all hardware items are on a per-unit basis. The service contract cost is expressed as a percentage of the costs of all hardware items. The installation and software costs are overall costs for the entire network.

Price Quotes for Network Components by Vendor

Item	Vendor: CompuStore	Computers Are Us
Hardware		
File server PC unit	$2,240	$2,305
Participant PC unit	1,245	1,265
Laser printer	1,350	1,335
Network communications card	280	275
Two-year service contract (% of total hardware cost)	25%	20%
Installation	$1,200	$1,100
Network software (six-station license)	2,475	2,500

a. Prepare a spreadsheet comparing the costs of acquiring this network from each of the two alternative suppliers.

b. Based upon cost alone, which of the two suppliers would you select?

c. If you were actually making a recommendation about this type of purchase, what factors, in addition to cost, would you want to consider?

Review Quiz Answers

1. *28*
2. *25b*
3. *31*
4. *15*
5. *5*
6. *29*
7. *20*
8. *30*
9. *10*
10. *8*
11. *7*
12. *1*
13. *21a*
14. *27*
15. *9*
16. *23*
17. *11*
18. *2*
19. *26*
20. *24*
21. *16*
22. *17*
23. *13*
24. *12*
25. *18*
26. *25a*
27. *19*
28. *3*
29. *14*

Selected References

1. Arthur Andersen & Co. *Trends in Information Technology*. 3rd ed. 1987.
2. Berline, Gary, and Ed Perratore. "Portable, Affordable, Secure: Wireless LANs." PC Magazine, February 11, 1992.
3. *Computer Networks for All Your Computers*. EDP Analyzer Special Report, Canning Publications, 1986.
4. Donovan, John. "Beyond Chief Information Officer to Network Manager." *Harvard Business Review*, September/October 1988.
5. Gilder, George. "Into the Telecosm." *Harvard Business Review*, March/April 1991.
6. Hammer, Michael, and Glenn Mangurian. "The Changing Value of Communications Technology." *Sloan Management Review*, Winter 1987.
7. Keen, Peter. *Computing in Time: Using Telecommunications for Competitive Advantage*. New York: Ballinger Publishing Co., 1988.
8. Keen, Peter. *Shaping the Future: Business Design Through Information Technology*. Boston: Harvard Business School Press, 1991.
9. Roche, Edward M. *Telecommunications and Business Strategy*. Chicago: Dryden Press, 1991.
10. Rush, Jr., Wayne. "Managing the LAN." *Byte*, July 1991.
11. Stamper, David. *Business Data Communications*. 3rd ed. Redwood City: Benjamin Cummings Publishing Co., Inc., 1992.
12. Stephenson, Peter. "Create a WAN." *Byte*, July 1991.

Introduction to Database Management

CHAPTER OUTLINE

CHAPTER 5

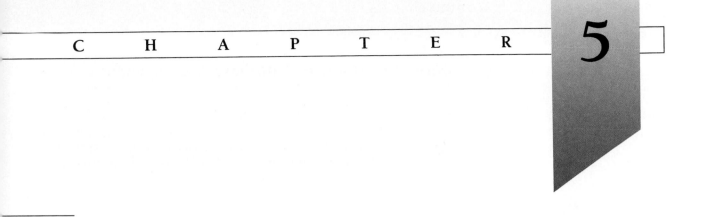

LEARNING OBJECTIVES

The purpose of this chapter is to give you an understanding of how data resources are managed in information systems by analyzing the managerial implications of basic concepts and applications of database management.

Section I of this chapter introduces the concept of data resource management and stresses the advantages of the database management approach versus the file processing approach in information systems. It also stresses the role of database management system software and the database administration function. Finally, it outlines the implications of the database management approach for managerial end users.

Section II surveys some of the more technical concepts in database management, including basic concepts of database organization, development, and access.

After reading and studying this chapter, you should be able to:

1. Explain the importance of data resource management and how it is implemented by methods such as database administration, data administration, and data planning.
2. Outline the advantages of the database management approach versus file processing methods.
3. Explain the functions of database management software in terms of end users, programmers, and database management applications.
4. Provide examples to illustrate each of the following concepts:
   a. Logical data elements.
   b. Fundamental database structures.
   c. Major types of databases.
   d. Database development.

SECTION I

A Manager's View of Database Management

Data Resource Management

Data is a vital organizational resource, which needs to be managed like other important business assets. Most organizations could not survive or succeed without quality data about their internal operations and external environment. That's why organizations and their managers need to practice **data resource management**—a managerial activity that applies information systems technology and management tools to the task of managing an organization's data resources. Managing data as organizational assets is an important focus for today's managers. Consider the following statement.

> Today, corporations are placing increasing emphasis on the management of data. A number of factors, including a significantly more competitive environment, more powerful workstations, and more computer-literate personnel, have led to a demand for more and better data. The forces underlying the growing importance of data management . . . will require the management of all organizations to have up-to-date information from multiple sources at whatever level of aggregation is desired. In order to survive, organizations will need improved designs for information acquisition and distribution. Acknowledging this, more and more companies are trying . . . to manage data as a resource [3].

This chapter will show you the managerial implications of some early attempts to manage data with information systems technology (file processing), as well as with more current technologies and methods (database management). We will also introduce the broader data resource management concepts of database administration, data administration, and data planning.

A Manager's View of File and Database Processing

How would you feel if you were an executive of a computer-using company and were told that some information you wanted about your employees was too difficult and too costly to obtain? Suppose the vice president of information services gave you the following reasons:

- The information you want is in several different files, each organized in a different way.
- Each file has been organized to be used by a different application program, none of which produces the information you want in the form you need.
- No application program is available to help get the information you want from these files.

Figure 5.1 shows a summary of the information you want and its related files and programs.

As a company executive, you would probably be frustrated and disenchanted with computer-based processing if it could not provide you with information for such a simple request. Well, that's how end users can be frustrated when an organization relies on **file processing** systems in which data are organized, stored, and processed in independent files of data records. In the **database management approach,** on the other hand, files are consolidated into a common pool, or *database*, of records available to many different application programs. In addition, an important software package called a *database management system* (DBMS) serves as a software interface between users and databases. This helps users easily access the

Information Requested	File	Application Program
Employee salary	Payroll file	Payroll program
Educational background	Employee skills file	Skills inventory program
Salary increases and promotions	Personnel action file	Personnel action program

FIGURE 5.1
An example of independent files and programs for information on employees.

records in a database. For example, if all data about an employee were stored in a common database, you could use the *query language* feature of a DBMS to easily obtain the employee information you want. See Figure 5.2.

Management Problems of File Processing

For many years, information systems had a file processing orientation, as illustrated in the previous example. Data needed for each user application was stored in independent data files. Processing consisted of using separate computer programs that updated these independent data files and used them to produce the documents and reports required by each separate user application. This file processing approach is still being used, but it has several major problems that limit its efficiency and effectiveness for end user applications.

Data Duplication

Independent data files include a lot of duplicated data; the same data (such as a customer's name and address) is recorded and stored in several files. This *data redundancy* causes problems when data has to be updated, since separate *file maintenance* programs have to be developed and coordinated to ensure that each file is properly updated. Of course, this proves difficult in practice, so a lot of inconsistency occurs among data stored in separate files. File maintenance is a time-consuming and costly process, and it increases the secondary storage space requirements of computer systems.

Lack of Data Integration

Having data in independent files makes it difficult to provide end users with information for ad hoc requests that require accessing data stored in several different files. Special computer programs have to be written to retrieve data from each independent file. This is so difficult, time-consuming, and costly for some organizations that it is impossible to provide end users or management with such information. If necessary, end users have to manually extract the required information from the various reports produced by each separate application and prepare customized reports for management.

Data Dependence

In file processing systems, major components of a system—the organization of files, their physical locations on storage hardware, and the application software used to access those files—depend on one another in significant ways. For example, application programs typically contain references to the specific *format* of the data stored in the files they use. Thus, changes in the format and structure of data and records in a file require that changes be made to all of the programs that use that file. This *program maintenance* effort is a major burden of file processing systems. It proves difficult to do properly, and it results in a lot of inconsistency in the data files.

Other Problems

In file processing systems, it is easy for data elements such as stock numbers and customer addresses to be defined differently by different end users and applications. This causes serious inconsistency problems in the development of programs to access such data. In addition, the *integrity* (i.e., the accuracy and completeness) of

FIGURE 5.2
Using a natural query language. Note how this database management capability allows you to easily specify the employee information you need.

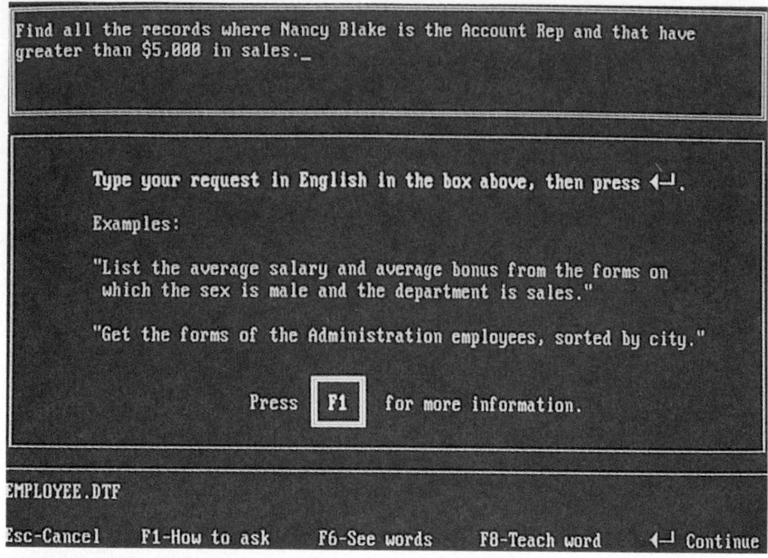

Find all the records where Nancy Blake is the Account Rep and that have greater than $5,000 in sales._
Type your request in English in the box above, then press ↵.
Examples:
"List the average salary and average bonus from the forms on which the sex is male and the department is sales."
"Get the forms of the Administration employees, sorted by city."
Press F1 for more information.
EMPLOYEE.DTF
Esc-Cancel F1-How to ask F6-See words F8-Teach word ↵ Continue

Frederick D. Bodin/Offshoot.

the data is suspect because there is no control over their use and maintenance by authorized end users. Such inconsistency and lack of integrity are extremely difficult to control, as there is no central *dictionary* to keep track of data definitions and their authorized use in the organization. Thus, a lack of standards causes major problems in application program development and maintenance, and in the security and integrity of the data files needed by the organization.

The Database Management Solution

The concepts of *databases* and *database management* were developed to solve the problems of file processing systems. A **database** is an integrated collection of logically related records and files. It consolidates records previously stored in independent files so that it serves as a common pool of data to be accessed by many different application programs. The data stored in a database is independent of the computer programs using it and of the type of secondary storage devices on which it is stored. **Database management** involves the control of how databases are created, interrogated, and maintained to provide information needed by end users and the organization.

Figures 5.3 and 5.4 contrast the file processing and database management approaches with examples from the banking industry. Note that it would be difficult to selectively gather information from three differently organized files about bank customers in the file processing approach. The database management approach, on the other hand, could easily handle such an assignment, because of how it accomplishes the *storage* and *processing* of data.

The Database Approach

Common databases are developed in the database management approach. A *data dictionary,* which describes the data contents and relationships of the databases, is established to ensure integrity, consistency, and reliability. The data needed by many different applications in an organization are consolidated and integrated into several common databases, instead of being stored in many independent data files. For example, customer records and other common types of data are needed for

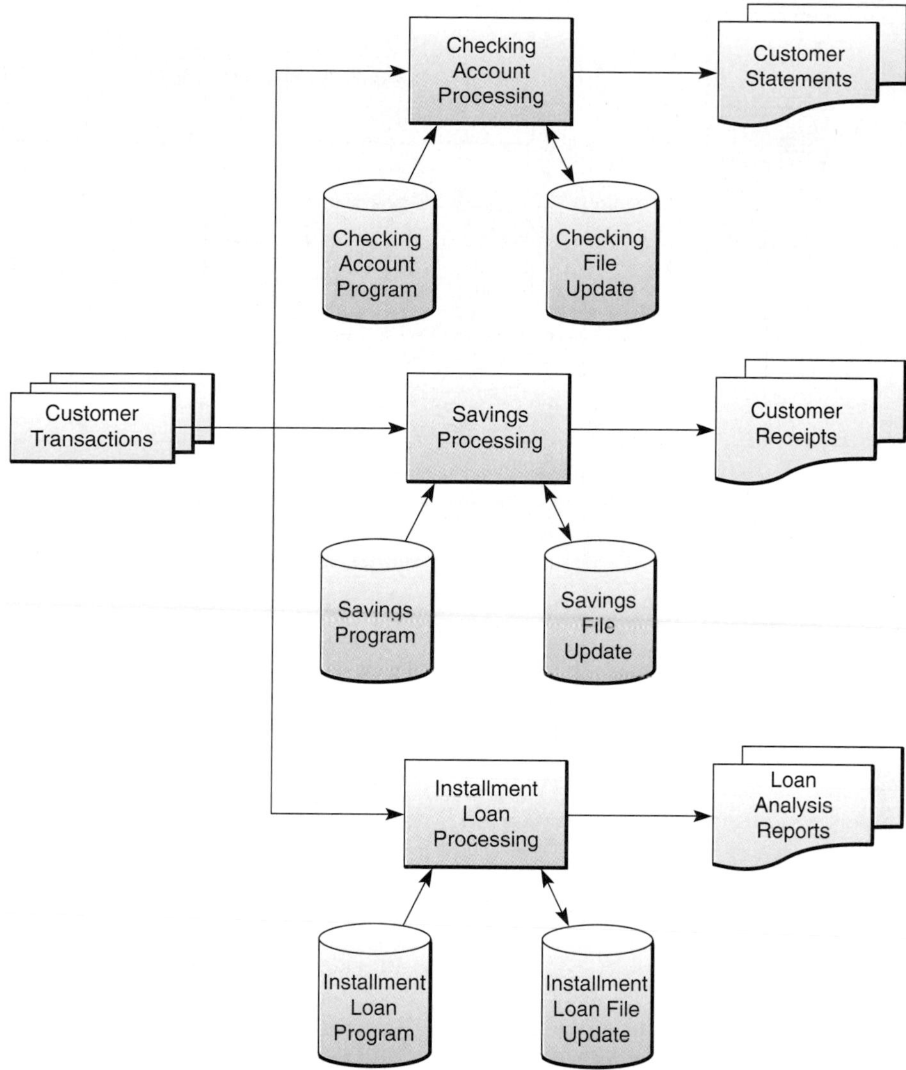

FIGURE 5.3
Examples of file processing systems in banking. Note the use of separate computer programs and independent data files in a file processing approach to the savings, installment loan, and checking account applications.

several different applications in banking, such as check processing, automated teller systems, bank credit cards, savings accounts, and installment loan accounting. This data can be consolidated into a common *customer database,* rather than being kept in separate files for each of those applications.

Database Processing

File processing involves updating and using independent data files to produce information needed for each user's application. However, database processing consists of three basic activities:

- Updating and maintaining common databases to reflect new business transactions and other events requiring changes to an organization's records.
- Providing information needed for each end user's application by using computer programs that share the data in common databases. This is accomplished through a common software interface provided by a database management system package. Thus, end users and programmers do not have to know where or how data are physically stored.

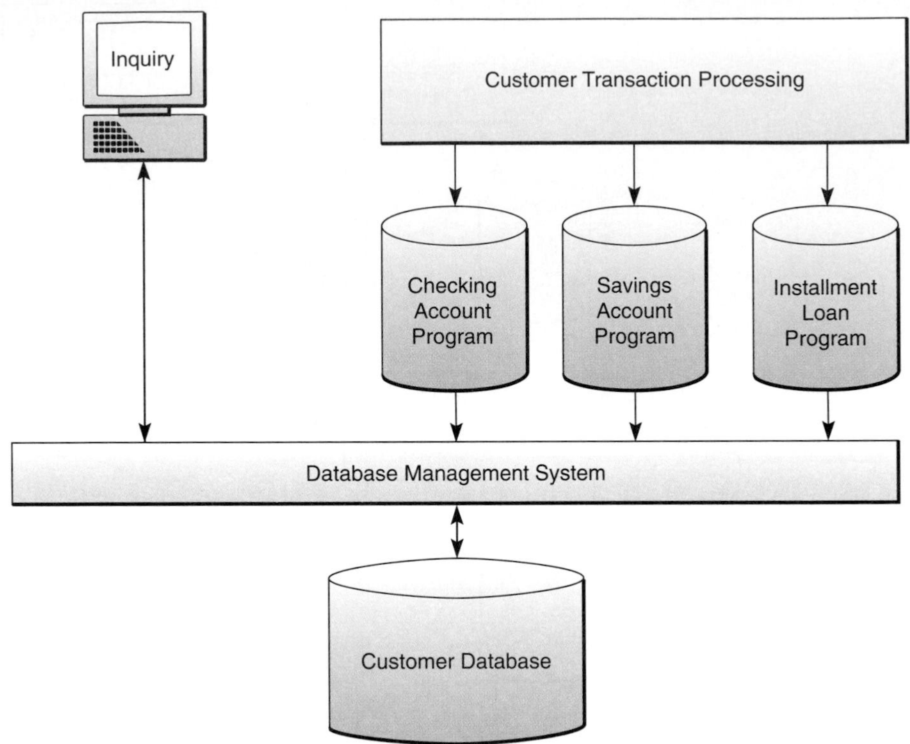

FIGURE 5.4
An example of a database management approach in a banking information system. Note how the savings, checking, and installment loan programs use a database management system to share a customer database. Note also that the DBMS allows a user to make a direct, ad hoc interrogation of the database without using application programs.

- Providing an inquiry/response and reporting capability through a DBMS package so that end users can easily interrogate databases, generate reports, and receive quick responses to their ad hoc requests for information.

Using Database Management Software

Let's take a closer look at the capabilities provided by database management software. A **database management system** (DBMS) is a set of computer programs that controls the creation, maintenance, and use of the databases of an organization and its end users. As we said in Chapter 3, database management packages are available for micro, mini, and mainframe computer systems. The four major uses of a DBMS are illustrated in Figure 5.5. Let's take a look at each of them now.

Database Development

Database management packages allow end users to easily develop the databases they need. However, a DBMS allows organizations to place control of organizationwide **database development** in the hands of **database administrators** (DBAs) and other specialists. This improves the integrity and security of organizational databases. The database administrator uses a *data definition language* (DDL) to develop and specify the data contents, relationships, and structure of each database. The database administrator also uses the DDL to modify these database specifications when necessary. Such information is cataloged and stored in a database of data definitions and specifications called a *data dictionary,* which is maintained by the DBA.

The Data Dictionary

Data dictionaries have become a major tool of database administration. A **data dictionary** is a computer-based catalog or directory containing *metadata,* that is, data about data. A data dictionary includes a software component to manage a database of *data definitions,* that is, metadata about the structure, data elements, and

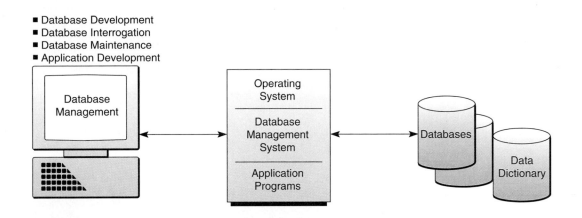

FIGURE 5.5
The four major uses of a DBMS package are database development, database interrogation, database maintenance, and application development.

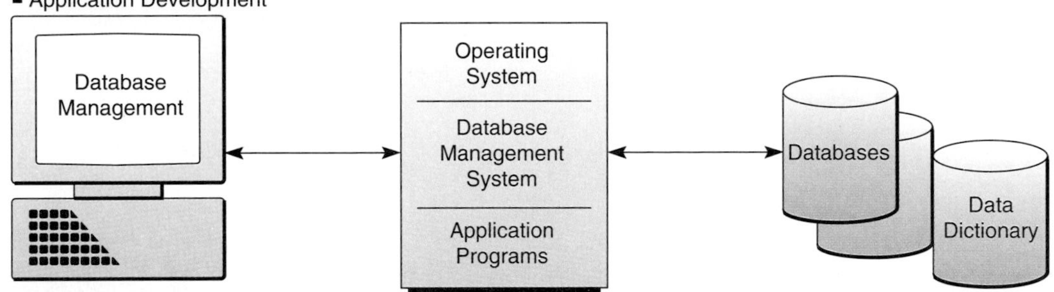

other characteristics of an organization's databases. For example, it contains the names and descriptions of all types of data records and their interrelationships, as well as information outlining requirements for end users' access, use of application programs, and database maintenance and security. See Figure 5.6.

Data dictionaries can be queried by the database administrator to report the status of any aspect of a firm's metadata. The administrator can then make changes to the definitions of selected data elements. Some *active* (versus *passive*) data dictionaries automatically enforce standard data element definitions whenever end users and application programs use a DBMS to access an organization's databases. For example, an active data dictionary would not allow a data entry program to use a nonstandard definition of a customer record, nor would it allow a data entry operator to enter a name of a customer that exceeded the defined size of that data element.

Database Interrogation

End users can use a DBMS by asking for information from a database using a *query language* or a *report generator*. They can receive an immediate response in the form of video displays or printed reports. No difficult programming is required. This **database interrogation** capability is a major benefit to ordinary end users. The **query language** feature lets you easily obtain immediate responses to ad hoc inquiries: you merely key in a few short inquiries. The **report generator** feature allows you to quickly specify a report format for information you want presented as a report. Figure 5.7 illustrates the use of a DBMS report generator.

SQL and QBE

Figure 5.2 illustrated the use of a query language for a simple request for employee information using *natural language* inquiries. Figure 5.8 shows the use of SQL and QBE, two popular forms of query languages. SQL, or Structured Query Language, is a query language found in many database management packages. The basic form of an SQL query is:

```
SELECT . . . FROM . . . WHERE . . .
```

After SELECT you list the data fields you want retrieved. After FROM you list the files or tables from which the data must be retrieved. After WHERE you specify

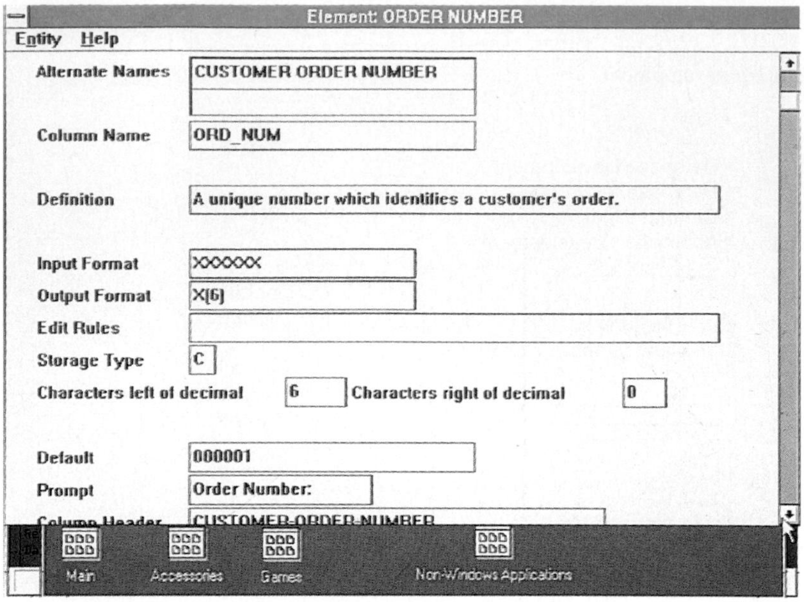

FIGURE 5.6
A display of part of the information in a data dictionary for a customer order number data element.

Courtesy Intersolv Inc.

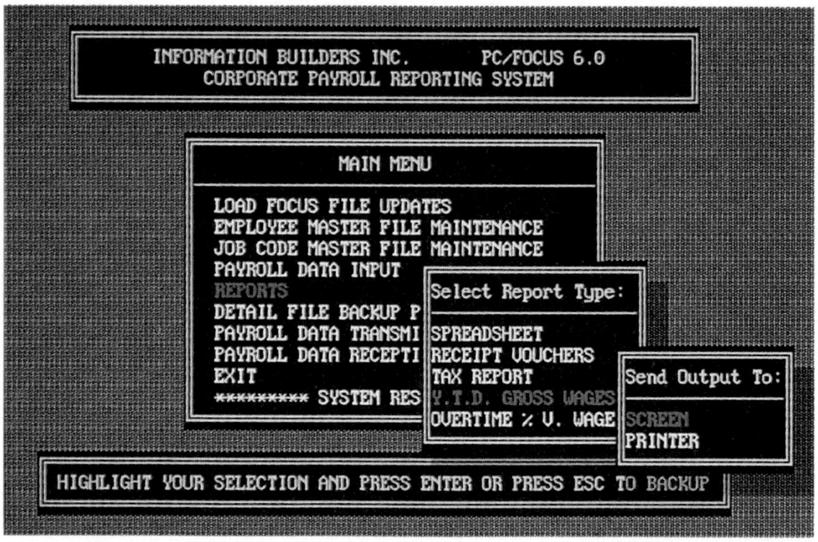

FIGURE 5.7
Using the report generator of PC/FOCUS to produce payroll reports.

Courtesy of Information Builders Inc.

conditions which limit the search to only those data records in which you are interested. For example, suppose a financial manager wanted to retrieve the names, social security numbers, departments, and salaries of all employees who are financial analysts from the employee and payroll files in the company's *human resources* database. Then he or she might use the following SQL query to display such information:

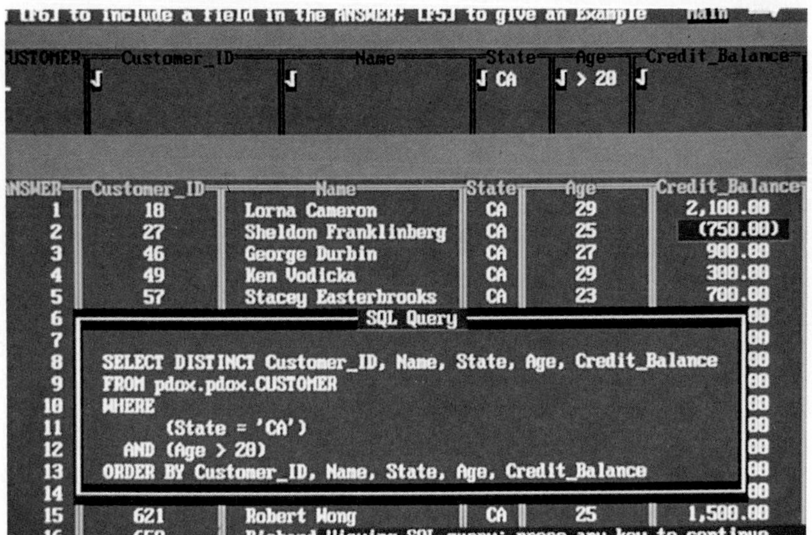

Courtesy Borland International.

FIGURE 5.8
Using the Paradox DBMS package to make QBE and SQL queries about customers.

```
SELECT NAME, SSNO, DEPARTMENT, SALARY
FROM EMPLOYEE, PAYROLL
WHERE EMPLOYEE.SSNO = PAYROLL.SSNO
AND CLASSIFICATION= "FINANCIAL ANALYST"
```

Another popular query language found in many database management packages is QBE, or *query by example*. This method displays boxes for each of the data fields in one or more files. You then use your keyboard or mouse to fill in or check boxes to indicate which information you want. For example, a QBE query that would retrieve information similar to the previous SQL query might be:

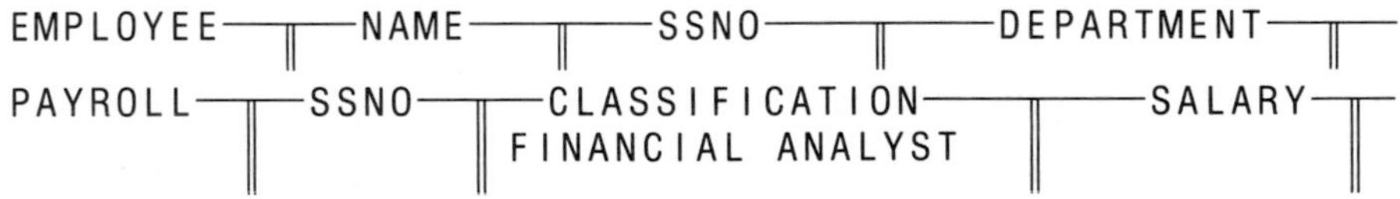

EMPLOYEE NAME SSNO DEPARTMENT
PAYROLL SSNO CLASSIFICATION SALARY
FINANCIAL ANALYST

Database Maintenance

The databases of an organization need to be updated continually to reflect new business transactions and other events. Other miscellaneous changes must also be made to ensure accuracy of the data in the databases. This **database maintenance** process is accomplished by transaction processing programs and other end user application packages, with the support of the DBMS. End users and information specialists can also employ various *utilities* provided by a DBMS for database maintenance.

Application Development

DBMS packages play a major role in **application development**. A DBMS makes the job of application programmers easier, since they do not have to develop detailed data-handling procedures using a conventional programming language (a host language, such as COBOL) every time they write a program. Instead, they can include *data manipulation language* (DML) statements in their application programs, which let the DBMS perform necessary data-handling activities. Programmers can also use the internal programming language provided by many DBMS packages or a built-in application generator to develop complete application programs.

Types of Databases

The growth of distributed processing, end user computing, and decision support and executive information systems has caused the development of several major types of databases. Figure 5.9 illustrates six major types of databases that may be found in computer-using organizations.

- **Operational databases.** These databases store detailed data needed to support the operations of the entire organization. They are also called *subject area databases* (SADB), *transaction databases,* and production *databases*. Examples are a customer database, personnel database, inventory database, and other databases containing data generated by business operations.
- **Management databases.** These databases store data and information extracted from selected operational and external databases. They consist of summarized data and information most needed by the organization's managers and other end users. Management databases are also called *information databases*. These are the databases accessed by executive end users as part of decision support systems and executive information systems to support managerial decision making.
- **Information warehouse databases.** An *information warehouse* stores data from current and previous years that has been extracted from the various operational and management databases of an organization. It is a central source of data that has been standardized and integrated so it can be used by managers and other end user professionals from throughout an organization. For example, a major use of information warehouse databases is *pattern processing*, where operational data is processed to identify key factors and trends in historical patterns of business activity [8].

FIGURE 5.9
Examples of the major types of databases used by organizations and end users.

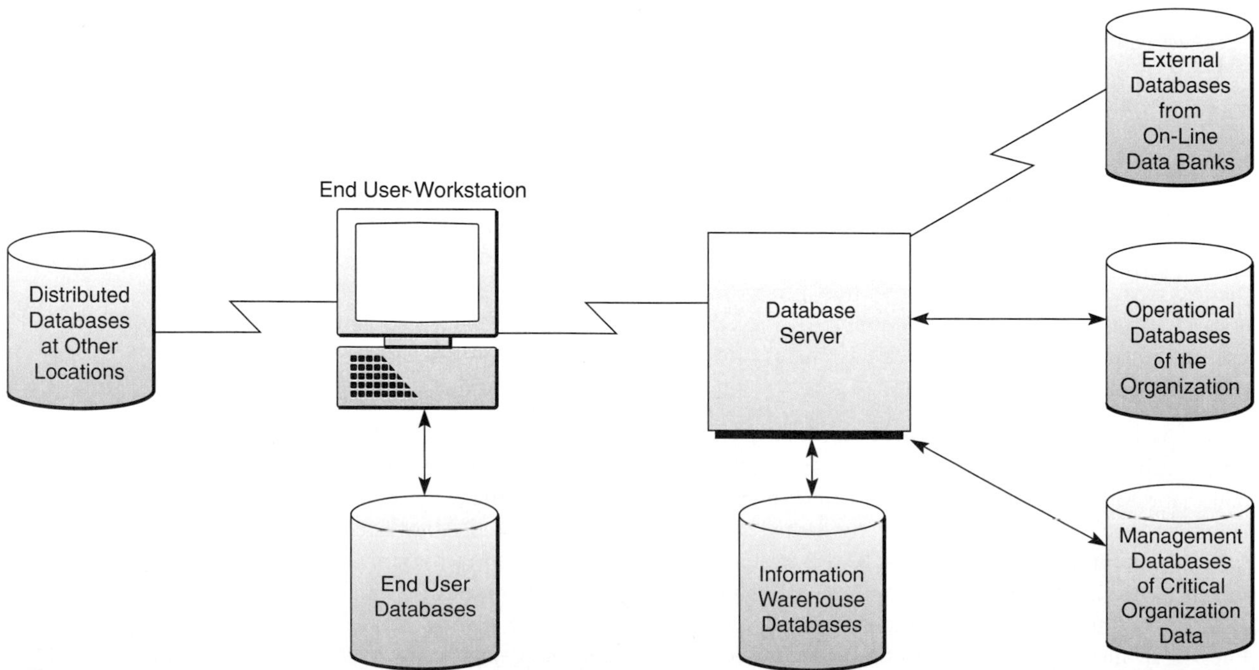

- **Distributed databases.** These are databases of local work groups and departments at regional offices, branch offices, manufacturing plants, and other work sites. These databases can include segments of both common operational and common user databases, as well as data generated and used only at a user's own site. Ensuring that all of the data in an organization's distributed databases are consistently and concurrently updated is a major consideration of data resource management.
- **End user databases.** These databases consist of a variety of data files developed by end users at their workstations. For example, users may have their own electronic copies of documents they generated with word processing packages or received by electronic mail. Or they may have their own data files generated from using spreadsheet and DBMS packages.
- **External databases.** Access to external, privately owned *online databases* or *data banks* is available for a fee to end users and organizations from commercial information services. Data is available in the form of statistics on economic and demographic activity from *statistical* data banks. Or you can receive abstracts from hundreds of newspapers, magazines, and other periodicals from *bibliographic* data banks. See Figure 5.10.

Text Databases

Text databases are a natural outgrowth of the use of computers to create and store documents electronically. Thus, online database services store bibliographic information such as publications in large text databases. Text databases are also available on CD-ROM optical disks for use with microcomputer systems. Major corporations and government agencies have developed large text databases containing documents of all kinds. They use *text database management systems* software to help create, store, search, retrieve, modify, and assemble documents and other information stored as text data in such databases. Microcomputer versions of this software have been developed to help users manage their own text databases on CD-ROM disks.

FIGURE 5.10
Examples of the information available in the online databases of commercial information services.

Dow Jones Information Service. Provides statistical data banks on stock market and other financial market activity, and on all corporations listed on the New York and American stock exchanges, plus 800 selected other companies. Its Dow Jones News/Retrieval system provides bibliographic data banks on business, financial, and general news from *The Wall Street Journal, Barron's*, the Dow Jones News Service, The Associated Press, Wall Street Week, and the 21-volume American Academic Encyclopedia.

Mead Data Central. Its bibliographical data bank *Lexis* provides legal research information, such as case law, court decisions, federal regulations, and legal articles. *Nexis* provides a full text bibliographic database of over 100 newspapers, magazines, newsletters, news services, government documents, and so on. It includes full text and abstracts from the *New York Times* and the complete 29-volume Encyclopædia Britannica.

Lockheed Information Systems. Its DIALOG system offers over 75 different data banks in agriculture, business, economics, education, energy, engineering, environment, foundations, general news publications, government, international business, patents, pharmaceuticals, science, and social sciences.

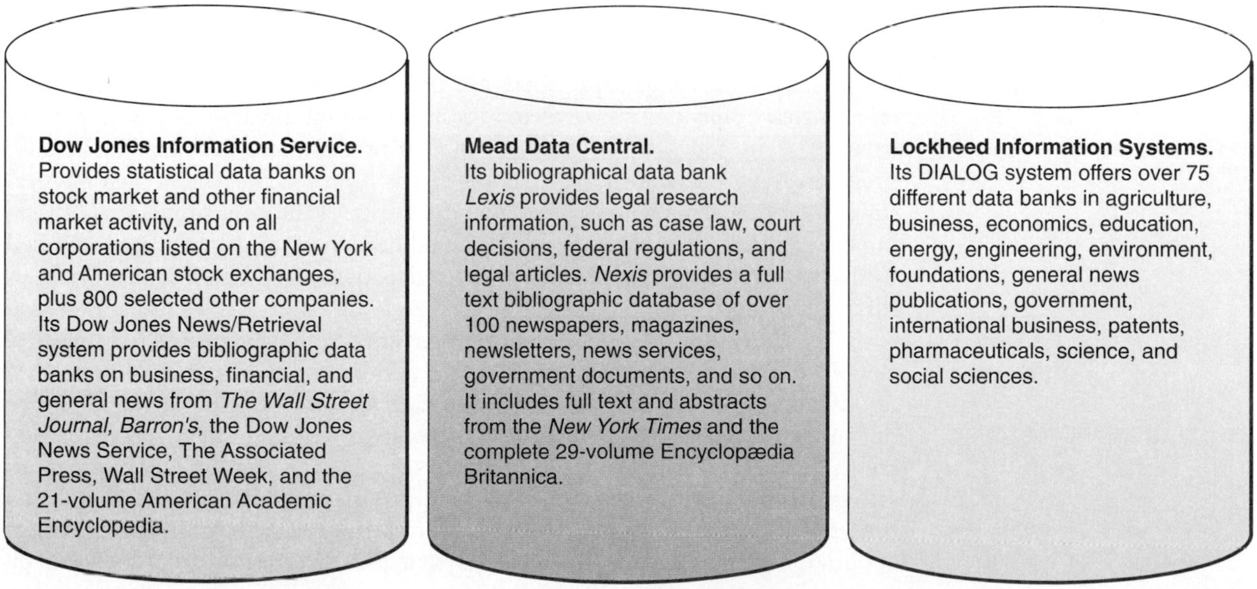

Image Databases

Up to this point, we have discussed databases which hold data in traditional alphanumeric records and files or as documents in text databases. But a wide variety of images can also be stored electronically in **image databases.** For example, *electronic encyclopedias* are available on CD-ROM disks which store thousands of photographs and many animated video sequences as digitized images, along with thousands of pages of text. The main appeal of image databases for business users is in *document image processing.* Thousands of pages of business documents, such as customer correspondence, purchase orders and invoices, as well as sales catalogs and service manuals, can be optically scanned and stored as document images on a single optical disk. Image database management software allows employees in many companies to quickly retrieve and display documents from image databases holding millions of pages of document images. Workers can view and modify documents at their workstations and electronically route them to the workstations of other end users in the organization.

Managerial Considerations for Data Resource Management

Managerial end users should view data as an important resource that they must learn to manage properly to ensure the success and survival of their organizations. But this is easier said than done. Consider this statement:

> A rapidly growing amount of data is now available in electronic form—most of it designed and organized to meet the needs of specific applications, with little thought given to compatibility of data across applications or business functions. Managing this data in a manner that best contributes to business objectives has become a complex problem [3].

Database management is an important application of information systems technology to the management of a firm's data resources. However, other major data resource management efforts are needed in order to offset some of the problems that can result from the use of a database management approach. Those are (1) database administration, (2) data administration, and (3) data planning. See Figure 5.11.

Benefits and Limitations of Database Management

The database management approach provides managerial end users with several important benefits. Database management reduces the duplication of data and integrates data so that they can be accessed by multiple programs and users. Programs are not dependent on the format of the data and the type of secondary storage hardware being used. Users are provided with an inquiry/response and reporting capability that allows them to easily obtain information they need without having to write computer programs. Computer programming is simplified, because programs are not dependent on either the logical format of the data or their physical storage location. Finally, the integrity and security of the data stored in databases can be increased, since access to data and modification of the database are controlled by database management system software, a data dictionary, and a database administrator function.

The limitations of database management arise from its increased technological complexity. Thus, a database management approach can pose problems in data resource management. Developing a large database and installing a DBMS can be difficult and expensive. More hardware capability is required, since storage requirements for the organization's data, overhead control data, and the DBMS programs are greater. Longer processing times may result from high-volume transaction processing applications since an extra layer of software (the DBMS) exists between application programs and the operating system. Finally, if an organization relies on

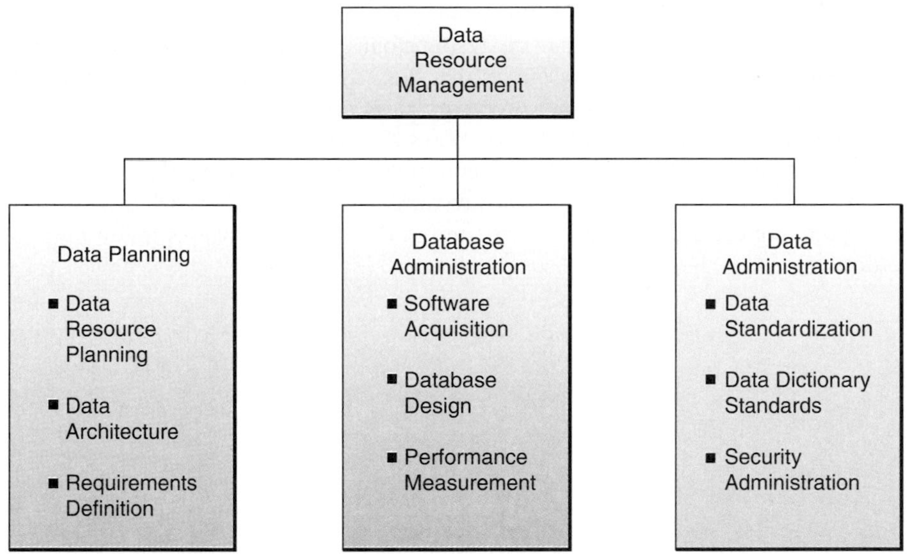

FIGURE 5.11
Data resource management includes data planning, database administration, and data administration activities.

Source: Adapted from Paul L. Tom, *Managing Information as a Corporate Resource*, 2nd ed. (New York: HarperCollins, 1991), p. 87.

centralized databases, their vulnerability to errors, fraud, and failures is increased. Yet problems of inconsistency of data can arise if a distributed database approach is used. Therefore, the security and integrity of an organization's databases are major concerns of an organization's data resource management effort.

Database Administration

Database administration is an important data resource management function responsible for the proper use of database management technology. Database administration has more operational and technical responsibilities than other data resource management functions. These include responsibilities for developing and maintaining the organization's data dictionary, designing and monitoring the performance of databases, and enforcing standards for database use and security. Database administrators work with systems analysts, programmers, and end users to provide their expertise to major systems development projects.

Data Administration

Data administration is another vital data resource management function. It involves the establishment and enforcement of policies and procedures for managing data as a strategic corporate resource. This means that the collection, storage, and dissemination of all types of data are administered in such a way that data become a standardized resource available to all end users in the organization. Thus, a data administrator must learn to work with the diverse business units and work groups in an organization, many of whom are uncomfortable with any attempt to dictate the use of "their data."

Data administration typically is an organizationwide managerial function without the operational and technical focus of database administration. Its focus is the planning and control of data in support of an organization's business functions and strategic business objectives. A major thrust of data administration, therefore, is the establishment of a data-planning activity for the organization. Data administration may also include responsibility for developing policies and setting standards for corporate database design, processing, and security arrangements, and for selecting database management and data dictionary software.

Data Planning

Data planning is a corporate planning and analysis function that focuses on data resource management. It includes the responsibility for developing an overall *data architecture* for the firm's data resources that ties in with the firm's strategic mission and plans, and the objectives and processes of its business units. Data planning is thus a major component of an organization's strategic planning process. It shows that an organization has made a formal commitment to long-range planning for the strategic use and management of its data resources. In Section II we will discuss how data planning is also an important first step in developing databases for an organization.

REAL WORLD CASE

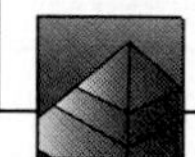

Spalding Sports: Reengineering Data Management

Spalding Sports produces a broad range of sporting equipment, including 1 million golf balls a day. Now it is time for Spalding to reinvent its business processes, according to Bard White, chief information officer. The technology and business procedure it uses to pump out baseball equipment, golf balls, clubs, basketballs, tennis balls, and an assortment of other equipment are now in the midst of a major overhaul. "We were on the same treadmill as everyone else, with a mainframe and just a zillion terminals hooked in," White said, "and when the machine got slow, you just went out and got a bigger one."

Spalding stopped the treadmill in 1990, when it officially launched a strategy to move from a Hewlett-Packard host-based environment to a client/server architecture using newer HP equipment. At the same time, it is redesigning critical procedures, such as order processing, to more quickly respond to major customers such as Wal-Mart Stores, Inc., Kmart Corp., and Sears, Roebuck and Co.

But both efforts revolve around one key issue: better data management. The client/server migration will eventually result in an information systems framework that includes a host data server, high-powered HP I486-based servers, and IBM PC clones on the desktop. All corporate data will reside on the HP host, where it will be secured and maintained. Applications will run on servers and PCs.

The new business procedures were designed to make better use of inventory data so the company can ship products more quickly. The strategy grew out of an observation in the late 1980s: PCs will slowly but surely alter the use of information in the company. "We started to acquire PCs, 10 here and 15 there," White said. "Pretty soon we were up to 400 PCs. We were losing control of corporate data." Copies of data were being maintained in departments. So, to answer a question as simple as how many customers Spalding had, the company could come up with "four or five answers," White said. "Marketing counted one way, credit counted another," White said. "We decided we needed a strategy [for IS] to be the official keeper of the data."

That set in motion a plan to move applications off the mainframe systems. The company installed a newer HP mainframe at the end of 1992 to function as the corporate data server. Applications are now being developed to run on PCs and servers. White said the company is about 20 percent client/server, and it should take several years to complete the switch. Spalding is writing and licensing application software to run on desktops and access corporate data. In some cases, the software is written from scratch. In other cases, the company is licensing microcomputer software and then writing interfaces to the host databases.

CASE STUDY QUESTIONS

1. How is Spalding Sports practicing better data management?
2. Why does reengineering business processes require better data management?
3. Why does changing to client/server computing require better data management?

Source: Adapted from Rosemary Cafasso, "Spalding Tees Up Client/Server," *Computerworld*, March 22, 1993, p. 51. Used with permission.

SECTION II
Technical Foundations of Database Management

Just imagine how difficult it would be to get any information from an information system if data were stored in an unorganized way, or if there was no systematic way to retrieve it. Therefore, in all information systems, data resources must be organized and structured in some logical manner so that they can be accessed easily, processed efficiently, retrieved quickly, and managed effectively. Thus, *data structures* and *access methods* ranging from simple to complex have been devised to efficiently organize and access data stored by information systems. In this section, we will explore these and other, more technical concepts of database management.

Logical Data Elements

As we first mentioned in Chapter 1, a hierarchy of several levels of data has been devised that differentiates between the most simple groupings, or *elements,* of data, and more complex data elements. Thus, data are logically organized into **characters, fields, records, files,** and **databases,** just as writing can be organized in letters, words, sentences, paragraphs, and documents. Examples of these **logical data elements** are shown in Figure 5.12.

Character

The most basic logical data element is the **character**, which consists of a single alphabetic, numeric, or other symbol. One might argue that the *bit* or *byte* is a more elementary data element, but remember that those terms refer to the *physical* storage elements provided by the computer hardware, discussed in Chapter 2. From a user's point of view (i.e., from a *logical* as opposed to a *physical* or *hardware* view of data), a character is the most basic element of data that can be observed and manipulated.

Field

The next higher level of data is the **field** or *data item*. A field consists of a grouping of characters. For example, the grouping of alphabetic characters in a person's name

FIGURE 5.12
Examples of the logical data elements in information systems. Note especially the examples of how data fields, records, files, and databases are related.

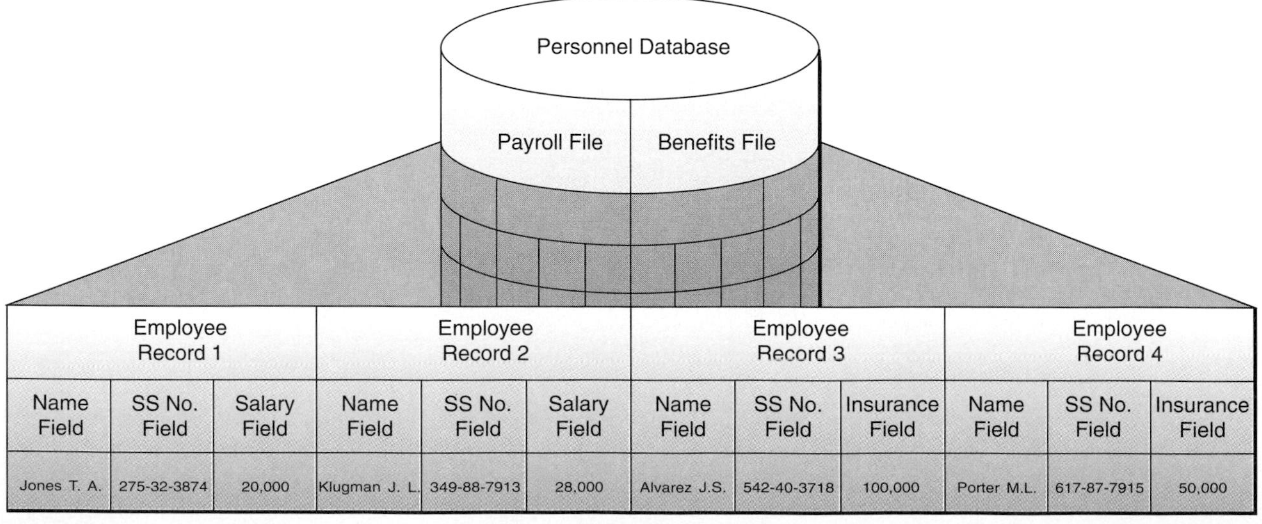

forms a *name field,* and the grouping of numbers in a sales amount forms a sales *amount field*. Specifically, a data field represents an **attribute** (a characteristic or quality) of some **entity** (object, person, place, or event). For example, a person's age could be a data field that represents one of the many attributes of an individual.

Record

Related fields of data are grouped to form a **record.** Thus, a record represents a collection of attributes that describe an entity. An example is the payroll record for a person, which consists of data fields such as the person's name, social security number, and rate of pay. *Fixed-length* records contain a fixed number of fixed-length data fields. *Variable-length* records contain a variable number of fields and field lengths.

File

A group of related records is known as a data **file.** Thus, an *employee file* would contain the records of the employees of a firm. Files are frequently classified by the application for which they are primarily used, such as a *payroll file* or an *inventory file*. Files are also classified by their permanence—for example, a payroll *master file* versus a payroll *weekly transaction file*. A **transaction file,** therefore, would contain records of all transactions occurring during a period and would be used periodically to update the permanent records contained in a **master file.** A *history file* is an obsolete transaction or master file retained for backup purposes or for long-term historical storage called *archival storage*.

Database

A **database** is an integrated collection of logically related records or files. A database consolidates records previously stored in separate files into a common pool of data records for many applications. For example, a personnel database consolidates data formerly segregated in separate files such as payroll files, personnel action files, and employee skills files. See Figure 5.13.

Database Structures

The relationships among the many individual records stored in databases are based on one of several logical *data structures* or *models*. Database management system packages are designed to use a specific data structure to provide end users with quick, easy access to information stored in databases. Three fundamental database

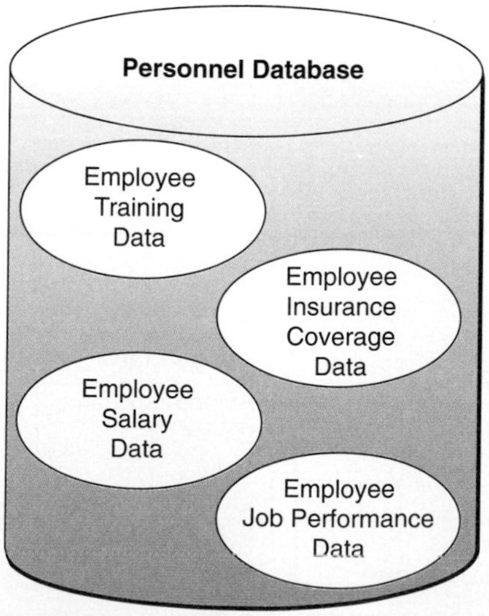

FIGURE 5.13
A personnel database consolidates data formerly kept in separate files.

structures are the **hierarchical**, **network**, and **relational** models. Simplified illustrations of these three database structures are shown in Figure 5.14.

Hierarchical Structure

Early mainframe DBMS packages used the **hierarchical** structure, in which the relationships between records form a *hierarchy* or treelike structure. In the traditional hierarchical model, all records are dependent and arranged in multilevel structures, consisting of one *root* record and any number of *subordinate* levels. Thus, all of

FIGURE 5.14
Examples of three fundamental database structures. They represent three basic ways to develop and express the relationships among the data elements in a database.

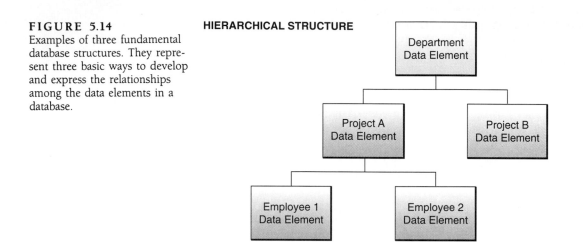

HIERARCHICAL STRUCTURE

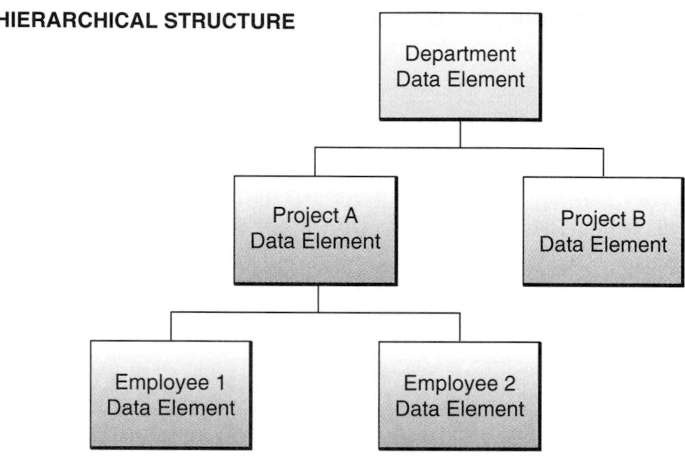

NETWORK STRUCTURE

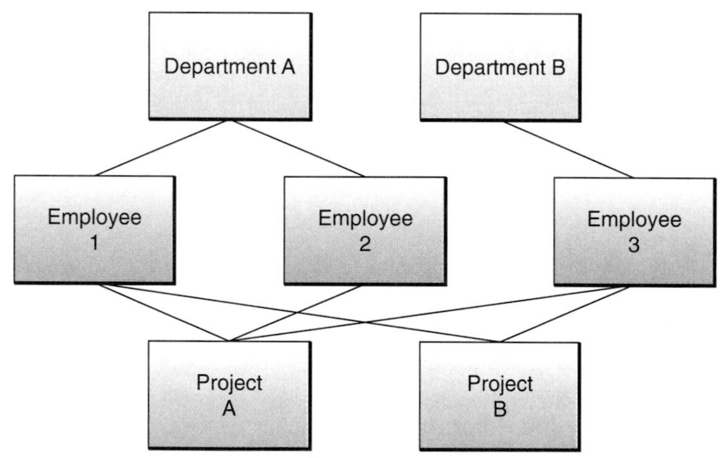

RELATIONAL STRUCTURE

Department Table

Deptno	Dname	Dloc	Dmgr
Dept A			
Dept B			
Dept C			

Employee Table

Empno	Ename	Etitle	Esalary	Deptno
Emp 1				Dept A
Emp 2				Dept A
Emp 3				Dept B
Emp 4				Dept B
Emp 5				Dept C
Emp 6				Dept B

the relationships among records are *one-to-many,* since each data element is related only to one element above it. The data element or record at the highest level of the hierarchy (the department data element in this illustration) is called the *root* element. Any data element can be accessed by moving progressively downward from a root and along the *branches* of the tree until the desired record (e.g., the employee data element) is located.

Network Structure

The **network** structure can represent more complex logical relationships, and is still used by many mainframe DBMS packages. It allows *many-to-many* relationships among records—that is, the network model can access a data element by following one of several paths, because any data element or record can be related to any number of other data elements. For example, in Figure 5.14, departmental records can be related to more than one employee record, and employee records can be related to more than one project record. Thus, one could locate all employee records for a particular department, or all project records related to a particular employee.

Relational Structure

The **relational** model has become the most popular of the three database structures. It is used by most microcomputer DBMS packages, as well as many minicomputer and mainframe systems. In the relational model, all data elements within the database are viewed as being stored in the form of simple **tables.** Figure 5.14 illustrates the relational database model with two tables representing some of the relationships among departmental and employee records. Other tables, or *relations,* for this organization's database might represent the data element relationships among projects, divisions, product lines, and so on. Database management system packages based on the relational model can link data elements from various tables to provide information to users. For example, a DBMS package could retrieve and display an employee's name and salary from the employee table in Figure 5.14, and the name of his or her department from the department table, by using their common department number field (Deptno) to link, or *join,* the two tables.

Object-Oriented Structure

Other database models are being developed to provide capabilities missing from the hierarchical, network, and relational structures. One example is the **object-oriented** database model. We introduced the concept of objects when we discussed *object-oriented programming* in Chapter 3. An object consists of data values describing the attributes and relationships of an entity, plus the methods and processes that can be performed upon the data. This capability is called *encapsulation,* and it allows the object-oriented model to better handle more complex types of data (graphics, pictures, voice, text) than other database structures. The object-oriented model also supports *inheritance;* that is, new objects can be automatically created by replicating some or all of the characteristics of one or more *parent objects.* Such capabilities have made object-oriented database management systems (OODBMS) popular in computer-aided design (CAD) and similar applications. For example, they allow designers to develop product designs, store them as objects in an object-oriented database, and replicate and modify them to create new product designs.

Evaluation of Database Structures

The hierarchical data structure is a natural model for the databases used for many of the structured, routine types of transaction processing characteristic of many business operations. Data for many of these operations can easily be represented by groups of records in a hierarchical relationship. However, there are many cases where information is needed about records that do not have hierarchical relationships. For example, it is obvious that, in some organizations, employees from more than one department can work on more than one project (see Figure 5.14). A network data structure could easily handle this many-to-many relationship. It is thus more flexible than the hierarchical structure in support of databases for many types of business operations. However, like the hierarchical structure, because its relationships must be specified in advance, the network model cannot easily handle ad hoc requests for information.

Relational databases, on the other hand, allow an end user to easily receive information in response to ad hoc requests. That's because not all of the relationships between the data elements in a relationally organized database need to be specified when the database is created. Database management software (such as Oracle, DB2, dBase IV, and Paradox) create new tables of data relationships using parts of the data from several tables. Thus, relational databases are easier for programmers to work with and easier to maintain than the hierarchical and network models. The major limitation of the relational model is that database management systems based on it cannot process large amounts of business transactions as quickly and efficiently as those based on the hierarchical and network models, in which all data relationships are prespecified. However, this performance gap is narrowing with the development of advanced relational DBMS software, including some with object-oriented capabilities. The use of database management software based on the object-oriented model is growing steadily, but this technology is still not developed fully enough for broad business use.

Database Development

Developing small personal databases is relatively easy using microcomputer database management packages. However, developing a large database can be a complex task. In many companies, developing and managing large corporate databases is the primary responsibility of the database administrator and database design analysts. They work with end users and systems analysts to determine (1) what data definitions should be included in the database and (2) what structure or relationships should exist among the data elements.

Data Planning and Modeling

As Figure 5.15 illustrates, database development must start with a top-down **data planning** process. Database administrators and designers work with corporate and end user management to develop an *enterprise model* that defines the basic business processes of the enterprise. Then they develop *entity relationship* models that define the relationships among the many entities involved in business processes. For example, Figure 5.16 illustrates some of the relationships in a purchasing/receiving system. At this point, logical *subject area databases* can be identified. For example, subject area databases for customers, employees, vendors, and products could support many basic business operations.

Next, end users must identify the key data elements in the SADBs that are needed to perform specific business activities. For example, they would need to identify what customer and product data are necessary in the order entry process. These *user views* are the basis for a **data modeling** step where the relationships between data elements are identified. Each data model defines the logical relationships among the data elements needed to support a basic business process. For example, can a customer have more than one type of account with us? Can an employee have several pay rates or be assigned to several project work groups? Answering such questions will identify data relationships that have to be represented in a data model.

These data models then serve as logical frameworks (called *schemas* and *subschemas*) on which to base the *physical design* of databases and the development of application programs to support the business processes of the organization. A

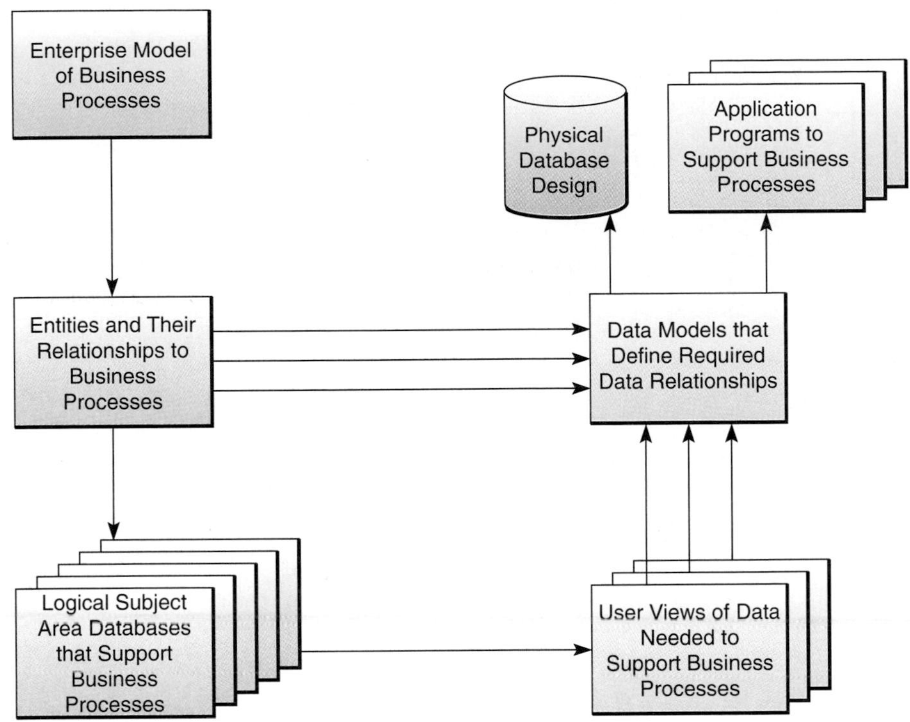

Source: Adopted from Dale Godhue, Judith Quillard, and John Rockhart, "Managing the Data Resource: A Contingency Perspective," *MIS Quarterly*, September 1988, p. 381.

FIGURE 5.15
Data planning ties a model of the business enterprise to data models used to develop databases and application programs for end users in the organization.

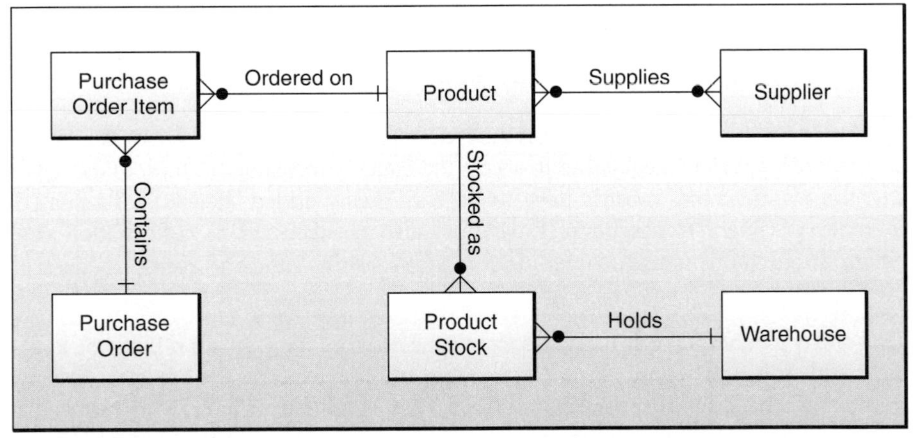

Courtesy of Texas Instruments.

FIGURE 5.16
This entity relationship diagram illustrates some of the relationships among entities in a purchasing/receiving system.

schema is an overall logical view of the relationships between data in a database, while the *subschema* is a logical view of the data relationships needed to support specific end user application programs that will access that database.

Remember that data models represent *logical views* of the data and relationships of the database. Physical database design takes a *physical* view of the data (also called the *internal* view) which describes how data is to be physically arranged, stored, and accessed on the magnetic disks and other secondary storage devices of a computer system. For example, Figure 5.17 shows these different database views and the software interface of a bank database processing system.

FIGURE 5.17
Examples of the logical and physical database views and the software interface of a database processing system in banking.

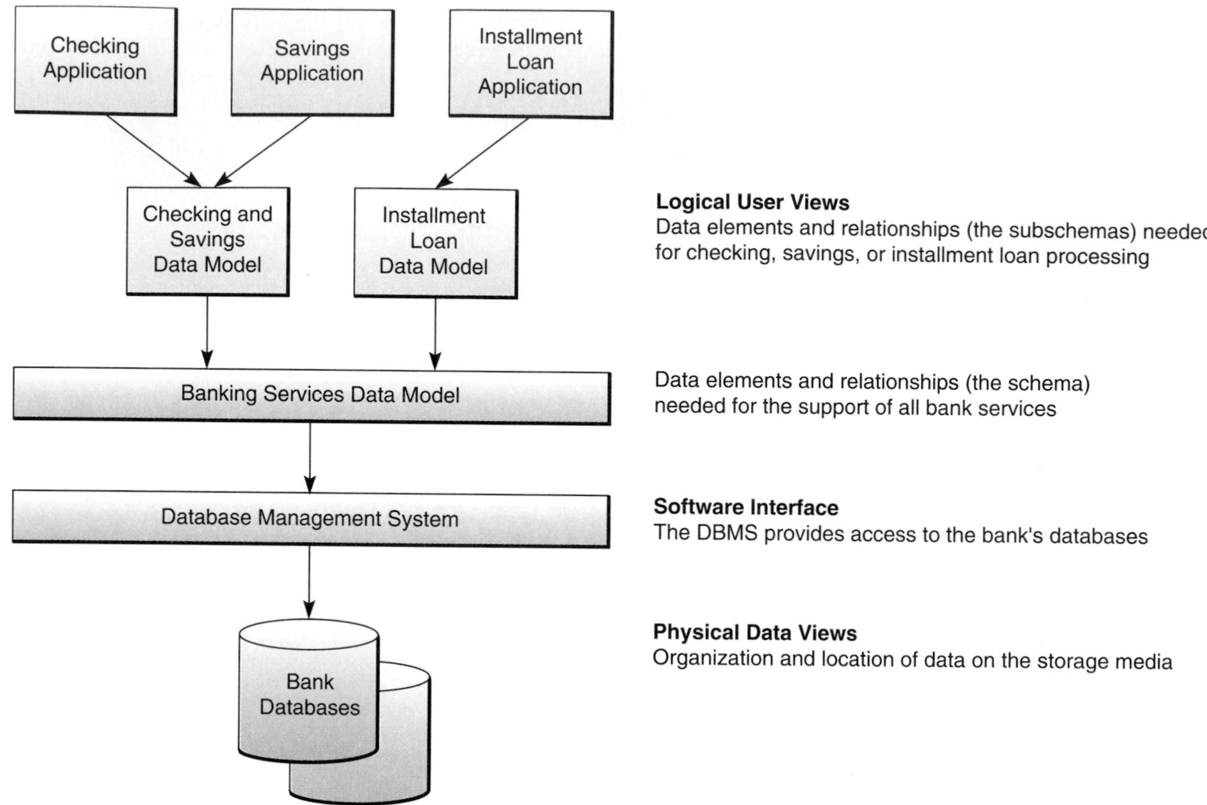

Accessing Files and Databases

Databases and files are stored on various types of storage media and are organized in a variety of ways to make it easier to access the data records they contain. In database and file maintenance, records have to be continually added, deleted, or updated to reflect business transactions. Data must also be accessed so information can be produced in response to end user requests. Thus, efficient access to data is important.

Key Fields

That's why all data records usually contain one or more identification fields or keys, which identify the record so it can be located. For example, the social security number of a person is often used as a *primary key* field which uniquely identifies the data records of individuals in student, employee, and customer files and databases. Other methods can be used to identify and link data records stored in several different database files. For example, hierarchical and network databases may use *pointer fields*. These are fields within a record that indicate (point to) the location of another record that is related to it in the same file, or in another file. Hierarchical and network database management systems use this method to link records so they can retrieve information from several different database files.

Relational database management packages use primary keys to link records. Each table (file) in a relational database must contain a primary key. This field (or fields) uniquely identifies each record in a file and must also be found in other related files. For example, in Figure 5.14, department number (Deptno) is the

FIGURE 5.18
Joining the employee and department tables in a relational database allows you to selectively access data in both tables at the same time.

Department Table

Deptno	Dname	Dloc	Dmgr
Dept A			
Dept B			
Dept C			

Employee Table

Empno	Ename	Etitle	Esalary	Deptno
Emp 1				Dept A
Emp 2				Dept A
Emp 3				Dept B
Emp 4				Dept B
Emp 5				Dept C
Emp 6				Dept B

primary key in the department table and is also a field in the employee table. As we mentioned earlier, a relational database management package could easily provide you with information from both tables to *join* the tables and retrieve the information you want. See Figure 5.18.

Sequential Organization and Access

One of the basic ways to access data is to use a **sequential organization**, in which records are stored in a specified order according to a key field in each record. For example, payroll records could be placed in a payroll file in a numerical order based on employee social security numbers. **Sequential access** is fast and efficient when dealing with large volumes of data that need to be processed periodically. However, it requires that all new transactions be sorted into the proper sequence for *sequential access processing*. Also, most of the database or file may have to be searched to locate, store, or modify even a small number of data records. Thus, this method is too slow to handle applications requiring immediate updating or responses.

Direct Organization and Access

When using **direct access** methods, records do not have to be arranged in any particular sequence on storage media. However, the computer must keep track of the storage location of each record using a variety of **direct organization** methods so that data can be retrieved when needed. New transactions data do not have to be sorted, and processing that requires immediate responses or updating is easily handled. There are a number of ways to directly access records in the direct organization method. Let's take a look at three widely used methods to accomplish such *direct access processing*.

One common technique of direct access is called **key transformation.** This method performs an arithmetic computation on a key field of record (such as a product number or social security number) and uses the number that results from that calculation as an address to store and access that record. Thus, the process is called *key transformation* because an arithmetic operation is applied to a key field to transform it into the storage location address of a record. Another direct access method used to store and locate records involves the use of an **index** of record keys and related storage addresses. A new data record is stored at the next available location, and its key and address are placed in an index. The computer uses this index whenever it must access a record.

In the **indexed sequential access method** (ISAM), records are physically stored in a sequential order on a magnetic disk or other direct access storage device based on the key field of each record. In addition, each file contains an index that references one or more key fields of each data record to its storage location address. Thus, an individual record can be directly located by using its key fields to search and locate its address in the file index, just as you can locate key topics in this book by looking them up in its index. As a result, if a few records must be processed quickly, the file index is used to directly access the record needed. However, when large numbers of records must be processed periodically, the sequential organization provided by this method is used. For example, processing the weekly payroll for employees or producing monthly statements for customers would be done using sequential access processing of the records in the file or database.

REAL WORLD CASE

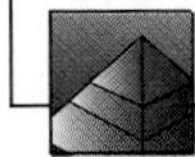

J. J. Kenny: Cooperative Client/Server Database Management

J. J. Kenny, the nation's largest municipal bond information and brokerage organization, solved its IS architectural crisis with a cooperative client/server database management technology. At Kenny, the database system is not just an adjunct to its business. Given the database-intensive nature of rating, tracking, and trading the database is at the core of the company.

Prior to implementing this technology, Kenny's IS infrastructure was typical of the traditional, heterogeneous conglomeration found in today's larger IS organizations. An IBM mainframe running DB2 was surrounded by Digital Equipment VAXs running the Oracle database, Hewlett-Packard processors running the Image database, and Concurrent Systems running a homegrown database.

"I had four separate operations going on, and the overhead was killing us. A good portion of our yearly expenses was related to IS. We knew we had to simplify our IT architecture," Zielinski said. Chief Information Officer Thomas Zielinski believed that migrating to a cooperative client/server database approach would provide a considerable short-term cost savings and long-term competitive advantage, because it would allow his firm to offer better online products and services. Zielinski's wish list was not inconsiderable. He wanted to:

- Centralize database management.
- Improve database performance.
- Fit into the existing satellite delivery system.
- Allow for incremental growth in processing power and application development.

His new technology plan was approved in 1990, and he was on track to have the first of the new systems out of test and into production before the end of 1992. Most of the old systems are being replaced by a pair of fault-tolerant Sequent computers running the ORACLE7 cooperative-server DBMS under UNIX. In this open systems environment, the Sequent systems are linked to PCs running Microsoft Windows with the Gupta 4GL database front-end package. Connectivity is provided by the Novell Netware network operating system and the Tuxedo transaction processing monitor from UNIX System Labs.

Zielinski's IS group found ORACLE7 to be better, tighter, and more bug-free than production releases of predecessor software products. A 2 million-row table filled with production data was loaded into the new system as a performance test. Skeptics predicted that it would take days to load. As it turned out, using the new ORACLE7 SQL*Loader, the table was loaded in about 12 minutes. It seemed too good to be true, so the table was emptied and loaded again—with the same results. Upon further testing, it was discovered that the bane of Kenny's IS existence, a portfolio update taking 18 to 19 hours on the old system, could be done in about 30 minutes on the new system.

Kenny now has a technology platform that offers substantial new decision support capabilities to its customers. Kenny is translating this capability into more products and services. For example, before a Kenny online customer buys a bond, the new system will allow the customer to purchase a history of the bond's performance. This kind of service keeps customers coming back.

CASE STUDY QUESTIONS

1. Why is the database "at the core of the company" for J. J. Kenny?
2. What is a cooperative/client/server approach to database management?
3. Why did J. J. Kenny switch to a cooperative client/server approach to database management?

Source: Adapted from Richard Skrinde, "Cooperative-Server: An Enterprise Solution," *Computerworld*, Special Advertising Supplement, February 1, 1993, p. 6. Used with permission.

Summary

- **Data Resource Management.** Data resource management is a managerial activity that applies information systems technology and management tools to the task of managing an organization's data resources. It includes the database administration function which focuses on developing and maintaining standards and controls for an organization's databases. Data administration, however, focuses on the planning and control of data to support business functions and strategic organizational objectives. This includes a data planning effort which focuses on developing an overall data architecture for a firm's data resources.
- **File Processing.** For many years, information systems had a file processing orientation, in which separate computer programs were used to update independent data files and produce the documents and reports required by each end user application. This caused problems of data duplication, unintegrated data, and data dependence. The concepts of databases and database management were developed to solve these problems.
- **Database Management.** The database management approach affects the storage and processing of data. The data needed by different applications is consolidated and integrated into several common databases, instead of being stored in many independent data files. Also, the database management approach emphasizes updating and maintaining common databases, having users' application programs share the data in the database, and providing a reporting and an inquiry/response capability so end users can easily receive reports and quick responses to requests for information.
- **Database Software.** Database management systems are software packages that simplify the creation, use, and maintenance of databases. They provide software tools so end users, programmers, and database administrators can create and modify databases, interrogate a database, generate reports, do application development, and perform database maintenance.
- **Types of Databases.** Several types of databases are used by computer-using organizations, including central, distributed, end user, management, information warehouse, and online databases. Text databases consist of data in text form, while image databases contain digitized images of documents, photographs, and other visual media. Special database management software is used to catalog and index such databases for quick retrieval of text and images of documents or other forms of information.
- **Database Development.** The development of databases can be easily accomplished using microcomputer database management packages for small end user applications. However, the development of large corporate databases requires a top-down data planning effort. This may involve developing enterprise and entity relationship models, subject area databases, and data models which reflect the logical data elements and relationships needed to support the operation and management of the basic business processes of the organization.
- **Data Organization and Access.** Data must be organized in some logical manner on physical storage devices so that they can be efficiently processed. For this reason, data is commonly organized into logical data elements such as characters, fields, records, files, and databases. Database structures, such as the hierarchical, network, relational, and object-oriented models, are used to organize the relationships among the data records stored in databases. Databases and files can be organized in either a sequential or direct manner and can be accessed and maintained by either sequential access or direct access processing methods.

Key Terms and Concepts

These are the key terms and concepts of this chapter. The page number of their first explanation is in parentheses.

1. Data administration (169)
2. Data dictionary (162)
3. Data modeling (176)
4. Data planning (170)
5. Data resource management (158)
6. Database administration (169)
7. Database administrator (162)
8. Database management approach (160)
9. Database management system (162)
10. Database structures (173)
    a. Hierarchical (174)
    b. Network (175)
    c. Object-oriented (175)
    d. Relational (175)
11. Database and file access (178)
    a. Direct (179)
    b. Sequential (179)
12. DBMS uses (162)
    a. Application development (165)
    b. Database development (162)
    c. Database interrogation (163)
    d. Database maintenance (165)
13. File processing limitations (159)
    a. Data duplication
    b. Lack of data integration
    c. Data dependence
14. Key field (178)
15. Logical data elements (172)
    a. Character
    b. Field
    c. Record

d. File
e. Database
16. Query language (163)
17. Report generator (163)
18. Types of databases
a. Distributed (167)
b. End user (167)
c. External (167)
d. Image (168)
e. Information warehouse (166)
f. Management (166)
g. Operational (166)
h. Text (167)

Review Quiz

Match one of the key terms and concepts listed above with one of the brief examples or definitions listed below. Try to find the best fit for answers that seem to fit more than one term or concept. Defend your choices.

____ 1. Marked by data duplication, unintegrated data, and dependency between programs and data formats.
____ 2. The use of integrated collections of data records and files for data storage and processing.
____ 3. A DBMS allows you to create, interrogate, and maintain a database, create reports, and develop application programs.
____ 4. A specialist in charge of the databases of an organization.
____ 5. This DBMS feature allows users to easily interrogate a database.
____ 6. Defines and catalogs the data elements and data relationships in an organization's database.
____ 7. Helps you specify and produce reports from a database.
____ 8. The main software package that supports a database management approach.
____ 9. Databases are dispersed throughout an organization.
____ 10. Your own personal databases.
____ 11. Databases of documents.
____ 12. Applies information systems technology and management tools to the management of an organization's data resources.
____ 13. Developing and maintaining standards and controls for an organization's databases.
____ 14. The planning and control of data to support organizational objectives.
____ 15. A top-down effort that ties database development to the support of basic business processes.
____ 16. Developing conceptual views of the relationships among data in a database.
____ 17. A customer's name.
____ 18. A customer's name, address, and account balance.
____ 19. The names, addresses, and account balances of all of your customers.
____ 20. An integrated collection of all of the data about your customers.
____ 21. An identification field in a record.
____ 22. A treelike structure of records in a database.
____ 23. A tabular structure of records in a database.
____ 24. Transactions are sorted in ascending order by social security number before processing.
____ 25. Unsorted transactions can be used to immediately update a database.
____ 26. Databases that support the major business processes of an organization.
____ 27. A centralized and integrated database of current and historical data about an organization.
____ 28. Databases provided by online information services.

Discussion Questions

1. Organizations could not survive or succeed without quality data about their internal operations and external environment. Do you agree? What examples can you give to defend your position?
2. If data is an important resource and asset to a firm, it must be managed properly. What role does database management and data administration play in managing data?
3. What is the difference between the file processing and database management approaches? Give examples to illustrate your answer.
4. What is a database management system? What functions does it enable end users and IS professionals to accomplish?
5. Databases of information about a firm's internal operations were formerly the only databases that were considered to be important to a business. What other kinds of databases are there? What is their importance to end users and their organizations?
6. Why has the relational database model become more important than the hierarchical and network structures? Why

do you think object-oriented database models are gaining in popularity?

7. Why would developing an organization's database require a data planning effort that was part of a strategic planning process of an organization?
8. What is a data model? What is data modeling? Give several business examples to support your answers.
9. Refer to the Real World Case on Spalding Sports in the chapter. Why does the use of PCs "slowly but surely alter the use of information in the company"?
10. Refer to the Real World Case on J. J. Kenny in the chapter. What are the challenges to good data management of client/server computing? How can these challenges be met by a business?

Real World Problems

1. Helene Curtis: Responsive SQL Database Queries

Quality code and high levels of database performance are design targets at Helene Curtis, Inc., as the personal care products firm puts IBM's DB2 database management system through its paces. Lately database designers at the firm have been trying to squeeze out better mainframe performance by testing SQL statements even as they are being written. While DB2 is widely used, most of its estimated 7,000 sites monitor the cost of lengthy queries against large DB2 databases that run to millions of rows. Users must find ways to submit efficient queries for execution by the DB2 database system or pay the costs of slowed response time.

At Helene Curtis, response time is a key consideration. One new pricing application will allow product-line managers to access DB2 directly. Response time is made even more critical by the fact that the 3,100-person, $1.02 billion firm wants to stay lean and mean in its competitive battles against large rivals: $29 billion Procter & Gamble Co., the Lever Brothers subsidiary of $40 billion Unilever Group, and $7 billion Colgate-Palmolive Co. Bill Kellow, a senior technical specialist, is leading an information systems team in testing the companywide pricing application. When the application goes online, it will invoke many thousands of database transactions per day. Sometime this month, end users will try out the application to make sure it meets Helene Curtis's business requirements. "The pricing strategy is being changed to provide greater flexibility for our merchandisers and our product-line managers," Kellow said.

a. How do you think SQL queries of a database can be made more efficient?

b. What benefits result from more efficient SQL queries?

Source: Adapted from Jean Bozeman, "Helene Curtis Pushes DB2 Envelope," *Computerworld*, January 18, 1993, pp. 53–54. Used with permission.

2. Kash n' Karry: Object-Oriented Database Systems

Kash n' Karry, the $1.2 billion grocery store chain based in Tampa, Florida, plans to roll out point-of-sale systems and in-store Unix-based processors in its 115 stores starting later this year. The goal of their Store 2000 project is to extend Kash n' Karry's new object-oriented information architecture to the stores, providing a seamless information flow from the cashier level to the chief executive officer. "We're more than just your typical grocery store," said Jim Stikeleather, director of systems development at Kash n' Karry. "We got as far as we did with object technology because we basically jumped off the bridge and started doing it. Most people really don't understand what we're doing because it's so far [out] in left field from data processing," Stikeleather said. "But they recognize the results."

Among those results is an object-oriented warehousing system in production today at Kash n' Karry's Returns Processing Center (RPC), which Stikeleather's 17-person staff built in four months. The new software system, which processes up to 50,000 transactions a day through a Sun Microsystems SPARCstation workstation, led to a 35 percent productivity savings and eliminated the $90,000 annual bill for the third-party vendor system it replaced. Another result is a promotional pricing system, called PromoMan, which 60 store buyers are now using. It was built in six weeks using Kash n' Karry's object technology, after two mainframe programmers abandoned a two-year effort to create the same sort of application. "PromoMan has allowed me to do things like pull information from the disparate databases throughout the organization," said Einar Seadler, director of marketing at Kash n' Karry. "Instead of my people being scared to have a computer on their desk, they're demanding to have one."

a. What is object-oriented programming? Object-oriented database management systems?

b. What are the benefits of object-oriented technology to Kash n' Karry?

Source: Maryfran Johnson, "Kash n' Karry Shops in New Technology Aisles," *Computerworld*, March 1, 1993, pp. 1, 24. Used with permission.

3. Principal Financial Group: Graphing Sales Data

The Principal Financial Group has moved summary sales data from an IBM mainframe—where users previously could retrieve only canned output—to a client/server environment, where they can now get their hands on the underlying data. The firm said the move has saved expensive mainframe cycles and disk storage while offering users greater flexibility for sales analysis. The company, a $10.4 billion family of financial services concerns, used to devote 24 hours of IBM 4381 processing at month's end to produce 2,100 sales graphs of managers in the group and pension sales department. The graphs, generated by software from SAS Institute, were then reported out on IBM's Executive Decisions data presentation tool. Because the system gave users the ability to view only predefined output, every combination of sales representative, office, and region had to be plotted in advance in case someone might want to view that slice of the data. "The majority of them were not looked at in any given month," said Nancy Carley, compensation and research analyst. "How could you look at that many graphs?"

Now, monthly sales data is summarized in minutes on the mainframe and passed to a Novell local-area network, where it is preprocessed by the SAS software and stored in a special database on a PC server. Sales managers with OS/2-based PCs then used SAS/AF, SAS's tool for interactive applications development, generating only the needed sales graphs. Users who are not technically trained use a mouse to select a series of icons defining the graph to be generated, which then "pops up in a couple of seconds," Carley said. Sales histories going back five years and data, such as current period sales goals, are available, she said. However, although the new system is far more efficient and moves the data closer to the user, the data sets available for generating graphs are still predefined. The firm will soon test a copy of SAS/EIS for OS/2, an object-oriented development environment for building executive information systems. That will allow users to tailor their own graphs and produce ad hoc reports and queries, Carley said.

a. Why did Principal move the graphing of sales data off its mainframe to a LAN database.

b. Why are they planning to move to an object-oriented system?

Source: Adapted from Gary Anthes, "Client/Server Serves Up Data," *Computerworld*, March 1, 1993, p. 60. Used with permission.

4. Reynolds Metals Co. and Miller Brewing Co.: Using a DBMS for Application Development

Reynolds Metals Co. wanted to provide one of its customers, Miller Brewing Co.'s Can Division, with a system that would let it more closely monitor orders for raw materials as part of an expanded quality management program. The need for the application came about when Miller asked Reynolds, based in Richmond, Virginia, to help reduce its inventory of aluminum coils used at the can manufacturing plants and monitor the quality of the aluminum it received. The result was a Paradox for Windows application that let Miller perform tasks including tracking remote in-transit and in-house inventories, materials forecasting and ordering, and quality control monitoring.

The most important feature the Reynolds/Miller project team found in Paradox for Windows was its ability to efficiently create and modify screens and forms. Brent Kannady, team leader, would have users critique an interface. Then, because of the product's development tools, he could tell them, "Go back to your desk and it'll be ready in five minutes." The tools in Paradox for Windows include Object Inspectors, which let the developer point at an object and click the right mouse button to bring up a menu of properties that can be modified. The product also includes point-and-click relational table linking. "We normally spend 20 percent of our time getting specifications and 80 percent of our time coding," Kannady said. However, with tools such as those in Paradox for Windows, he said he foresees a time when he will spend 80 percent of his time being "a good business analyst," with minimal time spent coding.

a. How can a database management package be used for application development?

b. Why might a DMBS package like Paradox for Windows let Brent Kannady spent 80 percent of his time being "a good business analyst"?

Source: Adapted from Christopher Lindquist, "Miller Finds Paradox Brew Tasty," *Computerworld*, February 8, 1993, p. 51. Used with permission.

Application Exercises

1. Creating and Using a Database File

Use a database management software package to create a Student Exam Scores file to store the set of sample data shown below. Each student record includes the student's name, social security number, gender, and grades for three exams.

Sample Student Exam Scores

Name	Soc. Sec. #	Gender	Exam 1	Exam 2	Exam 3
Bevins, M.	386-27-1894	Female	88	84	91
Davidson, P.	684-76-9013	Male	72	79	74
Gorton, A.	713-23-9870	Male	93	90	94
Jones, J.	593-94-7826	Female	57	63	61
Miller, G.	774-92-6927	Female	96	94	98
Perkins, P.	657-83-6204	Male	53	59	64
Shaw, J.	546-68-0632	Female	76	74	79

a. Create the student exam scores file, enter the data records for the seven students shown below, and get a printed listing of the Student Exam Scores file.

b. Edit the Student Exam Scores file by changing at least two exam scores and add at least one new student record. Choose any values you want for these changes and additions. When you have completed these changes, get another printed listing of the Student Exam Scores file.

c. Retrieve a printed listing of all students whose score on the first exam was 85 or higher.

d. Create and print a report showing the exam scores and total points earned by students aggregated into male and female categories.

2. Baxter Lawn Products Company

John Davis is in charge of the assembly department at Baxter Lawn Products Company. The company produces wheelbarrows, and John's department is responsible for the final assembly of the wheelbarrows and their packing for shipment. Two identical assembly lines are used, and each line is operated on two shifts daily. The total number of units assembled is reported to upper management on a weekly basis. This information is collected on a daily basis by each shift's supervisor and recorded on a simple paper form like those shown below. At the end of the week, John adds up the daily figures and reports only a single weekly total, which is recorded in the organization's database and used by upper management.

Week#: 14

		Units Produced					
Shift	**Line**	**Mon.**	**Tue.**	**Wed.**	**Thur.**	**Fri.**	**Total**
Day	A	1426	1602	1574	1611	1538	
Day	B	1507	1564	1533	1498	1551	
Eve.	A	1588	1602	1618	1574	1498	
Eve.	B	1528	1517	1563	1548	1502	

Week#: 15

		Units Produced					
Shift	**Line**	**Mon.**	**Tue.**	**Wed.**	**Thur.**	**Fri.**	**Total**
Day	A	1523	1584	1593	1602	1577	
Day	B	1569	1602	1566	1592	1599	
Eve.	A	1558	1581	1583	1599	1563	
Eve.	B	1523	1543	1576	1567	1507	

Week#: 16

		Units Produced					
Shift	**Line**	**Mon.**	**Tue.**	**Wed.**	**Thur.**	**Fri.**	**Total**
Day	A	1498	1583	1569	1593	1573	
Day	B	1538	1592	1607	1572	1584	
Eve.	A	1611	1619	1607	1593	1592	
Eve.	B	1558	1538	1547	1539	1503	

In recent weeks, output of the assembly department has declined. When John discussed these problems with the shift supervisors and some of the assembly line workers, he found considerable disagreement about where the problems lay. Each shift and production line seemed to feel that another shift or line was responsible, and some workers specifically suggested that there were problems with the condition of workers and their performance on the Monday day shift and the Friday evening shift.

John decided to create his own database file to determine where the problems lay and to track performance on a day-by-day basis for each line. He plans to enter a record every week for each line of each shift, showing the output for that line for each day of the week. Each record will have the following variables: Week#, line, Shift, Mon_out, Tues_out, Wed_out, Thur_out, Fri_out and Tot_out.

a. Use a database package to create a database to store this data, enter the data, and check it for accuracy.

b. Create one or more reports providing comparisons of the performance of each line and shift and showing how production on each shift varied over the days of the week.

Review Quiz Answers

1. *13*
2. *8*
3. *12*
4. *7*
5. *16*
6. *2*
7. *17*
8. *9*
9. *18a*
10. *18b*
11. *18h*
12. *5*
13. *6*
14. *1*
15. *4*
16. *3*
17. *15b*
18. *15c*
19. *15d*
20. *15e*
21. *14*
22. *10a*
23. *10c*
24. *11b*
25. *11a*
26. *18g*
27. *18e*
28. *18c*

Selected References

1. Brancheau, James; Larry Schuster; and Salvatore March. "Building and Implementing an Information Architecture." *Data Base*, Summer 1989.
2. Courtney, James, and David Paradice. *Database Systems for Management*. 2nd ed. Homewood, Ill.: Richard D. Irwin, 1992.
3. Date, C. J. *An Introduction to Data Base Systems*. 5th ed. Reading, Mass.: Addison-Wesley, 1990.
4. Goodhue, Dale; Judith Quillard; and John Rockart. "Managing Data Resources: A Contingency Perspective." *MIS Quarterly*, September 1988.
5. Grover, Varun, and James Teng. "How Effective Is Data Resource Management? Reassessing Strategic Objectives." *Journal of Information Systems Management*, Summer 1991.

6. Hazzah, Ali. "Objects Are Taking Shape in a Flat Relational World." *Software*, June 1990.
7. Kim, Won. *Introduction to Object-oriented Databases*. Cambridge, Mass.: MIT Press, 1990.
8. Lazos, James. "Unleashing the Power of Your Marketing Database." *The Bankers Magazine*, March/April 1991.
9. McLeod, Dennis. "Perspective on Object Databases." *Information and Software Technology*, January/February 1991.
10. Petreley, Nicholas; Judy Duncan; Linda Slovick; and Zoreh Banapour. "Analyzing Relational Databases." *Infoworld*, January 8, 1990, and June 25, 1990.
11. Tasker, Daniel. "Object Lesson." *Computerworld*, April 22, 1991.
12. Vasta, Joseph. *Understanding Database Management Systems*. 2nd ed. Belmont, Calif.: Wadsworth, 1989.

Continuing Real World Case

Omaha Vision Center—Part 2: Hardware and Software Options

Hardware and Software Requirements

Carl Weber, administrator of the Omaha Vision Center, began to develop a shopping list of requirements for the computer system he felt was needed. He listed what he thought were necessary items of hardware and software as priorities, and then what he considered to be luxuries. He knew that cost would be a major factor in the search, as it would be a prime concern to Dr. Jerry Creighton. Swallowing the pill of computerization would be hard enough for the doctor without adding the bad taste of a large capital outlay. Medical management articles and discussions with other medical administrators provided Weber with a ballpark figure of between $15,000 and $20,000 for the total package. With this estimate and his shopping list, the search began.

Figure 2 displays the results of the search and the hardware and software options from which Weber had to choose. Proposals had been elicited from all vendors following full operational demonstrations of the equipment and software. Four finalists had been selected, each with different costs and capabilities for the hardware, software, and telecommunications networks that might be needed. These alternatives are summarized in Figure 2.

Case Study Questions

1. Should the Omaha Vision Center use stand-alone PCs or networked microcomputers? Explain your reasoning.
2. How important to the final selection decision are the differences among the software packages proposed by the four vendors? Explain.
3. If you had to make a decision at this point, which of the four proposals would your select? Explain.

FIGURE 2
Hardware and Software Systems Considered by the Omaha Vision Center.

1. **Nielson Computer Company, Wilmington, Delaware**
   Hardware: Altos Multiuser PC (file server). Wyse terminals, fully networked. Printer (letter-quality, high-speed).

   Software: Nielson proprietary software for general medical usage.

   Functions: All accounting, records, scheduling. Fully integrated. Very complete.

   Capacity: 10,000+ patients, easily expandable to handle any conceivable growth in the practice.

   Cost: $50,000 all inclusive.
2. **Ivy Technologies Company, St. Louis, Missouri**
   Hardware: IBM PC clones fully networked. Printer (dot-matrix, very-high-speed).

   Software: Ivy Technology proprietary software. Developed by an ophthalmologist for use exclusively in ophthalmologic practices.

   Functions: Billing accounts receivable, records, scheduling. Not a full accounting package.

   Capacity: 10,000 patients

   Cost: $19,200
3. **Data Systems Corporation, Omaha, Nebraska**
   Hardware: IBM PC clones, no network. Printer (dot-matrix, high-speed)

   Software: DSC proprietary General medical office system.

   Functions: Accounts receivable, billing, scheduling, records. Not a full accounting package.

   Capacity: 16,000 patients

   Cost: $12,500
4. **Advanced Software Company, Sioux City, Iowa**
   Hardware: IBM PC clones, no network.

   Software: ASC software proprietary. Full accounting package adapted for medical use.

   Functions: All accounting functions.

   Capacity: 10,000 patients

   Cost: $11,000

M O D U L E **III**

Applications

How are information systems used to support end user computing, business operations, managerial decision making and strategic advantage? The four chapters of this module show you how such applications are accomplished in modern organizations.

Chapter 6, "Information Systems in Business Management," introduces the major operations and management roles of information systems and emphasizes the strategic role that information systems can play in gaining competitive advantages for an organization.

Chapter 7, "End User and Office Information Systems," discusses the resource requirements and managerial challenges of end user and work group computing applications. It also discusses the benefits and limitations of major types of office automation information systems.

Chapter 8, "Transaction Processing and Business Information Systems," shows the various ways that information systems support the processing of transactions generated by business operations. It also describes how information systems support the business functions of marketing, manufacturing, human resource management, accounting, and finance.

Chapter 9, "Management Information and Support Systems," shows how decision support systems and executive information systems have been developed and applied to business decision-making situations faced by managers. It also shows how artificial intelligence and expert systems are being used to support business operations and management.

Information Systems in Business Management

CHAPTER OUTLINE

CHAPTER 6

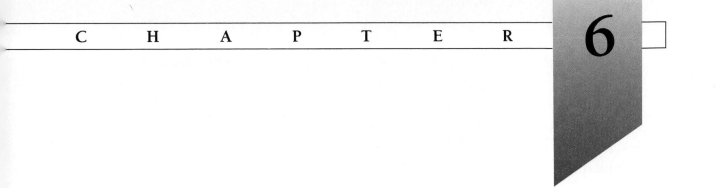

LEARNING OBJECTIVES

The purpose of this chapter is to give you an understanding of the roles played by information systems in organizations by analyzing (1) the operations and management support roles of information systems and (2) the role of information systems in helping an organization achieve a strategic advantage over its competitors.

Section I of this chapter presents an overview of the major operational and managerial support roles of information systems, emphasizing their role in supporting the functions, roles, and levels of management and the stages of managerial decision making.

Section II emphasizes competitive strategy concepts and the three major strategic roles information systems can play in gaining competitive advantages for an organization.

After reading and studying this chapter, you should be able to:

1. Give examples of how the roles of information systems have expanded to provide support for a firm's business operations, managerial decision making, and strategic advantage.
2. Identify how three major types of operations information systems support the operations of a business.
3. Identify the major types of management information systems, and discuss how each supports the managers of an organization.
4. Briefly explain how information systems can support some of the functions, roles, and levels of management, and the stages of decision making.
5. Identify three strategic roles of information systems and give examples of how they can provide competitive advantages to a business.

SECTION I

Information Systems for Operations and Management

The Expanding Roles of Information Systems

The roles given to the information systems function in an organization have expanded significantly over the years. Figure 6.1 summarizes these changes. Until the 1960s, the role of information systems was simple: transaction processing, record-keeping, accounting, and other *electronic data processing* (EDP) applications. Then another role was added, as the concept of *management information systems* (MIS) was conceived. This new role focused on providing managerial end users with predefined management reports that would give managers the information they needed for decision-making purposes.

By the 1970s, it was evident that the prespecified information products produced by such *information reporting systems* were not adequately meeting many of the decision-making needs of management. So the concept of *decision support systems* (DSS) was born. The new role for information systems was to provide managerial end users with ad hoc and interactive support of their decision-making processes. This support would be tailored to the unique decision-making styles of managers as they confronted specific types of problems in the real world.

In the 1980s, several new roles for information systems appeared. First, the rapid development of microcomputer processing power, application software packages, and telecommunication networks gave birth to the phenomenon of *end user computing*. Now end users can use their own computing resources to support their job requirements instead of waiting for the indirect support of corporate information services departments.

Next, it became evident that most top corporate executives did not directly use either the reports of information reporting systems or the analytical modeling capabilities of decision support systems, so the concept of *executive information systems* (EIS) was developed. These information systems attempt to give top executives an easy way to get the critical information they want, when they want it, tailored to the formats they prefer.

Third, breakthroughs were made in the development and application of artificial intelligence (AI) techniques to business information systems. *Expert systems* (ES) and other *knowledge-based systems* forged a new role for information systems. Today, expert systems can serve as consultants to users by providing expert advice in limited subject areas.

Finally, an important new role for information systems appeared in the 1980s and continues into the 1990s. This is the concept of a strategic role for information systems, sometimes called *strategic information systems* (SIS). In this concept, information systems are expected to play a direct role in achieving the strategic objectives of a firm. This places a new responsibility on the information systems function of a business. No longer is IS merely an *information utility*, a service group providing information processing services to end user departments within the firm. Now it must become a *producer of information-based products and services* that earn profits for the firm and also give it a competitive advantage in the marketplace.

All these changes have increased the importance of the information systems function to the success of a firm. However, as we will see in this text, they also present new challenges to end users to effectively capitalize on the potential benefits of information technology.

Data Processing: 1950s–1960s
Electronic data processing systems
Transaction processing, record keeping, and traditional accounting applications
Management Reporting: 1960s–1970s
Management information systems
Management reports for prespecified information to support decision making
Decision Support: 1970s–1980s
Decision support systems
Interactive ad hoc support of the managerial decision-making process
Strategic and End User Support: 1980s–1990s
End user computing systems
Direct computing support for end user productivity
Executive information systems
Critical information for top management
Expert systems
Knowledge-based expert advice for end users
Strategic information systems
Strategic products and services for competitive advantage

FIGURE 6.1
The expanding roles of information systems. Note how the roles of computer-based information systems have expanded over time. Also, note the impact of these changes on the end users and managers of an organization.

Operations and Management Classifications

Information systems perform important operational and managerial support roles in businesses and other organizations. Therefore, several types of information systems can be classified conceptually as either *operations* or *management* information systems. Figure 6.2 illustrates this conceptual classification of information systems. Information systems are categorized this way to spotlight the major roles each plays in the operations and management of a business.

Information Systems for Business Operations

Information systems have always been needed to process data generated by and used in business operations. Such **operations information systems** produce a variety of information products for internal and external use. However, they do not emphasize producing the specific information products that can best be used by managers. Further processing by management information systems is usually required. The role of a business firm's operations information systems is to efficiently process business transactions, control industrial processes, support office communications and productivity, and update corporate databases. Figure 6.3 is an example of an operations information system. It illustrates the components and activities of a sales transaction processing system that captures sales transaction data, updates databases, and responds to end user inquiries.

Transaction Processing Systems

Operations information systems include the major category of **transaction processing systems** (TPS). Transaction processing systems record and process data resulting from business transactions. Typical examples are information systems that process sales, purchases, and inventory changes. The results of such processing are used to update customer, inventory, and other organizational databases. These databases then provide the data resources that can be processed and used by information reporting systems, decision support systems, and executive information systems.

Transaction processing systems also produce a variety of information products for internal or external use. For example, they produce customer statements, employee paychecks, sales receipts, purchase orders, dividend checks, tax forms, and financial statements. Transaction processing systems process transactions in two

FIGURE 6.2
Operations and management classifications of information systems. Note how this conceptual overview emphasizes the main purpose of information systems that support business operations or managerial decision making.

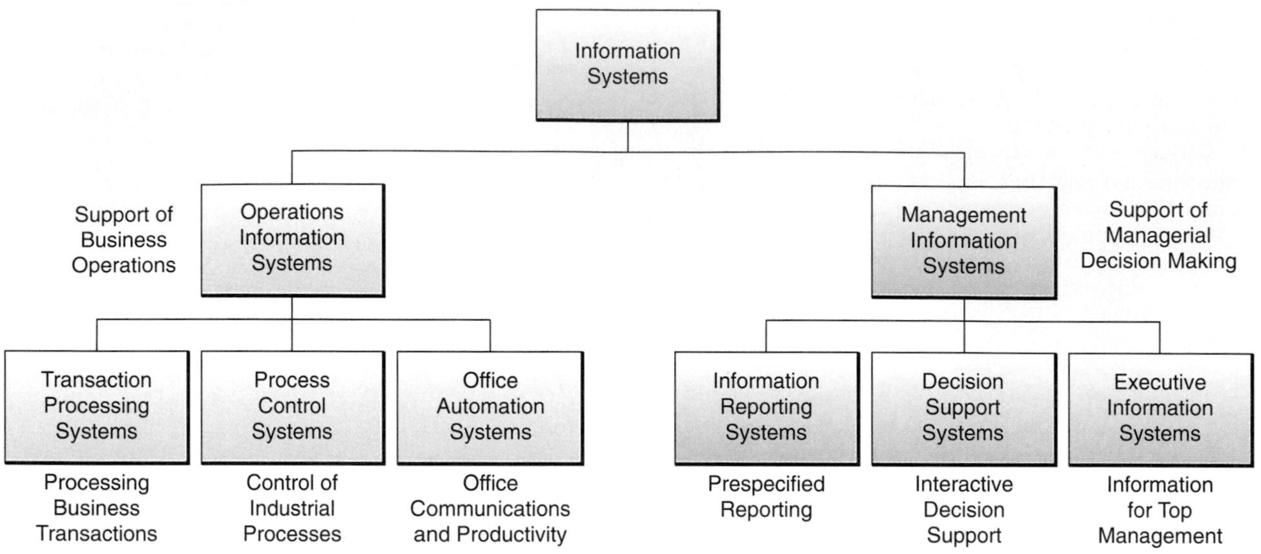

FIGURE 6.3
A sales transaction processing system is an example of an operations information system.

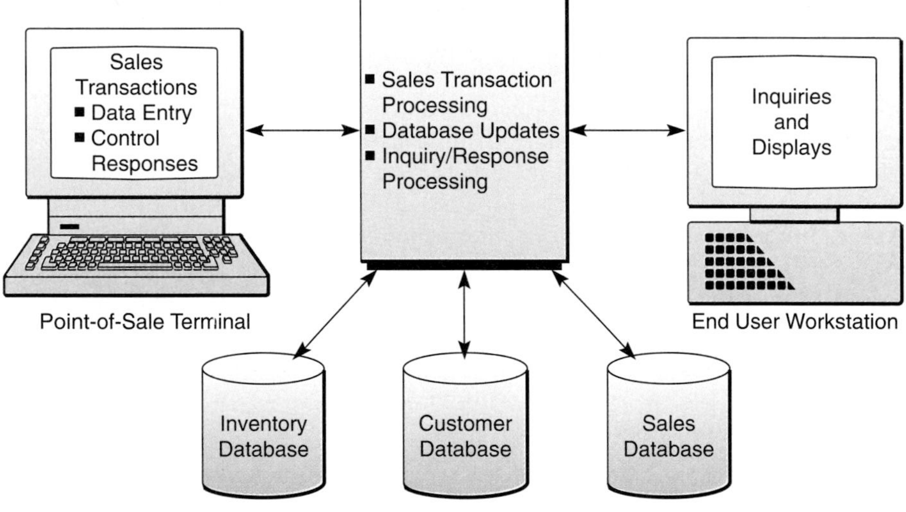

basic ways. In **batch processing**, transactions data is accumulated over a period of time and processed periodically. In **realtime** (or *online*) **processing**, data is processed immediately after a transaction occurs. For example, point-of-sale (POS) systems at retail stores may use electronic cash register terminals to capture and transmit sales data over telecommunications links to regional computer centers for immediate (realtime) or nightly (batch) processing. See Figure 6.4. We will discuss transaction processing systems in more detail in Chapter 8.

Bill Varie/The Image Bank.

FIGURE 6.4
This sales transaction processing system captures sales transactions data, updates databases, and responds to end user inquiries.

Process Control Systems

Operations information systems also make routine decisions that control operational processes. Examples are automatic inventory reorder decisions and production control decisions. This includes a category of information systems called **process control systems** (PCS), in which decisions adjusting a physical production process are automatically made by computers. For example, petroleum refineries and the assembly lines of automated factories use such systems. They monitor a physical process, capture and process data detected by sensors, and make realtime adjustments to a process. We will discuss process control systems further in Chapter 8.

Office Automation Systems

Another major role of operations information systems is the transformation of traditional manual office methods and paper communications media. **Office automation systems** (OAS) collect, process, store, and transmit information in the form of electronic office communications. These automated systems rely on text processing, telecommunications, and other information systems technologies to enhance office communications and productivity. For example, a business may use word processing for office correspondence, electronic mail to send and receive electronic messages, desktop publishing to produce a company newsletter, and teleconferencing to hold electronic meetings. We will discuss office automation systems in detail in Chapter 7.

Information Systems and Management

Information systems can significantly support managerial decision making. That is the goal which the information systems industry has been working toward since the concept of **management information systems** were developed. Developing effective MIS requires understanding how information systems can contribute to the decision-making process, as well as to the many functions and roles performed by managers.

In order to understand what information system support a manager needs, we need to review what management means. Figure 6.5 summarizes three fundamental conceptual frameworks that answer the question, "What does a manager do?" Let's take a closer look at each of these concepts to see how information systems can help meet the information needs of managers.

IS and the Functions of Management

Management is traditionally described as a process of leadership involving the management functions of planning, organizing, directing, and controlling. These functions of management are based on those expounded in the early 1900s by Henri

FIGURE 6.5
What a manager does. This figure summarizes (1) the four functions of management, (2) the 10 major roles played by managers, and (3) the three levels of management activity.

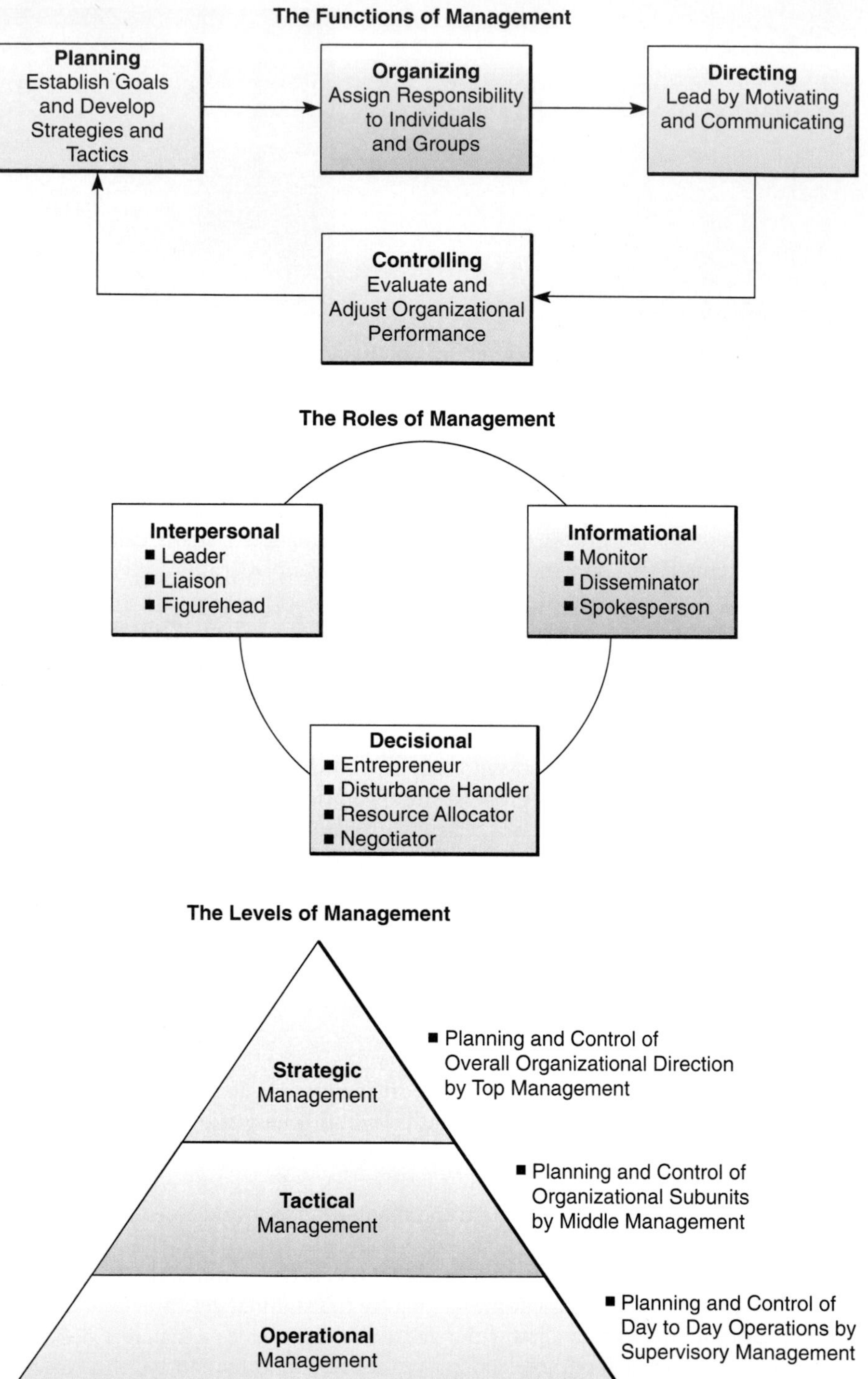

Fayol of France, a pioneer of management theory [11]. They give us a valuable way to think about what managers do. A manager should plan the activities of his or her organization, organize its personnel and their activities, direct its operations, and control its direction by evaluating feedback and making necessary adjustments.

- Planning involves the development of long- and short-range plans requiring the formulation of goals, objectives, strategies, policies, procedures, and standards. Planning also involves the perception and analysis of opportunities, problems, and alternative courses of action and the design of programs to achieve selected objectives.
- Organizing involves making assignments for the accomplishment of tasks to individuals and groups by delegating authority, assigning responsibility, and requiring accountability.
- Directing is the leadership of an organization through communication, inspiration, and motivation of organizational personnel.
- Controlling involves observing and measuring organizational performance and environmental activities and modifying the plans and activities of the organization when necessary.

Information systems can assist managers by providing information needed to accomplish each of these managerial functions. For example, information systems can help managers plan by providing both planning data and planning models. A typical example is the use of capital-budgeting models to develop long-range plans for the major expenditures needed to build new factories or retail stores or to make other major additions to plant and equipment. Information systems could provide data on internal-resource needs and external factors such as interest rates, as well as financial-modeling software.

Information systems can help managers organize and staff their organizations with human resources. For example, information from a personnel database and software for personnel requirements forecasting and an employee skills inventory can help managers organize present and proposed work groups and project teams. This helps ensure that employees with the necessary skills will be available when needed. Information systems can also help managers direct their organizations. For example, the electronic mail capabilities of office automation systems make it easier for managers to communicate with people in their organizations. Finally, information systems play a major role in the control function of management. Through such information products as exception reports, they help managers recognize deviations in performance from standards, forecasts, and budgets. This kind of feedback helps managers adjust a firm's operations to meet organizational objectives.

IS and the Roles of Management

Another useful management model was developed by management scholar Henry Mintzberg in the early 1970s [11]. This model views management as the performance of a variety of managerial roles. A manager has the authority and status to play the following roles:

- **Interpersonal roles.** A manager should be (1) a leader of subordinates, (2) a liaison with the external environment, and (3) a figurehead when ceremonial duties arise.
- **Information roles.** A manager should be (4) a monitor of information on organizational performance, (5) a disseminator of information within the organization, and (6) a spokesperson to the external environment.

- **Decision roles.** A manager should be (7) an entrepreneur in making innovative changes that affect the organization, (8) a disturbance handler when unanticipated events occur, (9) a resource allocator in determining the distribution of financial and other resources within the organization, and (10) a negotiator who resolves both internal and external disputes.

What information do managers need to perform these roles? How can information systems help? Mintzburg's studies of top-level executives showed that they did not get much help from computer-based information systems. Instead, they relied primarily on verbal information gathered from telephone calls, personal contacts, and meetings. However, improvements in office automation systems and executive information systems have been aimed at making information systems more attractive, easy to use, and helpful to top executives and other managers. For example, electronic mail systems allow electronic messages to be sent, stored, and forwarded among managerial and staff workstations. Executive information systems can make it easy for executives to gather critical information about organizational performance.

Another point to remember is that many of the 10 roles of management can be related to the four managerial functions. For example, the interpersonal role of a leader is directly related to the management functions of organizing, staffing, and directing. The information roles of a monitor and disseminator are directly related to the functions of directing and controlling. The decisional roles of an entrepreneur and resource allocator are directly related to the planning function. So, since information systems can supply information to support these managerial functions, they can also supply the information needed to perform the diverse roles of management.

IS and the Levels of Management

The information requirements of management depend heavily on the management level involved. Figure 6.5 emphasized that the activities of management can be subdivided into three major levels: (1) strategic management, (2) tactical management, and (3) operational management. These levels are related to the traditional management levels of top management, middle management, and operating or supervisory management. This "managerial pyramid" model of management was introduced in Chapter 1. It was popularized in the 1960s by Robert N. Anthony, another pioneer of management theory. It answers the question, "What does a manager do?" by emphasizing that management consists of planning and control activities determined by the manager's specific level in an organization [4].

- **Strategic planning and control.** Top executives develop overall organizational goals, strategies, policies, and objectives through long-range strategic planning. They also monitor the strategic performance of the organization and its overall direction.
- **Tactical planning and control.** Middle managers develop short- and medium-range plans and budgets and specify the policies, procedures, and objectives for subunits of the organization. They also acquire and allocate resources and monitor the performance of organizational subunits, such as departments, divisions, and other work groups.
- **Operational planning and control.** Supervisory managers develop short-range planning devices such as production schedules. They direct the use of resources and the performance of tasks according to established procedures and within budgets and schedules established for the work groups of the organization.

FIGURE 6.6
Information requirements by management level. The type of information required by managers is directly related to their level of management and the structure of decision situations they face.

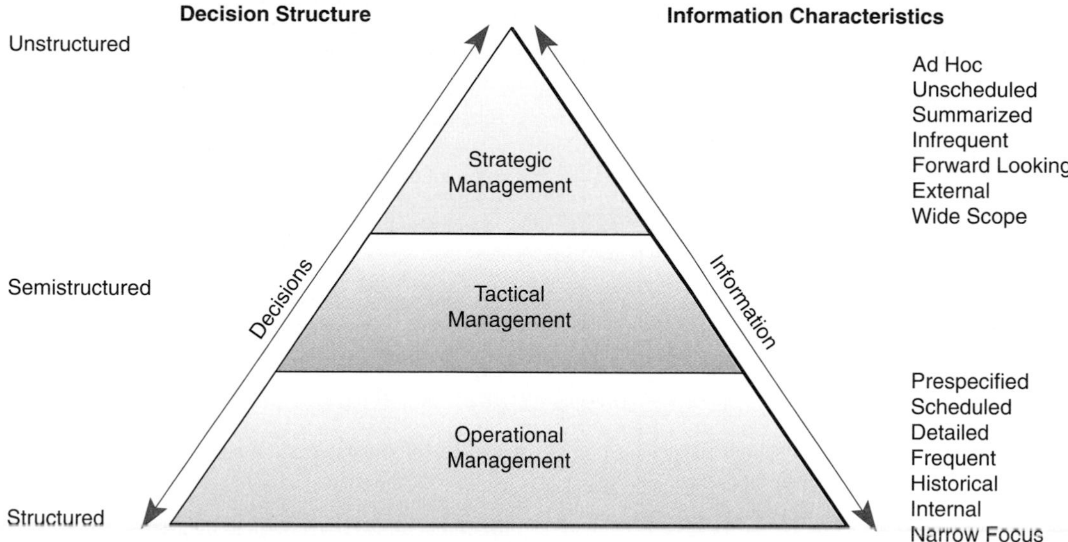

Figure 6.6 emphasizes that the type of information required by managers is directly related to the level of management and the amount of structure in the decision situations they face. For example, the strategic-management level requires more summarized, ad hoc, unscheduled reports, forecasts, and external intelligence to support its more unstructured planning and policy-making responsibilities. The operational-management level, on the other hand, may require more regular internal reports emphasizing detailed current and historical data comparisons that support its more structured control of day-to-day operations. Thus, we can generalize that higher levels of management require more ad hoc, unscheduled, infrequent summaries, with a wide, external, forward-looking scope. On the other hand, lower levels of management require more prespecified, frequently scheduled, and detailed information, with a more narrow, internal, and historical focus.

IS and Decision Making

The most widely used model of the decision-making process was developed by Herbert A. Simon, a Nobel Prize–winning economist and scholar of management decision making. His model is a conceptual framework that divides the decision-making process into intelligence, design, and choice activities [15]. Other researchers have emphasized that since managerial decision making is typically a problem-solving process, the implementation of a decision is as important to its success as the steps that lead up to making it [4]. Therefore, we can use a model of decision making that consists of four stages:

- **Intelligence activities.** Search the environment and identify events and conditions requiring decisions.
- **Design activities.** Develop and evaluate possible courses of action.
- **Choice activities.** Select a particular course of action.
- **Implementation activities.** Implement the decision and monitor its success.

As Figure 6.7 shows, this four-stage decision-making process includes the ability to cycle back to a previous stage if the decision maker is dissatisfied with the

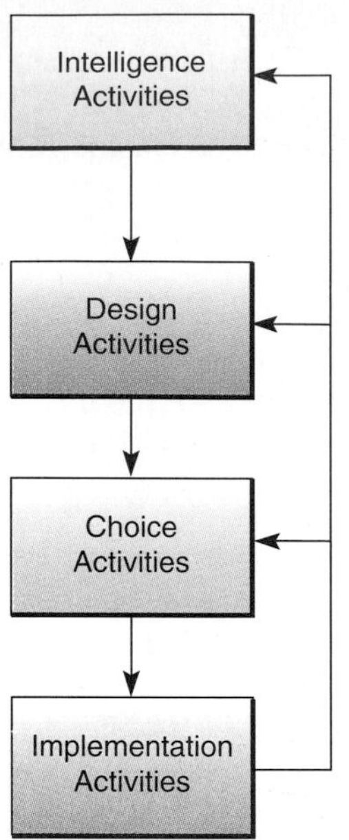
Intelligence Activities
Design Activities
Choice Activities
Implementation Activities
■ Search for and identify conditions requiring a decision.
■ Information systems should scan the internal organization and the external environment and help identify problems and opportunities.
■ Develop and evaluate alternative courses of action.
■ Information systems should help generate and evaluate decision alternatives.
■ Select a course of action.
■ Information systems should help emphasize and prioritize decision alternatives.
■ Implement and monitor the success of the decision.
■ Information systems should provide feedback on the implemented decision.

FIGURE 6.7
A model of the decision-making process. Note that the decision-making process is a four-stage process of intelligence, design, choice, and implementation activities that may cycle back to previous stages. Also note how information systems can support each stage of this process.

intelligence gathered, the alternatives developed, or the success of implementation activities. Also note that each of these stages of decision making has unique information requirements, which we will now explore.

Information for the Intelligence Stage

Information systems can help in the intelligence stage by providing information about internal and external conditions that might require decision making by appropriate managers. Thus, information systems can be used to scan the operations of an organization or the activities taking place in the business environment. Information systems can also scan the external environment to identify potential decision situations. Sales analysis reports can be furnished to managers periodically, when exceptional sales situations occur, or on demand. These help managers identify the status of sales performance, sales trends, and exceptional sales conditions for the firm. Information from market research studies and external databases could also help managers identify changes in consumer preferences or competitive products.

An important information system capability is needed in this stage. Managers should have the ability to make ad hoc inquiries, that is, unique, unscheduled, situation-specific information requests. The prespecified reports typically provided by information reporting systems periodically, on an exception basis, or even on demand may not be satisfactory. Such information products may not give a manager enough information to recognize whether a problem or opportunity exists.

A disturbing sales trend can be brought to a manager's attention by a weekly sales report that spotlights unusual or exceptional sales activity. However, the manager may need to make further inquiries to isolate the sales problem. Therefore, information systems frequently provide a query language capability to allow a manager to make ad hoc inquiries of a sales database to get the exact sales information he or she needs.

Information for the Design Stage

The design stage of decision making involves developing and evaluating alternative courses of action. A major consideration introduced by Simon for this stage (as well

FIGURE 6.8
Examples of decisions by the type of decision structure and by level of management.

Decision Structure	Operational Management	Tactical Management	Strategic Management
Unstructured		Work group reorganization	New business planning
	Cash management	Work group performance analysis	Company reorganization
Semistructured	Credit management	Employee performance appraisal	Product planning
	Production scheduling	Capital budgeting	Mergers and acquisitions
	Daily work assignment	Program budgeting	Site location
Structured	Inventory control	Program control	

as for the other stages) is whether the decision situation is programmable or nonprogrammable, or, more popularly, structured or unstructured.

Figure 6.8 shows the amount of structure in typical decisions faced by each level of management, based on the work of G. Anthony Gorry and Michael Scott Morton [4]. Their work emphasized that many of the changes in managers' information needs can be attributed to the degree of decision structure at each level of management. Decisions at the operational level tend to be more structured, those at the tactical level more semistructured, and those at the strategic level more unstructured. Therefore, information systems must be designed to produce a variety of information products to meet the changing decision needs of managers at different levels of an organization.

Structured Decisions

Structured decisions (also called *programmable decisions*) involve situations where the procedures to follow when a decision is needed can be specified in advance. Therefore, such decisions are structured or programmed by the decision procedures, or decision rules, developed for them. A structured decision may involve what is known as a *deterministic*, or *algorithmic*, *decision*. In this case, a decision's outcome can be determined with certainty if a specified sequence of activities (an algorithm) is performed. Or a structured decision may involve a probabilistic decision situation. In this case, enough probabilities about possible outcomes are known that a decision can be statistically determined with an acceptable probability of success.

The inventory reorder decisions faced by most businesses are frequently quantified and automated. Inventory control software includes decision algorithms that outline the computations to perform and the steps to take when quantities in inventory are running low. Computing economic order points and quantities is a typical example. Thus, one way that information systems can support structured decisions is by quantifying and automating a decision-making process. In other cases, prespecified information products such as periodic reports can provide most of the information needed by a decision maker faced with a structured decision situation.

Unstructured Decisions

Unstructured decisions (also called *nonprogrammable decisions*) involve decision situations where it is not possible or desirable to specify in advance most of the decision procedures to follow. Many decision situations in the real world are unstructured because they are subject to too many random or changeable events or involve too many unknown factors or relationships. At most, many decision situations are semistructured. That is, some decision procedures can be prespecified, but not enough to lead to a definite recommended decision.

Decisions involved in starting a new line of products or making major changes to employee benefits would probably range from unstructured to semistructured. The many unknown or changeable factors involved would require a less structured approach leading to subjective judgments by managers. Information systems can support such decisions by providing (1) the ability to make ad hoc inquiries for information in company databases and (2) the ability to reach a decision in an interactive process using a decision support system.

As we mentioned earlier, decision support systems and expert systems can give managers such assistance. Models of business operations can be developed with decision support software, including advanced statistical, management science, and modeling packages, or less complex spreadsheet programs. These packages and models can then be used to manipulate information collected in the intelligence stage to develop and evaluate a variety of alternatives. Figure 6.9 is a sales analysis display generated by a popular executive information system with DSS capabilities.

An electronic spreadsheet package can be used to build product performance models that incorporate some of the factors and relationships a product manager thinks are important. The product manager can then load the models with appropriate data and ask a series of what-if questions to see the effects on the spreadsheet display of a variety of alternatives. For example, "What would happen to the breakeven point if we cut advertising expense by 10 percent, 20 percent, and 25 percent?" Or goal seeking questions could be used. For example, "How much would we have to cut fixed costs to get a 10 percent decrease in the breakeven point?" As a product manager repeats this process, information is generated that helps develop and evaluate possible decision alternatives pertaining to product performance.

Information for the Choice Stage

Information systems should help managers select a proper course of action from the alternatives developed during the design stage. Of course, this assumes that enough information was gathered during the intelligence phase and that a sufficient number of alternatives were developed and evaluated during the design stage. If not, the manager may choose to return to those stages for more data or alternatives.

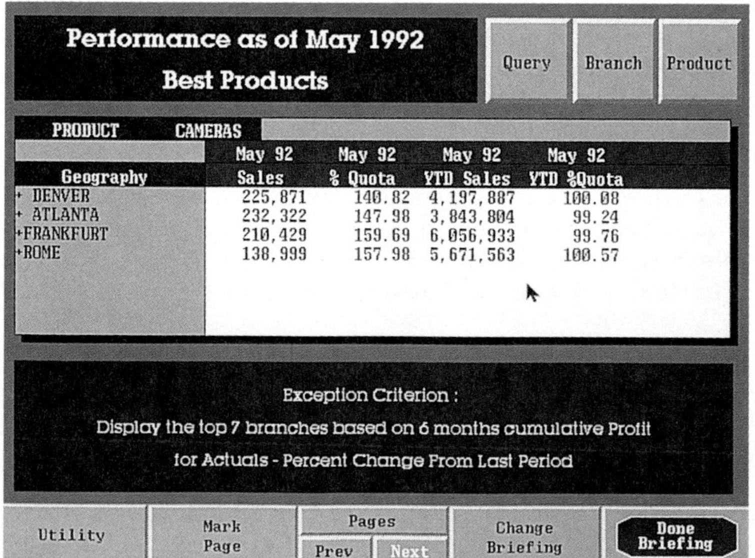

Courtesy of Information Resources, Inc.

FIGURE 6.9
Using EXPRESS/EIS—a decision support/executive information system package. This analysis of sales by product and branch can help a marketing manager evaluate decision alternatives.

However, given the time and resource constraints of the real world, most decision makers will choose to *satisfice* rather than optimize when faced with a decision situation. That is, they will rarely act as rational economic beings who insist that all relevant information be gathered, that all rational alternatives be considered, and that only the optimum alternative be chosen. Instead, they will act with what Simon calls *bounded rationality*. That is, they will be satisfied to make a decision based on incomplete information and a limited number of alternatives if it meets some of their subjective preferences and produces an acceptable level of results.

In any case, information systems can help managers in the choice stage in several ways. Managers can be provided with summarized and organized information emphasizing the main points (such as major assumptions, resource requirements, and expected results) of each decision alternative. Various financial and marketing ratios and other methods can also be used to prioritize alternatives and thus help managers select the best course of action.

An information system can provide calculations of the net present value, internal rate of return, and payback period to rank several competing proposals from a financial point of view. Other criteria, such as expected market share, number of new personnel required, and training requirements, could also be used to rank alternatives.

Information for the Implementation Stage

The implementation stage involves accomplishing activities that implement the decision alternative selected during the choice stage. It also involves monitoring the success of the decision after it is implemented. Information systems can help managers monitor the successful implementation of a decision. They can provide feedback about business operations affected by the decision that was made. This helps a manager assess a decision's success or failure and determine whether follow-up decisions are needed.

If a decision to cut promotion costs is made, a sales manager can monitor the decision's effects on sales activity. If a larger drop in sales occurs than was expected, the manager must then decide what actions to take to correct the problem. The decision-making process then begins all over again.

Management Information Systems

When information systems focus on providing information and support for effective decision making by managers, they are called **management information systems**. The concept of management information systems (MIS) originated in the 1960s and became the byword (and the *buzzword*) of almost all attempts to relate computer technology and systems theory to data processing in organizations. At that time, it became evident that computers were being applied to the solution of business problems in a piecemeal fashion, focusing almost entirely on the computerization of clerical and record-keeping tasks. The concept of management information systems was developed to counteract such inefficient development and ineffective use of computers. Though tarnished by early failures, the MIS concept is still recognized as vital to efficient and effective information systems in organizations for two major reasons:

- It emphasizes the **management orientation** of information technology in business. A major goal of computer-based information systems should be the support of *management decision making*, not merely the processing of data generated by business operations.
- It emphasizes that a **systems framework** should be used for organizing information systems applications. Business applications of information tech-

nology should be viewed as interrelated and integrated *computer-based information systems* and not as independent data-processing jobs.

Providing information and support for management decision making by all levels of management (from top executives to middle managers to supervisors) is a complex task. Conceptually, several major types of information systems are needed to support a variety of managerial end user responsibilities: (1) information reporting systems, (2) decision support systems, and (3) executive information systems. Figure 6.10 illustrates some of the resources needed and information products produced by several types of management information systems.

Information Reporting Systems

Information reporting systems (IRS) are the most common form of management information systems. They provide managerial end users with information products that support much of their day-to-day decision-making needs. Information reporting systems provide a variety of reports and displays to management. The contents of these information products are specified in advance by managers so that they contain information that managers need. Information reporting systems retrieve information about internal operations from databases that have been updated by transaction processing systems. They also obtain data about the business environment from external sources.

Information products provided to managers include displays and reports that can be furnished (1) on demand, (2) periodically, according to a predetermined schedule, or (3) whenever exceptional conditions occur. For example, sales managers could receive (1) instantaneous visual displays at their workstations in response to requests for information about the sales of a particular product; (2) weekly sales analysis reports evaluating sales results by product, salesperson, and sales territory; or (3) reports produced automatically whenever a salesperson fails to produce sales results during a specified period. We will discuss information reporting systems further in Chapter 9.

FIGURE 6.10
The components and activities of management information systems. Note some of the resources needed to provide information reporting, decision support, strategic information, and expert advice to managerial end users.

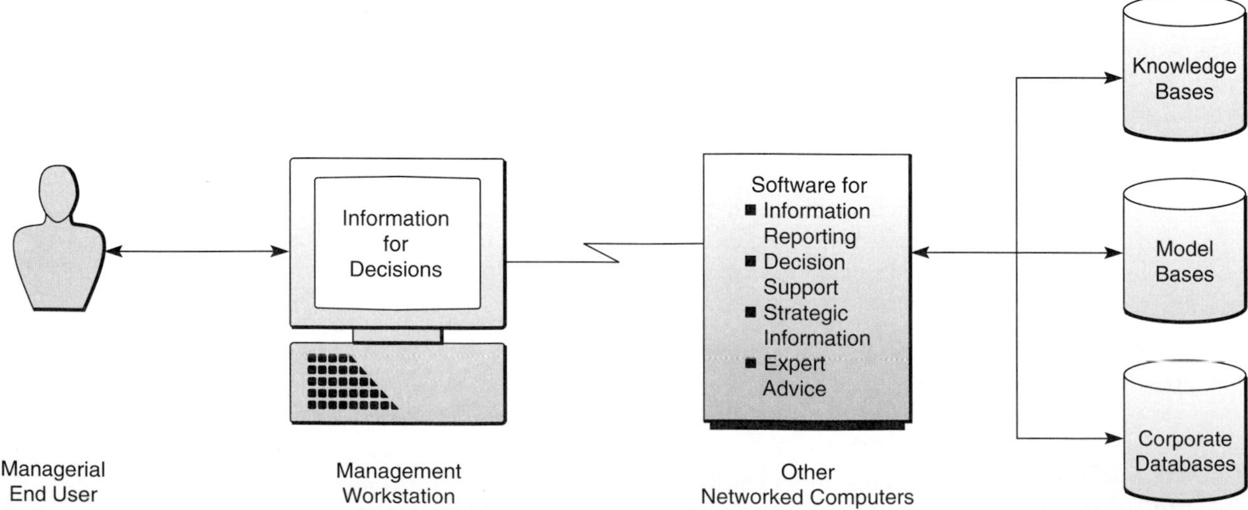

Decision Support Systems

Decision support systems (DSS) are a natural progression from information reporting systems and transaction processing systems. Decision support systems are interactive, computer-based information systems that use decision models and specialized databases to assist the decision-making processes of managerial end users. Thus, they are different from transaction processing systems, which focus on processing the data generated by business transactions and operations, though they extract data from corporate databases maintained by TPS. They also differ from information reporting systems, which focus on providing managers with prespecified information (reports) that can be used to help them make more effective, structured types of decisions.

Instead, decision support systems provide managerial end users with information in an interactive session on an ad hoc (as needed) basis. A DSS provides managers with analytical modeling, data retrieval, and information presentation capabilities. Managers generate the information they need for more unstructured types of decisions in an interactive, computer-based process. For example, electronic spreadsheets and other decision support software allow a managerial end user to pose a series of what-if questions and receive interactive responses to such ad hoc requests for information.

Thus, information from a DSS differs from the prespecified responses generated by information reporting systems. When using a DSS, managers are exploring possible alternatives and receiving tentative information based on alternative sets of assumptions. Therefore, managerial end users do not have to specify their information needs in advance. Instead, a DSS interactively helps them find the information they need. Decision support systems are discussed further in Chapter 9.

Executive Information Systems

Executive information systems (EIS) are management information systems tailored to the strategic information needs of top management. Top executives get the information they need from many sources, including letters, memos, periodicals, and reports produced manually as well as by computer systems. Other sources of executive information are meetings, telephone calls, and social activities. Thus, much of a top executive's information comes from noncomputer sources. Computer-generated information has not played a primary role in meeting many top executives' information needs.

The goal of computer-based executive information systems is to provide top management with immediate and easy access to selective information about key factors that are critical to accomplishing a firm's strategic objectives. Therefore, an EIS is easy to operate and understand. Graphics displays are used extensively, and immediate access to internal and external databases is provided. An EIS provides information about the current status and projected trends for key factors selected by top executives. Executive Information Systems have become so popular in recent years that their use is spreading into the ranks of middle management. Executive information systems are discussed again in Chapter 9. See Figure 6.11.

Other Classifications of Information Systems

Several other categories of information systems provide more unique or broad classifications than those we have just mentioned. That's because these information systems can support either operations or management applications. For example, *expert systems* can provide expert advice for operational chores like equipment diagnostics, or managerial decisions such as loan portfolio management. Another example is *end user computing systems*, which provide direct hands-on support of end users for either operational or managerial applications. Finally, information systems

FIGURE 6.11
Management information systems provide information and decision support to managers at all levels of an organization.

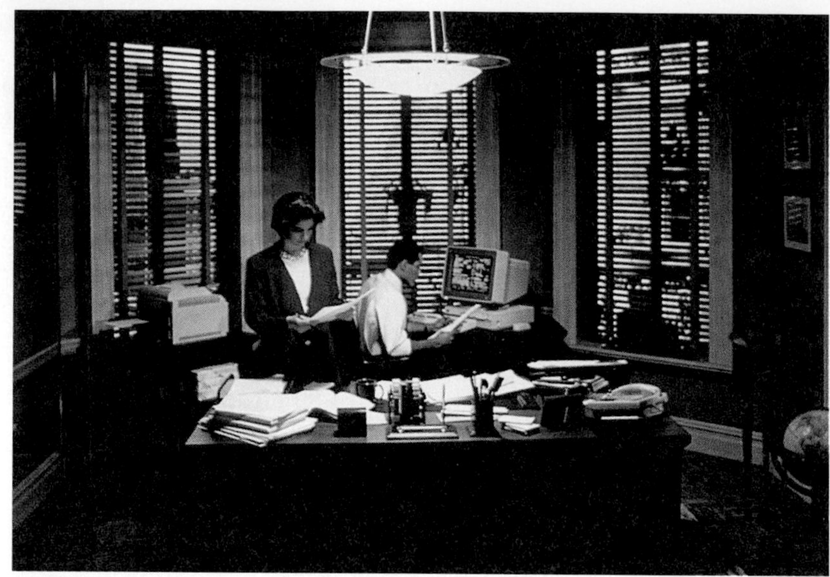

Courtesy IBM Corporation.

which focus on operational and managerial applications in support of basic business functions such as accounting or marketing are known as *business information systems*.

Expert Systems

The frontiers of information systems are being affected by developments in **artificial intelligence**. (AI) Artificial intelligence is an area of computer science whose long-range goal is to develop computers that can think, as well as see, hear, walk, talk, and feel. For example, AI projects involve developing natural computer interfaces, advanced industrial robots, and intelligent computer software. A major thrust is the development of computer functions normally associated with human intelligence, such as reasoning, learning, and problem solving.

One of the most practical applications of AI is the development of **expert systems**. An expert system is a *knowledge-based information system*; that is, it uses its knowledge about a specific area to act as an expert consultant to users. The components of an expert system are a knowledge base and software modules that perform inferences on the knowledge and offer answers to a user's questions. Expert systems are being used in many different fields, including medicine, engineering, the physical sciences, and business. For example, expert systems now help diagnose illnesses, search for minerals, analyze compounds, recommend repairs, and do financial planning. Expert systems can support either operations or management activities. We will discuss artificial intelligence and expert systems further in Chapter 9.

End User Computing Systems

End user computing systems are computer-based information systems that directly support both the operational and managerial applications of end users. You should think of end user computing primarily as the direct, hands-on use of computers by end users, instead of the indirect use provided by the hardware, software, and professional resources of an organization's information services department. In end user computing systems, end users typically use microcomputer workstations and a variety of software packages and databases for personal productivity, information retrieval, decision support, and application development. For example, users may do word processing, send electronic mail, retrieve information from a database, manipulate an analytical model, or develop a new business application. We will discuss end user computing systems in Chapter 7.

Business Information Systems

As a future managerial end user, it is important for you to realize that information systems directly support both operations and management activities in the business functions of accounting, finance, human resource management, marketing, and operations management. Such **business information systems** are needed by all business functions.

For example, marketing managers need information about sales performance and trends provided by marketing information systems. Financial managers need information concerning financing costs and investment returns provided by financial information systems. Production managers need information analyzing resource requirements and worker productivity provided by a variety of manufacturing information systems. Personnel managers need the information concerning employee compensation and professional development provided by human resource information systems. Thus, business information systems provide managers with a variety of information products to support their decision-making responsibilities in each of the functional areas of business. We will discuss these systems in more detail in Chapter 8.

Integrated Information Systems

It is also important to realize that information systems in the real world are typically integrated combinations of several types of information systems we have just mentioned. That's because conceptual classifications of information systems are designed to emphasize the many different roles of information systems. In practice, these roles are integrated into *composite* or *cross-functional* information systems that provide a variety of functions. Thus, most information systems are designed to produce information and support decision making for various levels of management and business functions, as well as do record-keeping and transaction processing chores.

For example, a payroll system that processes employee time cards and produces employee paychecks is an operations information system. An information system that uses payroll data to produce labor analysis reports showing variances and trends in labor costs is a human resource management information system. However, in most cases, these functions are combined in an integrated payroll/labor analysis system.

Another example involves sales order/transaction processing, which is an operations information system, and sales analysis, which is a marketing management information system. However, these two systems are typically integrated in a business. Thus, a sales order processing system would collect and record sales transaction data and provide input to a sales analysis system, which produces reports for sales managers concerning sales performance.

So whenever you analyze a business information system, you will probably see that it provides information for a variety of managerial levels and business functions. Figure 6.12 summarizes the major categories of information systems we have discussed in this section.

FIGURE 6.12
A summary of the major categories of information systems.

Operations information systems process data generated by business operations. Major categories are:

- **Transaction processing systems** process data resulting from business transactions, update operational databases, and produce business documents.
- **Process control systems** monitor and control industrial processes.
- **Office automation systems** automate office procedures and enhance office communications and productivity.

Management information systems provide information and support needed for effective decision making by managers. Major categories are:

- **Information reporting systems** provide information in the form of prespecified reports and displays to managers.
- **Decision support systems** provide interactive ad hoc support for the decision-making process of managers.
- **Executive information systems** provide critical information tailored to the information needs of top management.

Other categories of information systems can support either operations, management, or strategic applications.

- **Expert systems** are knowledge-based systems that provide expert advice and act as expert consultants to users.
- **End user computing systems** support the direct, hands-on use of computers by end users for operational and managerial applications.
- **Business information systems** support the operational and managerial applications of the basic business functions of a firm.
- **Strategic information systems** provide a firm with strategic products, services, and capabilities for competitive advantage.

REAL WORLD CASE

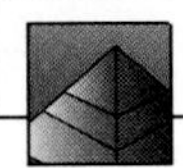

Chase Manhattan Bank: Banking on Information Systems

Chase Manhattan's 1,100 New York investment bankers used to spend hours scanning dozens of day-old newsletters on other business publications for company and financial information that could lead them to new clients. But all too often, the competition was beating the $97 billion financial institution to the table to make deals. To remedy the situation, Chase Manhattan Chief Information Officer Craig Goldman proposed an online information news-retrieval system that is part of CIX, a telecommunications network that links Chase Manhattan facilities worldwide.

The online news-retrieval system links Chase Manhattan investment bankers and their PCs with corporate data and breaking news from more than 70 online financial news and information sources. It also provides them with real-time analysis of events, ranging from a downturn in gold prices to the outbreak of a civil war—information that could impact an investment decision. Additionally, CIX furnishes all Chase Manhattan employees at its New York headquarters with access to a standardized office software, including electronic mail, the Lotus 1-2-3 spreadsheet, and WordPerfect word processor.

Chase Manhattan's IS team also went to work on an expert systems-based analysis system, which contains detailed models for measuring potential business risks associated with events such as a drop in a particular company's stock price or a freeze in Florida, which could adversely affect citrus crops, as well as the businesses that depend on them. Dealmakers are alerted to these events via a built-in warning system that issues a beeping sound and/or flashes breaking news in a screen-based alert window.

Goldman says CIX has been instrumental in winning new business and bolstering customer service. He relays the case of an investment banker who was at his desk late one Friday when the system alerted him to what looked like a hostile takeover of a Chase Manhattan client company in California. The banker called the client, then assembled a team to fly to the West Coast for a weekend strategy session. By Monday morning, the team had put together a package and worked out a satisfactory deal.

That incident was not an isolated one, according to Executive Vice President Mike Dacey, who heads Chase Manhattan's corporate finance and capital markets business in North America. "With CIX, it is not unusual at all for us to find out information on a given client before the company itself knows of the news," he says. "We can be on the phone with a solution before a VP of finance at a client company even knows they have a problem."

Since their inception four years ago, CIX and the online news system have been continually enhanced and expanded. Initially targeted to serve 1,100 employees in New York, the network now serves 4,000 Chase Manhattan employees worldwide. "What started as a system for North America has grown to be our global infrastructure," Goldman notes. "Over time, we've also consistently added new capabilities including Lotus' Notes work group software, more information products, and new models and analysis tools. We've gone from an information desert to a tropical forest," Dacey notes.

At the heart of the project's success is strong user involvement and support, Goldman says. Granted, at first banking executives new to PCs had to be "handheld and babysat" by in-house IS training groups. IS also confronted user resistance to standardizing on certain office application software, but in the end—thanks to a massive training effort—users came around, Goldman says.

CASE STUDY QUESTIONS

1. What types of information systems do you recognize in this case? Explain.
2. How does the CIX information system support Chase's business operations? Managerial decision making? Strategic advantage?
3. How could other types of business firms benefit from similar systems?

Source: Adapted from Julia King, "The Secret of Their Success," *Computerworld*, March 29, 1993, p. 100–101. Used with permission.

SECTION II
Information Systems for Strategic Advantage

Information systems can play a major role in support of the strategic objectives of an organization. This strategic role involves using information technology to develop products, services, and capabilities that give a firm a strategic advantage over the competitive forces it faces in the global marketplace. Let's look at several basic concepts that define the role of such **strategic information systems**.

Competitive Strategy Concepts

How should a business manager think about competitive strategies? How can competitive strategies be applied to the use of information systems by an organization? Several important conceptual frameworks for understanding and applying competitive strategies have been developed by Michael Porter [12, 13], Charles Wiseman [17, 18], and others. Figure 6.13 illustrates several important concepts. A firm can survive and succeed in the long run if it successfully develops strategies to confront five **competitive forces** that shape the structure of competition in its industry. These are (1) rivalry of competitors within its industry, (2) threats of new entrants, (3) threats of substitutes, (4) the bargaining power of customers, and (5) the bargaining power of suppliers.

Several **competitive strategies** can be developed to help a firm confront these competitive forces. These include the following:

- **Cost leadership strategy.** Becoming a low-cost producer of products and services in the industry. Also, a firm can find ways to help its suppliers or customers reduce their costs or to increase the costs of their competitors.
- **Differentiation strategy.** Developing ways to differentiate a firm's products and services from its competitors' or reduce the differentiation advantages of competitors. This may allow a firm to focus its products or services to give it an advantage in particular segments or niches of a market.
- **Innovation strategy.** Finding new ways of doing business. This may involve the development of new products and services, entry into new markets or market segments, or establishment of new business alliances. It may also involve finding new ways of producing or distributing products and services

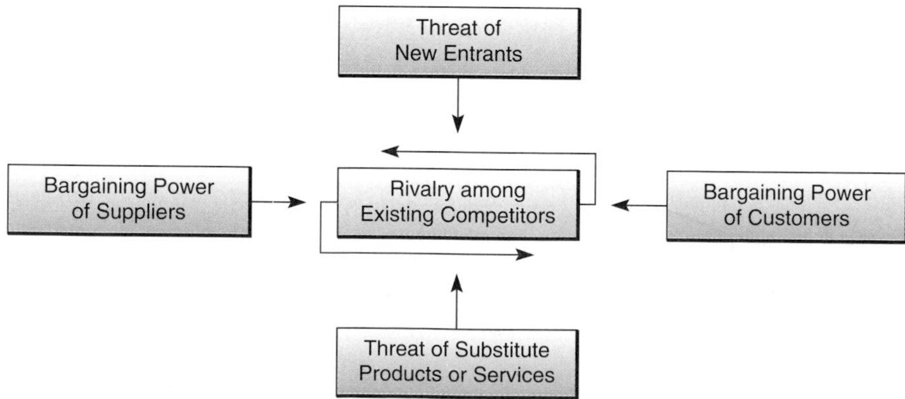

Source: Adapted from Michael E. Porter, *Competitive Advantage: Creating and Sustaining Superior Performance* (New York: Free Press, 1985), p. 5.

FIGURE 6.13
The competitive environment of an industry. Note the five competitive forces that determine the profitability and survival of the firms within an industry.

that are so different from the way business has been conducted that they alter the fundamental structure of an industry.

Figure 6.14 provides examples of how each of these three competitive strategies can be used to confront each of the competitive forces facing a firm. Such strategic alternatives can be generated as part of a strategic management process known as *SWOT analysis*, in which managers evaluate a firm's Strengths, Weaknesses, Opportunities, and Threats prior to making strategic choices.

Strategic Roles for Information Systems

How can the preceding competitive strategy concepts be applied to the strategic role of information systems in an organization? Put another way, how can managers use investments in information technology to directly support a firm's competitive strategies? These questions can be answered in terms of three key strategic roles that information systems can perform in a firm. Figure 6.15 emphasizes that strategic information systems can help a firm (1) improve its operational efficiency, (2) promote organizational innovation, and (3) build strategic IT resources. These three fundamental roles support a firm's use of competitive strategies against the competitive forces from competitors, customers, suppliers, substitutes, and new entrants.

Improving Operational Efficiency

Investments in information technology can help make a firm's operations significantly more efficient. *Re-engineering* its business processes could allow the firm to cut costs dramatically and improve the quality and delivery of its products and services. For example, manufacturing operations of many automobile manufacturers have been automated and significantly improved by computer-aided manufacturing (CAM) technology. The distribution of cars and parts, and the exchange of accounting information has also been improved by telecommunications networks that electronically connect a car manufacturer's distribution facilities with automobile

FIGURE 6.14
Examples of the use of competitive strategies to confront each of the competitive forces facing a firm and achieve strategic objectives. Information systems can directly support such strategic thrusts.

	Customers	Suppliers	Competitors	New Entrants	Substitutes
Strategic Objectives	Attract new customers and lock in present customers by creating switching costs	Lock in suppliers by creating switching costs	Lock out competitors by locking in customers and suppliers	Create barriers to entry into the industry	Make substitution unattractive
Cost Leadership Strategy	Offer lower prices	Help suppliers lower costs	Undercut competitor prices	Make entry investment unattractive	Make substitution economically unfeasible
Differentiation Strategy	Provide better quality, features, and service	Help suppliers improve services	Toughen competition with unique features	Complicate entry decision	Provide features of substitutes
Innovation Strategy	Provide new products and services to new markets	Develop unique supply services or alliances with suppliers	Provide unmatched products and services	Enter businesses of potential entrants	Produce substitutes

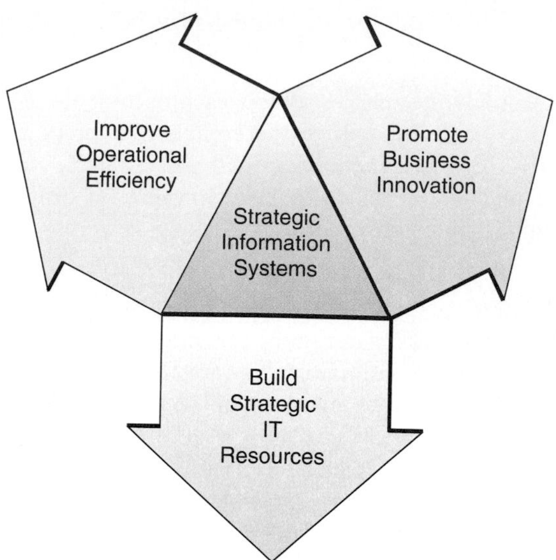

FIGURE 6.15
The strategic roles of information systems. Note that information systems give a firm three fundamental capabilities to confront the competitive forces that surround it.

dealers. Figure 6.16 outlines some of the major ways that information technology can improve the operational efficiency of business processes.

Operational efficiency may allow a firm to adopt a low-cost leadership strategy. However, a firm could decide instead to use its operational efficiency to increase quality and service by choosing a product differentiation strategy. This strategy would stress the unique quality of a firm's products and services. In either case, a firm would be better able to deter competitive threats. Its industry rivals and firms seeking to enter the industry using similar or substitute products would have a harder time beating an efficient competitor.

Barriers to Entry

By making investments in information technology that increased its operational efficiency, a firm could also erect **barriers to entry**. These could be made by increasing the amount of investment or the complexity of the technology required to compete in a market segment. Such actions would tend to discourage firms already in the industry and deter external firms from entering the industry. Thus, large investments in computer-based information systems can make the stakes too high for some present or prospective players.

Lock in Customers and Suppliers

Investments in information technology can also allow a business to **lock in customers and suppliers** (and lock out competitors) by building valuable new relationships with them. This can deter both customers and suppliers from abandoning a firm for its competitors or intimidating a firm into accepting less-profitable relationships. Early attempts to use information systems technology in these relationships focused on significantly improving the quality of service to customers and suppliers in a firm's distribution, marketing, sales, and service activities. Then businesses moved to more innovative uses of information technology.

For example, many telecommunications networks were designed to provide salespeople and customer service staff with up-to-date sales, shipping, inventory, and account status information for relay to their customers. Firms began to use the operational efficiency of such information systems to offer better-quality service and thereby differentiate themselves from their competitors. Then some firms began to extend these networks to their customers and suppliers in order to build innovative

IT Capability	Operational Improvements to Business Processes
Transactional	Transform unstructured processes into routine transactions
Geographical	Transform information quickly and easily across large distances, making processes independent of geography
Automational	Reduce or replace human labor in a process
Analytical	Bring complex analytical methods to bear on a process
Informational	Bring large amounts of detailed information into a process
Sequential	Enable changes in the sequence of tasks, often allowing multiple tasks to be worked on simultaneously
Knowledge	Allow the capture and dissemination of knowledge and expertise to improve a process
Tracking	Allow the detailed tracking of the status, inputs, and outputs of a process
Disintermediation	Connect two parties within a process that would otherwise communicate through an intermediary

Source: Adapted from Thomas H. Davenport and James E. Short, "The New Industrial Engineering: Information Technology and Business Process Redesign," *Sloan Management Review* (Summer 1990), p. 17.

FIGURE 6.16
How information technology can improve business processes.

relationships which would lock in their business. This creates **interorganizational information systems** in which telecommunications networks electronically link the terminals and computers of businesses with their customers and suppliers, resulting in new business alliances and partnerships.

Promoting Business Innovation

Investments in information systems technology can result in the development of new products, services, and processes. This can create new business opportunities, and enable a firm to expand into new markets or into new segments of existing markets. The use of automated teller machines (ATMs) in banking is an example of an innovative investment in information systems technology.

By employing ATMs, Citibank and several other large banks were able to gain a strategic advantage over their competitors that lasted for several years. ATMs lured customers away from other financial institutions by cutting the cost of delivering bank services and increasing the convenience of such services. The more costly and less-convenient alternative would have been to establish new bank branch offices. ATMs are also an example of product differentiation, since bank services are now provided in a new way. ATMs raised the cost of competition, which forced some smaller banks that could not afford the investment in new technology to merge with larger banks. ATMs represented an attractive and convenient new banking service produced and distributed to customers by making innovative changes in the delivery of bank services. Thus, information systems technology was used to develop a new distribution process for bank services.

Switching Costs

A major emphasis in strategic information systems is to build **switching costs** into the relationships between a firm and its customers or suppliers. That is, investments in information systems technology can make customers or suppliers dependent on the continued use of innovative, mutually beneficial interorganizational information systems. Then they become reluctant to pay the costs in time, money, effort, and inconvenience that it would take to change to a firm's competitors.

A good example is the computerized airline reservation systems offered to travel agents by several major airlines, such as the SABRE system of American Airlines and the APOLLO system of United Airlines. Once a travel agency has invested a substantial sum in installing such an interorganizational system, and travel agents have been trained in its use, the agency is reluctant to switch to another airline's reservation system. Thus, what seemed to be just a more convenient and efficient way of processing airline reservations has become a strategic weapon that gives these airlines a major competitive advantage. Not only does a specialized airline reservation system raise competitive barriers and increase switching costs, it also gives the airlines a built-in advantage in gaining reservations for themselves and provides them with a new information product that allows them to differentiate their services from other airlines. Finally, computer-based reservation services are a major source of revenue for these airlines, which charge a variety of fees to travel agencies and other airlines that use their systems. See Figure 6.17.

Building Strategic IT Resources

Information technology enables a firm to build strategic information resources that allow it to take advantage of strategic opportunities. In many cases, this results from a firm investing in advanced computer-based information systems to improve the efficiency of its own internal operations. Typically this means acquiring hardware and software, developing telecommunications networks, hiring information system specialists, and training end users. Then, armed with this resource base, the firm can **leverage investment in information technology** by developing new products and services. For example, the development by banks of remote banking services using automated teller machines was an extension of their expertise in teller terminal networks, which interconnect their branches.

A Strategic Information Base

Information systems also allow a firm to build a **strategic information base** that can provide information to support the firm's competitive strategies. Information in a firm's corporate databases has always been a valuable asset in promoting efficient operations and effective management of a firm. However, information about a firm's operations, customers, suppliers, and competitors, as well as other economic and demographic data, is now viewed as a strategic resource; that is, it is used to support strategic planning, marketing, and other strategic initiatives.

FIGURE 6.17
International airline reservation networks are an example of the strategic use of information technology.

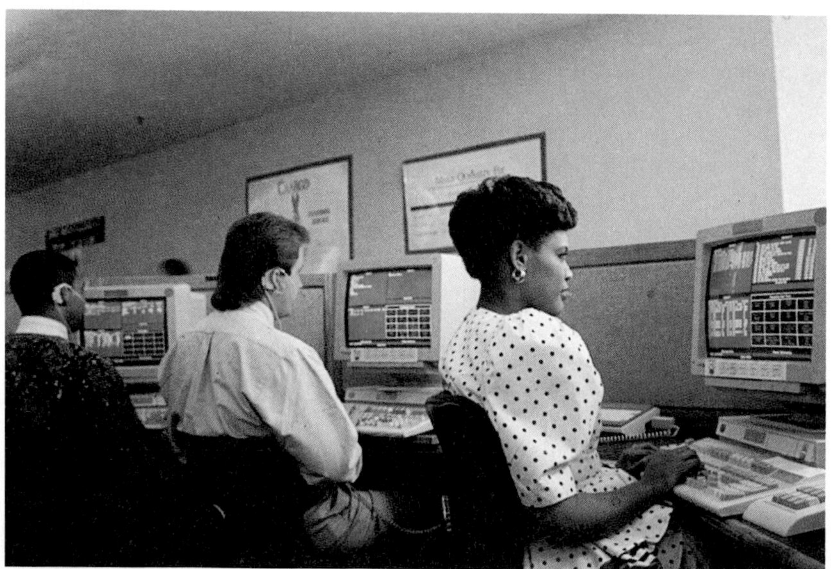

Courtesy of American Airlines.

For example, many businesses are now using computer-based information about their customers to help design marketing campaigns to sell customers new products and services. This is especially true of firms that include several subsidiaries offering a variety of products and services. For example, once you become a customer of a subsidiary of Sears, Roebuck & Co., you quickly become a target for marketing campaigns by their other subsidiaries, based on information provided by the Sears strategic information resource base. This is one way a firm can leverage its investment in transaction processing and customer accounting systems by linking its databases to its strategic planning and marketing systems. This strategy helps a firm create better marketing campaigns for new products and services, build better barriers to entry for competitors, and find better ways to lock in customers and suppliers.

A Managerial Perspective

The strategic role of information systems forces managers to look at information systems in a new light. No longer is the information systems function merely a necessary service group for processing transactions and keeping the books of a firm. It is also more than a helpful supplier of information and tools for decision making. Now the IS function can help managers develop competitive weapons that use information technology to meet challenges from the competitive forces that confront any organization.

Of course, strategic information systems are not easy to develop and implement. They may require major changes in the way a business operates and in a business's relationships with its employees, customers, suppliers, competitors, and others. The competitive advantages that strategic information systems produce can quickly fade away, and their failure can seriously damage a firm's performance. The case studies in this chapter demonstrate the challenges and problems as well as the benefits of strategic information systems. Thus, the effective use of strategic information systems presents managerial end users with a major managerial challenge. We will discuss the managerial implications of this challenge further in Chapter 11.

Figure 6.18 summarizes the variety of ways companies can use information systems technology to gain a strategic advantage over their competitors.

Improve Operational Efficiency
- Use IT to improve the efficiency of operational processes.
- Lower the cost of operational processes controlled by IT.
- Improve the quality of products and services produced with the support of IT.

Promote Business Innovation
- Provide new products and services that include IT components.
- Provide new IT features to differentiate existing products and services.
- Use IT to develop new markets, businesses, and business alliances.

Build Strategic IT Resources
- Build a strategic information base of internal and external data collected and analyzed by IT.
- Leverage investment in IT from its operational use into strategic applications.

Other IT Strategies
- Develop interorganizational information systems which create switching costs that lock in customers and suppliers.
- Use investment in IT to build barriers to entry against industry outsiders.
- Use IT components to make substitution of competing products and services unattractive.
- Apply IT to basic business processes to add value to a firm's products and services.

FIGURE 6.18
A summary of the strategic applications of information technology. These are examples of ways companies can gain a competitive edge with information systems.

REAL WORLD CASE

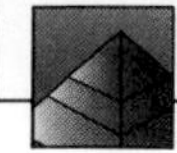

McFarlan and Companies: Using IT Strategically

F. Warren McFarlan of the Harvard Business School has been studying how companies use information technology strategically for many years. Here's just a sample of how he emphasizes the impact IT can have on organization structure, business processes, and managerial control.

Frito-Lay, Inc.: Organizational Restructuring

Our largest manufacturer of salty food snacks in the United States, Frito-Lay, has a large database that keeps track of every single bag of potato chips sold in every one of 300,000 stores every day for the last 365 days. It took them eight years to develop and install the system. At the center of the system, all 10,000 of their truck drivers have hand-held computers to record each transaction. That database supports how Frito-Lay's market planning department does its sophisticated pricing, discounting, and product selection strategy for its different stores.

In the last year and a half, Frito-Lay has built a wide-area, satellite-based system to drive the entire database down into the 21 sales regions of the United States. In every regional office, there is a local area network with large capacity personal computers working for them, using a very sophisticated user-friendly executive information system (the Commander package of Comshare). That has enabled them to decentralize production scheduling and product mix decision from Dallas, down into the region where the local knowledge is.

CNN and the Oil Company: Time-Based Competition

The most exciting time I spent last year [1990] was in October, when I spent a day at a major oil company. Two years before they had acquired a series of $20,000 workstations for their oil traders. Those workstations, in their judgment, paid for themselves at least tenfold over last August. Why? What was it that drove the worldwide oil prices last August? It was CNN network service that interconnected a hundred different countries, brought every rumor and action from around the globe to the public, causing prices to go up and down. In every one of these workstations, in the upper-right-hand window, was CNN News, live. The voice box connected to this machine had CNN News audio coming out, while the rest of the screen contained the normal buying/selling software. They believed that this gave them a 10-minute edge over normal competition in the fast-moving market. That was just enough time for them to pick the pocket of a large number of competitors.

People's Express versus American Airlines: Rapid Positioning

I had an interesting interview two years ago with Don Burr, the former chairman and founder of People's Express Airlines. He described in vivid detail how he believed this technology [IT] was used by American Airlines to drive his airline into bankruptcy. Don noted that, in his judgment, the day of his airline's demise began when American put in place its capacity to carry a different price on each individual seat on every aircraft they would fly every day for the next year. People's Express conversely had a very simple pricing strategy: one price for every seat in every plane on the route all week long—Boston to New York for $22, didn't matter whether it was for a 7 o'clock A.M. Monday flight, a noontime Tuesday flight, or some other time.

Don noted that on January 19, 1985, when American snapped this system into place, they were able to take dead aim at his airline. On every route they flew head to head with People's Express, depending on the loading factors of the planes, American opened between one and 120 deep, deep discount seats that were $5 less than the prevailing People's Express price. They launched a huge national advertising campaign where they advertised "call your travel agent and find out who the real low cost airline is . . . it's not People's Express, but rather American Airlines, and American Airlines will give you free drinks as well." Overnight, Don noted, People's Express planes began to empty out. As fast as People's Express would change a fare, 20 minutes later American would change its fare so they remained $5 beneath the new People's Express airfare. Don noted, "You don't win many of those battles."

Bergen Brunswig: Cost Reduction

Bergen Brunswig, a $4 billion wholesale drug distributor, is a remarkable story. In 1970, Bergen Brunswig's operating costs to sales ratio was 16 percent. As a result of sustained automation [with IT] year after year after year, by 1990 the ratio had dropped to 2 percent. You don't need a Ph.D. in accounting to figure out that when there's a 2 percent operating cost as a percentage of sales performance in the market place, there's no room left for the 16 percent firm.

CASE STUDY QUESTIONS

1. Do these examples show you that information technology can have a strategic impact on organizations and their operations and management? Explain.
2. What generic competitive forces and competitive strategies do you see in these examples?
3. What strategic roles does IT play in each of these companies?

Source: Adapted from F. Warren McFarlan, "The Experts' Opinion," *Information Resources Management Journal*, Fall 1991, pp. 39–41.

Summary

- **Categories of Information Systems.** Major conceptual categories of information systems include operations information systems, such as transaction processing systems, process control systems, and automated office systems, and management information systems, such as information reporting systems, decision support systems, and executive information systems. Other major categories are end user computing systems, expert systems, strategic information systems, and business function information systems. However, in the real world, these conceptual classifications are typically combined into integrated information systems which provide information and decision support for managers and also perform operational information processing activities. Refer to Figure 6.12 for a summary of the major categories of information systems.
- **Information Systems and Management.** Information systems can support a variety of management activities. These include the four functions of management (plan, organize, direct, and control), the 10 roles of management (leader, liaison, figurehead, monitor, disseminator, spokesperson, entrepreneur, disturbance handler, resource allocator, and negotiator), and the three levels of management activity (strategic, tactical, and operational planning and control).
- **Information Systems and Decision Making.** Information systems can support the intelligence, design, choice, and implementation activities of the decision-making process. To do this, information systems should (1) scan the internal organization and external environment to produce information that helps identify problems and opportunities, (2) help generate and evaluate decision alternatives, (3) provide information products that emphasize and prioritize decision alternatives, and (4) provide feedback on implemented decisions.
- **Decision Structure.** Decision can be classified as structured, semistructured, or unstructured. Structured decisions involve situations where decision procedures can be specified in advance. Unstructured decisions are subject to too many random, changeable, or unknown factors for decision procedures to be specified in advance. Information systems can provide a wide range of information products to support many types of decisions.
- **Strategic Information Systems.** Information systems can play three strategic roles in businesses. They can help a business improve operational efficiency, promote organizational innovation, or build strategic information resources, thereby giving the business a competitive advantage in its relationships with customers, suppliers, competitors, new entrants, and producers of substitute products. Thus, a firm can use information systems to improve productivity; lower costs; develop new products, services, and processes; lock in customers and suppliers; and build a strategic information base. Refer to Figure 6.18 for a summary of the uses of information technology for strategic advantage.

Key Terms and Concepts

These are the key terms and concepts of this chapter. The page number of their first explanation is in parentheses.

1. Artificial intelligence (208)
2. Business information systems (209)
3. Competitive strategy concepts (212)
   a. Barriers to entry (214)
   b. Competitive forces (212)
   c. Competitive strategies (212)
   d. Locking in customers and suppliers (214)
   e. Switching costs (215)
4. Classifications of information systems (195)
5. Decision-making process (201)
   a. Intelligence activities (201)
   b. Design activities (201)
   c. Choice activities (201)
   d. Implementation activities (201)
6. Decision support systems (207)
7. End user computing systems (208)
8. Executive information systems (207)
9. Expanding roles of information systems (194)
10. Expert systems (208)
11. Functions of management (197)
12. Information reporting systems (206)
13. Integrated information systems (209)
14. Interorganizational information systems (215)
15. Levels of management (200)
16. Management information systems (197)
17. Office automation systems (195)
18. Operations information systems (195)
19. Process control systems (197)
20. Roles of management (199)
21. Semistructured decision (203)
22. Strategic information systems (194)
23. Strategic roles of information systems (213)
   a. Operational efficiency (213)
   b. Business innovation (215)
   c. Strategic IT resources (216)
24. Structured decisions (203)
25. Transaction processing systems (195)
26. Unstructured decisions (203)

Review Quiz

Match one of the key terms and concepts listed above with one of the brief examples or definitions listed below. Look for the "best" fit for answers that seem to fit more than one key term or concept. Defend your choices.

___ 1. Information systems can be classified into operations, management, and other categories.

___ 2. Information systems have evolved from a data processing orientation to the support of decision making, end users, and strategic initiatives.

___ 3. Include transaction processing, process control, and office automation subsystems.

___ 4. Handle routine information processing generated by business activities.

___ 5. Control ongoing physical processes.

___ 6. Provide electronic office communications.

___ 7. Information systems should help identify problems and opportunities.

___ 8. Information systems should help generate and evaluate decision alternatives.

___ 9. Information systems should help emphasize and prioritize decision alternatives.

___ 10. Inventory reorder decisions can frequently be quantified and automated.

___ 11. Decisions involved in starting a new line of products might involve a lot of unknown factors.

___ 12. Managers should plan, organize, staff, direct, and control an organization.

___ 13. A manager is a leader, liaison, monitor, spokesperson, entrepreneur, and negotiator, among other things.

___ 14. Top managers concentrate on strategic planning for the organization, whereas operational managers control day-to-day operations.

___ 15. Include information reporting, decision support, and executive information.

___ 16. Provide information for managers in a variety of structured formats.

___ 17. Provide ad hoc, interactive support for decision making.

___ 18. Hopes to develop computers that can see, hear, walk, talk, feel, and think.

___ 19. Serve as consultants to end users.

___ 20. Provide direct computer support for the activities of end users.

___ 21. Support the functional areas of business in an organization.

___ 22. Perform traditional data processing activities and also provide information to the managers of an organization.

___ 23. A business must deal with customers, suppliers, competitors, new entrants, and substitutes.

___ 24. Cost leadership, differentiation of products, and development of new products are examples.

___ 25. Using investment in technology to keep firms out of an industry.

___ 26. Making it unattractive for a firm's customers or suppliers to switch to its competitors.

___ 27. Time, money, and effort needed for customers or suppliers to change to a firm's competitors.

___ 28. Information systems that support operational efficiency, promote business innovation, and build strategic information resources.

___ 29. Information systems can help a business develop new products, services, and processes.

___ 30. Information systems can help a business significantly reduce costs and improve productivity.

___ 31. Information systems can help a business build a strategic base of information.

___ 32. Information systems can help a business develop electronic links to its customers and suppliers.

Discussion Questions

1. In what major ways have the roles of information systems expanded during the last 40 years?
2. Can the same information system be used to support several of the functions, roles, and levels of management? Give a business example to support your answer.
3. How can information systems support the four stages of decision making? Give a business example to support your answer.
4. Why are there so many conceptual classifications of information systems? Why are they typically integrated in the information systems found in the real world?
5. How do decision support systems differ from information reporting systems and executive information systems in their support of a manager's decision making?

6. How can information systems promote business innovation, operational efficiency, and strategic information resources? Use business examples to support your answer.
7. Refer to the Real World Case on Chase Manhattan Bank in the chapter. How and why were end users involved in the CIX system's development?
8. How can information systems erect barriers to entry, increase switching costs, and lock in customers and suppliers? Use business examples to support your answers.
9. Refer to the Real World Case on Five Companies' Strategic Success in the chapter. What strategic roles do you see IT playing in each example? Explain.
10. How do strategic information systems affect the way managerial end users rely on information systems in a business? Explain.

Real World Problems

1. United Parcel Service: World Class Information Systems

Kent C. "Oz" Nelson, chairman and chief executive officer at Atlanta-based United Parcel Service, Inc., is the 11th winner of the Excellence in Technology Award, presented annually by Gartner Group and The Conference Board. "The wizardry of Oz played a key role in . . . transforming an operations-oriented company into a master of modern technology," said Gartner CEO Manny Fernandez. "Almost overnight, UPS built a world-class information system for international package deliveries." Prior to 1986, UPS—a worldwide company with revenue of approximately $16 billion and a package/document traffic volume recently estimated at 2.9 billion a year—did not rely on information technology to drive its distribution business, reportedly the largest in the world. Nelson, then a senior vice president, was named the head of a Technology Task Force and set out to forge a strategy aimed at "fundamentally overhauling technology at UPS," a company spokesman said.

UPS started out with a $1.5 billion budget and a five-year plan, the spokesman said. "But the fact is, we ended up spending that much well before the five years was up," he added. "The effort ended up costing multibillions." The plan came in on time. By 1991, UPS was able to boast a network that linked six mainframes, approximately 250 minicomputers, and 40,000 PCs and an estimated 75,000 handheld units, connecting some 1,300 worldwide distribution sites. Today, enabled by a cellular-based, nationwide, mobile service and a $100 million data center in Mahwah, New Jersey, the company relies on an electronic data storage and retrieval system to track an estimated 11 million packages a day delivered to destinations around the globe. The company is prepared to invest an additional $3 billion toward an expansion of the system that will make realtime package tracking a reality by 1997.

a. Why do you think UPS decided to begin investing heavily in information technology?

b. Do you think their multibillion dollar investment in IT has paid off? Explain.

Source: Adapted from Nell Margolis, "UPS Head Lauded for IS Use," *Computerworld*, March 1, 1993, p. 65. Used with permission.

2. Massachusetts Financial Services: Reengineering Business Processes

Massachusetts Financial is reaping the benefits of a companywide system based on IBM's OS/2 operating system, an IBM Application System/400 minicomputer, local-area networks and networking their PCs to an outsourcer company's mainframe. Massachusetts Financial's new electronic document imaging system, called their Automated Work Distribution System, and the process review that led to it have helped the mutual fund company reduce the number of business steps involved in servicing customers from 600 to 270. The system was built by DST Systems in Kansas City, Missouri, an outsourcer company that also provides transaction processing for several financial services firms including Massachusetts Financial.

Before committing to the DST system, however, Massachusetts Financial launched an internal business process review. That analysis showed that too many people were handling each business transaction. For example, a customer's request to redeem shares could involve 20 steps, 14 more than necessary. Massachusetts Financial has seen an early payback on its $5 million investment in operational efficiencies: The company can handle its $30 billion in funds using 100 fewer employees than before. Now Massachusetts Financial sees opportunities to build on the document management system. These include voice recognition and annotation, character recognition for reading account names and numbers, online customer access, and a telecommuting option in which customer service reps could work with the document image system from home.

a. Does reengineering business processes require new information technology? Explain.

b. Is the automated work distribution system a strategic information system? Explain.

Source: Adapted from James Connolly, "Financial Firm Banks on Imaging," *Computerworld*, April 5, 1993, p. 40. Used with permission.

3. UCAR Carbon Co: Reinventing a Company

UCAR Carbon Co., a maker of carbon and graphite products in Clarkesville, Tennessee, is hoping to "reinvent the company" through a series of reengineering projects. "This company is over 100 years old," says Bill Wiemels, vice president of U.S. operations. "The business ways were appropriate once, but they are not all appropriate today." Several projects of varying intensity advance the long-term goal of complete transformation. Some efforts call for a total redesign, while others focus mainly on restructuring management.

UCAR Carbon has already enjoyed some early success. A recent computer-based overhaul of ordering procedures, for example, reduced processing time from several days or weeks to as little as a few hours, according to Wiemels. Now, a single customer representative at a PC handles the process from start to finish. Estimated annual savings: $3.2 million. The company is also restructuring factory operations in hopes of trimming four or five levels of management between plan supervisors and workers. Workers carry more responsibility and use PC networks to handle tasks such as scheduling their own overtime. They "feel like they are part of the process now," Wiemels says.

a. What strategic role does IT play in "reinventing" UCAR?

b. Hot can IT help to trim "four or five levels of management"?

Source: Adapted from Rosemary Cafasso, "Step by Step, Companies Move Ahead," *Computerworld*, March 15, 1993, p. 104. Used with permission.

4. Key Corporation: Reengineering with IT

In 1991, Key Corporation, a $23 billion bank holding company launched a corporate information technology effort dubbed Vision 2001 and targeted its loan processing operation as a top priority. The company had been relying on a mix of outdated mainframe-based applications and manual procedures to handle its loan processing operation. According to Jay Ward, Key's chief information officer, the approach "wouldn't meet the goals we had for going into the future." Ward and the Vision 2001 crew are counting on big benefits from the project, including overall user productivity boosts of 20 percent. But Ward said he expects the real change to occur in customer relations, and he is predicting a 50 percent improvement in customer service processes. The loan origination system, for example, will replace a manual process that included filling out loan application forms and contacting credit bureaus.

For starters, the firm populated the project teams with users. Michael Quinn, project manager, comes from the user side, having spent 28 years in the commercial and consumer loan business. "You need to bring the end user into the development process as early as possible," he said. Second, Key elected to keep its mainframe platform in a central role. While the team was interested in a client/server architecture, it decided that using its mainframe provided the security and integrity that is essential to loan processing and was also less expensive and less risky. Third, Key did not consider in-house development to create the new loan processing applications software because it would have been too costly and time-consuming. Finally, Key is delivering ease-of-use features to users. For example, an attractive interface was designed to link the new loan origination program with an existing branch automation system so employees at the bank's branches could use their PCs to work on the loan origination system.

a. Is the Key Corporation using IS strategically? Explain.

b. How important are each of the four project development characteristics mentioned in the case to the success of this project? Explain your reasoning.

Source: Adapted from Rosemary Cafasso, "Re-Engineering Plan Preserves Mainframe Role," *Computerworld*, April 12, 1993, pp. 63, 68. Used with permission.

Application Exercises

1. Western Chemical Corporation

Western Chemical uses telecommunications systems that connect its computers to those of its customers and suppliers to capture data about sales orders and purchases. This data is processed immediately, and inventory and other databases are updated. Word processing and electronic mail services are also provided. Data generated by a chemical refinery process are captured by sensors and processed by a computer that also suggests answers to a complex refinery problem posed by an engineer. Managerial end users receive reports on a periodic, exception, and demand basis, and use computers to interactively assess the possible results of alternative decisions. Finally, top management can access text summaries and graphics displays that identify key elements of organizational performance.

Make an outline that identifies:

a. How information systems support (1) business operations, (2) management decision making, and (3) strategic advantage at Western Chemical.

b. There are many different types of information systems at Western Chemical. Identify as many as you can in the preceding scenario. Explain the reasons for your choices.

2. IBM Corporation

IBM has made massive investments in computer technology to automate its factories in a drive to become the low-cost producer in the computer industry. It spends billions of dollars annually for research and development to develop new production methods and new products. These include specialized microprocessors and advanced memory chips, since, unlike most of its U.S. competitors, IBM is determined not to be dependent on Japan for these vital components. IBM's factories and branch offices worldwide are connected by a telecommunications network to improve communications between its managers and other employees, as well as to provide vital information to top executives from corporate databases. Software developed for this network and other internal IBM operations (such as manufacturing expert systems) is now offered as software products for sale to its customers. With a major share of the U.S. computer market, IBM uses investments in information systems technology to help it keep its position as a full-service provider of high quality computer hardware, software, education, maintenance, and other services.

Make an outline that:

a. Identifies how strategic information systems (1) improve operational efficiency, (2) promote innovation, and (3) build strategic information resources at IBM.

b. Identifies each of the competitive forces involved and the generic competitive strategies IBM is using. Also identify any instances of barriers to entry, switching costs, and leveraging investment in information technology.

3. Al's Appliance City

The sales staff at Al's Appliance City are paid on a commission basis. The amount of commission earned is based on two components. A standard commission of 2 percent is paid on all sales. An additional bonus is paid on sales of items that have been identified as "high-priority items." These generally are items that are overstocked. At the beginning of each week Al distributes to his sales staff a list of the high-priority items for that week and indicates the bonus percentage that will be paid for sales of those items. Al often varies this bonus percentage from week-to-week, as needed, to move overstocked items.

Because of the complexity and changing nature of the commission system used, commissions have always been hand calculated. Al's Appliance City uses a PC-based accounting package to handle its order processing. That package is used to produce weekly sales totals for each salesperson. The total dollar amount of all sales and the dollar amount of sales of high-priority items by each salesperson is reported. A listing of this data for the most recent week is shown below.

Al's Appliance City Weekly Sales Data

Salesperson	Total Sales	High Priority Sales
Caldwell, C.	$15,725	$4,250
Flowers, R.	18,240	5,340
Garrett, P.	17,835	3,890
Howard, M.	21,065	6,275
Johnson, A.	16,240	3,100
Lerner, V.	14,270	4,275
Masters, T.	23,500	6,950
Miller, J.	19,730	4,635
Sanderson, T.	12,040	2,830
Ward, W.	20,140	5,115

Al has requested that you create a spreadsheet for him that will allow him to calculate the total bonus owed each employee. The bonus rate for high-priority sales should appear on the spreadsheet as a parameter that Al can change when necessary.

a. Based on the sample data, create a spreadsheet to calculate the commission earned by each salesperson and total commissions earned. Assume a bonus rate for high-priority items of 3 percent. Get a printed listing of your results.

b. Suppose the bonus rate for high-priority items had been 5 percent. Change the bonus rate parameter on your spreadsheet and print a revised set of commissions.

c. What type of information system does this application represent? Explain your reasoning.

4. Monroe City School District

The Monroe City School District currently operates four high schools. Enrollment in three of these schools is significantly above their planned capacity. The school board will meet soon to examine proposals to alleviate overcrowding. The superintendent of the Monroe City School District has collected data showing planned capacity and actual enrollment for each high school over the past five years. These data are shown blow.

Your task is to summarize these data in graphical form in a way that will highlight the nature of the problem for the school board members. Your graphs should give an overall picture of the problem and also allow more detailed examination of the situation faced by individual schools. The data you present should highlight the magnitude of the current problem but should also give the board members a feel for the historical trends that are at work.

Enrollment in Monroe City High Schools

School	Planned Capacity	Actual Enrollment by Year 1989	1990	1991	1992	1993
Washington	680	642	628	631	618	620
Jefferson	750	715	743	761	766	791
Lincoln	660	652	679	701	722	737
Roosevelt	900	830	848	887	934	986

a. Create a spreadsheet application incorporating the data shown. Perform any calculations on the raw data that are needed to generate useful information for graphic display. (For example, enrollment as a percentage of capacity or enrollment minus capacity might be an appropriate item for a graph. Also, you might want to base one or more graphs on totals across all of the schools.)

b. Create a set of graphs highlighting the information discussed above and get a printout of each graph.

c. What type of information system does this application represent? Explain your reasoning.

Review Quiz Answers

1. *4*
2. *9*
3. *18*
4. *25*
5. *19*
6. *17*
7. *5a*
8. *5b*
9. *5c*
10. *24*
11. *26*
12. *11*
13. *20*
14. *15*
15. *16*
16. *12*
17. *6*
18. *1*
19. *10*
20. *7*
21. *2*
22. *13*
23. *3b*
24. *3c*
25. *3a*
26. *3d*
27. *3e*
28. *22*
29. *23b*
30. *23a*
31. *23c*
32. *14*

Selected References

1. Bakos, J. Yannis. "A Strategic Analysis of Electronic Marketplaces," *MIS Quarterly*, September 1991.
2. Cash, James, Jr.; F. Warren McFarlan; James McKenney; and Lynda Applegate. *Corporate Information Systems Management.* 3rd ed. Homewood, Ill.: Richard D. Irwin, 1992.
3. Clemons, Eric, and Michael Row. "Sustaining IT Advantage: The Role of Structural Differences." *MIS Quarterly*, September 1991.
4. Gorry, G. Anthony, and Michael Scott Morton. "A Framework for Management Information Systems." *Sloan Management Review*, Fall 1971; republished Spring 1989.
5. Hopper, Max. "Rattling SABRENew Ways to Compete on Information." *Harvard Business Review*, May/June 1990.
6. Johnston, H. Russell, and Michael Vitale. "Creative Competitive Advantage with Interorganizational Systems." *MIS Quarterly*, June 1988.
7. Keen, Peter. *Shaping the Future: Business Design through Information Technology*. Cambridge, Massachusetts: Harvard Business School Press, 1991.
8. Konsynski, Ben, and F. Warren McFarlan. "Information Partnerships Shared Data, Shared Scale." *Harvard Business Review*, January/February 1991.
9. Lederer, Albert, and Aubrey Mendelow. "Convincing Top Management of the Strategic Potential of Information Systems." *MIS Quarterly*, December 1988.
10. McFarlan, Warren. "Information Technology Changes the Way You Compete." *Harvard Business Review*, May/June 1984.
11. Mintzberg, Henry. *The Nature of Managerial Work*. New York: Harper & Row, 1983.
12. Porter, Michael. *Competitive Advantage*. New York: Free Press, 1985.
13. Porter, Michael, and Victor Milar. "How Information Gives You Competitive Advantage." *Harvard Business Review*, July/August 1985.
14. Reid, Richard, and William Bullers, Jr. "Strategic Information Systems Help Create Competitive Advantage." *Information Executive*, Spring 1990.
15. Simon, Herbert A. *The New Science of Management Decision*. Revised ed. Englewood Cliffs, N.J.: Prentice Hall, 1977.
16. Sullivan-Trainor, Michael, and Joseph Maglitta. "Competitive Advantage Fleeting." *Computerworld*, October 8, 1990.
17. Wiseman, Charles, and Ian MacMillan. "Creating Competitive Weapons from Information Systems." *Journal of Business Strategy*, Fall 1984.
18. Wiseman, Charles. *Strategic Information Systems*. Homewood, Ill.: Richard D. Irwin, 1988.

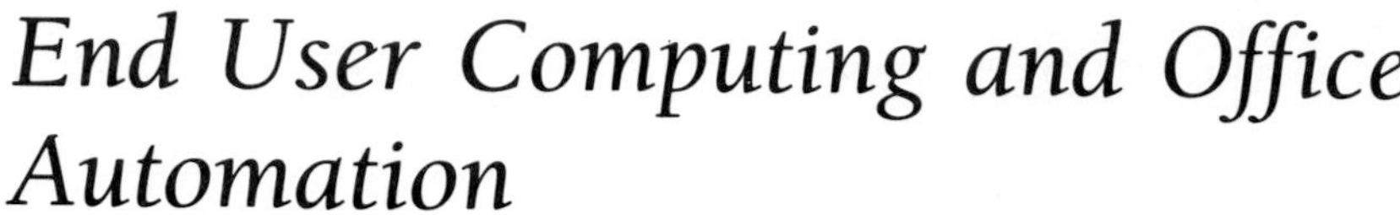

End User Computing and Office Automation

CHAPTER OUTLINE

CHAPTER 7

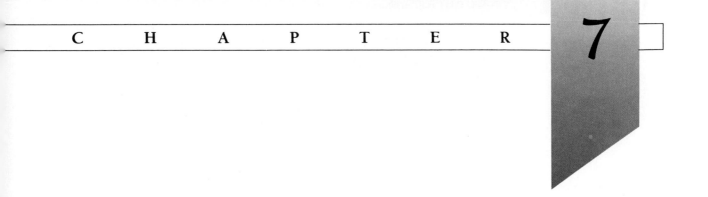

LEARNING OBJECTIVES

The purpose of this chapter is to give you an understanding of the role played in organizations by information systems in end user computing and office automation.

Section I of this chapter explores the reasons for end user computing and work group computing and analyzes the resources needed to accomplish major end user computing applications. It also discusses the role of information centers, as well as the potential risks of end user computing and the resulting challenges posed to managerial end users.

Section II describes the major types of information systems that fall under the office automation umbrella. The benefits and limitations of such systems to end users are also emphasized.

After reading and studying this chapter, you should be able to:

1. Discuss the reasons for the growth of end user and work group computing.
2. Identify the major components and resources needed to support end user computing.
3. Identify and give examples for each of the major application categories of end user and work group computing.
4. Give examples of several risks in end user computing and possible managerial solutions to reduce such risks.
5. Discuss the purposes and activities of the major types of office automation systems.
6. Identify several types of electronic office communications and their benefits for end users.
7. Discuss the benefits and limitations of office automation systems.

SECTION I
End User Computing

The days of relying primarily on information systems professionals to meet our information processing needs are over. Most organizations can't keep up with the information demands of their end users. So more and more people are learning to use microcomputers as professional workstations to get the information they need to accomplish their jobs successfully. That's what **end user computing** is all about. It's the direct, hands-on use of computers by end users, instead of the indirect use provided by the hardware, software, and professional resources of an organization's information services department.

This doesn't mean that end users don't rely on IS resources. However, in end user computing, an information services department plays only a supportive role to an end user's own computing resources and efforts. Figure 7.1 outlines the typical levels in an organization where traditional and end user computing are concentrated. Notice that end user computing is concentrated at the individual, work group, and departmental levels of an organization. However, both types of computing can be found at all levels.

The Growth of End User Computing

Why treat end user computing as such a major development in information systems? Because it is a revolutionary change in how computer-based information processing is accomplished in most organizations. End user computing began in the 1970s and is expected to continue to accelerate during the 1990s. Various studies have tried to estimate the growth of end user computing by estimating its share of (1) the total number of machine cycles of central processing units, (2) information processing budgets, and (3) keyboards installed. These results are compared to the share of traditional data processing groups in an organization. Such studies show end user computing growing from about 25 percent in the early 1980s to at least 40 percent in the mid-1980s, for each of these factors. Estimates indicate that end user computing will grow to represent 75 to 90 percent of all computer-based information processing activity in the organizations of the 1990s [18]. So end user computing is a major development that is here to stay.

The Hidden Backlog

Why has end user computing grown? Because information services departments have shown that they cannot keep up with the information demands of end users. Remember the process of systems development we discussed in Chapter 3? Developing computer-based information system solutions for users by teams of systems analysts and programmers is costly and time-consuming. Thus, many organizations estimate they have a backlog of unfilled user requests for information systems development of two to five years. This backlog includes the development of new applications as well as the changes made to improve existing information systems in the systems maintenance activity. To make matters worse, the backlog discourages users from making additional requests for systems development. Experts estimate that this creates a *hidden backlog* of unsubmitted requests that is even greater than the apparent backlog of formal user requests.

The Microcomputer Revolution

Another major reason for the growth of end user computing lies in the dramatic improvements in the capabilities and availability of computer hardware and software. The developments of minicomputers and microcomputers have brought computing power down to the departmental, work group, and individual levels.

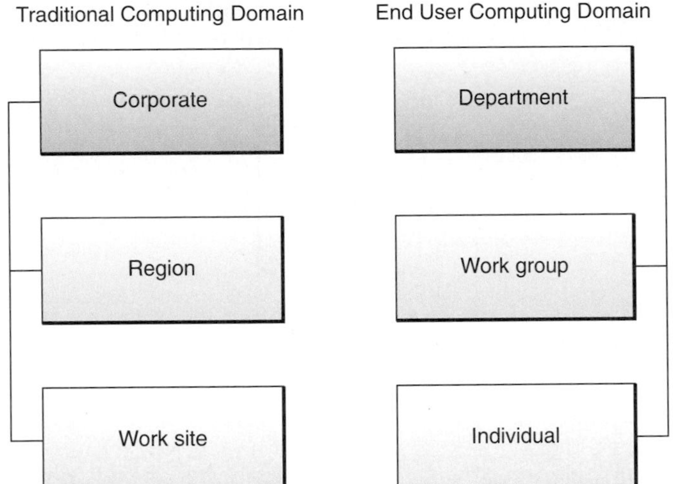

Source: Adapted from Ralph Sprague and Barbara McNurin, *Information Systems Management in Practice* (Englewood Cliffs, N.J.: Prentice-Hall, 1986), p. 117.

FIGURE 7.1
The domains of traditional and end user computing. Note the levels in an organization where each type of computing is concentrated.

Also, software packages for end users for all types of applications have proliferated and improved in their power and ease of use. These improvements have made hardware and software affordable and attractive to many individuals and organizations. These developments are reinforced by the growing familiarity of many end users with computers, caused by their longtime and widespread use in schools, businesses, and other organizations. Thus, end users are able to turn to the direct use of information technology to solve their information processing problems.

Components of an End User Computing System

It is important to think of end user computing in an information system context. Figure 7.2 shows the resource components and application outputs of an end user computing system. It illustrates the major categories of end user computing applications, and the hardware, software, people, and data resources required. As you can see, end user computing systems are microcomputer-based information systems that directly support both the operational and managerial applications of end users.

Figure 7.2 also shows that many end users do not rely solely on their own microcomputer workstations, software packages, and databases. They can also rely on the support of software packages, databases, and computer systems at the work group, departmental, and corporate levels. In addition, many organizations provide *information centers* as another source of support for end user computing. Information center specialists serve as consultants to users who need assistance in their computing efforts. In this way, organizations hope to improve the efficiency and effectiveness of end user computing.

Resources for End User Computing

Figure 7.2 emphasizes that hardware, software, people, and data resources are needed for end user computing. Let's briefly consider each of these resources.

Hardware Resources: End User Workstations

The hardware resources for end user computing consist primarily of microcomputer workstations. Microcomputer systems (including their peripheral devices) provide the information processing capabilities needed for most user applications. Though dumb terminals connected to minicomputers or mainframes are sometimes used,

FIGURE 7.2
An end user computing system. Note the major categories of end user computing applications and the hardware, software, people, and data resources required.

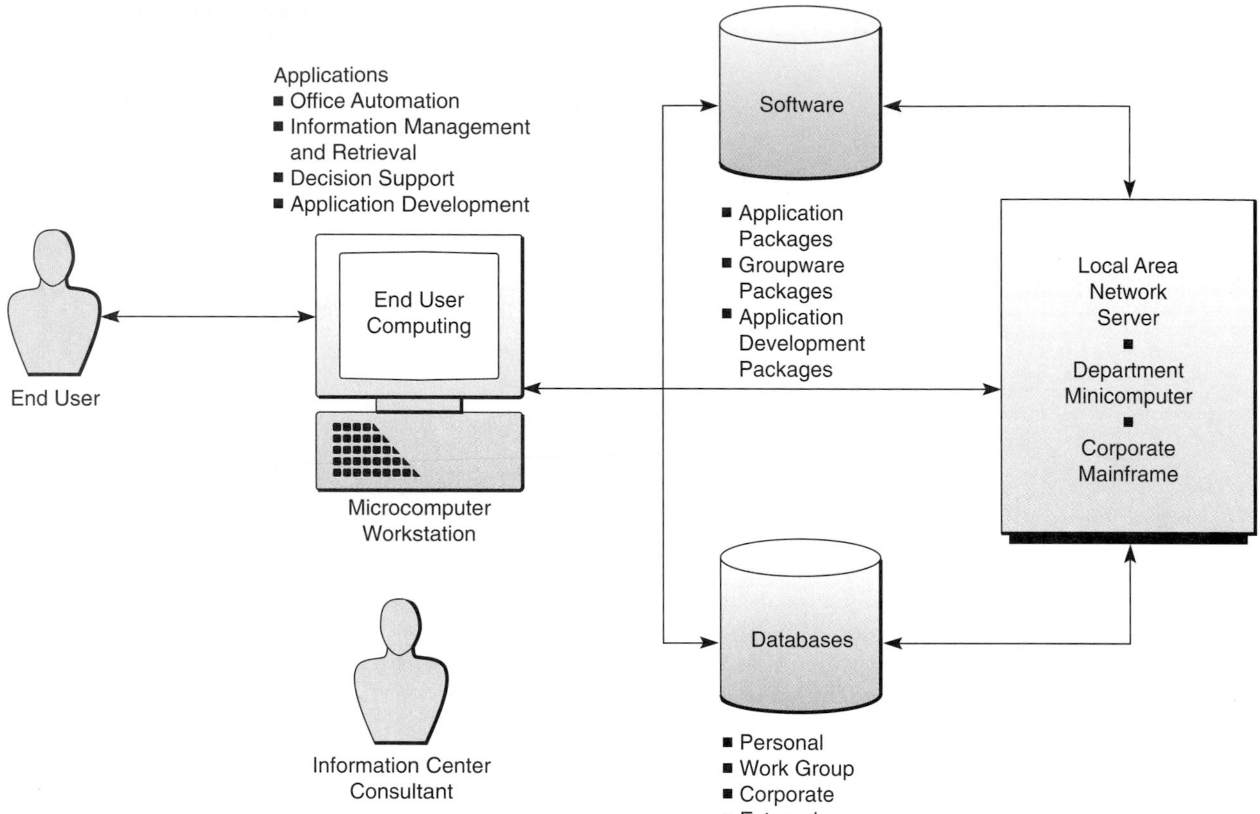

they are rapidly being replaced by microcomputers with telecommunications capabilities. Therefore, as Figure 7.2 shows, microcomputer workstations may be tied by telecommunications links to other workstations in a local area network, with a more powerful microcomputer operating as a network server. Or they may be connected to larger networks, using departmental minicomputers or corporate mainframes as hosts. These computer systems (1) help control communications in the network including serving as gateways between networks, (2) oversee the sharing of software packages and databases among the workstations in the network, and (3) perform time-sharing processing services for jobs that are too big for the workstations to handle.

Software Resources: End User Packages

Application software packages for microcomputer systems are the primary software resources needed for end user computing. These include general-purpose *productivity packages* for word processing, electronic spreadsheets, database and information management, graphics, data communications, and integrated packages, as discussed in Chapter 3. Other software resources include packages for *office automation* applications such as desktop publishing, electronic mail, and office support services. We will discuss such packages in Section II of this chapter. Of course, many other types of application software can be used, depending on the business needs of end users.

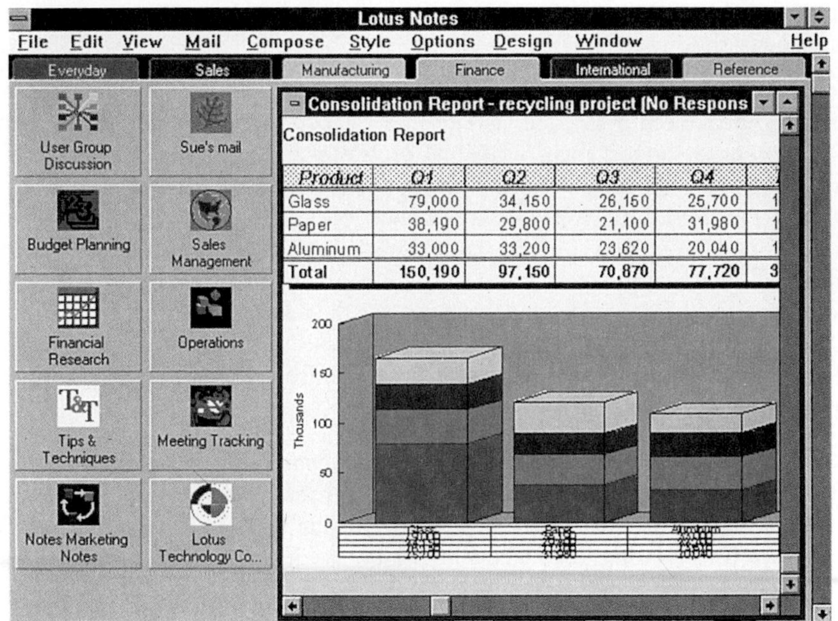

Courtesy of Lotus Development Corporation.

FIGURE 7.3
Lotus Notes is a popular groupware package. Notice how it organizes end user activities to support work group computing.

Groupware is a fast-growing category of software for end user computing. Groupware is *collaboration software*, that is, software that helps work groups of end users work together to accomplish group assignments. Typically, this includes software for applications like electronic mail, joint word processing and spreadsheet analysis, file sharing, computer conferencing, scheduling meetings, project management, and so on. See Figure 7.3.

Application development packages are another major category of software resources shown in Figure 7.2. This includes fourth-generation languages and other application development tools. As discussed in Chapter 3, 4GL packages allow users to specify what information they want, rather than how the computer system should do it. Major categories of 4GLs include natural and structured query languages such as Intellect and SQL, and the report generators found in many spreadsheet programs, integrated packages, database management systems, and decision support system packages. Such 4GL tools allow end users to make ad hoc inquiries and generate their own reports. The application generators found in database management and other application development packages are also included in this category. These packages provide programming tools that allow experienced end users to interactively develop their own application programs, instead of relying on professional systems analysts and programmers.

People Resources: The Information Center

Figure 7.2 emphasizes that many organizations have made a major commitment of human resources to end user computing. This commitment usually takes the form of an **information center**, which is an organizational unit that supports the end users in an organization. The information center's biggest contribution to end user computing is a staff of user consultants consisting of systems analysts, programmers, and technicians. Their primary role is to educate and assist users in the effective use of microcomputer systems and their many software packages. They also work as consultants to end users to help them develop new applications using a variety of application development tools. We will have more to say about the role of information centers shortly.

Data Resources: Multiple Databases

Figure 7.2 emphasized that end user computing relies on several major types of databases introduced in Chapter 7. Personal databases are created and maintained by end users to support their individual professional activities. For example, personal databases may have files of correspondence created by word processing or spreadsheets created by electronic spreadsheet packages. End users may also have access to work group and corporate databases through telecommunications network links. This allows end users to transfer data files among themselves and work group and corporate offices. Finally, end users can use the telecommunications capabilities of their workstations to access external databases. This allows them to access a wealth of economic and other types of information from the data banks of commercial information services.

End User Computing Applications

Figure 7.2 listed four major categories of end user computing applications: (1) office automation, (2) information management and retrieval, (3) decision support, and (4) application development. These categories define what end users do when they do their own computing. Let's take a brief look at what's involved in each of them.

Office Automation

Office automation (OA) applications are a major category of end user computing, since much end user and work group computing takes place in office settings. Office automation will be discussed in detail in Section II of this chapter. OA applications enhance end user productivity and communications within work groups, organizations, and with external contacts such as customers and suppliers. This typically involves applications such as word processing, electronic mail, desktop publishing, and presentation graphics. For example, you could compose a business letter using word processing, send electronic messages to colleagues using electronic mail, and prepare graphic displays for a formal presentation using the hardware and software capabilities of your microcomputer workstation.

Information Management and Retrieval Applications

End users are inundated with data and information that must be organized, stored, and retrieved. Thus, one major application of end user computing is the use of database management packages to manage the creation, access, and maintenance of databases and files. In Chapters 3 and 5, we discussed how DBMS packages help end users create data files and databases to store data and retrieve information. The query languages and report generators of such packages allow end users to retrieve information from personal, work group, corporate, and external databases. Query languages allow simple inquiries to be made quickly and easily by end users. Report generators help end users prepare reports that extract, manipulate, and display information in a variety of formats. In Chapter 5, we saw how end users can make inquiries using a query language like SQL or QBE and receive immediate displays of information.

Another software package used for information management and retrieval is the **personal information manager** (PIM). These packages help end users store, organize, and retrieve text and numerical data in the form of notes, lists, clippings, tables, memos, letters, reports, and so on. For example, information can be entered randomly about people, companies, deadlines, appointments, meetings, projects, and financial results. The PIM package will automatically organize such data with minimal instructions from the end user. Then portions of the stored information can be retrieved in any order, and in a variety of forms, depending on the relationships established among pieces of data by the software and the user. For example, information can be retrieved as a list of appointments, meetings, or other things to do; the timetable for a project; or a display of key facts and financial data about a competitor [18]. See Figure 7.4.

In Chapter 9, we will discuss how executive information systems (EIS) enable end users who are corporate executives to easily retrieve information tailored to their strategic information needs. So end user computing allows managerial end users at all levels to bypass the periodic reporting process of traditional information system applications. Instead, they can receive directly at their workstations much of the information they need.

Decision Support Applications

Software packages such as electronic spreadsheets, integrated packages, and other decision support system (DSS) software allow end users to build and manipulate analytical models of business activities. End users can thus create their own decision support systems with the use of such tools and the variety of databases previously mentioned. As we will discuss in Chapter 9, this allows end users to pose *what-if* questions by entering different alternatives into a spreadsheet or other model. They can then see the results displayed immediately on their workstation screens.

Thus, managerial end users can use an interactive modeling process to analyze alternatives and help them make or recommend decisions. Besides spreadsheet programs, a variety of 4GL products and financial, statistical, and mathematical analysis packages can be used by end users for decision support applications. This includes group decision support system (GDSS) software which enhances the joint decision making of work groups and other organizational units.

End User Application Development

Another major category of end user computing is the development of new or improved applications by users. That is, end users can develop new or improved ways to perform their jobs without the direct involvement of professional systems analysts. Users themselves can accomplish the steps of the traditional or prototyping methods of information systems development discussed in Chapter 10. The primary reasons for this phenomenon are the growing capabilities and availabilities of

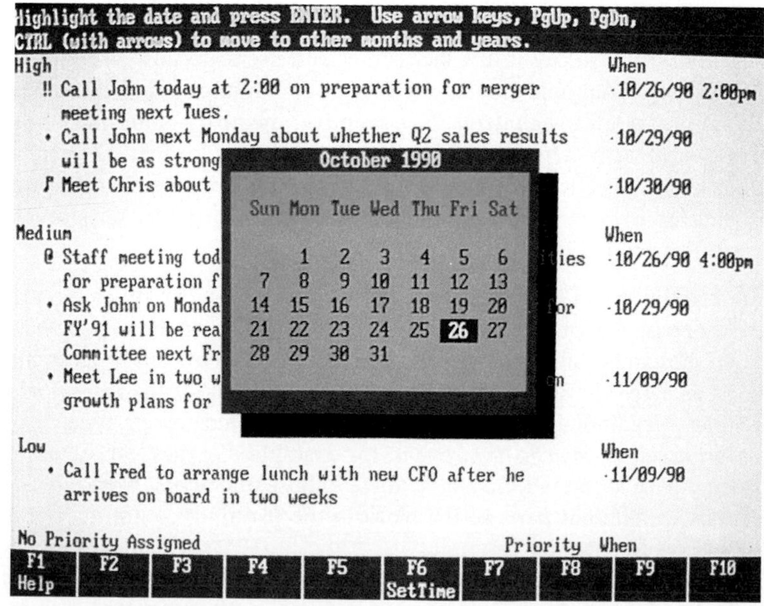

Courtesy of Lotus Development Corporation.

FIGURE 7.4
An example of a personal information manager (PIM). Notice the variety of ways that information is recorded and presented by Lotus Agenda.

FIGURE 7.5
Using PC/Focus for end user application development.

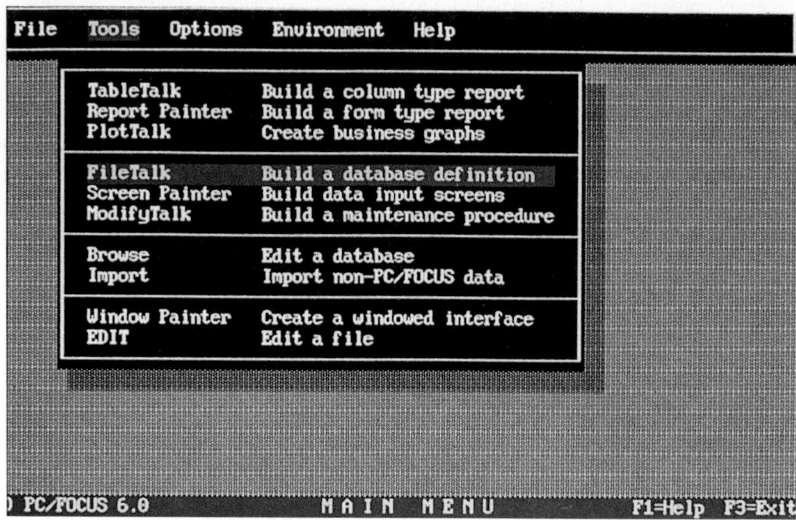

Courtesy of Information Builders, Inc.

microcomputer workstations and a variety of end user application development tools. The application generation capabilities of electronic spreadsheet and database management packages and fourth-generation languages have been a driving force for end user development. These hardware and software resources make it easier for end users to develop their own limited, but highly functional, computer-based information systems. See Figure 7.5.

Work Group Computing

Work is fundamentally social. Most activity, and certainly its meaning, arises in a context of cooperation [12].

Much end user computing is a group effort known as **work group computing**. More formal terms include *computer-supported collaboration* (CSC), *computer-based systems for collaborative work* (CSCW), or *collaborative work support systems* (CWSS). But no matter what you call it, the fact is that end users are now using computers, software, and telecommunications networks to communicate and coordinate with each other about work assignments. For example, members of an office sales team may use a local area network and software packages known as *groupware* to communicate with electronic mail and jointly do the word processing, spreadsheet analysis, and report generation needed to accomplish a particular sales presentation assignment. See Figure 7.6.

Electronic Work Groups

There are many types of work groups, each with its own work styles, agendas, and computing needs. A **work group** can be defined as two or more people working together on the same task or assignment. Thus, a work group can be as small as two persons or as large as 30 or more people. Work groups can be as formal and structured as a traditional office or department dedicated to one type of business activity—an *accounts payable department*, for example. Or they can be as informal and unstructured as an ad hoc task force whose members work for different organizations in different parts of the world—the planning committee for a major international conference, for example.

Therefore, the members of a work group don't have to work in the same physical location. They can be members of a *virtual work group*, that is, one whose

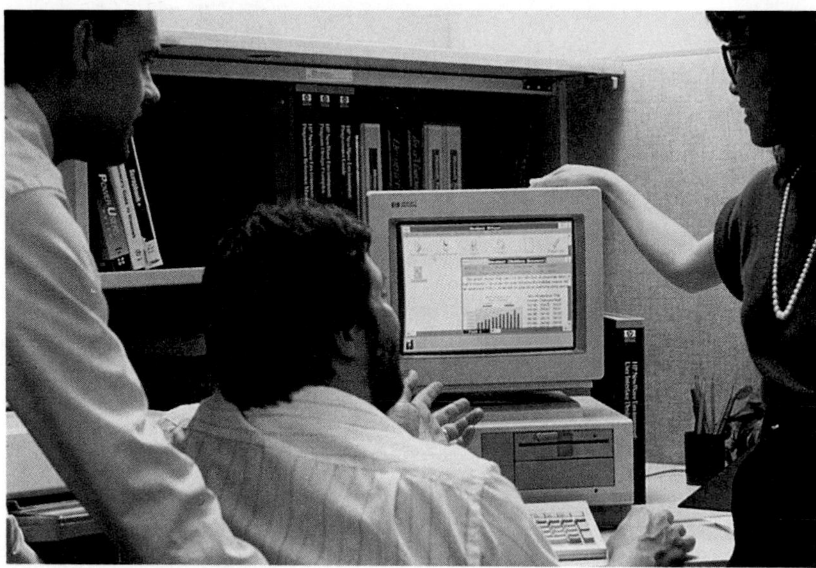

Courtesy of Hewlett-Packard.

FIGURE 7.6
Much end user computing is a work group effort.

members are united by the tasks on which they are collaborating, not by geography or membership in a larger organization. In sociology and cultural anthropology, these work groups are called *social fields*—semiautonomous and self-regulating associations of people with their own work agendas, rules, relationships, and norms of behavior. Work group computing makes *electronic social fields* possible. Computers, groupware, and telecommunications allow end users to work together without regard to time constraints, physical location, or organizational boundaries [19]. See Figure 7.7.

The Role of Groupware

As Figure 7.7 shows, work group computing is possible without groupware. Work groups can accomplish their work assignments using traditional organizational and end user computing software; telecommunications services such as the telephone, electronic mail, and facsimile; and, of course, company, postal, and express mail systems. But Figure 7.7 also shows that groupware can dramatically increase the scope of work group computing. That's because groupware is designed to make communication and coordination of work group activities significantly easier, no matter where the members of the work group are located.

So, though groupware packages can accomplish many important jobs, their key feature is the work group communication and coordination they make possible. That's why groupware is also known as *collaboration software*. It helps the members of a work group collaborate on group projects, while it also provides some of the office automation, information management and retrieval, decision support, and application development tools they need to accomplish specific work assignments.

Figure 7.8 outlines the major types of work group computing applications that may be supported by groupware packages. Some groupware packages support only one of these application areas, while others attempt to integrate several applications in one groupware package. For example, a software package like Topic by Verity, Inc., is used primarily for document retrieval, while Lotus Notes, a top-selling groupware package, supports E-mail, document management, computer conferencing, and many other functions.

FIGURE 7.7
The impact of groupware on the computing activities of work groups.

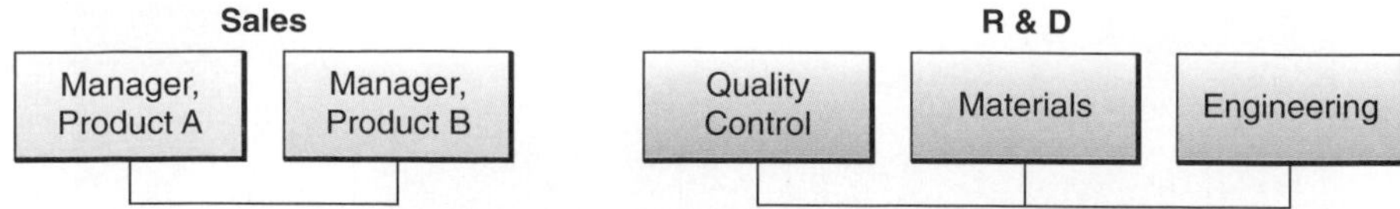

Traditionally, workgroup computing has been limited by departmental boundaries or the physical proximity of employees.

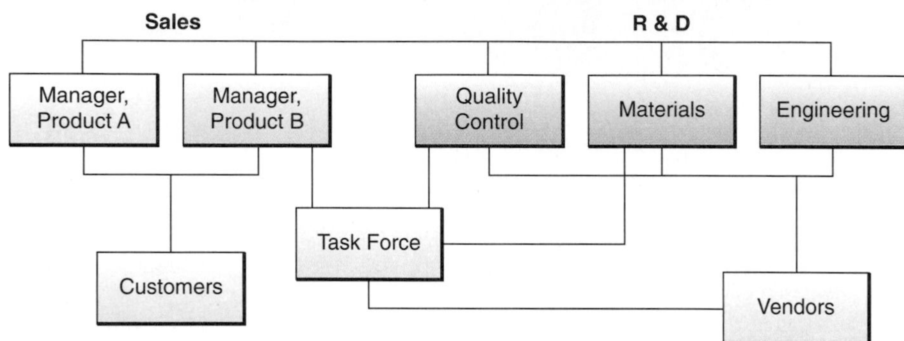

Today, groupware applications enable workgroup computing to go beyond traditional boundaries. Permanent and interim links may be forged among employees throughout an enterprise as well as with business contacts outside the company.

Source: Adapted from Doug Dayton, "Groupware Provides Competitive Edge," *PC Week*, October 14, 1991, p. S/4.

FIGURE 7.8
Applications of groupware for work group computing.

- **Electronic Messaging**
  Sending electronic messages to work group members using electronic mail, voice mail, bulletin board systems, and facsimile.
- **Electronic Meetings**
  Holding electronic meetings of work groups using computer conferencing and teleconferencing systems.
- **Scheduling Management**
  Scheduling work group appointments and meetings using electronic calendars and appointment books.
- **Task and Project Management**
  Managing work group tasks and projects by project scheduling, resource allocation, tracking, reminding, and record-keeping.
- **Document Creating and Management**
  Joint work group editing and annotation of documents. Electronic filing, retrieval, and routing of documents to work group members.
- **Data Management**
  Managing the storage and retrieval of work group data files and databases.
- **Decision Support**
  Joint work group spreadsheet development and analysis. Using other types of group decision software.

The Information Center

An **information center** is an organizational subunit that provides hardware, software, and people support to end users in an organization. It typically has been part of an organization's information services department, but it can also be found in individual end user departments. Beginning at IBM-Canada in 1974, the concept of providing support facilities for end user computing has grown so popular that it has become a dominant factor in organizational computing. In recent years, many organizations have distributed responsibility for end user support to their business units and have abolished their centralized information centers. However, information centers still play a major role in end user support [21]. Most information centers provide:

- **Hardware support** for end users who need it by providing the use of microcomputers, intelligent terminals, advanced graphic terminals, high-speed printers, plotters, and so on.
- **Software support** by offering the temporary use of advanced software packages for application development, desktop publishing, presentation graphics, database management, and so on.
- **People support** by a staff of end user consultants—systems analysts and programmers who are trained to educate and help end users apply their own hardware and software resources to improve the efficiency and effectiveness of their work activities.

The Role of the Information Center

What do information centers do? Information centers provide a variety of services, depending on the type and size of the organization and the age and mission of each center [17]. Figure 7.9 summarizes many of the services provided by information centers. As you can see, most of the services can be categorized as dealing with end user education and training, assistance with applications development, hardware/software sharing and evaluation, or the development of administrative control methods for end user applications.

Another way to view the role of the information center in an organization is shown in Figure 7.10. In this context, the information center serves as a source of application consultation, software distribution, and help services. These services can be provided by the information center's end user consultants, with the assistance of specialized expert system packages. Thus, an information center can provide expertise in application development consulting, software distribution, and problem resolution [1, 18].

Management Implications of End User Computing

Managers face significant challenges in managing end user computing in their organizations. Managing the hardware, software, people, and data resources of end user computing systems is a major challenge. Workstations, computers, telecommunication networks, and software packages must be evaluated and acquired. End users must be properly trained and assisted. The integrity and security of the databases that are created and available to end users must be ensured. Finally, the applications end users develop and implement must be evaluated for their efficiency and effectiveness in using organizational resources and helping to meet organizational objectives.

The Risks of End User Computing

There is no question that end user computing has improved the development and use of computer-based information systems for the end users of an organization. It has also relieved the burden of end user demands on information services departments. However, end user computing can also pose major problems and risks to an organization. Figure 7.11 outlines some of the serious potential risks of end user computing. Notice that it categorizes the risks to an organization based on the major stages of the systems development life cycle. The development and use of applications by end users instead of by professional systems analysts is seen as a major risk factor in today's organizations. Inadequate analysis, poor design, improper implementation, and lack of controls can easily result from an end user's rush to develop and implement new applications.

FIGURE 7.9
Information center services. Note the variety of services that may be provided.

Basic Services	Enhanced Services
▪ Computer literacy education ▪ Training on use of products ▪ Hardware/software sharing ▪ Application consulting ▪ Help center with hotline telephone service ▪ Hardware/software evaluation ▪ Hardware and software standards ▪ Support for standard products ▪ Security support	▪ Development of telecommunications software ▪ Data administration ▪ Installing and testing new software product releases ▪ Maintenance of PC equipment ▪ Project management for user-development projects ▪ Quality assurance of user-written software ▪ Prototype development for end users

Source: Adapted from Ralph Sprague and Barbara McNurlin, *Information Systems Management in Practice*, 2nd ed. (Englewood Cliffs, N.J.: Prentice-Hall, 1989), pp. 328–29.

FIGURE 7.10
The roles of an information center. An information center can provide application consultation, software distribution and help services.

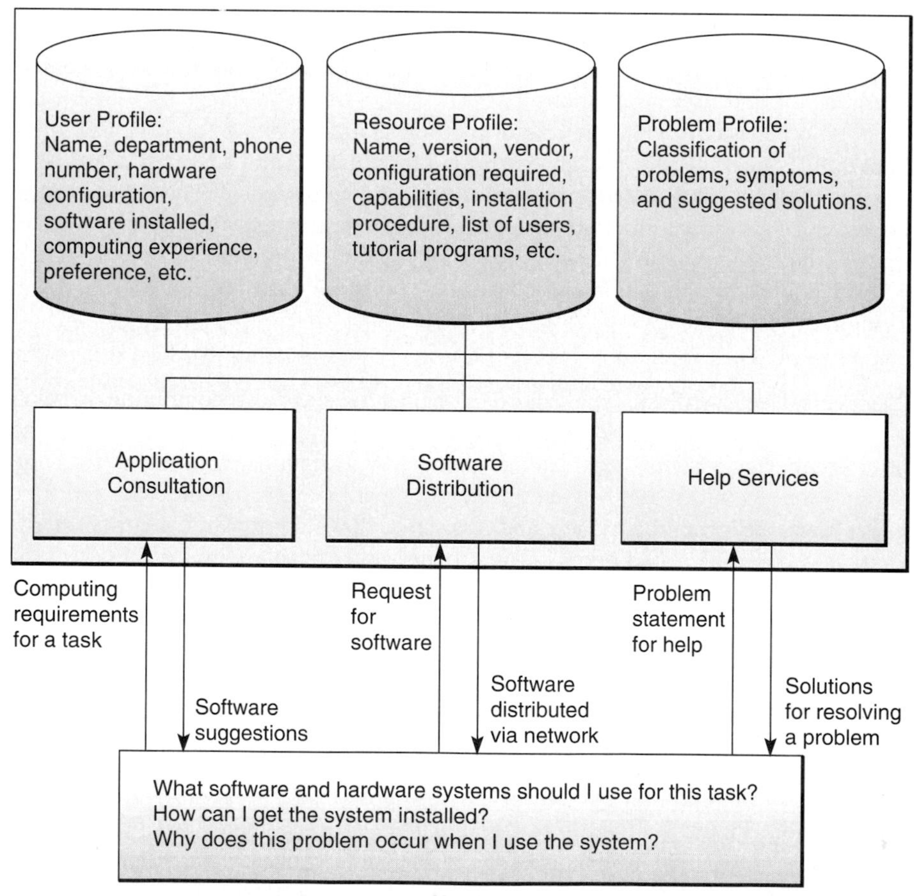

Source: Adapted from Jay Nunamaker, Ben Konsynski, Minder Chen, Ajay Vinze, Y. Irene Liou Chen, and Mari Heltne, "Knowledge-based Systems Support for Information Centers," *Journal of Management Information Systems*, Summer 1988, p. 9.

FIGURE 7.11
The risks of end user computing and suggested managerial solutions.

End User Life Cycle Stages		Organizational Risks	Control Methods
Analysis	Use of development tools	Ineffective use of monetary resources	Cost/benefit analysis
		Incompatible end user tools	Hardware/software standards
		Threats to data security and integrity	Policy for end user access to corporate database
	Analysis of end user application	Overanalysis and insufficient search for the solution	Provide user training in problem solving and modeling
		Solving the wrong problem	Involve analysts in the design process for review
Design	Conceptual design of end user application	Applying the wrong model	Technical training Reviews Policy for technical reviews
	Development of end user application	Little or no documentation	Enforce documentation standards Include documentation in development process
		Lack of extensive testing	Testing/validation standards User training in application quality assurance
		Lack of validation and quality assurance	Analyst/auditor "walk-through" Auditor reviews
		Redundant development effect	End user training in modeling application development Common application library
		Inefficient expenditure of end user time	Management policy for limits on allocation of end user time Support from analyst
Implementation	Operation of end user application	Threats to data integrity	Input data validation routines User training in data integrity issues
		Taxing mainframe computer resources	Management policy on the role of end user computing Integrating EUC and IS planning Control of EUC growth through budgets and chargebacks
		Threats to security	Access control via passwords Physical access control (restricted areas) Standards for backups
Maintenance		Failure to document and test modifications	Maintenance review by analyst
		Failure to upgrade the application	Periodic system review by end user analyst

Source: Adapted from Maryam Alavi and Ira Weiss, "Managing the Risks Associated with End User Computing," *Journal of MIS*, Winter 1985, pp. 18–19.

Managerial Solutions

However, as Figure 7.11 also indicates, there are many specific managerial solutions to the potential risks of end user computing. The challenge to end user managers is to develop and enforce the policies and procedures needed to implement appropriate solutions to the problems of end user computing. So managing end user computing is not an easy job. However, it is a responsibility shared by every managerial end user, as well as by the management of an organization's information systems function. Computer-using organizations typically make a variety of organizational, policy, and procedural changes to support and control end user computing. Previously mentioned was the creation of information centers with staffs of user consultants to support end user computing efforts. Organizations also develop policies that establish an organizational role for end user computing. In some organizations, end user computing plays a major role in improving operational efficiency and productivity and promoting innovation in products and services by end user departments. In other organizations, end user computing is relegated to a more supportive role in the centralized information systems function of the organization [1, 18].

Managing end user computing requires the development of policies and procedures concerning hardware and software acquisition and application development by end users. Corporate guidelines regulating the cost and types of hardware and software end users can purchase are common. What managers are trying to do is to avoid the proliferation of hardware and software while ensuring compatibility with the organization's computing and telecommunications resources. Application development guidelines encourage end users to develop well-documented information systems with built-in controls that make efficient use of computing resources and do not threaten the integrity of the organization's databases. Information center consultants and other services are provided to help end users develop applications that meet such standards.

The creation and access of data resources by end users make the integrity and security of end user and corporate databases another major concern of end user computing. For example, passwords and other safeguards for proper access to sensitive corporate data must be developed. Also, end user databases extracted from corporate databases may become out-of-date or incorrect if they are not properly updated and maintained. Thus, managing end user data resources has become a major managerial challenge.

These and other planning and control issues of end user computing will be discussed further in Chapters 11 and 12. However, you should realize that it is the responsibility of every managerial end user to ensure the effective use of computing resources in his or her work group or department. So, the effective management of end user computing will one day be one of your major managerial responsibilities.

REAL WORLD CASE

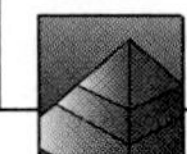

Alaska Airlines: End User Computing

It's a typical day at Alaska Air Group, Inc., and hundreds of employees in accounting, maintenance, flight operations, and other departments log on to the corporate IBM mainframe. Once online, they access and analyze information that at many other organizations would be considered sacrosanct to all but the highest level executives.

Even more striking is that many white-collar workers at the $1.1 billion Seattle-based holding company of Alaska Airlines routinely work with the information systems department to develop or customize department software. At a company that sees highly skilled users as the best way to boost productivity and contain technology costs, it's all part of the job.

"The idea is for workers to do end-user computing as a means to leverage themselves," explains Leif Haslund, assistant vice president of administrative services at the airline. The strategy works to hold down IS costs—even as the airline continues to expand—because workers who do their own computing require fewer IS professionals to support them, he says.

According to Haslund's own "unscientific study," Alaska Airlines used to employ an IS professional for every $18 million in revenue it generated. Now, with end users doing much of the computing themselves, there is one IS staff member for every $25 million in sales. What's more, in the seven years that end-user computing has been deployed, IS spending has held steady at less than 1 percent of company revenue. Meanwhile, the most widely used barometer of airline passenger business—passenger revenue miles—has climbed by more than 50 percent, Haslund says.

The notion of cashing in on end-user computing began evolving soon after personal computers, spreadsheets, early desktop publishing software, and fourth-generation languages arrived at Alaska Airlines in 1985. The new technology, combined with a desire to "take the IS department out of the operations loop whenever possible," made end-user computing a natural choice for the company, Haslund says.

Since then, Alaska Airlines has installed approximately 550 Apple Computer, Inc. Macintoshes and 150 IBM PCs and compatibles. These desktop devices are networked to each other, as well as to the corporate IBM mainframe and the System One reservation system used by the airline. The result is that any and all information can be transferred to and from all of the airline's computing platforms.

Most data can be directly accessed by all employees, 300 of whom have been trained to use Information Builders, Focus, the language adopted for end-user computing. For example, the airline's in-house frequent-flier application regularly samples data from the reservation system, from forecasted travel patterns to scheduling requirements. Similarly, in-house staff members use data accessed from the System One reservation system to determine the correct number of airline meals needed on a particular flight. "We basically allow end users to get a substantial number of corporate files in whatever way they want," Haslund says.

A key goal is to free the 84-member IS department from routine data processing in order to focus on application development and other strategic projects. Today, IS sees itself primarily as a support group, Haslund says. Indeed one of the chief benefits is decreased reliance on IS for routine analyses and reports, which workers throughout the company now prepare themselves.

The approach seems to work very well. Since 1986, Alaska Air Group has kept ISA costs under $10 million, thanks largely to its end-user focus, Haslund says.

"IS isn't growing as fast as the airline, yet we're still putting in more applications. The moves we've made so far have brought phenomenal productivity. We'll stay on this course."

CASE STUDY QUESTIONS

1. What categories of end user computing applications do you recognize at Alaska Airlines? Give an example of each.
2. What end user computing resources do you recognize? Explain your choices.
3. What are the business benefits and risks of end user computing at Alaska Airlines.

Source: Adapted from Julia King, "Users Help Alaska Air Soar," *Computerworld*, January 2, 1992, p. 16. Used with permission.

SECTION II
Office Automation Systems

Introduction

Office automation (OA) is changing the equipment and work habits of today's end users. Of course, none of us would like to work in an office where all information processing activities are done manually. Office machines such as electric typewriters, copying machines, and dictation machines have made office work easier and more productive. But the *mechanized office* is giving way to the *automated office*. Investment in computer-based workstations and other automated equipment is transforming traditional manual office methods and paper communications media. This transformation has resulted in the development of automated systems that rely on text processing, image processing, telecommunications, and other information technologies.

Office automation systems are computer-based information systems that collect, process, store, and transmit electronic messages, documents, and other forms of communications among individuals, work groups, and organizations. Such systems can increase the productivity of managerial end users and other professional and staff personnel by significantly reducing the time and effort needed to produce, access, and receive business communications. Figure 7.12 outlines major office automation systems.

Information System Activities

You should think of office automation systems as computer-based information systems. This concept is illustrated in Figure 7.13. Hardware resources (intelligent workstations), software resources (automated office programs), and people resources (knowledge workers) convert text, voice, and image data resources into finished information products using the information system activities of input, processing, output, storage, and control.

Thus, ideas can be expressed in words, numbers, symbols, sounds, and images and entered into a computer as text, voice, or image data (input); edited and manipulated electronically (processing); stored and filed electronically on magnetic, optical, micrographic, or paper media (storage); directed by various office automation programs (control); and communicated electronically in voice, video, or on paper to a recipient (output). For example, one can speak into a telephone (input) and have the voice message digitized (processing), temporarily placed on a magnetic disk (storage), then transmitted to another end user's telephone as a voice mail message when requested (output), under the direction of a voice mail program (control).

Word Processing

Word processing was the first, and is still the most common, office automation application. **Word processing** is the use of computer systems to create, edit, revise, and print text material. As we mentioned in Chapter 3, word processing involves manipulating **text data** (characters, words, sentences, and paragraphs) to produce information products in the form of **documents** (letters, memos, forms, and reports).

Figure 7.14 illustrates a word processing application that might take place in a large office. These figures show how a personnel department responds to inquiries concerning employment opportunities with a personal letter which merges standard paragraphs (called *boilerplate*) with variable information specific to the person who applied for employment.

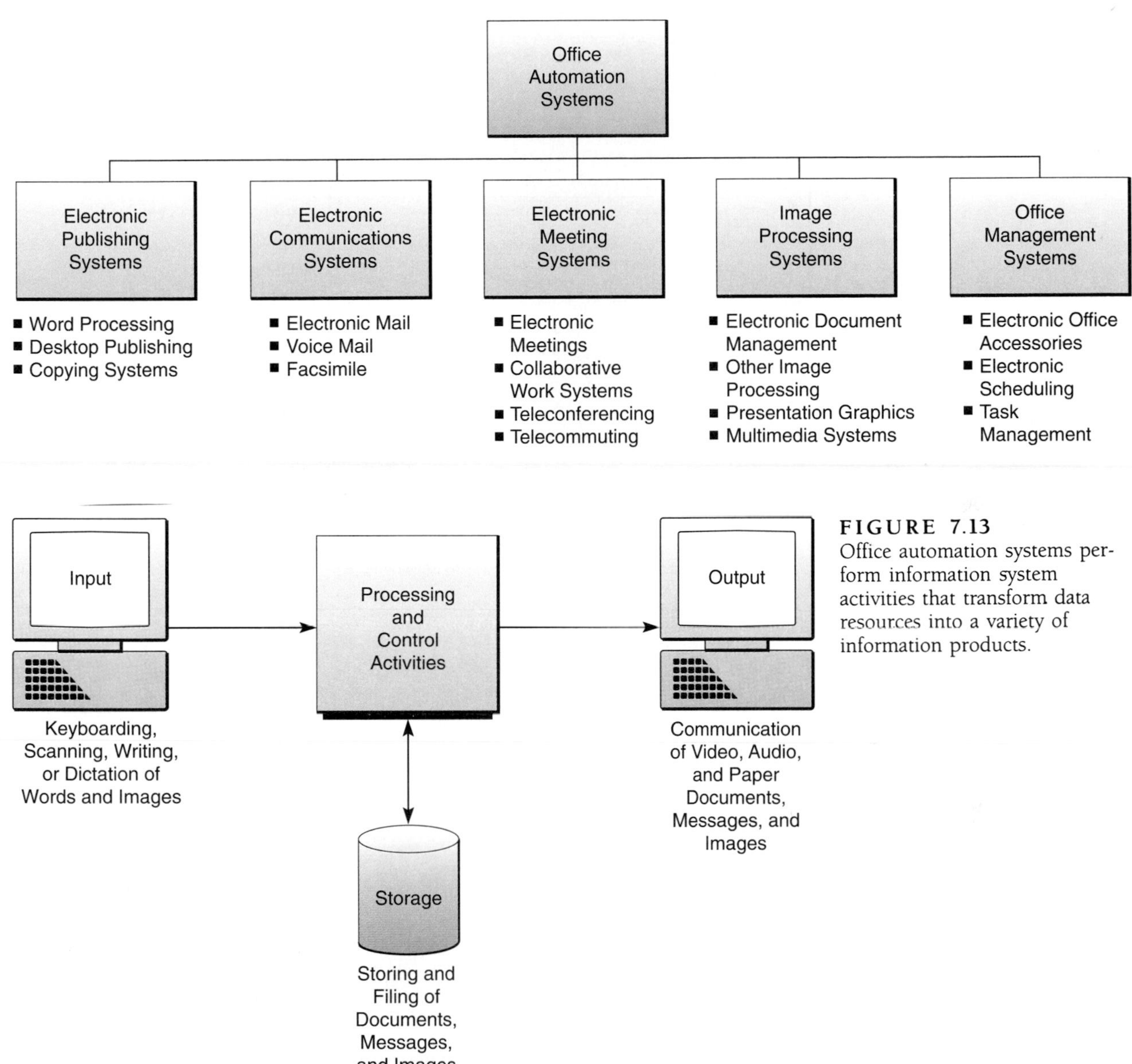

FIGURE 7.12
An overview of office automation systems.

FIGURE 7.13
Office automation systems perform information system activities that transform data resources into a variety of information products.

Desktop Publishing

One of the major applications in office automation is **desktop publishing**. Organizations can use desktop publishing systems to produce their own printed materials. They can design and print their own newsletters, brochures, manuals, and books with several type styles, graphics, and colors on each page. What constitutes a desktop publishing system? Minimum hardware and software requirements include:

- A personal computer with a hard disk.
- A laser printer or other printer capable of high-quality graphics.
- Software that can do word processing, graphics, and page makeup.

FIGURE 7.14
Steps in an office word processing application. Note the use of standard paragraphs to produce a personalized letter for the personnel department.

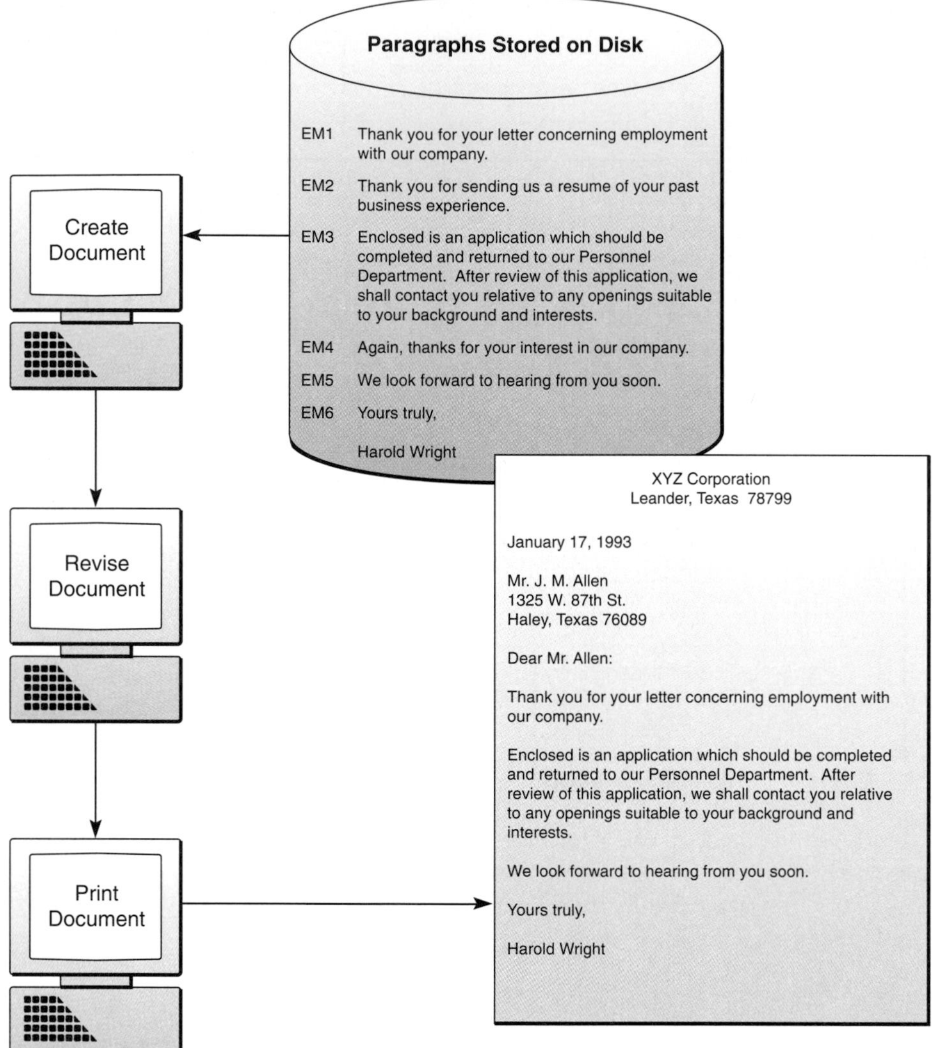

Word processing packages and **page composition** packages are typically used to do word processing, graphics, and page makeup functions. For higher-quality printing, end users need to invest in a more powerful computer with advanced graphic capabilities, a more expensive graphics and page makeup package with more extensive features, and a laser or other printer with a greater variety of capabilities.

How does desktop publishing work? Here are the major steps in the process.

1. Prepare your text and illustrations with a word processing program and a graphics package. Use an optical scanner to input text and graphics from other sources. You can also use files of **clip art**, predrawn graphic illustrations provided by your software or available from other sources.

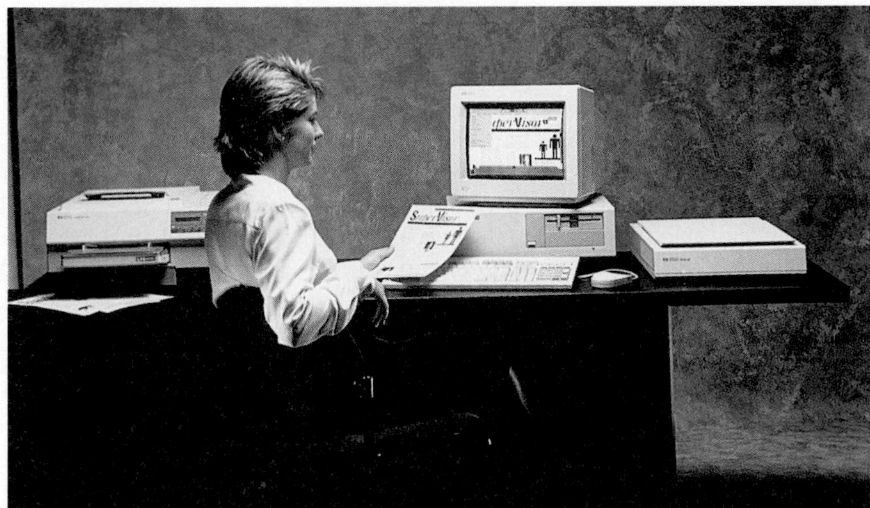

Courtesy of Hewlett-Packard.

FIGURE 7.15
Desktop publishing in action. The video Display shows the use of page makeup software to produce a newsletter on a laser printer.

2. Use the page composition program to develop the format of each page. This is where desktop publishing departs from standard word processing and graphics. Your video screen becomes an *electronic pasteup board* with rulers, column guides, and other page design aids.
3. Now merge the text and illustrations into the page format you designed. The page composition software will automatically move excess text to another column or page and help size and place illustrations and headings. Most page composition packages provide WYSIWYG (What You See Is What You Get) displays so you can see what the finished document will actually look like.
4. When the pages look the way you want them on the screen, you can store them electronically on your hard disk, then print them on a laser printer or other printer to produce the finished printed material. See Figure 7.15.

Many word processing packages now provide limited desktop publishing features. However, the desktop publishing process is not as easy as it sounds for the casual end user. Projects involving complex layouts require experience, skill, and a knowledge of graphics design techniques. However, advances in software have made the job easier in terms of ease of use and helping end users do a better job of graphics design. For example, predesigned forms for various types of printed material (called *templates* or *style sheets*) are frequently provided by many software packages [3, 21].

Image Processing

Image processing is another fast-growing area of office automation. It allows end users to electronically capture, store, process, and retrieve images of documents that may include numeric data, text, handwriting, graphics, and photographs. **Electronic document management** (EDM) is based on image processing technology. However, it views a document as "something that has been authored for human comprehension." Thus an electronic document is not just an electronic image of traditional documents as described earlier. It may also take the form of a digitized "voice note" attached to an electronic mail message, or electronic images for a color graphics presentation [6, 21].

Electronic document management may interface with other electronic document preparation systems such as word processing, desktop publishing, electronic mail, and voice mail. However, one of the fastest growing application areas is *transaction document image processing*. Documents such as customer correspondence, sales orders, invoices, application forms, and service requests are captured electronically and routed to end users throughout the organization for processing. For example, a customer application form for a bank loan can be captured by optical scanning, indexed by the image database management system, stored on optical disk drives, electronically routed to various end user workstations for editing and financial and credit analysis, and then rerouted to a loan officer's workstation where the loan application decision is made. Such image processing and document management systems have shown productivity improvements of 20 to 25 percent, as well as significant cost savings [6, 13, 21]. See Figure 7.16.

Computer Graphics

Which type of output would you rather see: columns of numbers or a graphics display of the same information? Most people find it difficult to quickly and accurately comprehend numerical or statistical data that is presented in a purely numerical form (such as rows or columns of numbers). That is why presentation graphics methods, such as charts and graphs, are typically used in technical reports and business meetings. As we mentioned in Chapter 5, microcomputer and graphics software packages give end users a variety of computer graphics capabilities, ranging from computer-aided design to computer art to presentation graphics. Graphics can be presented as video displays, printed material, transparencies, and color slides. Computer-based presentations containing many different graphics display screens are common and the use of multimedia presentations with sound, animation, and video clips is growing. See Figure 7.17.

Computer graphics has been used for many years in design applications called *computer-aided design* (CAD). Engineers use CAD to design complex mechanical and electronic products and physical structures. Architects use CAD to help them design buildings, work spaces, and other environments. Computer graphics also assists

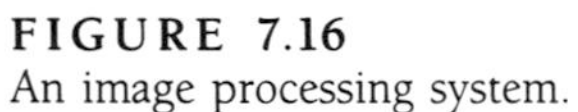

FIGURE 7.16
An image processing system.

Courtesy of IBM Corporation.

researchers in analyzing volumes of data and process control technicians in monitoring industrial processes.

The use of color is also steadily replacing monochrome (one-color) displays of graphics. Color displays provide a more natural user interface. This makes using video displays a more attractive and comfortable experience and can result in fewer errors and greater productivity. Color is a very effective way of categorizing displayed information. Color helps draw attention to selected items, and it can be used to link related items in a display. For example, if an end user changes a data item that affects other data items in a display, then affected data items can change color, alerting the user.

FIGURE 7.17
Business graphics displays. Note the use of color, geographic images, line and bar graphs, three-dimensional graphics, and other graphics images.

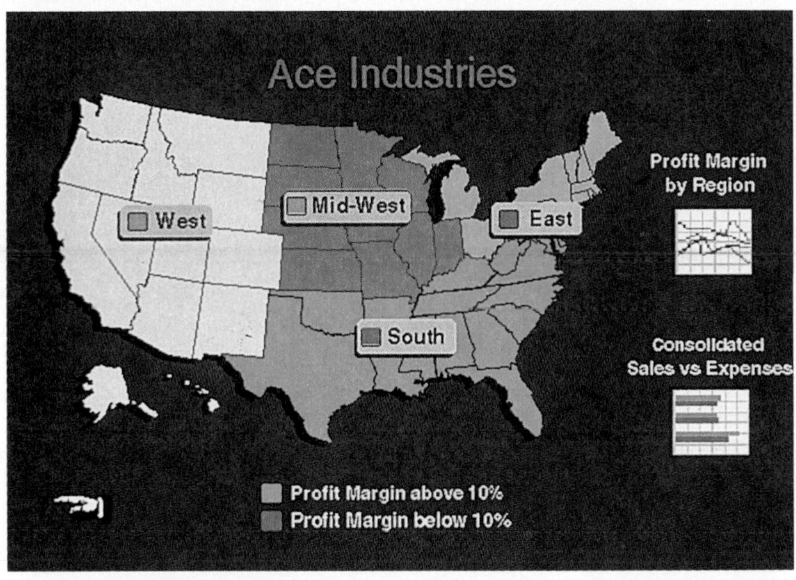

Courtesy of Information Builders, Inc.

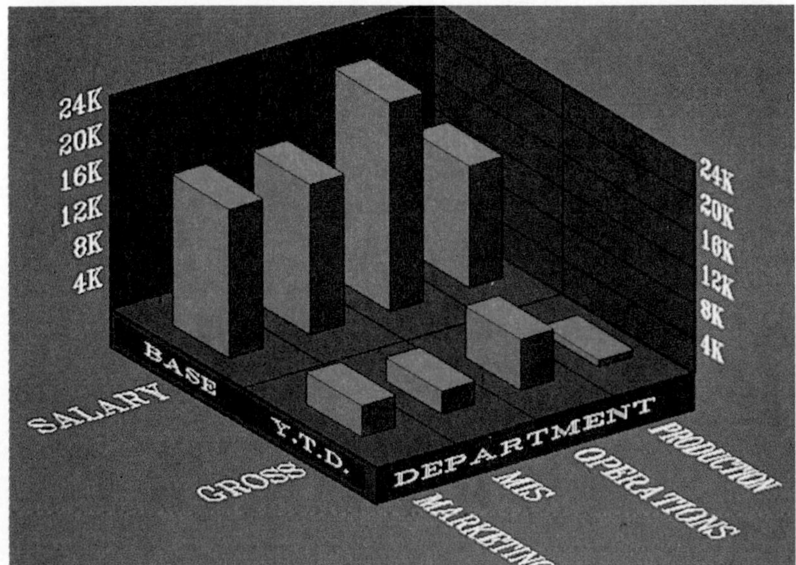

Courtesy of Information Builders, Inc.

Presentation Graphics

The goal of presentation graphics is to provide information in a graphical form that helps end users and managers understand business proposals and performance and make better decisions about them. This includes the use of line and bar graphs, pie charts, and pictorial charts using a variety of symbols. So instead of being overwhelmed by large amounts of computer-produced data, graphics displays can assist managers in analyzing and interpreting information presented to them.

Presentation graphics does not totally replace reports and displays of numbers and text material. Such methods are still needed to present the detailed information that many applications require. However, presentation graphics is becoming the usual method of presenting business information in reports, meetings, and other business presentations. That's because trends, problems, and opportunities hidden in data are easier to spot and communicate when using graphics displays. For example, presentation graphics makes it easier for a marketing manager to see complex market trends and communicate potential market problems and opportunities to the members of a sales team. Figure 7.18 outlines the advantages and disadvantages of various presentation graphics methods.

Multimedia Presentations

Information technology is enabling multimedia presentations to go far beyond traditional forms of numeric, text, and graphics presentations. Multimedia methods of presentation give end users information in a variety of media, including text and graphics displays, voice and other digitized audio, photographs, and video clips. However, many multimedia systems go beyond one-way information presentations. They allow end users to select the form and content of the information presented and browse through the information in a random way, instead of being tied to the sequential access of information. Let's take a closer look now at several of these information presentation technologies.

FIGURE 7.18
The advantages and disadvantages of four types of presentation graphics.

	Line Charts	Bar Charts	Pie Charts	Pictorial Charts
Advantages	1. Shows time and magnitude of relationships well	1. Good for comparisons	1. Good for monetary comparisons	1. Very easily understood
	2. Can show many points	2. Emphasizes one point	2. Good for part versus whole comparison	2. Easily constructed
	3. Degree of accuracy adjustable	3. Accurate	3. Very easily understood	
	4. Easily read	4. Easily read		
Disadvantages	1. Limited to less than four lines without adding complexity	1. Limited to one point	1. Limited usage	1. Limited usage
	2. Limited to two dimensions	2. Spacing can mislead	2. Limited precision	2. Limited precision
	3. Spacing can mislead		3. Tends to oversimplify	3. Tends to oversimplify

Source: John Burch and Gary Grudnitski, *Information Systems Theory and Practice*, 5th ed. (New York: John Wiley & Sons, 1989). Used by permission.

Hypertext and Hypermedia

Hypertext is an important methodology for the construction and interactive use of text databases. A hypertext document is a body of text of any size in electronic form that is indexed so that it can be quickly searched by the reader. For example, if you highlight a term on a hypertext document displayed on your computer video screen and press a key, the computer could instantly bring up a display of a passage of text related to that term. Once you finished reading that pop-up display, you could return to what you were reading originally, or jump to another part of the document instantly. Thus, the use of hypertext provides an environment for interactive reading of a document.

There are several software packages available for the development of hypertext documents. One of the most widely used is the HyperCard package for the Apple Macintosh microcomputer. In HyperCard, the basic unit of text is called a card. A hypertext document consists of stacks, or collections, of interrelated and indexed cards; thus, hypertext document packages are known as stackware. Hypertext documents can be programmed to let a reader navigate through a document by following one or more scripts. This creates a hypertext document that can lead the reader through the document several different ways [12].

By definition, hypertext contains only text and a limited amount of graphics. Hypermedia are electronic documents that contain multiple forms of media, including text, graphics, video, and so on. Proponents of hypertext and hypermedia expect such "electronic books" to become as popular as more traditional paper documents such as books, magazines, and newspapers. Figure 7.19 shows the display of a hypermedia package that combines text, graphics, video, and audio to make hypermedia presentations [4, 6].

Interactive Video

Interactive video or multimedia systems integrate image processing with text, audio, and video processing technologies. Software for developing such digital video interactive (DVI) applications requires microcomputer systems with more processing power and memory, add-on circuit boards, and hard disk and CD-ROM optical

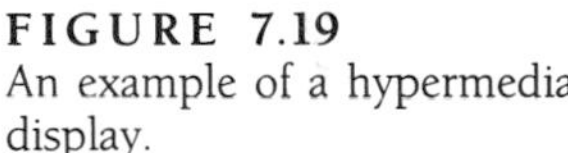

FIGURE 7.19
An example of a hypermedia display.

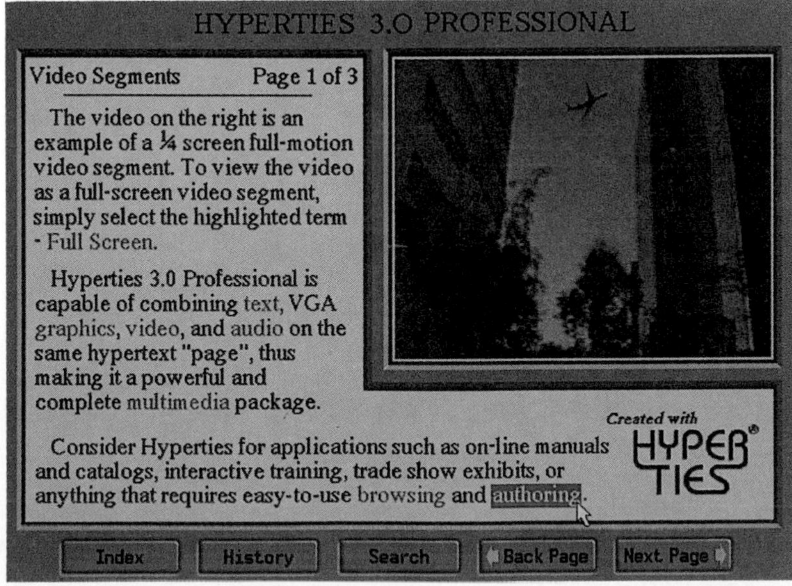

Courtesy Digital Equipment Corporation.

disk storage. This allows end users to digitally capture, edit, and combine text, pictures, and sound into multimedia business and educational presentations. For example, an interactive video session for training auto mechanics can be produced on optical disks. It could combine animated graphics displays of engine parts, electronic diagnostic charts, lists of major topics and facts, video clips of mechanics working on vehicles, and engine sounds helpful in engine diagnostics [15].

Interactive video sessions allow end users with microcomputers and optical disk drives to see and hear prepared material interactively. That is, they do not have to view a program sequentially. They can move among various segments randomly or according to preestablished paths indicated by menus and prompts. When interactive video uses hypertext technology it becomes hypermedia. Though expensive to produce, interactive video is being used for education and training purposes by large business firms, government agencies, schools, and other organizations.

Electronic Communications Systems

Electronic communications systems are one of the major application areas of office automation. **Electronic mail, voice mail**, and **facsimile** allow organizations to send messages in text, video, or voice form or transmit copies of documents and do it in seconds, not hours or days. Such systems involve the transmission and distribution of text and images in electronic form over telecommunications networks, thus reducing the flow of paper messages, letters, memos, documents, and reports that floods our present interoffice and postal systems.

Electronic Mail

Electronic mail has changed the way people work and communicate. Millions of end users now depend on electronic mail (E-mail) to send and receive electronic messages. You can send E-mail to anyone else on your network for storage in their *electronic mailboxes* on magnetic disk drives. Whenever they are ready, they can read their electronic mail by displaying it on the video screens at their workstations. So, with only a few minutes of effort (and a few microseconds of transmission), a message to one or many individuals can be composed, sent, and received. Thus, many organizations and work groups depend on E-mail packages and their wide and local area networks for electronic mail. Communications companies such as GTE, TELENET, and MCI also offer such services, as do personal computer networks such as CompuServe, Genie, and Prodigy. Figure 7.20 shows a video display provided by an electronic mail package.

Many E-mail packages can route messages to multiple end users based on predefined mailing lists, and provide password security, automatic message forwarding, and remote user access. They also may allow you to store messages in *folders* with provisions for adding attachments to message files. Other E-mail packages may allow you to edit and send graphics as well as text, and provide bulletin board and computer conferencing capabilities. Finally, some E-mail packages can automatically filter and sort incoming messages (even news items from online services such as Dow Jones News/Retrieval Service) and route them to appropriate user mailboxes and folders [9].

Voice Mail

Another variation of electronic mail is **voice mail** (also called *voice store-and-forward*) where digitized voice messages, rather than electronic text, are used. In this method, you first dial the number of the voice mail service. In some secure systems, you may be asked to enter an identification code. Once you are accepted, you dial the voice mail number of the person you wish to contact and speak your message. Your analog message is digitized and stored on the magnetic disk devices of the

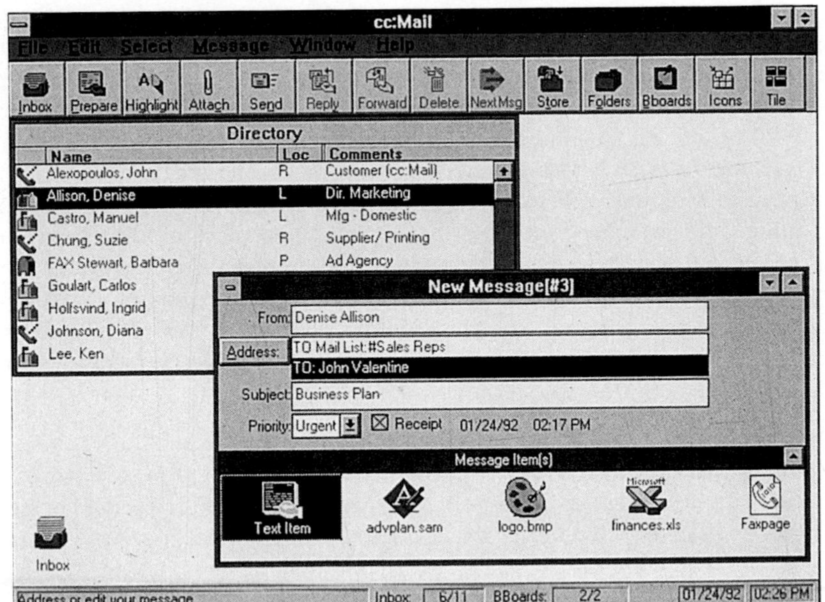

Courtesy of Lotus Development Corporation.

FIGURE 7.20
Using an electronic mail package, cc: Mail, by Lotus.

voice mail computer system. Whenever you want to hear your voice mail, you simply dial your mailbox and listen to the stored message, which the computer converts back into analog voice form.

Facsimile

Facsimile (fax) is not a new office telecommunications service. However, advances in digital imaging technology and microelectronics have caused a sharp drop in prices and a significant increase in capabilities. As a consequence, sales of fax machines have skyrocketed in the last few years, and faxing has become a commonplace business term. Facsimile allows you to transmit images of important documents over telephone or other telecommunication links. Thus, "long-distance copying" might be an appropriate nickname for this telecommunications process.

Usually a fax machine at one office location transmits to a fax machine at another location, with both units connected to high-speed modems. Transmission speeds for digital office fax machines range from one to four pages per minute, with quality equivalent to an office copier. A more recent development is the availability of facsimile circuit boards for microcomputers. Installing a fax board and using a fax software package allows a personal computer to transmit digital copies of text files to fax machines anywhere. Thus, fax machines can now become remote dial-up printers for microcomputer systems [5].

Electronic Meeting Systems

Why do people have to spend travel time and money to attend meetings away from their normal work locations? They don't have to if they use several types of **electronic meeting systems** (EMS), a growing method of electronic office telecommunications. Electronic meeting systems involve the use of video and audio communications to allow conferences and meetings to be held with participants who may be scattered across a room, a building, a country, or the globe. Reducing the need to travel to and from meetings should save employee time, increase productivity, and reduce travel expenses and energy consumption. Electronic meeting systems are also being promoted as a form of group decision support systems (GDSS), because they promote more efficient and effective decision making by groups of people [8].

There are several variations of electronic meeting systems, as illustrated in Figure 7.21. In some versions, participants at remote sites key in their presentations and responses whenever convenient from their online terminals or workstations connected to a central conference computer. Since not all participants have to do this at the same time, this form of EMS is called *computer conferencing* and is like a form of interactive electronic mail. Group decision support systems for small groups may use a network of workstations and large screen projection in a *decision room* while a GDSS for large groups constitutes a *legislative session*. Both of these forms of electronic meeting systems provide extensive computer and video facilities for their participants. See Figure 7.22.

Teleconferencing

Teleconferencing is an important form of EMS. Sessions are held in realtime, with major participants being televised while participants at remote sites usually take part with voice input of questions and responses. See Figure 7.23. Teleconferencing can also consist of using closed circuit television to multiple small groups, instead of television broadcasting to reach large groups at multiple sites.

Several major communications carriers and hotel chains now offer teleconferencing services for such events as sales meetings, new-product announcements, and employee education and training. However, organizations have found that teleconferencing and some forms of EMS are not as effective as face-to-face meetings, especially when important participants are not trained in how to communicate using these systems. Also, the cost of providing some electronic meeting services and facilities can be substantial and make EMS not as cost-effective as traditional meetings.

Telecommuting

Telecommuting is the use of telecommunications by workers to replace commuting to work from their homes. It is also used to describe the use of telecommunications to carry on work activities from temporary locations other than offices and homes. Some people refer to telecommuting as the creation of *virtual offices*. Workers use a computer terminal or microcomputer with telecommunications capability to access their company's computer network and databases. Telecommuting workers and their colleagues also use electronic mail or voice mail to communicate with each other about job assignments.

Telecommuting is being tried by several major corporations and is used by many independent professionals. It seems to be most popular with people whose jobs involve a lot of individual work, such as programmers, systems analysts, writers, consultants, and so on. It is especially helpful for handicapped persons and working parents of young children. However, studies have shown that telecommuting is not appropriate for many jobs and people. Productivity and job satisfaction seem to suffer unless workers spend several days each week at the office or other work sites with their colleagues. So telecommuting is considered only a temporary or partial work alternative for many knowledge workers [3, 19].

Office Management Systems

Office management systems is an office automation category that integrates electronic calendars, tickler files, electronic mail directories, schedulers, and task management systems. This provides computer-based support services to managers and other office professionals to help them organize their work activities. Office management software computerizes manual methods of planning such as paper calendars,

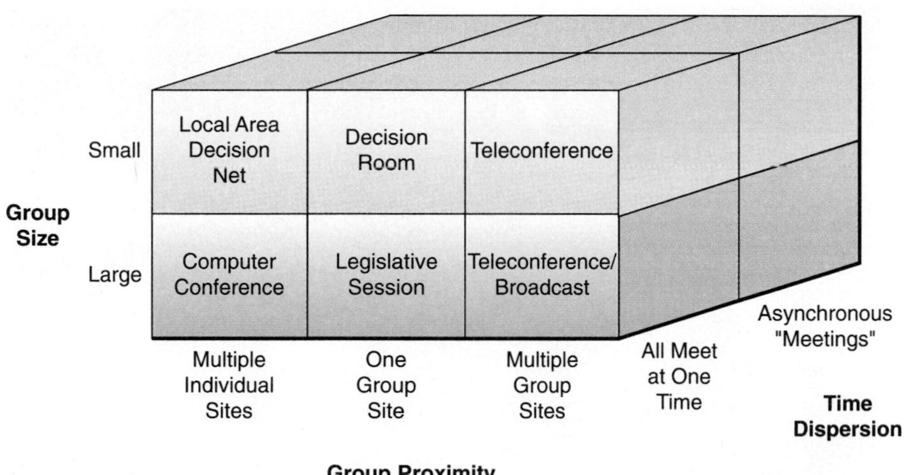

Adapted from Alan Dennis, Joey George, Len Jessup, Jay Nunamaker, and Douglas Vogel, "Information Technology to Support Group Meetings," *MIS Quarterly*, December 1988, p. 609.

FIGURE 7.21
A taxonomy of electronic meeting system environments. Note the place of teleconferencing and other forms of EMS.

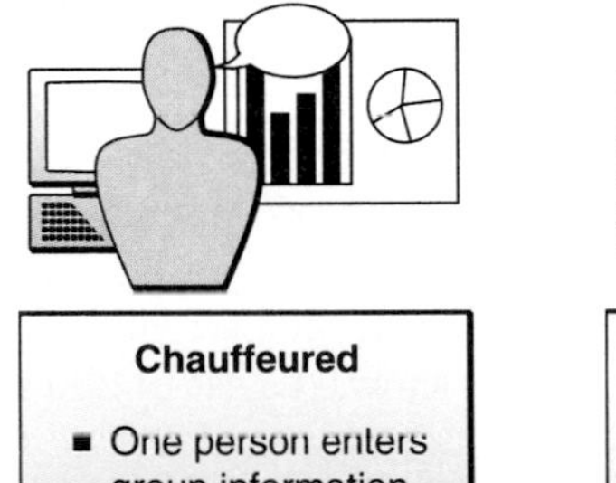

Source: Jay Nunamaker, Alan Dennis, Joseph Valacich, Douglas Vogel, and Joey George, "Electronic Meeting Systems to Support Group Work," *Communications of the ACM*, July 1991, p. 50.

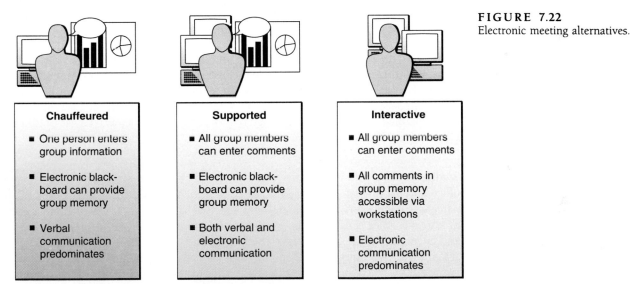

FIGURE 7.22
Electronic meeting alternatives.

appointment books, directories, file folders, memos, and notes. Microcomputer users can get some of the benefits of mainframe office systems by using **desktop accessory** software packages. *Groupware* packages are also available which allow members of work groups on local area networks to share a variety of office services and other OA applications such as word processing and electronic mail. Thus, office management systems can help end users and work groups organize routine office tasks.

For example, you could enter the date and time of a meeting into an electronic calendar. An electronic tickler file will automatically remind you of important events. Electronic schedulers use the electronic calendars of several people to help you schedule meetings and other activities with them. Desktop accessories provide

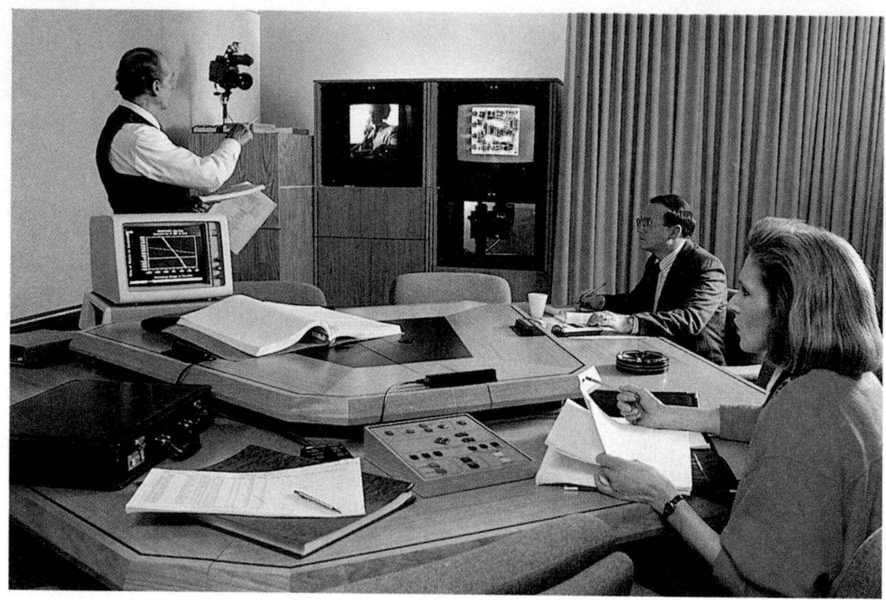

FIGURE 7.23
Teleconferencing in action.

Gabe Palmer/The Stock Market.

features such as a calculator, notepad, alarm clock, phone directory, and appointment book that pop up in a window on the display screen of your workstation at the touch of a key. Electronic mail directories help you contact people easily. And electronic task management packages help you plan a series of related activities so that scheduled results are accomplished on time. Figure 7.24 shows the use of IBM's Officevision office management system.

Management Implications of Office Automation

Studies made of how knowledge workers spend their time have determined that office automation can save a significant amount of a knowledge worker's time (15 percent is one estimate). The major areas that can be improved include less-productive office activities such as seeking information, waiting for appointments and meetings, organizing work, scheduling, and filing. More productive office activities, such as meetings, telephone calls, and creating documents, can also be improved by office automation systems. Studies have also shown that office workers have less plant and equipment invested per worker ($2,000/worker) than factory workers ($25,000/worker) or agricultural workers ($50,000/worker). Thus, increased investment in office automation systems promises increased productivity by office workers [3, 17].

OA Benefits

Office automation systems help end users achieve the benefits of (1) more cost-effective communications and (2) more *time-effective* communications than traditional written and telephone communications methods. For example, electronic mail and facsimile systems are designed to minimize *information float* and *telephone tag* **Information float** is the time (at least several days) when a written letter or other document is in transit between the sender and receiver, and thus unavailable for any action or response. **Telephone tag** is the process of (1) repeatedly calling people, (2) finding them unavailable, (3) leaving messages, and (4) finding out later you were unavailable when they finally returned your calls.

Courtesy IBM Corporation.

FIGURE 7.24
A display of IBM's Officevision office support system.

Electronic mail, voice mail, and facsimile systems can also eliminate the effects of mail that is lost in transit or phone lines that are frequently busy. They can also reduce the costs of labor, materials, and postage for office communications (from more than $5 for a written message to less than 50 cents for an electronic message is one estimate). Also, the amount of time wasted in regular phone calls can be reduced (by one third, according to another estimate) [3, 20].

Thus, office automation systems can:

- Increase the productivity of secretarial personnel and reduce the costs of creating, reviewing, revising, and distributing office documents and messages.
- Shorten the turnaround time between the preparation and receipt of messages and documents by moving information quickly and efficiently to the people who need it.
- Reduce the frustration, expense, and errors involved in revising text and images for attractive and effective documents and presentations.
- Store, retrieve, and transmit electronic documents, images, and messages quickly and efficiently.
- Increase the productivity of executives, professionals, and other knowledge workers who are heavy users of office communications. For example, most of the managerial roles discussed in Chapter 10 involve extensive information transfer activities, which can be effectively supported by office automation systems. [14]

OA Limitations

Of course, these advantages are not acquired without some negative effects. First, the cost of automated office hardware is significantly higher than the equipment it replaces. Another limitation is less obvious. Office automation can disrupt traditional office work roles and work environments. For example, some word processing systems have caused significant employee dissatisfaction because they give some secretaries nothing but typing to do, and isolate them from other employees [17].

The ease of use and lack of security of many office automation systems have also caused problems. Inefficient and unauthorized use of electronic mail, voice mail, and facsimile services can significantly impair office productivity. One example is sending copies of electronic messages to people who do not need or want them. Another is "junk fax"—receiving unauthorized advertisements and unrequested documents that disrupt the normal use of an office fax machine. These problems of office automation must be solved before knowledge workers can fully accept and cooperate with a technology that significantly changes their work roles, processes, and environment. Only then will office automation's promises of increased productivity and job satisfaction be fulfilled.

REAL WORLD CASE

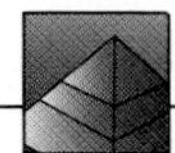

JC Penney Co.: Electronic Document Imaging

To help handle significant growth in its life insurance unit, JC Penney Co. is developing an electronic document imaging and work-flow system. The system, from New York-based Image Business Systems, uses IBM Risc System/6000 Unix servers and PCs with Microsoft Windows. It will initially support 250 customer service representatives at the insurance group's facility in Plano, Texas. But the installation will likely grow to nearly twice that size, said David Evans, vice president of information systems at JC Penney.

If it reaches 450 seats, JC Penney's facility would be among the largest 100 imaging systems in the country. The deal would also be one of Image Business Systems' five largest from among its 35 customers, most of which have applications supporting 30 to 50 image-enabled workstations. Last year, the company made headlines with the announcement of a $10 million, two-year project to image-enable some 700 or 800 insurance claims clerks at Louisville, Kentucky-based insurer Humana, Inc.

Evans said he visited Humana and awarded the competitively bid contract to Image Business Systems based in part on the success of that project. Humana officials reached last week confirmed that the effort to streamline three service centers with imaging is on track, although they said only about 120 users have been put on the system so far. "We probably won't be as big as Humana in any one place, but we might have large numbers of users in 10 or 20 locations," Evans said, adding that JC Penney plans to evaluate the project with an eye toward putting Image Business Systems imaging in customer services operations elsewhere within the retailing giant.

JC Penney already has two other imaging applications. The first system, built in 1984 using a minicomputer and dedicated terminals, supports high-volume processing of credit-card remittance forms; the other application, a two-year-old client/server system using Windows-based workstations and a Sun Microsystem server, handles the processing of new credit applications. According to Evans, while the new Image Business Systems application will manage a much lower volume of documents than the two other systems, it will offer significantly more sophisticated work-flow features. "In the long terms, we think it'll be critical to have image as part of an application and be able to control the work queues and work flow," he said.

The Image Business Systems deployment at JC Penney will be in three areas: claims, customer service, and specialty insurance products. The vendor is deploying the systems in all three areas simultaneously. JC Penney is specifically looking for an improvement in productivity to accommodate growth in business at JC Penney Insurance, which posted income of $101 million last year, up from $79 million in 1991 and $55 million in 1990. But JC Penney is also looking at extending the life of a series of applications resident on an IBM mainframe by adding an imaging component and off-loading some portions of these applications to the RS/6000 image server system.

CASE STUDY QUESTIONS

1. Why is JC Penney moving to document imaging?
2. Why would Humana, Inc. need document image processing?
3. What other types of business could use document imaging?

Source: Adapted from Ellis Booker, "Imaging, Work Flow Expand at JC Penney," *Computerworld*, April 12, 1993, p. 52. Used with permission.

Summary

- **End User Computing.** End user computing is the direct, hands-on use of computers by end users to perform the information processing needed to accomplish their work activities. End user computing has grown dramatically because information services have not been able to keep up with the information processing requests of users. Also, dramatic improvements in microcomputer hardware and software capabilities have made personal computing attractive, affordable, and effective for end users in many organizations. End user computing application areas include office automation, information management and retrieval, decision support, and application development.
- **End User Computing Systems.** End user computing should be viewed as systems of hardware, software, people, and data resources. Hardware resources include microcomputer workstations, local area network servers, departmental minicomputers, and corporate mainframes. Software resources consist of application packages, groupware packages, and application development packages. People resources include end users and information center consultants. Data resources include personal, work group, corporate, and external databases.
- **Work Group Computing.** Much of end user computing is a group effort known as work group computing. End users are using networked computers and groupware packages to collaborate on work assignments without regard to time constraints, physical location, or organizational boundaries. Groupware packages can accomplish many applications, as summarized in Figure 7.8. However, the key features of such collaboration software are the work group communications and coordination that it makes possible.
- **Office Automation.** Office automation systems combine text processing, image processing, telecommunications, and other information technologies to develop computer-based information systems that collect, store, and transmit electronic messages, documents, and other forms of communications. Office automation systems include word processing, desktop publishing, graphics and multimedia presentations, electronic mail, voice mail, facsimile, image processing, electronic meeting systems, and office management systems.
- **OA Benefits and Limitations.** Automated office systems increase the productivity of office personnel and reduce the costs of office communications. They shorten the turnaround time between the preparation and receipt of documents and messages, reduce the expense and errors involved in producing documents, and increase the productivity of executives and professionals who are heavy users of office communications. However, the cost of automated office hardware is higher than the equipment it replaces. Office automation may also disrupt traditional office work roles and work environments and impair organizational productivity. Therefore, managerial end users must establish policies to support the security and effectiveness of office automation services.

Key Terms and Concepts

These are the key terms and concepts of this chapter. The page number of their first explanation is in parentheses.

1. Computer graphics (246)
2. Desktop accessories (253)
3. Desktop publishing (243)
4. Document (242)
5. Electronic document management (245)
6. Electronic mail (250)
7. Electronic meeting systems (250)
8. End user computing (228)
   a. Rationale (228)
   b. Management implications (234)
   c. Resources (229)
9. End user computing Applications (232)
   a. Office automation (232)
   b. Information management and retrieval (232)
   c. Decision support (233)
   d. Application development (233)
10. Facsimile (251)
11. Groupware (235)
12. Hypermedia (249)
13. Hypertext (249)
14. Information center (236)
15. Information float (254)
16. Image processing (245)
17. Interactive video (249)
18. Multimedia presentations (248)
19. Office automation (242)
   a. Benefits and limitations (254)
   b. Information system activities (242)
   c. Types of systems (242)
20. Office management systems (252)
21. Personal information manager (232)
22. Presentation graphics (248)
23. Telecommuting (252)
24. Teleconferencing (252)
25. Telephone tag (254)
26. Text data (242)
27. User consultant (229)
28. Voice mail (250)
29. Word processing (242)
30. Work group (234)
31. Work group computing (234)

Review Quiz

Match one of the key terms and concepts listed above with one of the brief examples or definitions listed below. Try to find the best fit for answers that seem to fit more than one term or concept. Defend your choices.

____ 1. The direct, hands-on use of computers by users.

____ 2. End user applications frequently lack adequate controls.

____ 3. Examples are microcomputer workstations, application packages, information center consultants, and external databases.

____ 4. Using your workstation to prepare documents and communicate with your colleagues.

____ 5. Managing databases and generating reports.

____ 6. Using an electronic spreadsheet for what-if analysis.

____ 7. Developing new ways to use computers to perform jobs for you.

____ 8. Software that helps people collaborate on group work assignments.

____ 9. Members of a work group share computer resources to jointly accomplish work assignments.

____ 10. Organizations have established these end user support groups.

____ 11. Optical scanning input, image processing, interactive video output.

____ 12. Automates office work activities and communications, but may disrupt traditional work roles.

____ 13. Includes word processing, desktop publishing, electronic mail, and teleconferencing.

____ 14. Text data is manipulated and documents are produced.

____ 15. Characters, words, sentences, and paragraphs.

____ 16. Letters, memos, forms, and reports.

____ 17. Users can produce their own brochures and manuals.

____ 18. Includes computer-aided design, presentation graphics, and computer art.

____ 19. Easier to understand than columns of numbers.

____ 20. Presenting information in a variety of forms of media.

____ 21. Helps you interactively browse through a text database.

____ 22. A multimedia form of hypertext technology.

____ 23. Allows end users to capture video and sound for computer-based presentations.

____ 24. Use your workstation to send and receive messages.

____ 25. Use your telephone as an electronic message terminal.

____ 26. The time a document is in transit between sender and receiver.

____ 27. You and the person you want to contact repeatedly miss each other's phone calls.

____ 28. Transmitting images of documents electronically.

____ 29. Saves travel time and money spent on meetings.

____ 30. Realtime televised electronic meetings at remote sites.

____ 31. Using telecommunications so you can work at home.

____ 32. End users can electronically capture, store, process, and retrieve images.

____ 33. Customer correspondence and sales orders can be optically captured and routed to end users for processing.

____ 34. Helps end users store information in a variety of forms and retrieve it in many different ways.

____ 35. Integrates calculator, calendar, address book, notepad, and other functions.

____ 36. Provides a variety of office automation services such as electronic calendars and meeting scheduling.

Discussion Questions

1. What developments are responsible for the growth of end user computing? Do you expect this growth to continue? Explain.
2. What changes do you expect in the future in the types of hardware, software, people, and data resources typically used in end user computing systems? In the four major application areas of end user computing?
3. Refer to the Real World Case on Alaska Airlines in the chapter. Is their decreasing reliance on their IS staff a good trend? Explain.
4. Why is work group computing becoming an increasingly important form of end user computing? What is the role of groupware in supporting this trend?
5. Why do you think some organizations are closing their information centers and distributing end user support to departments and other business units?
6. Refer to the Real World Case on JC Penney in the chapter. Which is more important, the data on a document or an image of the document? Explain.

7. If you were a manager, how would you manage some of the risks of end user computing?
8. What office automation developments are moving us toward a "paperless" electronic office? What circumstances inhibit movement in that direction?
9. How will the growth of graphics and multimedia presentations affect the information presentation preferences of managers? Explain.
10. Would you like to take part in electronic meetings such as teleconferences? Would you like to telecommute to work? Why or why not?

Real World Problems

1. Ann Palermo of DataCorporation: The Office of 2001

Ann Palermo, director of workgroup and messaging research at International DataCorporation, says that by the end of the century ubiquitous PCs, workstations, and computer networks will be marshaled to automate group tasks using sophisticated work-flow software. Already, she noted, the first application on this local-area network infrastructure—electronic mail—is being enhanced with calendaring and scheduling systems. "The most significant difference we'll see in the way people work 10 years from now will be the greater use of collaborative technologies," Palermo said. Different types of information will also come together, which will make multimedia and compound documents at the desktop commonplace. Likewise, she said, the distinction between the computer system and the phone system in an office will fade away.

Naturally, integrating these ways of communicating will require building a telecommunication network infrastructure, which Palermo said will be a major challenge. Automation of routine business processes will also serve to sweep a clear path for users, many of whom complain about the glut of information and E-mail on their desktops. For this reason, Palermo was optimistic about office productivity. "We're going to see a huge jump in productivity by 2001," she predicted. "We're getting smart and starting to automate business processes instead of just tasks."

a. Will you like to work in the office environment predicted by Ann Palermo? Why or why not?

b. Why does Ann Palermo feel that there will be a big jump in office productivity? Do you agree? Explain.

Source: Adapted from Ellis Booker, "Looking Forward to Office 2001," *Computerworld*, January 11, 1993, p. 28. Used with permission.

2. Joseph Duncan of Dun and Bradstreet: Presentation Graphics

When Joseph Duncan consults the oracles of the economy, people listen. And they watch. As vice president and chief economist at The Dun & Bradstreet Corp. in New York, Duncan presents his views throughout the United States and the world as many as three times a week. But unlike many economists, who are often technology-shy, Duncan has trained himself to be an expert in computer-generated graphics and animation. For example, when Duncan made a November presentation to his most important audience, the D&B board of directors, he was able to dress it up not only with static graphics but also with videotape digitized to fit the CD-ROM drive in the PC that supports his presentations. In one instance—as part of a D&B team overseeing a joint venture in the former Soviet Union—he included in his core presentation footage of Russians lining up for food and commodities.

Duncan uses Harvard Graphics, a package that includes several support programs including Linkway, which captures digitized video. Among the benefits of using multimedia is that Duncan no longer has to pay a commercial film lab for each image in his presentation. He was spending $8 to $10 for each slide. Nor does he have to worry about updating his visuals every time something changes in the economy. He keeps his data updated daily on a Microsoft Excel spreadsheet, which drives the graphics. Says John Wu, a New York multimedia consultant who works on contract with D&B: "Harvard Graphics uses 'hyperlinks' to let you go from slide to slide within a presentation instead of being bound by the normal linear sort of program like you get with a 35mm slide presentation." Wu continues, "With hyperlinks and a set of backup slides, Joe can go to a particular graphic if he needs to, especially during question-and-answer sessions."

a. What computer graphics capabilities are used by Joseph Duncan?

b. What other graphics technologies could he use in his presentations? Explain how.

Source: Adapted from Robert Knight, "Sound, Vision Add Presentation Punch," *Computerworld*, January 25, 1993, p. 69. Used with permission.

3. RE/Max Mexico: Multimedia in Real Estate

At RE/Max Mexico's real estate headquarters, the curtain is rising on what sales agents call "The Hollywood Show" as a network of Sun Microsystems workstations take center stage. This week, the real estate franchise corporation will announce a $4 million contract with Sun for the installation of more than 600 SPARCstations and SPARCservers to run a custom-built, multimedia application that showcases property listings via color pictures and walk-through videos. "When customers come into a RE/Max office, they'll be given 'The Hollywood Show,'" said Peter Bowthorpe, general manager of RE/Max Mexico. "We believe this is the way real estate offices in general will be going. The human eye is so much more useful in absorbing information than the ear."

The multimedia application is called CLI/Max, which in Spanish is the acronym for *Consolidacion de Listados Interactiva/Maxima*. The system was developed for RE/Max by one of Sun's distribution partners, Cromasoft SA de C.V., here. It uses database query capabilities to search for a customer's ideal property, then displays a series of photos or videos in windows on the computer screen. "This is a tremendous time-saver for buyers and sellers. It can take all day to see three houses here," said Steve Tirado, general manager and director of Sun Microsystems of Mexico. When RE/Max test-marketed the software in one resort area office and a Guadalajara shopping center, the reaction to it was gratifyingly intense, Bowthorpe said. "It nearly stopped the traffic, and we realized we were on to something," he said.

a. How will CLI/Max benefit RE/Max Mexico?

b. What other businesses could benefit from multimedia systems like CLI/Max?

Source: Adapted from Maryfran Johnson, "Mexican Real Estate Firm Goes Hollywood," *Computerworld*, February 15, 1993, p. 37–38. Used with permission.

4. Carolina Freight and the Travelers: Using Electronic Communications Systems

Carolina Freight Corp. in Cherryville, North Carolina, which is using a whole family of electronic technologies to give customers a window into the trucking company's operations. The business goal, simply put, is to make it easier for customers to do business with Carolina Freight than with its competitors, says John Rudasill, president of the firm's computer services subsidiary. The company's suite of technologies includes an EDI network for its high-end customers, a PC-based software package for mid-size customers, and a voice-response system that allows smaller customers to use a push-button phone to access the shipper's computer systems. The voice-response system provides information about rates and routes and even allows customers to trace their shipments by the waybill number, Rudasill says. Customers can also get a shipment status report faxed to them.

The Travelers Corp. in Hartford, Connecticut, has a variety of voice response systems. "I'm absolutely convinced we have to do this because customers are going to expect it. Otherwise, they're going to think something is wrong with us," says Gus Bender, vice president of telecommunications. Travelers has 12 voice-response applications running on 50 voice-response units, which now handle 30 percent of the company's incoming calls. Callers use their telephones to get status reports on their latest insurance claims and to check eligibility information. If the caller then needs a live operator, Travelers uses "automatic screen transfer" technology to ensure that the caller and the caller's computerized records arrive at the customer service agent's terminal at the same instant. Customers do not have to identify themselves once again, which shaves 20 seconds off each call.

a. Why does Carolina Freight use different information technologies for different types of customers?

b. Why does Travelers think that voice response systems are a necessity? Do you agree? Explain.

Source: Adapted from Mitch Betts, "Serve or Else," *Computerworld*, January 4, 1993, pp. 29–30. Used with permission.

Application Exercises

1. End User Office Automation

Match one of the following office automation systems with the examples listed below.

a. Desktop publishing
b. Electronic mail
c. Office management systems
d. Teleconferencing
e. Voice mail
f. word processing
g. Image processing
h. Facsimile
i. Electronic meetings

____ 1. Composing, editing, and printing a letter to a customer.

____ 2. Producing a company newsletter with text and graphics.

____ 3. Being prompted that you have scheduled a meeting.

____ 4. Visually displaying messages that have been sent to you.

____ 5. Listening to a computer-generated message from an associate.

____ 6. Participating in a companywide TV workshop.

____ 7. Conducting a meeting where all participants use computers.

____ 8. Sending a copy of a letter electronically using the telephone system.

____ 9. Optically capturing and using document images instead of paper documents.

2. ABC Department Stores: End User Development

The Marketing Department at ABC Department Stores maintains a small library of periodicals and reference works for their staff. This library has been run on an honor system. The employee checking out an item is to write his or her name, the date, and the title and issue of the publication checked out on a cardboard form and put it in a box beside the library shelves. Employees are asked to keep a publication no longer than one week. When they return the publication, they so indicate on the cardboard form and put it in a different box.

This system has not always worked well; most employees do remember to fill out the form, but many forget to return the items they have borrowed. Also, whenever someone needs to get information from a publication that is checked out, they have to search through all of the cards to find out which employee has the publication they want.

Suppose you were asked to develop a simple computer-based application to manage checkouts from this library. You can assume that it is not necessary to keep an inventory of the books in the library; only a listing for checked-out books is to be maintained. A sample set of data is listed in Figure 7.25. Use a database management package or an integrated package to do the following:

a. Create a database file to store the appropriate data for this application, and enter the sample data shown in Figure 7.25.

b. Retrieve information needed to satisfy the following end user requests. Get printed listings of your results.

(1) An employee wants to know who has checked out *Statistics Made Simple*.

(2) Sue Smith (Smith, S.) wants to know which books she has checked out.

(3) You want to know how many books are currently checked out.

(4) You want a list of each publication that has been checked out longer than one week and the name of the employee who checked it out. (Assume the current data is 9/28/93).

3. Anderson Products Software Training

Anderson Products Company encourages its workers to seek training in the use of common software packages. Anderson does not provide the training internally but pays the fees for training provided by a local university. The company will pay the full cost for up to 15 days of software training for each employee. For any additional training beyond 15 days, the employee must pay half of the fee.

You have been assigned the responsibility for managing the software training in your department. You decide to create a database file to keep track of training. You want to keep information identifying the employee's name, the length of the training, the type of software that the training addresses, and an indication of whether or not the training has been completed. When an employee informs you that they plan to enroll for a training session, you will add a new record to the database filling in all information and placing an "N" in the Completed field. Once an employee completes the training session, they submit a request for reimbursement. At that time, the value for the Completed field is changed to a "Y." A set of historical data for this database file is shown below.

Anderson Product Employee Software Training History

Employee Name	Software Type	Number of Training Days	Training Completed?
Evans, D.	Database	2	Y
Andrews, A.	Word Processing	3	Y
Barnes, W.	DOS	2	Y
Evans, D.	Spreadsheet	3	Y
Barnes, W.	Word Processing	3	Y
Norris, B.	DOS	2	N
Andrews, A.	Spreadsheet	3	Y
Evans, D.	DOS	2	N
Dale, E.	Database	2	N
Barnes, W.	Spreadsheet	3	Y
Barnes, W.	DOS	2	N
Norris, B.	Spreadsheet	3	Y

FIGURE 7.25
Sample employee checkout data.

Employee Name	Checkout Date	Periodical Name	Returned
Smith S.	9/19/93	Marketers Guide	No
Wick J.	9/20/93	Lotus Users Guide	No
Adams A.	9/17/93	Media Week, 25-2	Yes
Smith S.	9/21/93	A Guide to BEA Data	No
Smith S.	9/24/93	Media Week, 24-7	No
Bates N.	9/19/93	Ad Era, 39-14	No
Davis R.	9/20/93	Statistics Made Simple	No
Law V.	9/25/93	Ad Era, 40-2	Yes
Davis R.	9/27/93	Ratings Rater, 34-7	No
Morris M.	9/26/93	Media Week, 25-4	No
Adams M.	9/27/93	Sampling Methods	No
Wick J.	9/27/93	Retail Trends 32-17	No
Law V.	9/28/93	Marketer's Guide	No
Bates N.	9/28/93	A DBASE Primer	No

a. Create a database file to store the data needed for this application and enter the set of historical data shown.
b. Create a report listing all of your training data sorted by employee name. Your report should have subtotals showing the total days of training for each employee and a grand total for training days.
c. Using the retrieval capabilities of your database software package, perform the following retrievals:
(1) Get a list of the names of employees who have completed spreadsheet training sessions.
(2) Retrieve the total number of days of training that Barnes, W. has completed.
(3) Retrieve the total number of days of DOS training that is pending (Completed = "N").

Review Quiz Answers

1. *8*	10. *14*	19. *22*	28. *10*
2. *8b*	11. *19b*	20. *18*	29. *7*
3. *8c*	12. *19a*	21. *13*	30. *24*
4. *9a*	13. *19c*	22. *12*	31. *23*
5. *9b*	14. *29*	23. *17*	32. *16*
6. *9c*	15. *26*	24. *6*	33. *5*
7. *9d*	16. *4*	25. *28*	34. *21*
8. *11*	17. *3*	26. *15*	35. *2*
9. *31*	18. *1*	27. *25*	36. *20*

Selected References

1. Alavi, Maryam; R. Ryan Nelson; and Ira Weiss. "Strategies for End User Computing: An Integrative Framework." *Journal of Management Information Systems*, Winter 1988.
2. Amoroso, Donald, and Paul Cheney. "Testing a Causal Model of End User Application Effectiveness." *Journal of Management Information Systems*, Summer 1991.
3. Barcomb, David. *Office Automation: A Survey of Tools and Technology*. 2nd ed. Boston, Mass.: Digital Press, 1988.
4. Christoff, Kurt. *Managing the Information Center*. Glenview, Ill.: Scott, Foresman/Little Brown, 1990.
5. Dennis, Alan; Joey George; Len Jessup; Jay Nunamaker; and Douglas Vogel. "Information Technology to Support Group Meetings." *MIS Quarterly*, December 1988.
6. Doll, William, and Gholamreza Torkzadeh. "A Congruence Construct for User Involvement." *Decision Science Journal*, Spring 1991.
7. "Electronic Document Management." *I/S Analyzer*, May-June 1989.
8. Grohowski, Ron; Chris McGoff; Doug Vogel; Ben Martz; and Jay Nunamaker. "Implementing Electronic Meeting Systems at IBM: Lessons Learned and Success Factors." *MIS Quarterly*, December 1990.
9. "Groupware: The Team Approach." *Supplement to PC Week*, October 14, 1991.
10. Hershey, Gerald, and Donna Kizzier. *Planning and Implementing End User Information Systems*. Cincinatti, Ohio: South Western, 1992.
11. Kling, Rob "Cooperation, Coordination and Control in Computer Supported Work." *Communications of the ACM*, December 1991.
12. Kyng, Morten. "Designing for Cooperation: Cooperating in Design." *Communications of the ACM*, December 1991.
13. Lasher, Donald; Blake Ives; and Sirkka Jarvenpaa. "USAA-IBM Partnership in Information Technology: Managing the Image Project." *MIS Quarterly*, December 1991.
14. Millman, Zeeva, and John Hartwick. "The Impact of Automated Office Systems on Middle Managers and Their Work." *MIS Quarterly*, December 1987.
15. Nelson, R. Ryan, ed. *End User Computing: Concepts, Issues, and Applications*. New York: John Wiley & Sons, 1988.
16. Nunamaker, Jay; Alan Dennis; Joseph Valacich; Douglas Vogel; and Joey George. "Electronic Meeting Systems to Support Group Work." *Communications of the ACM*, July 1991.
17. Olson, Margarethe, and Jon Turner. "Rethinking Office Automation." *Data Base*, Summer 1986.
18. Panko, Raymond. *End User Computing: Management, Applications, and Technology*. New York: John Wiley & Sons, 1988.
19. Perin, Constance. "Electronic Social Fields in Bureacracies." *Communications of the ACM*, December 1991.
20. Sassone, Peter, and A. Perry Schwartz. "Cost-Justifying OA." *Datamation*, February 15, 1986.
21. Sprague, Ralph, and Barbara McNurlin, eds. *Information Systems Management in Practice*. 2nd ed. Englewood Cliffs, N.J.: Prentice-Hall, 1989.

Transaction Processing and Business Information Systems

CHAPTER OUTLINE

CHAPTER 8

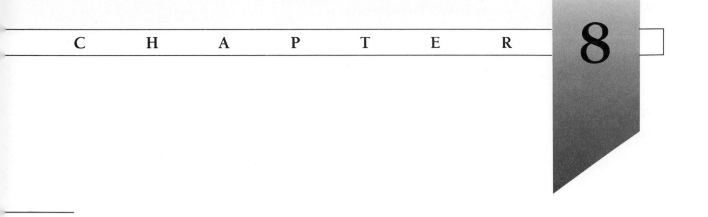

LEARNING OBJECTIVES

The purpose of this chapter is to give you an understanding of how information systems support the processing of business transactions and the information needs of the functional areas in business.

Section I of this chapter outlines the major functions of transaction processing systems. It also discusses major changes taking place in transaction processing, as well as the advantages and disadvantages of major types of transaction processing systems.

Section II discusses information systems in marketing, manufacturing, and human resource management, and the most widely used types of accounting information systems, as well as information systems needed for the effective financial management of a firm.

After reading and studying this chapter, you should be able to:

1. Identify the major activities of transaction processing systems, and give examples of how they support the operations of a business.
2. Identify the advantages and disadvantages of traditional data entry versus source data automation, and batch processing versus realtime processing.
3. Provide business examples that demonstrate the benefits and limitations of electronic data interchange and online transaction processing systems.
4. Give examples of how information systems support the business functions of accounting, finance, human resource management, marketing, and production and operations management.

SECTION I
Transaction Processing Systems

Transaction Processing

Transaction processing systems (TPS) are information systems that process data resulting from the occurrence of business transactions. Figure 8.1 illustrates this concept. *Transactions* are events that occur as part of doing business, such as sales, purchases, deposits, withdrawals, refunds, and payments. Think, for example, of the data generated whenever a business sells something to a customer on credit. Data about the customer, product, salesperson, store, and so on, must be captured and processed. This in turn causes additional transactions, such as credit checks, customer billing, inventory changes, and increases in accounts receivable balances, which generate even more data. Thus, transaction processing activities are needed to capture and process such data, or the operations of a business would grind to a halt. Therefore, transaction processing systems play a vital role in supporting the operations of an organization.

Strategic TPS

However, remember that transaction processing systems can play strategic roles in gaining competitive advantages for a business. For example, many firms have developed *interorganizational* transaction processing systems that tie them electronically to their customers or suppliers with telecommunications network links. *Electronic data interchange* (EDI) systems (which exchange electronic copies of transaction documents) are an important example that we will discuss in this chapter. Many companies have also found that *realtime* or *online* transaction processing (OLTP) systems, which capture and process transactions immediately, can help them provide superior service to customers. This capability *adds value* to their products and services, and thus gives them an important way to differentiate themselves from their competitors [11].

The Transaction Processing Cycle

Transaction processing systems capture and process data describing business transactions. Then they update organizational files and databases, and produce a variety of information products for internal and external use. You should think of these activities as a cycle of basic transaction processing activities. As Figure 8.2 illustrates, transaction processing systems go through a five-stage cycle of (1) data entry activities, (2) transaction processing activities, (3) file and database processing activities, (4) document and report generation, and (5) inquiry processing activities.

The Data Entry Process

The input activity in transaction processing systems involves a **data entry** process. In this process, data is captured or collected by recording, coding, and editing activities. Then data may be converted to a form that can be entered into a computer system. Data entry activities have always been a bottleneck in the use of computers for transaction processing. It has always been a problem getting data into computers accurately and quickly enough to match their awesome processing speeds. Thus, traditional *manual* methods of data entry that make heavy use of *data media* are being replaced by *direct automated* methods. These methods are more efficient and reliable and are known as *source data automation*. Let's take a look at both types of data entry. See Figure 8.3.

Traditional Data Entry

Traditional methods of data entry typically rely on the end users of an information system to capture data on **source documents** such as purchase orders, payroll time sheets, and sales order forms. These source documents are then usually accumulated into batches and transferred to data processing professionals specializing in data

FIGURE 8.1
The role of transaction processing systems in a business. Note how business transactions such as sales to customers and purchases from suppliers are generated by the physical operations systems of this manufacturing firm. Documents describing such transactions are subsequently processed by the firm's transaction processing systems, resulting in updated databases and a variety of information products.

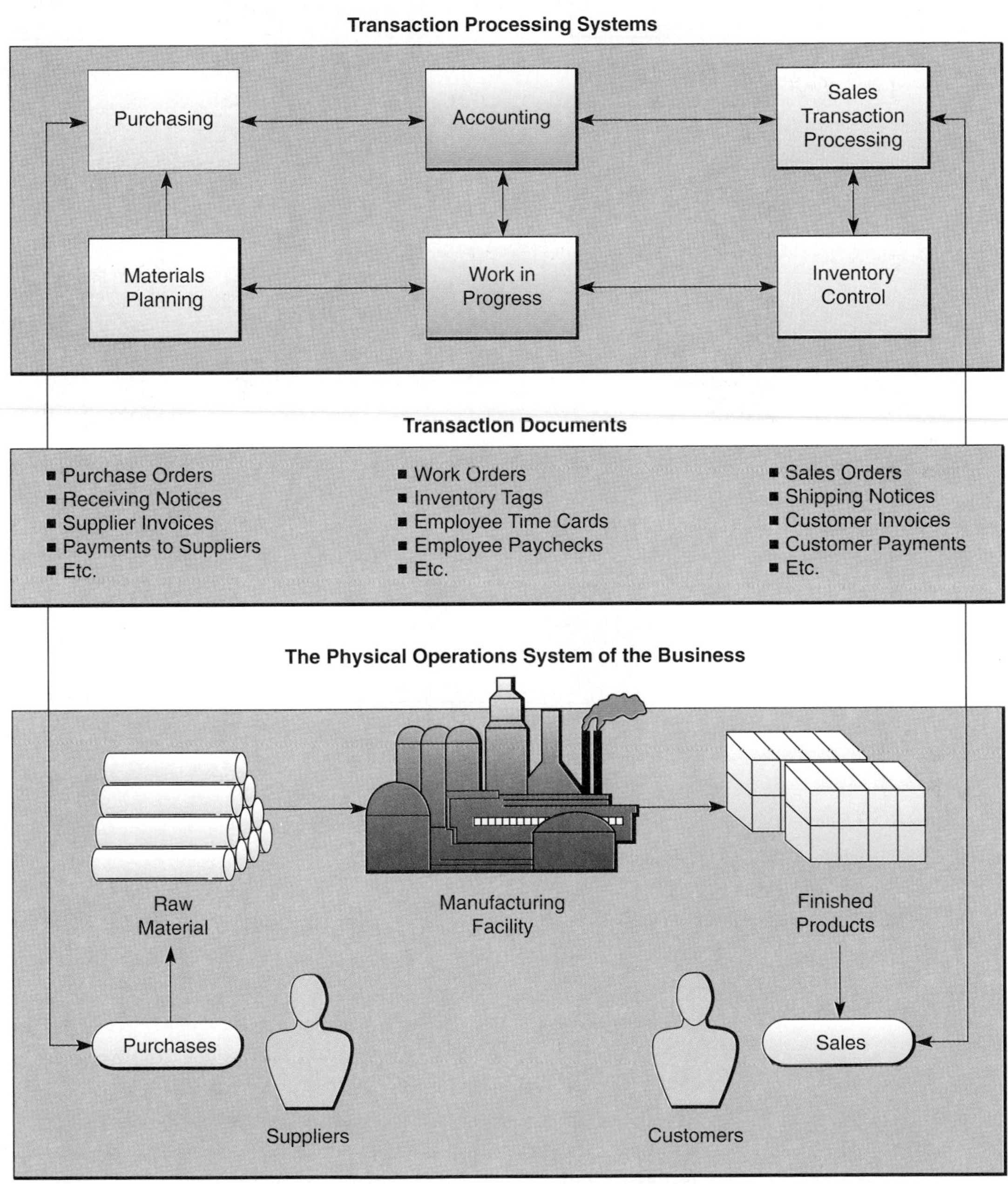

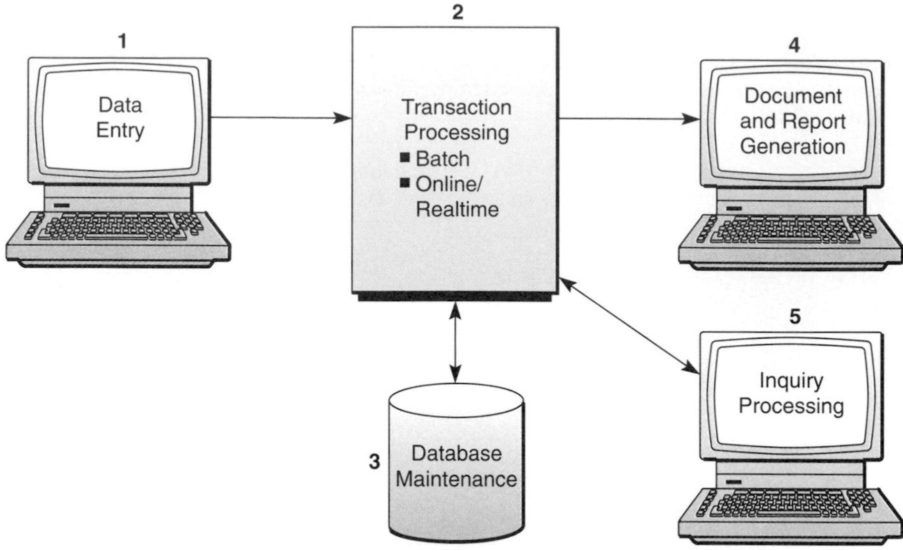

FIGURE 8.2
The transaction processing cycle. Note that transaction processing systems use a five-stage cycle of data entry, transaction processing, database maintenance, document and report generation, and inquiry processing activities.

Jon Feingersh/The Stock Market.

FIGURE 8.3
Traditional computer-based data entry involves keying data from source documents into a computer system.

entry. Periodically, the source documents are subjected to one of the following additional data entry activities:

- The data is converted into a machine-readable medium, such as magnetic tape or magnetic disks. Typically, this means using such devices as key-to-tape machines and key-to-disk systems. These media are then read by input devices that enter the data into a computer system.
- The data from source documents could alternatively be directly entered into a computer system, using a direct input device (such as the keyboard of a video terminal) without the use of machine-readable media.

Figure 8.4 illustrates this traditional data entry process, using sales transaction processing as an example. Note the use of sales forms as source documents, and their conversion to magnetic tape media. Note also the many data entry activities involved. It should not be surprising, then, to discover that there has been a major shift away from traditional data entry. First, it requires too many activities, people, and data media. Second, it results in high costs and increases the potential for errors.

FIGURE 8.4
A traditional data entry example: sales transaction processing. Note that source documents are (1) manually edited, (2) batched, (3) converted to another medium, (4) entered into a computer system, (5) edited again, (6) corrected where necessary and reentered, (7) sorted, and (8) accepted into the computer system.

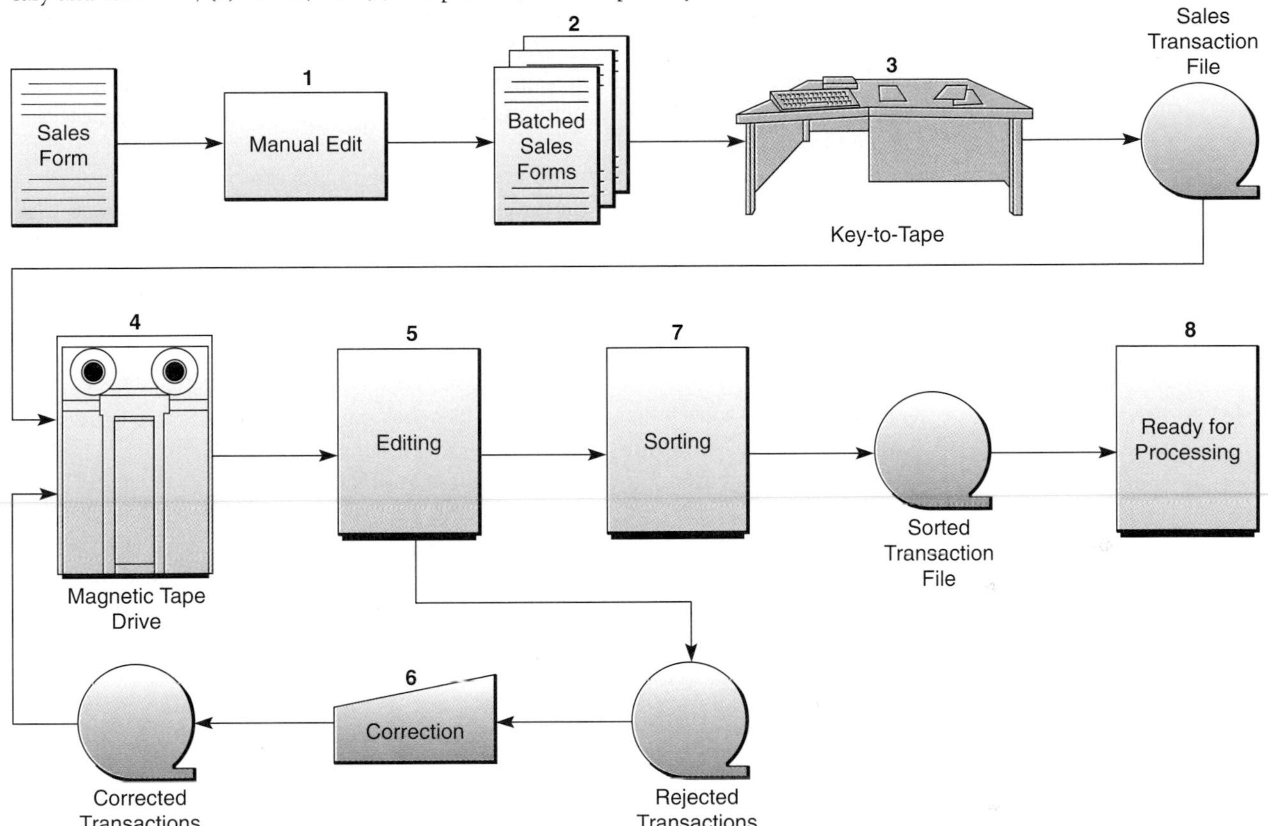

Therefore, the response of both users and the computer industry has been to move toward *source data automation.*

Source Data Automation

The use of automated methods of data entry is known as **source data automation**. Several methods have been developed to accomplish this automation, though very few completely automate the data entry process. They are all based on trying to reduce or eliminate many of the activities, people, and data media required by traditional data entry methods. Figure 8.5 is an example of source data automation. Notice that this sales transaction processing system:

- Captures data *as early as possible* after a transaction or other event occurs by using POS terminals.
- Captures transaction data *as close as possible* to the source that generates the data. Salespersons at POS terminals capture and edit data right on the sales floor.
- Captures data by using *machine-readable media* initially (bar-coded tags and mag stripe credit cards), instead of preparing written source documents.
- Captures data that rarely changes by *prerecording* it on machine-readable media, or by storing it in the computer system.

- Captures data directly *without the use of data media* by optical scanning of bar code packaging.

The example in Figure 8.5 reveals some of the many types of devices used in source data automation. This includes *transaction terminals*, such as POS terminals and automated teller machines (ATMs), and *optical character recognition* (OCR) devices, such as optical scanning wands and grocery checkout scanners. Many other input/output devices and telecommunications technologies discussed in Chapters 4 and 6 also play a role in source data automation. These include the use of PCs with cash drawers as intelligent POS terminals, portable digital radio terminals and pen-based tablet PCs for remote data entry, or touch screens and voice recognition systems for data entry. Organizations may also use local area networks of microcomputer workstations to accomplish data entry activities at regional centers, and then upload the data to corporate mainframes for further processing. Other organizations depend on LANs of networked PCs to accomplish their transaction processing activities [11].

Electronic Data Interchange

The ultimate in source data automation in many transaction processing systems is called **electronic data interchange**, or EDI. This involves the electronic transmission of business transaction data over telecommunications links between the computers of *trading partners* (organizations and their customers and suppliers). Data representing a variety of business *transaction documents* (such as purchase orders, invoices, requests for quotations, and shipping notices) are electronically transmitted using standard document message formats. Thus, EDI is an example of the almost complete automation of the data entry process.

Formatted transaction data is transmitted over telecommunications links directly between computers, without paper documents or human intervention. Besides direct network links between the computers of trading partners, third-party services are widely used. Value-added telecommunications carriers like GE Information Services, IBM, Control Data, and McDonnell Douglas offer EDI services, including an *electronic mailbox* for EDI documents [4]. If necessary, EDI software is used to convert a company's own document formats into standardized EDI formats as specified by various industry and international protocols.

FIGURE 8.5
An automated data entry example: sales transaction processing. Note how few steps are needed compared to a traditional data entry.

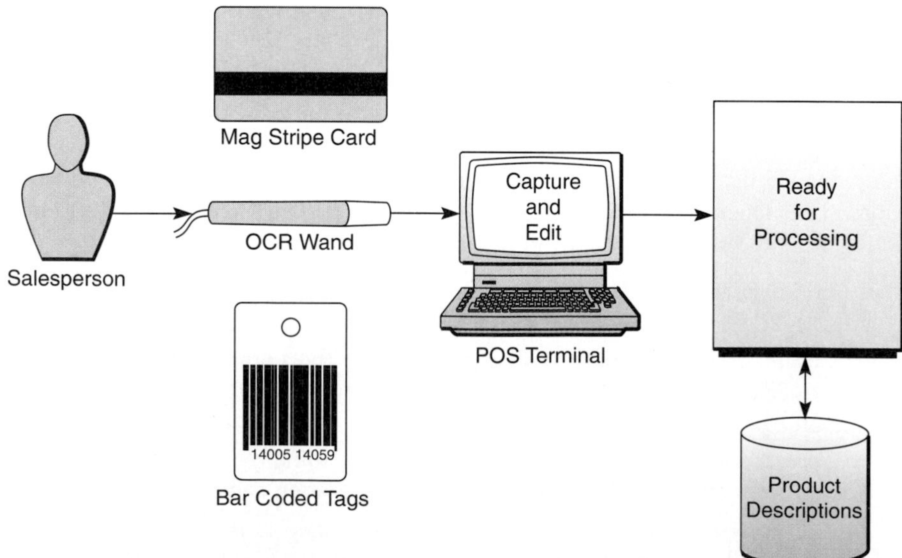

Figure 8.6 is an example of EDI in action. In this example, Motorola Codex has EDI links with its supplier, Texas Instruments, for the exchange of a variety of electronic transaction documents. In addition, it "closes the loop" by using *electronic funds transfer* (EFT) links to its banks so it can make electronic payments to its supplier [16].

Benefits of EDI

EDI eliminates the printing, mailing, checking, and handling by employees of numerous multiple-copy forms of business documents. Also, since standard document formats are used, the delays caused by mail or telephone communication between businesses to verify what a document means are drastically reduced. Some of the benefits of EDI that result are reductions in paper, postage, and labor costs; faster flow of transactions; reductions in errors; increases in productivity; support of just-in-time (JIT) inventory policies; reductions in inventory levels; and better customer service. For example, decreases of 25 to 50 percent in the total time it takes to receive, process, package, and ship customer orders are reported. Annual savings of $300 million in the grocery industry and $12 billion in the textile industry are expected. RCA expects the cost of processing a purchase order to drop from $50 to $4, and EDI is estimated to save $200 per automobile in the auto industry [4].

However, EDI is more than a way to increase efficiency, cut costs, and provide better service. In many industries, it has become an absolute business requirement. EDI is now a *strategic application* of information systems in many industries, where the message is "link up or lose out." Or, as IBM vice president Edward Lucente says, "Doing business without EDI will soon be like trying to do business without a

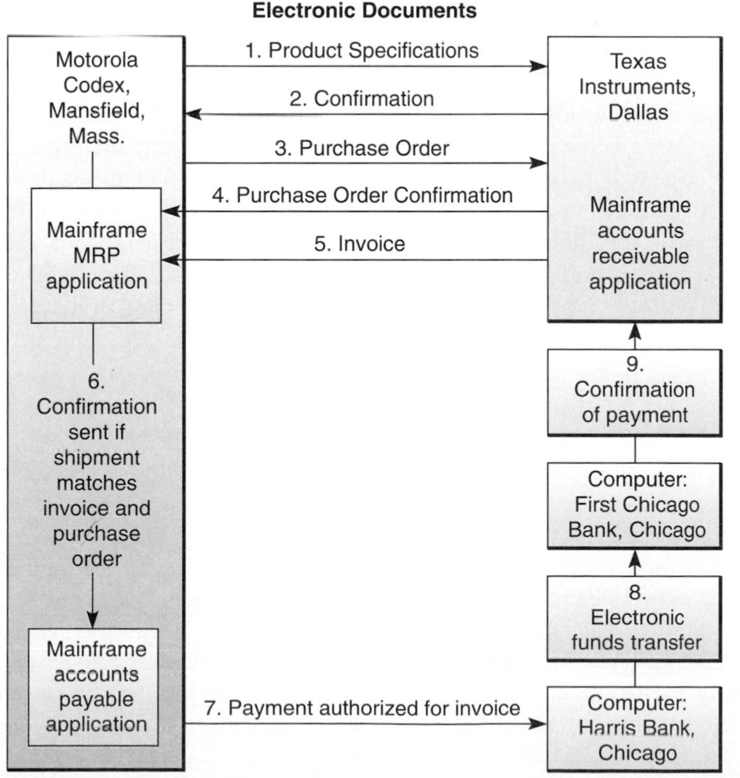

Source: Adapted from Clinton Wilder, "Codex Goes Paperless with EDI," *Computerworld*, January 13, 1992, p. 6.

FIGURE 8.6
An example of EDI. Motorola Codex uses EDI links to its supplier, Texas Instruments, for the exchange of business documents. Codex also makes electronic funds transfers to its banks to pay its suppliers.

telephone. No EDI, no business." General Motors proved that point when it made EDI a requirement for thousands of its suppliers, as did the U.S. Department of Defense. Experts predict that, by 1995, one third of all business documents will involve EDI. Thus, EDI promises to revolutionize data entry in many transaction processing systems while promoting strategic relationships between industry trading partners [4, 16].

Batch Processing

Transaction processing systems process data in two basic ways: (1) **batch processing**, where transactions data is accumulated over a period of time and processed periodically, and (2) **realtime processing** (also called *online processing*), where data is processed immediately after a transaction occurs. Transaction processing systems still make heavy use of batch processing. However, the use of realtime processing is growing, and it is expected to eventually become the primary form of transaction processing.

Batch Processing Activities

In **batch processing**, transactions data are accumulated over a period of time and processed periodically. Batch processing usually involves:

- Gathering *source documents* originated by business transactions, such as sales orders and invoices, into groups called *batches*.
- Recording transaction data on some type of input medium, such as magnetic disks or magnetic tape.
- Sorting the transactions in a *transaction file* in the same sequence as the records in a sequential *master file*.
- Processing transaction data and creating an updated master file and a variety of *documents* (such as customer invoices and paychecks) and reports.
- Capturing and storing batches of transaction data at remote sites, and then transmitting it periodically to a central computer for processing. This is known as *remote job entry*, or RJE.

In batch processing, not only are the transaction data for a particular application accumulated into batches, but a number of different transaction processing jobs are run (processed) periodically (daily, weekly, monthly). The rationale for batch processing is that the grouping of data and the periodic processing of jobs uses computer system resources more efficiently, compared to allowing data and jobs to be processed in an unorganized, random manner. Of course, this efficiency, economy, and control are accomplished by sacrificing the immediate processing of data for end users.

EXAMPLE

In a typical example of batch processing, the banking industry usually accumulates all checks deposited during the day into batches for processing each evening. Thus, customer bank balances are updated on a daily basis and many management reports are produced daily. Figure 8.7 illustrates a batch processing system where transaction data in the form of batches of deposited checks are captured each day by MICR reader/sorters, which read the data recorded in magnetic ink on the bottom of each check. This transaction data is then processed to update customer and other databases and produce a variety of customer documents and management reports.

FIGURE 8.7
A batch processing system example. Batches of deposited checks are accumulated and processed daily in the banking industry.

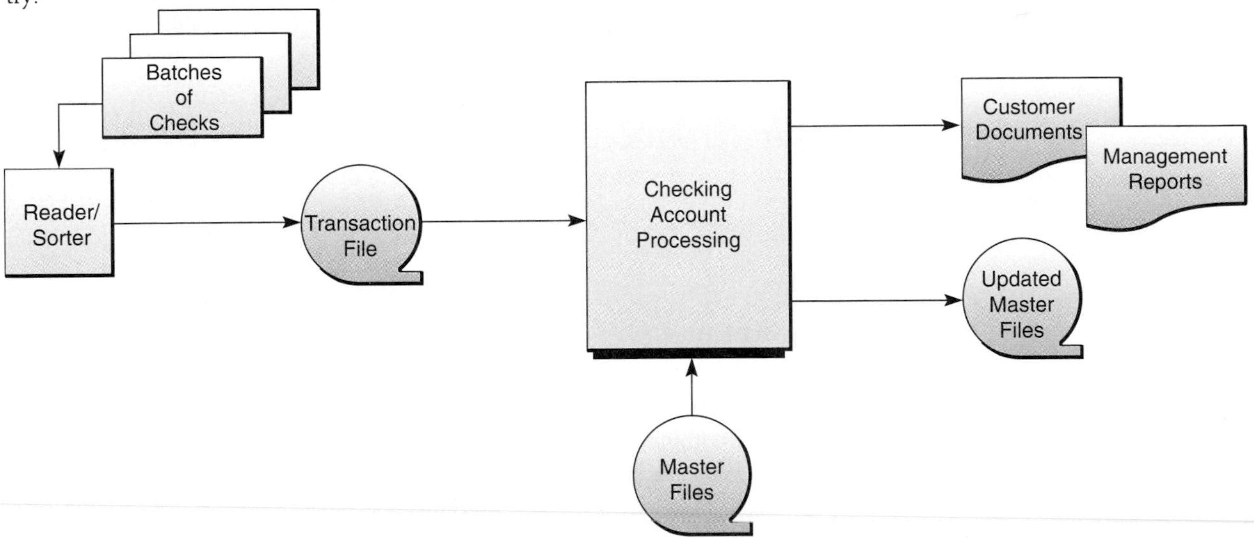

Advantages and Disadvantages

Batch processing is an economical method when large volumes of transactions data must be processed. It is ideally suited for many applications where it is not necessary to update databases as transactions occur, and where documents and reports are required only at scheduled intervals. For example, customer statements may be prepared on a monthly basis, whereas payroll processing might be done on a weekly basis.

However, batch processing has some real disadvantages. Master files are frequently out-of-date between scheduled processing, as are the periodic scheduled reports that are produced. Also, immediate updated responses to inquiries cannot be made. For these reasons, more and more computer applications use realtime processing systems. However, batch processing systems are still widely used, and some of their disadvantages are overcome by using realtime processing for some transaction processing functions, such as data entry or inquiry processing.

Realtime Processing

In transaction processing systems, a **realtime processing** capability allows transaction data to be processed immediately after they are generated and can provide immediate output to end users. Full-fledged realtime systems for transaction processing are popularly called **online transaction processing** (OLTP) systems. Transaction data are processed as soon as they are originated or recorded, without waiting to accumulate batches of data. Data are fed directly into the computer system from online terminals, without being sorted, and they are always stored online in direct access files. Files and databases are always up-to-date since they are updated whenever data are originated, regardless of their frequency. Responses to end users' inquiries are immediate, since information stored on direct access devices can be retrieved almost instantaneously. Realtime processing depends on wide area and local area networks to provide telecommunications links between transaction terminals, workstations, and other computers. A summary of the important capabilities differentiating batch processing and realtime processing is shown in Figure 8.8.

FIGURE 8.8
Batch versus realtime processing. Note the major differences.

Characteristic	Batch Processing	Realtime Processing
Processing of transactions	Transaction data is recorded, accumulated into batches, sorted, and processed periodically	Transaction data is processed as generated
File update	When batch is processed	When transaction is processed
Response time/turnaround time	Several hours or days after batches are submitted for processing	A few seconds after each transaction is captured

EXAMPLE

An example of a realtime sales transaction processing system is shown in Figure 8.9. Note how POS terminals are connected by telecommunications links to a computer for immediate entry of sales data and control responses (such as customer credit verification). The customer, product, and sales databases are stored on online direct access devices (typically magnetic disk drives) and can be updated immediately to reflect sales transactions. Finally, an inquiry processing capability and telecommunication links to employee workstations allow them to make inquiries and display responses concerning customers, sales activity, inventory status, and so on.

Fault Tolerant Processing

Many airlines, banks, telephone companies, and other organizations depend on **fault tolerant** computer systems to protect themselves against failure of their strategic online transaction processing applications. For example, airline reservation systems and bank electronic funds transfer systems use fault tolerant computers that provide a nonstop realtime transaction processing capability that allows them to continue operating even if parts of the system fail. As we mentioned in Chapter 2, fault tolerant computers may use a multiprocessor design of several coupled CPUs or a parallel processor design of many networked microprocessors to provide a built-in backup capability in case one or more processors fail. In addition, fault tolerant computers have redundant memory units, disk drives, and other devices, as well as duplicate copies of software, including, in some cases, redundant operating systems [13]. See Figure 8.10.

Advantages and Disadvantages

Realtime processing provides immediate updating of files and immediate responses to user inquiries. Realtime processing is particularly important for applications where a high frequency of changes must be made to a file during a short time to keep it updated. Only the specific records affected by transactions or inquiries need to be processed, and several files can be processed or updated concurrently.

Realtime processing has its disadvantages. Because of the online, direct access nature of realtime processing, special precautions must be taken to protect the contents of databases. Thus, many realtime systems use magnetic tape files as *control logs* (to record all transactions made) or as *backup files* (by periodically making a magnetic tape copy of a file). Also, more controls have to be built into the software and processing procedures to protect against unauthorized access or the accidental destruction of data. In addition, organizations with critical OLTP applications have to pay a high cost premium for the security of fault tolerant computer systems. Thus,

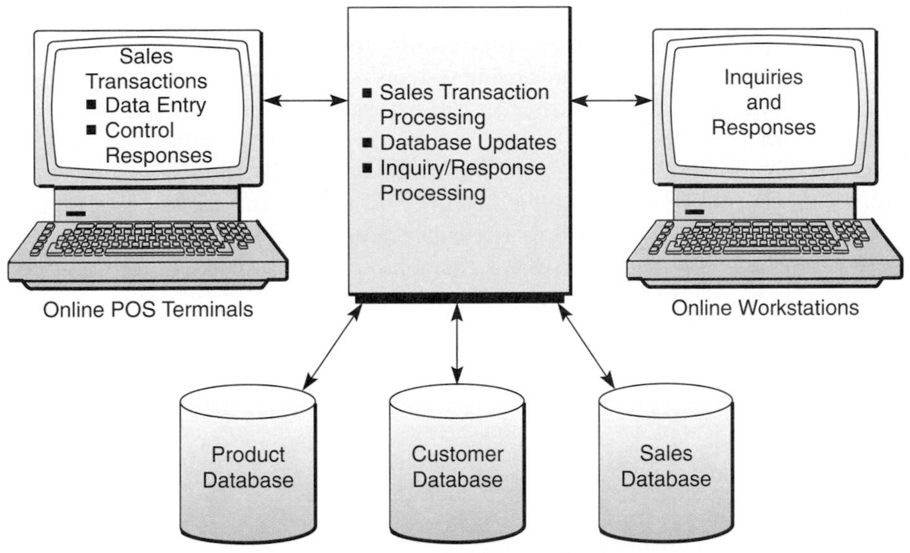

FIGURE 8.9
Example of a realtime sales processing system. Note that sales transaction processing, inquiries and responses, and database updates are accomplished immediately using online devices.

FIGURE 8.10
The securities industry depends on fault tolerant transaction processing to keep their securities trading systems running around the clock.

the many advantages of realtime processing must be balanced with the extra costs and security precautions that are necessary. However, many computer-using firms are willing to pay this price for the speed, efficiency, and superior service that realtime processing provides.

Database Maintenance

Database maintenance is a major activity of transaction processing systems. An organization's databases must be maintained by its transaction processing systems so that they are always correct and up to date. Therefore, transaction processing systems update the corporate databases of an organization to reflect changes resulting from day-to-day business transactions. For example, credit sales made to customers will cause customer account balances to be increased and the amount of inventory on hand to be decreased. Database maintenance ensures that these and other changes are reflected in the data records stored in the company's databases.

In addition, transaction processing systems process data resulting from miscellaneous adjustments to the records in a file or database. For example, name and address changes may have to be made to customer records, and tax withholding changes may have to be made to employee payroll records. Thus, one of the major functions of transaction processing systems is to update and make changes to an organization's corporate databases. These databases then provide the data resources that can be processed and used by information reporting systems, decision support systems, and executive information systems.

Document and Report Generation

The final stage in the transaction processing cycle is the generation of information products such as documents and reports. Figure 8.11 illustrates several examples. Documents produced by transaction processing systems are called **transaction documents**.

There are several major types of such documents:

- **Action documents.** These are documents that initiate actions or transactions on the part of their recipient. For example, a purchase order authorizes a purchase from a supplier, and a paycheck authorizes a bank to pay an employee.
- **Information documents.** These documents relate, confirm, or prove to their recipients that transactions have occurred. Examples are sales receipts, sales order confirmations, customer invoices and statements, and credit rejection notices. Information documents can be used as control documents, since they document the fact that a transaction has occurred.
- **Turnaround documents.** Some types of transaction documents are designed to be read by magnetic or optical scanning equipment. Forms produced in this manner are known as turnaround documents because they are designed to be returned to the sender. For example, many computer-printed invoices consist of a turnaround portion, which is returned by a customer along with his or her payment. The turnaround document can then be automatically processed by optical scanning devices. Thus, turnaround documents combine the functions of an action document (the turnaround portion) and an information document (the receipt portion).

Transaction processing systems also produce several types of reports and displays designed to document and monitor the results of business transactions occurring or processed during a specific time period. They are not specifically tailored for management use, though they may be used by managers. Such reports can provide an audit trail for transaction control purposes. Examples are:

- **Control listings.** These are detailed reports that describe each transaction occurring during a period. They are also called *transaction logs*. For example, a listing known as a payroll register lists every paycheck printed on a specified payday by a payroll system.
- **Edit reports.** These are reports that describe errors detected during processing. For example, invalid account numbers, missing data, and incorrect control totals would be presented in edit reports.

FIGURE 8.11
Examples of information products produced by transaction processing systems. Transaction documents such as customer statements must be prepared and mailed to customers on a monthly basis. The cash requirements register is a control listing that lists the checks that must be prepared in payment of amounts owed to vendors.

LANG
CORPORATION

STATEMENT OF CUSTOMER ACCOUNT

CUSTOMER NO.
554386

HITTON CORPORATION
138 MARSHALL DR.
PO BOX 851
LONG PORT, CA 94134

DATE
9/30/--

DATE			INVOICE NUMBER	REFERENCE NUMBER	DESCRIPTION	AMOUNT
MO	DY	YR				
					PRIOR BALANCE	$7,565.46
09	08	--	185163		INVOICE	1,685.91
09	10	--	075126		PAYMENT	1,865.00CR
09	15	--		091531	LC ADJUSTMENT	13.00CR
09	30	--			LATE CHARGES	8.00

CURRENT AMOUNT	30 DAYS	60 DAYS & OVER	BALANCE DUE
$1,693.91	$696.46		$2,390.37

K KRAUSZ MANUFACTURING COMPANY
ACCOUNTS PAYABLE

CASH REQUIREMENTS REGISTER

DATE APR 12 19

VENDOR	VENDOR NUMBER	DUE DATE	INVOICE AMOUNT	DISCOUNT	CHECK AMOUNT
SOLVAY GEN SUP	1016	4/16	$ 773.30	$ 15.47	$ 757.83
ROCHESTER PR CO	1021	4/16	1,620.18	32.40	1,587.78
CALABRIA CONT	1049	4/16	143.65	2.87	140.78
ONONDAGA STL CO	1077	4/16	5,982.82	119.66	5,863.16
BLACK & NICHOLS	1103	4/16	14.25	.71	13.54
AUSTERHOLZ INC	1240	4/16	624.77	12.50	612.27
AUSTERHOLZ INC	1240	4/16	1,833.19	36.66	1,796.53
CHRISTIE & CO	1366	4/16	745.54		754.54
WILSON & WILSON	2231	4/16	2,936.12	58.72	2,877.40
CLAR. HIGGINS	2590	4/16	1,000.00		1,000.00
HONOUR BROS	3101	4/16	97.36	1.95	95.41
BASTIANI & SON	3112	4/16	3,580.85	71.62	3,509.23
DRJ WIRE CO	3164	4/16	256.90	5.14	251.76
HASTING-WHITE	3258	4/16	1,144.42	22.89	1,121.53
DARONO ART MET	3427	4/16	32.75	.66	32.09
DARONO ART MET	3427	4/16	127.52	2.55	124.97
DARONO ART MET	3427	4/16	96.60	1.93	94.67

- **Accounting statements.** These are reports that legally document the financial performance or status of a business. Examples are general ledger summaries, statements of cash flow, balance sheets, and income statements.

Inquiry Processing

Transaction processing and information reporting systems frequently support the realtime interrogation of online files and databases by end users. As we have previously mentioned, this **inquiry processing** capability can be provided by either batch or realtime processing. End users at workstations in wide area and local area networks can use database management query languages to make inquiries and receive responses concerning the results of transaction activity. Typically, responses are displayed in a variety of prespecified formats or *screens*. For example, employees can check on the status of a sales order, the balance in an account, or the amount of stock in inventory and receive immediate responses at their workstations. Or managers can receive responses and reports on demand concerning the performance of their employees, work groups, or departments. See Figure 8.12.

FIGURE 8.12
A multiple-window customer order status display provided by a transaction processing system.

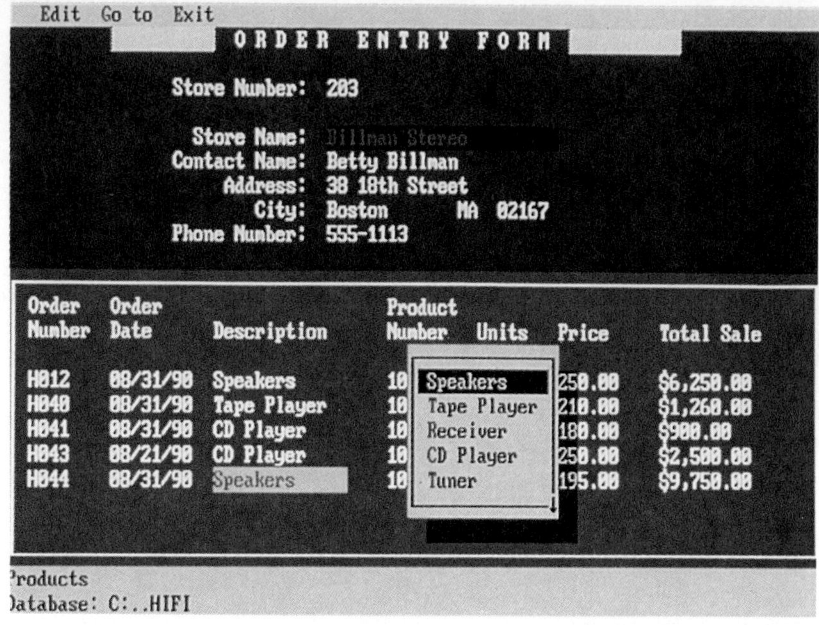

Courtesy Micorim Inc.

REAL WORLD CASE

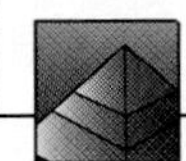

New York State Department of Civil Service: Online Transaction Processing

The Employee Benefits Division of the New York State Department of Civil Service can now handle online claim transactions from more than 1.2 million employees. Implemented in 1990, the solution chosen by the benefits division includes an employee management system based on financial accounting software from PeopleSoft, Inc., and a mainframe-to-PC client/server computing platform. The new system generates an estimated $1 million savings annually by reducing the maintenance and administrative costs associated with maintaining the previous paper-based system. Created in the 1970s, the older terminal-based system was tied to an IBM mainframe.

"In government, you only get a chance to make significant changes once in a while. So when you get the chance, you make as big a jump as you can without jumping off the cliff," said Henry J. Nahal, director of telecommunications and information management at the department.

Over 150 PCs in Albany, the state capital, are linked in a local area network that is connected to an IBM mainframe in Omaha, Nebraska, as are over 275 PCs located in various state agencies throughout the state. The mainframe belongs to First Data Corporation, which provides time-sharing computing services to the system. The mainframe uses the DB2 database management system and accounting software to help benefits administrators at their PCs access an employee benefits database.

The costs of accessing the mainframe are reduced by having users first process the data on their PCs using end user versions of the PeopleSoft software assisted by Microsoft Windows. "Because a benefits administrator is typically working online with the employee, we can make sure all the data required is entered correctly the first time. These claims usually require 20 to 30 pieces of data spanning four or five screens," Nahal said. "We now have an ad hoc query capability we never had before, and the data is more reliable because it was processed online. It used to take up to six weeks to make any kind of change to the day. We wanted an electronic paperless system to process claims," he said.

The new system allows benefits administrators to process employee claims online, including verifying their eligibility for various state benefits. This is particularly important because each labor union has a different contract with the state providing different levels of coverage and deductibles. Since deploying the system, Hahal has expanded it by linking pharmacies directly with the benefits office in Albany. His long-term goal is to bring doctors' offices and hospitals online as well.

Like most IS professionals, Nahal has struggled with the issues created by running Windows on PCs and the performance issues created by splitting the processing applications across various computers on a network. Nahal said he has two people dedicated to maintaining PC applications in the Albany office. Also, to reduce the costs associated with maintaining PCs at remote sites, Nahal has mandated that those PCs be restricted to running only PeopleSoft client software for now.

"The most important thing you have to remember [is] that client/server computing is a cultural change. You can train people all you want, but if somebody has been doing a job one way for a lot of time, it takes time for them to master the new system. You have to set up help desks, make people PC-literate and realize you're essentially running a customer service application," Nahal said.

CASE STUDY QUESTIONS

1. Is the employee benefits system an example of source data automation? Explain.
2. What stages of the transaction processing cycle can you recognize in the case? Explain.
3. What are the benefits and limitations of this transaction processing system?

Source: Adapted from Michael Vizard, "N.Y. Saves Big with Client/Server," *Computerworld*, March 8, 1993, pp. 87, 89. Used with permission.

SECTION II
Business Information Systems

IS in Business

There are as many ways to use information systems in business as there are business activities to be performed, business problems to be solved, and business opportunities to be pursued. As a prospective business end user, you should have a general understanding of the major ways information systems are used to support each of the **functions of business**. We will use the term **business information systems** to describe a variety of types of information systems (transaction processing, information reporting, decision support, etc.) that support a business function such as accounting, finance, marketing, or human resource management. Thus, applications of information systems in the functional areas of business are called *accounting information systems, marketing information systems, human resource information systems*, and so on.

As a business end user, you should also have a *specific* understanding of how information systems affect a particular business function (e.g., marketing) or a particular industry (e.g., banking) that is directly related to your career objectives. For example, someone whose career objective is a marketing position in banking should have a basic understanding of how information systems are used in banking and how they support the marketing activities of banks and other firms.

Cross-Functional Information Systems

Figure 8.13 illustrates how information systems can be grouped into business function categories. Information systems in this section will be analyzed according to the business function they support to give you an appreciation of the variety of business information systems that both small and large business firms may use. However, as we emphasized in Chapter 6, information systems in the real world are typically integrated combinations of functional information systems. There is a strong emphasis in many organizations to develop such *composite* or **cross-functional information systems**. These organizations view cross-functional information systems as a strategic way to share information resources and improve the efficiency and effectiveness of a business, thus helping it attain its strategic objectives.

Marketing Information Systems

The business function of **marketing** is concerned with the planning, promotion, and sale of existing products in existing markets, and the development of new products and new markets to better serve present and potential customers. Thus, marketing performs a vital function in the operation of a business enterprise. Business firms have increasingly turned to computers to help them perform vital marketing functions in the face of the rapid changes of today's environment. Computers have been a catalyst in the development of **marketing information systems**, which integrate the information flows required by many marketing activities.

Figure 8.14 illustrates how marketing information systems provide information for planning, control, and transaction processing in the marketing function. Strategic, tactical, and operational information systems assist marketing managers in product planning, pricing decisions, advertising and sales promotion strategies and expenditures, forecasting market potential for new and present products, and determining channels of distribution. Control reporting systems support the efforts of marketing managers to control the efficiency and effectiveness of the selling and distribution of products and services. Analytical reports provide information on a

FIGURE 8.13
Examples of business information systems. Note how they support the major functional areas of business.

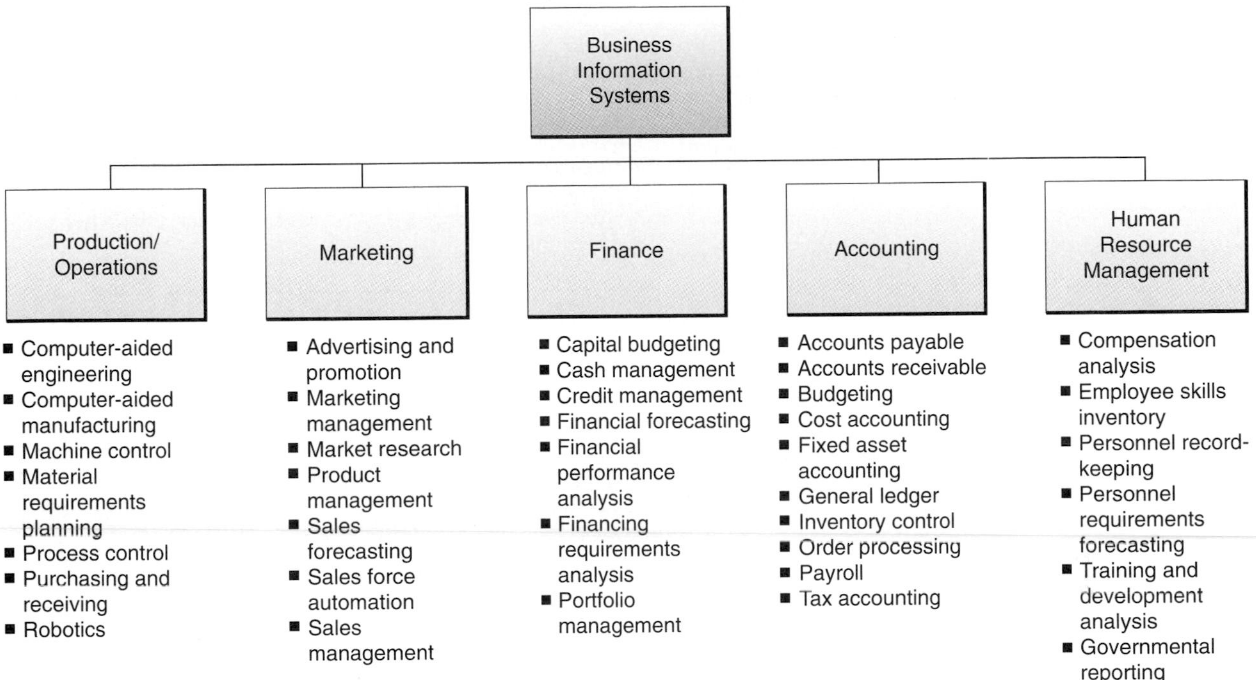

firm's actual performance versus planned marketing objectives. Figure 8.15 summarizes several important ways that computer-based information systems could be used to support the marketing function.

Sales Management

Sales managers must plan, monitor, and support the performance of the salespeople in their organizations. So in most firms, computer-based systems produce sales analysis reports (such as Figure 8.16), which analyze sales by product, product line, customer, type of customer, salesperson, and sales territory. Such reports help marketing managers monitor the sales performance of products and salespeople and help them develop sales support programs to improve sales results.

Sales Force Automation

However, sales analysis is only one aspect of the use of computers for sales management and support. Increasingly, computer-based information systems are providing the basis for **sales force automation**. In many companies, the sales force is being outfitted with laptop computers, hand-held PCs, or even pen-based tablet computers. This not only increases the personal productivity of salespeople, but dramatically speeds up the capture and analysis of sales data from the field to marketing managers at company headquarters. In return, it allows marketing and sales management to improve the support they provide to their salespeople. Therefore, many companies are viewing sales force automation as a way to gain a strategic advantage in sales productivity and marketing responsiveness.

For example, salespeople use their PCs to record sales data as they make their calls on customers and prospects during the day. Then each night sales reps in the field can connect their computers by modem and telephone links to the mainframe computer at company headquarters and upload information on sales orders, sales calls, and other sales statistics, as well as send electronic mail messages and other

FIGURE 8.14
Marketing information systems provide information for the planning and control of major components of the marketing function.

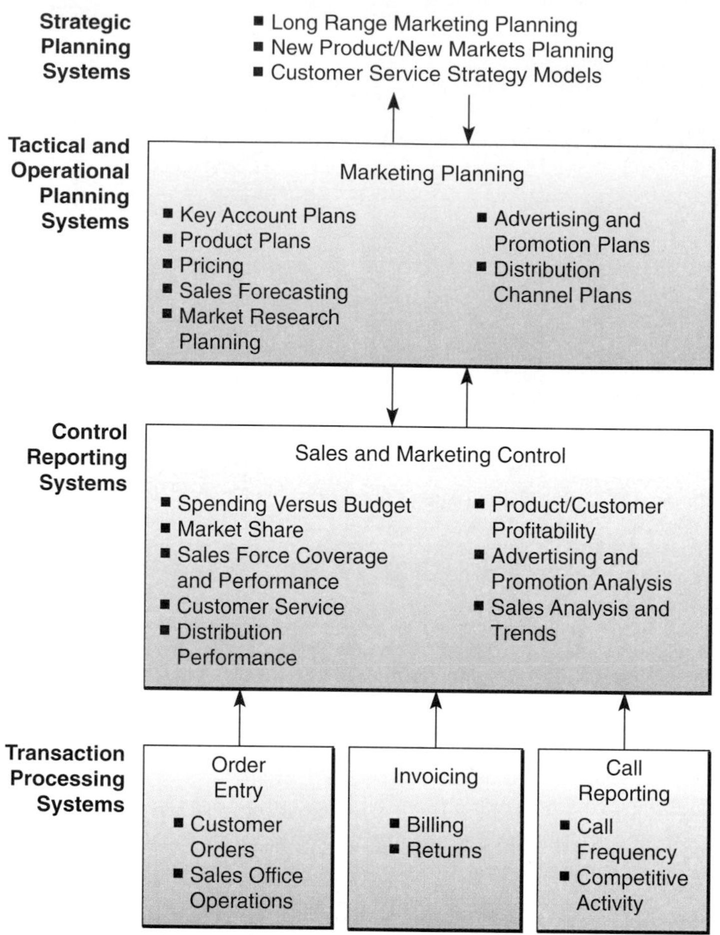

Source: Adapted from Andersen Consulting, *Foundations of Business Systems,* 2nd ed. (Fort Worth, Tex: Dryden Press, 1992) p. 124.

FIGURE 8.15
Examples of important computer-based information systems in marketing.

Sales Management
Plan, monitor, and support the performance of salespeople and sales of products and services.

Sales Force Automation
Automate the recording and reporting of sales activity by salespeople and the communications and sales support from sales management.

Product Management
Plan, monitor, and support the performance of products, product lines, and brands.

Advertising and Promotion
Help select media and promotional methods and control and evaluate advertising and promotion results.

Sales Forecasting
Produce short- and long-range sales forecasts.

Market Research
Collect and analyze internal and external data on market variables, developments, and trends.

Marketing Management
Develop marketing strategies and plans based on corporate goals and market research and sales activity data, and monitor and support marketing activities.

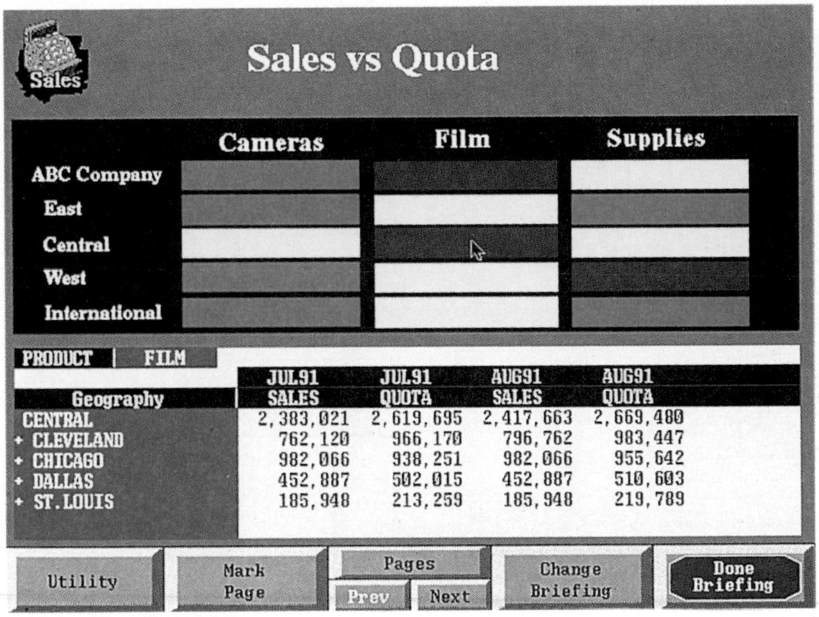

Sales vs Quota

	Cameras	Film	Supplies
ABC Company			
East			
Central			
West			
International			

PRODUCT | FILM

Geography	JUL91 SALES	JUL91 QUOTA	AUG91 SALES	AUG91 QUOTA
CENTRAL	2,383,021	2,619,695	2,417,663	2,669,480
+ CLEVELAND	762,120	966,170	796,762	983,447
+ CHICAGO	982,066	938,251	982,066	955,642
+ DALLAS	452,887	502,015	452,887	510,603
+ ST.LOUIS	185,948	213,259	185,948	219,789

Utility | Mark Page | Pages Prev Next | Change Briefing | Done Briefing

Courtesy of Information Resources, Inc.

FIGURE 8.16
An example of a sales analysis display produced by an executive information system.

queries. In return, the host computer may download product availability data, *prospect lists* of information on good sales prospects, E-mail messages, and other sales support information. Figure 8.17 illustrates IBM's sales force automation system.

Product Management

Product managers need information to plan and control the performances of specific products, product lines, and brands. Computers can help provide price, revenue, cost, and growth information for existing products and new product development. Providing information and analysis for pricing decisions is a major function of this system. Information is also needed on the manufacturing and distribution resources proposed products will require. Computer-based models may be used to evaluate the performances of current products and the prospects for success of proposed products.

Advertising and Promotion

Marketing managers need information to help them achieve sales objectives at the lowest possible costs for advertising and promotion. Computers use market research information and promotion models to help (1) select media and promotional methods, (2) allocate financial resources, and (3) control and evaluate results of various advertising and promotion campaigns. For example, a marketing analyst may develop an electronic spreadsheet model to analyze the sales response of advertising placed in a variety of media.

Sales Forecasting

The basic functions of sales forecasting can be grouped into the two categories of short-range forecasting and long-range forecasting. Short-range forecasting deals with forecasts of sales for periods up to one year, whereas long-range forecasting is concerned with sales forecasts for a year or more into the future. Marketing managers use market research data, historical sales data, promotion plans, and statistical forecasting models to generate short-range and long-range sales forecasts.

FIGURE 8.17
IBM's sales force automation system. Note the complete cycle of sales and marketing support activities.

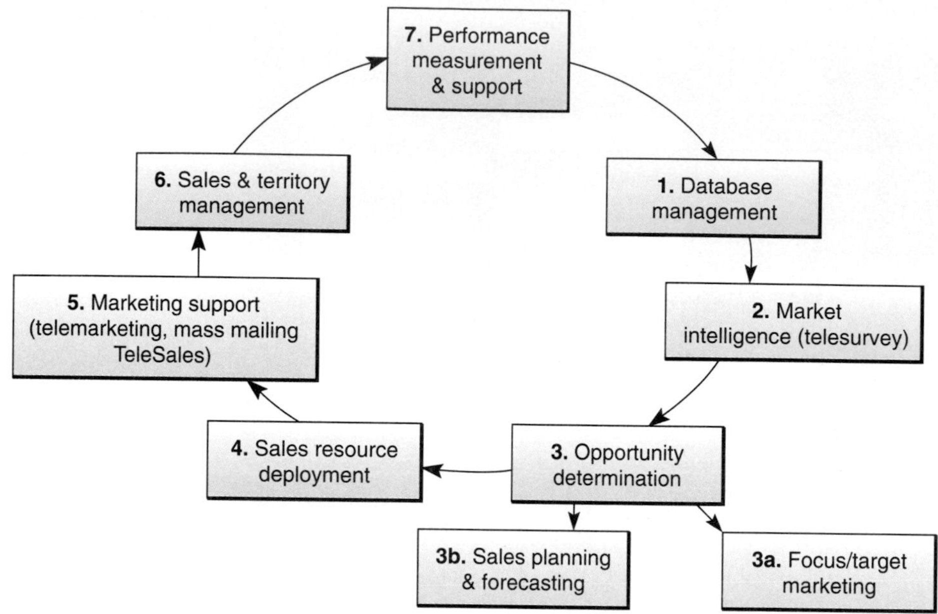

Source: Adapted from Ned Snell, "Software to Tame the Sales Force," *Datamation*, June 1, 1991, p. 67.

Market Research

The market research information system provides marketing intelligence to help managers make more effective marketing decisions. It also provides marketing managers with information to help them plan and control the market research projects of the firm. Computers help the market research activity collect, analyze, and maintain an enormous amount of information on a wide variety of market variables that are subject to continual change. This includes information on customers, prospects, consumers, and competitors. Market, economic, and demographic trends are also analyzed. Data can be purchased in computer-readable form from external sources, or computers can help gather data through telemarketing and computer-aided telephone interviewing techniques. Finally, statistical analysis software packages help managers analyze market research data and spot important marketing trends.

Marketing Management

Marketing managers use computer-based information systems to develop short- and long-range plans outlining product sales, profit, and growth objectives. They also provide feedback and analysis concerning performance-versus-plan for each area of marketing. Computer-based marketing models in decision support systems and expert systems are also being used to investigate the effects of alternative marketing plans. In addition, the fast capture of sales and marketing data by sales force automation systems helps marketing management respond faster to market shifts and sales performance trends and develop more timely marketing strategies.

Manufacturing Information Systems

Manufacturing information systems support the **production/operations** function, which includes all activities concerned with the planning and control of the processes that produce goods or services. Thus, the production/operations function is concerned with the management of the *operational systems* of all business firms.

FIGURE 8.18
Production/operations management information systems for a manufacturing company. Note the levels of planning, control, and transaction processing information systems.

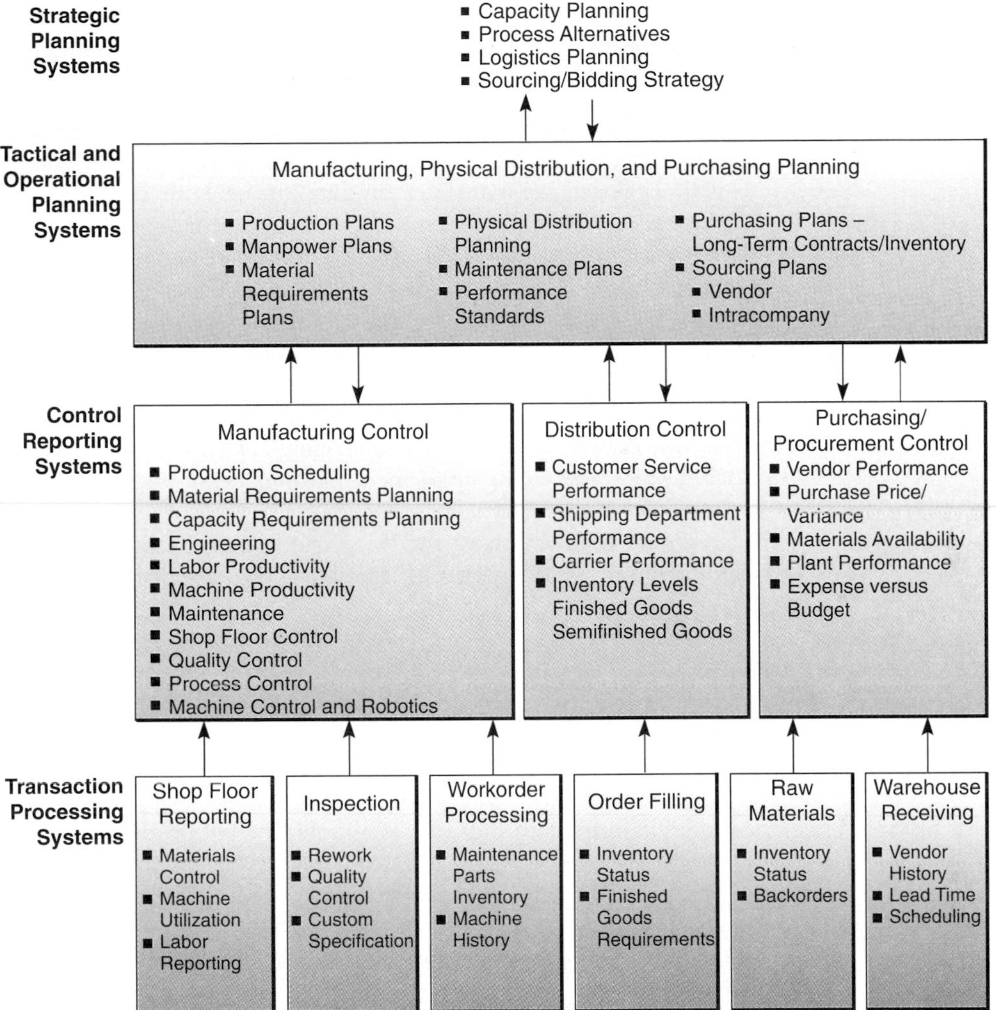

Source: Adapated from Andersen Consulting, *Foundations of Business Systems*, 2nd ed. (Fort Worth, Tex.: Dryden Press, 1992), p. 124.

Planning and control information systems are used for operations management and transaction processing, as illustrated in Figure 8.18. However, some of these systems are needed by *all* firms that must plan, monitor, and control inventories, purchases, and the flow of goods and services. Therefore, firms such as transportation companies, wholesalers, retailers, financial institutions, and service companies must use production/operations information systems to plan and control their operations. In this section, we will concentrate on computer-based manufacturing applications to illustrate information systems that support the production/operations function.

Computer Integrated Manufacturing

Computer-based manufacturing information systems use several major techniques to support **computer integrated manufacturing** (CIM). CIM is an overall concept that stresses that the goals of computer use in factory automation must be to:

- **Simplify** production processes, product designs, and factory organization as a vital foundation to automation and integration.
- **Automate** production processes and the business functions that support them with computers and robots.
- **Integrate** all production and support processes using computers and telecommunications networks [2].

Thus, computers are simplifying, automating, and integrating many of the activities needed to produce products of all kinds. For example, computers are used to help engineers design better products using both *computer-aided engineering* (CAE) and *computer-aided design* (CAD), and better production processes with *computer-aiding processing planning* (CAPP). They are also used to help plan the types of material needed in the production process, which is called *material requirements planning* (MRP), and to integrate MRP with production scheduling and shop floor control, which is known as *manufacturing resource planning* (MRPII). *Computer-aided manufacturing* (CAM) may be used to help manufacture products. This could be accomplished by monitoring and controlling the production process in a factory (*shop floor control*) or by directly controlling a physical process (*process control*), a machine tool (*machine control*), or a machine with some humanlike capabilities (robots). See Figure 8.19.

Figure 8.20 illustrates the three major dimensions of computer integrated manufacturing. CIM focuses its simplification, automation, and integration efforts on:

- The three basic manufacturing functions to be performed: engineering, manufacturing administration, and factory operations.
- The workplace environment, from the entire enterprise, factory facility, and shop floor to small work cells, individual workstations, and equipment.
- The manufacturing resources available, which are people, computers, telecommunications networks, factory floor equipment, and databases of manufacturing information.

FIGURE 8.19
Examples of computer-based systems in manufacturing.

Computer-Aided Design.
Creates designs for products and manufacturing processes.
Computer-Aided Manufacturing.
Fabricates metals, plastics, and other materials by molding, machining, welding, etc.
Assembly and Packaging.
Uses robots to put together parts fabricated on-site or purchased from outside.
Logistics and Storage.
Purchases and distributes materials, inventory control, removal of materials, management of supplies.
Maintenance.
Monitors equipment and processes, makes adjustments when needed, fault diagnosis, preventive and corrective maintenance.
Quality Control.
Tests incoming materials and outgoing products, tests of process in progress, quality assurance.
Factory Management.
Coordinates incoming orders, requests components and material, planning and scheduling, overseeing cost control, arranges deliveries.

Source: Adapted from Efraim Turban, *Decision Supoort and Expert Systems: Management Support Systems* (New York: Macmillan, 1990), p. 820.

Some of the benefits of computer integrated manufacturing systems are:

- Increased efficiency through work simplification and automation, better production schedule planning, and better balancing of production workload to production capacity.
- Improved utilization of production facilities, higher productivity, and better quality control resulting from continuous monitoring, feedback, and control of factory operations, equipment, and robots.
- Reduced investment in production inventories and facilities through work simplification, just-in-time inventory policies, and better planning and control of production and finished goods requirements.
- Improved customer service by drastically reducing out-of-stock situations and producing high-quality products that better meet customer requirements.

Process Control

Process control is the use of computers to control an ongoing physical process. Process control computers are used to control physical processes in petroleum refineries, cement plants, steel mills, chemical plants, food product manufacturing plants, pulp and paper mills, electric power plants, and so on. Many process control computers are special-purpose minicomputer systems. A process control computer

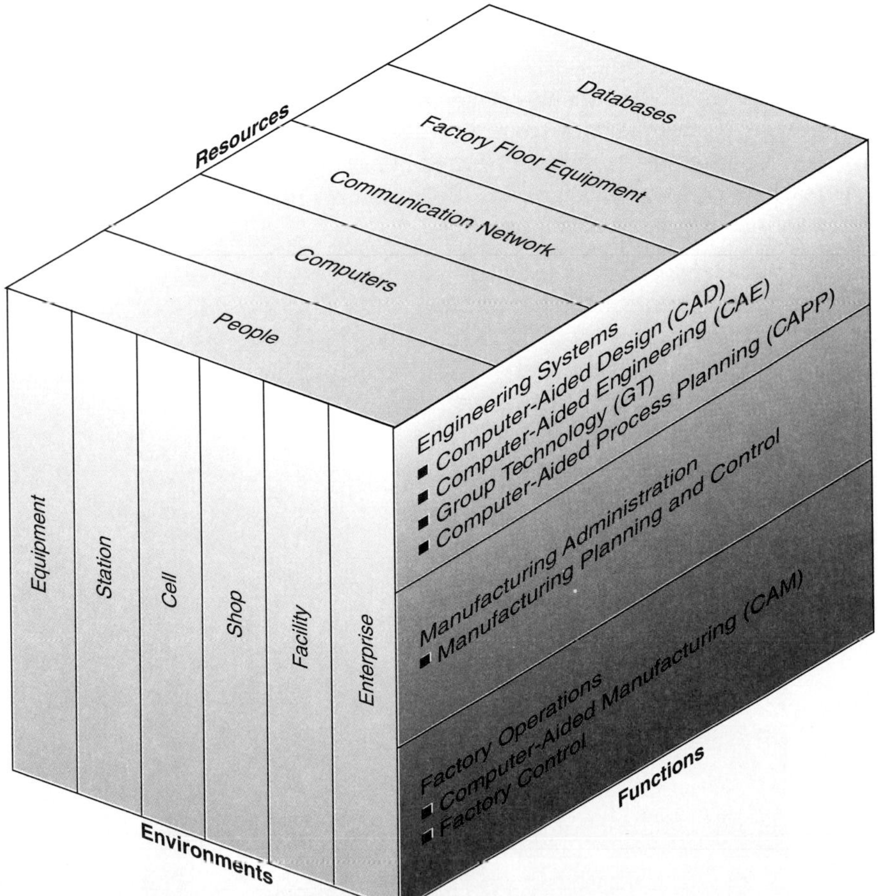

Source: Adapted from Arthur Andersen & Co., *Trends in Information Technology*, 3rd ed., 1987, p. 72.

FIGURE 8.20
The three major dimensions of computer integrated manufacturing. CIM focuses on simplifying, automating, and integrating the major functions, environment, and resources of modern manufacturing.

system requires the use of special sensing devices that measure physical phenomena such as temperature or pressure changes. These continuous physical measurements are converted to digital form by analog-to-digital converters and relayed to computers for processing.

Process control software uses mathematical models to analyze the data generated by the ongoing process and compare them to standards or forecasts of required results. Then the computer directs the control of the process by adjusting control devices such as thermostats, valves, switches, and so on. The process control systems also provide messages and displays about the status of the process so that a human operator can take appropriate measures to control the process. In addition, periodic and on-demand reports analyzing the performance of the production process can be produced. Personal computers have become a popular method of analyzing and reporting process control data. See Figure 8.21.

Machine Control

Machine control is the use of a computer to control the actions of a machine. This is also popularly called *numerical control*. The control of machine tools in factories is a typical numerical control application, though it also refers to the control of typesetting machines, weaving machines, and other industrial machinery.

Numerical control computer programs for machine tools convert geometric data from engineering drawings and machining instructions from process planning into a numerical code of commands that control the actions of a machine tool. Machine control may involve the use of special-purpose microcomputers called *programmable logic controllers* (PLCs). These devices operate one or more machines according to the directions of a numerical control program. Specially equipped personal computers that can withstand a factory environment are being used to develop and install numerical control programs in PLCs. They are also used to analyze production data furnished by the PLCs. This analysis helps engineers fine-tune machine performance. Figure 8.22 shows how machine control can be integrated with computer-aided design.

Robotics

An important development in machine control and computer-aided manufacturing is the creation of smart machines and robots. These devices directly control their own activities with the aid of microcomputers. **Robotics** is the technology of building and using machines (robots) with computer intelligence and computer-

Dan McCoy/Rainbow.

FIGURE 8.21
Process control computer systems control the paper-making process at this automated Weyerhaeuser paper mill in Longview, Washington.

controlled humanlike physical capabilities (dexterity, movement, vision, etc.). Robotics has also become a major thrust of research and development efforts in the field of artificial intelligence.

Robots are used as "steel-collar" workers to increase productivity and cut costs. For example, one robot regularly assembles compressor valves with 12 parts at the rate of 320 units per hour, which is 10 times the rate of human workers. Robots are also particularly valuable for hazardous areas or work activities. Robots follow programs loaded into separate or on-board special-purpose microcomputers. Input is received from visual and/or tactile sensors, processed by the microcomputer, and translated into movements of the robot. This typically involves moving its arms and hands to pick up and load items or perform some other work assignment such as painting, drilling, or welding. Robotics developments are expected to make robots more intelligent, flexible, and mobile by improving their computing, visual, tactile, and navigational capabilities [16]. See Figure 8.23.

Computer-Aided Engineering

Manufacturing engineers use **computer-aided engineering** to simulate, analyze, and evaluate the models of product designs they have developed using **computer-aided design** methods. Powerful *engineering workstations* with enhanced graphics and computational capabilities are used to analyze and design products and manufacturing facilities. Products are designed according to product specifications determined in cooperation with the product design efforts of marketing research and product development specialists. One of the final outputs of this design process is the *bill of materials* (specification of all required materials) used by the MRP application. The engineering subsystem is frequently responsible for determining standards for product quality (i.e., *quality assurance*). It also is responsible for the design of the production processes needed to manufacture the products it designs. This function depends heavily on the use of computers to perform the necessary analysis and design, and it is known as *computer-aided process planning*.

Computer-aided design packages and engineering workstations are the software and hardware resources that make computer-aided engineering possible. Engineers use these high-powered computing and advanced graphics workstations for the design and testing of products, facilities, and processes. Input is by light pen, joystick, or keyboard, with the CAD package refining an engineer's initial drawings. Output is in two- or three-dimensional graphics that can be rotated to display all sides of the object being designed. The engineer can zoom in for close-up views of a

FIGURE 8.22
From computer-aided design to direct machine control. Computers can be involved from the design stage to the actual production process of a product.

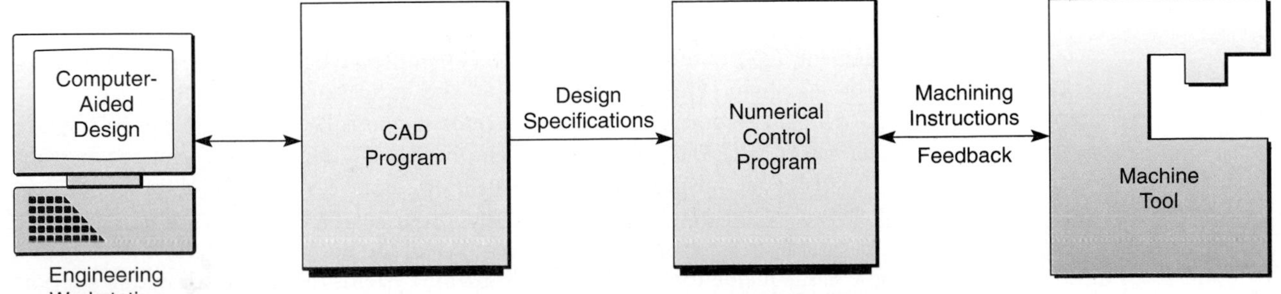

FIGURE 8.23
This robot is checking electronic circuit boards being assembled at an IBM plant in Poughkeepsie, New York.

Charles Harbutt/Actuality Inc.

specific part and even make parts of the product appear to move as they would in normal operation. The design can then be converted into a finished mathematical model of the product. This is used as the basis for production specifications and machine tool programs.

Human Resource Information Systems

The **human resource management** (or personnel) function involves the recruitment, placement, evaluation, compensation, and development of the employees of an organization. Originally, businesses used computer-based information systems to (1) produce paychecks and payroll reports, (2) maintain personnel records, and (3) analyze the use of personnel in business operations. Many firms have gone beyond these traditional functions and have developed **human resource information systems** (HRIS), which also support (1) recruitment, selection, and hiring, (2) job placement, (3) performance appraisals, (4) employee benefits analysis, (5) training and development, and (6) health, safety, and security. See Figure 8.24.

Human resource information systems support the concept of *human resource management.* This business function emphasizes (1) *planning* to meet the personnel needs of the business, (2) *development* of employees to their full potential, and (3) *control* of all personnel policies and programs. The goal of human resource management is the effective and efficient use of the human resources of a company. Some of the major applications of information systems that could be used to support human resource management are summarized in Figure 8.25.

FIGURE 8.24
Human resource information systems support the strategic, tactical, and operational use of the human resources of an organization.

	Staffing	Training/ Development	Performance Review and Appraisal	Compensation Administration
Strategic information systems	Manpower planning Labor force tracking	Succession planning	Performance appraisal planning	Contract costing Salary forecasting Benefits tracking
Tactical information systems	Budget analysis Turnover analysis Turnover cost Absenteeism/ performance	Training effectiveness Career matching	Performance/ training correlation	Compensation effectiveness Benefit preference models
Operational information systems	Recruiting Structured interview/ assessment Workforce planning Scheduling Selection models	Skill assessment	Computer-based evaluation programs	Compensation equality

Source: Adapted from David Meinert and Donald Davis, "Human Resource Decision Support Systems (HRDSS): Integrating Decision Support and Human Resource Information Systems," *Information Resources Management Journal*, Winter 1989, p. 45.

FIGURE 8.25
Human resource information systems support the four major functions of human resource management.

Staffing.
Record and track human resources through personnel record-keeping, skills inventories, and personnel requirements forecasting.
Training and Development.
Plan and monitor employee recruitment, training, performance appraisals, and career development.
Compensation.
Analyze, plan, and monitor policies for employee wages, salaries, incentive payments, and fringe benefits.
Governmental Reporting.
Reporting to government agencies concerning equal opportunity policies and statistics, employee health, workplace accidents and hazards, safety procedures, and so on.

Staffing

These information systems record and track human resources within a company to maximize their use. For example, a *personnel record-keeping* system keeps track of additions, deletions, and other changes to the records in a personnel database. Changes in job assignments and compensation, or hirings and terminations, are examples of information that would be used to update the personnel database. Another example is an *employee skills inventory* system which uses the employee skills data from a personnel database to locate employees within a company who have the skills required for specific assignments and projects.

A final example is doing *personnel requirements forecasting* to assure a business of an adequate supply of high-quality human resources. This application provides information required for forecasts of personnel requirements in each major employment category for various company departments or for new projects and other ventures being planned by management. Such long-range planning may use a computer-based simulation model to evaluate alternative plans for recruitment, reassignment, or retraining programs.

Training and Development

Information systems help human resource managers plan and monitor employee recruitment, training, and development programs by analyzing the success history of present programs. They also analyze the career development status of each employee to determine whether development methods such as training programs and periodic performance appraisals should be recommended. Computer-based training programs, and appraisals of employee job performance are available to help support this area of human resource management. See Figure 8.26.

Compensation Analysis

Information systems can help analyze the range and distribution of employee compensation (wages, salaries, incentive payments, and fringe benefits) within a company and make comparisons with compensation paid by similar firms or with various economic indicators. This information is useful for planning changes in compensation, especially if negotiations with labor unions are involved. It helps keep the compensation of a company competitive and equitable, while controlling compensation costs.

Governmental Reporting

Nowadays, reporting to government agencies is a major responsibility of human resource management. So organizations use computer-based information systems to keep track of the statistics and produce reports required by a variety of government laws and regulations. For example, in the United States, statistics on employee recruitment and hiring must be collected for possible use in Equal Employment Opportunity Commission hearings; statistics for employee health, workplace hazards, accidents, and safety procedures must be reported to the Occupational Safety Health Administration (OSHA); and statistics on the use of hazardous materials must be reported to the Environmental Protection Agency (EPA). Software packages to collect and report such statistics are available from a variety of software vendors.

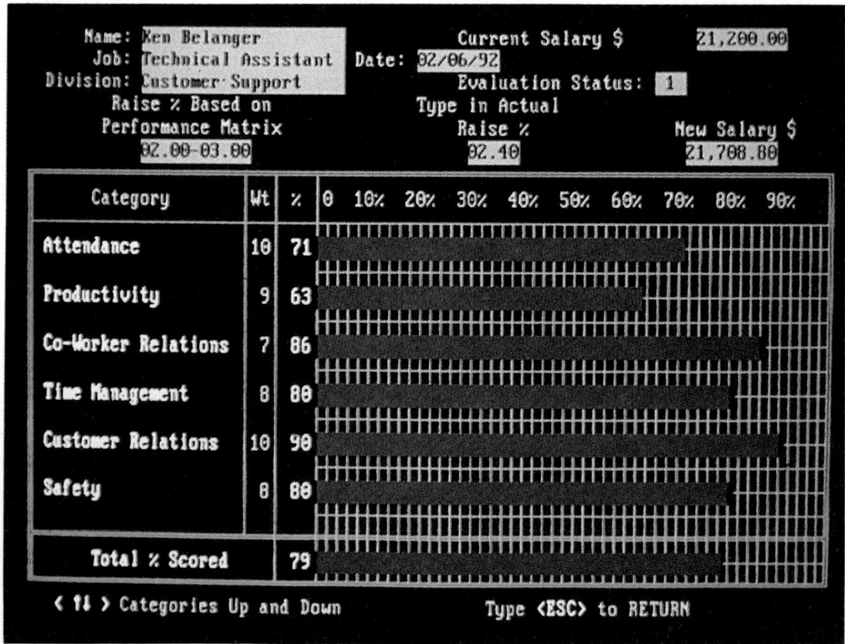

Courtesy of Hi Tech Enterprises.

FIGURE 8.26
An example of a performance evaluation display. Note how this employee is rated on six key areas of performance.

Accounting Information Systems

Accounting information systems are the oldest and most widely used information systems in business. They record and report business transactions and other economic events. Accounting information systems are based on the double-entry bookkeeping concept, which is hundreds of years old, and other, more recent accounting concepts such as responsibility accounting and profitability accounting. Computer-based accounting systems record and report the flow of funds through an organization on a historical basis and produce important financial statements such as balance sheets and income statements. Such systems also produce forecasts of future conditions such as projected financial statements and financial budgets. A firm's financial performance is measured against such forecasts by other analytical accounting reports.

Operational accounting systems emphasize legal and historical record-keeping and the production of accurate financial statements. Typically, these systems include transaction processing systems such as order processing, inventory control, accounts receivable, accounts payable, payroll, and general ledger systems. *Management accounting systems* focus on the planning and control of business operations. They emphasize cost accounting reports, the development of financial budgets and projected financial statements, and analytical reports comparing actual to forecasted performance.

Figure 8.27 illustrates the interrelationships of several important accounting information systems commonly computerized by both large and small businesses.

FIGURE 8.27
Important accounting information systems for transaction processing and financial reporting. Note how they are related to each other in terms of input and output flows.

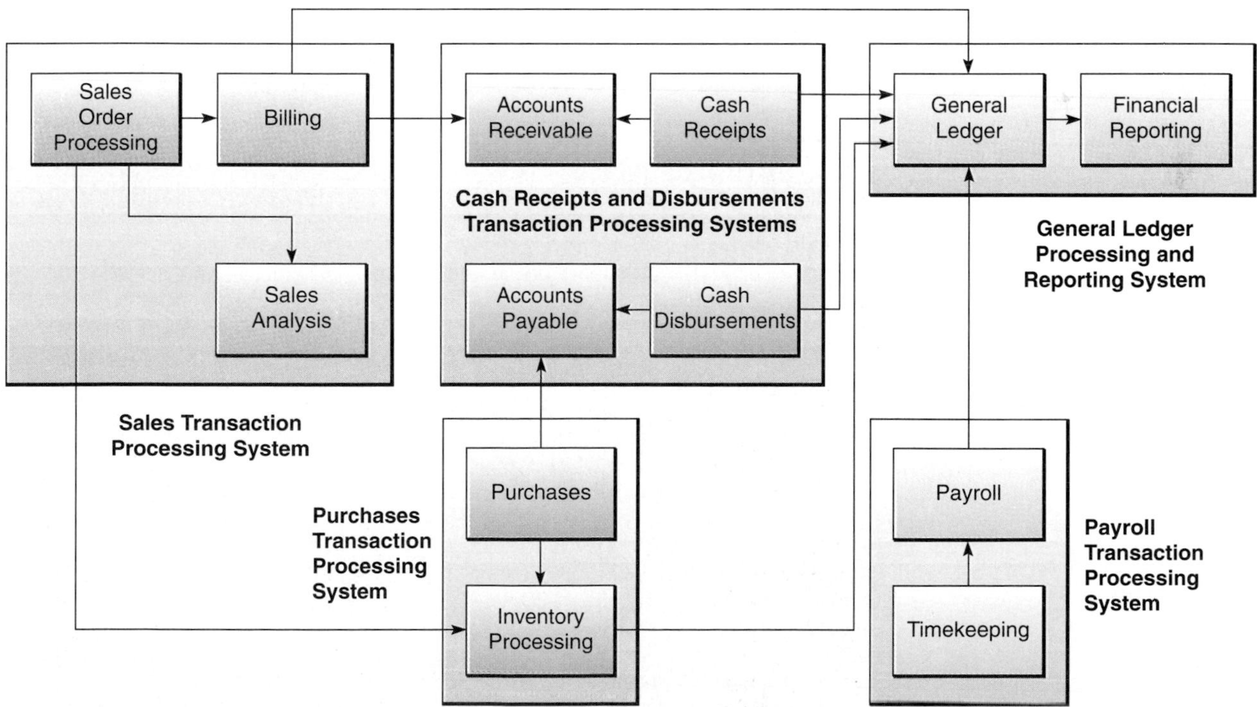

Source: Adapted from Joseph W. Wilkinson, *Accounting Information Systems: Essential Concepts and Applications* (New York: John Wiley & Sons, 1989), p. 184.

Many accounting software packages are available for these applications. Let's briefly review how several of these systems support the operations and management of a business firm. Figure 8.28 summarizes the purpose of six common, but important, accounting information systems.

Order Processing

Order processing, or *sales order processing*, is an important transaction processing system which captures and processes customer orders and produces invoices for customers and data needed for sales analysis and inventory control. In many firms, it also keeps track of the status of customer orders until goods are delivered. Computer-based sales order processing systems provide a fast, accurate, and efficient method of recording and screening customer orders and sales transactions. They also provide inventory control systems with information on accepted orders so they can be filled as quickly as possible.

Inventory Control

Inventory control systems process data reflecting changes to items in inventory. Once data about customer orders is received from an order processing system, a computer-based inventory control system records changes to inventory levels and prepares appropriate shipping documents. Then it may notify managers about items that need reordering and provide them with a variety of inventory status reports. Computer-based inventory control systems thus help a business provide high-quality service to customers while minimizing investment in inventory and inventory carrying costs.

Accounts Receivable

Accounts receivable systems keep records of amounts owed by customers from data generated by customer purchases and payments. They produce monthly customer statements and credit management reports, as were illustrated in Figure 8.12. Computer-based accounts receivable systems stimulate prompt customer payments by preparing accurate and timely invoices and monthly statements to credit customers. They provide managers with reports to help them control the amount of credit extended and the collection of money owed. This activity helps to maximize profitable credit sales while minimizing losses from bad debts.

FIGURE 8.28
A summary of six widely used accounting information systems.

Order Processing
Captures and processes customer orders and produces customer invoices.

Inventory Control
Processes data reflecting changes in inventory and provides shipping and reorder information.

Accounts Receivable
Records amounts owed by customers and produces monthly customer statements and credit management reports.

Accounts Payable
Records purchases from, amounts owed to, and payments to suppliers, and produces cash management reports.

Payroll
Records employee work and compensation data and produces paychecks and other payroll documents and reports.

General Ledger
Consolidates data from other accounting systems and produces the periodic financial statements and reports of the business.

Accounts Payable

Accounts payable systems keep track of data concerning purchases from and payments to suppliers. They prepare checks in payment of outstanding invoices and produce cash management reports. Computer-based accounts payable systems help ensure prompt and accurate payment of suppliers to maintain good relationships, ensure a good credit standing, and secure any discounts offered for prompt payment. They provide tight financial control over all cash disbursements of the business. They also provide management with information needed for the analysis of payments, expenses, purchases, employee expense accounts, and cash requirements.

Payroll

Payroll systems receive and maintain data from employee time cards and other work records. They produce paychecks and other documents such as earnings statements, payroll reports, and labor analysis reports. Other reports are also prepared for management and government agencies. Computer-based payroll systems help businesses make prompt and accurate payments to their employees, as well as reports to management, employees, and government agencies concerning earnings, taxes, and other deductions. They may also provide management with reports analyzing labor costs and productivity.

General Ledger

General ledger systems consolidate data received from accounts receivable, accounts payable, payroll, and other accounting information systems. At the end of each accounting period, they close the books of a business and produce the general ledger trial balance, the income statement and balance sheet of the firm, and various income and expense reports for management. Computer-based general ledger systems help businesses accomplish these accounting tasks in an accurate and timely manner. They typically provide better financial controls and management reports and involve fewer personnel and lower costs than manual accounting methods. Figure 8.29 is an example of a journal entry display of a general ledger package.

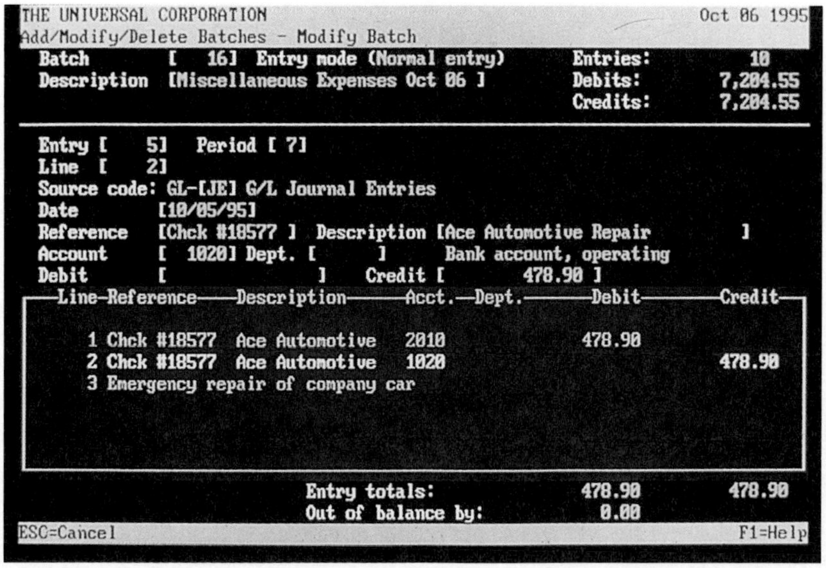

```
THE UNIVERSAL CORPORATION                                      Oct 06 1995
Add/Modify/Delete Batches - Modify Batch
  Batch        [   16] Entry mode (Normal entry)       Entries:          10
  Description  [Miscellaneous Expenses Oct 06 ]        Debits:     7,204.55
                                                       Credits:    7,204.55

  Entry [     5]  Period [ 7]
  Line  [     2]
  Source code: GL-[JE] G/L Journal Entries
  Date         [10/05/95]
  Reference    [Chck #18577 ] Description [Ace Automotive Repair          ]
  Account      [  1020] Dept. [      ]      Bank account, operating
  Debit        [               ]  Credit [       478.90 ]
 -Line-Reference---Description------Acct.-Dept.--------Debit----------Credit-

      1 Chck #18577  Ace Automotive   2010             478.90
      2 Chck #18577  Ace Automotive   1020                             478.90
      3 Emergency repair of company car

                          Entry totals:                478.90          478.90
                          Out of balance by:             0.00
ESC=Cancel                                                          F1=Help
```

Courtesy of Computer Associates International Inc.

FIGURE 8.29
An example of a journal entry display of a popular general ledger software package.

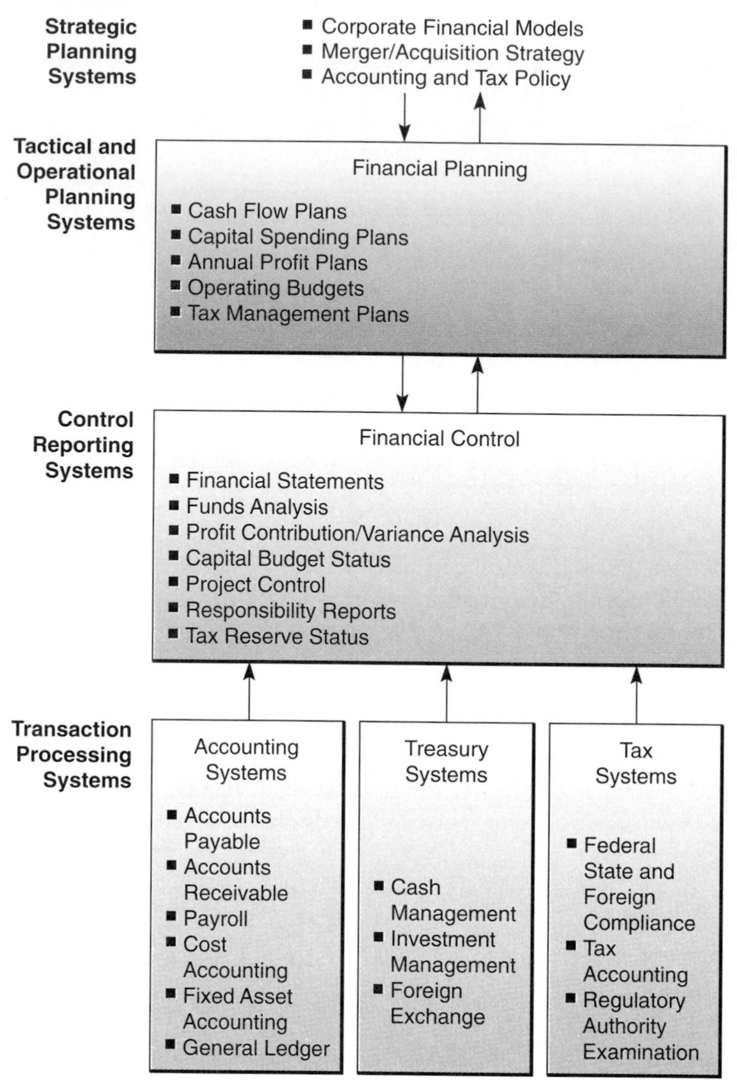

FIGURE 8.30
Financial planning, reporting, and transaction processing information systems support decisions concerning the financing and the allocation and control of funds within a business.

Source: Adapted from Andersen Consulting, *Foundations of Business Systems,* 2nd ed. (Fort Worth, Tex.: Dryden Press, 1992), p. 133.

Financial Information Systems

Computer-based **financial information systems** support financial managers in decisions concerning (1) the financing of a business and (2) the allocation and control of financial resources within a business. Major financial information system categories include cash and securities management, capital budgeting, financial forecasting, and financial planning. Accounting information systems are frequently included as a vital category of financial information systems. Figure 8.30 illustrates that the financial manager of a business may rely on a variety of financial planning, reporting, and transaction processing information systems to make financing, investment, and accounting decisions. Let's take a brief look at the functions of these computer-based financial systems. Figure 8.31 summarizes examples of important financial information systems.

Cash and Securities Management
Record data and produce forecasts of cash receipts and disbursements and manage investment in short-term securities.
Capital Budgeting
Evaluate the profitability and financial impact of proposed capital expenditures.
Financial Forecasting
Forecast business and economic trends and financial developments.
Financial Planning
Evaluate the present and projected financial performance and financing needs of the business.

FIGURE 8.31
Examples of important financial information systems.

Cash and Securities Management

Information systems collect information on all cash receipts and disbursements within a company on a realtime or periodic basis. Such information allows businesses to deposit or invest excess funds more quickly, and thus increase the income generated by deposited or invested funds. These systems also produce daily, weekly, or monthly forecasts of cash receipts or disbursements (cash flow forecasts), which are used to spot future cash deficits or surpluses. Mathematical models are frequently used to determine optimal cash collection programs and to determine alternative financing or investment strategies for dealing with forecasted cash deficits or surpluses.

Many businesses invest their excess cash in short-term marketable securities (such as U.S. Treasury bills, commercial paper, or certificates of deposit) so that investment income may be earned until the funds are required. The portfolio of such securities can be managed by portfolio management software. It helps a financial manager make buying, selling, or holding decisions for each type of security so that the optimum mix of securities is developed that minimizes risk and maximizes investment income.

Capital Budgeting

The capital budgeting process involves evaluating the profitability and financial impact of proposed capital expenditures. Long-term expenditure proposals for plants and equipment can be analyzed using a variety of techniques incorporating present value analysis of expected cash flows and probability analysis of risk. This application makes heavy use of spreadsheet models that are designed for corporate financial planning.

Financial Forecasting

A business must make financial and other forecasts of economic trends. A variety of statistical forecasting packages provide analytical techniques that result in economic or financial forecasts of national and local economic conditions, wage levels, price levels, and interest rates. This forecasting may involve the use of data about the external business environment obtained from proprietary financial and demographic data banks provided by the information services described in Chapter 6.

Financial Planning

Financial planning systems use *planning models* to evaluate the present and projected financial performance of a business or of one of its divisions or subsidiaries. They also help determine the financing needs of a business and analyze alternative methods of financing the business. Information concerning the economic situation, business operations, types of financing available, interest rates, and stock and bond prices are used to develop an optimal financing plan for the business. Electronic

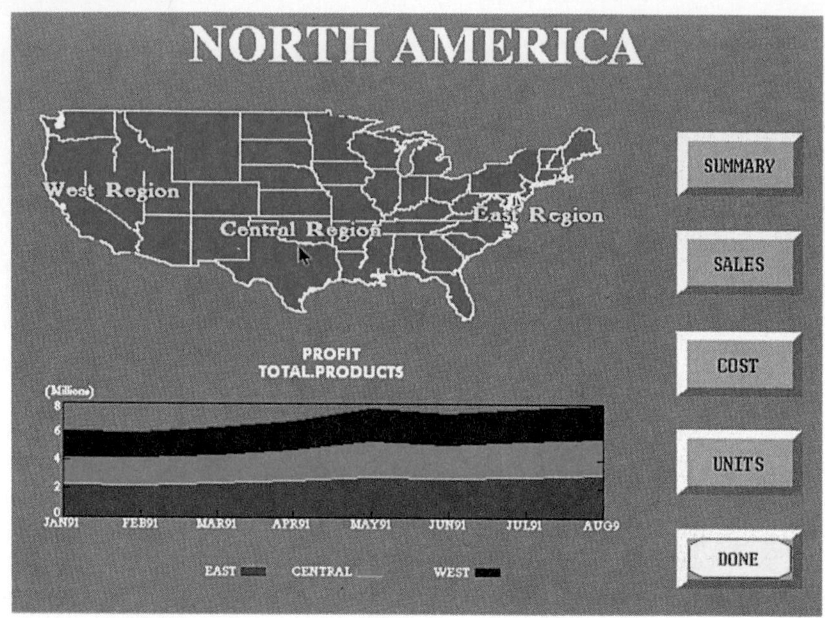

FIGURE 8.32
An example of a graphical analysis of a company's profits generated by a DSS/EIS package.

Courtesy of Information Resources, Inc.

spreadsheet packages and DSS generators are frequently used to build and manipulate these models. Answers to what-if and goal-seeking questions can be explored as financial analysts and managers evaluate their financing and investment alternatives. Figure 8.32 displays a graphical analysis of profits for a company generated by a DSS/EIS package.

REAL WORLD CASE

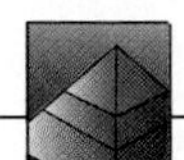

Buick Motor Division: PC-Based Marketing

The Buick Motor Division of General Motors is turning customer information into a more productive and useful asset. In the past, automakers used the names and addresses of car buyers mainly for recalls. Now, Buick, which is headquartered in Flint, Michigan, is analyzing its customer information and other sales data using Compass software from Claritas/NPDC.

Compass is a PC-based market analysis system that contains a Claritas database called PRIZM, which categorizes every neighborhood in the United States by including it in one of 40 clusters. Each cluster encompasses a distinct lifestyle, which includes demographics such as occupation, income, housing, ethnic group, and household composition (that is, whether it is a traditional family or one that is composed of unrelated adults).

Using these clusters, Compass can tell marketers where —by ZIP code, census tract, or block group—the highest concentrations of certain lifestyle groups reside. The software works like radar to home in on potential customers. "You can slice and dice the market data according to the type of product you sell or the type of consumer you are trying to reach," explains Michael Reinemer, director of communications for Claritas.

Buick uses Compass in its target marketing. It also uses the program to guide the companies that manage its field market-research projects. Buick can tell these researchers whom to recruit for new-model test drives, focus groups, and phone interviews.

The capability to zero in on potential customers has become more important lately, as market segments have gotten thinner. For example, when Buick was launching its Roadmaster estate wagon (an automobile line expected to sell only about 12,000 cars per year) and sedan, it used Compass data to selectively bind an ink-jet-printed card in Time-Warner magazines. The insertion cards were sent only to the 4,900 ZIP codes (out of the 39,000 in this country) that contained people who had demonstrated a propensity to buy station wagons.

The combination of Compass research and selective binding technology is a "marketing manager's dream," says Patrick Harrison, marketing line manager for Buick luxury cars. "Our reply rate was triple what we had predicted—at a fraction of the cost. We then used the information we obtained to refine our customer database."

Customers may not know, or care, about the technology investments that help create and distribute the various products they buy. But manufacturers that understand how markdowns can sabotage earnings do realize that IT can shift the odds back in their favor. It's like paying wholesale to get just the right customers.

CASE STUDY QUESTIONS

1. How does Buick use information technology like Compass to support the marketing function?
2. What is Compass? Why are the capabilities of Compass, called a "marketing manager's dream"?
3. How could other types of business use software packages like Compass? Give a specific example.

Source: Adapted from Raymond Boggs and John Hulak, "To Market, to Market," *Beyond Computing*, January/February 1993, pp. 47–48.

Summary

- **Transaction Processing.** Transaction processing systems play a vital role in processing data resulting from business transactions. They involve the basic activities of (1) data entry, (2) transaction processing, (3) database maintenance, (4) document and report generation, and (5) inquiry processing. However, transaction processing systems can also play a strategic role in gaining competitive advantages for a business.
- **Data Entry.** Traditional data entry methods in transaction processing systems requiring too many activities, people, and forms of data media are being replaced by more direct, automated methods known as source data automation. The high cost and potential for errors characteristic of traditional data entry methods can be minimized with source data automation that captures data as early and as close as possible to the source generating the data. Data is captured by using machine-readable media, prerecording data, or by capturing data directly without the use of data media. Electronic data interchange methods allow the direct electronic transmission of source documents between companies.
- **Batch and Realtime Processing.** Two basic categories of transaction processing systems are batch processing, in which data is accumulated and processed periodically, and realtime (or online) processing, which processes data immediately. Realtime processing can be subdivided into several levels: inquiry, data entry, file processing, full capability, and process control.
- **IS in Business.** Business information systems support the functional areas of business (marketing, production/operations, accounting, finance, and human resource management) through a wide variety of computer-based operational and management information systems.
- **Marketing.** Marketing information systems provide information for the planning and control of the marketing function. Marketing planning information assists marketing managers in product planning, pricing decisions, planning advertising and sales promotion strategies and expenditures, forecasting the market potential for new and present products, and determining channels of distribution. Marketing control information supports the efforts of management to control the efficiency and effectiveness of the selling and distribution of products and services. The major types of marketing information systems are sales management, sales force automation, product management, advertising and promotion, sales forecasting, market research, and market management systems.
- **Manufacturing.** Computer-based manufacturing information systems use several major subsystems to achieve computer-aided manufacturing. Computers are automating many of the activities needed to produce products in manufacturing industries. For example, computers help engineers design products using computer-aided design. Then they help plan the types of material needed in the production process using material requirements planning. Finally, they may be used to directly manufacture the products on the factory floor by directly controlling a physical process (process control), a machine tool (numerical control), or machines with some humanlike physical capabilities (robotics).
- **Human Resource Management.** Human resource information systems support human resource management in organizations. They include information systems for staffing, training and development, compensation administration, and performance appraisal.
- **Accounting and Finance.** Accounting information systems record and report business transactions and events for business firms and other organizations. Operational accounting systems emphasize legal and historical record-keeping and the production of accurate financial statements. Management accounting systems focus on the planning and control of business operations. Common operational accounting information systems include order processing, inventory control, accounts receivable, accounts payable, payroll, and general ledger systems. Information systems in finance support financial managers in decisions regarding the financing of a business and the allocation of financial resources within a business. Financial information systems include cash and securities management, capital budgeting, financial forecasting, and financial planning.

Key Terms and Concepts

These are the key terms and concepts of this chapter. The page number of their first explanation is in parentheses.

1. Accounting information systems (293)
2. Accounts payable (295)
3. Accounts receivable (294)
4. Batch processing (272)
5. Business information systems (280)
6. Computer-aided design (289)
7. Computer-aided engineering (289)
8. Computer-aided manufacturing (286)
9. Computer graphics (289)
10. Computer integrated manufacturing (285)
11. Control listing (276)
12. Cross-functional information systems (280)

13. Edit report (276)
14. Electronic data interchange (270)
15. Fault tolerant system (274)
16. Financial information systems (296)
17. Financial planning models (297)
18. General ledger (295)
19. Human resource information systems (290)
20. Inquiry processing (278)
21. Inventory control (294)
22. Machine control (288)
23. Manufacturing information systems (284)
24. Marketing information systems (280)
25. Material requirements planning (286)
26. Online transaction processing (273)
27. Order processing (294)
28. Payroll (295)
29. Process control (287)
30. Realtime processing (272)
31. Robotics (288)
32. Sales force automation (281)
33. Source data automation (269)
34. Source document (266)
35. Strategic transaction processing systems (266)
36. Traditional data entry (266)
37. Transaction (266)
38. Transaction document (276)
39. Transaction processing cycle (266)
40. Transaction processing system (266)
41. Turnaround document (276)

Review Quiz

Match one of the key terms and concepts listed above with one of the brief examples or definitions listed below. Try to find the best fit for answers that seem to fit more than one term or concept. Defend your choices.

____ 1. An example is making a sale or a payment.

____ 2. They process data resulting from business transactions.

____ 3. Data entry, transaction processing, database maintenance, document and report generation, and inquiry processing.

____ 4. Has too many activities, people, media, costs, and errors.

____ 5. The automatic capture of data at the time and place of transactions.

____ 6. The electronic transmission of source documents between companies.

____ 7. Collecting and periodically processing transaction data.

____ 8. Processing transaction data immediately after it is captured.

____ 9. A sales order form is an example.

____ 10. Examples are paychecks, customer statements, and sales receipts.

____ 11. Part of a customer's invoice is returned for automated data entry.

____ 12. A payroll register is an example.

____ 13. Reports that identify errors occurring during transaction processing.

____ 14. Allows end users to check on the status of an order or the balance in an account and receive an immediate response.

____ 15. A nonstop transaction processing capability.

____ 16. A popular name for realtime transaction processing.

____ 17. Transaction processing systems can build strong relationships with customers and suppliers.

____ 18. Support marketing, production, accounting, finance, and human resource management with computer-based information systems.

____ 19. Information systems must integrate the activities and resources of the functional areas of a business.

____ 20. Information systems for sales management, product management, and promotion management.

____ 21. Uses computers to automate sales recording and reporting by salespeople.

____ 22. Information systems which support manufacturing operations and management.

____ 23. Using computers in a variety of ways to help manufacture products.

____ 24. Helps the design process using advanced graphics, workstations, and software.

____ 25. Helps engineers evaluate products and processes.

____ 26. A conceptual framework for all aspects of factory automation.

____ 27. Using computers to operate a petroleum refinery.

____ 28. Using computers to help operate machine tools.

____ 29. Computerized devices can take over some production activities from human workers.

____ 30. Translates the production schedule into a detailed plan for all materials required.

____ 31. Information systems to support staffing, training and development, and compensation administration.

____ 32. Accomplish legal and historical record-keeping and

gather information for the planning and control of business operations.

____ 33. Handles sales orders from customers.

____ 34. Keeps track of items in stock.

____ 35. Keeps track of amounts owed by customers.

____ 36. Keeps track of purchases from suppliers.

____ 37. Produces employee paychecks.

____ 38. Produces the financial statements of a firm.

____ 39. Information systems for cash and securities management, capital budgeting, and financial forecasting.

____ 40. Provides a DSS capability for financial planning.

Discussion Questions

1. How can transaction processing systems play a strategic role in gaining competitive advantages for a business?
2. Why would electronic data interchange be "the ultimate in source data automation?"
3. Refer to the Real World Case on the New York State Department of Civil Service. Why does transaction processing using client/server computing "create performance issues"? How can such problems be addressed?
4. What are several reasons for the continued growth of online transaction processing? When would an OLTP system need a fault tolerant capability?
5. What is sales force automation? How does it affect salesperson productivity, marketing management, and competitive advantage?
6. Refer to the Real World Case on the Buick Motor Division. What are other ways computers are used to support the marketing function?
7. What is computer integrated manufacturing? What is the role of computer-aided manufacturing, computer-aided engineering, and robotics in CIM?
8. How can computer-based information systems support human resource management in a business? Give a few examples.
9. What are the most common applications of computers in accounting? Why do most businesses computerize these accounting systems?
10. What are cross-functional information systems? Why is there a trend toward such systems?

Real World Problems

1. Wisconsin Power and Light: Transacting Customer Service

Customer service has been reenergized at Wisconsin Power & Light Co. by a distributed application that has cut response time to customers from minutes down to seconds. "Our goal was to answer 80 percent of the calls in three rings, which is about 20 seconds, " said Dennis Vickers, director of information planning and operations at the Madison, Wisconsin based concern. "Before, in some cases, customers were hanging on for 15 minutes. That doesn't happen anymore." For example, for the month of October, customer service representatives achieved the 20-second goal 79 percent of the time, Vickers said.

The center handles about a half million calls per year. Customers call in with problems ranging from emergency power outages to billing questions and change-of-address requests. Employees can access a customer file on the mainframe, answer questions, issue a work order, and update the host file. The customer service center is in Janesville, 40 miles away from the corporate data center in Madison, where an IBM mainframe is housed. Employees, mostly part-timers, use IBM Personal System/2 PCs connected to the mainframe via LAN Gateway to access a database with the help of the host's IMS database management system.

a. What steps of the transaction processing cycle do you see in Wisconsin Power's customer service application?

b. How could source data automation be used to improve the response in this application?

Source: Adapted from Johanna Ambrosio, "Distributed App Reduces Customer Response Time," *Computerworld*, January 11, 1993, pp. 63–64. Used with permission.

2. Weirton Steel: Computer Integrated Manufacturing

Weirton Steel needed to update many of the decades-old processes employed by the company, which is the nation's eighth largest steel manufacturer. Weirton was suffering some hard times, and the pressure was on to simultaneously produce higher quality products and reduce costs. Therefore, in 1989 the 83-year old enterprise decided to plow some of its profits into the development of a multimillion-dollar Integrated Manufacturing Information System (IMIS). The project involved placing nonprogrammable color terminals at each of its 32 production lines. These terminals would be linked to four DEC-VAX computers on the plant floor.

By 1994 some 2,000 users—mostly steel workers—will utilize the DEC plant system to capture production information and pass the information through to the DB2 database software running on the IBM ES/3090 mainframe at corporate headquarters. The system will give managers real-time information about the status of any work being done in the plant. The IMIS project is just the first phase of the planned massive plant management system that will help Weirton cut costs through more efficient production scheduling, more timely deliveries to customers, and reduced inventories. The final phase will involve connecting the system to a process control system that monitors quality characteristics (such as the thickness and hardness of steel) to ensure that customer specifications are met.

a. How is Weirton Steel practicing computer integrated manufacturing?

b. Is Weirton making strategic use of information technology? Explain.

Source: Adapted with permission from *Beyond Computing*, January/February 1993.

3. Staples, Inc.: Marketing and the Customer Database

Staples, the discount office products retailing chain headquartered in Framingham, Massachusetts, is making the most out of its customer database. When customers shop at Staples, they can get extra savings by joining the Staples Saving Program. The application forms provide information about customers and their companies. Afterward, whenever members shop at Staples, cashiers ask for their Staples number and log all the items purchased against that number. This enables Staples to develop a database on each customer's buying habits. By analyzing the database, Staples can find out more about customers—and use that information to find new ones. For example, if the database reveals that Staples is doing a lot of business with doctors and lawyers, it can buy lists of people in those professions and target marketing efforts at them.

Staples also uses their database to exploit geographic areas more fully. For example, by comparing sales in various ZIP codes around each store, the company can determine which ZIP codes have not been penetrated as well as others. Then it can buy business listings to market to companies in those target areas. When sales to a steady customer diminish, Staples can act quickly to prevent a defection. "The lazy way to handle this is to send the customer a coupon," says James Forbush,vice president of marketing. "The smart way is to include the customer in a focus group or research study in order to find out where we're falling down on the job." The database also provides store managers with a list of Staples' top customers. The managers call the customers to thank them for their business, to inquire if they have any problems or suggestions, and to give the customers their phone number so they can call if anything comes up later. "We then track the people we called for the next six months," says Forbush, "and usually experience increased purchases."

a. How does Staples' use of its customer database support the marketing function?

b. Can Staples' use of its customer database give it a competitive advantage? Explain.

Source: Adapted with permission from *Beyond Computing*, January/February 1993.

4. Internal Revenue Service: Computerized Tax Accounting

The Internal Revenue Service reports a sharp increase in automated tax return filing and promises fewer processing errors and speedier refunds as a result. About 5 million returns—more than one third of all those filed—have been filed with electronic assistance. The 1040PC alternative posted the biggest percentage gain over last year. The 1040PC is a condensed paper format printed from one of several commercially available PC software packages certified by the IRS. The software computes taxes due and prints only those lines from the 1040 and supporting schedules that contain taxpayer data. Most returns fit on one page. The IRS said 1040PCs are filed by taxpayers and processed by the IRS faster and with fewer errors than traditional forms. The form also provides for direct deposit of a refund to the taxpayer's bank account. A spokesman for the IRS said the IRS is expecting some 6.7 million 1040PCs this year, compared with 1.5 million last year.

Electronic filing of federal returns by CPAs and other accountants and tax preparers for individuals so far this year is up to 4.8 million. In addition, some 300,000 returns were combined federal and state returns from 12 states that offer that option. The IRS expects 14 million electronic returns this year, compared with 10.9 million last year. In another filing option, called Telefile, taxpayers can call a toll-free number and enter tax return information through a Touch-Tone telephone during a computerized "interview." The IRS will compute the tax and any refund or tax due while the filer is on the phone. The option is being tested in Ohio for the second year. In last year's test of TeleFile, taxpayers still had to mail in a special form containing W-2s as well as the taxpayer's signature. In Southern Ohio this year, taxpayers will enter all W-2 data via telephone and will send in a "voice signature"—the taxpayer's name and social security number—attesting to the accuracy of the return. The signature will be stored on laser disk.

a. What are the benefits and limitations of the three types of computerized tax accounting alternatives approved by the IRS?

b. Which alternative would you prefer to use? Explain.

Source: Adapted from Gary Anthes, "Electronic Tax Filings Up," *Computerworld*, March 1, 1993, p. 38. Used with permission.

Application Exercises

1. **ABC Department Stores**
   ABC Department Stores uses POS terminals connected to a minicomputer in each store to capture sales data immediately and store them on a magnetic disk unit. Each night, the central computer in Phoenix polls each store's minicomputer to access and process the day's sales data, update the corporate database, and produce management reports. The next morning, managers use their terminals to interrogate the updated corporate databases.
   Identify how each of the following types of computer processing is occurring in the example above:
   a. Batch
   b. Realtime
   c. Online
   d. Transaction
   e. Data entry
   f. Database maintenance
   g. Inquiry processing
2. **Business Information Systems**
   Which business information systems should be improved if the following complaints were brought to your attention? Identify the business function (accounting, finance, marketing, production/operations, or human resource management) and the specific information system in that functional area that is involved. (Refer to Figure 8.13)
   a. "Nobody is sure which of our sales reps is our top producer."
   b. "Why was this part left out of the bill of materials?"
   c. "I don't know why I didn't get a raise this year."
   d. "Why were we overinvested in short-term securities?"
   e. "Why are the balance sheet and income statement late this month?"
   f. "Our sales reps are spending too much time on paperwork."
   g. "The ROI and payback on this deal are all wrong."
   h. "Which of our managers have overseas experience?"
   i. "We need a workstation to design this product."
   j. "Why are we being stuck with home office overhead expenses?"
3. **Accounting Information Systems**
   Which common accounting information systems should be improved if the following complaints were brought to your attention? (Refer to Figure 8.28)
   a. "Month-end closings are always late."
   b. "We are never sure how much of a certain product we have on the shelves."
   c. "Many of us didn't get an earnings and deductions statement this week."
   d. "We're tired of manually writing up a receipt every time a customer orders something."
   e. "Our suppliers are complaining that they are not being paid on time."
   f. "Our customers resent being sent notices demanding payment when they have already paid what they owe."
4. **Designing Information Products**
   a. In your day-to-day living, you are a user of many transaction processing systems, including those used by banks, department stores, supermarkets, utility companies, and universities to process data generated by various end user transactions. Design a mockup of a report, document, or display that could be produced by a transaction processing system of your choice. Use a report generator from a database management or other software package to develop the report mockup if possible.
   b. Evaluate how well the transaction processing system you chose performs its basic transaction processing activities. Write up a brief evaluation based on the activities illustrated in Figure 8.2.

FIGURE 8.33
Sample Rental Transactions for One Customer for One Month

Customer Name	Acct. #	Item Description	Rental Date	Daily Rental Rate	Rental Days	Total Charge
Builtrite	117	Backhoe	10/02/93	$150	2.5	$375
Builtrite	117	Cement Mixer	10/03/93	100	1.0	100
Builtrite	117	Port. Blower	10/03/93	50	2.0	100
Builtrite	117	Ditch Devil	10/06/93	175	1.0	175
Builtrite	117	Cement Mixer	10/07/93	100	0.5	50
Builtrite	117	Compressor	10/10/93	90	3.0	270
Builtrite	117	Nail Gun	10/10/93	30	3.0	90
Builtrite	117	Backhoe	10/15/93	150	1.0	150
Builtrite	117	Ditch Devil	10/16/93	175	2.0	350
Builtrite	117	Cement Mixer	10/21/93	100	1.5	150
Builtrite	117	Port. Blower	10/22/93	50	0.5	25
Builtrite	117	Backhoe	10/27/93	150	1.5	225
Builtrite	117	Compressor	10/28/93	90	2.0	180

5. Ron's Rentals Customer Billing Report
Ron's Rentals rents construction equipment to contractors. Approved customers are allowed to charge their rentals and are sent billings on a monthly basis. Ron would like to use database software to record information about each rental as it occurs and print up monthly billings to be sent to each customer. A set of rentals by one customer over a sample month is shown in Figure 8.33. You are to use this sample data to design a billing report that Ron's can send to its customers.

The report should be as informative as possible. You will certainly want to report the total amount billed, but your report should also give subtotals spent on different items.

a. Based on the sample data below, build a database file to store rental transaction records, and enter the sample data shown.

b. Using the report generation feature of your database package, create a monthly billing report for a customer. This report should be laid out as nicely as possible and be as informative as possible. Print a copy of your report based on the sample data.

c. Critique your report. Are there elements of the report that you would like to have laid out differently, or features that you would like to have added? Did the database package you used limit your options in formatting this report?

Review Quiz Answers

1. *37*	11. *41*	21. *32*	31. *19*
2. *40*	12. *11*	22. *23*	32. *1*
3. *39*	13. *13*	23. *8*	33. *27*
4. *36*	14. *0*	24. *6*	34. *21*
5. *33*	15. *15*	25. *7*	35. *3*
6. *14*	16. *26*	26. *10*	36. *2*
7. *4*	17. *35*	27. *29*	37. *28*
8. *30*	18. *5*	28. *22*	38. *18*
9. *34*	19. *12*	29. *31*	39. *16*
10. *38*	20. *24*	30. *25*	40. *17*

Selected References

1. Andersen Consulting. *Foundations of Business Systems*. 2nd ed. Fort Worth, Tex.: Dryden Press, 1992.
2. Bakos, J. Yannis. "A Strategic Analysis of Electronic Marketplaces." *MIS Quarterly*, September 1991.
3. Bray, Olin. *Computer Integrated Manufacturing: The Data Management Strategy*. Bedford, Mass.: Digital Press, 1988.
4. Burch, John. "EDI: The Demise of Paper." *Information Executive*, Winter 1989.
5. Cushing, Barry, and Marshal Romney. *Accounting Information Systems*. 5th ed. Reading, Mass.: Addison-Wesley Publishing, 1990.
6. Douglass, David. "Computer Integrated Manufacturing." *SIM Executive*, First Quarter 1991.
7. Dams, Leila. "On the Fast Track to HR Integration." *Datamation*, September 15, 1991.
8. Eliason, Alan. *Online Business Computer Applications*. 3rd ed. New York: Macmillan, 1991.
9. Hansen, James, and Ned Hill. "Control and Audit of Electronic Data Interchange." *MIS Quarterly*, December 1989.
10. "Integration Strategies: Manufacturing." *Computerworld*, October 28, 1991.
11. Lindholm, Elizabeth. "Transactions on the Desktop." *Datamation*, August 1, 1991.
12. Meinert, David; and Donald Davis. "Human Resource Decision Support Systems (HRDSS): Integrating Decision Support and Human Resource Information Systems." *Information Resources Management Journal*, Winter 1989.
13. Moad, Jeff. "Relational Takes on OLTP." *Datamation*, May 15, 1991.
14. Snell, Ned. "Software to Tame the Sales Force." *Datamation*, June 1, 1991.
15. Trippi, Robert, and Efraim Turban. *Investment Management: Decision Support and Expert Systems*. Boston: Boyd & Fraser Publishing Co., 1990.
16. Wilder, Clinton. "Codex Goes Paperless with EDI." *Computerworld*, January 13, 1992.

Managerial Information and Support Systems

CHAPTER OUTLINE

SECTION I Executive Information and Decision Support Systems

Information Reporting Systems

Attributes of Information Quality

Information Reporting Alternatives

Information Reporting versus Decision-making Support

Decision Support Systems

Examples of DSS Applications

Components of a Decision Support System

Models for Decision Support

Software for Decision Support

DSS and Electronic Spreadsheets

Using Decision Support Systems

Analytical Modeling Alternatives

Group Decision Support Systems

Group Decision Making

GDSS Packages

Executive Information Systems

Rationale for EIS

Components of an EIS

Example of an EIS

Developing DSS and EIS

Real World Case: Mazda and Ford Motor Companies: Information Systems for Quality Management

SECTION II Artificial Intelligence and Expert Systems

An Overview of Artificial Intelligence

The Domains of Artificial Intelligence

Knowledge-based Information Systems

Expert-assisted IS

Components of an Expert System

Examples of Expert Systems

Expert System Applications

Developing Expert Systems

Expert System Suitability

Expert Systems: Make or Buy?

Knowledge Engineering

A Managerial Perspective

Benefits of Expert Systems

Limitations of Expert Systems

Real World Case: Red Lobster Restaurants, Royal Bank of Canada, and St. Luke's Episcopal Hospital: Knowledge-Based Systems

CHAPTER 9

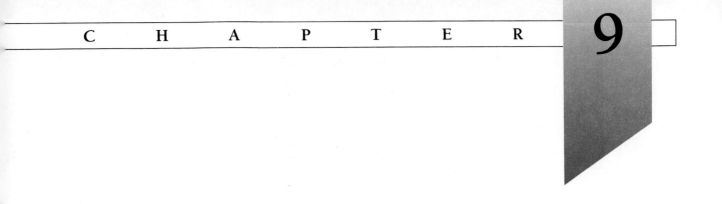

LEARNING OBJECTIVES

The purpose of this chapter is to give you an understanding of how information reporting, decision support, executive information, and expert systems support managerial decision making and business operations.

Section I discusses basic concepts and components of information reporting, decision support and executive information systems and provides examples of DSS and EIS applications.

Section II of this chapter gives an overview of artificial intelligence application areas and explores the fundamentals of expert systems, including their relationship to decision support systems, and provides examples of the business use of expert systems.

After reading and studying this chapter, you should be able to:

1. Identify the major components of a decision support system and explain how it differs from traditional information reporting systems.
2. Explain how decision support systems help managers do analytical modeling to support decision making.
3. Explain how executive information systems can support the information needs of top and middle managers.
4. Identify the present and future impacts of artificial intelligence on business operations and management.
5. Identify the major components of an expert system and explain how expert systems are developed.
6. Give examples of several ways expert systems can be used in business decision-making situations.

SECTION I

Executive Information and Decision Support Systems

Previous chapters of this text have emphasized that information systems can support the diverse information and decision-making needs of managers. Figure 9.1 emphasizes the differing conceptual focuses of major types of information systems. In this section, we will explore in more detail how this is accomplished by information reporting, decision support, and executive information systems. We will concentrate our attention on how these information technologies have significantly strengthened the role information systems play in supporting the decision-making activities of managerial end users. See Figure 9.2.

Information Reporting Systems

Information reporting systems were the original type of management information systems, and they are still a major category of MIS. They produce information products that support many of the day-to-day decision-making needs of management. Reports, displays, and responses produced by such systems provide information that managers have specified in advance as adequately meeting their information needs. Such predefined information products satisfy the information needs of managers at the operational and tactical levels of the organization who are faced with more structured types of decision situations. For example, sales managers

FIGURE 9.1
The differing focuses of major types of information systems.

Type of Information System	Focus
Expert systems	Knowledge—from experts
Decision support systems	Decisions—interactive support
Executive information systems	Information—for top management
Information reporting systems	Information—for managerial end users
Transaction processing systems	Data—from business operations

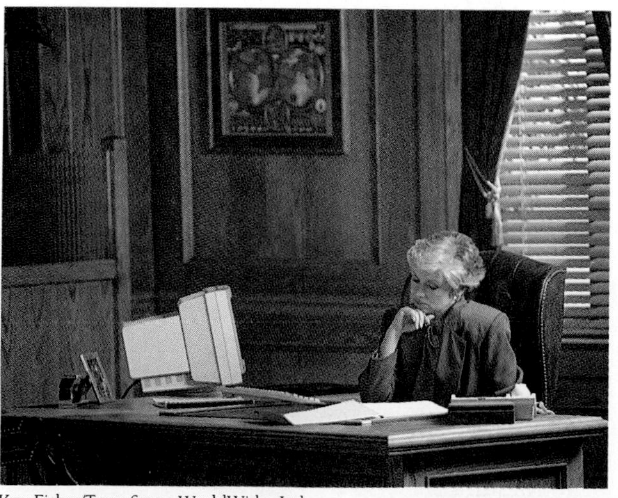

Ken Fisher/Tony Stone WorldWide, Ltd.

FIGURE 9.2
Every manager relies on information systems for information and decision support.

rely heavily on sales analysis reports to evaluate differences in performance among salespeople who sell the same types of products to the same types of customers. They have a pretty good idea of the kinds of information about sales results they need to manage sales performance effectively.

Figure 9.3 illustrates the components of an information reporting system. Managers can receive information at their workstations that supports their decision-making activities. This information takes the form of periodic, exception, and demand reports and immediate responses to inquiries. Application programs and database management software provide access to information in the corporate databases of the organization. Remember, these databases are maintained by transaction processing systems. Data about the business environment is obtained from external databases when necessary.

Attributes of Information Quality

What characteristics make information meaningful and useful to managers? What qualities give it value for end users? One way to answer these important questions is to examine the characteristics or *attributes* of *information quality*.

Information that is outdated, inaccurate, or hard to understand would not be very meaningful, useful, or valuable to managers. They want information of high quality, that is, *information products* whose characteristics, attributes, or qualities help make it valuable to them. It is useful to think of information as having the three dimensions of time, content, and form. Figure 9.4 summarizes the important attributes of information and groups them into these three dimensions.

Information Reporting Alternatives

Information reporting systems provide a variety of information products to managers. The three major reporting alternatives provided by such systems are summarized below. See Figure 9.5.

- **Periodic scheduled reports.** This traditional form of providing information to managers uses a prespecified format designed to provide managers with information on a regular basis. Typical examples of such periodic scheduled reports are weekly sales analysis reports and monthly financial statements.
- **Exception reports.** In some cases, reports are produced only when exceptional conditions occur. In other cases, reports are produced periodically but contain information only about these exceptional conditions. For example, a credit manager can be provided with a report which contains only information on customers who exceed their credit limits. Such exception reporting promotes *management by exception*, instead of overwhelming management with periodic detailed reports of business activity.

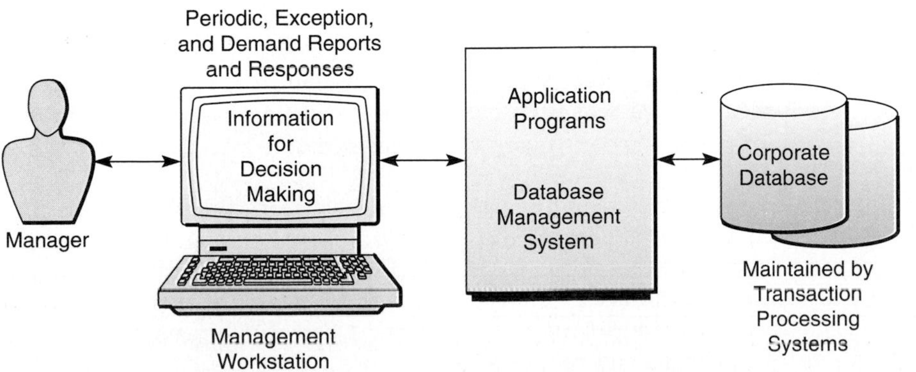

FIGURE 9.3
The information reporting system concept. Note especially that periodic, exception, and demand reports and responses are the information products produced for managers by this type of information system.

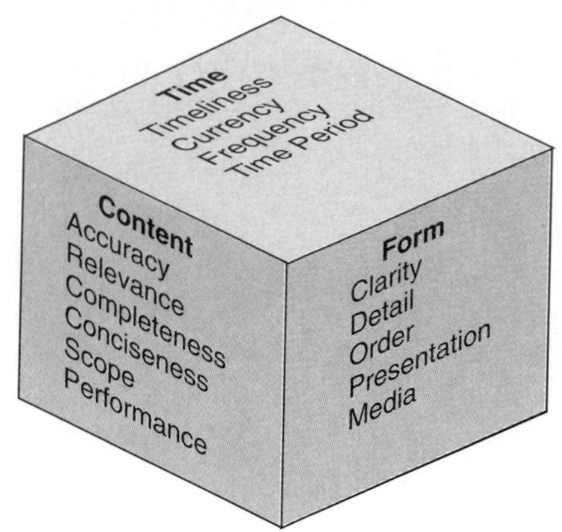

FIGURE 9.4
A summary of the attributes of information quality. This outlines the attributes that should be present in high-quality information products.

Time Dimension	
Timeliness	Information should be provided when it is needed
Currency	Information should be up-to-date when it is provided
Frequency	Information should be provided as often as needed
Time Period	Information can be provided about past, present, and future time periods
Content Dimension	
Accuracy	Information should be free from errors
Relevance	Information should be related to the information needs of a specific recipient for a specific situation
Completeness	All the information that is needed should be provided
Conciseness	Only the information that is needed should be provided
Scope	Information can have a broad or narrow scope, or an internal or external focus
Performance	Information can reveal performance by measuring activities accomplished, progress made, or resources accumulated
Form Dimension	
Clarity	Information should be provided in a form that is easy to understand
Detail	Information can be provided in detail or summary form
Order	Information can be arranged in a predetermined sequence
Presentation	Information can be presented in narrative, numeric, graphic, or other forms
Media	Information can be provided in the form of printed paper documents, video displays, or other media

- **Demand reports and responses.** Information is provided whenever a manager demands it. For example, DBMS query languages and report generators allow managers at online workstations to get immediate responses or reports as a result of their requests for information. Thus, managers do not have to wait for periodic reports to arrive as scheduled.

Information Reporting versus Decision-making Support

Information reporting systems focus on providing managers with prespecified information products that report on the performance of the organization. Decision support systems, however, focus on providing information interactively to support specific types of decisions by individual managers. Managers at the tactical and strategic levels of an organization need ad hoc types of information products to support their planning and control responsibilities. Decision support systems help

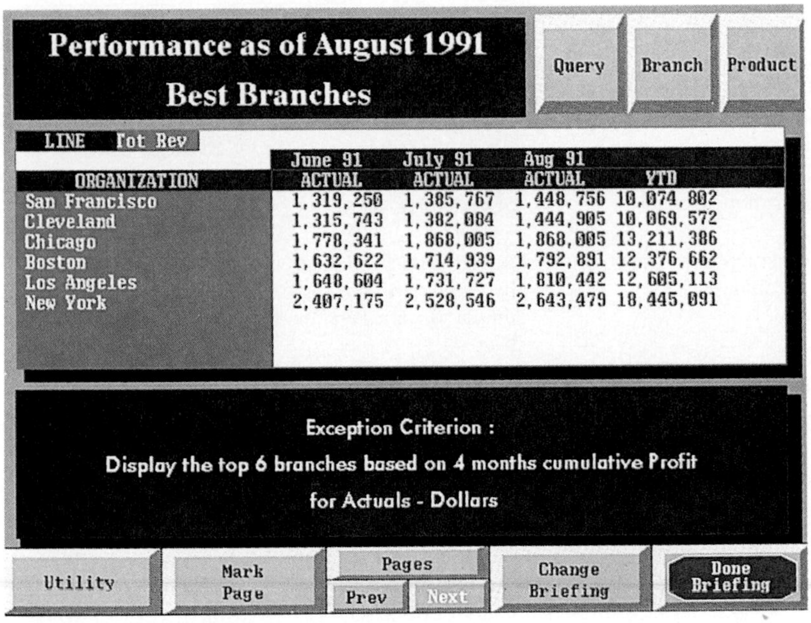

Performance as of August 1991

Best Branches

Query | Branch | Product

LINE Tot Rev

ORGANIZATION	June 91 ACTUAL	July 91 ACTUAL	Aug 91 ACTUAL	YTD
San Francisco	1,319,250	1,385,767	1,448,756	10,074,802
Cleveland	1,315,743	1,382,084	1,444,905	10,069,572
Chicago	1,778,341	1,868,005	1,868,005	13,211,386
Boston	1,632,622	1,714,939	1,792,891	12,376,662
Los Angeles	1,648,604	1,731,727	1,810,442	12,605,113
New York	2,407,175	2,528,546	2,643,479	18,445,091

Exception Criterion :

Display the top 6 branches based on 4 months cumulative Profit for Actuals - Dollars

Utility | Mark Page | Pages Prev Next | Change Briefing | Done Briefing

Courtesy of Information Resources, Inc.

FIGURE 9.5
This video display is an example of a report available on demand using exception criteria to display monthly and year-to-date information.

such managers solve the semistructured and unstructured problems they typically face in the real world. In contrast, information reporting systems are designed to indirectly support the more structured types of decisions involved in operational and tactical planning and control.

Figure 9.6 summarizes and contrasts the differences between decision support systems and information reporting systems. Note that the objective of decision support systems is to provide information and decision support techniques needed to solve specific problems or pursue specific opportunities. In contrast, the objective of information reporting systems is to provide information about the performance of basic organizational functions and processes, such as marketing, manufacturing, and finance. Thus, decision support systems have a much more specific role in the decision-making process. Note also that a DSS is designed to support all four stages (intelligence, design, choice, and implementation) of decision making. Information reporting systems, on the other hand, are designed to provide information for the intelligence phase, which starts the decision-making process, and the implementation stage, which monitors its success.

EXAMPLE

An example might help at this point. Sales managers typically rely on information reporting systems to produce sales analysis reports. These reports contain sales performance figures by product line, salesperson, sales region, and so on. A decision support system, on the other hand, would also interactively show a sales manager the effects on sales performance of changes in a variety of factors (such as promotion expense and salesperson compensation). The DSS could then use several criteria (such as expected gross margin and market share) to evaluate and rank several alternative combinations of sales performance factors.

FIGURE 9.6
Comparing decision support systems and information reporting systems. Note the major differences in the information and decision support they provide.

	Information Reporting Systems	Decison Support Systems
Information provided		
Information form and frequency	Periodic, exception, and demand reports and responses	Interactive inquiries and responses
Information format	Prespecified, fixed format	Ad hoc, flexible, and adaptable format
Information processing methodology	Information produced by extraction and manipulation of operational data	Information produced by analytical modeling of operational and external data
Decision support provided		
Type of support	Provide information about the performance of the organization	Provide information and decision support techniques to confront specific problems or opportunities
Stages of decision making supported	Support the intelligence and implementation stages of decision making	Support the intelligence, design, choice, and implementation stages of decision making
Types of decisions supported	Structured decisions for operational and tactical planning and control	Semistructured and unstructured decisions for tactical and strategic planning and control
Type of decision maker supported	Indirect support designed for many managers	Direct support tailored to the decision making styles of individual managers

Decision Support Systems

Decision support systems are a major category of management information systems. They are computer-based information systems that provide interactive information support to managers during the decision-making process. Decision support systems use (1) analytical models, (2) specialized databases, (3) a decision maker's own insights and judgments, and (4) an interactive, computer-based modeling process to support the making of semistructured and unstructured decisions by individual managers. Therefore, they are designed to be ad hoc, quick-response systems that are initiated and controlled by managerial end users. Decision support systems are thus able to directly support the specific types of decisions and the personal decision-making styles and needs of individual managers [25].

Examples of DSS Applications

Decision support systems are used for a variety of applications in both business and government. When a DSS is developed to solve large or complex problems that continually face an organization, it is called an *institutional* DSS. Decision support systems used for strategic corporate planning are an example of this type of DSS. Other DSS applications are developed quickly to solve smaller or less-complex problems that may be one-time situations facing a manager. These are called *ad hoc* DSS. Also, many decision support systems are developed to support the types of decisions faced by a specific industry (such as the airline, banking, or automotive industry) or by a specific functional area (such as marketing, finance, or manufacturing). Let's take a brief look at three examples to demonstrate the variety of DSS applications.

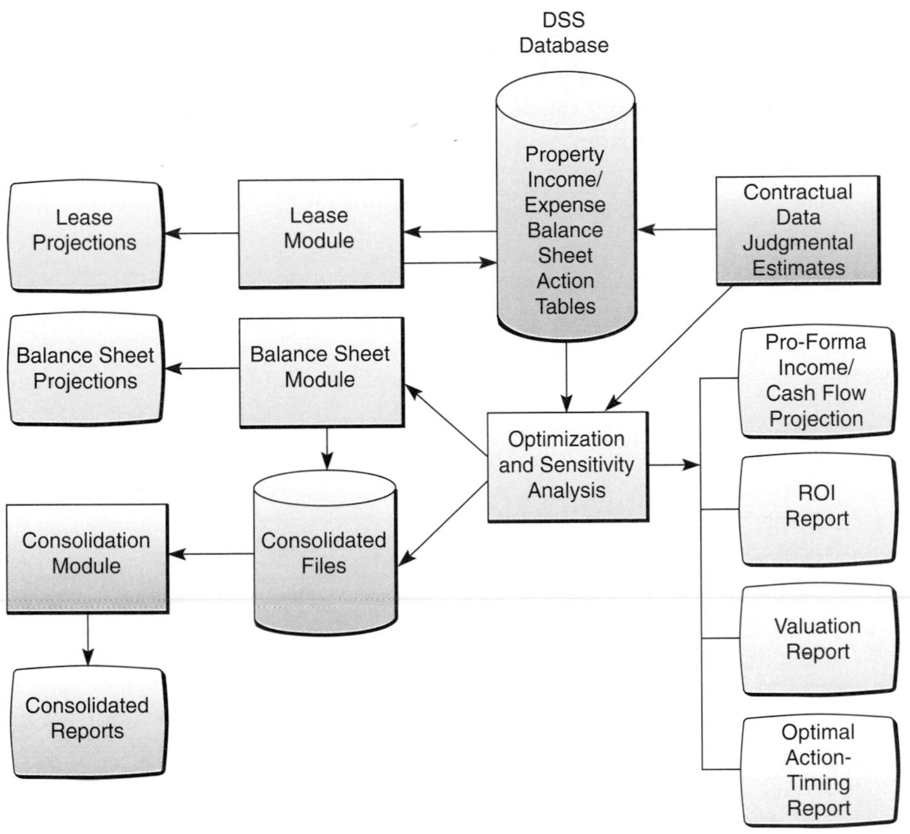

FIGURE 9.7
An example of analytical modeling for decision support. The RealPlan DSS helps decision makers evaluate proposed commercial real estate investments.

Source: Adapted from Efraim Turban, *Decision Support and Expert Systems: Management Support Systems*, 2nd Ed. (New York: Macmillan, 1990), p. 000.

An Airline DSS

The Analytical Information Management System (AAIMS) is a decision support system used in the airline industry. It was developed by American Airlines but is used by other airlines, aircraft manufacturers, airline financial analysts, consultants, and associations. AAIMS supports a variety of airline decisions by analyzing data collected on airline aircraft utilization, seating capacity and utilization, and traffic statistics. For example, it produces forecasts of airline market share, revenue, and profitability. Thus, AAIMS helps airline management make decisions on aircraft assignments, route requests, ticket classifications, pricing, and so on [25].

A Real Estate DSS

RealPlan is a DSS used in the real estate industry to do complex analyses of investments in commercial real estate. For example, investing in commercial real estate properties typically involves highly detailed income, expense, and cash flow projections. RealPlan easily performs such analyses, even for properties with multiple units, lease terms, rents, and cost of living adjustments. Since RealPlan can also make forecasts of property values up to 40 years into the future, it helps decision makers not only with acquisition decisions but with real estate improvement and divestment decisions as well [25]. See Figure 9.7.

A Geographic DSS

Geographic information systems (GIS) are a special category of DSS that integrate computer graphics and geographic databases with other DSS features. IBM's GeoManager is a GIS which constructs and displays maps and other graphics displays that support decisions affecting the geographic distribution of people and other resources. For example, it can analyze and display the geographic distribution of crimes and thus help public safety officials decide how to assign police to geographic areas of a city. GeoManager can also be used for urban growth studies, defining legislative district boundaries, and emergency vehicle deployment. GIS are also being used in business for decision support in electrical power distribution, forest management, and railroad maintenance applications [22].

Components of a Decision Support System

Figure 9.8 illustrates the components present in any decision support system. Note the hardware, software, data, model, and people resources needed to provide interactive decision support for managers. Let's first outline the functions of these components and then discuss DSS model and software requirements in more detail.

- **Hardware resources.** Personal computer workstations provide the primary hardware resource for a DSS. They can be used on a stand-alone basis, but are typically connected by wide area or local area networks to other computer systems for access to other DSS software, model, and data resources.
- **Software resources.** DSS software packages (*DSS generators*) contain software modules to manage DSS databases, decision models, and end user/system dialogue.
- **Data resources.** A DSS database contains data and information extracted from the databases of the organization, external databases, and a manager's personal databases. It includes summarized data and information most needed by managers for specific types of decisions.
- **Model resources.** The *model base* includes a library of mathematical models and analytical techniques stored as programs, subroutines, spreadsheets, and command files.
- **People resources.** A DSS can be used by managers or their staff specialists to explore decision alternatives. Decision support systems can also be developed by such end users. However, the development of large or complex decision support systems and DSS generator software packages is typically left to information systems specialists.

FIGURE 9.8
The decision support system concept. Note that hardware, software, data, model, and people resources provide interactive decision support for managers.

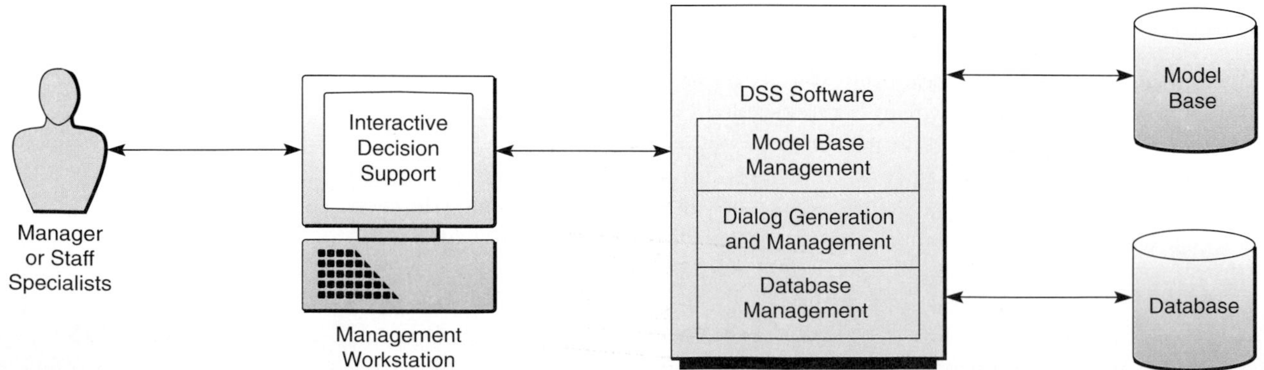

Models for Decision Support

Unlike information reporting systems, decision support systems rely on model bases as well as databases as vital system resources. A DSS **model base** is an organized collection of mathematical models. It includes models developed to support specific decisions as well as general-purpose models. The model base can include models representing simple computational and analytical routines, or models that mathematically express complex relationships among many variables.

For example, models might express simple accounting relationships among variables, such as revenue − expenses = profit. Or the DSS model base could include models and analytical techniques used to express much more complex relationships among variables. For example, it might contain linear programming models, multiple regression forecasting models, and capital budgeting present value models. Such models may be stored in the form of spreadsheet models or *templates*, programs and program modules, and command files. Model base management software packages can combine models and model components to create integrated models that support specific types of decisions.

Software for Decision Support

The software resources needed by decision support systems must integrate the management and use of the model bases, databases, and dialogue generation capabilities of a decision support system. They range from special-purpose and full-featured **DSS generators** to more modest electronic spreadsheet and integrated packages.

Figure 9.9 is a display provided by EXPRESS/EIS, a popular DSS/EIS generator. Notice how it compares the revenue of a company's three product lines. Several other DSS software packages (such as IFPS/PLUS, ENCORE, STRATEGEM, and System W) are available from independent consulting firms and computer manufacturers. Many are now available in microcomputer versions (e.g., PC/FOCUS, IFPS Personal, and ENCORE). In addition, statistical software packages (such as the SAS System and SPSS-X) are used as DSS generators for decision support that requires extensive statistical analysis.

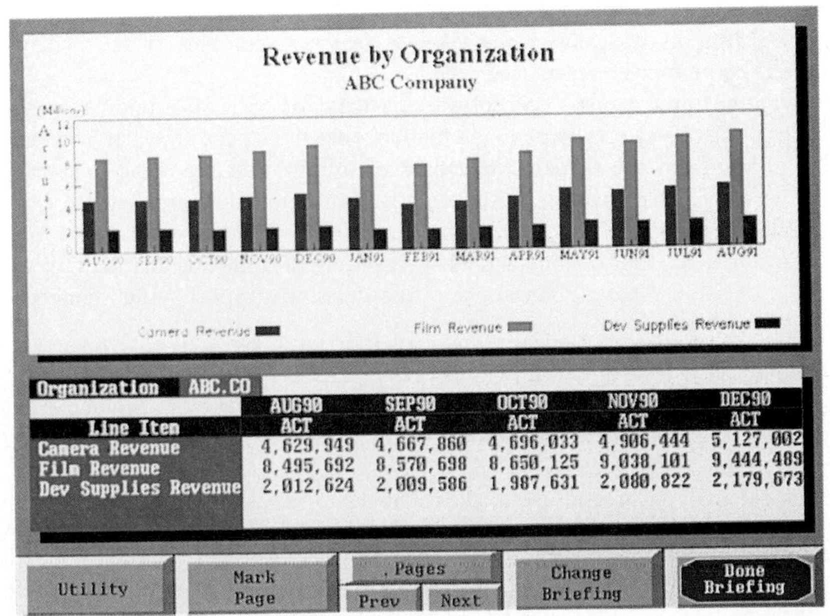

Courtesy of Information Resources, Inc.

FIGURE 9.9
Using a DSS/EIS package helps a manager compare the revenue of a company's product lines as an aid to decision making.

DSS and Electronic Spreadsheets

Don't forget that electronic spreadsheet packages (such as Lotus 1-2-3, Excel, and Quattro Pro) and integrated packages (such as Microsoft Works, Enable, and Framework) are limited DSS generators. They provide some of the model building (spreadsheet models), analytical modeling (*what-if* and *goal seeking* analysis), database management, and dialogue management (menus, icons, and prompts) offered by more powerful DSS generators. For example, we have discussed several times how a product manager could use a spreadsheet package to support his or her decision making.

An electronic spreadsheet package allows you to build models by entering the data and relationships (formulas) of a problem into the columns and rows of a worksheet format. Then you can do what-if analysis by making a variety of changes to data and formulas and visually evaluating the results of such changes either in worksheet or graphics displays. Spreadsheet programs provide many commands to manipulate the worksheet and also include built-in *functions* that perform common arithmetic, statistical, and financial computations needed for decision support. Figures 9.10, 9.11 and 9.12 provide examples of a simple spreadsheet, the formulas and functions that constitute the spreadsheet model, and graphics generated by the spreadsheet package.

An electronic spreadsheet package is a valuable tool for both business analysis and decision support. It can be used to solve problems that require the comparison, projection, or evaluation of alternatives. Therefore, spreadsheets are used for many applications. Typical business uses include sales forecasting, profit and loss analysis, product pricing, investment analysis, budget development, cash flow analysis, financial statement preparation, construction bidding, real estate investment, and bank loan analysis.

Using Decision Support Systems

Using a decision support system involves an interactive **analytical modeling** process. Typically, a manager or staff specialist uses a DSS software package at his or her workstation. This allows managers to make inquiries and responses and issue commands using a keyboard, an electronic mouse, a touch screen, or possibly voice input. Output is typically in the form of text and graphics visual displays, but printed reports may be produced.

For example, using a DSS software package for decision support may result in a series of displays in response to alternative what-if changes keyed in by a manager. This differs from the demand responses of information reporting systems, since managers are not demanding prespecified information. Rather, they are exploring possible alternatives. Thus, they do not have to specify their information needs in advance. Instead, the DSS interactively helps them find the information they need to make a decision. That is the essence of the decision support system concept.

Analytical Modeling Alternatives

Using a decision support system involves four basic types of analytical modeling activities: (1) what-if analysis, (2) sensitivity analysis, (3) goal seeking analysis, and (4) optimization analysis [16]. Let's briefly look at each type of analytical modeling that can be used for decision support. See Figure 9.13.

What-if Analysis

In what-if analysis, an end user makes changes to variables, or relationships among variables, and observes the resulting changes in the values of other variables. As we mentioned earlier, a spreadsheet user might change a revenue amount (a variable) or a tax rate formula (a relationship among variables) in a simple financial spreadsheet model. Then he or she could command the spreadsheet program to instantly

FIGURE 9.10
An example of a simple spreadsheet.

ABC Company: Financial Performance					
	1991	1992	1993	Total	Average
Revenue	$1,000.00	$1,100.00	$1,200.00	$3,300.00	$1,100.00
Expenses	$600.00	$660.00	$720.00	$1,980.00	$660.00
Profit	$400.00	$440.00	$480.00	$1,320.00	$440.00
Taxes	$160.00	$176.00	$192.00	$528.00	$176.00
Profit after taxes	$240.00	$264.00	$288.00	$792.00	$264.00

FIGURE 9.11
These formulas and functions constitute the spreadsheet model for the spreadsheet in Figure 9.10.

ABC Company: Financial Performance					
	1991	1992	1993	Total	Average
Revenue	(C5)	(C5*(1.1)	(C5*(1.2)	@SUM(C5..E	@AVG(C5..E
Expenses	(C5*0.6)	(D5*0.6)	(E5*0.6)	(F5*0.6)	@AVG(C6..E
Profit	(C5-C6)	(D5-D6)	(E5-E6)	(F5-F6)	@AVG(C8..E
Taxes	(C8*0.4)	(D8*0.4)	(E8*0.4)	(F8*0.4)	@AVG(C9..E
Profit after taxes	(C8-C9)	(D8-D9)	(E8-E9)	(F8-F9)	@AVG(C11..E

FIGURE 9.12
Examples of a bar graph and a pie chart of the data in the spreadsheet shown in Figure 9.10.

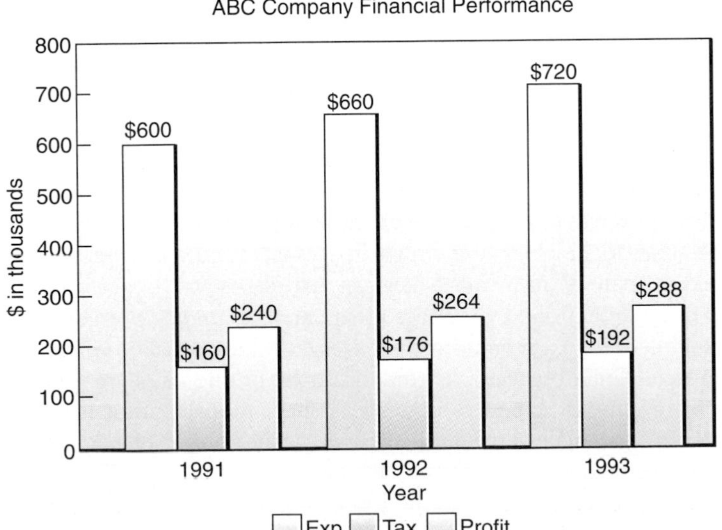

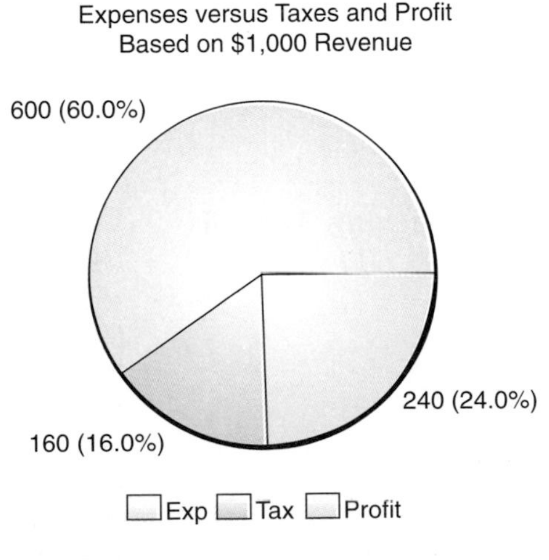

FIGURE 9.13
Activities and examples of the major types of analytical modeling.

Type of Analytical Modeling	Activities and Examples
What-if analysis	Observing how changes to selected variables affect other variables. *Example:* What if we cut advertising by 10 percent? What would happen to sales?
Sensitivity analysis	Observing how repeated changes to a single variable affects other variables. *Example:* Let's cut advertising by $100 repeatedly so we can see its relationship to sales.
Goal seeking analysis	Making repeated changes to selected variables until a chosen variable reaches a target value. *Example:* Let's try increases in advertising until sales reach $1 million.
Optimization analysis	Finding an optimum value for selected variables given certain constraints. *Example:* What's the best amount of advertising to have, given our budget and choice of media?

recalculate all affected variables in the spreadsheet. A managerial user would be very interested in observing and evaluating any changes that occurred to the values in the spreadsheet, especially to a variable such as net profit after taxes. To many managers, net profit after taxes is an example of the bottom line, that is, a key factor in making many types of decisions. This type of analysis would be repeated until the manager was satisfied with what the results revealed about the effects of various possible decisions. Figure 9.14 is an example of what-if analysis.

Sensitivity Analysis

Sensitivity analysis is a special case of what-if analysis. Typically, the value of only one variable is changed repeatedly, and the resulting changes on other variables are observed. So sensitivity analysis is really a case of what-if analysis involving repeated changes to only one variable at a time. Some DSS packages automatically make repeated small changes to a variable when asked to perform sensitivity analysis. Typically, sensitivity analysis is used when decision makers are uncertain about the assumptions made in estimating the value of certain key variables. In our previous spreadsheet example, the value of revenue could be changed repeatedly in small increments, and the effects on other spreadsheet variables observed and evaluated. This would help a manager understand the impact of various revenue levels on other factors involved in decisions being considered.

Goal Seeking Analysis

Goal seeking analysis reverses the direction of the analysis done in what-if and sensitivity analysis. Instead of observing how changes in a variable affect other variables, goal seeking analysis (also called *how can* analysis) sets a target value (a goal) for a variable and then repeatedly changes other variables until the target value is achieved. For example, a manager could specify a target value or goal of $2 million for net profit after taxes for a business venture. Then he or she could repeatedly change the value of revenue or expenses in a spreadsheet model until a result of $2 million is achieved. The manager would discover what amount of revenue or level of expenses the business venture needs to achieve in order to reach the goal of $2 million in after-tax profits. Therefore, this form of analytical modeling would help answer the question, "How can we achieve $2 million in net profit after taxes?" instead of the question, "What happens if we change revenue or expenses?" Thus, goal seeking analysis is another important method of decision support.

Profit and Loss Report
ABC Company – April 1992

	Actuals	Budget	$ Variance	% Variance
Camera Revenue	4,587,960.0	3,423,956.0	1,164,003.0	33.996
Film Revenue	8,461,277.0	6,887,128.0	1,574,150.0	22.856
Dev Supplies Revenue	2,073,848.0	1,622,587.0	451,261.40	27.811
Total Revenue	15,095,07			
Cost of Goods Sold	16,13			
Total Equipment Costs	66,14			
Total Facility Costs	243,06			
Total Labor Expenses	949,11			
Total T&E	398,62			
Total Marketing	936,92			
Miscellaneous Expenses	102,16			
Total Expenses	2,623,16			
Profit	12,471,91			

Assumptions

Data: ACTUALS

Camera Revenue % gross:	0.05
Film Revenue % gross:	0.05
Supplies Rev. % gross:	0.05
Total Expenses % gross:	0.05

CANCEL RESET CALC

Print Edit Org Time What-If Done

Courtesy of Information Resources, Inc.

FIGURE 9.14
The EXPRESS/EIS package can use a spreadsheet format to do what-if analysis.

Optimization Analysis

Optimization analysis is a more complex extension of goal seeking analysis. Instead of setting a specific target value for a variable, the goal is to find the optimum value for one or more target variables, given certain constraints. Then one or more other variables are changed repeatedly, subject to the specified constraints, until the best values for the target variables are discovered. For example, a manager could try to determine the highest possible level of profits that could be achieved by varying the values for selected revenue sources and expense categories. Changes to such variables could be subject to constraints such as the limited capacity of a production process or limits to available financing. Optimization is typically accomplished by special-purpose software packages for optimization techniques such as linear programming, or by advanced DSS generators. Figure 9.7 illustrated how the RealPlan DSS uses optimization and sensitivity analysis to support commercial real estate investment decisions.

Group Decision Support Systems

Decision making by groups of people is an important dimension of managerial decision making. In the real world, many decisions are not made by solitary decision makers. Instead, decisions are frequently made by groups of people coming to an agreement on a particular issue. Between these two extremes is a consultative type of decision making, combining both individual and group characteristics. For example, a manager may ask advice from other people individually before making a particular decision. Or the manager may bring a group of people together to discuss an issue but still makes the final decision.

Group Decision Making

Thus, managers are frequently faced with decision-making situations that require interaction with groups of people. Figure 9.15 outlines some of the major factors that affect group decision making. The success of group decision making depends on such factors as (1) the characteristics of the group itself, (2) the characteristics of the task on which the group is working, (3) the organizational context in which the group decision-making process takes place, (4) the use of information technology such as electronic meeting systems and group decision

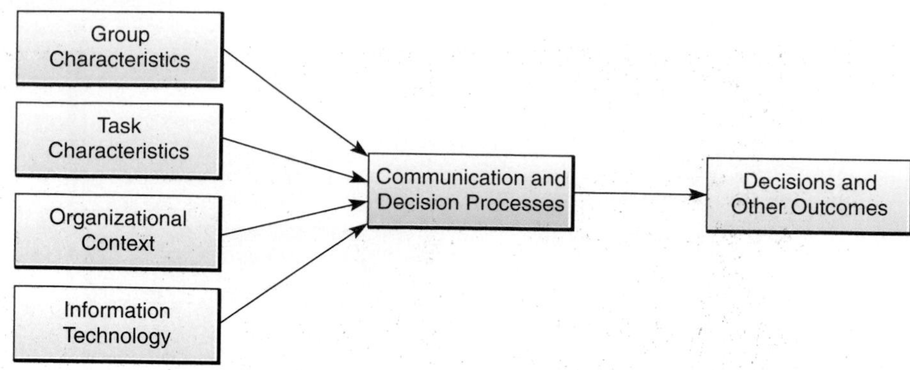

FIGURE 9.15
Important factors affecting the success of group decision making.

Source: Adapted from Jay Nunamaker et al., "Electronic Meetings to Support Group Work," *Communications of the ACM*, July 1991, p. 44.

support systems, and (5) the communication and decision-making processes the group utilizes [4, 15].

Information technology can provide a variety of computer-based tools to increase the effectiveness of group decision making. This includes **group decision support systems** (GDSS), electronic meeting systems (EMS), and computer-based systems for cooperative work (CSCW). We discussed these systems in Chapter 7 in the context of work group computing and office automation. Research studies indicate that EMS and GDSS produce significant improvements in factors such as ease of communication, anonymity, and public recording of communications (group memory). This significantly improves the efficiency and effectiveness of group decision making in business meetings [10, 15].

GDSS Packages

The unique needs of decision making by groups of people have spawned a variety of software packages for group decision support systems. For example, extensive electronic meeting systems packages are available which support the various group activities that may take place in a group decision-making situation. Other GDSS software may be designed to support a specific application or task, such as a package for labor/management negotiations or a package that merely supports anonymous voting by members of a group. Figure 9.16 is an example of the group decision-making activities supported by the software tools in the GroupSystems EMS software package developed at the University of Arizona [15].

Groupware packages which support work group computing activities may also support group decision making for members of a work group whose workstations are interconnected by a local area network. As we mentioned in Chapter 7, these packages are designed to support work group collaboration and communications in *computer-based systems for cooperative work* (CSCW) or *collaborative work support systems* (CWSS). Thus, they can support group decision making, document preparation, communications, and other work group activities. For example, some groupware packages support joint what-if analysis of a spreadsheet model and electronic mail among members of a work group to accomplish group decision making.

Executive Information Systems

Executive information systems (EIS) are information systems that combine many of the features of information reporting systems and decision support systems. However, their focus is on meeting the strategic information needs of top management. Thus, the goal of executive information systems is to provide top management

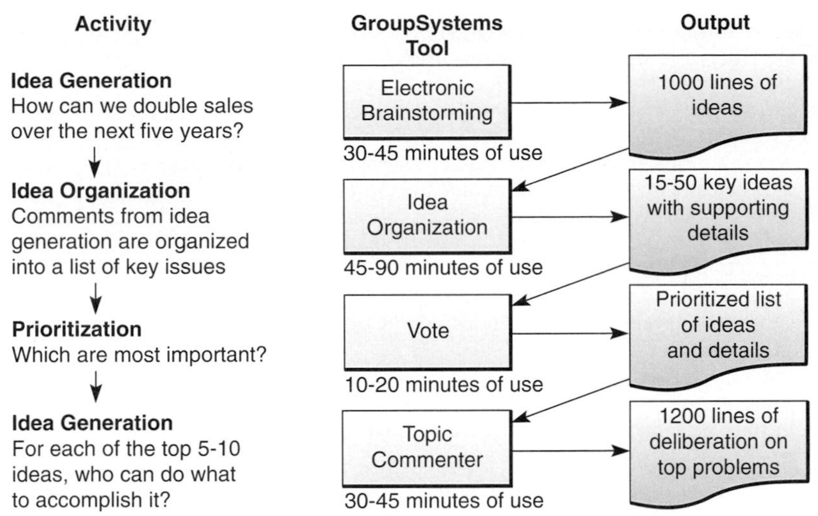

Source: J. F. Nunamaker et at., "Electronic Meetings to Support Group Work," *Communications of the ACM*, July 1991, p. 44.

FIGURE 9.16
An example of the use of the software tools in the Group-Systems software package for conducting electronic meetings. Note the various group activities support by the modules of the GDSS package.

with immediate and easy access to information about a firm's *critical success factors* (CSFs), that is, key factors that are critical to accomplishing an organization's strategic objectives. For example, the executives of a department store chain would probably consider factors such as its sales promotion efforts and its product line mix to be critical to its survival and success.

Rationale for EIS

Studies have shown that top executives get the information they need from many sources. These include letters, memos, periodicals, and reports produced manually or by computer systems. Other major sources of executive information are meetings, telephone calls, and social activities. Thus, much of a top executive's information comes from noncomputer sources. Computer-generated information has not played a major role in meeting many top executives' information needs [20].

Therefore, computer-based executive information systems have been developed which meet the information needs of top management that are not being met by other forms of MIS. Executives and IS specialists have capitalized on advances in computer technology to develop attractive, easy-to-use ways to provide executives with the information they need. Software packages are now available that support EIS on mainframe, minicomputer, and networked microcomputer systems.

Executive information systems are still faced with resistance by some executives, plagued by high costs, and have had many publicized failures. However, the use of executive information systems is growing rapidly. They are spreading even into the ranks of middle management as more executives come to recognize their feasibility and benefits, and as less expensive microcomputer-based systems for local area networks become available. Also, more features, such as DSS and expert system capabilities, electronic mail, and personal productivity aids such as electronic calendars, are being added to many systems to make them more attractive to executives. That is why the term **executive support system** (ESS) is being used to describe such EIS [20, 26]. See Figure 9.17.

Components of an EIS

As Figure 9.18 illustrates, executive workstations in an EIS are typically networked to mainframe or minicomputer systems or LAN servers for access to EIS software. The EIS package works with database management and telecommunications soft-

FIGURE 9.17
Capabilities of executive information and support systems.

Executive Information Systems (EIS)
- are tailored to individual executive users
- extract, filter, compress, and track critical data
- provide online status access, trend analysis, exception reporting, and "drill-down" capabilities
- access and integrate a broad range of internal and external data
- are user-friendly and require minimal or no training to use
- are used directly by executives without intermediaries
- present graphical, tabular, and/or textual information

Executive Support Systems (ESS)
- are EIS with additional capabilities
- support electronic communications (e.g., E-mail, computer conferencing, and word processing)
- provide data analysis capabilities (e.g., spreadsheets, query languages, and decision support systems)
- include personal productivity tools (e.g., electronic calendars, rolodex, and tickler files)

Source: Adapted from Hugh Watson, R. Kelly Ranier, and Chang Koh, "Executive Information Systems: A Framework for Development and a Survey of Current Practices," *MIS Quarterly*, March 1991, p. 14.

ware to provide easy access to internal, external, and special databases with almost instantaneous response times. Executive information systems provide information about the current status and projected trends in a company's critical success factors, as determined by its top executives. An analytical modeling capability to evaluate alternatives for decision support is also being provided by newer EIS packages, as are some expert system features, such as an *explain* capability.

Of course, in an EIS, information is presented in forms tailored to the preferences of the executives using the system. For example, most executive information systems stress the use of a graphical user interface and graphics displays that can be customized to the information preferences of executives using the EIS. Other information presentation methods used by an EIS include exception reporting and trend analysis. The ability to "drill down," which allows executives to quickly retrieve displays of related information at lower levels of detail, is another important capability of an EIS [5, 20, 26].

Example of an EIS

Figure 9.19 shows actual displays provided by the Commander executive information system. Notice how simple and brief these displays are. Also note how they provide executives with the ability to drill down quickly to lower levels of detail in areas of particular interest to them. This drill-down capability is related to the hypertext technology (discussed in Chapter 7) which allows end users to interactively retrieve related pieces of information from text databases. That is why many EIS packages for microcomputers are based on hypertext systems. Besides the drill-down capability, the Commander also stresses trend analysis and exception reporting. Thus, an executive can quickly discover the direction key factors are heading and the extent to which critical factors are deviating from expected results [5, 26].

Developing DSS and EIS

Decision support and executive information systems must be created by a developmental process that differs in several major respects from that used to develop other types of information systems. One reason for this is that a DSS or EIS must have unique capabilities in handling internal and external data, analytical models, and user dialogue. Another reason is that the decision support or strategic orientation of

FIGURE 9.18
The executive information system concept. Note the hardware, software, and data resources involved.

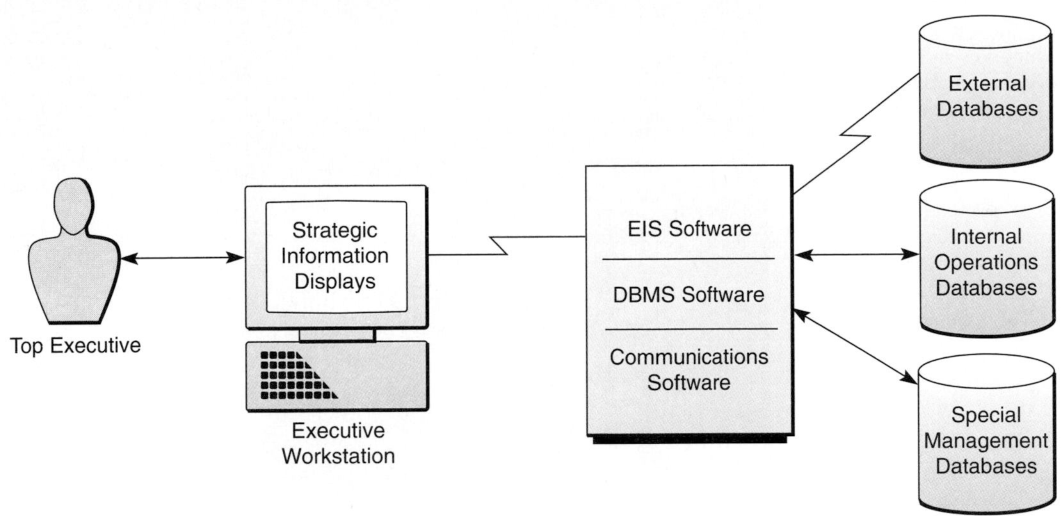

a DSS or EIS makes it harder to specify user requirements in advance, compared to the prespecified information focus of information reporting systems or the transaction data focus of transaction processing systems. Also, especially in the case of DSS, they must be designed to support specific types of decisions faced by end users, and support all four stages of the decision-making process. An EIS also has unique information presentation requirements and usually needs a member of top management to sponsor its development [25, 26]. Figure 9.20 outlines key factors that must be considered in developing a successful EIS. Alternative approaches for developing decision support or executive information systems include:

- **Acquire a special-purpose DSS or EIS package.** Acquiring a fully developed, commercial DSS or EIS package specifically designed for particular types of decision making is one option. For example, a real estate investment firm could purchase or lease the RealPlan package, mentioned earlier for real estate investment analysis. A government agency could acquire the GeoManager package from IBM for law enforcement resource allocation decisions. Or an airline company could license the AAIMS package from American Airlines to support decisions common to the airline industry.
- **Use a DSS or EIS development package.** Another possibility is acquiring DSS generators and other packages as tools for developing a decision or executive support system. As we mentioned earlier, full-capability DSS generators such as IFPS/Plus, FOCUS, and EXPRESS could be used to develop the capabilities needed by a DSS. This process includes building the user interface and the data and model bases needed by the DSS. EIS packages like Commander by Comshare or Command Center by Pilot enable IS specialists to customize an EIS for a company's executives. Other packages, such as statistical analysis or linear programming packages, could be acquired if they are needed for decision support, instead of developing those capabilities from scratch.

FIGURE 9.19
Displays provided by the Commander executive information system. Note the simplicity and clarity in which key information is provided, and the ability to drill down to lower levels of detail.

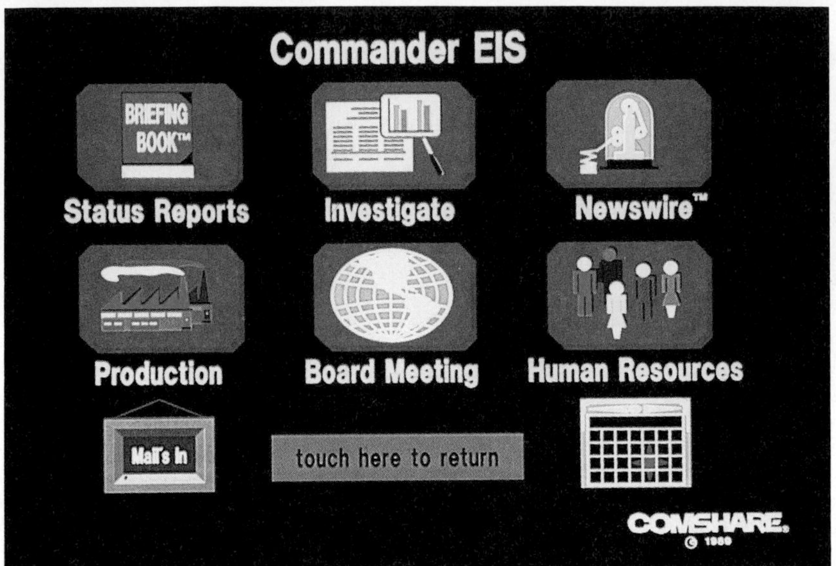

Courtesy Comshare Corporation.

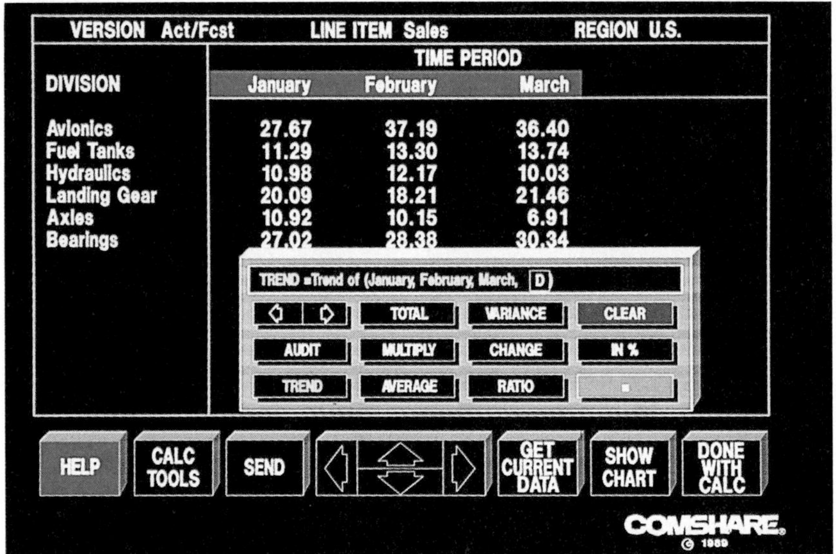

Courtesy Comshare Corporation.

- **Use end user application packages.** Deserving special mention is the use of electronic spreadsheet packages, integrated packages, and other microcomputer packages to provide some DSS or EIS features. For example, spreadsheet packages have become a popular way for users to build and manipulate analytical models for decision support. Integrated packages may add features such as database management, graphics, electronic mail, and desktop accessories to a spreadsheet capability to provide a simple, but effective, managerial support system.

FIGURE 9.20
Key factors needed for a successful EIS.

Commitment and Involvement from Top-Level Management
If executives are not visibly 100 percent behind the project, it will not get the priority or ongoing use.

Understanding Data Sources
A successful EIS implementation depends on the availability of accurate and complete data. For many organizations, this could mean that a significant investment in existing business systems is needed prior to implementing EIS.

Focusing on What Is Important
Organization CSFs, exception reporting, accessing information with drill-down capability are a key to success of an EIS.

Response Time
A successful EIS will increase in use, functionally and scope over time. Ongoing system performance monitoring is key.

Understanding of Computer Literacy Level of Executives
Dictates presentation format, degree of use of graphics, text, mouse, touch screen, etc. The EIS must be easy to use.

Learning Curve for Development Team
Tools to be used are key, especially if developing a system. Familiar tools are best. Vendor support for an EIS package is essential.

Flexibility
Executives' needs will continue to evolve and change with time. As much flexibility as possible should be included.

Ongoing Support
EIS cannot be implemented and forgotten. Continuing support is critical to satisfy changing needs.

Source: John Southcott and Bruch Hooey, "EIS Big League Decision Support," *Edge*, November/December 1989, p. 29.

- **Develop a custom DSS or EIS.** Finally, a DSS or EIS can be developed from scratch using a variety of systems development and software development tools and programming languages. Custom development can be appropriate for simple or complex systems, depending on the unique type of decisions or executives involved. The expertise of the decision makers and the availability of support from systems development specialists are major factors to consider when deciding on this approach.

REAL WORLD CASE

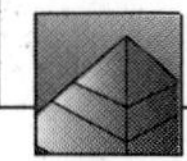

Mazda and Ford Motor Companies: Information Systems for Quality Management

The word *kaizen* is Japanese for a business philosophy of constant improvement. You can find the word written on bulletin boards and the concept depicted in murals on the manufacturing floor at Auto Alliance International, Inc. (AAI), the venture between Mazda Motor Corp. and Ford Motor Co. that produces the Ford Probe, Mazda 626, and Mazda MX-6.

To help implement kaizen, the alliance has launched a quality information management system (QIMS). The system instantly delivers information collected by inspectors on the plant floor about problems that prevent cars from shipping. The information is compiled every six minutes and made available to managers, engineers, analysts, and executives via nodes on a local-area network.

Although this was a big improvement over previous paper and pencil systems, the company has gone one step further and found a way to get the data into the hands of 70 managers and executives wherever they are, using pagers. "There are some people that say, 'You aren't going to change manufacturing or make an improvement with just the data.' That is correct," says Kasey Kasemodel, an analyst at Mazda Systems Service of North America, the group in charge of developing QIMS. "But you also aren't going to make any changes unless you have the information, so this is just one step in being able to improve the quality of the vehicles."

Before QIMS, it took roughly 30 hours for data collected on the production line to reach decision makers who could address problems, Kasemodel said. In addition, it was difficult or impossible to study the history of problems because the reports were rigidly formatted and distributed on paper. Now, information is available almost immediately, and custom reports can be generated in minutes.

While the impact of getting data faster is hard to measure precisely, response time to problems "has definitely improved," according to Joe Silvestri, senior staff engineer at AAI. In addition, the company saves administrative and personnel costs because fewer people are needed to collect and distribute the data. The half-million-dollar investment in hardware, software, and programming hours will pay back in less than eight months, Silvestri estimated.

Inspectors check every vehicle and record problems on a ticket that accompanies the vehicles to the end of the production line. There, final inspectors speak into headsets equipped with Task Manager voice recognition software. The inspectors have a 600-word vocabulary to describe what is wrong with the vehicle. Every time a car is completed, the information is transmitted by radio frequency to a PC workstation 70 feet away. The station is connected to a local area network via fiber cabling that runs to the ceiling of the production area and continues on to a "task processor" PC in a computer room.

At intervals of one minute, the task processor PC polls the workstation on the plant floor, uploads the data, generates reports, and creates database files. A database server lifts the data from the task processor, and users throughout the network query the database and generate reports using the Excel spreadsheet program. Using the Excel program, users can click on a certain field, such as Top 20 concerns, do "what-if" modeling, and generate custom reports in a matter of minutes.

Meanwhile, condensed data, such as the number of cars that come through the system, is sent every two hours via modem from a page server to a host computer and then is broadcast to roughly 70 unit leaders, managers, and executives carrying pagers. "The way we are disseminating information is changing how people look at data," Kasemodel said. "They don't have to seek out a PC; the data comes to them, and that keeps people focused on quality."

CASE STUDY QUESTIONS

1. Is QIMS an information reporting system or a decision support system? Explain.
2. What are the benefits of QIMS to Mazda and Ford compared to previous systems?
3. What other types of business firms could use a system like QIMS? Give several examples.

Source: Adapted from Lynda Radosevich, "Ford, Mazda Put Quality On-Line," *Computerworld*, March 1, 1993, pp. 51–52. Used with permission.

SECTION II
Artificial Intelligence and Expert Systems

An Overview of Artificial Intelligence

The field of information systems and its applications in business and society are being increasingly affected by developments in the field of artificial intelligence. Developments such as natural languages and user interfaces, industrial robots, expert systems, and "intelligent" computers are some examples of this impact. As a future business end user, you should be aware of the importance of such developments. Businesses and other organizations are significantly increasing their attempts to assist the human intelligence and productivity of their knowledge workers with artificial intelligence tools and techniques.

But what is artificial intelligence? **Artificial intelligence** (AI) is a science and technology based on disciplines such as computer science, biology, psychology, linguistics, mathematics, and engineering. The goal of AI is to develop computers that can think, as well as see, hear, walk, talk, and feel. A major thrust of artificial intelligence is the development of computer functions normally associated with human intelligence, such as reasoning, learning, and problem solving, as summarized in Figure 9.21. That's why the term *artificial intelligence* was coined by John McCarthy at MIT in 1956. Besides McCarthy, AI pioneers included Herbert Simon and Allen Newell at Carnegie-Mellon, Norbert Wiener and Marvin Minsky at MIT, Warren McCulloch and Walter Pitts at Illinois, Frank Rosenblatt at Cornell, Alan Turing at Manchester, Edward Feigenbaum at Stanford, Roger Shank at Yale, and many others [24].

Debate has raged around artificial intelligence since serious work in the field began in the 1950s. The possibility of intelligent, "thinking" machines involves not only technological questions, but moral and philosophical questions as well. For example, British AI pioneer Alan Turing in 1950 proposed a test for determining if machines could think. According to the Turing test, a computer could demonstrate intelligence if a human interviewer, conversing with an unseen human and an unseen computer, could not tell which was which [27].

Though much work has been done in many of the subgroups that fall under the AI umbrella, critics believe that no computer can truly pass the Turing test. They claim that developing intelligence to impart true humanlike capabilities to computers is simply not possible. But progress continues, and only time will tell if the ambitious goals of artificial intelligence will be achieved and equal the popular images found in science fiction.

The Domains of Artificial Intelligence

Figure 9.22 illustrates the major domains of AI research and development. Note that AI applications can be grouped under the four major areas of cognitive science, computer science, robotics, and natural interfaces, though these classifications do overlap each other and other classifications can be used. Also note that expert systems are just one of many important AI applications. Let's briefly review each of these major areas of AI and some of their current applications.

Cognitive Science

This area of artificial intelligence is based on research in biology, neurology, psychology, mathematics, and many allied disciplines. It focuses on researching how the human brain works and how humans think and learn. The results of such research in *human information processing* are the basis for the development of a variety of computer-based applications in artificial intelligence.

FIGURE 9.21
Attributes of intelligent behavior. AI is attempting to duplicate these capabilities in computer-based systems.

- Think and reason.
- Use reason to solve problems.
- Learn or understand from experience.
- Acquire and apply knowledge.
- Exhibit creativity and imagination.
- Deal with complex or perplexing situations.
- Respond quickly and successfully to new situations.
- Recognize the relative importance of elements in a situation.
- Handle ambiguous, incomplete, or erroneous information.

FIGURE 9.22
The major application areas of artificial intelligence. Note that the many applications of AI can be grouped into the four major areas of cognitive science, computer science, robotics, and natural interfaces.

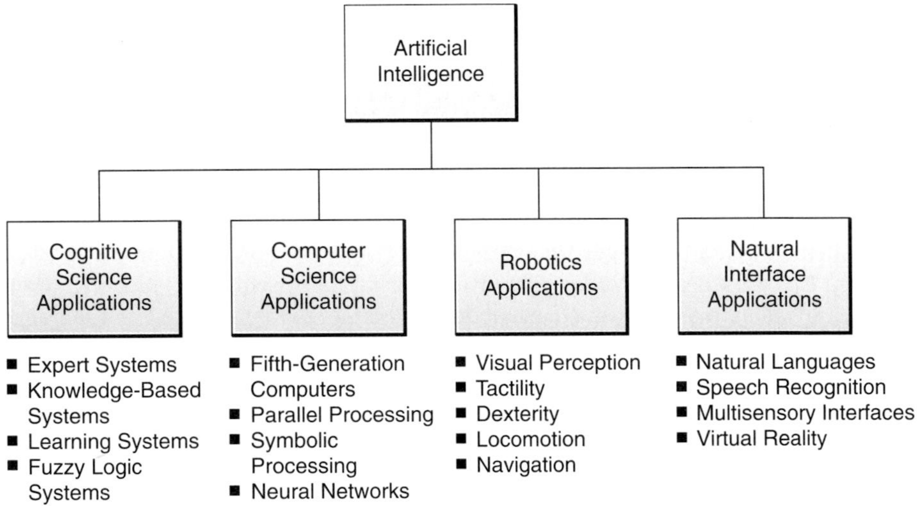

Applications in the cognitive science area of AI include the development of *expert systems* and other *knowledge-based* systems that add a knowledge base and some reasoning capability to information systems. Also included are *adaptive learning* systems that can modify their behaviors based on information they acquire as they operate. Chess-playing systems are primitive examples of such applications, though many more applications are being implemented. **Fuzzy logic** systems can process data that are incomplete or approximate, that is, *fuzzy* data. Thus, they can solve unstructured problems with incomplete knowledge by providing approximate answers, as humans do [21].

Computer Science

This area of AI applications focuses on the computer hardware and system software needed to produce the powerful supercomputers required for many AI applications. At the forefront of this area are efforts to create a *fifth* generation of intelligent computers, which use the *parallel processing* architecture discussed in Chapter 2. Such computers will be designed for optimum *logical inference* processing, which depends on *symbolic* processing instead of the numeric processing of traditional computing. Other attempts are being made to develop **neural networks**, including massively parallel, *neurocomputers* and software whose architecture is based on the human brain's meshlike neuron structure. Neural network computers can process many different pieces of information simultaneously. Neural network software for traditional computers can learn by being shown sample problems and their solutions. As they start to recognize patterns, they can begin to program themselves to solve related problems on their own [23].

Robotics

AI, engineering, and physiology are the basic disciplines of robotics. This technology produces **robot** machines with computer intelligence and computer-controlled, humanlike physical capabilities. This area thus includes applications designed to give robots the powers of sight, or *visual perception*; touch, or *tactile* capabilities; *dexterity*, or skill in handling and manipulation; *locomotion*, or the physical ability to move over any terrain; and *navigation*, or the intelligence to properly find one's way to a destination [24]. The use of robotics in computer-aided manufacturing was discussed in Chapter 8.

Natural Interfaces

The development of *natural interfaces* is considered a major area of AI applications and is essential to the natural use of computers by humans. The development of *natural languages* is a major thrust of this area of AI. Being able to talk to computers and robots in conversational human languages and have them understand us as easily as we understand each other is the goal of many AI researchers. Thus, this application area involves research and development in linguistics, psychology, computer science, and other disciplines. Applications include human language understanding, speech recognition, and the development of multisensory devices that use a variety of body movements to operate computers. Thus, this area of AI drives developments in the voice recognition and response technology discussed in Chapter 2, and the natural programming languages discussed in Chapter 3. Finally, an emerging application area in AI is **virtual reality** or *artificial reality*. This field is developing multisensory human/computer interfaces (such as video/stereo headsets and fiber-optic gloves and body suits) that enable human users to experience computer-simulated objects, spaces, and activities, and enter "virtual worlds" as if they actually exist [19]. Virtual reality video games are an early example.

Knowledge-based Information Systems

One of the most practical and widely implemented applications of artificial intelligence in business is the development of expert systems and other knowledge-based information systems. **A knowledge-based information system** (KBIS) adds a knowledge base to the major components found in other types of computer-based information systems. An **expert system** (ES) is a knowledge-based information system that uses its knowledge about a specific, complex application area to act as an expert consultant to end users. As we said in Chapter 6, expert systems can be used for either operational or management applications. Thus, they can be classified conceptually as either *operations* or *management* information systems, depending on whether they are giving expert advice to control operational processes or to help managerial end users make decisions. See Figure 9.23.

Expert systems are related to *knowledge-based decision support systems*, which add a knowledge base to the database and model base of traditional decision support systems. However, unlike decision support systems, expert systems provide answers to questions in a very specific problem area by making humanlike inferences about knowledge contained in a specialized knowledge base. They must also be able to explain their reasoning process and conclusions to a user. So expert systems can provide decision support to managers in the form of advice from an expert consultant in a specific problem area [25]. Figure 9.24 outlines the differences between expert systems and decision support systems.

FIGURE 9.23
Using an expert system at General Electric to diagnose electronic control problems for GE's large, land-based gas turbines.

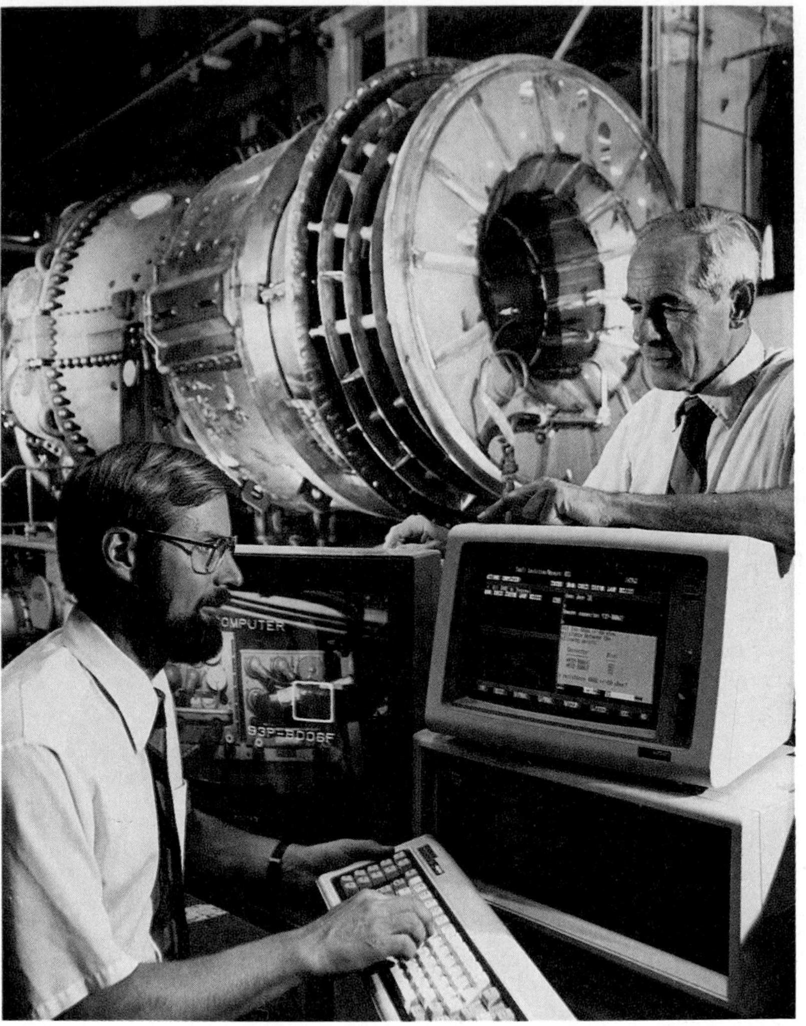

Courtesy of General Electric Research and Development Center.

Expert-assisted IS

The integration of expert systems into decision support systems and other types of information systems is expected to become a major characteristic of a trend toward *expert-assisted* information systems. This integration adds expertise as well as a knowledge base to information systems. For example, fifth-generation computer-aided systems engineering (CASE) packages are available that include expert system components. This integration promises to make the application development process easier and faster for end users and other developers who do not have a lot of systems development experience and expertise.

Another example is the integration of expert systems and decision support systems into a new generation of executive information systems. For example, Figure 9.25 illustrates how the expert system capability of an *explain* feature has been built into an EIS. This executive information system can automatically select and arrange relevant data and produce explanatory text and graphics. Therefore, it can explain the meaning of previously displayed results to an executive upon request.

Attribute	DSS	ES
Objectives	Assist human decision maker	Replicate a human advisor and replace him/her
Who makes the recommendations (decisions)?	The human and/or the system	The system
Major orientation	Decision making	Transfer of expertise (human-machine-human) and rendering of advice
Major query direction	Human queries the machine	Machine queries the human
Nature of support	Personal, groups, and institutional	Personal and groups
Data manipulation method	Numerical	Symbolic
Characteristics of problem area	Complex, broad	Narrow domain
Type of problems treated	Ad hoc, unique	Repetitive
Content of database	Factual knowledge	Procedural and factual knowledge
Reasoning capability	No	Yes, limited
Explanation capability	Limited	Yes

Source: Efraim Turban and Paul Watkins, "Integrating Expert Systems and Decision Support Systems," *MIS Quarterly*, June 1986, p. 123.

FIGURE 9.24
Differences between expert systems and decision support systems.

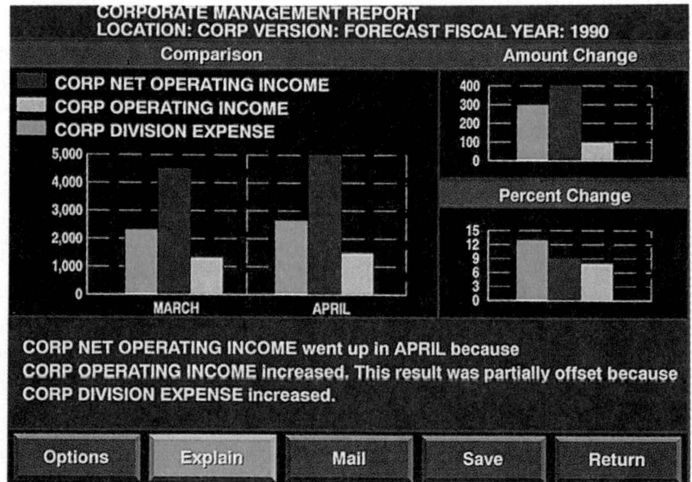

Source: Courtesy of Comshare Inc.

FIGURE 9.25
A display of an expert-assisted EIS. This executive information system will explain the reasons for previously displayed results with explanatory text and graphics upon request.

Components of an Expert System

The components of an expert system include a knowledge base and software modules that perform inferences on the knowledge and communicate answers to a user's questions. Figure 9.26 illustrates the interrelated components of an expert system. Note the following components:

- **Knowledge base.** The knowledge base of an expert system contains (1) facts about a specific subject area (e.g., *John is an analyst*) and (2) heuristics (rules of thumb) that express the reasoning procedures of an expert on the subject (e.g., *IF John is an analyst, THEN he needs a workstation*). Figure 9.27 illustrates the contents of a knowledge base in a rule-based expert system. Notice that the expert system's knowledge base consists of a *rule base* of if-then rules and a *fact base* of facts and other information about a subject, which is processed by a software component called the *inference engine*.
- **Software resources.** An expert system software package contains an **inference engine** and other programs for refining knowledge and communicating with users. The inference engine program processes the knowledge (such as rules and facts) related to a specific problem. It then makes associations and inferences resulting in recommended courses of action for a user. User interface programs for communicating with end users are also needed, including an explanation program to explain the reasoning process to a user if requested.

Inferences can be made using *forward chaining* (reaching a conclusion by applying rules to facts). For example, if a search of the rules and facts in the knowledge base found that analysts need workstations and John is an analyst, then the conclusion that "John needs a workstation" would be made.

Some expert systems use *backward chaining* (justifying a proposed conclusion by determining if it results from applying rules to facts). For example, the hypothesis that "John should have a workstation" would be accepted only if a search of the knowledge base found that analysts need workstations and John is an analyst.

Knowledge acquisition programs are not part of an expert system but are software tools for knowledge base development. Other software packages, such as expert system *shells*, are important software resources for developing expert systems.

- **Hardware resources.** These include stand-alone microcomputer systems, as well as microcomputer workstations and terminals connected to minicomputers or mainframes in a telecommunications network. Sometimes, complex expert systems are developed with powerful, special-purpose computers specifically designed for advanced expert system development packages or the LISP or PROLOG programming languages.
- **People resources.** An expert system provides expert advice to end users. This expertise is captured in a knowledge base by a *knowledge engineer* from facts and rules provided by one or more experts. Or experts and end users can be their own knowledge engineers and use expert system shells as development tools to build their own knowledge bases and expert systems.

Examples of Expert Systems

Using an expert system involves an interactive computer-based session, in which the solution to a problem is explored with the expert system acting as a consultant to an end user. The expert system asks questions of the user, searches its knowledge base for facts and rules or other knowledge, explains its reasoning process when asked, and gives expert advice to the user in the subject area being explored. For example,

FIGURE 9.26
Components of an expert system. The software modules perform inferences on a knowledge base built by an expert and/or knowledge engineer. This provides expert answers to an end user's questions in an interactive process.

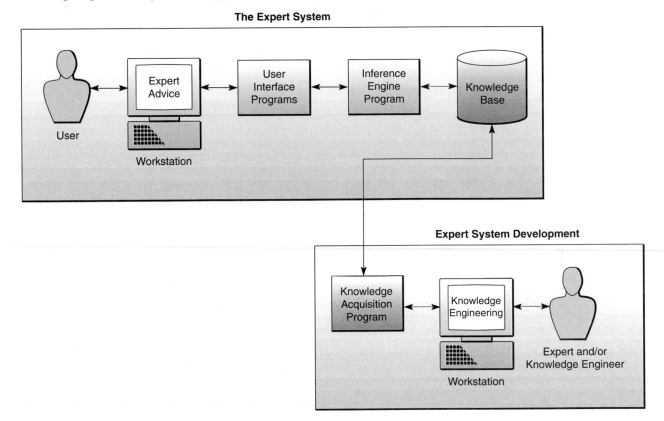

The Expert System

User
Expert Advice
Workstation
User Interface Programs
Inference Engine Program
Knowledge Base

Expert System Development

Knowledge Acquisition Program
Knowledge Engineering
Workstation
Expert and/or Knowledge Engineer

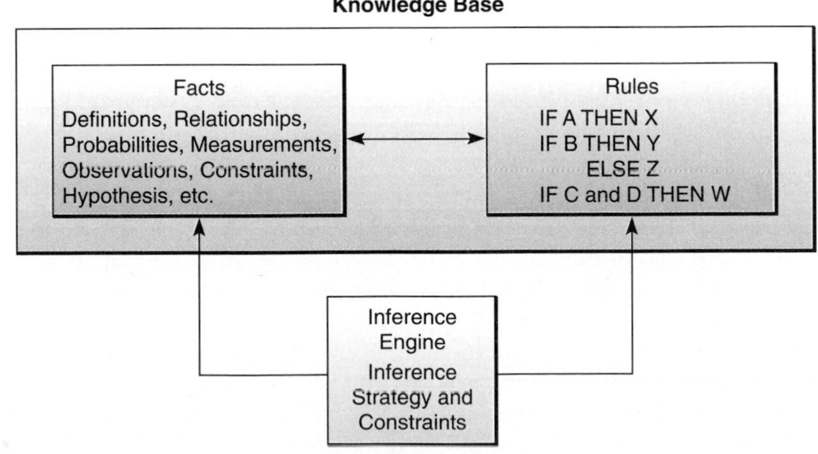

FIGURE 9.27
A rule-based expert system. Note that such systems have an inference engine program that manipulates a knowledge base consisting of facts and rules in order to reach conclusions.

FIGURE 9.28
One of the displays of the Shipping Advisor expert system. Note how it recommends the selection of a shipping alternative.

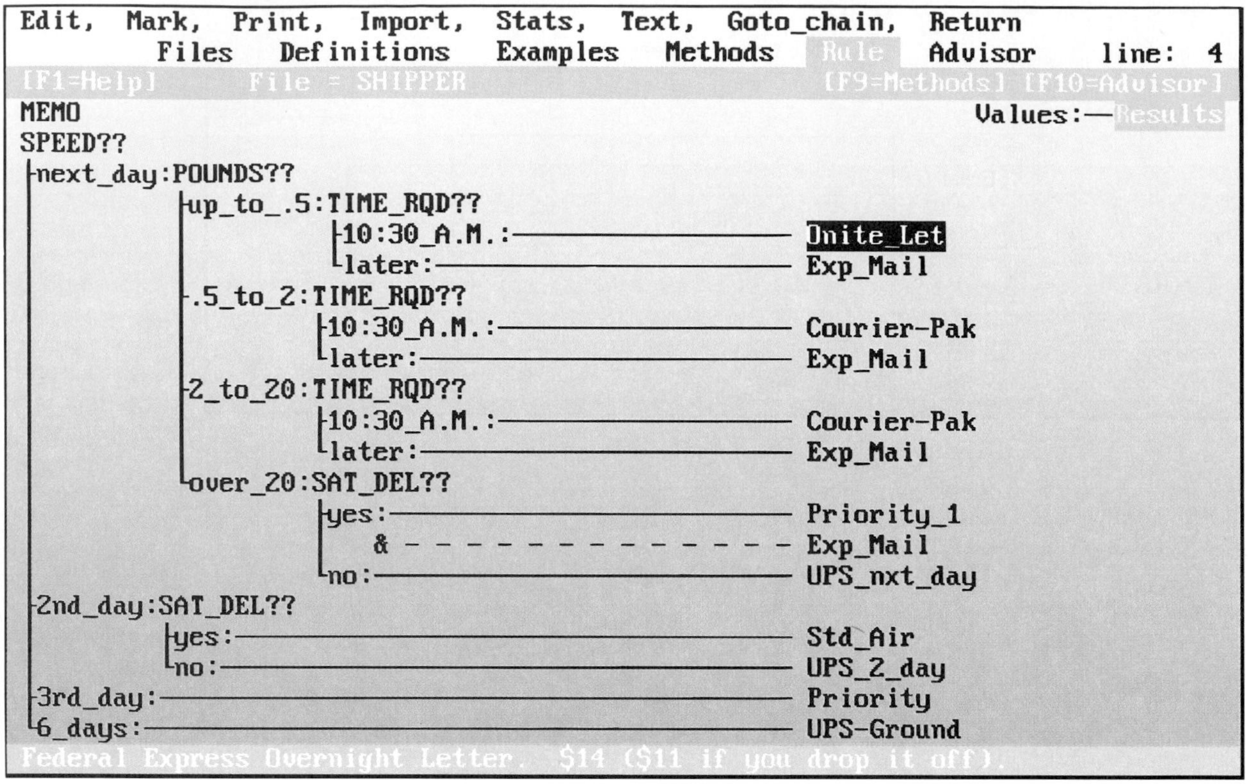

```
Edit,  Mark,  Print,  Import,  Stats,  Text,  Goto_chain,  Return
       Files   Definitions   Examples   Methods   Rule   Advisor    line:  4
[F1=Help]       File = SHIPPER                    [F9=Methods] [F10=Advisor]
MEMO                                                          Values:—Results
SPEED??
├next_day:POUNDS??
│         ├up_to_.5:TIME_RQD??
│         │          ├10:30_A.M.:─────────────────── Onite_Let
│         │          └later:──────────────────────── Exp_Mail
│         ├.5_to_2:TIME_RQD??
│         │          ├10:30_A.M.:─────────────────── Courier-Pak
│         │          └later:──────────────────────── Exp_Mail
│         ├2_to_20:TIME_RQD??
│         │          ├10:30_A.M.:─────────────────── Courier-Pak
│         │          └later:──────────────────────── Exp_Mail
│         └over_20:SAT_DEL??
│                    ├yes:────────────────────────── Priority_1
│                    │  & - - - - - - - - - - - - - Exp_Mail
│                    └no:─────────────────────────── UPS_nxt_day
├2nd_day:SAT_DEL??
│       ├yes:─────────────────────────────────────── Std_Air
│       └no:──────────────────────────────────────── UPS_2_day
├3rd_day:─────────────────────────────────────────── Priority
└6_days:──────────────────────────────────────────── UPS-Ground
Federal Express Overnight Letter.  $14 ($11 if you drop it off).
```

Courtesy AI Corp.

Figure 9.28 illustrates one of the displays of Shipping Advisor, a simple expert system built with the 1st CLASS expert system shell. It advises mailroom employees how to ship and mail packages based on time, weight, security, and other factors.

Expert System Applications

Expert systems are being used for many different types of applications, and the variety of applications is expected to continue to grow. However, you should realize that expert systems typically accomplish one or more generic uses. Figure 9.29 outlines seven generic categories of expert system activities, with specific examples of actual expert system applications. As you can see, expert systems are being used in many different fields, including medicine, engineering, the physical sciences, and business. Expert systems now help diagnose illnesses, search for minerals, analyze compounds, recommend repairs, and do financial planning. Figure 9.30 emphasizes that, from a strategic business standpoint, expert systems can and are being used to improve every step of the product cycle of a business, from finding customers to shipping products to them. Let's look at three actual examples more closely.

Credit Management

At ITT Commercial Finance Corporation, every manager who makes credit decisions can use the experience and knowledge of its senior credit experts that has been captured in the Expert Credit System (ECS). Installed throughout ITT's 23 offices in the United States, Canada, and the United Kingdom, ECS has over 250 users. ECS analyzes credit information, identifies credit proposal strengths and weaknesses, and

Application Categories and Typical Uses
Decision management—Systems that appraise situations or consider alternatives and make recommendations based on criteria supplied during the discovery process: ▪ Loan portfolio analysis ▪ Employee performance evaluation ▪ Insurance underwriting ▪ Demographic forecasts
Diagnostic/troubleshooting—Systems that infer underlying causes from reported symptoms and history: ▪ Equipment calibration ▪ Help desk operations ▪ Software debugging ▪ Medical diagnosis
Maintenance/scheduling—Systems that prioritize and schedule limited or time-critical resources: ▪ Maintenance scheduling ▪ Production scheduling ▪ Education scheduling ▪ Project management
Intelligent text/documentation—Systems that take existing legislation or established policies and procedures and recast them into a knowledge base system: ▪ Building Regulations ▪ OSHA Safety Standards ▪ Employee Benefits ▪ EEO Employment Codes
Design/configuration—Systems that help configure equipment components, given existing constraints: ▪ Computer option installation ▪ Manufacturability studies ▪ Communications networks ▪ Optimum assembly plan
Selection/classification—Systems that help users choose products or processes, often from among large or complex sets of alternatives: ▪ Material selection ▪ Delinquent account identification ▪ Information classification ▪ Suspect identification
Process monitoring/control—Systems that monitor and control procedures or processes: ▪ Machine control (including robotics) ▪ Inventory control ▪ Production monitoring ▪ Chemical testing

Source: Courtesy Information Builders, Inc.

FIGURE 9.29
Major application categories and examples of typical expert systems. Note the variety of applications that can be supported by such systems.

offers credit recommendations to ITT managers. Because ECS is user-friendly, managers can easily go through the whole process of gathering and inputting information, and receive consistent credit recommendations on a daily basis. After several years of use, the careful planning that went into the development of ECS has paid great dividends. ECS was awarded ITT's 1990 Corporate Quality Award. In the two-and-a-half years since it was installed, ECS has saved ITT approximately $500,000 in hard costs. In addition, a million-dollar savings in bad loan write-offs has been attributed to ECS [6].

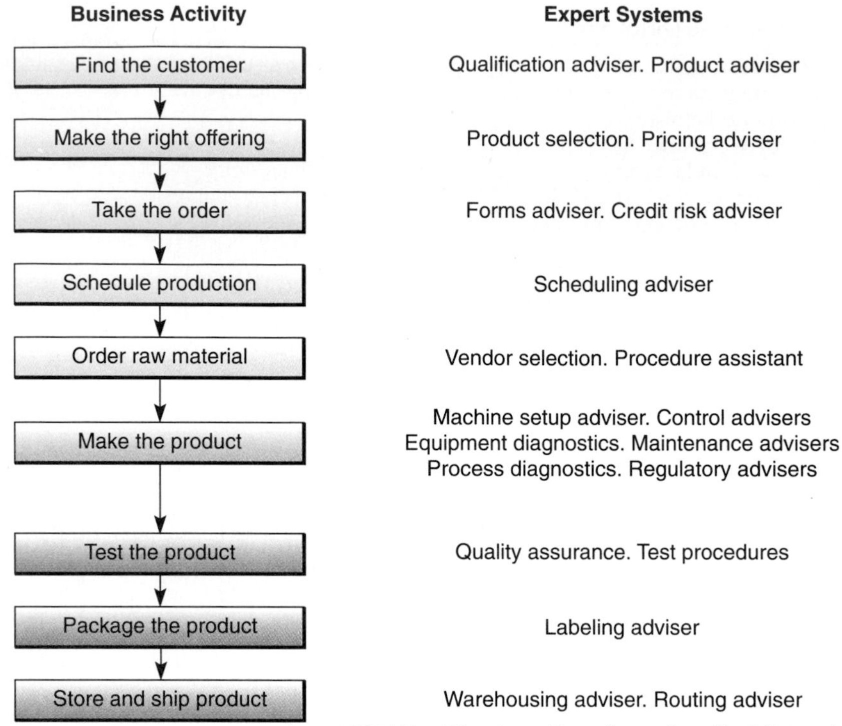

FIGURE 9.30
Expert systems can be used at every step of the product cycle of a business.

Source: Adapted from C. Lawrence Meador and Ed Mahler, "Choosing an Expert System Game Plan," *Datamation*, August 2, 1990, p. 66.

Customer Service

Texas Instruments (TI) established a customer support group for its widely used mainframe-based computer-aided software engineering (CASE) software product, the Information Engineering Facility (IEF). The customer support group was set up to minimize response time to customer questions. However, TI soon realized that the complex new product presented new problems, and not everyone in the support group was familiar with every problem.

To ensure consistent levels of quality of support and service across its entire staff, TI created the Information Engineering Facility Customer Response Expert System (IEFCARES). This expert system handles complex user problems, such as those involving system difficulties affecting printer and plotter operation. Now that the system is operational, TI expects that support personnel will be able to handle 250 percent more questions and problems by using IEFCARES [14].

Production Management

Stone & Webster Engineering has developed Production Scheduling Advisor, a production-scheduling expert system. The Advisor helps users plan daily production for a forecast period of as long as one year. It can accommodate facilities with multiple units, storage, and production streams that produce intermediate raw materials as well as finished products. It uses an interactive Gantt chart that lets users manipulate their production schedules within given constraints. Inventories, production constraints, and production cycles may be shortened, lengthened, or rescheduled. Users model their production processes with a spreadsheet module that accepts specifications by week, month, order, or in any combination. The

Suitability Criteria
Domain: The domain, or subject area, of the problem is relatively small and limited to a well-defined problem area.
Expertise: Solutions to the problem require the efforts of an expert. That is, a body of knowledge, techniques, and intuition is needed that only a few people possess.
Complexity: Solution of the problem is a complex task that requires logical inference processing, which would not be handled as well by conventional information processing.
Structure: The solution process must be able to cope with ill-structured, uncertain, missing, and conflicting data, and a problem situation that changes with the passage of time.
Availability: An expert exists who is articulate and cooperative, and who has the support of the management and end users involved in the development of the proposed system.

FIGURE 9.31
Criteria for applications that are suitable for expert systems development.

Advisor's optimization module satisfies production constraints, minimizes inventory violations, and prioritizes tasks as efficiently as possible. For example, Union Carbide, one of the first corporate users of Advisor, reports that production scheduling time has been shortened and many more alternatives are possible. They can now make last minute scheduling changes and have become much more responsive to the marketplace [11].

Developing Expert Systems

As the previous examples show, many organizations are developing expert system solutions to business problems. However, before developing an expert system, the following questions need to be answered:

- What applications are suitable for expert systems?
- What benefits and limitations of expert systems should be considered?
- Should the expert system be (1) purchased as a completely developed system, (2) developed with an expert system shell, or (3) developed from scratch as a custom system?

Expert System Suitability

Obviously, expert systems are not the answer to every problem facing an organization. People using other types of information systems do quite well in many problem situations. So what types of problems are most suitable to expert system solutions? One way to answer this is to look at examples of the applications of current expert systems, including the generic tasks being accomplished, as summarized in Figure 9.29. Another way is to identify criteria that make a problem situation suitable for an expert system. Figure 9.31 outlines some important criteria [7, 13].

Figure 9.31 should emphasize that many real world situations do not fit the suitability criteria for expert system solutions. Therefore, expert systems should be developed cautiously, especially if sensitive or strategic applications are involved. Hundreds of rules may be required to capture the assumptions, facts, and reasoning that are involved in even simple problem situations. For example, a task that might take an expert a few minutes to accomplish might require an expert system with hundreds of rules and take several months to develop. A task that may take a human expert several hours to do may require an expert system with thousands of rules and take several years to build [9, 13].

Expert Systems: Make or Buy?

Once the suitability and feasibility of a proposed expert system application have been evaluated, it's time to confront the make-or-buy decision. As you saw in a previous example, complete expert system packages like the Production Scheduling Advisor can be purchased by manufacturing companies and other businesses. Many other packages are available in a variety of application areas, and the number is increasing each year. As in other make-or-buy decisions, the suitability of the expert system package for an end user's needs must be balanced against the cost in time and money of developing a custom system.

Expert System Shells

The easiest way to develop your own expert system is to use an **expert system shell** as a developmental tool. An expert system shell is a software package consisting of an expert system without its *kernel*, that is, its knowledge base of facts and rules. This leaves a shell of software (the inference engine and user interface programs) with generic inferencing and user interface capabilities. Other development tools (such as rule editors and user interface generators) are added to make the shell a powerful expert system development tool.

Expert systems shells are now available as relatively low cost software packages that help users develop their own expert systems on microcomputers. They allow trained users to develop the knowledge base for a specific expert system application. For example, one shell uses a spreadsheet format to help end users develop if-then rules, automatically generating rules based on examples furnished by a user. Once a knowledge base is constructed, it is used with the shell's inference engine and user interface modules as a complete expert system on a specific subject area. Expert system shells have accelerated the widespread development and use of expert systems. See Figure 9.32.

Custom Expert System Development

Instead of using an expert system shell, an expert system can be developed from scratch. This requires using one or more programming languages to develop the inference engine and user interface programs and build the knowledge base of facts

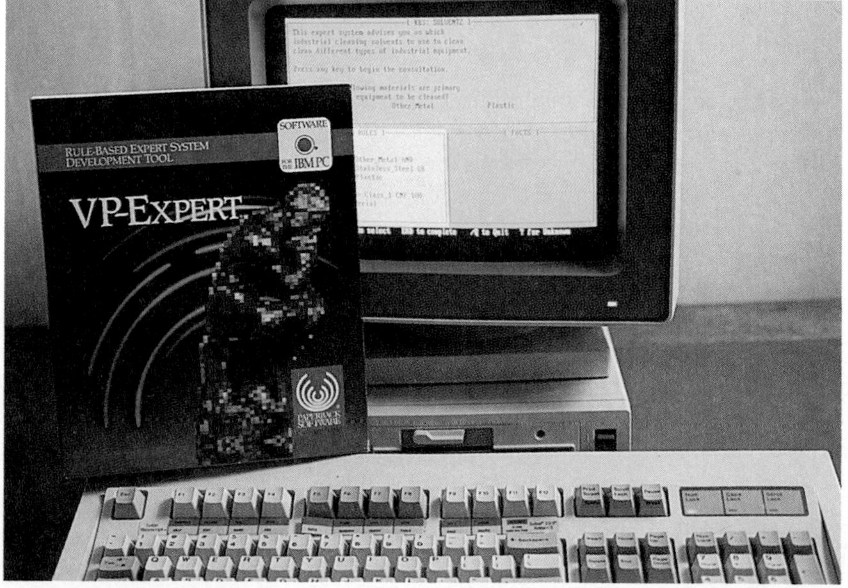

FIGURE 9.32
Using the VP-Expert system shall to develop an expert system.

Fredrik D. Bodin/Offshoot.

and rules. Obviously, this is a much more difficult, time-consuming, and costly undertaking. However, early expert systems were developed this way, as are many large expert system projects. Their developers are not satisfied with the generic nature and basic capabilities of many shells. Thus they prefer to develop an expert system tailored to their specific needs.

Two programming languages, LISP and PROLOG, have long been used for expert systems development. LISP is a procedural, list processing language specifically designed to handle many types of logical text processing (symbolic processing). PROLOG is a nonprocedural language that uses statements defining values and relationships between objects to produce logical inferences. It thus is more efficient than LISP in constructing rule-based knowledge bases. Microcomputer and minicomputer workstations designed specifically to develop and run programs written in LISP or PROLOG are sometimes used because their speed and power significantly improve the development process. However, improvements in the capabilities of computer systems and programming tools have made other languages (especially C and C++) quite popular for developing expert systems.

Knowledge Engineering

Developing expert systems is different from developing other types of information systems because it results in the development of a knowledge base, and it frequently requires the services of a knowledge engineer.

A **knowledge engineer** is a professional who works with experts to capture the knowledge (facts and rules of thumb) they possess. The knowledge engineer then builds the knowledge base (and the rest of the expert system if necessary), using an iterative, prototyping process until the expert system is acceptable. Thus, knowledge engineers perform a role similar to that of systems analysts in conventional information systems development. Obviously, knowledge engineers must be able to understand and work with experts in many subject areas. Therefore, this new information systems specialty requires good people skills, as well as a background in artificial intelligence and information systems.

Once the decision is made to develop an expert system, a team of one or more domain experts and a knowledge engineer may be formed. Or experts skilled in the use of expert system shells could develop their own expert systems. If a shell is used, facts and rules of thumb about a specific domain can be defined and entered into a knowledge base with the help of a rule editor or other tool. A limited working prototype of the knowledge base is then constructed, tested, and evaluated using the inference engine and user interface programs of the shell. The knowledge engineer and domain experts can add and revise facts and decision rules in the knowledge base, then retest the system and evaluate the results. This process is repeated until the knowledge base and the shell result in an acceptable expert system.

A Managerial Perspective

Before deciding to acquire or develop an expert system, it is important that managerial end users evaluate its benefits and limitations. In particular, they must decide whether the benefits of a proposed expert system will exceed its costs [7, 13, 27].

Benefits of Expert Systems

An expert system captures the expertise of an expert or group of experts in a computer-based information system. Thus, it can outperform a single human expert in many problem situations. That's because an expert system is faster and more consistent, can have the knowledge of several experts, and does not get tired or distracted by overwork or stress.

Expert systems also help preserve and reproduce the knowledge of experts. They allow a company to preserve the expertise of an expert before he or she leaves

REAL WORLD CASE

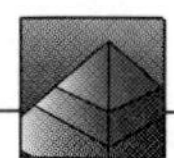

Red Lobster Restaurants, Royal Bank of Canada, and St. Luke's Episcopal Hospital: Knowledge-Based Systems

According to users and analysts, a new and improved generation of artificial intelligence technology—sold under the guise of "business process automation" or "knowledge-based systems"—is accruing gains where nothing else will work. "People think AI died years ago," said Neena Buck, vice president and director of applied intelligent systems at New Science Associates, a Westport, Connecticut consultancy. Rumors of AI's death are bolstered by "the very negative reactions of people who haven't been exposed to the new technology," Buck added. But for those who have examined and implemented the revampled development tools and languages, AI—by any name—is paying off.

A six-month development effort at General Mills Restaurants, Inc., in Orlando, Florida, helped reduce food costs by $2 million to $3 million per year, said programmer/analyst Kurt Navratil. Responsible for the operations of more than 600 Red Lobster Restaurants in the United States and Canada, the firm brought to Knowledge Base Management System (KBMS) a development tool from Palo Alto, California-based Trinzic Corp.

Called the Waste and Inventory Control System, the General Mills expert system is run monthly to determine whether each restaurant is meeting general guidelines for efficient use of its food inventory. If the amount of waste—food lost to spoilage or preparation inefficiencies—exceeds guidelines, the application performs additional inventory analysis to determine which food items might be the source of the problem. Then it generates a set of suggestions from its database for use by the local restaurant manager. The suggestions are forwarded to the local back-office computer at each restaurant. Managers are free to improve on or reject the suggestions made by the application. "You don't want to clamp down so tight that you're adversely affecting your managers," Navratil said.

Yet some applications were designed specifically to adversely affect their subjects. At Toronto's Royal Bank of Canada, a KBMS-based "fraud detection system" now in place for more than a year has reduced credit-card fraud. Although reticent to discuss the specific fraud reductions or the means by which they are achieved, Elo Laugesen, manager of technology products, said the applications "give us tools to detect fraud faster and earlier."

Like other developers, Laugesen said knowledge-based applications are easier than more-conventional applications to modify and improve, which is important for adjusting to new criminal tactics. "There are always new techniques for defrauding banks," he said. With a knowledge-based system, "we can add changes very rapidly," Laugesen said.

Change is also a keynote at St. Luke's Episcopal Hospital in Houston. The hospital's cardiac catheter laboratory serves more than 50 patients a day, as well as 70 support staff members and 80 cardiologists. According to Robert Marsh, the hospital's manager of decision support, scheduling the patients, staff, and physicians to use equipment, diagnostic rooms, and lab facilities had become a nightmare. "We were desperate to alleviate the situation," which required the full time attention of two managers. "It was difficult recruiting for the position," Marsh added.

After using the KBMS development tools on a research and development basis during a six-month period to develop a scheduling expert system, Bruce Boley, St. Luke's senior analyst, said the scheduling managers "now have time to spend 15 percent to 20 percent of their day answering questions that are managerial in nature."

CASE STUDY QUESTIONS

1. What business problems are solved by the expert systems used at Red Lobster Restaurants, the Royal Bank, and St. Lukes?
2. How were these expert systems developed?
3. What other types of business firms or organizations could use similar systems? Give several examples.

Source: Adapted from Garry Ray, "AI: New Name, Better Game," *Computerworld*, January 11, 1993, p. 69. Used with permission.

the organization. This expertise can then be shared by reproducing the software and knowledge base of the expert system. This allows novices to be trained and supported by copies of an expert system distributed throughout an organization. Finally, expert systems can have the same competitive advantages as other types of information technology. That is, the effective use of expert systems can allow a firm (1) to improve the efficiency of its operations, (2) to produce new products and services, (3) to lock in customers and suppliers with new business relationships, and (4) to build knowledge-based strategic information resources.

Limitations of Expert Systems

The major limitations of expert systems arise from their limited focus, inability to learn, maintenance problems, and developmental cost. Expert systems excel only in solving specific types of problems in a limited domain of knowledge. They fail miserably in solving problems requiring a broad knowledge base and subjective problem solving. They do well with specific types of operational or analytical tasks, but falter at subjective managerial decision making. For example, an expert system might help a financial consultant develop alternative investment recommendations for a client. But it could not adequately evaluate the nuances of current political, economic, and societal developments, or the personal dynamics of a session with a client. These important factors would still have to be handled by the human consultant before a final investment decision could be reached.

Expert systems may also be difficult and costly to develop and maintain properly. The costs of knowledge engineers, lost expert time, and hardware and software resources may be too high to offset the benefits expected from some applications. Also, expert systems can't maintain themselves. That is, they can't learn from experience but must be taught new knowledge and modified as new expertise is needed to match developments in their subject areas. However, some of these limitations can be overcome by the use of expert system shells and other developmental tools that make the job of development and maintenance easier.

Summary

- **Information Reporting.** Information reporting systems are management information systems that produce information products that meet many of the day-to-day information needs of management. Reports, displays, and responses provide prespecified information on demand, according to a schedule, or on an exception basis.
- **Information Quality.** Managers have to be provided with information products that possess many attributes of information quality in each of the three dimensions of time (timeliness, currency, frequency, and time period), content (accuracy, relevance, completeness, conciseness, scope, and performance), and form (clarity, detail, order, presentation, and media).
- **Decision Support Systems.** Decision support systems are interactive, computer-based information systems that use a model base and a database to provide information tailored to support semistructured and unstructured decisions faced by individual managers. They are designed to use a decision maker's own insights and judgments in an ad hoc, interactive, analytical modeling process leading to a specific decision.
- **DSS Components.** A decision support system consists of hardware, software, data, model, and people resources. Hardware resources include management workstations, departmental minicomputers, and corporate mainframes. Software resources include software packages such as DSS generators and spreadsheet packages that perform database management, model base management, and dialogue generation and management. Data and model resources include a database extracted from internal, external, and personal databases, and a model base that is a collection of mathematical models and analytical techniques. People resources include managers and staff specialists who explore decision alternatives with the support of a DSS.
- **Analytical Modeling.** Using a decision support system is an interactive, analytical modeling process, consisting of what-if analysis, sensitivity analysis, goal seeking analysis, and optimization analysis activities. Decision support system applications may be institutional or ad hoc but are typically developed to support the types of decisions faced by specific industries, functional areas, and decision makers.

- **Group Decision Support.** Managers are frequently faced with decision-making situations that require interactions with groups of people. Also, many decisions are made by groups of people coming to an agreement on a particular issue. The success of group decision making depends on many factors that can be enhanced by group decision-making methodologies and facilitated by using the computer-based facilities and software tools of electronic meeting systems and group decision support systems.
- **Executive Information Systems.** Executive information systems are management information systems designed to support the strategic information needs of top management. However, their use is spreading to lower levels of management. An EIS is easy to use and enables an executive to retrieve information tailored to his or her needs and preferences. Thus, an EIS can provide information about a company's critical success factors to executives to support their planning and control responsibilities.
- **DSS and EIS Development.** Decision support and executive information systems need unique capabilities in handling internal and external data, analytical models, information presentation, and user dialogue. These capabilities can be provided by acquiring a special-purpose package, using a DSS or EIS development package, using end user application packages, or developing a custom DSS or EIS.
- **Artificial Intelligence.** The major application domains of artificial intelligence include a variety of applications in cognitive science, computer science, robotics, and natural interfaces. The goal of AI is the development of computer functions normally associated with human physical and mental capabilities, such as robots that see, hear, talk, feel, and move, and software capable of reasoning, learning, and problem solving. Thus AI is being applied to many applications in business operations and management, as well as in many other fields.
- **Expert Systems.** Expert systems are knowledge-based information systems that use a knowledge base about a specific, complex application area and an inference engine program to act as an expert consultant to users. An expert system consists of hardware, software, knowledge, and people resources. Hardware includes workstations and other computers. Software includes an inference engine program that makes inferences based on the facts and rules stored in a knowledge base. Other software includes user interface programs and expert system shells for expert system development. A knowledge base consists of facts about a specific subject area and heuristics (rules of thumb) that express the reasoning procedures of an expert. Users, domain experts, and knowledge engineers are the people resources of an expert system.
- **Expert System Development.** Expert systems can be purchased or developed if a problem situation exists that is suitable for solution by expert systems rather than by conventional experts and information processing. The benefits of expert systems (such as preservation and replication of expertise) must be balanced with their limited applicability in many problem situations. If the decision is made to develop an expert system, the use of an expert system shell should be considered. It allows end users to develop their own expert systems in an interactive prototyping process.

Key Terms and Concepts

These are the key terms and concepts of this chapter. The page number of their first explanation is in parentheses.

1. Analytical modeling (316)
   a. Goal seeking analysis (318)
   b. Optimization analysis (319)
   c. Sensitivity analysis (318)
   d. What-if analysis (316)
2. Artificial intelligence (327)
   a. Application areas (327)
3. Components of a DSS (314)
4. Decision support versus information reporting (310)
5. Decision support system (312)
6. Developing DSS and EIS (322)
7. DSS generator (315)
8. DSS model base (315)
9. Executive information system (320)
10. Executive support system (321)
11. Expert system (329)
    a. Benefits and limitations (339)
    b. Components (332)
    c. Generic applications (334)
    d. Suitable applications (337)
12. Expert system development (337)
13. Expert system shell (338)
14. Group decision making (319)
15. Group decision support system (320)
16. Inference engine (332)
17. Information quality (309)
18. Information reporting system (308)
19. Information reporting alternatives (309)
    a. Demand
    b. Exception
    c. Periodic
20. Knowledge base (332)
21. Knowledge-based systems (329)
22. Knowledge engineer (339)

Review Quiz

Match one of the key terms and concepts listed above with one of the brief examples or functions listed below. Try to find the best fit for answers that seem to fit more than one term or concept. Defend your choices.

____ 1. Provide an interactive modeling capability tailored to the specific information needs of managers.

____ 2. Interactive responses to ad hoc inquiries versus prespecified information.

____ 3. A management workstation, DSS generator, database, model base, and manager or staff specialist.

____ 4. A collection of mathematical models and analytical techniques.

____ 5. The software component that provides database management, model base management, and dialogue generation and management.

____ 6. Analyzing the effect of changing variables and relationships and manipulating a mathematical model.

____ 7. Changing revenues and tax rates to see the effect on net profit after taxes.

____ 8. Changing revenues in many small increments to see revenue's effect on net profit after taxes.

____ 9. Changing revenues and expenses to find how best to achieve a specified amount of net profit after taxes.

____ 10. Changing revenues and expenses subject to certain constraints in order to achieve the highest net profit after taxes.

____ 11. People coming to an agreement on an issue.

____ 12. Computer-based tools can enhance the effectiveness of group decision making.

____ 13. Management information systems for the strategic information needs of top management.

____ 14. Executive information systems that may have DSS, expert system, and office automation features.

____ 15. Acquire a special-purpose package, use a development package, use an application package, or develop a custom system.

____ 16. Information technology that focuses on the development of computer functions normally associated with human physical and mental capabilities.

____ 17. Applications in cognitive science, computer science, robotics, and natural interfaces.

____ 18. An information system that has a knowledge base as a major system component.

____ 19. A knowledge-based information system that acts as an expert consultant to users in a specific application area.

____ 20. A workstation, user interface programs, inference engine, knowledge base, and an end user.

____ 21. Applications such as diagnosis, design, prediction, interpretation, and repair.

____ 22. Small, well-defined problem areas that require experts and logical inference processing for solutions.

____ 23. They can preserve and reproduce the knowledge of experts but have a limited application focus.

____ 24. A collection of facts and reasoning procedures in a specific subject area.

____ 25. A software package that manipulates a knowledge base and makes associations and inferences leading to a recommended course of action.

____ 26. A software package consisting of an inference engine and user interface programs used as an expert system development tool.

____ 27. One can either buy a completely developed expert system package, develop one with an expert system shell, or develop one from scratch by custom programming.

____ 28. An analyst who interviews experts to develop a knowledge base about a specific application area.

____ 29. Whether information is valuable and useful to you.

____ 30. Provide information for managers in a variety of prespecified formats.

____ 31. Information provided on a scheduled basis.

____ 32. Information provided on a selective basis.

____ 33. Information provided whenever you want it.

Discussion Questions

1. What is the difference between the ability of a manager to retrieve information instantly on demand using a networked workstation, and the capabilities provided by a DSS?
2. Refer to the Real World Case on Mazda and Ford Motor Companies. What types of information should be transmitted to managers' pagers? Explain.
3. In what ways does using an electronic spreadsheet package provide you with the components and capabilities of a decision support system?

4. How do electronic meeting systems support group decision making? What benefits and limitations do you see to using an EMS for group decision support?
5. Why is the use of executive information systems expanding into the ranks of middle management?
6. Can computers think? Will they ever be able to? Explain why or why not.
7. What are some of the most important applications of AI in business? Defend your choices.
8. Refer to the Real World Case on Red Lobster Restaurants, Royal Bank of Canada, and St. Luke's Hospital. Why do you think knowledge-based systems would be easy to modify?
9. What are several good applications of expert systems in business? Defend your choices based on the content of Figures 9.29 and 9.30.
10. How are expert systems developed? What is the role of a knowledge engineer and an expert system shell?

Real World Problems

1. Arby's, Walgreen, and Levi Strauss: Geographic Information Systems

Serious interest in geographic information systems (GIS) is stirring in the business community as more companies turn to this technology to choose new retail site locations, optimize distribution routes, or analyze the demographics of their target audiences. Companies such as Levi Strauss & Co., Arby's, Inc., Consolidated Rail Corp., Federal Express Corp., and Wisconsin Power & Light Co. are using GIS to integrate mapping, graphics, and spatial data with traditional business data such as spreadsheets and statistics. "Business interest is much higher now," said Hal Reid, vice president of development research at Arby's in Miami Beach. Yet it is often marketing, planning, or operations divisions rather than IS departments that seem more attuned to what GIS can offer, he added. Reid has two urban geographers using PC-based GIS applications for strategic development planning, franchise administration, and demographics analysis. The results, he added, have been reduced costs and increased capabilities in managing Arby's franchise territories.

At Walgreen Co. in Deerfield, Illinois, the drugstore chain is using GIS applications running on a trio of Intel 486-based PCs for planning and site development work. But like Arby's, it operates apart from the information system group. "MIS people don't embrace this stuff very much," said Joseph Mercurio, director of planning and research at Walgreen. Levi Strauss took its plunge into GIS in the mid-1980s by integrating geodemographic analysis, mapping, and internal shipment data with marketing analyses. Its first application was a distribution analysis and tracking system that made it possible to "anticipate change rather than just react to it," according to P. J. Santoro, a target marketing specialist at Levi Strauss. The jeans maker is now developing GIS applications to help determine what merchandise mix is best for stores in particular trading areas, and it is integrating video images of its store displays into analysis and querying capabilities.

a. Are geographic information systems a form of decision support systems? Why or why not?

b. What are the business benefits of such systems?

Source: Adapted from Maryfran Johnson, "GIS Popularity Growing," *Computerworld*, March 22, 1993, pp. 41–42. Used with permission.

2. American Airlines: Operations Research and Decision Support Systems

"If IS departments had more participation from operations research analysts, they would be building much better, richer IS solutions," declares Ron J. Ponder, chief information officer at Sprint Corp. in Kansas City, Missouri, and former CIO at Federal Express Corp. Thomas M. Cook, president of American Airlines Decision Technologies, Inc., in Fort Worth, Texas, puts it in even stronger terms. IS departments typically believe their job is done if they deliver accurate and timely information. But Cook says that adding operations research skills to the team can produce *intelligent* systems that actually recommend *solutions* to business problems.

One of the big success stories at Cook's operations research shop is a "yield management" system, which decides how much to overbook and how to set prices for each seat so that a plane is filled up and profits are maximized. The yield management system, which deals with more than 250 decision variables, accounts for a whopping 5 percent of American Airlines' revenue. The airline's Sabre reservation system "got a lot of great press, but the value of things like yield management might even dwarf Sabre's benefits," Cook says.

a. What is operations research? How can it improve information systems?

b. Does American Airlines' yield management system sound like an expert system or a decision support system? Explain.

Source: Adapted from Mitch Betts, "Efficiency Einsteins," *Computerworld*, March 22, 1993, pp. 63–64. Used with permission.

3. Fox Valley Technical College: Group Decision Support

Fox Valley Technical College faculty and staff are using a

new tool to help them achieve their goal of total quality management, thanks to TeamFocus® software from IBM. TeamFocus dramatically helps groups brainstorm, prioritize, and evaluate in order to solve problems with maximum efficiency, using networked computers to enhance traditional meetings. TeamFocus software includes 11 tools that can be used alone or in combination. Using teamFocus, participants sit at computers around a U-shaped table. A facilitator introduces the agenda. In one popular tool called Topic Commenter, computer screens display a question at the top of the screen, and participants anonymously type their comments in at the bottom of the screen. A projection screen at the front of the room shows the facilitator's screen of compiled comments. Team members can open each category on their screens and read the various responses and add their own. Since no one knows who made a particular comment, an idea is evaluated on its own merit, independent of personalities. There is no need to take notes—a program record is provided on paper and in electronic media form immediately after the session.

The Fox Valley system is made up of 20 PS/2® computers connected by a local area network. A facilitator and keyboard operator work together to run the meetings. Carol Mishler, project and research services manager, works with her clients to establish the agenda and the questions that will be addressed. Participants receive the agenda and any background material prior to the meeting so that they are prepared to comment. The facilitator starts the meeting, takes questions, leads participants through the exercises, interprets information, and prints the report. According to Ms. Mishler, "The real benefit of TeamFocus is that it allows us to generate and organize a lot of data in a short period of time with input from everyone, including those who don't usually participate in meetings. The anonymity of the program allows people to say what they really think."

a. What are the benefits of TeamFocus to an organization?
b. Would you like to attend meetings supported by TeamFocus? Why or why not?

Source: Adapted from "TeamFocus: Breaking Down Barriers for Better Communications," *Columns*, Spring 1993, p. 9.

4. **Compaq Computer Corporation**

Compaq Computer Corporation, one of the largest manufacturers of personal computers, has an expert system called Support Management Automated Reasoning Technology (SMART). SMART is in use throughout North America and will soon be deployed worldwide. Any customer who contacts Compaq customer support can speak with an operator equipped with SMART.

Compaq customer-support personnel face a quandary that many companies with large product lines experience regularly. These personnel must contend not only with problems about the use and integration of Compaq products, but these problems more often than not involve non-Compaq equipment. Consequently, Compaq customer-support representatives must be prepared to handle not only product-specific questions but those that involve the larger issues of system integration, as well.

SMART captures knowledge about the entire Compaq product line, as well as that about products from Novell, Banyan, Microsoft, and other companies, using case-based reasoning—capturing knowledge as a series of cases based on experience. Like other expert systems, SMART provides "intelligent" information to customer-support representatives and thereby minimizes the number of customer questions that are kicked upstairs to the next-level help desk. But SMART picks up where other applications leave off, because users can add new information to the knowledge base themselves. This new information can be accessed and used almost immediately by other reps. According to Gus Kolias, director of Compaq customer support training, "SMART lets us support the most extensive range of products possible . . . It has also increased the productivity of our help-desk staff and will ultimately help us reduce support costs."

a. What were Compaq's reasons for developing SMART? What are its advantages?
b. How was SMART's knowledge base developed? How is it maintained?

Source: Adapted from Justin Kesletyn, "A Reasonable Case, Too," *AI Expert*, May 1992, p. 56.

Application Exercises

1. **ABC Company: Spreadsheets for Decision Support**

Use an electronic spreadsheet or integrated package available on the microcomputer or mainframe systems at your university to create the ABC Company Financial Performance spreadsheet as shown in Figure 9.10, using the formulas shown in Figure 9.11. Start by entering formulas for 1991 entries, which assume that expenses are 60 percent of revenue, profit is revenue minus expenses, taxes are 40 percent of profit, and profit after taxes equals profit minus taxes. Complete the 1992 and 1993 columns of the spreadsheet, which assume that 1992 revenue is 110 percent of 1991, and 1993 revenue is 120 percent of 1991. Assume that all other formula relationships for 1991 entries also apply to 1992 and 1993. Then use SUM and AVERAGE functions to complete the final two columns of the spreadsheet.

a. Enter $1,000 for 1991 sales. Notice how the spreadsheet shown in Figure 9.10 is instantly generated and displayed. Store and print this spreadsheet as shown in Figure 9.10.

b. Then print out a version of the spreadsheet with all formulas displayed to document the formulas you used. See Figure 9.11.

c. Use the spreadsheet you created to perform what-if analyses. For example, change revenue, expense, or tax values or formulas in the ABC Company Financial Performance spreadsheet. (For example, increase revenue for 1991 by $1,000, increase expenses to 65% of revenue, and decrease taxes to 25% of profit.) What happens to the company's profit in each year? Print a copy of the spreadsheet with the results of these changes.

d. Create graphics displays of parts of the spreadsheet you developed. For example, develop a pie chart of profit after taxes, or a bar graph of expenses. See Figure 9.12. Make changes to entries in the spreadsheet and use graphics displays to help you perform what-if analyses.

e. Write a short explanation of what happened when you did what-if analysis and its implications for a managerial end user. What features need to be added or improved to make this package easier to use and a more effective DSS generator? Explain how and why you think this should be done.

2. **Designing Information Products**

a. Design a mock-up of a report or display that could be produced by an information reporting, decision support or executive information system for managers in a business or other organization.

b. Use a report generator from a database management or other software package to develop the report mock-up.

c. Evaluate the information quality of the information product you design. Write up a brief evaluation based on the attributes outlined in Figure 9.4.

3. **Evaluating Expert Systems**

Evaluate the Expert Credit System of either ITT Commercial Finance or Stone & Webster Engineering and Union Carbide, on pages 334 and 336 in the chapter. Write up your evaluation based on the following points:

a. The components of an expert system that you recognize (see Figure 9.26).

b. How well it fits the suitability criteria and application categories for expert systems (see Figures 9.29 and 9.30).

c. The benefits and limitations of this expert system.

Review Quiz Answers

1. 5
2. *4*
3. *3*
4. *8*
5. *7*
6. *1*
7. *1d*
8. *1c*
9. *1a*
10. *1b*
11. *14*
12. *15*
13. 9
14. *10*
15. 6
16. 2
17. *2a*
18. *21*
19. *11*
20. *11b*
21. *11c*
22. *11d*
23. *11a*
24. *20*
25. *16*
26. *13*
27. *12*
28. 22
29. *17*
30. *18*
31. *19c*
32. *19b*
33. *19a*

Selected References

1. "Artificial Intelligence," *The Economist*, March 14, 1992.
2. Barsanti, Joanne. "Expert Systems." *Information Executive*, Winter 1990.
3. Carlson, Eileen. "What Color Is Your EIS?" *Computerworld*, July 16, 1990.
4. Dennis, Alan; Joey George; Len Jessup; Jay Nunamaker; and Douglas Vogel. "Information Technology to Support Electronic Meetings." *MIS Quarterly*, December 1988.
5. *EIS II: Benefits Analysis Guide*. Chicago: Information Resources, Inc., 1991.
6. Enrado, Patty. "Giving Credit Where It Is Due." *AI Expert*, September 1991.
7. Gallagher, John. *Knowledge Systems for Business: Integrating Expert Systems and MIS*. Englewood Cliffs, N.J.: Prentice-Hall, 1988.
8. Guimaraes, Tor; Magid Igbaria; and Ming-Te Lu. "The Determinants of DSS Success: An Analytical Model." *Decision Sciences Journal*, March/April 1992.
9. Harmon, Paul; Rex Maus; and William Morrissey. *Expert Systems Tools and Applications*. New York: John Wiley & Sons, 1988.
10. Jessup, Leonard, and David Tansuk. "Decision Making in an Automated Environment: The Effects on Anonymity and Proximity with a Group Decision Support System." *Decision Sciences Journal*, Spring 1991.
11. Kestelyn, Justin. "Scheduling Advisor." *AI Expert*, May 1991.

12. Kirkpatrick, David. "Here Comes the Payoff on PCs." *Fortune*, March 23, 1992.
13. Nelson, Carl, and R. Balchandra. "Choosing the Right Expert System Building Approach." *Decision Sciences Journal*, Spring 1991.
14. Newquist, Harvey. "New and Improved." *AI Expert*, December 1991.
15. Nunamaker, Jay; Alan Dennis; Joseph Valacich; Douglas Vogel; and Joey F. George. "Electronic Meetings to Support Group Work." *Communications of the ACM*, July 1991.
16. Panko, Raymond. *End User Computing: Management, Applications, and Technology*. New York: John Wiley & Sons, 1988.
17. Pigford, D. V., and Greg Bauer. *Expert Systems for Business*. Boston: Boyd & Fraser, 1990.
18. Raisbeck, Gordon. *Information Theory*. Cambridge, Mass.: MIT Press, 1964.
19. Rheingold, Howard. "How Real Is Virtual Reality?" *Beyond Computing*, March/April 1992.
20. Rockart, John, and David DeLong. *Executive Support Systems: The Emergence of Top Management Computer Use*. Homewood, Ill.: Dow Jones–Irwin, 1988.
21. Savage, J. A. "Fuzzy Logic? Maybe; We're Not Sure." *Computerworld*, January 29, 1990.
22. Sigloh, Dennis. "Geographic Information Systems: Toward the Intelligent Super Map." *IBM Update*, November/December 1990.
23. Tafti, Mohammed. "Neural Networks: A New Dimension in Expert System Applications." *Data Base*, Winter 1992.
24. The Editors. *Artificial Intelligence*. Alexandria, Va.: Time-Life Books, Inc., 1988.
25. Turban, Efraim. *Decision Support and Expert Systems: Management Support Systems*. 2nd ed. New York: Macmillan, 1990.
26. Watson, Hugh; R. Kelly Ranier; and Chang Koh. "Executive Information Systems: A Framework for Development and a Survey of Current Practices." *MIS Quarterly*, March 1991.
27. Zeichick, Alan. "The Turing Test." *AI Expert*, January 1992.

Continuing Real World Case

Omaha Vision Center—Part 3: IS Applications

Application Areas

The new computer system being considered by the Omaha Vision Center is to be put to work to improve the center's business operations in four major application areas: accounts receivable, billing, medical recordkeeping, and scheduling. Carl Weber, the center administrator, was sure that automating those areas would greatly increase the efficiency and effectiveness of the clerical staff, thus significantly improving the quality of customer service and the support of Dr. Creighton and his medical staff.

Accounts Receivable

Carl Weber viewed the accounts receivable application as the key problem area of the center's operations. Information on the status of an individual customer's account, on accounts with overdue balances, and on the age of all outstanding accounts was difficult to obtain and was very time-consuming to extract. Weber would wait for days to get an aging analysis of accounts receivable, and even then it was vague. Data on amounts due from customers was the most vital need of the practice and the main reason for purchasing the computer system.

Billing

The billing process would also be streamlined with the computer, hopefully eliminating the manual statements that were generated each month. Probably most interesting for the future was the ability to automatically transmit claims to Medicare; that feature alone should reduce the account turnover by weeks and end the need for Adams to mail claims to Medicare.

Medical Recordkeeping

The center's operations were also bogged down by the need to work with over 8,000 handwritten medical charts for its patients. This made the job of the medical staff more difficult, as well as slowing down the billing, accounts receivable, and scheduling activities. Hopefully, electronic patient records would rectify this situation.

Scheduling

As mentioned in Module I, the center manually scheduled appointments and surgeries for more than 4,500 patients each year. The medical secretary had to record and integrate information from written patient records and a written appointment log book, with messages received by telephone from customers. Weber knew that computerizing this application would help the whole center to run more smoothly.

The Center's Staff

The administrative staff of the Omaha Vision Center was small, yet they would be the ones utilizing the system. The medical technicians at the center would have little use for computers except in isolated circumstances. The practice had always been run on manual systems and was relatively successfully at that; it was evident that

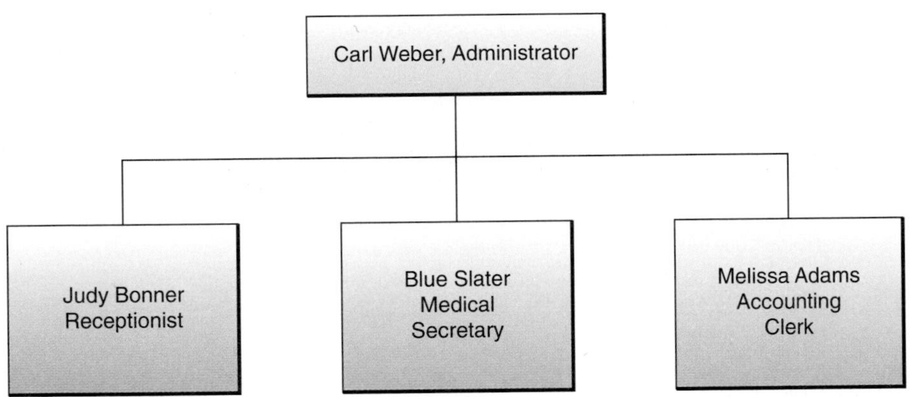

FIGURE 3
The Administrative Staff

there would be some resistance from the staff to the changes brought about by the new computer system, and the level of resistance would vary. See Figure 3.

Melissa Adams

Melissa Adams was the accounting clerk and had been with the practice for nearly two years. She had been doing billing and receivable work at different practices for over 10 years, however, and was very competent. Adams was silent about the entire plan but was obviously not thrilled with the advent of a computer system. She said that she would try to work with it; she was very dedicated to her work and conscientious. Weber felt that he could depend on her but was hoping to see more enthusiasm from the person whom the system would benefit most.

Blue Slater

The practice's medical secretary, Blue Slater, was the strongest supporter of computerization. Slater was enthusiastic from the first and participated in many of the discussions about the system. She saw the value of the system for scheduling, a task she performed, as well as for word processing. Slater attended college at night and was majoring in management. She felt that the computer experience would help her significantly in other areas.

Judy Bonner

The practice receptionist, Judy Bonner, was the least involved in the computer selection and installation. She was senior to the others in age and showed little interest in automation. If anything, she seemed fearful at the first sight of the boxes. However, Bonner would have to learn how to operate the computer, since she was the backup to Adams and Slater when either was out of the office. Weber noticed almost a belligerence on Bonner's part when she—or anyone, for that matter—discussed the computer. He felt that she would be the most difficult to sway in her opinion of the system.

Case Study Questions

1. Which of the four applications of the computer-based information systems at the Omaha Vision Center will be the most beneficial to the center's business operations? To Dr. Creighton and Carl Weber's decision making? Explain.
2. What future applications of computer-based information systems should be investigated by Carl Weber? How would they benefit the business operations, managerial decision making, or competitive position of the Omaha Vision Center?
3. How would you approach each of the three clerical staff members to help you successfully implement the proposed computer system?

M O D U L E **IV**

Development and Management

How can information system solutions be developed to solve business problems or pursue business opportunities? What managerial challenges do information systems pose for the managers of modern organizations? The three chapters of this module are designed to emphasize how managers and end users can plan, develop, implement, and control the use of information technology in a global information society.

Chapter 10, Developing Information System Solutions, introduces the traditional and prototyping approaches to the development of information system solutions to business problems, discusses important issues in the implementation of information systems, and demonstrates the use of several systems development tools.

Chapter 11, Managing Information Technology, emphasizes the impact of information technology on management and organizations, the importance of information resource management, and the managerial implications of global information technology.

Chapter 12, Security and Ethical Challenges of Information Technology, discusses the controls needed for information system performance and security, as well as the ethical implications and societal impacts of information technology.

Developing Information System Solutions

CHAPTER OUTLINE

CHAPTER 10

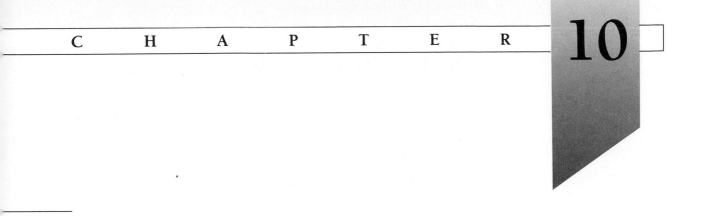

LEARNING OBJECTIVES

The purpose of this chapter is to give you an understanding of how end users can apply the methodology of systems development to develop and implement information system solutions to business problems.

Section I describes the activities involved and products produced in each of the stages of the information systems development cycle, including information systems planning, and the use of computer-aided and prototyping approaches to systems development.

Section II explores major activities and management considerations in the implementation process for information systems.

Section III demonstrates the form and use of several systems development tools such as system flowcharts and data flow diagrams.

After reading and studying this chapter, you should be able to:

1. Describe how the steps of the information systems development cycle can be used to provide information system solutions to business problems.
2. Explain how computer-aided systems engineering and prototyping have affected the process of information systems development for end users and information systems specialists.
3. Use the systems development cycle and a model of information system components as a framework to help you propose information systems solutions to simple business problems.
4. Identify the activities involved in the information systems implementation process and give examples of some of the major management techniques and issues involved.
5. Discuss several evaluation factors that should be considered in evaluating the acquisition of hardware, software, and IS services.
6. Identify how end user resistance to information systems can be minimized by end user involvement in systems development and implementation.
7. Identify how several systems development tools can be used for systems analysis and design.

SECTION I

Developing Information System Applications

Suppose the chief executive of a firm where you are the sales manager asks you to find a better way to get information to the salespeople in your company. How would you start? What would you do? Would you just plunge ahead and hope you could come up with a reasonable solution? How would you know whether your solution was a good one for your company? Do you think there might be a systematic way to help you develop a good solution to your chief executive's request? There is. It's a systematic problem-solving process called **the systems approach**.

The Systems Approach

The systems approach is a modification of the scientific method. It stresses a *systematic process* of problem solving. Problems and opportunities are viewed in a *systems context*. Studying a problem and formulating a solution becomes an organized system of interrelated activities, such as:

1. Define a problem or opportunity in a systems context.
2. Gather data describing the problem 'or opportunity.
3. Identify alternative solutions.
4. Evaluate each alternative solution.
5. Select the best solution.
6. Implement the selected solution.
7. Evaluate the success of the implemented solution.

The Systems Development Cycle

The systems approach can be applied to the solution of many types of problems. When this involves the development of information system solutions to business problems, it is called **information systems development**, or *application development*. Most computer-based information systems are conceived, designed, and implemented using some form of systematic development process. In this process, end users and information specialists *design* information systems based on an analysis of the information requirements of an organization. Thus, a major part of this process is known as *systems analysis and design*. However, as Figure 10.1 shows, several other major activities are involved in a complete development cycle.

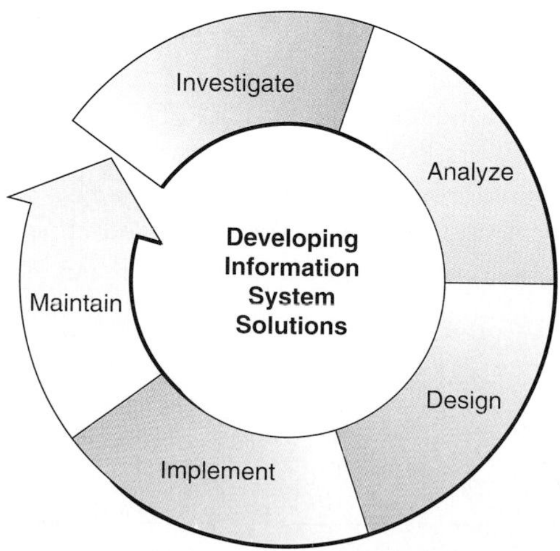

FIGURE 10.1
Developing information systems solutions to business problems is typically a multistep process or cycle.

When the systems approach is applied to the development of information system solutions, a multistep process or cycle emerges. This is frequently called the *systems development cycle*, or *systems development life cycle* (SDLC). Figure 10.2 summarizes what goes on in each stage of the traditional **information systems development cycle**, which includes the steps of (1) investigation, (2) analysis, (3) design, (4) implementation, and (5) maintenance.

You should realize, however, that all of the activities involved are highly related and interdependent. Therefore, in actual practice, several developmental activities can occur at the same time. So, different parts of a development project can be at different stages of the development cycle. In addition, analysts may recycle back at any time to repeat previous activities in order to modify and improve a system they are developing.

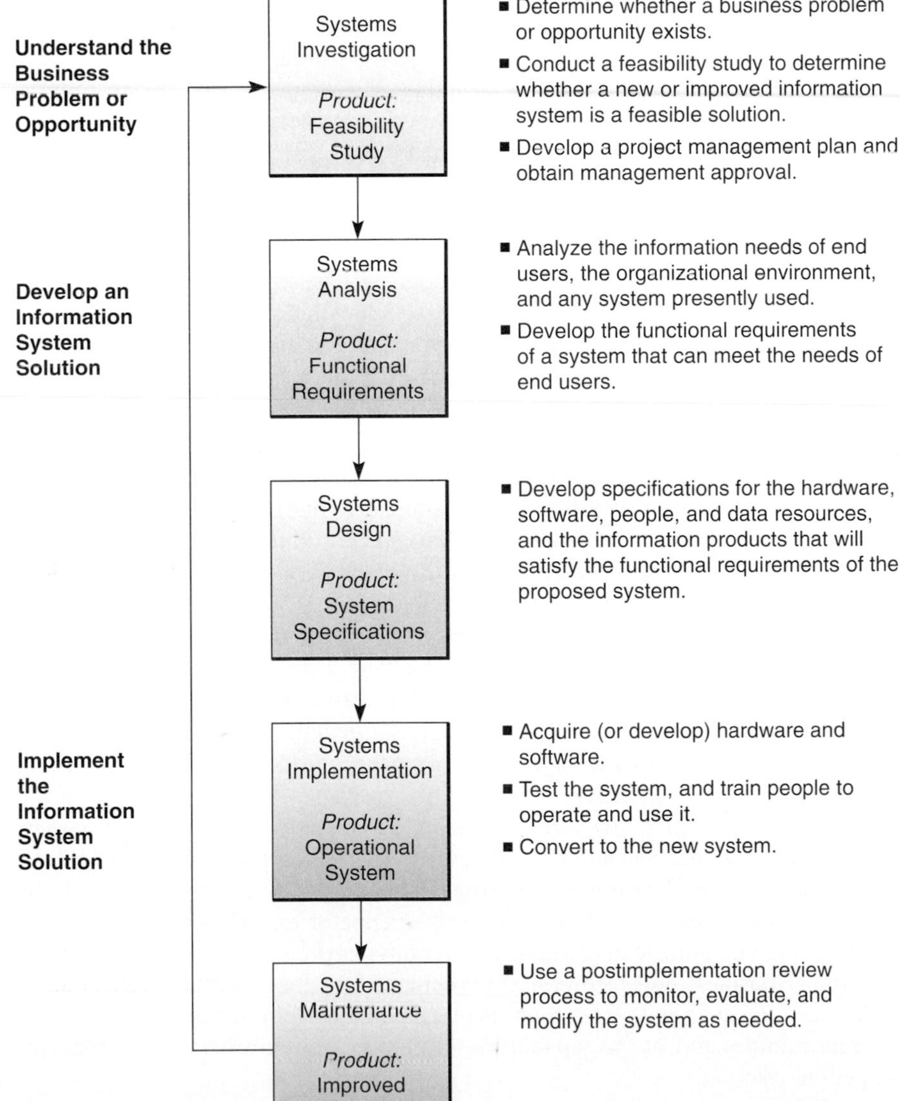
Understand the Business Problem or Opportunity
Systems Investigation
Product: Feasibility Study
■ Determine whether a business problem or opportunity exists.
■ Conduct a feasibility study to determine whether a new or improved information system is a feasible solution.
■ Develop a project management plan and obtain management approval.
Develop an Information System Solution
Systems Analysis
Product: Functional Requirements
■ Analyze the information needs of end users, the organizational environment, and any system presently used.
■ Develop the functional requirements of a system that can meet the needs of end users.
Systems Design
Product: System Specifications
■ Develop specifications for the hardware, software, people, and data resources, and the information products that will satisfy the functional requirements of the proposed system.
Implement the Information System Solution
Systems Implementation
Product: Operational System
■ Acquire (or develop) hardware and software.
■ Test the system, and train people to operate and use it.
■ Convert to the new system.
Systems Maintenance
Product: Improved System
■ Use a postimplementation review process to monitor, evaluate, and modify the system as needed.

FIGURE 10.2
The traditional information systems development cycle. Note that the five steps of the cycle fit into the three stages of the systems approach. Also note the products that result from each step in the cycle.

Finally, you should realize that developments such as computer-aided systems engineering (CASE), prototyping, and end user development are automating and changing some of the activities of information systems development. These developments are improving the quality of systems development and making it easier for IS professionals, while enabling more end users to develop their own systems. We will discuss them shortly. Now, let's take a look at each step of this development process.

Systems Investigation

Do we have a business problem (or opportunity)? What is causing the problem? Would a new or improved information system help solve the problem? What would be a *feasible* information system solution to our problem? These are the questions that have to be answered in the systems investigation stage—the first step in the systems development process. This stage includes the screening, selection, and preliminary study of proposed information system solutions to business problems.

Information Systems Planning

The investigation stage may involve the study of information systems development proposals generated by a formal **information systems planning** process. A formal information systems planning process that is part of the regular business planning process of the organization is highly desirable. There are typically many opportunities to use information systems to support an organization's end users and its business operations, management decision making, and strategic objectives. However, in the real world, end users, departments, and the organization itself have only limited amounts of human and financial resources to allocate to the development of new information systems, no matter how desirable they may be. Therefore, business and information systems planning helps to generate, screen, and select potential information systems for development. Figure 10.3 illustrates how strategic information systems planning fits into an organization's planning process. It emphasizes the activities and outputs of strategic planning and its interrelationship with the business unit and IT planning processes.

Strategic Information Systems Planning

A strategic IS plan formulates policies, objectives, and strategies for delivering information services and allocating information systems resources. It involves a study of how the information systems function can contribute to the achievement of the goals contained in the strategic plan for the entire organization. This process is sometimes called *enterprise analysis*. The emphasis is on planning computer-based information systems that will improve the firm's performance and competitive position. Enterprise analysis frequently includes *stage analysis*. This is an analysis of the information systems needs of an organization based on its current stage in the growth cycle that is typical of most organizations Obviously, a firm's IS needs may differ depending on whether it is a start-up company, enjoying rapid growth, or has reached maturity in its industry.

A strategic IS plan frequently contains an analysis of a firm's *application portfolio*. It helps a firm plan an IS investment strategy, since it spotlights the types of IS applications being developed, the business functions being supported, and the resources being allocated (as a percentage of revenue or assets) to the information systems function. Strategic IS planning also requires *environmental analysis*, in which the external business and technical environments and the internal organizational environment are analyzed. Assessment is made of information technology problems and opportunities and of the capabilities of the organization's hardware, software, and people resources.

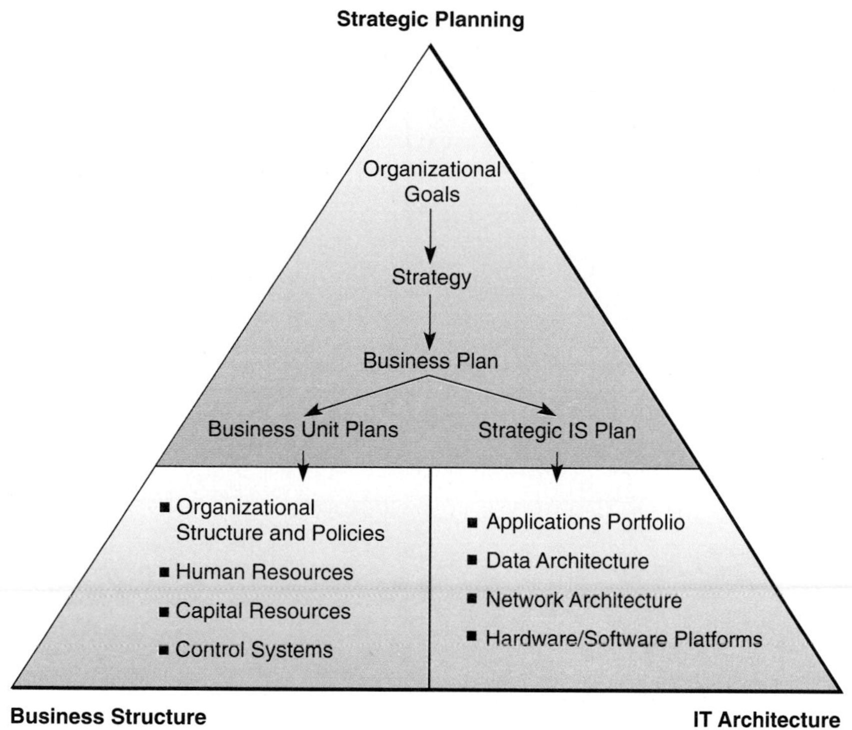

Source: Adapted from Lewis Leeburg and Bill Mann, "Managing the Integration of Information Technologies," *Handbook of IS Management*, 3rd ed. (Boston: Auerbach, 1991), p. 40.

FIGURE 10.3
How strategic planning leads to business unit and strategic IS planning.

Planning for Competitive Advantage

Especially important at this stage is an analysis of the potential the firm has for using information technology for competitive advantage. In Chapter 6, we introduced Porter's model of competitive forces (competitors, customers, suppliers, new entrants, and substitutes) and competitive strategies (cost leadership, differentiation, and innovation), as well as his value chain model of basic business activities. These models can be used in the strategic planning process to help generate ideas for the strategic use of IT. Also popular in strategic IS planning is a strategic thrusts approach, by Wiseman and others, that adds growth by acquisitions and alliances with other organizations as competitive strategies. This approach builds on Porter's ideas to construct a strategic thrusts/targets matrix, as illustrated in Figure 10.4. SWOT analysis (Strengths, Weaknesses, Opportunities, and Threats) is used to evaluate the impact that each possible strategic thrust or target can have on the business.

Tactical and Operational Planning

Tactical information systems planning starts with a specific assessment of an organization's current and projected information requirements. These requirements are then subdivided into individual project proposals for the development of new or improved information systems. These projects are then evaluated, ranked, and fitted into a multiyear development plan. Finally, a resource allocation plan is developed to specify the hardware, software, and personnel resources, telecommunications facilities, and financial commitments needed to implement the master development plan.

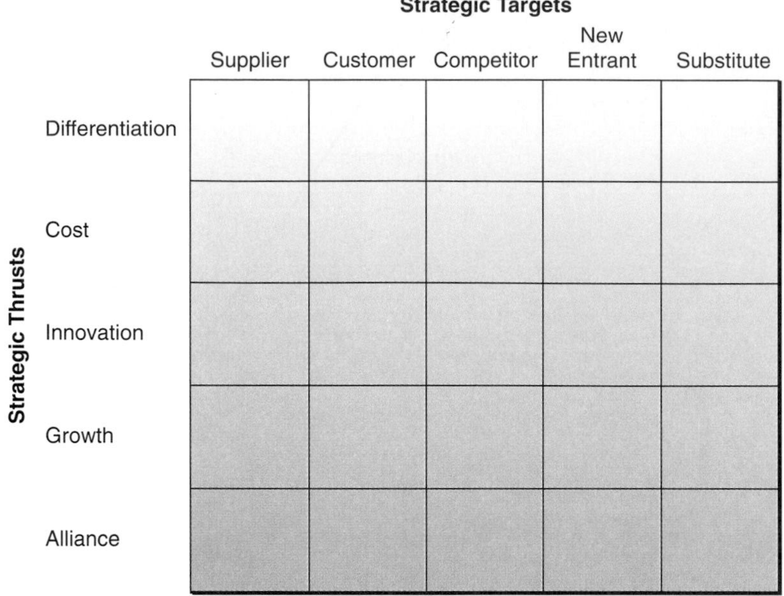

FIGURE 10.4
A strategic thrusts/targets matrix. This matrix helps planners identify strategic uses of IT.

Operational information systems planning involves the preparation of annual operating budgets and the planning for individual information systems development projects. Annual operating budgets specify the allocation of financial and other resources needed to support the organization's information services department in day-to-day operations and systems development and maintenance activities. This also holds true for end user departments and other work groups that do a lot of their own information processing and application development.

Project planning is an important operational planning function. It involves the development of plans, procedures, and schedules for an information systems development project. Such planning is an important part of a **project management** effort that plans and controls the implementation of systems development projects. This is necessary if a project is to be completed on time and within its proposed budget and if it is to meet its design objectives.

Several techniques of project management produce charts to help plan and control projects. One is the Gantt chart, which specifies the times allowed for the various activities required in information systems development. Another is produced by network methodologies such as the PERT system (Program Evaluation and Review Techniques), which develops a network diagram of required activities. Network methodologies view a project as a network of distinct tasks and milestones and specify the amount of time budgeted for the completion of each task. Figure 10.5 is an example of a Gantt chart prepared by a personal information management software package.

Feasibility Studies

Because the process of developing a major information system can be costly, the systems investigation stage frequently requires a preliminary study called a **feasibility study**. A feasibility study is a preliminary study to investigate the information needs of prospective users and determine the resource requirements, costs, benefits, and feasibility of a proposed project. The methods of gathering information summarized in Figure 10.6 are used to collect data for a feasibility study. The findings of this study are usually formalized in a written report. It includes prelimi-

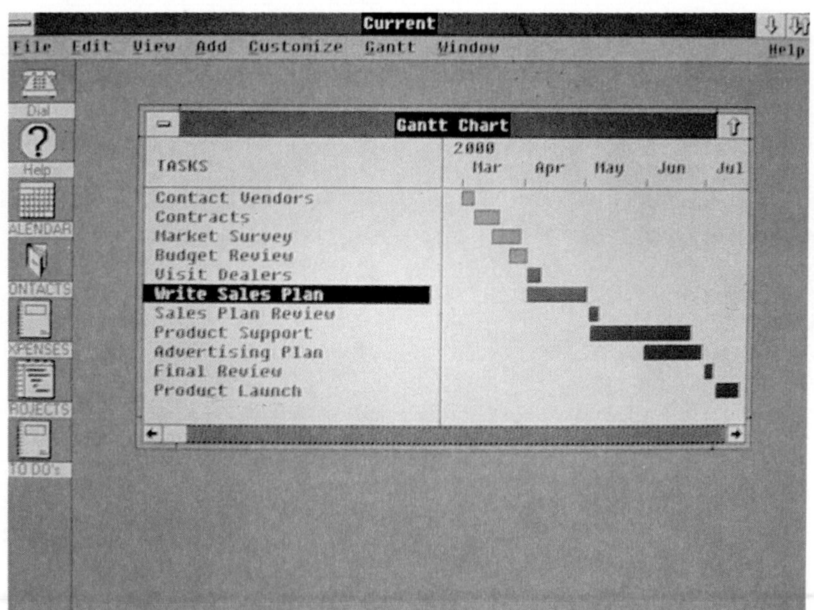

Courtesy of IBM Corporation.

FIGURE 10.5
A Gantt chart for a business project produced by a personal information management package.

- Interviews with employees, customers, and managers.
- Questionnaires to appropriate end users in the organization.
- Personal observation or involvement in business operations.
- Examination of documents, reports, procedures manuals, and other documentation.
- Development, manipulation, and observation of a model of the business operations.

FIGURE 10.6
Ways to gather information for systems development.

nary specifications and a developmental plan for the proposed system. This report is submitted to the management of the firm for its approval before development can begin. If management approves the recommendations of the feasibility study, the *systems analysis* stage can begin.

Cost/Benefit Analysis

Feasibility studies typically involve **cost/benefit analysis**. If costs and benefits can be quantified, they are called *tangible*; if not, they are called *intangible*. Examples of tangible costs are the costs of hardware and software, employee salaries, and other quantifiable costs needed to develop and implement an IS solution. Intangible costs are difficult to quantify; they include the loss of customer goodwill or employee morale caused by errors and disruptions arising from the installation of a new system.

Tangible benefits are favorable results, such as the decrease in payroll costs caused by a reduction in personnel or a decrease in inventory carrying costs caused by a reduction in inventory. Intangible benefits are harder to estimate. Such benefits as better customer service or faster and more accurate information for management fall into this category. Figure 10.7 lists typical tangible and intangible benefits with examples. Possible tangible and intangible costs would be the opposite of each benefit shown.

FIGURE 10.7
Possible benefits of computer-based information systems, with examples. Note that an opposite result for each of these benefits would be a cost or disadvantage of computer-based information systems.

Tangible benefits	Example
Increase in sales or profits	Development of computer-based products and services
Decrease in information processing costs	Elimination of unnecessary procedures and documents
Decrease in operating costs	Reduction in inventory carrying costs
Decrease in required investment	Decrease in inventory investment required
Increased operational ability and efficiency	Improvement in production ability and efficiency; for example, less spoilage, waste, and idle time
Intangible benefits	**Example**
New or improved information availability	More timely and accurate information and new types of information
Improved abilities in computation and analysis	Analytical modeling
Improved customer service	More timely service response
Improved employee morale	Elimination of burdensome and boring job tasks
Improved management decision making	Better information and decision analysis
Improved competitive position	Systems which lock in customers and suppliers
Improved business and community image	"Progressive" image as perceived by customers, suppliers, and investors

The Feasibility of a System

The goal of feasibility studies is to evaluate alternative systems and to propose the most feasible and desirable systems for development. The feasibility of a proposed system can be evaluated in terms of four major categories, as illustrated in Figure 10.8.

The focus of **organizational feasibility** is on how well a proposed information system supports the objectives of the organization and its strategic plan for information systems. For example, projects that do not directly contribute to meeting an organization's strategic objectives are typically not funded. **Economic feasibility** is concerned with whether expected cost savings, increased revenue, increased profits, reductions in required investment, and other types of benefits will exceed the costs of developing and operating a proposed system. For example, if a project can't cover its development costs, it won't be approved unless mandated by government regulations or other considerations. **Technical feasibility** can be demonstrated if reliable hardware and software capable of meeting the needs of a proposed system can be acquired or developed by the business in the required time. Finally, **operational feasibility** is the willingness and ability of the management, employees, customers, suppliers, and others to operate, use, and support a proposed system. For example, if the software for a new system is too difficult to use, employees may make too many errors and avoid using it. Thus, it would fail to show operational feasibility.

Organizational feasibility	**Economic feasibility**
▪ How well the proposed system supports the strategic objectives of the organization	▪ Cost savings ▪ Increased revenue ▪ Decreased investment ▪ Increased profits
Technical feasibility	**Operational feasibility**
▪ Hardware and software capability, reliability, and availability	▪ End user acceptance ▪ Management support ▪ Customer, supplier, and government requirements

FIGURE 10.8
Organizational, economic, technical, and operational feasibility factors. Note that there is more to feasibility than cost savings or the availability of hardware and software.

Systems Analysis

What is **systems analysis**? Whether you want to develop a new application quickly or are involved in a long-term project, you will need to perform several basic activities of systems analysis. Many of these activities are an extension of those used in conducting a feasibility study. Some of the same information-gathering methods are used, plus some new tools that we will discuss shortly. However, systems analysis is not a preliminary study. It is an in-depth study of end user information needs which produces **functional requirements** that are used as the basis for the design of a new information system. Systems analysis traditionally involves a detailed study of:

- The information needs of the organization and its end users.
- The activities, resources, and products of any present information systems.
- The information system capabilities required to meet the information needs of end users.

Organizational Analysis

An **organizational analysis** is an important first step in systems analysis. How can you improve an information system if you know very little about the organizational environment in which that system is located? You can't. That's why you have to know something about the organization, its management structure, its people, its business activities, the environmental systems it must deal with, and its current information systems. You must know this information in more detail for the specific end user departments that will be affected by the new or improved information system being proposed. For example, you cannot design a new inventory control system for a chain of department stores until you learn a lot about the company and the types of business activities that affect its inventory.

Analysis of the Present System

Before you design a new system, it is important to study the system that will be improved or replaced (if there is one). You need to analyze how this system uses hardware, software, and people resources to convert data resources, such as transactions data, into information products, such as reports and displays. Then you should document how the information system activities of input, processing, output, storage, and control are accomplished. For example, you might note the format, timing, volume, and quality of input/output activities that provide *user interface* methods for interaction between end users and computers. Then, in the systems design stage, you can specify what the resources, products, and activities *should be* in the system you are designing.

FIGURE 10.9
Functional requirements specify information system capabilities required to meet the information needs of users. Note the examples of functional requirements for a sales transaction processing system.

- **User interface requirements.** The input/output needs of end users that must be supported by the information system, including sources, formats, content, volume, and frequency of each type of input and output.
  Example: Automatic entry of product data and easy-to-use data entry screens for sales people.
- **Processing requirements.** Activities required to convert input into output. Includes calculations, decision rules, and other processing operations, and capacity, throughput, turnaround time, and response time needed for processing activities.
  Example: Fast, automatic calculation of sales totals and sales taxes for each sales transaction.
- **Storage requirements.** Organization, content, and size of databases, types and frequency of updating and inquiries, and the length and rationale for record retention.
  Example: Fast retrieval and updating of data from product and customer databases.
- **Control requirements.** Accuracy, validity, safety, security, and adaptability requirements for system input, processing, output, and storage functions.
  Example: Signals and messages for data entry errors, and easy-to-read receipts for customers.

Functional Requirements Analysis

This step of systems analysis is one of the most difficult. You need to work with systems analysts and other end users to determine your specific information needs. For example, you need to determine what type of information you require; what its format, volume, and frequency should be; and what response times are necessary. Second, you must try to determine the information processing capabilities required for each system activity (input, processing, output, storage, control) to meet these information needs. Your main goal should be to identify what should be done, not how to do it. Finally, you should try to develop **functional requirements**. Functional requirements are end user information requirements that are not tied to the hardware, software, and people resources that end users presently use or might use in the new system. That is left to the design stage to determine. For example, Figure 10.9 outlines some of the key areas where functional requirements should be developed. Figure 10.9 also shows examples of functional requirements for a sales transaction processing system.

Systems Design

Systems analysis describes what a system should do to meet the information needs of users. **Systems design** specifies *how* the system will accomplish this objective. Systems design consists of design activities which produce **system specifications** satisfying the functional requirements developed in the systems analysis stage. These specifications are used as the basis for software development, hardware acquisition, system testing, and other activities of the implementation stage. A variety of tools and methods which can be used for systems design are discussed in Section III of this chapter.

User Interface, Data, and Process Design

A useful way to look at systems design is illustrated in Figure 10.10. This concept focuses on three major products, or *deliverables*, that should result from the design stage. In this framework, systems design consists of three activities: user interface, data, and process design. This results in specifications for user interface methods and products, database structures, and processing and control procedures [1].

User Interface Design

The user interface design activity focuses on designing the interactions between end users and computer systems. Designers concentrate on input-output methods and

FIGURE 10.10
Systems design can be viewed as the design of user interfaces, data, and processes.

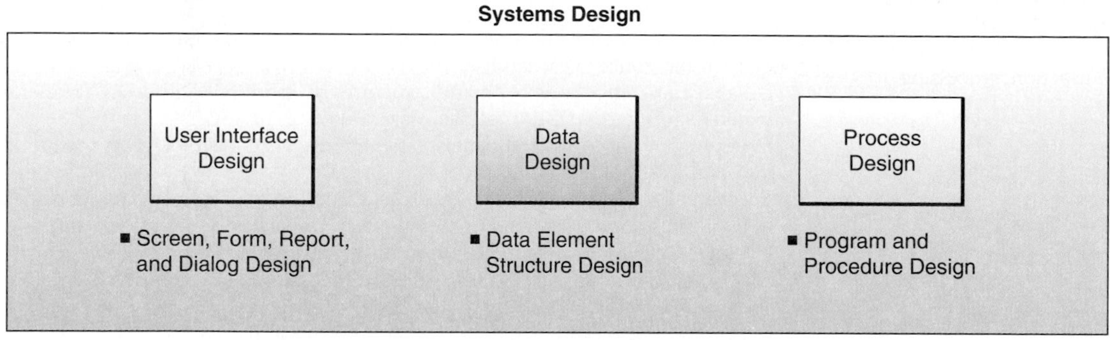

the conversion of data and information between human-readable and machine-readable forms. As we will see shortly, user interface design is frequently a *prototyping* process, where working models, or *prototypes*, of user interface methods are designed and modified with feedback from end users. Thus, user interface design produces detailed specifications for information products such as display screens, interactive user/computer dialogues (including the sequence or flow of dialogue), audio responses, forms, documents, and reports.

Data Design

The data design activity focuses on the design of the structure of databases and files to be used by a proposed information system. Data design frequently produces a *data dictionary*, which catalogs detailed descriptions of:

- The *attributes* or characteristics of the *entities* (objects, people, places, events) about which the proposed information system needs to maintain information.
- The relationships these entities have to each other.
- The specific data elements (databases, files, records, etc.) that need to be maintained for each entity tracked by the information system.
- The integrity rules that govern how each data element is specified and used in the information system.

Process Design

The process design activity focuses on the design of *software resources*, that is, the programs and procedures needed by the proposed information system. It concentrates on developing detailed specifications for the program modules that will have to be purchased as software packages or developed by custom programming. Thus, process design produces detailed program specifications and procedures needed to meet the user interface and data design specifications that are developed. Process design must also produce specifications that meet the functional control and performance requirements developed in the analysis stage.

System Specifications

The design of user interface methods and products, database structures, and processing and control procedures results in hardware, software, and personnel specifications for a proposed system. Systems analysts work with you so they can use your knowledge of your own work activities and their knowledge of computer-based systems to specify the design of a new or improved information system. The final design must specify what types of hardware resources (machines and media), software resources (programs and procedures), and people resources (end users and

FIGURE 10.11
System specifications specify the details of a proposed information system. Note the examples of system specifications for a sales transaction processing system.

- **User interface specifications:** The content, format, and sequence of user interface products and methods such as display screens, interative dialogues, audio responses, forms, documents, and reports.
  Example: Use hand-held optical scanning wands to automatically capture product data on bar-coded merchandise.
- **Database specifications**: Content, structure, distribution, and access, response, maintenance, and retention of databases.
  Example: Develop relational databases which organize customer and product data into multiple tables for easy access.
- **Software specifications**: The required software package or programming specifications of the proposed system, including performance and control specifications.
  Example: Develop or acquire a sales transaction processing program which can accept optical scanning of bar codes, retrieve necessary data, compute sales amounts, and update product databases in less than two seconds per transaction.
- **Hardware and facilities specifications**: The physical and performance characteristics of the equipment and facilities required by the proposed system.
  Example: Install point-of-sale terminals at each checkout station in each store, and interconnect them in a local area network that is also connected to the corporate wide area network.
- **Personal specifications**. Job descriptions of persons who will operate the system.
  Example: All hardware and software must be easy to operate by regular store personnel with minimal training requirements.

information systems staff) will be needed. It must specify how such resources will convert data resources (stored in files and databases they design) into information products (displays, responses, reports, and documents). These specifications are the final product of the systems design stage, and are called the **system specifications**. Figure 10.11 outlines some of the key characteristics that should be included in system specifications. It also shows examples of system specifications that could be developed for a sales transaction processing system.

Computer-aided Systems Engineering

Major changes are occurring in the traditional process of systems development that we described in this chapter. That's because the SDLC process has often been too inflexible, time-consuming, and expensive. In many cases, end user requirements are defined early in the process, and then end users are locked out until the system is implemented. Also, the backlog of unfilled user requests has grown to two to five years in many companies. Therefore, a **computer-aided systems engineering** process has emerged due to the availability of a variety of software packages for systems and software development. CASE (which also stands for **computer-aided software engineering**) involves using software packages, called *CASE tools*, to perform many of the activities of the systems development life cycle. For example, software packages are available to help do business planning, project management, user interface design, database design, and software development. Thus, CASE tools make a computer-aided systems development process possible. See Figure 10.12.

Some of the capabilities of CASE tools are also found in the application development capabilities of end user productivity software such as electronic spreadsheet and database management packages. That's why **end user development** has become a major category of end user computing. Thus, computer-aided systems engineering allows systems analysts and end users to use microcomputer workstations and CASE tools to help accomplish (and, in some cases, automate) activities of the systems development process. The use of CASE tools is discussed

FIGURE 10.12
The components of CASE. This is an example of the CASE software tools and repositories in an integrated CASE product: IEF by Texas Instruments.

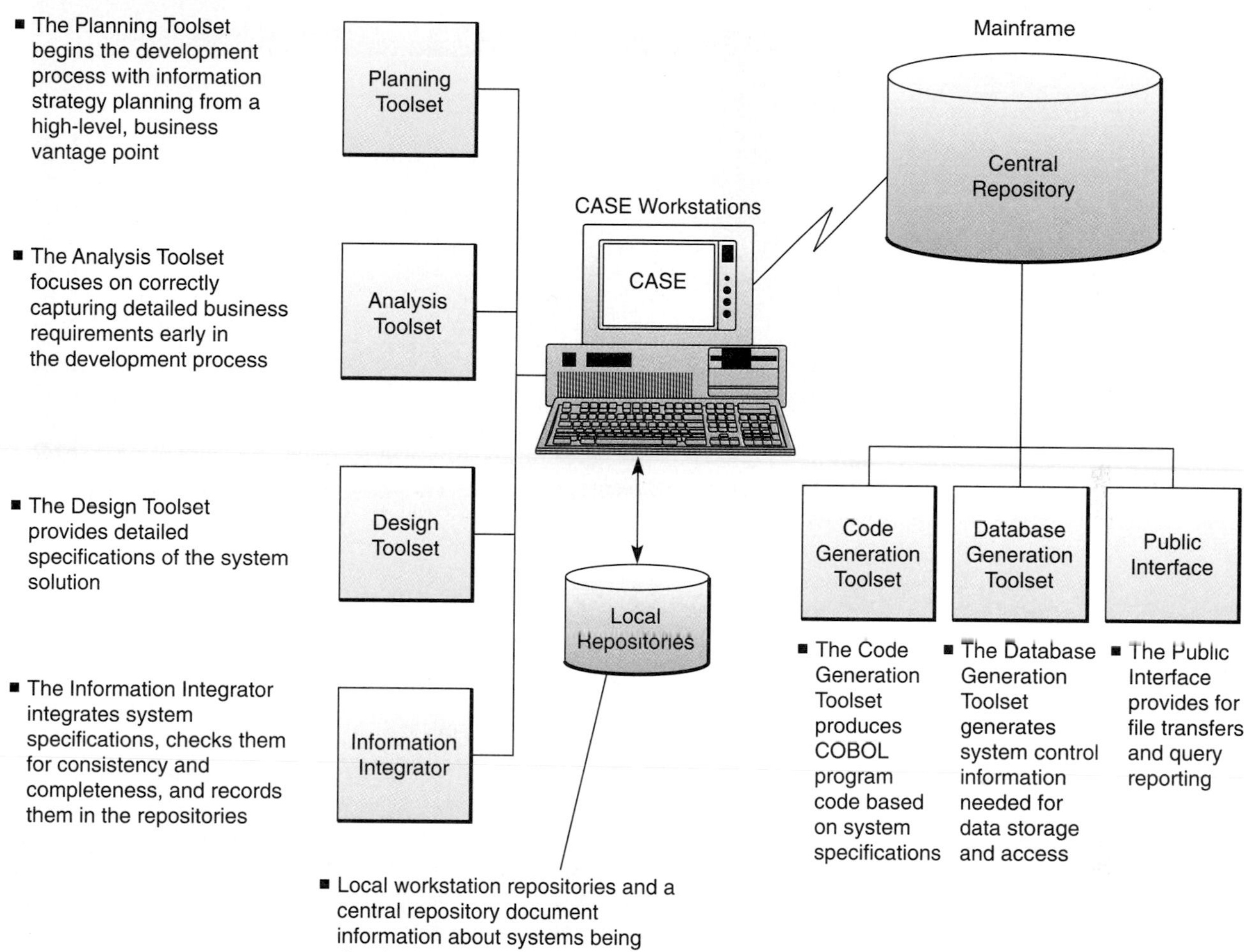

CASE Software Tools
■ The Planning Toolset begins the development process with information strategy planning from a high-level, business vantage point
■ The Analysis Toolset focuses on correctly capturing detailed business requirements early in the development process
■ The Design Toolset provides detailed specifications of the system solution
■ The Information Integrator integrates system specifications, checks them for consistency and completeness, and records them in the repositories
Planning Toolset
Analysis Toolset
Design Toolset
Information Integrator
CASE Workstations
CASE
Local Repositories
Mainframe
Central Repository
Code Generation Toolset
Database Generation Toolset
Public Interface
■ The Code Generation Toolset produces COBOL program code based on system specifications
■ The Database Generation Toolset generates system control information needed for data storage and access
■ The Public Interface provides for file transfers and query reporting
■ Local workstation repositories and a central repository document information about systems being developed or in use

Source: Adapted Courtesy of Texas Instruments.

further in Section III. Figure 10.13 is an example of a display generated by a widely used CASE software package.

Prototyping

Microcomputer workstations and a variety of CASE and other software packages allow the rapid development and testing of working models, or **prototypes**, of new applications in an interactive, iterative process involving both systems analysts and end users. **Prototyping** not only makes the development process faster and easier for systems analysts, especially for projects where end user requirements are hard to define, but it has opened up the application development process to end users. These developments are changing the roles of end users and information systems specialists in systems development.

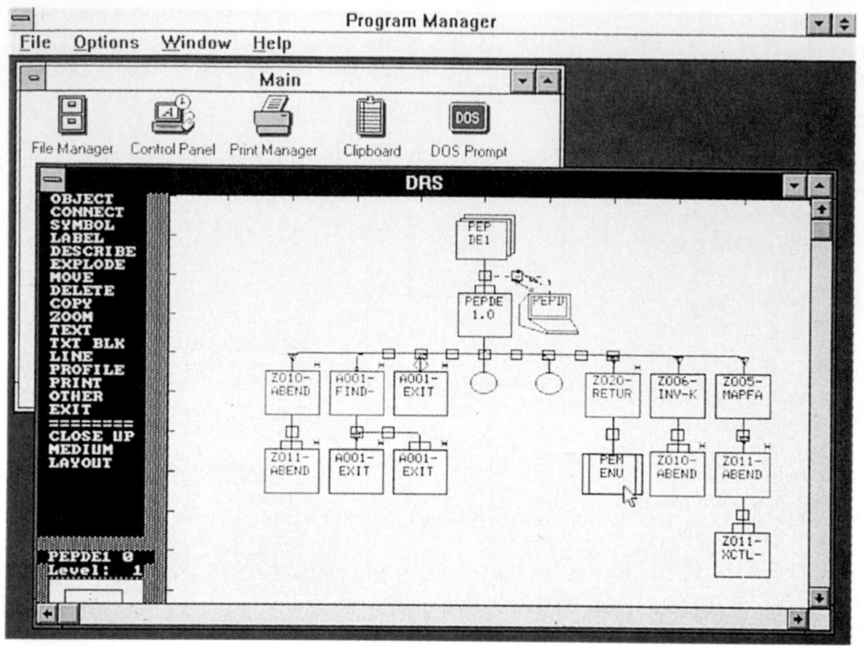

Courtesy Intersolv Inc.

FIGURE 10.13
Displays of a CASE software package. The Excellerator package allows a system analyst to interactively develop system specifications, use a variety of analysis and design tools, and design the format of screens and reports.

The Prototyping Process

Prototyping can be used for both large and small applications. Typically, large systems still require using the traditional system development approach, but parts of such systems can frequently be prototyped. A prototype of an information system needed by an end user is developed quickly using a variety of application development packages. The prototype system is then repeatedly refined until it is acceptable to an end user.

As Figure 10.14 illustrates, prototyping is an iterative, interactive process that combines steps of the traditional systems development cycle. End users with sufficient experience with application development packages can do prototyping themselves. Alternatively, an end user can work with a systems analyst to develop a prototype system in a series of interactive sessions. For example, they could develop prototypes of management reports or data entry screens, such as the one illustrated in Figure 10.15. The prototype is usually modified several times until the end user finds it acceptable. Any program modules not directly developed by the CASE software can then be coded by programmers using conventional programming languages. The final version of the system is then turned over to the end user for operational use.

Checklist for Systems Analysis and Design

Figure 10.16 outlines key questions you can use as a checklist to begin the process of analysis and design. Also included are answers that identify generic system components which are typically found in most computer-based information systems in business. Use this checklist as a tool to identify such components yourself in any information system you are studying. Then use it again as a source of design features you may want to suggest for a new or improved system.

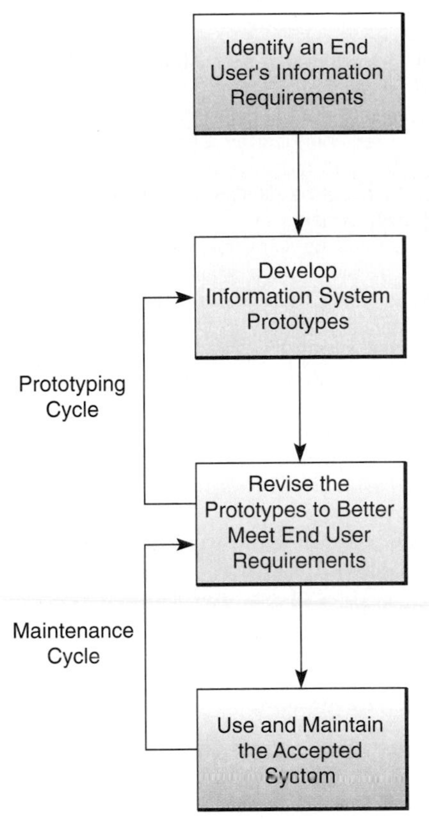

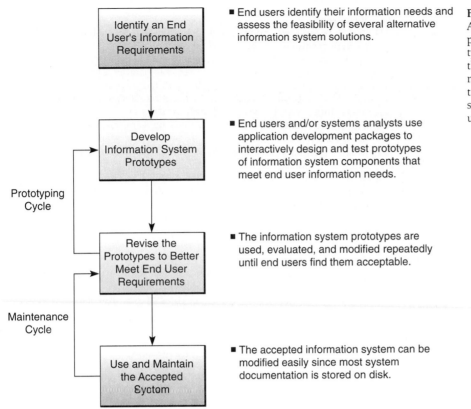

- End users identify their information needs and assess the feasibility of several alternative information system solutions.
- End users and/or systems analysts use application development packages to interactively design and test prototypes of information system components that meet end user information needs.
- The information system prototypes are used, evaluated, and modified repeatedly until end users find them acceptable.
- The accepted information system can be modified easily since most system documentation is stored on disk.

FIGURE 10.14
Application development using prototyping. Note how prototyping combines the steps of the traditional systems development cycle and changes the traditional roles of information systems specialists and end users.

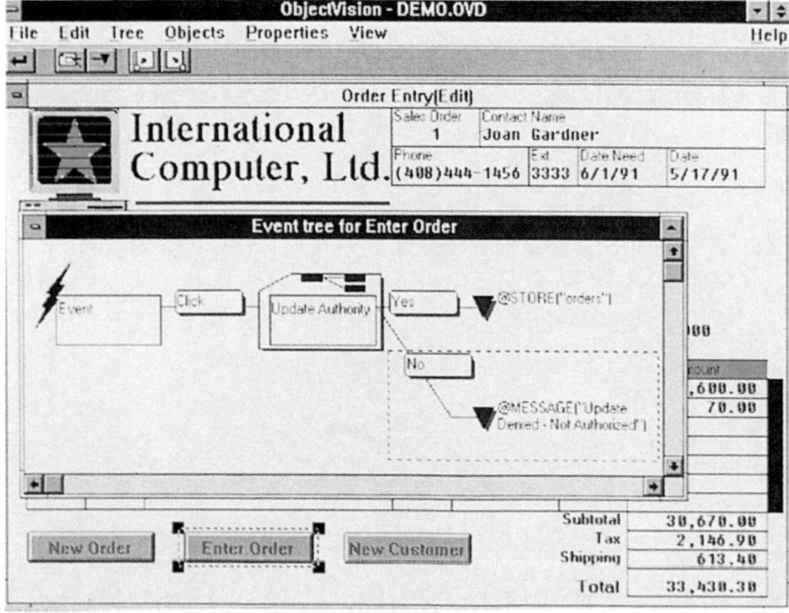

Courtesy of Borland International Inc.

FIGURE 10.15
Using an application development package to design a prototype data entry screen for an order processing system.

FIGURE 10.16
A checklist for systems analysis and design.

Input of Data Resources

Question: How is data captured and prepared for processing? How should it be? What **data resources** are or should be captured?

Answers: Input data is frequently collected from *source documents* (such as payroll time cards) and converted to machine-sensible data by a *keyboarding* data entry process. Other input data may be captured directly by transaction terminals (such as point-of-sale terminals) using devices such as optical scanners. Input into the system typically consists of:

- **Transaction data.** *Example:* Data describing sales transactions is captured by a point-of-sale terminal.
- **Database adjustments.** *Example:* A change in a customer's credit limit, using an online terminal in the credit department or processing a "credit increase request form" mailed in by a customer.
- **Inquiries.** *Example:* What is the balance owed on a customer's account?
- **Output of other systems.** *Example:* The output of a sales transaction processing system includes data needed as input by an inventory control system to reflect transactions that change the amount of inventory on hand.

Processing of Data Resources

Question: How is data manipulated and transformed into information? How should it be? What processing alternatives should be considered?

Answers: Data resources are subjected to sorting, summarizing, calculating, and other manipulation activities. Processing alternatives include batch processing and realtime processing and result in:

- The production of a variety of information products.
- The updating of information stored in databases.
  Example: Sales data captured by point-of-sale terminals at several retail stores are transmitted to and processed at a regional computer center. Company databases are updated, and sales documents and reports are produced.

Output of Information Products

Question: How is information communicated to users? How should it be? What **information products** are and should be produced?

Answers: Output typically takes the form of the following information products:

- **Reports.** *Example:* A sales analyis report outlining the sales made during a period by sales territory, product, and salesperson.
- **Documents.** *Example:* A paycheck or sales receipt.

FIGURE 10.16
Continued

- **Displays or responses.** *Example:* A video terminal displays the balance owed on a customer's account. The same information can be transmitted to a telephone by a computer audio-response unit.
- **Control listings.** *Example:* Each time an employee paycheck is printed, a line on a listing known as a payroll register is also printed and recorded on magnetic tape. This helps provide an *audit trail* for control purposes.
- **Input to other systems.** *Example:* Part of the output of a payroll system serves as input to a labor-cost accounting system and the general ledger system of the firm.

Storage of Data Resources

Question: How are **data resources** organized, stored, updated, and retrieved? How should they be?

Answers: Data resources are stored for later processing. They are typically organized into files and databases. This facilitates:

- Supplying data needed by the organization's information system applications.
- The updating of files and databases to reflect the occurrence of new business transactions.
  Example: The current credit balances of customers are supplied in response to inquiries from sales personnel. Also, credit sales transactions cause some customer credit balances to be increased in the customer database.

Control of System Performance

Question: How are input, processing, output, and storage activities monitored and controlled? How should they be? What control methods should be considered?

Answers: Input, processing, output, and storage activities must be controlled so that an information system produces proper information products and achieves its other objectives. Typical control methods include:

- **Input controls.** *Example:* Formatted data entry screens warn users if input data exceed specified parameters.
- **Processing controls.** Software may contain checkpoint routines that check the accuracy of intermediate results during processing.
- **Output controls.** *Example:* Computer users may check the accuracy of specified control totals in reports.
- **Storage controls.** *Example:* Databases may be protected by security programs that require proper identification and authorization codes by end users.

REAL WORLD CASE

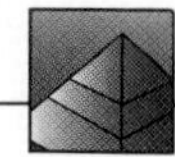

Florida Power Corporation: Developing Systems with CASE

Florida Power Corporation is smack dab in the middle of a three-year, $48 million overhaul of a mission-critical customer service application. Florida Power serves 1.2 million electricity users in the central and northern regions of the state. However, the company said it can serve Floridians better by transforming a 20-year-old, mainframe-based customer service system into a more efficient client/server application geared for the Windows NT or OS/2 operating systems.

The system, which handles tasks such as billing customers and troubleshooting power failures during Florida's hurricane months, "is really the cornerstone of how we do business," said Mitch Hull, manager of information systems. The company plans to move 60 percent or more of its business processing off an IBM mainframe by enabling over 1,000 PC users to hunt down data on the mainframe and collect and work with it on the desktop.

The linchpin of the undertaking is Andersen Consulting's Windows version of Foundation for Cooperative Processing (FCP), a computer-aided software engineering (CASE) workbench. With analysis and design completed, the customer service application is now in the construction phase, with more than 680 windows painted to date by Hull and a 90-member crew. They have also constructed about 50 dialogues, which are macros that automatically provide options and solutions to the most common customer calls received by Florida Power's service desk.

But do not think the going has been glitch-free. At $48 million, the switch is not cheap. Plus, network security is an unresolved issue. FCP provides a certain level of security, as will Windows NT if Microsoft comes through on its promises. "But we don't want our users having to log on to five different nodes or four different systems levels to get their work done," Hull said. "We've still got that floating over our heads."

Andersen claimed that FCP is better suited to client/server development than previous versions because of the following enhancements:

- Improved communication between mainframes and OS/2 or Windows clients.
- Stronger security features that developers can include in other case-built programs.
- Better application programming interfaces for moving between OS/2 and Windows.

Also important to Florida Power's plans is the fact that the FCP developers do not have to target a specific operating system for the finished application right from the beginning. That means programmers can analyze, design, and create prototypes of applications without regard for platform. Then, at construction, they click a box to choose the operating system: Windows, Windows NT, or OS/2.

Florida Power's relationship with Andersen goes back to 1991, when the utility's staff did not quite believe Andersen's client/server claims. So it put the vendor's feet to the fire with a rigorous test of FCP that yielded impressive results. "We did a prototype of a large sales application in only two months with COBOL programmers who had never used the tool before, never mind programmed in C," Hull explained.

CASE STUDY QUESTIONS

1. How is Florida Power using the FCP CASE "workbench"?
2. What are the benefits of FCP for systems developers?
3. Do you think it's a good idea for Florida Power to have network security as "an unresolved issue" after its analysis and design phases are completed? Explain.

Source: Adapted from Kim Nash, "Utility Powers Up with Client Server," *Computerworld*, February 15, 1993, pp. 75, 77. Used with permission.

SECTION II
Implementing Information System Solutions

Implementing Information Systems

Implementation is an important managerial responsibility. Implementation is doing what you planned to do. You should view implementation as a process that carries out the operational plans developed at the end of the information systems planning process. More specifically, the implementation process is a major stage that follows the investigation, analysis, and design stages of the systems development process. Therefore, implementation is an important activity in the deployment of information technology to support an organization and its end users.

Implementation involves a variety of acquisition, testing, documentation, installation, and conversion activities. It also involves the training of end users in the operation and use of a new information system. Thus, implementation is a vital step in ensuring the success of new systems. Even a well-designed system can fail if it is not properly implemented. Figure 10.17 illustrates the major activities of the implementation process. In this section, we will concentrate on the acquisition and installation of IS resources and other managerial implementation issues.

Acquiring Hardware, Software, and Services

Acquiring hardware, software, and external IS services is a major implementation activity. These resources can be acquired from many sources in the computer industry. For example, Figure 10.18 lists the top 10 mainframe, microcomputer, minicomputer, software, services, and data communications companies in 1992. Of course, there are many other firms in the computer industry that supply hardware, software, and services. For example, you can buy microcomputer hardware and software from mail-order firms like Dell and Gateway, or retail chains like Computerland and MicroAge, while thousands of small consulting firms provide a broad range of IS services.

Hardware and Software Suppliers

The major computer manufacturers shown in Figure 10.18 produce many types of computer systems, as well as peripheral equipment and software. Of course, you can buy software packages directly from large software developers such as Microsoft and Lotus Development, or through computer retailers and mail-order companies. Many

FIGURE 10.17
An overview of the implementation process. Implementation activities are needed to transform a newly developed information system into an operational system for end users.

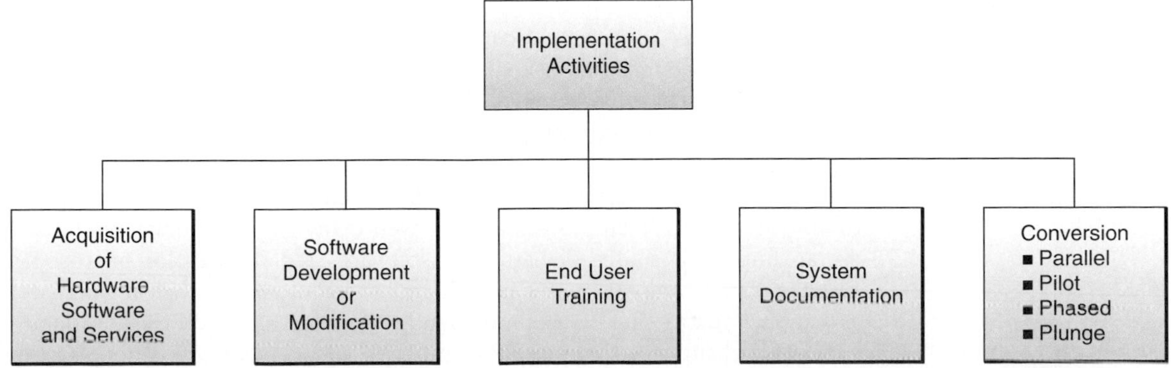

FIGURE 10.18
Major companies in the computer industry that provide mainframes, minicomputers, microcomputers, software, services, and data communications products. Note the major presence of IBM and international corporations.

Mainframe Systems

Rank	Company	Revenues ($ millions)
1	IBM	9,100.0
2	Fujitsu	4,446.1
3	Hitachi	3,501.9
4	NEC	3,063.5
5	Amdahl	987.2
6	Nihon Unisys	965.4
7	Siemens Nixdorf	964.4
8	Unisys	850.0
9	Groupe Bull	830.2
10	Cray	682.0

Minicomputer Systems

Rank	Company	Revenues ($ millions)
1	IBM	5,870.0
2	Digital	2,730.0
3	Fujitsu	2,609.7
4	NEC	1,838.1
5	Toshiba	1,332.1
6	Unisys	945.0
7	Siemens Nixdorf	934.3
8	Hewlett-Packard	832.0
9	Tandem	790.0
10	AT&T	550.0

Microcomputer Systems

Rank	Company	Revenues ($ millions)
1	IBM	8,505.0
2	Apple	4,900.0
3	NEC	4,135.8
4	Compaq	3,271.4
5	Fujitsu	2,319.7
6	Toshiba	2,093.5
7	Olivetti	1,586.1
8	Unisys	1,061.0
9	Intel	1,050.0
10	Commodore	1,038.5

Computer Software

Rank	Company	Revenues ($ millions)
1	IBM	10,525.0
2	Fujitsu	2,513.0
3	Microsoft	2,045.9
4	NEC	1,761.5
5	Computer Associates	1,437.8
6	Oracle	1,085.0
7	Siemens Nixdorf	964.4
8	Hitachi	959.1
9	Lotus	828.9
10	Digital	796.0

IS Services

Rank	Company	Revenues ($ millions)
1	EDS	3,666.1
2	Andersen Consulting	2,083.0
3	IBM	2,018.0
4	CSC	1,944.7
5	TRW	1,839.0
6	ADP	1,810.0
7	Digital	1,570.3
8	Fujitsu	1,546.5
9	Cap Gemini	1,492.1
10	NTT	996.9

Data Communications

Rank	Company	Revenues ($ millions)
1	IBM	2,000.0
2	AT&T	1,790.0
3	NTT	1,495.4
4	Northern Telecom	1,460.0
5	Matsushita	1,267.2
6	Ricoh	892.2
7	Racal	679.0
8	Toshiba	639.5
9	Fujitsu	579.9
10	Mitsubishi	550.0

Source: Adapted from "Global Leaders," *Datamation*, June 15, 1992, pp. 26–27.

larger business and professional organizations, educational institutions, and government agencies have employee purchase plans that let you buy computer hardware and software at substantial discounts. These *corporate buying plans* are arranged through negotiations with hardware manufacturers and software companies.

Original equipment manufacturers (OEMs) produce and sell computers by assembling components produced by other hardware suppliers. *Plugcompatible manufacturers* (PCMs) manufacture computer mainframes and peripheral devices that are specifically designed to be compatible (by just plugging in) with the computers made by IBM, Digital Equipment Corporation, and others. *Value-added resellers* (VARs) specialize in providing industry-specific hardware and software from selected manufacturers.

Computer retailers and mail-order firms sell microcomputers and peripherals to individuals and small businesses, and even many large corporate accounts. They are an important source of hardware, software, and services for microcomputer systems. Retail computer stores include thousands of independent retailers, as well as national chains such as Computerland, MicroAge, and JWP Businessland, and superstore chains like CompuAdd, CompUSA, and Tandy Corporation's Computer

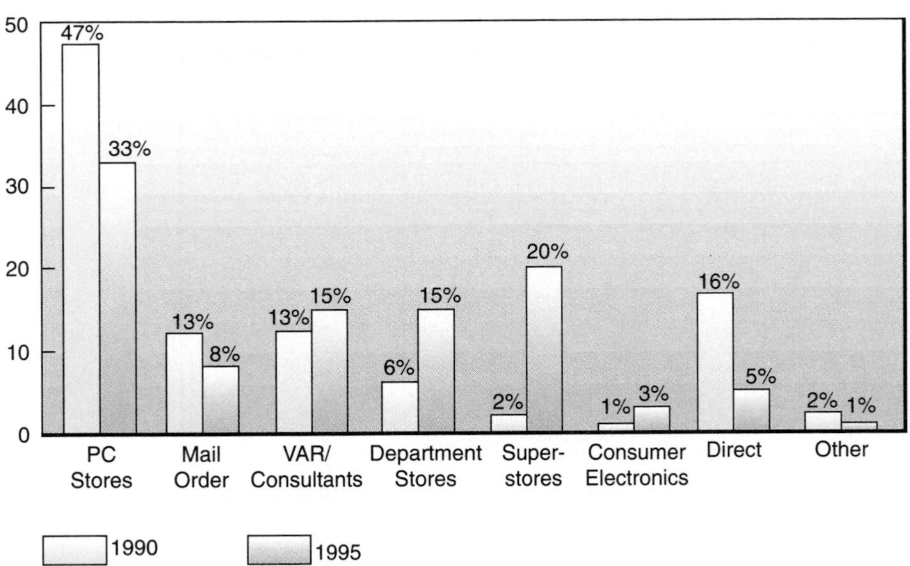

Source: Adapted from Bob Francis, "Why PC Managers Still Want Services," *Datamation*, November 15, 1991, p. 40.

FIGURE 10.19
Present and future sources of PC purchases by business.

City SuperCenters. Mail-order firms include Dell, Gateway, and Zeos, to name a few. Figure 10.19 illustrates the results of a survey of 1,200 corporate buyers that shows the many sources used by businesses for PC purchases.

Suppliers of IS Services

The major sources of external information systems services are computer manufacturers, computer retailers, computer service centers, time-sharing companies, systems integrators, and independent consultants. These and other types of firms in the computer industry offer a variety of services. For example, computer service centers (or service bureaus) provide off-premises computer processing of customer jobs, and time-sharing companies provide realtime mainframe computing via wide area networks to subscribers. Systems integrators take over complete responsibility for an organization's computer facilities when an organization outsources its computer operations. They may also assume responsibility for developing and implementing large systems development projects that involve many vendors and subcontractors. Many other services are available to end users, including computer rentals, systems design services, contract programming, consulting, education, and hardware maintenance.

Evaluating Hardware, Software, and Services

How do computer-using organizations evaluate and select hardware and software? Typically, they require suppliers to present bids and proposals based on system specifications developed during the design stage of systems development. Minimum acceptable physical and performance characteristics for all hardware and software requirements are established. Most large business firms and all government agencies formalize these requirements by listing them in a document called an RFP (request for proposal) or RFQ (request for quotation). The RFP or RFQ is then sent to appropriate vendors, who use it as the basis for preparing a proposed purchase agreement. See Figure 10.20.

Computer users may use a scoring system of evaluation when there are several competing proposals for a hardware or software acquisition. Each evaluation factor is given a certain number of maximum possible points. Then each competing

FIGURE 10.20
Example of a request for proposal (RFP). Note how it specifies the capabilities that must be met in the supplier's bid for 10 dot matrix printers.

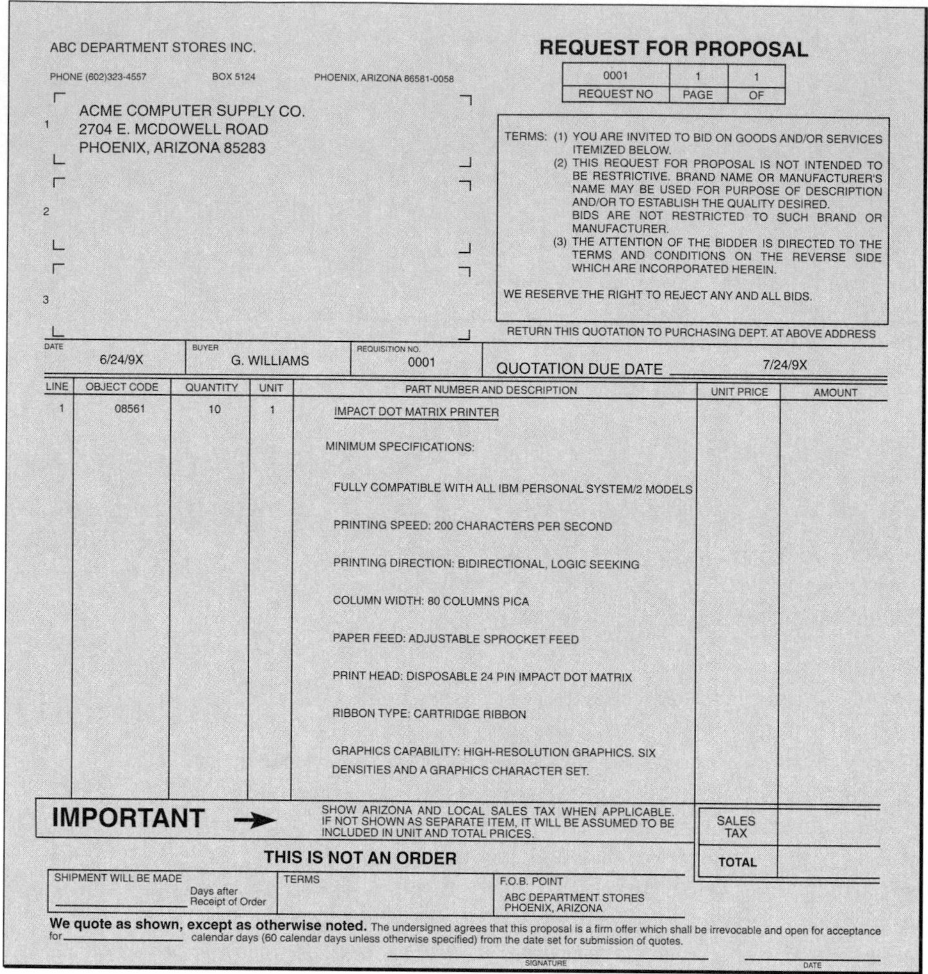

ABC DEPARTMENT STORES INC.

PHONE (602)323-4557 BOX 5124 PHOENIX, ARIZONA 86581-0058

REQUEST FOR PROPOSAL

REQUEST NO	PAGE	OF
0001	1	1

1 ACME COMPUTER SUPPLY CO.
2704 E. MCDOWELL ROAD
PHOENIX, ARIZONA 85283

2

3

TERMS: (1) YOU ARE INVITED TO BID ON GOODS AND/OR SERVICES ITEMIZED BELOW.
(2) THIS REQUEST FOR PROPOSAL IS NOT INTENDED TO BE RESTRICTIVE. BRAND NAME OR MANUFACTURER'S NAME MAY BE USED FOR PURPOSE OF DESCRIPTION AND/OR TO ESTABLISH THE QUALITY DESIRED. BIDS ARE NOT RESTRICTED TO SUCH BRAND OR MANUFACTURER.
(3) THE ATTENTION OF THE BIDDER IS DIRECTED TO THE TERMS AND CONDITIONS ON THE REVERSE SIDE WHICH ARE INCORPORATED HEREIN.

WE RESERVE THE RIGHT TO REJECT ANY AND ALL BIDS.

RETURN THIS QUOTATION TO PURCHASING DEPT. AT ABOVE ADDRESS

DATE	BUYER	REQUISITION NO.	QUOTATION DUE DATE
6/24/9X	G. WILLIAMS	0001	7/24/9X

LINE	OBJECT CODE	QUANTITY	UNIT	PART NUMBER AND DESCRIPTION	UNIT PRICE	AMOUNT
1	08561	10	1	IMPACT DOT MATRIX PRINTER MINIMUM SPECIFICATIONS: FULLY COMPATIBLE WITH ALL IBM PERSONAL SYSTEM/2 MODELS PRINTING SPEED: 200 CHARACTERS PER SECOND PRINTING DIRECTION: BIDIRECTIONAL, LOGIC SEEKING COLUMN WIDTH: 80 COLUMNS PICA PAPER FEED: ADJUSTABLE SPROCKET FEED PRINT HEAD: DISPOSABLE 24 PIN IMPACT DOT MATRIX RIBBON TYPE: CARTRIDGE RIBBON GRAPHICS CAPABILITY: HIGH-RESOLUTION GRAPHICS. SIX DENSITIES AND A GRAPHICS CHARACTER SET.		

IMPORTANT → SHOW ARIZONA AND LOCAL SALES TAX WHEN APPLICABLE. IF NOT SHOWN AS SEPARATE ITEM, IT WILL BE ASSUMED TO BE INCLUDED IN UNIT AND TOTAL PRICES.

SALES TAX

THIS IS NOT AN ORDER

TOTAL

SHIPMENT WILL BE MADE	TERMS	F.O.B. POINT
________ Days after Receipt of Order		ABC DEPARTMENT STORES PHOENIX, ARIZONA

We quote as shown, except as otherwise noted. The undersigned agrees that this proposal is a firm offer which shall be irrevocable and open for acceptance for ________ calendar days (60 calendar days unless otherwise specified) from the date set for submission of quotes.

SIGNATURE DATE

proposal is assigned points for each factor, depending on how well it meets the specifications of the computer user. Scoring each evaluation factor for several proposals helps organize and document the evaluation process. It also spotlights the strengths and weaknesses of each proposal. See Figure 10.21.

A formal evaluation process reduces the possibility of buying inadequate or unnecessary computer hardware or software. Badly organized computer operations, inadequate systems development, and poor purchasing practices may cause inadequate or unnecessary acquisitions. Therefore, it is necessary to use various methods of evaluation to measure key factors for computer hardware, software, and services. See Figures 10.22, 10.23, and 10.24.

Whatever the claims of hardware manufacturers and software suppliers, the performance of hardware and software must be demonstrated and evaluated. Independent hardware and software information services (such as the Datapro and Auerbach reporting services) should be used to gain detailed specification informa-

FIGURE 10.21
Evaluating Compaq's Deskpro/Microcomputer. Note the use of a scoring system and comments by computer industry magazines, analysts, and end users.

Compaq's Deskpro/M						
Reviews	**Performance**	**Ease of upgrade**	**Expandability**	**Service and support**	**Value**	**Overall**
Byte 10/91	Modest perform-ance for Compaq	Good board trade-in allowance	Smaller, simpler add-in boards	NC	Aggressive pricing	Affordable, up-gradable quality
PC Computing 11/91	Fast	Easy	Many options	NC	Very un-Compaq price	Flexible, modu-lar, good price
PC Magazine 10/29/91	Excellent	Easy	A good hedge against obsolescence	NC	Competitive pricing	Compaq quality, but no new innovation
Users						
Rick Upton, Egleston Children's Hospital	Very good	Very good	Very good	Good	Very good	Longer life span on computer
Tom Vayda, Kidder, Peabody & Co.	Very good	Good	Good	NC	Good	Most modular product yet
Jay Flatley, Molecular Dynamics	Very good	Very good	Good	Good	Very good	Architecture per-fect for upgrades
Jim Funari, Christian Broadcasting Network	Good	Very good	Good	Good	Good	Finally got ser-ious on price
Analysts						
Andrew Seybold, Dataquest, Inc.	Very good	Good	Good	Good	Fair	Workhorse mach-ine; premium price
Jerry Caron, Faulkner Technical Reports	Very good	Good	Very good	Good	Good	Always a solid PC

Key: Very good, Good, Fair, Poor

Courtesy *Computerworld.*

FIGURE 10.22
A summary of major hardware evaluation factors. Notice how you can use this to evaluate a computer system or a peripheral device.

Hardware Evaluation Factors	Rating
Performance What is its speed, capacity, and throughput?	
Cost What is its lease or purchase price? What will be its cost of operations and maintenance?	
Reliability What is the risk of malfunction and its maintenance requirements? What are its error control and diagnostic features?	
Availability When is the firm delivery date?	
Compatibility Is it compatible with existing hardware and software? Is it compatible with hardware and software provided by competing suppliers?	
Modularity Can it be expanded and upgraded by acquiring modular "add on" units?	
Technology In what year of its product life cycle is it? Does it use a new untested technology or does it run the risk of obsolescence?	
Ergonomics Has it been "human factors engineered" with the user in mind? Is it "user-friendly," designed to be safe, comfortable, and easy to use?	
Connectivity Can it be easily connected to wide area and local area networks of different types of computers and peripherals?	
Environmental Requirements What are its electrical power, air-conditioning, and other environmental requirements?	
Software Is system and application software available that can best use this hardware?	
Support Are the services required to support and maintain it available?	
Overall Rating	

tion and evaluations. Hardware and software should be demonstrated and evaluated. This can be done on the premises of the computer user or by visiting the operations of other computer users who have similar types of hardware or software. Other users are frequently the best source of information needed to evaluate the claims of manufacturers and suppliers. Vendors should be willing to provide the names of such users.

Large computer users frequently evaluate proposed hardware and software by requiring the processing of special benchmark test programs and test data. Users can then evaluate test results to determine which hardware device or software package displayed the best performance characteristics. Special software simulators may also be available that simulate the processing of typical jobs on several computers and evaluate their performances.

Software Evaluation Factors	Rating
Efficiency Is the software a well-written system of computer instructions that does not use much memory capacity or CPU time?	
Flexibility Can it handle its processing assignments easily without major modification?	
Security Does it provide control procedures for errors, malfunctions, and improper use?	
Language Is it written in a programming language that is used by our computer programmers and users?	
Documentation Is the software well documented? Does it include helpful user instructions?	
Hardware Does existing hardware have the features required to best use this software?	
Other Factors What are its performance, cost, reliability, availability, compatibility, modularity, technology, ergonomics, and support characteristics? (Use the hardware evaluation factor questions in Figure 14.6)	
Overall Rating	

FIGURE 10.23
A summary of selected software evaluation factors. Note that most of the hardware evaluation factors in Figure 10.22 can also be used to evaluate software packages.

Hardware Evaluation Factors

When you evaluate computer hardware, you should investigate specific physical and performance characteristics for each hardware component to be acquired. This is true whether you are evaluating mainframes, microcomputers, or peripheral devices. Specific questions must be answered concerning many important factors. These **hardware evaluation factors** and questions are summarized in Figure 10.22.

Notice that there is much more to evaluating hardware than determining the fastest and cheapest computing device. For example, the question of possible obsolescence must be addressed by making a *technology* evaluation. The factor of *ergonomics* is also very important. Ergonomic factors ensure that computer hardware and software are "user-friendly," that is, safe, comfortable, and easy to use. *Connectivity* is another important evaluation factor, since so many computer systems are now interconnected within wide area or local area telecommunications networks.

Software Evaluation Factors

You should evaluate software according to many factors that are similar to those used for hardware evaluation. Thus, the factors of performance, cost, reliability, availability, compatibility, modularity, technology, ergonomics, and support should be used to evaluate proposed software acquisitions. In addition, however, the software evaluation factors summarized in Figure 10.23 must also be considered. You should answer the questions they generate in order to properly evaluate software purchases. For example, some software packages are notoriously slow, hard to use, or poorly documented. They are not a good choice, even if offered at attractive prices.

Evaluating IS Services

Most suppliers of hardware and software products and many other firms offer a variety of IS services to end users and organizations. Examples include assistance

FIGURE 10.24
Evaluation factors for IS services. These factors focus on the quality of support services computer users may need.

Evaluation Factors for IS Services	Rating
Performance What has been their past performance in view of their past promises?	
Systems Development Are systems analysis and programming consultants available? What are their quality and cost?	
Maintenance Is equipment maintenance provided? What is its quality and cost?	
Conversion What systems development, programming, and hardware installation services will they provide during the conversion period?	
Training Is the necessary training of personnel provided? What is its quality and cost?	
Backup Are several similar computer facilities available for emergency backup purposes?	
Accessibility Does the vendor have a local or regional office that offers sales, systems development, and hardware maintenance services? Is a customer hotline provided?	
Business Position Is the vendor financially strong, with good industry market prospects?	
Hardware Do they have a wide selection of compatible hardware devices and accessories?	
Software Do they offer a variety of useful system software and application packages?	
Overall Rating	

during installation or conversion of hardware and software, employee training, customer hot lines, and hardware maintenance. Some of these services are provided without cost by hardware manufacturers and software suppliers. Other types of services can be contracted for at a negotiated price. Evaluation factors and questions for IS services are summarized in Figure 10.24.

Other Implementation Activities

Testing

Testing, documentation, and training are keys to successful implementation of a new system. See Figure 10.25. The testing of a newly developed system is an important implementation activity. **System testing** involves testing hardware devices, testing and debugging computer programs, and testing information processing procedures. Programs are tested using test data, which attempts to simulate all conditions that may arise during processing. In good programming practice (*structured programming*), programs are subdivided into levels of modules to assist their development, testing, and maintenance. Program testing usually proceeds from higher to lower levels of program modules until the entire program is tested as a unit. The program is then tested along with other related programs in a final *systems test*. If computer-aided software engineering (CASE) methodologies are used, such program testing is

John Coletti/Stock Boston.

FIGURE 10.25
Testing, documentation, and training are keys to successful implementation.

minimized, since any automatically generated program code is more likely to be error-free.

An important part of testing is the production of tentative copies of displays, reports, and other output. These should be reviewed by end users of the proposed systems for possible errors. Of course, testing should not occur only during the system's implementation stage, but throughout the system's development process. For example, input documents, screen displays, and processing procedures are examined and critiqued by end users when a *prototyping* methodology is used during the systems design stage. Immediate end user testing is one of the benefits of a prototyping process.

Documentation

Developing good user **documentation** is an important part of the implementation process. Examples include manuals of operating procedures and sample data entry display screens, forms, and reports. During the implementation stage, system documentation manuals may be prepared to finalize the documentation of a large system. When computer-aided systems engineering methods are used, documentation can be created and changed easily. Figure 10.26 illustrates the contents of system documentation stored by the Excellerator CASE package.

Documentation serves as a method of communication among the people responsible for developing, implementing, and maintaining a computer-based system. Installing and operating a newly designed system or modifying an established application requires a detailed record of that system's design. Documentation is extremely important in diagnosing errors and making changes, especially if the end users or systems analysts who developed a system are no longer with the organization.

Training

Training is a vital implementation activity. IS personnel, such as user consultants, must be sure that end users are trained to operate a new system or its implementation will fail. Training may involve only activities like data entry, or it may also involve all aspects of the proper use of a new system. In addition, managers and end users must be educated in the fundamentals of information systems technology and its application to business operations and management. This basic knowledge should be supplemented by training programs for specific hardware devices, software packages, and end user applications. As we mentioned in Chapter 7, this educational role is a typical service of an organization's *information center*. Figure

FIGURE 10.26
The contents of system documentation organized and stored using the Excellerator software package.

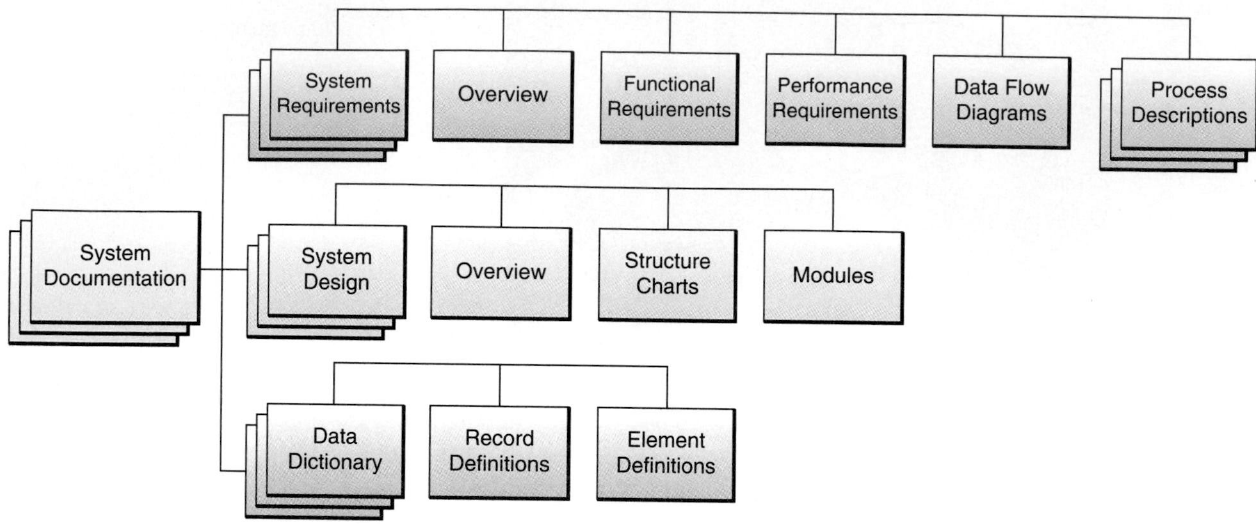

Source: Adapted courtesy of INTERSOLV Corporation.

10.27 shows the hierarchy of skill levels that end users can achieve with proper education and training.

Conversion Methods

The initial operation of a new computer-based system can be a difficult task. Such an operation is usually a **conversion** process in which the personnel, procedures, equipment, input/output media, and databases of an old information system must be converted to the requirements of a new system. Four major forms of system conversion are illustrated in Figure 10.28. They include:

- Parallel conversion.
- Phased conversion.
- Pilot conversion.
- Plunge or direct cutover.

Conversions can be done on a *parallel* basis, whereby both the old and the new system are operated until the project development team and end user management agree to switch completely over to the new system. It is during this time that the operations and results of both systems are compared and evaluated. Errors can be identified and corrected, and the operating problems can be solved before the old system is abandoned. Installation can also be accomplished by a direct *cutover* or *plunge* to the newly developed system. It can also be done on a *phased* basis, where only parts of a new application or only a few departments, branch offices, or plant locations at a time are converted. A phased conversion allows a gradual implementation process to take place within an organization. Similar benefits accrue from using a *pilot* conversion, where one department or other work site serves as a test site. A new system can be tried out at this site until developers feel it can be implemented throughout the organization.

Maintenance

Once a system is fully implemented and being operated by end users, the maintenance function begins. **System maintenance** is the monitoring, evaluating, and

FIGURE 10.27
Levels of end user skills. Note the skill level and knowledge that end users can gain with proper education and training.

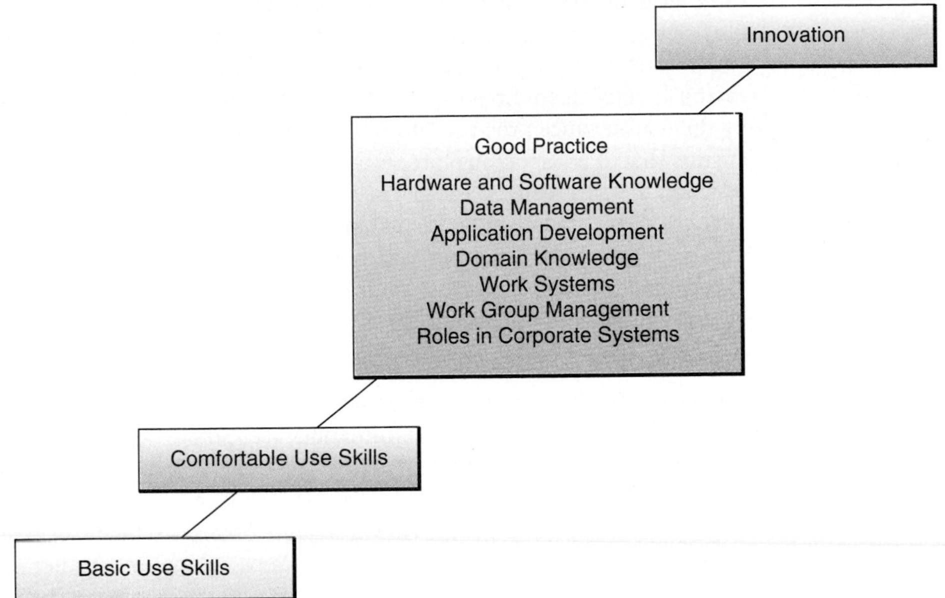

Source: Adapted from Raymond Panko, *End User Computing, Management, Applications, and Technology* (New York: John Wiley & Sons, 1988), p. 167.

FIGURE 10.28
The four major forms of conversion to a new system.

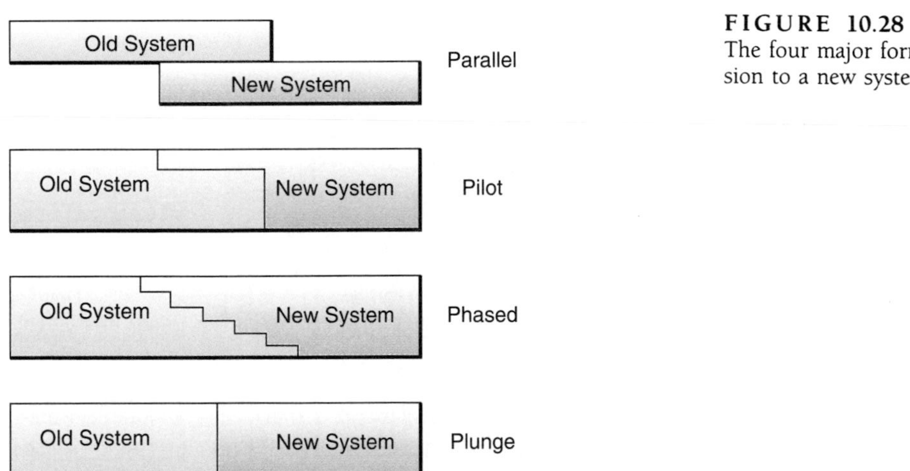

Source: Adapted from E. Wainwright Martin, Daniel DeHayes, Jeffrey Hoffer, and William Perkins, *Managing Information Technology: What Managers Need to Know* (New York: Macmillan, 1991), p. 299.

modifying of operational information systems to make desirable or necessary improvements. For example, the implementation of a new system usually results in the phenomenon known as the *learning curve*. Personnel who operate and use the system will make mistakes simply because they are not familiar with it. Though such errors usually diminish as experience is gained with a new system, they do point out areas where a system may be improved. Maintenance is also necessary for other failures and problems that arise during the operation of a system. End users and information systems personnel then perform a *troubleshooting* function to determine the causes of and solutions to such problems.

The maintenance activity includes a **postimplementation review** process to ensure that newly implemented systems meet the systems development objectives established for them. Errors in the development or use of a system must be corrected by the maintenance process. This includes a periodic review, or *audit*, of a system to ensure that it is operating properly and meeting its objectives. This audit is in addition to continually monitoring a new system for potential problems or necessary changes. Maintenance includes making modifications to a system due to changes in the business organization or the business environment. For example, new tax legislation, business reorganizations, and new business ventures usually require changes to current organizational information systems.

End Users and Implementation

Any new way of doing things generates some resistance by the people affected. Thus, the implementation of new information technology can generate a significant amount of end user fear and reluctance to change. There are many reasons for such *end user resistance*, some of which we explore in a discussion concerning societal impacts of IT in Chapter 12. However, end user resistance can be minimized by formal **technology implementation** programs which end user managers and IS consultants can develop to encourage user acceptance and productive use of new information technologies. So, the key to solving problems of end user resistance is proper end user education and training, improved communications with IS professionals, and end user involvement in systems development and implementation. See Figure 10.29.

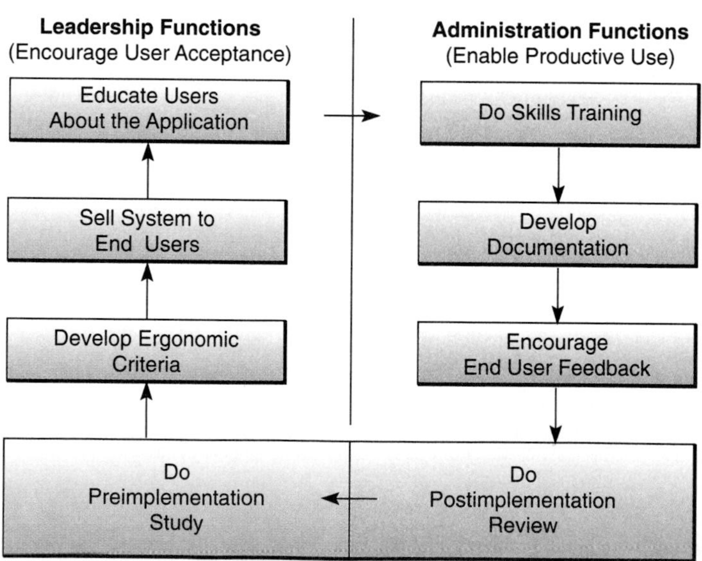

FIGURE 10.29
A technology implementation cycle. Technology implementation activities can minimize end user resistance to new information technology.

Source: Adapted from Vicki McConnel and Carl Koch, *Computerizing the Corporation* (New York: Van Nostrand Reinhold, 1990), p. 101.

Direct end user participation in systems development projects *before* a system is implemented is especially important in reducing the potential for end user resistance. This involvement helps ensure that end users "assume ownership" of a system, and that its design meets their needs. Systems that tend to inconvenience or frustrate their users cannot be effective systems, no matter how technically elegant they are and how efficiently they process data. Figure 10.30 is a tongue-in-cheek reminder of what may happen when end users are not involved in the development process.

As Stated in the Functional Requirements

As Outlined in the System Specifications

As Designed by the Systems Analyst

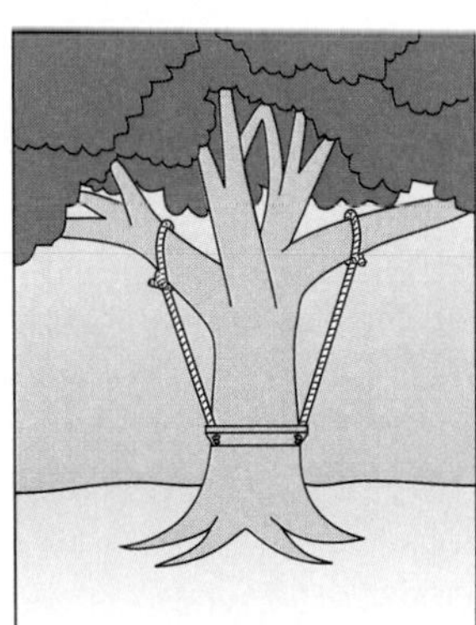

As Implemented by Information Services

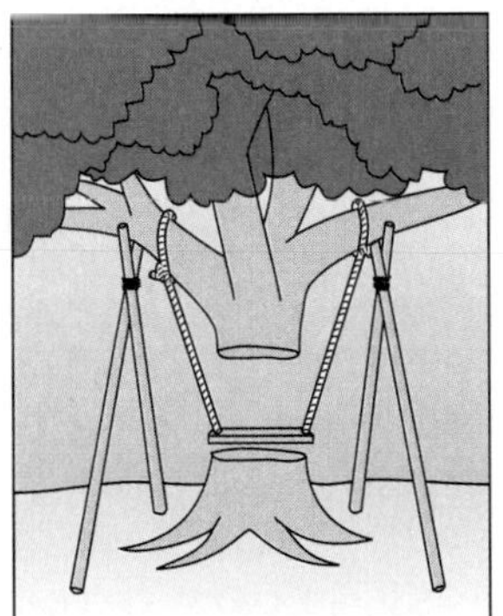

As Operated by the End User

What the End User Really Needed

FIGURE 10.30
Application development without end user involvement. Effective information systems cannot be developed without end user participation.

REAL WORLD CASE

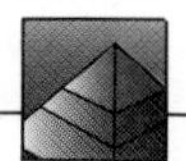

Quaker Oats Company: Implementing a New System

Quaker Oats Company recently installed a Unix-based system at its Jacksonville, Tennessee, Celeste Pizza plant. The business decision to replace its aging system of Burroughs, Hewlett-Packard, and Digital Equipment computers at the Celeste plant was tied to the need to replace its existing statistical process control software. In particular, the project sponsors wanted to streamline data collection and provide near-realtime feedback. The company believed the plant, which produces 45 million pizzas each year, could save money by more closely controlling its use of ingredients.

The need for a new system was also driven by the fact that the Food and Drug Administration and United States Drug Administration monitor separate areas in the plant. Representatives of the two agencies wanted to be able to review data without operating in each other's territory.

The old system was unable to efficiently deal with the daily reams of paper-based quality assurance data providing feedback on the preceding day's run. Someone back on the plant floor would view the data and then have someone else key it into a PC or similar repository. During this process of multiple individuals shuffling through the data, some errors were inevitably made.

In addition to realizing speedier, more accurate data handling, the group wanted to make the data more widely available and easier to use. Toward this goal, a number of employees from the plant floor were involved from the beginning of the project.

In specifying a new system, the decision was made to choose the best hardware and software, whether or not it was compatible with the old system. Among other things, the project team was looking for lower costs, more flexibility, and quicker access. Because the team wanted an open system, it decided to seek a Unix-based platform. It also wanted a hardware-independent system able to use packages that run on PCs from IBM and Compaq, as well as on computers from HP and Digital Equipment.

Although the team was seeking something new, it also wanted to draw on proven technology. With that in mind, it wanted an Oracle database that could be accessed through SQL. While shopping for software and the expertise to run it, the team examined some 29 packages, finally settling on Production/Management Information Systems (PMIS) from Bradley Ward. The package combines the process control and management functions required for the new system. After the hardware evaluation was finished, the team selected HP 9000 minicomputers to run the software. Telecommunications connectivity is provided by an HP Vectra PC.

PMIS allows operators on the plant floor to enter a product code and time frame and then monitor running conditions during that time frame. The plant lab, which samples and analyzes pizza has an HP 9000/345 workstation to provide similar access.

Since installing the system, Quaker Oats has realized the benefits it hoped for, including:

- Cost savings due to weighing accuracy.
- Improved quality due to weighing accuracy.
- Immediate quality feedback.
- Appropriate data readily available to government agencies.

Once the new system was implemented, the team took an initial group of 25 employees who had helped design it, trained them in operations, and gave them the responsibility for training the remaining employees. The project team is also reviewing other software packages for future improvements. It is also building on this system by allowing the old Digital Equipment VAXes to interface with the new HP system. When this is accomplished, anyone with a terminal or PC will be able to interface with the new system.

CASE STUDY QUESTIONS

1. What functional requirements did Quaker Oats specify for their new process control system? What benefits have resulted?
2. What selection criteria for hardware and software were used by Quaker Oats?
3. What implementation activities do you recognize in this case? Give several examples.

Source: Adapted from "Quaker Oats Looks for Better Systems Mix," *Computerworld*, Special Advertising Supplement, February 15, 1993, p. 10. Used with permission.

SECTION III
Using Systems Development Tools

This section provides material on systems development tools that may be assigned at the option of your instructor. Read it if you want to know more about several types of traditional and CASE tools used by information systems professionals during the systems development process.

Systems Development Tools

Many tools and techniques have been developed to help improve current information systems or develop new ones. Such tools help end users and systems analysts:

- Conceptualize, clarify, document, and communicate the activities and resources involved in an organization and its information systems.
- Analyze the present business operations, management decision making, and information processing activities of an organization.
- Propose and design new or improved information systems to solve business problems or pursue business opportunities that have been identified.

Many **systems development tools** take the form of diagrams and other graphic representations. That's because they are easier to understand than narrative descriptions of a system. Good graphic tools can also represent the major activities and resources of a system without a lot of detail and yet be able to show various levels and modules of detail when needed. They also can be modified during the course of analysis and design, as you specify more features of a present or proposed information system. Finally, graphics and other tools serve as documentation methods. For example, they document the results of the analysis stage for use in the design stage, then they document the results of the design stage to assist in the implementation and maintenance of a new system.

Overview of Systems Development Tools

Figure 10.31 outlines some of the major types of tools used for systems development. Notice that the tools can be grouped into four categories based on the system features each typically documents: (1) the components and flows of a system, (2) the user interface, (3) data attributes and relationships, and (4) detailed system processes. We will briefly describe these tools now, and then show you examples of how system flowcharts, data flow diagrams, and the system component matrix are used in a case study example: ABC Auto Parts.

Remember that such tools can be used in every stage of systems development as analytical tools, design tools, and documentation methods. For example, system

System Feature	Systems Development Tools Used
System components and flows	System flowcharts, presentation graphs, data flow diagrams, context diagrams, system component matrix.
User interface	Input/output layout forms and screens, dialogue flow diagrams.
Data attributes and relationships	Data dictionaries, entity-relationship diagrams, file layout forms, grid charts.
Detailed system processes	Decision trees and tables, structure charts, pseudocode, program flowcharts.

FIGURE 10.31
Examples of systems development tools. Note the four primary areas of use for these tools.

flowcharts and data flow diagrams can be used to (1) analyze an existing system, (2) express the design of a new system, and (3) provide the documentation for the implementation and maintenance of a newly developed system. You should also realize that software packages for computer-aided systems engineering (CASE) have computerized many of these tools. For example, many CASE packages will automatically draw and revise system flowcharts or data flow diagrams based on end user or analyst descriptions of a system, as well as create and maintain a data dictionary for the system.

System Components and Flows

These tools help you document the data flows among the major resources and activities of an information system. System flowcharts are typically used to show the flow of data media as they are processed by hardware devices and manual activities. Presentation charts are quite similar but use less-technical symbols. Data flow diagrams use a few simple symbols to illustrate the flow of data among external entities (such as people or organizations), processing activities, and data storage elements. A context diagram is the highest-level data flow diagram. It defines the boundaries of a system by showing a single major process and the data inputs and outputs and external entities involved. A system component matrix provides a matrix framework to document the resources used, the activities performed, and the information products produced by an information system.

The User Interface

Designing the interface between end users and computer systems is a major consideration in developing new systems. Layout forms and video screens generated by a variety of software development packages are used to construct the formats and generic content of input-output media and methods. Dialogue flow diagrams analyze the flow of dialogue between computers and people. They document the flows among different display screens generated by alternative end user responses to menus and prompts.

Data Attributes and Relationships

As mentioned in Chapter 5, the data resources in information systems are defined, catalogued, and designed by this category of tools. A data dictionary catalogs the definitions (descriptions) of the attributes (characteristics) of all data elements and their relationships to each other, as well as to external systems. Entity-relationship diagrams are used to document the number and type of relationships among the entities in a system. File layout forms document the type, size, and names of the data elements in a system. Grid charts help identify the use of each type of data element in the input, output, or storage media of a system.

Detailed System Processes

This final group of tools is used to help programmers develop the detailed procedures and processes required in the design of computer programs. Decision trees and decision tables use a network or tabular form to document the complex conditional logic involved in choosing among the information processing alternatives in a system. Structure charts document the purpose, structure, and hierarchical relationships of the modules in a program. Pseudocode expresses the processing logic of a program module in a series of short phrases. Program flowcharts are used to illustrate the detailed sequence of processing steps required in a computer program.

* * * * *

A Case Study Example: ABC Auto Parts

ABC Auto Parts is a chain of auto parts stores in southern California, with headquarters in Los Angeles. The firm has grown to 14 stores in just 10 years, and it offers a wide variety of automotive parts and accessories. Sales and profits have increased each year, but the rate of sales growth has failed to meet forecasts in the last three years. Early results for 1992 indicate that the rate of sales growth is continuing to drop, even with the addition of two new stores in 1991. Adding the new stores was the solution decided on by corporate management last year to reverse the trend in sales performance.

Now, the company is faced with finding another solution to its problem. In recent meetings of corporate and store managers, the issue of computer use has been raised. ABC Auto Parts uses computers for various information processing jobs, such as sales transactions processing, analysis of sales performance, employee payroll processing, and accounting applications. However, sales transactions by customers are still written up by salespeople. Also, corporate and store managers depend on daily sales analysis reports that contain information that is always several days old.

The Retail Automation Issue

Most store managers, along with the vice presidents of marketing and information systems, argue that retail automation is a key to reversing ABC's sales trends. They believe in using point-of-sale (POS) terminals in each store would drastically shorten the time needed by a salesperson to write up a sale. This would not only improve customer service, it would free salespeople to sell to more customers. The managers consider these the "selling floor" benefits of retail automation.

Another major point raised is that retail automation would allow immediate capture and processing of sales transaction data. Up-to-date sales performance information could then be made available to managers at management workstations, which would be personal computers connected into the company's data communications network. This would provide the capability for information on sales performance to be tailored to each manager's information needs. Currently, managers have to depend on daily sales analysis reports that use the same report format. Too much of a manager's time is being used to generate sales performance information not provided by the system. Managers complain they don't have enough time to plan and support sales efforts unless they make decisions without enough information.

The president of ABC Auto Parts has resisted previous proposals to automate the selling process. He knows automation would involve a large initial investment and resistance to the technology by some salespeople and managers. He fears the loss of salesperson/customer interactions. He also fears that managers will become too dependent on computers if they have them in their offices. However, the continued disappointing sales performance has softened his position. Also, the president realizes that POS systems have become commonplace in all types of retail stores. ABC's major competitors have installed such systems, and their growth continues to outpace his own firm's. The company is failing to achieve its goal of increasing its share of the automotive parts market.

Planning and Investigation

Long-range planning sessions with the managers and a management consulting group identified a strategic role for information systems in the company. A long-range strategic plan was developed that stressed the need to use information systems technology to reduce the company's cost of doing business and to enhance the products and services the firm offers. Retail automation is identified as one possible thrust of this role for information systems. Other possibilities include advanced systems in marketing, distribution, and a number of other areas. The plan also stresses that the top priorities of new information systems must be (1) support of personal selling, (2) tailoring of information to managers' needs, and (3) integration of information systems resources and services.

A group of store managers and systems analysts from the information services department were commissioned to conduct a feasibility study of the retail automation options facing the firm. However, the president insisted that they include the option of keeping the present system. This alternative would involve adding more salespeople to improve personal selling and customer service. Staff assistants would also be hired for each store manager. Their duties would include information analysis, thus freeing managers for more hands-on management.

The systems analysts made personal observations of the sales processing system in action, and interviewed managers, salespeople, and other employees. The following description of the present sales processing system is a summary of information gathered by the systems analysts. The information is presented in sequential order, to make it easier to follow the events that occur in a sales transaction.

The Present System

The present sales processing system at ABC Auto Parts includes the following activities:

1. When a customer wants to buy an auto part, a salesclerk writes up a sales order form. Recorded on this form is customer data, such as name, address, and account number, and product data, such as name, product number, and price. A copy of the sales order form is given to the customer as a receipt.
2. Sales order forms are sent at the end of each day to the information services department. The next day they are recorded on magnetic tape using key-to-tape data entry devices.
3. The file of sales transactions is now ready for computer processing. One of the important information processing jobs that needs to be done is the updating of the sales files and the preparation of sales analysis reports. One of the first jobs the store's mainframe computer does is sort the sales transactions by product number.
4. The sorted sales transactions are used by a sales processing program to update a sales master file to reflect the new sales. A new sales master file is created on magnetic tape.
5. Sales processing also produces a sales analysis file. This file contains historical data on previous sales, as well as new sales data. The computer uses this file and a sales analysis program to perform sales analysis. Sales analysis reports are produced that tell management the trends in sales performance of various products.

The Proposed System

Based on a preliminary analysis of user requirements, the systems analysts proposed a new sales processing system. This new system features a telecommunications network of point-of-sale (POS) terminals and management workstations. A brief description of part of this proposed system follows.

1. When a customer wishes to buy an auto part, the salesclerk enters customer and product data using an online POS terminal. The POS terminal has a keyboard for data entry and a video screen for display of input data, as well as data entry menus, prompts, and messages. POS terminals are connected in a telecommunications network to the store's mainframe computer, which uses a comprehensive sales transaction processing program.
2. The POS terminal prints out a sales receipt for the customer that contains customer and product data and serves as a record of the transaction.
3. Errors in data entry may cause an error indication to be displayed by the POS terminal. The salesclerk must follow various error procedures to correct such errors.

4. The POS terminal transmits sales transaction data to the store's mainframe computer. This immediately updates the sales records in the company's database, which is stored on magnetic disk units.
5. The computer performs sales analyses using the updated sales records in the company database. Afterward, sales performance information is available to corporate and store managers in a variety of report formats at their management workstations.
6. Database management software also supports ad hoc database inquiries by managers, who can receive instantaneous responses about sales performance in displays at their management workstations.

* * * * *

System Flowcharts

A **system flowchart** is a graphic diagraming tool that documents and communicates the flow of data media and the information processing procedures taking place in an information system. This is accomplished by using a variety of labeled symbols connected by arrows to show the sequence of information processing activities. System flowcharts typically emphasize the media and hardware used and the processes that take place within an information system. They thus represent a graphic model of the *physical* information system that exists or is proposed. Figure 10.32 illustrates some common system flowchart symbols.

System flowcharts are widely used to communicate the overall structure and flows of a system to end users because they can offer a *physical view* that emphasizes the hardware and data media involved. However, in many cases, they have been

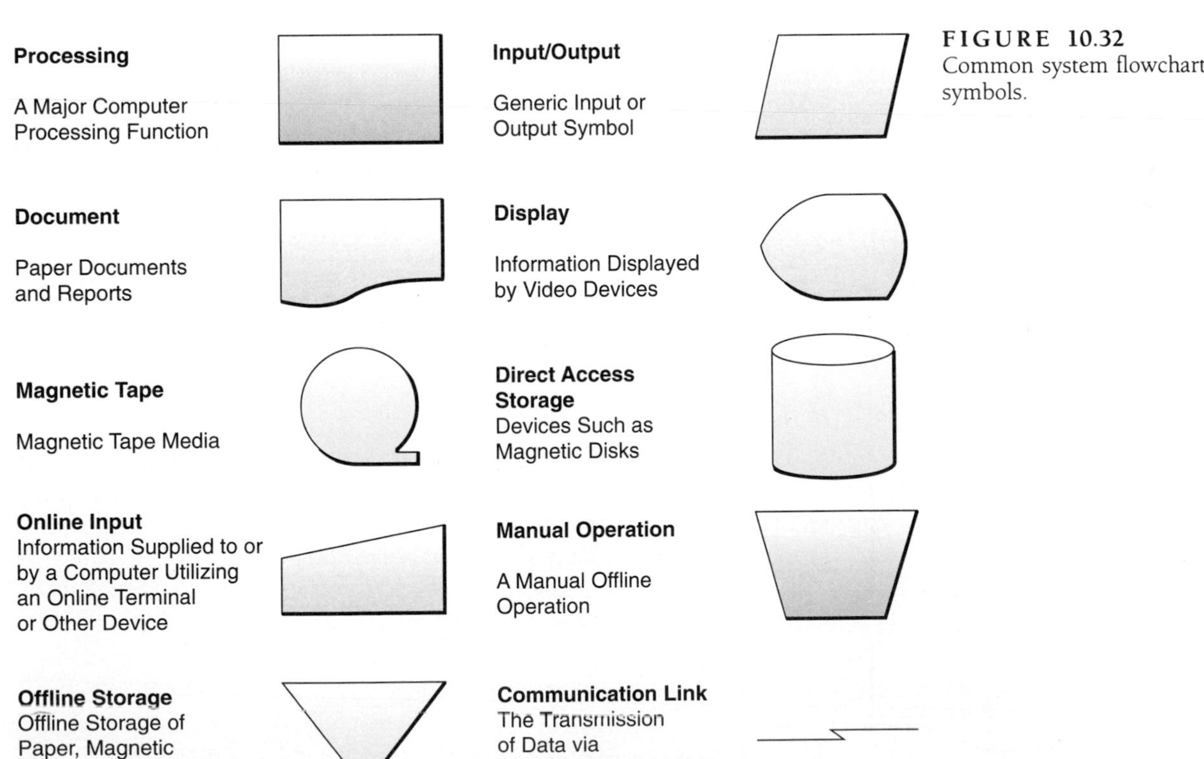

FIGURE 10.32
Common system flowchart symbols.

FIGURE 10.33
Flowcharts of a present and proposed sales transaction processing system.

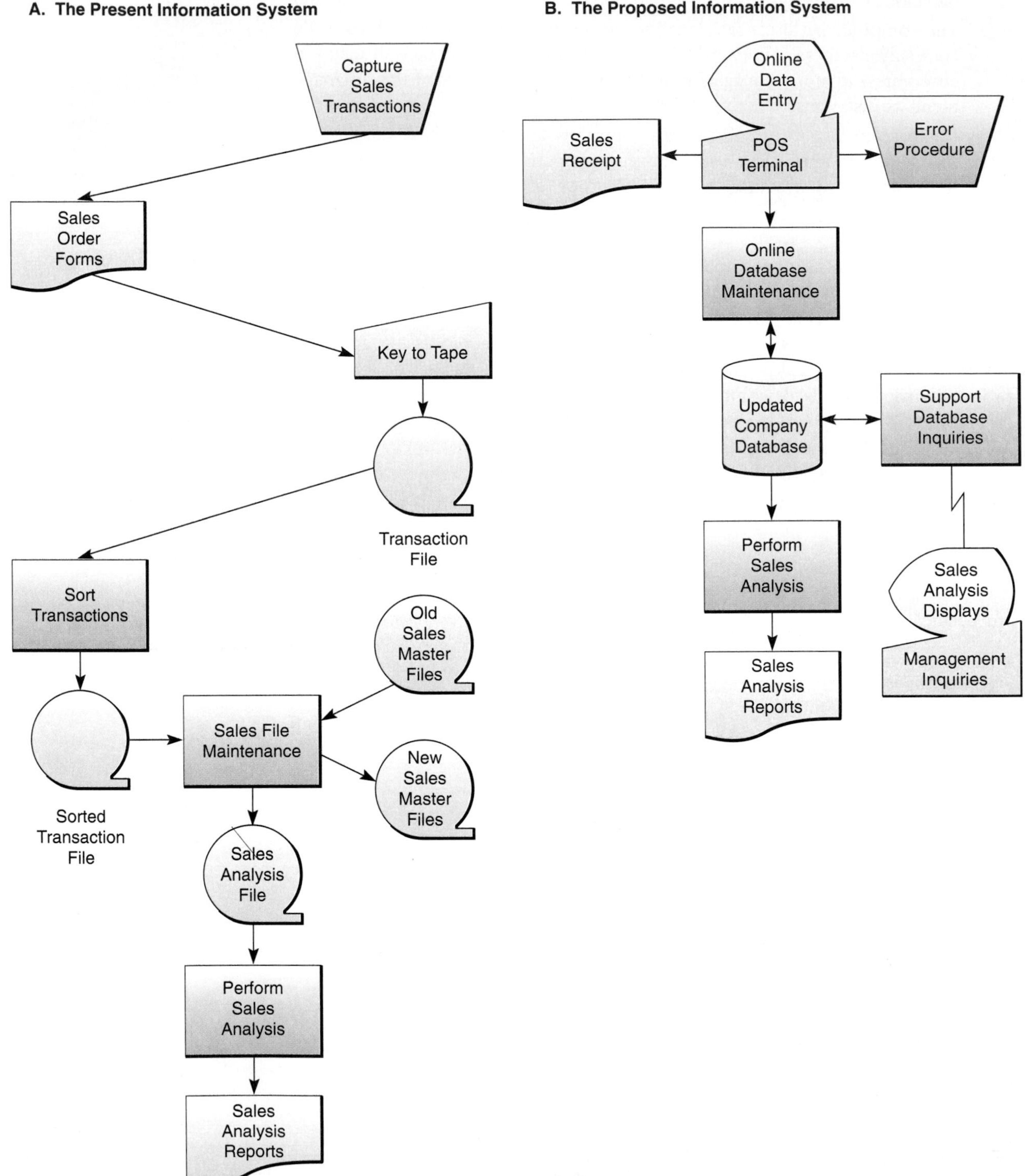

displaced by data flow diagrams for use by professional systems analysts, and by presentation graphs for communicating with end users.

Figure 10.33(A) shows how a system flowchart is used as a tool for the analysis of the present sales processing system at ABC Auto Parts. It graphically portrays the flow of data media and the major information processing tasks taking place. Note how the flowchart symbols indicate the physical equipment and media used for input, output, and storage. For example, symbols and labels indicate the use of many paper documents and reports, a key-to-tape data entry device, and magnetic tape storage.

Figure 10.33(B) is also a system flowchart, but it is being used to illustrate the design of the proposed sales processing system for ABC Auto Parts. This is a new system that might replace the system illustrated in Figure 10.33(A). Note how it shows an online data entry terminal, magnetic disk storage, and several printed reports. This is obviously a physical design, because the hardware devices and media that will be used in the new system are specified.

Data Flow Diagrams

A **data flow diagram** (DFD) can help you identify the flow of data in a system without specifying the media or hardware involved. Data flow diagrams use a few simple symbols connected by arrows to represent such flows. Data flow diagrams can easily illustrate the *logical* relationships among data, flows, external entities (sources and destinations), and stores. Figure 10.34 illustrates the four basic symbols used in data flow diagrams and summarizes some helpful information for their use.

External Entities

Example: Customers

- Organizations, departments, persons, other systems
- Originate input or receive output
- May be duplicated

Processes

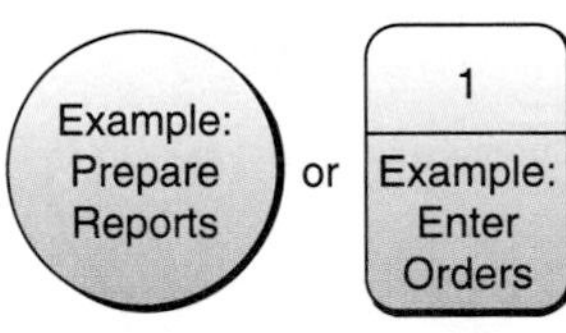

- Transform inputs into outputs
- Represent manual or automated activities
- Must have at least one input and one output data flow
- May be numbered

Data Stores

Example: Customer File

- Store data between processes
- Must be connected only to processes (by data flows)
- Must have at least one input and one output data flow
- May be duplicated

Data Flows

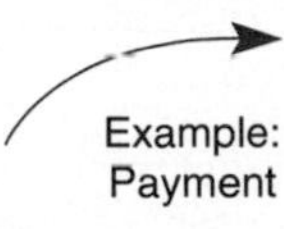

- Represent transfers of data among entities, processes, and stores
- Arrows represent direction of flows
- Must begin or end at a process
- Must be labeled to describe data being transferred

FIGURE 10.34
Data flow diagram symbols. Note how they should be used when developing data flow diagrams.

This graphic tool is widely used for several reasons. It is simple to draw (mostly circles connected by arrows) and easily depicts the basic components and flows of a system. DFDs can also be drawn in increasing levels of detail, starting with a summary high-level view and proceeding to more detailed lower-level views. This supports a *modular, structured, top-down* view of system components and flows. For example, Figure 10.35 illustrates the highest level of data flow diagram, called a *context diagram* or level-0 DFD.

Figures 10.36 and 10.37 show the next level of detail in data flow diagrams used as a tool for both analysis and design. (These are level-1 DFDs.) Note that data flow diagrams can portray the *logical flow* of data in both the present and proposed sales processing system of ABC Auto Parts. That's because they do not specify the media and equipment involved. These DFDs illustrate only the logical relationships among the data flows, external entity sources and destinations, processes, and data stores in present and proposed sales processing systems similar to the ones portrayed by previous system flowcharts.

However, data flow diagrams can also be used to represent a physical view of a system. These *physical data flow diagrams* reveal the actual form of the data media used, the people and hardware involved in processing, and the devices in which data is stored. This is done simply by additional labeling of the symbols for the data flows, processing, and data stores in a logical data flow diagram. For example, adding labels such as "sales invoice" to a data flow arrow, "data entry by clerks using POS terminals" to a processing symbol, or "customer file on magnetic disk" to a data store symbol would begin to change a data flow diagram from a logical to a physical view.

Figure 10.38 illustrates another level of system detail that data flow diagrams can represent. Figure 10.38 is a portion of a *level-2* DFD for the sales processing system illustrated in the level-1 DFD in Figure 10.36. Notice how process symbol 1.0 (Capture Sales Transactions) in Figure 10.36 is *exploded* or *decomposed* in Figure 10.38 into three distinct processes: 1.0 (Capture Sales Orders), 2.0 (Convert Source Documents), and 3.0 (Sort Transactions), as well as three different data stores and the many data flows between them. Thus, the DFD in Figure 10.38 gives us more details on how data about sales transactions are captured and made ready for sales processing in the sales processing system.

FIGURE 10.35
A context diagram of a sales processing system. This level-0 DFD is the highest-level view of this system.

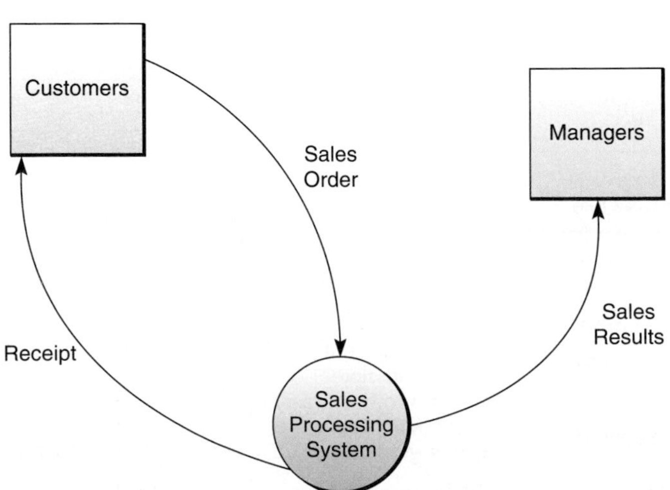

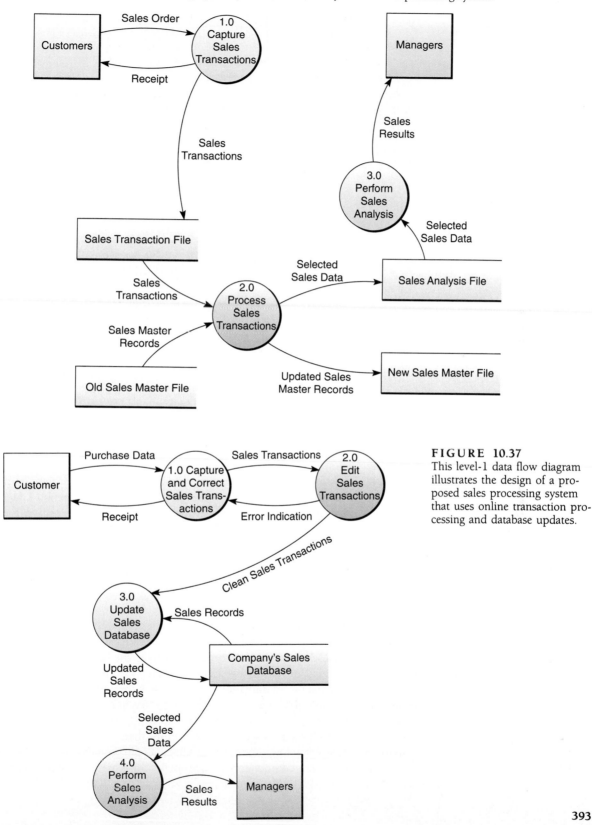

FIGURE 10.36
Using data flow diagrams. This level-1 DFD graphically illustrates the analysis of a sales processing system.

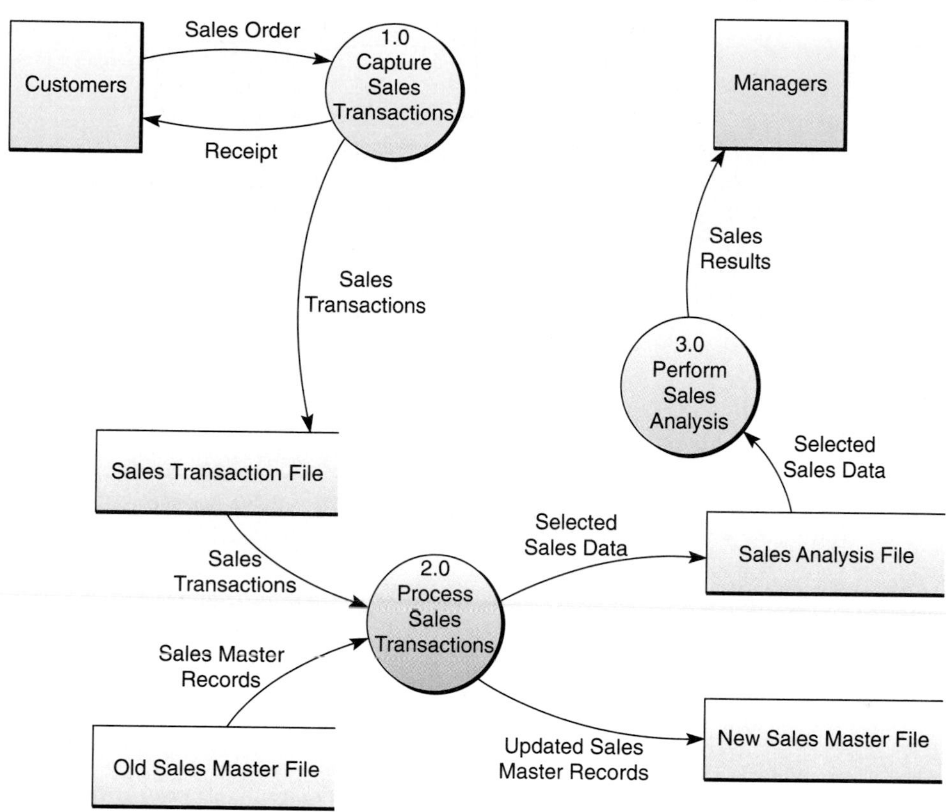

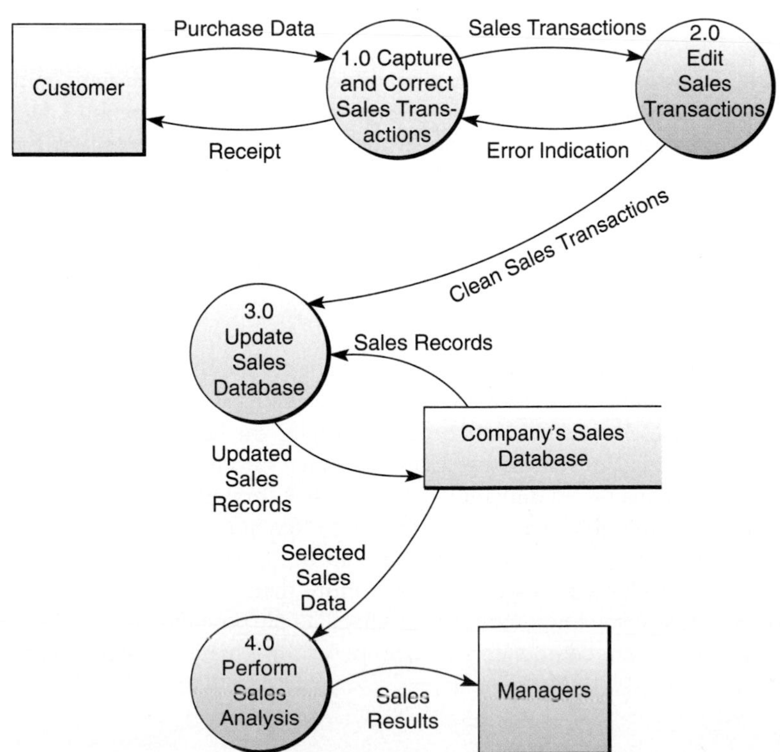

FIGURE 10.37
This level-1 data flow diagram illustrates the design of a proposed sales processing system that uses online transaction processing and database updates.

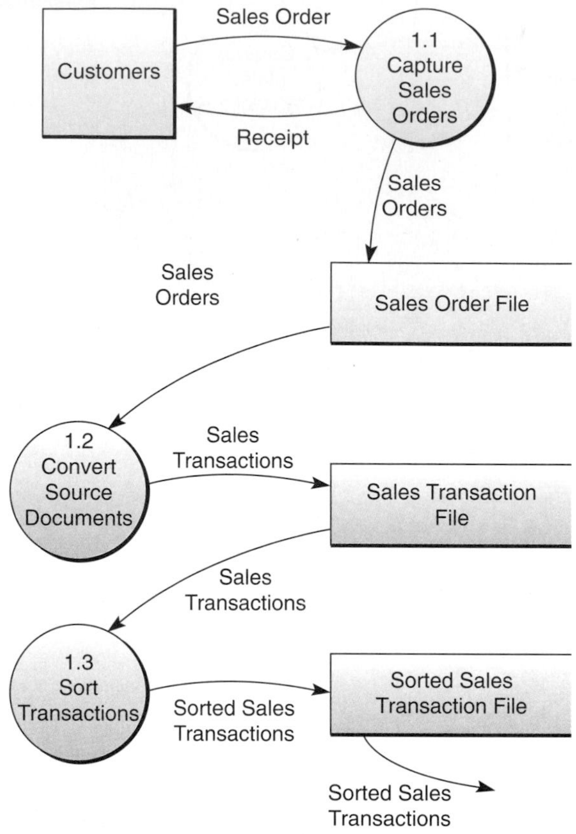

FIGURE 10.38
A level-2 data flow diagram of the Capture Sales Transactions process (1.0) of Figure 10.36.

System Component Matrix

The **system component matrix** is based on the conceptual framework of the model of information system components introduced in Chapter 1. As shown in Figure 10.39, a system component matrix can be used as an information system framework for both systems analysis and systems design. It views an information system as a matrix of components that highlights how the basic information systems activities of input, processing, output, storage, and control are accomplished, and how the use of people, hardware, and software resources can convert data resources into information products. It poses the following fundamental question that should be answered in the information systems development process: What information system resources are needed to accomplish the information processing activities that can produce the information products required by end users?

Figure 10.40 illustrates the use of a system component matrix to document the basic components of a proposed sales processing system similar to the one described for ABC Auto Parts. Note how it spotlights the basic information processing activities needed, resources used, and products produced by this information system. This tool may seem difficult to use because information for each cell may not be available or applicable. Thus, blank cells are often appropriate and unavoidable. However, duplicate cell entries can be made in the matrix, because many systems resources and products are used to support more than one information processing activity. Still, a system component matrix serves its purpose by emphasizing the use of information system components in a proposed information system solution.

FIGURE 10.39
A system component matrix used as an information system framework for systems analysis and design. It highlights the resources needed to accomplish activities that produce information products needed by end users.

Information System Activities	Hardware Resources		Software Resources		People Resources		Data Resources	Information Products
	Machines	Media	Programs	Procedures	Specialists	Users		
Input								
Processing								
Output								
Storage								
Control								

Using CASE Tools

How can end users (and systems analysts) take advantage of computer-aided tools for systems analysis and design? In Section I, we discussed how computer-aided software engineering packages, and even end user application packages can be used in a prototyping process of systems development. For example, end users, alone or working with systems analysts, can use the screen and report generators in database management packages to develop user interface prototypes such as data entry screens or management reports. CASE tools also help automate the use of graphics tools such as flowcharts and data flow diagrams, as well as the creation of data dictionaries. See Figure 10.41.

Figure 10.42 emphasizes that CASE packages provide many computer-based tools for both the *front end* of the systems development life cycle (planning analysis and design) and the *back end* of systems development (implementation and maintenance). Note than a *system repository* and systems developers such as programmers and systems analysts help integrate the use of tools at both ends of the development cycle. Integrated CASE (I-CASE) tools are now available that can assist all of the stages of systems development. Some of these CASE tools support *joint application design* (JAD), where a group of systems analysts, programmers, and end users can jointly and interactively design new applications. Finally, if the development of new systems can be called *forward engineering*, some CASE tools support *backward engineering*. That is, they allow systems analysts to inspect the logic of a program code for old applications, and convert it automatically into more efficient programs that significantly improve system effectiveness.

System Repositories

Many CASE tools now include a **system repository** component that expands the role of the *data dictionary* as a catalog of data definitions. Instead, a repository provides systems analysts with computer-aided data descriptions and other cataloging facilities, beginning with their systems planning and systems analysis activities. They can continue to build and use the repository in the data design, process design, and user interface design activities of systems design. Finally, they can use the repository to ensure proper implementation and maintenance of a system.

FIGURE 10.40
An example of a system component matrix for a sales processing system. Note how it emphasizes the basic activities needed, resources used, and products produced by this information system.

Information System Activities	Hardware Resources		Software Resources		People Resources		Data Resources	Information Products
	Machines	**Media**	**Programs**	**Procedures**	**Specialists**	**Users**		
Input	POS terminals	Bar tags mag stripe credit cards	Data entry program	Data entry procedures		Salesclerks Customers	Customer data Product data	Data entry displays
Processing	Mainframe computer		Sales processing program Sales analysis program	Sales transaction procedures	Computer operators	Salesclerks Managers	Customer inventory, and sales databases	Processing status displays
Output	POS terminals Management workstations	Paper reports and receipts	Report generator program Graphics programs	Output use and distribution procedures		Salesclerks Managers Customers		Sales analysis reports and displays Sales receipts
Storage	Magnetic disk drives	Magnetic disk packs	Database management program		Computer operators		Customer, inventory, and sales databases	
Control	POS terminals Management workstations	Paper documents and control reports	Performance monitor program Security monitor program	Correction procedures	Computer operators Control clerks	Salesclerks Managers Customers	Customer, inventory, and sales databases	Data entry displays Sales receipts Error displays and signals

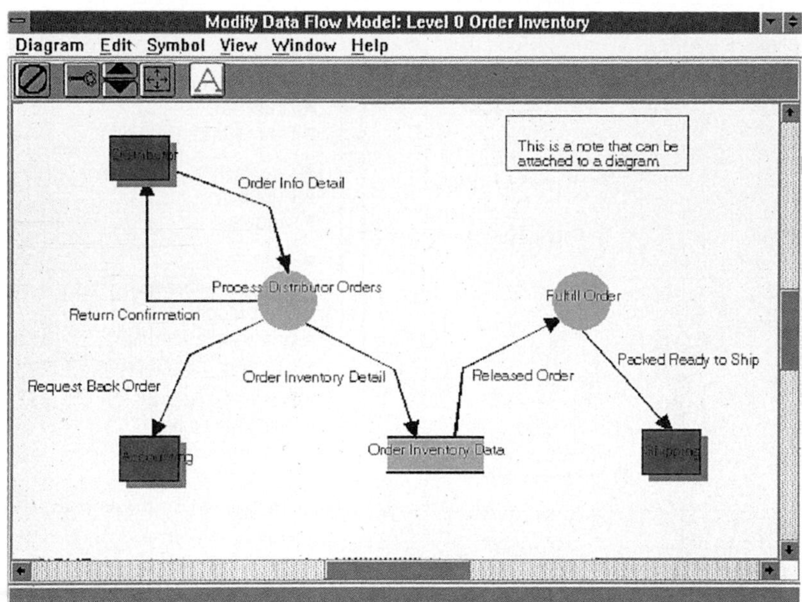

Courtesy of Intersolv Inc.

FIGURE 10.41
A data flow diagram drawn by the Excellerator CASE package.

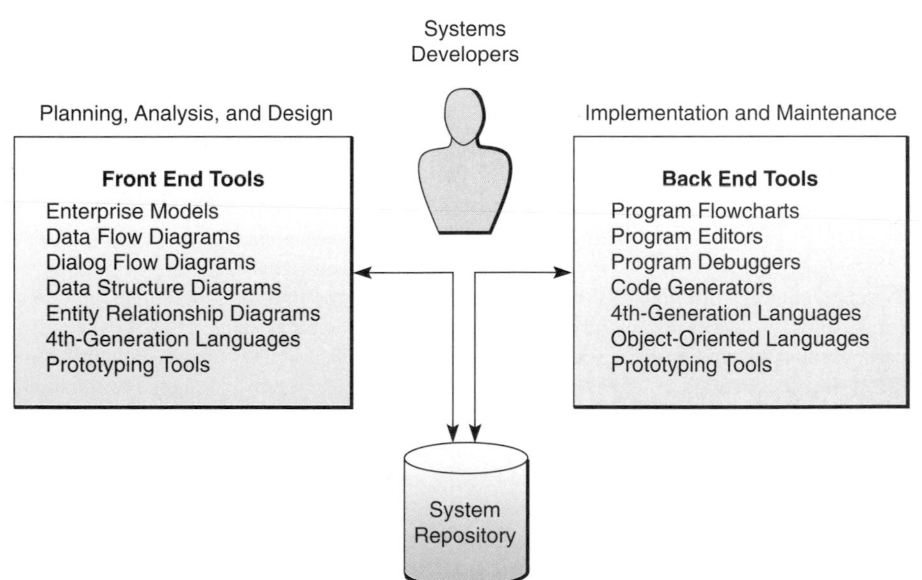

FIGURE 10.42
The role of CASE tools. Note their use in the stages of the systems development life cycle, and the integrative role of systems developers and system repositories.

Thus, the system repository has become a database for all of the details of a system generated with other systems development tools. More important, the repository itself has become a vital tool of systems development. That is, it supports and integrates the use of other tools, to ensure consistency and compatibility in the design of the data elements, processes, user interface, and other aspects of the system being developed. Figure 10.43 illustrates the contents of a system repository. Notice how it documents many forms of information about the computer-based information systems of an organization.

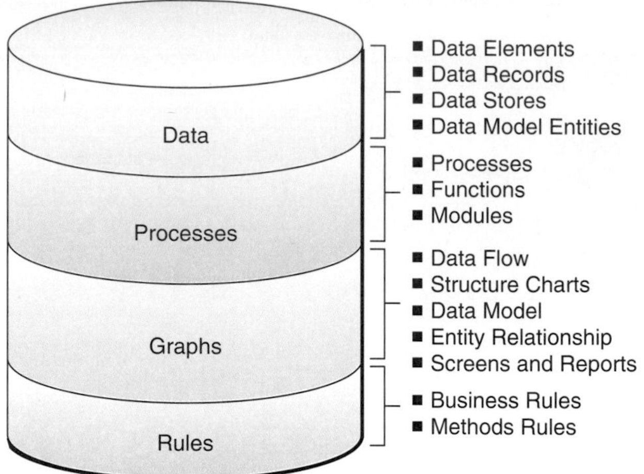

FIGURE 10.43
The contents of a system repository. Note how it contains a variety of descriptions of the components of an organization's information systems.

Source: Adapted from Carma McClure, "Modeling the Enterprise," *The Consultant Forum*, Special edition, 1991, p. 17.

Summary

- **The Systems Development Cycle.** End users and systems analysts should use a systems approach to help them develop information system solutions to business problems. This typically involves an information systems development cycle where IS specialists and end users conceive, design, and implement computer-based information systems. The stages, activities, and products of the information systems development cycle are summarized in Figure 10.2.
- **CASE and Prototyping.** Major changes occurring in the traditional information systems development cycle include computer-aided systems engineering software packages, which computerize and automate parts of the systems development process, and prototyping tools and methodologies, which promote an iterative, interactive process that develops prototypes of user interfaces and other information system components.
- **IS Planning.** Information systems planning includes strategic, tactical, and operational planning activities. Strategic IS planning involves activities that evaluate how information technology can contribute to strategic organizational goals such as reengineering business processes or gaining competitive advantages. It results in a strategic information systems plan that outlines a mission, goals, architecture, applications portfolio, and management philosophy for the IS function. Tactical information systems planning evaluates current and projected information needs of the organization; defines, prioritizes, and schedules information systems development projects; and develops allocation plans for hardware, software, personnel, telecommunications, facilities, and financial resources. Operational IS planning develops operational plans such as annual operating budgets and individual system development project plans.
- **Implementation.** The implementation process for information systems consists of activities that carry out the operational plans developed during the information systems planning process. As summarized in Figure 10.44, it involves acquisition, testing, documentation, training, installation, and conversion activities that transform a newly designed information system into an operational system for end users.
- **Evaluating Hardware, Software, and Services.** Managerial end users should know how to evaluate the acquisition of information system resources. Manufacturers and suppliers can be required to present bids and proposals based on system specifications developed during the design stage of systems development. A formal evaluation process reduces the possibility of incorrect or unnecessary purchases of computer hardware or software. Several major evaluation factors, summarized in Figures 10.22, 10.23, and 10.24, can be used to evaluate hardware, software, and IS services.

Acquisition
Evaluate and acquire necessary hardware and software resources and information system services. Screen vendor proposals.
Software Development
Develop any computer programs that will not be acquired externally as software packages. Make any necessary modifications to software packages that are acquired.
Training
Educate and train management, end users, and operating personnel. Use consultants or training programs to develop user competencies.
Testing
Test and make necessary corrections to the programs, procedures, and hardware used by a new system.
Documentation
Record and communicate detailed system specifications, including procedures for end users and IS personnel and examples of input/output displays and reports.
Conversion
Convert from the use of a present system to the operation of a new or improved system. This may involve operating both new and old systems in *parallel* for a trial period, operation of a *pilot* system on a trial basis at one location, *phasing in* the new system one location at a time, or an immediate *cutover* to the new system.

FIGURE 10.44
A summary of IS implementation activities.

Key Terms and Concepts

These are the key terms and concepts of this chapter. The page number of their first explanation is given in parentheses.

1. Computer-aided systems engineering (364)
2. Conversion alternatives (380)
3. Computer industry (371)
4. Cost/benefit analysis (359)
5. Documentation (379)
6. Economic feasibility (360)
7. Evaluation factors (377)
   a. Hardware
   b. Software
   c. IS services
8. External IS services (373)
9. Feasibility study (358)
10. Functional requirements (362)
11. Information systems planning (356)
    a. Strategic (356)
    b. Tactical (357)
    c. Operational (358)
12. Intangible (359)
    a. Benefits
    b. Costs
13. Operational feasibility (360)
14. Organizational analysis (361)
15. Organizational feasibility (360)
16. Planning for competitive advantage (357)
17. Postimplementation review (382)
18. Project management (358)
19. Prototype (365)
20. Prototyping (365)
21. Systems analysis (361)
22. Systems approach (354)
23. Systems design (362)
24. Systems development life cycle (354)
25. Systems implementation (371)
26. Systems investigation (356)
27. Systems maintenance (380)
28. System specifications (363)
29. System testing (378)
30. Tangible (359)
    a. Benefits
    b. Costs
31. Technical feasibility (360)
32. Technology implementation (382)
33. User interface, data, and process design (362)

Review Quiz

Match one of the key terms and concepts listed above with one of the brief examples or definitions listed below. Try to find the best fit for answers that seem to fit more than one term or concept. Defend your choices.

____ 1. Using an organized sequence of activities to study a problem or opportunity in a systems context.

____ 2. Evaluating the success of a solution after it has been implemented.

____ 3. Your evaluation shows that benefits outweigh costs for a proposed system.

____ 4. The costs of acquiring computer hardware, software, and specialists.

____ 5. Loss of customer goodwill caused by errors in a new system.

____ 6. Increases in profits caused by a new system.

____ 7. Improved employee morale caused by efficiency and effectiveness of a new system.

____ 8. Multistep process to conceive, design, and implement an information system.

____ 9. The first stage of the systems development cycle.

____ 10. Determines the organizational, economic, technical, and operational feasibility of a proposed information system.

____ 11. Cost savings and additional profits will exceed the investment required.

____ 12. Reliable hardware and software is available to implement a proposed system.

____ 13. Customers will not have trouble using a proposed system.

____ 14. The proposed system supports the strategic plan of the business.

____ 15. Studying in detail the information needs of users and any information systems presently used.

____ 16. A detailed description of user information needs and the input, processing, output, storage, and control capabilities required to meet those needs.

____ 17. The process that results in specifications for the hardware, software, people, and data resources and information products needed by a proposed system.

____ 18. Systems design should focus on developing end user input/output methods, data structures, and programs and procedures.

____ 19. A detailed description of the hardware, software, people, and data resources and information products required by a proposed system.

____ 20. Acquiring hardware and software, testing and documenting a proposed system, and training people to use it.

____ 21. Using software packages to computerize many of the activities in the systems development process.

____ 22. A working model of an information system.

____ 23. An interactive and iterative process of systems development.

____ 24. Outlines a mission, goals, architecture, and applications portfolio for the information systems function.

____ 25. Defines, prioritizes, and schedules information systems development projects for the organization.

____ 26. Develops operating budgets for the information systems function.

____ 27. Management of the development work for new information systems.

____ 28. IS planning should focus on developing strategies for using information technology to gain competitive advantages.

____ 29. Contracting with outside firms for computer processing, education, maintenance, and so on.

____ 30. Performance, cost, reliability, technology, and ergonomics are examples.

____ 31. Performance, cost, efficiency, language, and documentation are examples.

____ 32. Maintenance, conversion, training, and business position are examples.

____ 33. User resistance to the introduction of IT can be overcome by their involvement and training.

____ 34. Operate in parallel with the old system, use a test site, switch in stages, or cut over immediately to a new system.

____ 35. Checking whether hardware and software work properly for end users.

____ 36. A user manual communicates the design and operating procedures of a system.

____ 37. New business ventures or legislation will probably require changes to some of our information systems.

____ 38. The source of hardware, software, and IS services for end users.

Discussion Questions

1. Could you use the systems approach to problem solving as a way to solve a marketing problem? A financial problem? A human resource management problem? Explain.
2. Refer to the Real World Case of Florida Power Corporation. How do CASE tools affect prototyping?
3. Why have computer-aided systems development and prototyping methods become so popular? What are their limitations?
4. Refer to the Real World Case of Quaker Oats Comany. What are the advantages and disadvantages of "choosing the best hardware and software whether or not it was compatible with the old system"?
5. What applications software packages can be used by end users to do applications development? Give several examples.
6. Pick a task you would like to computerize. How could you use the steps of the information systems development cycle in Figure 10.2 and the checklist for systems analysis and design in Figure 10.16 to help you?
7. What kinds of companies produce hardware and software and provide IS services?
8. What are the three most important factors you would use in evaluating computer hardware? Explain why.
9. What are the three most important factors you would use in evaluating computer software? Explain why.
10. Assume that in your first week on a new job you are asked to use a type of software package that you have never used before. What kind of user training should your company provide to you before you start?

Real World Problems

1. Wausau Insurance Company: Determining Functional Requirements

The need for change of some sort was clear. Wausau Insurance Company's Group Retirement Division had been running its mainframe-based pension administration program for 15 years, and the program had grown so outdated that the market for managing corporate pension funds was passing the company by. Among other shortcomings, the mainframe system could manage only three funds in any one pension portfolio, and it could change funds only once a quarter at the most. "We couldn't compete," IS VP Dick Lund said. So Wausau decided to move an outdated, in-house-developed IBM 3090-based pension management system to a Unix client/server computing system. Moving the Unix meant asking Division VP Tom Erickson and his pension department to rely on an unproved technology for mission-critical operations. "Nobody likes to be the guinea pig, and we found ourselves in that role," Erickson said.

"I had formed a misconception that CASE tools that make programming faster also make overall development faster," Erickson said. "It doesn't. You still have to figure out what you're going to do. There are a lot of issues that have to be worked through before you go ahead and start programming." for instance, before programming the procedures for processing deposits into employee accounts, Wausau and its software development partner, Super Solutions Corp. in Minneapolis, first had to think through how they wanted to do it, what information the employees should see, and what sorts of editing features and controls the task should include. "It took us a good deal of time to determine what we wanted to do," Erickson said of the overall process. In the end, it was worth the agonizing, Erickson said. With the Unix system, pension portfolio administrators are able to perform their tasks 30 percent faster than on the old mainframe, he said.

a. What stages and activities of the systems development life cycle are mentioned in the case? Explain.

b. What types of functional requirements did Wausau investigate? What are some other they might have determined? Give several examples.

Source: Adapted from Mark Halper, "Move off Mainframe Requires More than New Equipment," *Computerworld*, March 29, 1993, p. 80. Used with permission.

2. Royal Bank of Canada: OS/2 and Application Development

The Royal Bank of Canada is currently moving into a second generation of LAN usage by implementing the OS/2 2.0 operating system on LAN servers at its branches. The resulting benefits according to George Oliver, manager of IT delivery, include:

- The addition of electronic mail gateways on the branch servers.
- Higher levels of remote system management, diagnostics, and software distribution by headquarters staff.
- Increased performance from existing hardware.
- Faster application development and customization of end user applications.

OS/2, Oliver notes, will also "take the handcuffs" off the bank's software developers, who have been working with a patchwork of purchased and home-grown DOS development tools.

"Another area where we like OS/2 2.0," says Oliver, "is in remote system management. If we have 2,000 LANs, we don't want 2,000 individuals in the branches having to become programmers. OS/2 2.0 allows us to do more from our end." But perhaps the biggest benefit of OS/2 for the bank is the freedom it provides programmers. Now they work less on developing system software and tools and more on developing applications. For example, LAN-based PCs are now used for executing branch office applications that are generally developed by headquarters IS staff and deployed in "workbenches" tailored for individuals. The applications include personal productivity, local processing, and access to large corporate databases and transactions system.

a. Why do you think OS/2 is changing application development at Royal Bank?

b. What business and systems development benefits can result from using operating systems like OS/2?

Source: Adapted from "The Royal Bank of Canada: 32 Bits at the Branches," *Computerworld*, Special Advertising Supplement, February 15, 1993, pp. 23-25. Used with permission.

3. Duke Power Company: Implementing a New System

Duke Power Company, based in Charlotte, North Carolina wanted to make realtime, online monitoring available to select groups of employees. The company, which operates a variety of nuclear, hydroelectric, and fuel-fired power plants in the Carolinas, also wanted to monitor online data at remote sites using only a portable PC with a modem. In order to realize its goals, Duke put together an open architecture-based system that runs DOS, OS/2, Unix, or VMS operating systems. It also employs multiple relational database products including OS/2-DBM, ORACLE, and DB2. The system was christened Total Operating Plant Process System (TOPPS).

Duke put together a multidisciplinary team that was involved in the project from the beginning to end. Team members came from different plants and included end users (operators), design engineers, maintenance staff, IS personnel, training staff, and technical support people. Duke insisted that its vendors—IBM, Intellution, and Computer Products Inc. (CPI)—work together to provide the solution it desired. The vendor contacts were also considered part of the company's development team. Duke chose Intellution's process control software product, the Fix, and also its networking software. One of the attractions of Intellution's product was that the software was already running on OS/2 and VMS. Adding OS/2 to VMS gave the team another option and made the overall system more open. A decision was made to first implement the system at one plant, where it could be fully implemented and tested before being extended to other plants. The project took less than a year to devise, build, and test.

a. What implementation activities do you recognize in this case? Explain.

b. What development strategies and selection criteria did Duke use to develop TOPPS?

Source: Adapted from "Duke Power Uses Team Approach to Achieve an Open System," *Computerworld*, Special Advertising Supplement, February 15, 1993, p. 16.

4. U.S. Army: Implementing a Large System

Any IS professional who has labored to set up a local-area network will sympathize with the task U.S. Army Maj. Gen. Gary A. Stemley faces: He has 9,000 of them to install during a five-year period under what some say is the largest client/server implementation ever attempted. And anyone who has ever met an alligator in the swamp of large systems development will appreciate another challenge facing Stemley: writing 2 million lines of Ada program code in order to replace a hodgepodge of automated and manual processes. Even by the unique yardstick of government programs, the Reserve Component Automation System (RCAS) is a whopper, from its $1.8 billion price tag to winning bidder (the Boeing Co.), to its 60,000 users at 5,000 locations and its 35,000 pages of requirements documentation. Nevertheless, after years of political wrangling, false starts, and protests, RCAS is off to a good start, observers agreed. Although many of the toughest challenges lie ahead, observers said the year-old project is a model of technological farsightedness. Stemley said success stems in part from the careful homework that preceded the contract award. Although requirements were very carefully detailed in the request for proposals, solutions were left up to the bidders.

RCAS is in test use now at 21 sites in California, Virginia, and Georgia. An additional 900 LANs will be installed during the next 10 months, with the balance to be put in at the rate of 1,000 to 2,000 per year, stemley said. Late this summer, RCAS will start to roll out the first of the Boeing-written, custom-developed Ada applications to support personnel management, equipment, tracking and maintenance, supply, payroll, training, and mobilization. As each LAN is installed, Unix-based Zenith servers are loaded with Informix relational database management systems and electronic-mail, work processing, and spreadsheet packages from Uniplex. At small installations, the Zenith servers run those software packages plus the custom Ada applications. At larger facilities, the Ada applications will reside on a minicomputer Digital Equipment 5500 server. All users will access the servers via diskless terminals, and connections to other locations will be made via the Federal Telecommunications system 2000 national network.

a. What types of implementation activities do you recognize in this case? Explain.

b. Why could solutions be "left up to the bidders" on such a large project?

Source: Adapted from Gary Anthes, "Army Enlists Client/Server," *Computerworld*, March 29, 1993, p. 12.

Application Exercises

1. **Village Inn Restaurants**

Develop a data entry screen that could take the place of the paper order form used at Village Inn restaurants to capture customer food orders. Assume the food servers would use a hand-held computer with a four-inch display screen. Also assume the information would be displayed on a 15-inch screen that could easily be read by the restaurant's cooks. Use your own experience and observations or interview a food server and cook. Prepare a mock-up of the proposed screen.

a. Use a paper layout form to plan your design.

b. Use the report-generation capabilities of a database management or other software package to generate a data entry screen prototype.

c. Write up a brief explanation of the advantages of your design.

2. **Laurentian Industries, Inc.**

Develop a display screen mock-up for a sales manager at Laurentian Industries who wants to analyze sales performance. Use a paper layout form or a database management package to develop a screen prototype. Figure 10.45 is an example of a sales analysis display. How would you improve it if you were one of their sales managers?

a. Change the display by adding or deleting some of the information shown.

b. Improve the layout or format of the screen.

c. Design two or more sales analysis screens to give you sales performance information. Link them together by using an opening menu and prompts.

d. Write up a brief explanation of the advantages of your design.

3. **Systems Maintenance at ABC Products**

Modifying systems in response to user requests is a major aspect of systems maintenance for the Information Systems Department at ABC Products Company. Users can request changes to information systems by filling out a change request form. The change request form is a manual form. A copy of the form is sent to the group charged with maintenance responsibilities for the affected system.

Many users have complained of long response times to their change requests and lack of follow-up to ensure that the changes made are acceptable. To expedite the processing of change requests, ABC Products has decided to assign a user, you, authority and responsibility for coordinating the processing of change requests.

To better track the processing of change requests, you

LAURENTIAN INDUSTRIES, INC.
COMPARATIVE SALES ANALYSIS BY CUSTOMER
FOR EACH SALESPERSON
PERIOD ENDING 07/31/--

SLP. NO.	CUST. NO.	SALESPERSON/CUSTOMER NAME	THIS PERIOD THIS YEAR	THIS PERIOD LAST YEAR
10		A R WESTON		
	1426	HYDRO CYCLES INC	3,210.26	4,312.06
	2632	RUPP AQUA CYCLES	7,800.02	2,301.98
	3217	SEA PORT WEST CO	90.00CR	421.06
		SALESPERSON TOTALS	10,920.28	7,035.10
12		H T BRAVEMAN		
	0301	BOLLINGER ASSOCIATES	100.96	0.00

FIGURE 10.45
An example of a sales analysis display.

have decided to maintain a database file providing summary information about each change request. You will record the name of the user requesting the change, the date of the request, the name of the information system that is to be modified, the member of the maintenance team assigned to the request, and data about the status of work on the request. A request will be listed as IP (for in-process) when you assign it to a maintenance team. Once the changes have been completed, you are to be notified. At that point the status is changed to PA (for pending-approval). You then will notify the user who submitted the work request that he or she is to evaluate the changes. When the evaluation is completed, the changes are either accepted (status AC) or rejected (status RE). If changes are rejected, the user submits a new change request from describing further modifications that are required. Sample data for this file are shown in Figure 10.46.

a. Create a database file to store this information and enter the sample records shown.

b. Create and print a report categorized by maintenance team number and summarize the status of all change requests.

c. Perform and get printed listings of the following retrievals:

(1) Retrieve all information for requests whose status is IP.

(2) Retrieve the request number, request date, and status of all requests addressed to the Acct. Rec. system.

(3) Retrieve a count of the number of change requests whose status is AP.

4. Assessing Vendor Service Performance at Morris Manufacturing

Morris Manufacturing Company purchases microcomputer hardware from a number of vendors. In order to do a better job of tracking the service performance of those suppliers, Morris Manufacturing surveys its employees annually to determine how satisfied they are with the service provided by these suppliers. Each employee who has microcomputer equipment is asked to rate the supplier of that equipment with respect to: (1) the *speed* with which they have responded to service requests and (2) the *quality* of the servicing provided. This information is to be stored in a database file. Sample ratings for a recent year are shown below.

a. Create a database file to store this information and enter the sample data shown.

b. Create a report that will show the average rating given to each supplier in each category. Get a printed listing of this report.

c. Perform the following data retrievals and produce printed listings of their results:

(1) Retrieve a list of the names of all employees who provided ratings for the supplier CompStar.

(2) Retrieve a count of the number of Quality ratings assigned a value of less than 6.

Sample of Microcomputer Hardware Supplier Ratings

Employee Name	Supplier Name	Speed Rating	Quality Rating
Jones, B.	CompStar	8	9
Bates, N.	Pcs Are We	7	3
Adams, A.	CompStar	8	7
Morris, M.	PC Power	9	10
Lewis, J.	PCs Are We	8	5
Jarvis, M.	CompStar	7	9
Dandes, K.	PC Power	9	9
Thomas, R.	PC Power	8	10
Ward, M.	PCs Are We	8	5
Evans, J.	CompStar	6	8
Eads, M.	PC Power	9	9

5. Chevy Chase Bank

Chevy Chase Bank developed a Mortgagevision loan application service that is set in motion once field-based loan officers transmit loan information to the bank's mainframe using their laptop computers. Then Mortgagevision notifies the bank's mortgage underwriter, who integrates mainframe-based data using a LAN micro workstation running the OS/2 operating system. This is done via IBM's Easel graphics package, which provides a graphical interface up front while dealing with the mainframe in the background. The user just points and shoots to select necessary data. Once the mortgage underwriter gets the credit and application data, it is sent off in realtime to the mortgage insurer via telecommunications links to their mainframe computer. Once the

FIGURE 10.46
Sample Change Request Records for ABC Products

Requesting User	Request ID. No.	Request Date	System Affected	Maint. Team Assigned	Completion Status
Davis, L.	7843	10/07/93	Payroll	PO3	AP
Evans, G.	7844	10/09/93	Acct. Rec.	PO2	RE
Morris, M.	7845	10/09/93	Inventory	PO1	PA
Allen, J.	7846	10/12/93	Payroll	PO3	IP
Jones, P.	7857	10/28/93	Order Proc.	PO2	AP
Lewis, R.	7872	11/07/93	Inventory	PO1	AP
Evans, G.	7879	11/18/93	Acct. Rec.	PO2	IP
Norton, M.	7886	11/22/93	Inventory	PO1	IP
Powers, R.	7889	11/24/93	Payroll	PO3	IP

mortgage insurer has responded, Easel goes back into the mainframe to grab additional applicant credit information and then sends all collected and processed data over to a mortgage expert system, which resides on a PS/2 microcomputer.

"We spend about a year training it," says IS Director Bob Spicer. "We took the problem of underwriting a loan and broke it into a number of problem sets and then trained the expert system to experience what we said were good and bad loans. Then we taught it how to render a final decision," Spicer explained. If the expert system encounters a decision it has not seen before, it logs it so that bank officers can study it to determine the proper reaction. The final decision is then relayed back to the field. Mortgagevision also utilizes a voice processing system from Syntellect Corp. Rather than chase loan officers with sometimes fruitless phone calls, users awaiting a loan decision can call into the host, punch in their applications numbers, and hear a computerized voice recite their current loan status.

a. What business problems and opportunities are being handled by the use of computer-based information systems at the Chevy Chase bank?

b. Use one or more tools of analysis and design (system flowchart, data flow diagram, system component matrix) to analyze the mortgage loan processing system at Chevy Chase Bank.

Source: Adapted from Patricia Keefe, "Taking OS/2 Benefits to the Bank," *Computerworld*, April 23, 1990, p. 37.

6. University of California at Los Angeles

UCLA uses a touch-tone telephone system for student registration. Each student is assigned two telephone registration appointments, with graduating seniors getting the first appointments. Each appointment is a 12-hour window during which a student can register for up to 10 credit hours. If a call is placed during the wrong window, the INFOBOT voice messaging computer checks the appointment schedule database, announces the correct appointment time, and hangs up. When students call at the appropriate time, they enter their student ID numbers and proceed to register. They can use the touch-tone phone to request courses, search for courses still open, register, and lock up their course schedules, from anywhere in the world. This has eliminated student registration lines, saved on mailing and clerical costs, and reduced transportation, traffic, and parking problems, since students do not have to come to campus to register.

a. Develop a context diagram (level-0 data flow diagram) for students enrolling in bachelor's degree programs at UCLA.

b. Draw a level-1 data flow diagram of the registration process at UCLA.

c. Draw a systems flowchart or develop a system component matrix of the registration system at UCLA.

Source: Adapted from Leila Davis, "Phone Mail Gets Stamp of Approval," *Datamation*, April 1, 1989, p. 78.

Review Quiz Answers

1. *22*
2. *17*
3. *4*
4. *30b*
5. *12b*
6. *30a*
7. *12a*
8. *24*
9. *26*
10. *9*
11. *6*
12. *31*
13. *13*
14. *15*
15. *21*
16. *10*
17. *23*
18. *33*
19. *28*
20. *25*
21. *1*
22. *19*
23. *20*
24. *11a*
25. *11b*
26. *11c*
27. *18*
28. *16*
29. *8*
30. *7a*
31. *7b*
32. *7c*
33. *32*
34. *2*
35. *29*
36. *5*
37. *27*
38. *3*

Selected References

1. Andersen Consulting. *Foundations of Business Systems*. 2nd ed. Chicago: Dryden Press, 1992.
2. Banker, Rajiv, and Robert Kauffman. "Reuse and Productivity in Integrated Computer-aided Software Engineering: An Empirical Study." MIS Quarterly, September 1991.
3. Burch, John. *Systems Analysis, Design, and Implementation*. Boston: Boyd & Fraser, 1992.
4. Cerveny, Robert; Edward Garrity; and Lawrence Sanders. "A Problem Solving Perspective on Systems Development." *Journal of Management Information Systems*, Spring 1990.
5. Chen, Minder; Jay Nunamaker; and E. Sue Weber. "Computer-aided Software Engineering: Present Status and Future Directions." *Data Base*, Spring 1989.
6. Cooprider, Jay, and John Henderson. "Technology-Process Fit:

Perspectives on Achieving Prototyping Effectiveness." *Journal of Management Information Systems*, Winter 1990/91.

7. Forte, Gene, and Ronald Norman. "CASE: A Self Assessment By the Software Engineering Community." *Communications of the ACM*, April 1992.
8. Hershey, Gerald, and Donna Kizzier. *Planning and Implementing End User Information Systems*. Dallas, Tex.: South Western Publishing, 1992.
9. Keen, Peter. *Shaping the Future: Business Design Through Information Technology*. Boston: Harvard Business School, 1991.
10. Lederer, Albert and Vijay Sethi. "Critical Dimensions of Information Systems Planning" *Decision Sciences Journal*, Winter 1991.
11. McClure, Carma. *CASE IS Software Automation*. Englewood Cliffs, N.J.: Prentice-Hall, 1989.
12. O'Brien, James, and Craig Van Lengen. "Using an Information System Status Model for Systems Analysis and Design: A Missing Dimension." *Journal of Information Systems Education*, December 1988.
13. Rochester, Jack, Ed. "Re-engineering Existing Systems." *I/S Analyzer*, October 1991.
14. Whitten, Jeffrey, Lonnie Bentley, and Vic Barlow. *Systems Analysis and Design Methods*. 3rd ed. Homewood, Ill.: Richard D. Irwin, 1993.

Managing Information Technology

CHAPTER OUTLINE

SECTION I Information Resource Management

Managers and Information Technology

Information Systems Performance

Management Involvement

Organizations and Information Technology

Centralization versus Decentralization

Changing Trends

Information Resource Management

Strategic Management

The Chief Information Officer

Functional Management

Managing Systems Development

Managing IS Operations

Resource Management

Data Administration

Technology Management

Telecommunications Management

Advanced Technology Management

Distributed Management

Managing End User Computing

Real World Case: Cigna Corporation: Eric Scheffler on Reengineering

SECTION II Global Information Technology Management

The International Dimension

Cultural, Political, and Geoeconomic Challenges

Global Business and IT Strategies

Global Business and IT Applications

Global IT Platforms

Global Data Issues

Global Systems Development

You and Global IT Management

Real World Case: ABB Power Generation and Hypo Bank: Global IT Management

CHAPTER 11

LEARNING OBJECTIVES

The purpose of this chapter is to give you an understanding of the managerial challenges that information technology presents to managerial end users by analyzing (1) the managerial implications of information technology and (2) how IT can support global business operations.

Section I of this chapter discusses the impact of information technology on managers and organizations and the use of an information resource management approach in managing the performance of the information systems function.

Section II discusses how cultural, political, and geoeconomic considerations affect global business and IT strategies, applications, technology platforms, data issues, and systems development.

After reading and studying this chapter, you should be able to:

1. Identify the major ways information technology has affected managers.
2. Explain how problems of information system performance can be solved by management involvement in IS planning and control.
3. Explain how information technology is affecting the structure and activities of organizations.
4. Identify the five major dimensions of the information resource management concept and explain their impact on the management of the information systems function.
5. Identify several cultural, political, and geoeconomic challenges that confront managers in the management of global information technology.
6. Explain the effect on global IT strategy of the trend toward a transnational business strategy by international business organizations.
7. Identify several considerations that affect the choice of IT applications, IT platforms, data definitions, and systems development methods made by a global business.

SECTION I
Information Resource Management

Who should manage MIS? Managers or technicians? End users or IS specialists? Somebody has to. Inadequate management of information technology by business firms and other organizations has been documented for many years. Thus, there is a real need for end users to understand how to manage this vital organizational function. In this section, we will explore how IT has affected managers and organizations, and stress the concept of *information resource management* as a key framework for managing information technology by both end user managers and IS managers. So whether you plan to be an entrepeneur and run your own business, a manager in a corporation, or a managerial level professional, managing information system resources and technologies will be one of your major responsibilities.

Managers and Information Technology

When computers were first introduced into business, predictions were made that there would be significant changes in management and organizations. The information processing power and programmed decision-making capability of computer-based information systems were supposedly going to cause drastic reductions in employees, including middle management and supervisory personnel. Centralized computer systems would process all of the data for an organization, control all of its operations, and make most of its decisions [19].

This did not prove to be the case. Changes in organizational structure and types of personnel did occur, but they were not as dramatic as predicted. Naturally, highly automated systems do not require as many people as manual methods. Therefore, there have been significant reductions in the number of people required to perform manual tasks in many organizations. For example, computerized accounting systems have drastically reduced the need for clerical accounting personnel, and factory automation has greatly reduced the demand for many types of factory workers. However, these reductions were countered by dramatic increases in sales and service personnel, knowledge workers, and managers as businesses increased the depth and scope of their operations. It was also countered to some extent by the need for more technicians and professionals to develop and run the computer-based information systems of organizations [21].

Now, however, a variety of forces seem to be causing a significant change in the structure and distribution of managers in organizations in which information technology plays a major role. For example, Peter Drucker, the visionary management scholar and author, predicts that, before the end of the 1990s, the typical large business will have fewer than half the levels of management and no more than one third of the managers it had in the 1980s. He also predicts that information technology will allow the structure of information-based organizations to be more like those of hospitals, universities, and symphony orchestras. They will be *knowledge-based*, "composed largely of specialists who direct and discipline their own performance through organized feedback from colleagues, customers, and headquarters" [10].

MIS researchers Rockart and Short see what Drucker and others are predicting as an opportunity for information technology to help managers *manage interdependence* in the 1990s [30]. As Figure 11.1 illustrates, their research shows that competitive pressures are forcing major firms to become global in scope, to decrease time to market, and to manage business risk, customer service, and operating costs

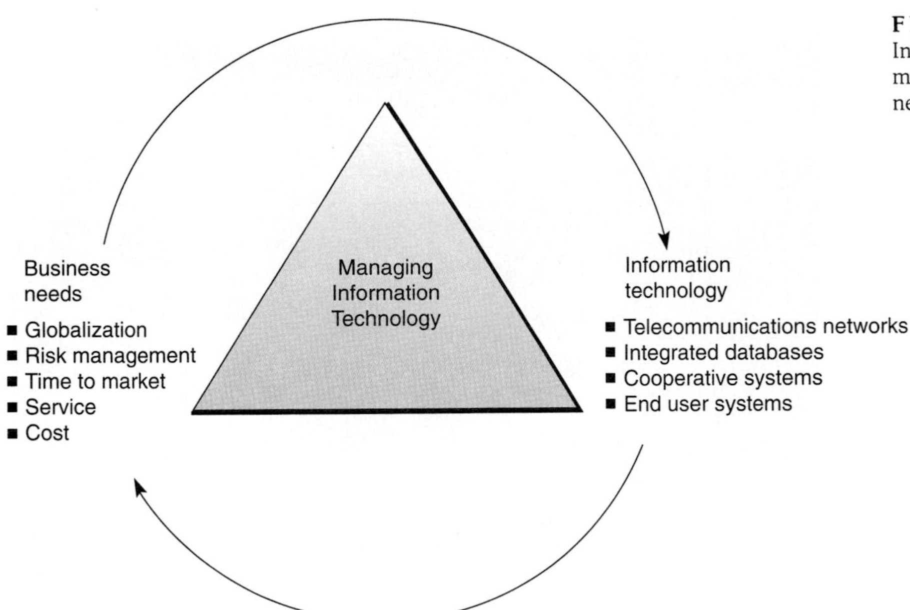

FIGURE 11.1
Information technology must be managed to meet business needs.

Source: Adapted from John Rockart and James Short, "IT in the 1990s: Managing Organizational Interdependence." *Sloan Management Review*, Winter 1989, p. 8.

like never before. They see information technology as an *enabling technology* for managing the interdependence that business units must have to successfully confront the competitive measures they face. For example, they see telecommunications networks and more cost-effective hardware and software as enabling individuals, business units, and organizations to be "wired together" in close business relationships that can provide the communication and coordination needed in today's competitive global marketplace.

Thus, **information technology**, that is, the technologies of modern computer-based information systems, is once again being portrayed as a major force for organizational and managerial change. Thanks to telecommunications networks and personal computers, computing power and information resources are now more readily available to more managers than ever before. In fact, these and other information technologies are already affecting managerial decision making, organizational structures, and work activities in companies around the world. See Figure 11.2.

For example, the decision support capability provided by information systems technology is changing the focus of managerial decision making. Managers freed from number crunching chores must now face tougher strategic policy questions in order to develop realistic alternatives for today's dynamic competitive environment. Telecommunications networks, electronic mail, and electronic meeting systems to coordinate work activity are other examples of the impact of information technology on management. Middle managers no longer need to serve as conduits for the transmission of operations feedback or control directives between operational managers and top management. Thus, drastic reductions in the layers and numbers of middle management, and the dramatic growth of work groups consisting of task-focused teams of specialists are forecast [10, 16, 21].

Finally, information technology presents managers with a major managerial challenge. Managing the information system resources of a business is no longer the

FIGURE 11.2
Information technology is having a major impact on the management, structure, and work activities of organizations.

Nubar Alexanian/Woodfin Camp & Associates.

sole province of information systems specialists. Instead, **information resource management** has become a major responsibility of all managers. That is, data and information, computer hardware and software, telecommunications networks, and IS personnel should be viewed as valuable resources that must be managed by all levels of management to ensure the effective use of information technology for the operational and strategic benefit of a business.

Information Systems Performance

> Despite all the current talk about the strategic use of information systems, a large number of top business executives feel that IS spending is out of control—and that their IS executives still fail to see technology in business terms [4].

The information systems function has performance problems in many organizations. The promised benefits of information technology have not occurred in many documented cases. Studies by management consulting firms, computer user groups, and university researchers have shown that many businesses have not been successful in managing their computer resources and information services departments. Figure 11.3 outlines the gap between the key goals of IS managers and their admitted poor performance, as identified in a survey by an international IS consulting group. Thus, it is evident that, in many organizations, information technology is not being used effectively, efficiently, or economically [4, 11, 16]. For example:

- Information technology is not being used *effectively* by companies that use IT primarily to computerize traditional business processes instead of using it for decision support and innovative processes and products to gain competitive advantages.
- Information technology is not being used *efficiently* by information services groups that provide poor response times, frequent downtimes, incompatible systems, unintegrated data, and applications development backlogs.
- Information technology is not being used *economically* in many cases. Information technology costs have risen faster than other costs in many businesses, even though the cost of processing each unit of data is decreasing due to

	Goals	Performance
Business/Strategy Issues		
Getting function managers involved in using IT to reshape business process	88%	30%
Integrating IT into corporate strategy	82%	31%
Developing a corporate wide strategy	79%	28%
Human Resource Issues		
Training and educating the work force in the use of IT	87%	34%
Managing and mastering change	81%	38%
Training and educating IS staff about the business	76%	36%
Defining the role and structure of IS in the organization	69%	36%
Technology Issues		
Developing a quick response capability to handle changing business conditions	76%	24%
Improving application development productivity	73%	23%
Defining an architecture that will enable integration of all information systems	69%	33%
Integrating systems across diverse organizational structures inside the company	57%	21%

Source: Adapted from Carroll Frenzel, *Management of Information Technology* (Boston: Boyd & Fraser, 1992), p. 26.

FIGURE 11.3
The performance gap in information technology. These goals and responses spotlight some of the problem areas in information systems performance.

dramatic price reductions and improvements in hardware and software technology.

What is the solution to problems of poor performance in the information systems function? There are no quick and easy answers. However, the experiences of successful organizations reveal that the basic ingredient of high-quality information systems performance is extensive and meaningful *involvement* of managers and end users in the planning, development, and operation of computer-based information systems [4, 25]. This should be the key ingredient in shaping the response of management to the challenge of improving the business value of information technology.

Management Involvement

Proper involvement of managers in the management of IT requires the active participation of managerial end users in the planning and control of the business uses of IT. Managers must manage the information system resources of their business units for operational efficiency, effectiveness, and competitive advantage. Then they will be able to improve the performance of their business units' information systems function in the key areas outlined in Figure 11.3. Without this high degree of involvement, managers will not be able to improve the business value of information technology. Figure 11.4 illustrates several major levels of management involvement.

- Many organizations use an executive information services committee of top management to do strategic information system planning and to coordinate the development of information systems projects. This committee includes senior management of the major divisions of the firm, as well as the chief information officer of the organization.
- A steering committee of business unit managers, operating managers, and management personnel from the information services department may be

FIGURE 11.4
Levels of management involvement. Successful information systems performance requires several levels of involvement by managers.

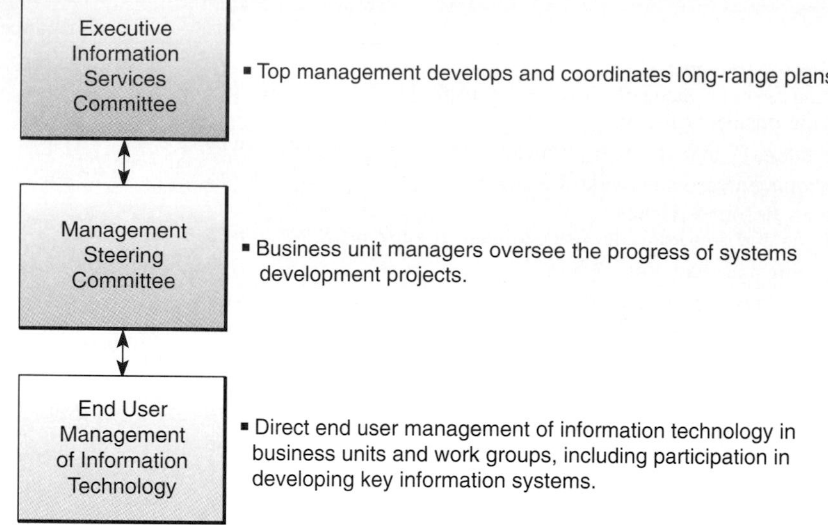
Executive Information Services Committee
▪ Top management develops and coordinates long-range plans.
Management Steering Committee
▪ Business unit managers oversee the progress of systems development projects.
End User Management of Information Technology
▪ Direct end user management of information technology in business units and work groups, including participation in developing key information systems.

created to oversee the progress of critical systems development projects. The committee meets on a regular basis to review progress made, to settle disputes, and, if necessary, to change priorities.

- Development of decision support and work group systems requires managerial involvement in the prototyping process for such projects. End user managers must also accept direct responsibility for managing the resources and quality of information services provided to their business units and work groups.

Organizations and Information Technology

One way to understand the organizational impact of information technology is to view an organization as a sociotechnical system. In this context, people, tasks, technology, culture, and structure are the basic components of an organization. Figure 11.5 illustrates this conceptual framework, which was first developed by Harold Leavitt [19]. This concept emphasizes that to improve an organization's performance, managers must (1) change one or more of these components and (2) take into account the relationships among these interdependent components. This is especially important for the proper use of information technology. In the past, people have used information systems technology to automate organizational tasks without giving sufficient consideration to its strategic impact on the organization. Thus, a major managerial challenge of information technology is to develop information systems that promote strategic improvements in how an organization supports its people, tasks, technology, culture, and structure.

People

Managers are individuals with a variety of preferences for information and diverse capabilities for effectively using information provided to them. As we pointed out in Chapter 9, information systems must produce information products tailored to meet managers' individual needs, as information reporting, decision support, and executive information systems can do.

Tasks

The tasks of many organizations have become quite complex and inefficient over time. In many cases, information technology has been used "to do the same old

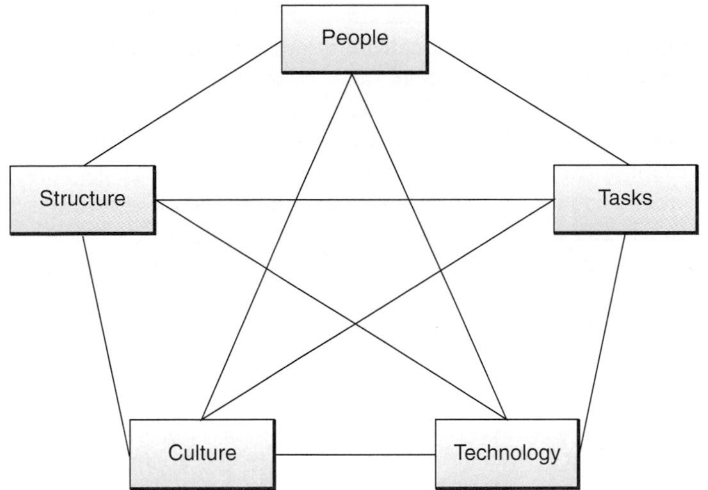

FIGURE 11.5
Organizations as sociotechnical systems. Information systems must accommodate the people, tasks, technology, culture, and structure components and relationships of an organization.

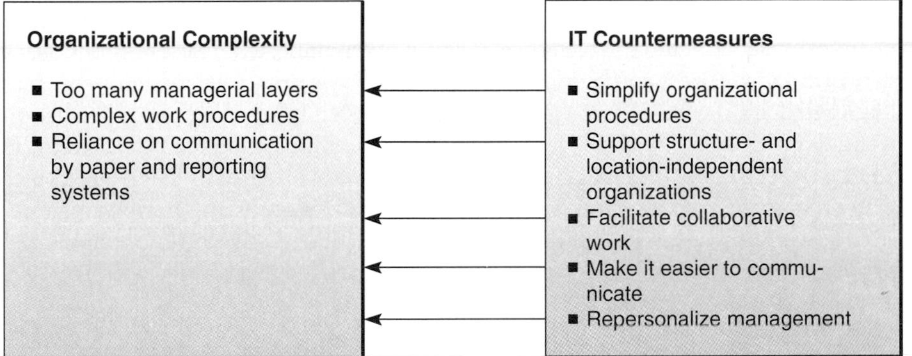

FIGURE 11.6
Information technology can counter organizational complexity and support the reengineering of business processes.

thing, only faster." However, it can play a major role in fighting organizational complexity by supporting the **reengineering of business processes**, also called *business process redesign* (BPR). For example, IT developments such as EDI and E-mail can dramatically reduce the need to prepare and mail paper documents and thus eliminate many manual tasks and required procedures, and significantly improve communication and coordination in an organization. Figure 11.6 shows some of the many ways IT can fight organizational complexity as emphasized by MIS researcher and consultant Peter Keen [15, 16].

Technology

The technology of computer-based information systems continues to grow more sophisticated and complex. However, this technology should not dictate the information needs of end users in the performance of their organizational tasks. It should accommodate the management culture and structure of each organization. For example, executive information systems have shown they can overcome many of the objections of top executives to the lack of individual and task flexibility of previous types of management information systems.

Culture

Organizations and their subunits have a culture which is shared by managers and other employees. That is, they have a unique set of organizational values and styles.

For example, managers at some organizations share an informal, collegial, entrepreneurial spirit that stresses initiative, collaboration, and risk taking. Managers at other organizations may stress a more formal "do it by the book," "go through the chain of command," or "don't risk the stockholders' money" approach. Naturally, the designs of information systems and information products must accommodate such differences. For example, managers in a corporate culture that encourages entrepreneurial risk taking and collaboration will probably favor information reporting systems that give them quick access to forecasts about competitors and customers, and E-mail and groupware systems that make it easy to communicate with colleagues anywhere.

Structure

Organizations structure their management, employees, and job tasks into a variety of organizational subunits. However, we have just mentioned how Drucker, Keen, Rockart, and others are emphasizing that information technology must support a process of *organizational redesign*. So the IS function must no longer assume a hierarchical, centralized, organizational structure which it supports by centralizing processing power, databases, and systems development at the corporate headquarters level. This type of structure emphasizes gathering data into centralized databases and producing reports to meet the information needs of functional executives.

Instead, IT must be able to support a more decentralized, collaborative type of organizational structure, which needs more interconnected telecommunications networks, downsized computers, databases, and systems development resources distributed to business unit and work group levels. For example, information technology must emphasize quick and easy communication and collaboration among the computer workstations of individuals and work groups using electronics instead of paper. Specific examples include E-mail, voice mail, groupware, electronic meeting systems, and so on. Figure 11.7 illustrates key features of the kind of organizational structure that many business firms are moving toward with the help of IT [5, 30].

Centralization versus Decentralization

Experience has shown that modern computer-based information systems can support either the centralization or decentralization of information systems, operations, and decision making within computer-using organizations. For example, centralized computer facilities connected to all parts of an organization by telecommunications networks allow top management to centralize decision making formerly done by lower levels of management. It can also promote centralization of operations, which reduces the number of branch offices, manufacturing plants, warehouses, and other work sites needed by the firm.

On the other hand, there is an increasing trend toward "downsized" and distributed networks of micro- and minicomputers at multiple work sites which allow top management to delegate more decision making to middle managers. Management can also decentralize operations by increasing the number of branch offices (or other company units) while still having access to the information and communications capabilities they need to control the overall direction of the organization.

Therefore, computer-based information systems can encourage either the centralization or decentralization of information systems, business operations, and management. The philosophy of top management, the culture of the organization, the need to reengineer its operations, and its use of aggressive or conservative competitive strategies all play major roles with information technology in shaping the firm's organizational structure and information systems architecture [2, 30].

FIGURE 11.7
The "tomorrow organization." Note the key features of the organizational structure that many firms are moving toward.

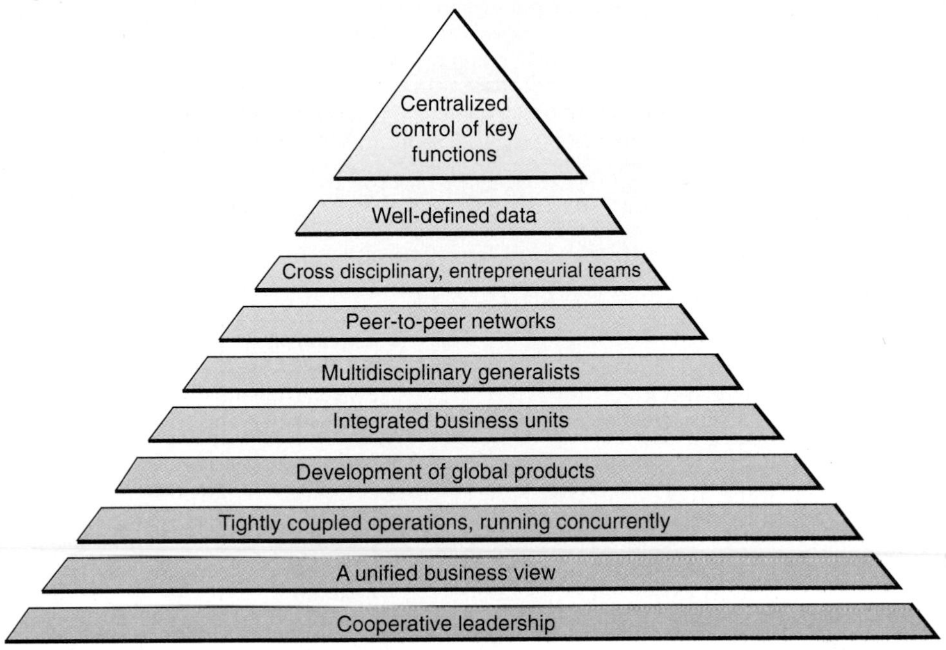

Source: Ralph Carlyle, "The Tomorrow Organization," *Datamation*, February 1, 1990, p. 25.

Changing Trends

Thus, companies continue to use a variety of organizational arrangements for the delivery of information services. In the early years of computing, when computers could barely handle a single department's work load, decentralization was the only option. Then the development of large mainframe computers and telecommunications networks and terminals caused a centralization of computer hardware and software, databases, and information specialists at the corporate level of organizations. Next, the development of minicomputers and microcomputers accelerated a **downsizing** trend which prompted a move back toward decentralization by many business firms. Distributed processing networks of micro- and minicomputers at the corporate, department, work group, and end user levels came into being. This promoted a shift of databases and information specialists to some departments, and the creation of information centers to support end user computing.

Lately, the trend has been to establish tighter control over the information resources of an organization, while still serving the strategic needs of its business units. This has resulted in a centralizing trend at some organizations and the development of hybrid structures with both centralized and decentralized components at others. Some companies have even spun off their information systems function into *IS subsidiaries* that offer information processing services to external organizations as well as to their parent company.

Other corporations have *outsourced*, that is, turned over all or part of their information systems operation to outside contractors known as *systems integrators* or facilities management companies. Such changes in the organizational alignment of the information systems function are expected to continue into the future. Organizations will continue to experiment with ways to control and encourage the use of

FIGURE 11.8
The role of the central IS function. Most of the IS executives surveyed agreed on the content and inevitability of a central IS function.

The central IS function will:

- Manage the computing and telecommunications utility.
- Manage and administer central databases accessible to all corners of the corporation.
- Operate high-volume applications.
- Set standards and policies.
- Perform IS strategic planning and opportunity finding.
- Coordinate computing efforts in business units or departments.
- Offer consulting services to departments.
- Conduct IT research and development.

Source: Adapted from Robert Morison, "The Shape of IS to Come," *Indications*, July/August 1990, p. 2

FIGURE 11.9
The information resource management (IRM) concept. Note that the job of managing information systems resources has five major dimensions.

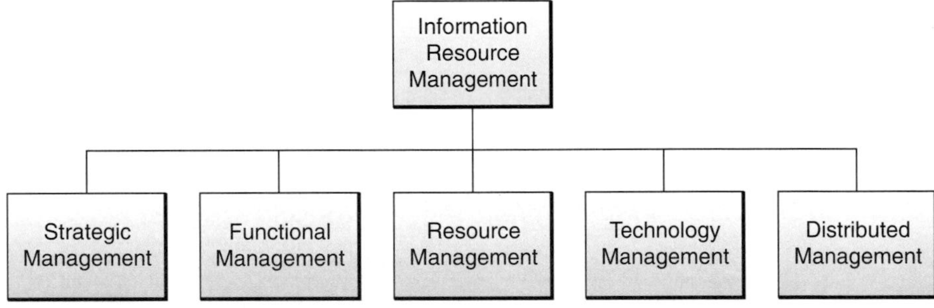

Source: Adapted from James A. O'Brien and James N. Morgan, "A Multidimensional Model of Information Resource Management," *Information Resources Management Journal*, Spring 1991, p. 4.

information system resources to promote end user productivity and the achievement of their strategic objectives. Figure 11.8 summarizes the responses of a recent survey of top IS executives in the United States, Canada, and Europe on the potential and extent of a central IS function [23].

Information Resource Management

Information resource management (IRM) has become a popular way to emphasize a major change in the management and mission of the information systems function in many organizations. IRM can be viewed as having five major dimensions. Figure 11.9 illustrates this conceptual framework [26].

- **Strategic management.** Information technology must be managed to contribute to a firm's strategic objectives and competitive advantages, not just for operational efficiency or decision support.
- **Resource management.** Data and information, hardware and software, telecommunications networks, and IS personnel are vital organizational resources that must be managed like other business assets.
- **Functional management.** Information technology and information systems can be managed by functional organizational structures and managerial techniques commonly used throughout other business units.
- **Technology management.** All technologies that process, store, and communicate data and information throughout the enterprise should be managed as integrated systems of organizational resources.
- **Distributed management.** Managing the use of information technology and information system resources in business units or work groups is a key responsibility of their managers, no matter what their function or level in the organization.

Strategic Management

The IRM concept emphasizes a strategic management view that we first discussed in Chapter 6 and have stressed throughout this text. That is, the IS function must manage information technology so that it makes major contributions to the profitability and strategic objectives of the firm. Thus, the information systems' function must change from an *information services utility* focused only on serving a firm's transaction processing or decision support needs. Instead, it must become a producer or packager of information products or an *enabler* of organizational structures and business processes that can give a firm a comparative advantage over its competitors. As we saw in Chapter 6, companies can develop strategic information systems to gain a competitive edge. Thus, information resource management focuses on developing and managing information systems that significantly improve operational efficiency, promote innovative products and services, and build strategic business alliances and information resources that can enhance the competitiveness of an organization.

The Chief Information Officer

Many companies have created a senior management position, the chief information officer (CIO), to oversee all use of information technology in their organizations. Thus, all traditional computer services, telecommunications services, office automation systems, and other IS technology support services are the responsibility of this executive. Also, the CIO does not direct day-to-day information service activities. Instead, CIOs concentrate on long-term planning and strategy. They also work with other top executives to develop strategic information systems that help make the firm more competitive in the marketplace. Several firms have filled the CIO position with executives from outside the IS field to emphasize the strategic business role of information technology.

Functional Management

The IRM concept stresses that managerial functions and techniques common to most businesses and organizational structures must be used to manage information technology. Managers must use managerial techniques (such as planning models, management by objectives, financial budgets, project management, and functional organization) just as they do with other major resources and activities of the business. The information systems' function is no longer treated as a special-case department that is too technically complex and dynamic to be managed effectively. Instead, it is treated like other functions and expected to use the managerial techniques employed by other business units to manage its resources and activities.

In many large organizations, the information systems function is organized into a departmental or divisional unit. We will use the name *information services department* for this group, though such names as information systems, computer services, data processing, EDP, MIS, and IRM department are also used. Information services departments perform several basic functions and activities. These can be grouped into three basic functional categories: (1) systems development, (2) operations, and (3) technical services. Figure 11.10 illustrates this grouping of information services functions and activities in a functional IS organizational structure.

Managing Systems Development

Managing the investigation, analysis, design, implementation, and maintenance of information systems within computer-using organizations is a big responsibility. As discussed in Chapter 10, managing systems development means managing activities such as systems analysis and design, prototyping, applications programming, project management, quality assurance, and system maintenance for all major systems development projects. Planning, organizing, and controlling the systems development function of an information services department is a major managerial responsibility. It requires managing the activities of systems analysts, programmers, and

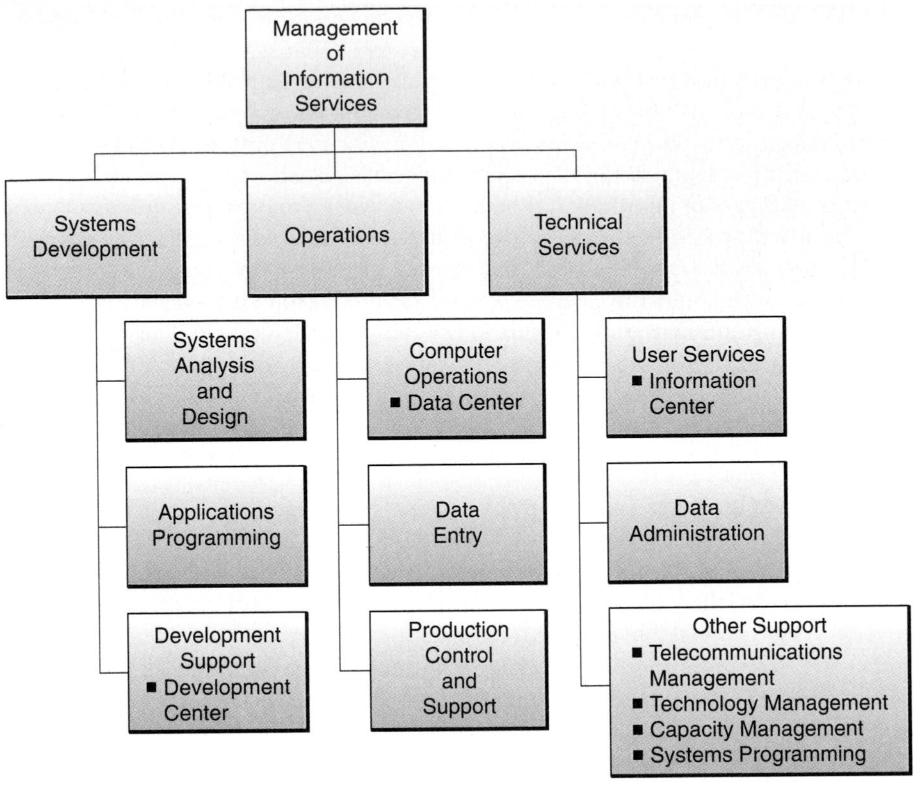

FIGURE 11.10
A functional organizational structure for an information services department. Note the activities that take place under each of the major functions of information services.

end users working on a variety of information systems development projects. Managing systems development thus requires a project management effort, which we discussed in the previous chapter. In addition, many systems development groups have established **development centers**, staffed with consultants to the professional programmers and systems analysts in their organizations. Their role is to evaluate new applications development tools and help information systems specialists use them to improve their application development efforts.

Managing IS Operations

IS operations management is concerned with the use of hardware, software, and personnel resources in the corporate or busines unit **data centers** (computer centers) of an organization. Operational activities that must be managed include data entry, equipment operations, production control, and production support. For example, data entry operators convert input source documents into machine-sensible form using a variety of data entry devices. This requires continual checking and monitoring of input data and output reports to ensure their accuracy, completeness, and timeliness. The activities of computer operators, who are responsible for the operation of large computer systems, also need supervision.

Many operations management activities are being automated by the use of software packages for computer system performance management. These **system performance monitors** monitor the processing of computer jobs, help develop a planned schedule of computer operations that can optimize computer system performance, and produce detailed statistics that are invaluable for effective planning and control of computing capacity. Such information is used to evaluate computer system utilization, costs, and performance. This evaluation provides information for capacity planning, production planning and control, and hardware/

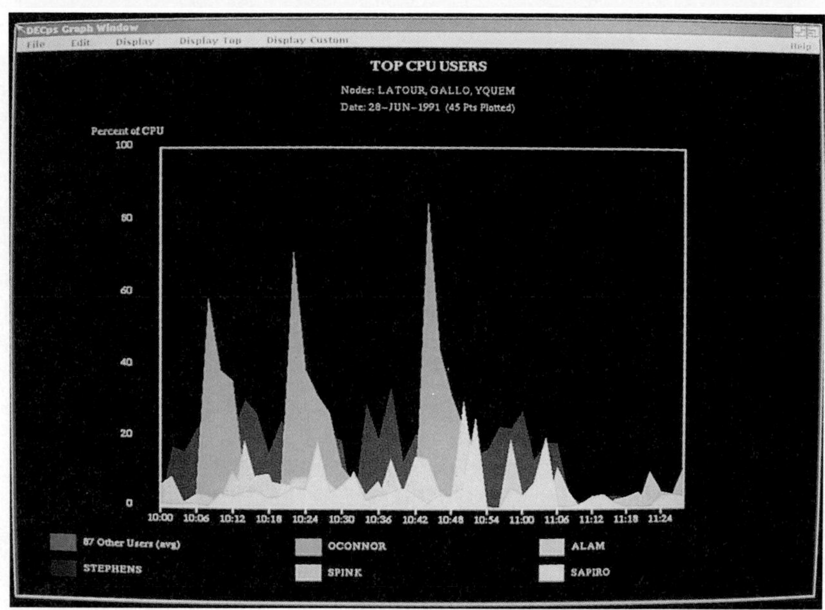

Courtesy of Digital Equipment Corporation.

FIGURE 11.11
A computer system performance monitor in action. Note how it tracks the use of mainframe CPU time by individual end users.

software acquisition planning. It is also used in *quality assurance* programs, which stress quality control of services to end users.

System performance monitors also supply information needed by **chargeback systems**, which allocate costs to users based on the information services rendered. All costs incurred are recorded, reported, allocated, and charged back to specific end user departments, depending on their use of system resources. Under this arrangement, the information services department becomes a service center whose costs are charged directly to computer users, rather than being lumped with other administrative service costs and treated as an overhead cost. See Figure 11.11.

Many performance monitors also feature process control capabilities. Such packages not only monitor, but automatically control computer operations at large data centers. Some use built-in expert system modules based on knowledge gleaned from experts in the operations of specific computer systems and operating systems. These performance monitors provide more efficient computer operations than human-operated systems. They also are leading toward the goal of "lights-out" data centers, where large mainframe systems can be operated unattended, especially after normal business hours.

Resource Management

From an information resource management point of view, data and information, hardware and software, telecommunications networks, and IS personnel are valuable resources that should be managed for the benefit of the entire organization. If plant and equipment, money, and people are considered vital organizational resources, so should its data, information, and other information system resources. This is especially true if the organization is committed to building a strategic information resource base to be used for strategic planning, and if it wants to develop innovative products and services that incorporate information systems technology and develop a top staff of IS professionals.

Data Administration

In Chapter 5, we discussed the need to manage the widespread use of common and specialized databases for corporate, work group, and end user information systems. This has made managing data resources a major dimension of information resource management. Since the databases of an organization are used by many different applications, they need to be centrally coordinated and controlled by a *data resource management* philosophy and a *data administration* function.

Data administration involves the establishment and enforcement of policies and procedures for managing data as a strategic corporate resource. This means that the collection, storage, and dissemination of data are administered in such a way that data becomes a standardized resource available to all information systems in the organization. Data administration typically results in long-range data planning and the development of common databases and standards. This includes a *database administration* function to enforce the use of a common data dictionary and standards for database use and security. Chapter 5 discussed such topics in data resource management. In industry practice, the major functions of data administration are performed in a variety of ways, many times with less than satisfactory results. However, the momentum in industry is toward adopting a data resource management philosophy, and a data administration function [13, 31].

Technology Management

An information resource management philosophy emphasizes that all technologies that process, store, and deliver data and information must be managed as integrated systems of organizational resources. Such technologies include telecommunications and office systems, as well as traditional computer-based information processing. These islands of technology are bridged by IRM and become a primary responsibility of the CIO, the executive in charge of all information technology services. Thus, the information systems function becomes a business within a business, whose chief executive is charged with strategic planning, research and development, and coordination of all information technologies for the strategic benefit of the organization [5, 6].

Telecommunications Management

The rapid growth of telecommunications networks in computer-using firms has made **telecommunications management** a major technology management function. This function manages the wide area networks for applications such as online transaction processing, electronic data interchange, and electronic mail, and the local area networks for work group and end user computing. These networks require a major commitment of hardware and software resources, as outlined in Chapter 4. They also require the creation of managerial and staff positions to manage their use. Thus, telecommunications management is responsible for overseeing all telecommunications services provided to end users and the information services function.

Telecommunications managers are usually responsible for evaluating and recommending the acquisition of communications media, communications carriers, and communications hardware and software for end user, departmental, and corporate telecommunications networks. They work with end user managers to improve the design, operational quality, and security of an organization's telecommunications networks and services. Network managers typically manage the operation of specific wide area and local area telecommunications networks. They monitor and evalute telecommunications processors (such as network and file servers), network control software (such as network operating systems), and other common network hardware and software resources to ensure a proper level of service to the users of a network [15].

Advanced Technology Management

The management of rapidly changing technology is important to any organization. Changes in information technology have come swiftly and dramatically and are expected to continue into the future. Developments in information systems technology have had, and will continue to have, a major impact on the operations, costs, management work environment, and competitive position of many organizations. Therefore, many firms have established separate groups to identify, introduce, and monitor the assimilation of new information systems technologies into their organizations, especially those with a high payoff potential [5]. These organizational units are called *technology management, emerging technologies*, or *advanced technology* groups.

Such advanced technology groups (ATGs) typically report to the chief information systems officer and are staffed with former senior systems analysts and other specialists in information systems technology. Their job is to monitor emerging technological developments and identify innovative developments that have high potential payoffs to the firm. Then they work with end user managers and information services management to introduce new technologies into the firm. They also audit a firm's current applications of technology so they can recommend improvements. Figure 11.12 illustrates the forces that need to be confronted in the management of information technology.

Distributed Management

Responsibility for managing information technology is increasingly being distributed to the managers of an organization at all levels and in all functions. Information resource management is not just the responsibility of an organization's chief information officer. If you're a manager, IRM is one of your responsibilities, whether you manage a company, a department, a work group, or a functional area. This is especially true as telecommunications networks and developments such as cooperative processing, end user computing, work group computing, and interorganizational information systems drive the responsibility for managing information systems out to all of an organization's functional and work group managers [1, 30].

Managing End User Computing

As we saw in Chapter 7, the number of people in organizations who use or want to use computers to help them do their jobs has outstripped the capacity of many information services departments. As a result, a revolutionary change to **end user computing** has developed. End users now use personal computer workstations, software packages, and local area networks to develop and apply computer-based information systems to their own business activities. Organizations have responded

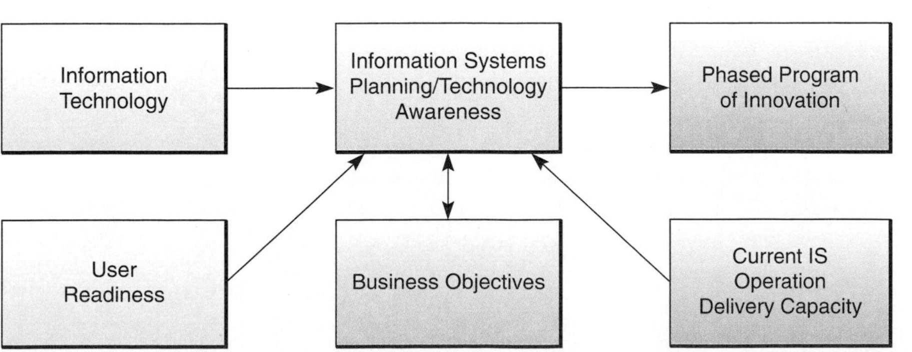

Source: Adapted from James Cash, Jr.; F. Warren McFarlan; James McKenney; and Lynda Applegate, *Corporate Information Systems Management: Text and Cases*, 3rd ed. (Homewood, Ill.: Richard D. Irwin, 1992), p. 481.

FIGURE 11.12
Forces to be confronted in the management of information systems technology.

FIGURE 11.13
Three strategies for managing end user computing.

User Autonomy
Equipment (primarily microcomputers) is purchased without corporate standards. End users are fully responsible for design and support of systems. End users totally control the budget.

User Partnership
Equipment and software are purchased by end users using a corporate standard. Applications are developed by end users. Systems training and support are given by the IS function. Budget responsibility is shared.

Central Control
Equipment and software are purchased by the IS function. Applications are developed by both end users and IS staff. The IS staff provides support and training. The budget is controlled by the IS function.

Source: Adapted from Thomas Clark, "Corporate Systems Management: An Overview and Research Perspective," *Communications of the ACM*, February 1992, p. 65.

by creating a **user services**, or *client services*, function to support and manage this explosion in end user computing.

End user computing provides both opportunities and problems for end user management. Establishing an **information center** in an organization or end user department is one solution. However, other organizations have dismantled their information centers and distributed end user support specialists to departments and other work groups. For example, some firms create user liaison positions, or "help desks," with end user hot lines. IS specialists with titles such as *user consultant*, *account executive*, or *business analyst* may be assigned to end user work groups. These specialists perform a vital role by troubleshooting problems, gathering and communicating information, coordinating educational efforts, and helping end users with application development. Their activities improve communication and coordination between end user work groups and the corporate information services department and avoid the runaround that can frustrate end users.

In addition to these measures, most organizations must still establish and enforce policies concerning the acquisition of hardware and software by end users. This ensures their compatibility with existing hardware and software systems. Even more important is the development of applications with proper controls to promote correct performance and safeguard the integrity of corporate and departmental databases. We will discuss such IS controls in the next chapter. Figure 11.13 summarizes three basic strategies organizations use to manage end user computing [8].

REAL WORLD CASE

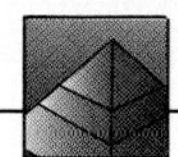

Cigna Corporation: Eric Scheffler on Reengineering

Coining of the term "reengineering" is generally credited to management guru Michael Hammer, but Cigna Corporation Chief Information Officer Raymond Caron may well go down in information systems history as one of the first to turn the word into action. Caron's ambitious attempt to align Cigna Systems with the business goals of its reinsurance business, Cigna RE, met near-legendary success, resulting in a 52 percent head count reduction, a 1,200 percent transaction time improvement, and a 42 percent operating cost reduction. Today, some 20 reengineering projects are afoot at the firm.

Senior Vice President Eric Scheffler was IS head of the Property and Casualty Division when the reengineering bandwagon began to roll. Scheffler recognized early on that "we had to find a different way of thinking about what we were doing or else be struck with a smokestack juggernaut." That led him to the "team training" concept, which in turn, he says, is leading him and his teammates through an unsparing and often painful reexamination of how they act and why. Here's what Scheffler has to say.

"The first problem you hit when you start team training isn't that nobody wants to do it. It's just the opposite. Everybody believes they're already working as a team. That's the beginning of the process of unlearning, which can be pretty traumatic stuff.

"For instance, before, I thought of myself as a manager. I thought my job entailed top-down direction and lots of reports and meetings. Suddenly I'm not a "manager"—I'm a "counselor," and I'm supposed to be "guiding" rather than "controlling." You're used to having three or four levels of people reporting to you, and overnight, all that's gone. Tell me you're not going to feel dislocated.

"This brings you right up against the issue that's key to the success of a transition to teamwork: rewards. Like virtually all companies, our rewards have traditionally been based on individual contribution. In IS, for instance: Say you were working on a unique project and came up with a creative way to do it; you might get extra money over and above your salary.

"But now you're part of a team. All the old rules are off. Uh-oh—so are the old rewards. Beating your colleague to the punch got you a bonus; beating your teammate to the punch is meaningless, if not bad.

"If there's no way at all to get rewarded, people aren't going to accept the team concept. But if you preach teamwork and keep rewarding individual action, you're attempting the impossible. The only choice left is to come up with an entirely new reward system. That's what we did, and why.

"Under our old structure, each individual was reviewed periodically, based on a five-grade performance system: basically, 1 meant that you walked on water and 5 meant that you passed water. No way could that system be adapted to the team model. So we threw away the grading system. All the numbers went away. So did individual reviews. Now, an entire teams's effort is considered as one performance.

"What else went away? Huge chains of control that created middle-management layers. For instance, our research, testing, and training department used to test code. This was replaced by a soup-to-nuts development process that requires the people who developed the code to test it and the business partners for whom it's being developed to be involved at every step.

"Great? Sure—for the developers, for the users, for the end product. But you can see why reengineering is very threatening to large groups of people. If testing is taken out of the mix, how do they fit in? The fact is, some don't.

"And there's another hard part of the reengineering process: layoffs. This issue isn't pretty. It isn't nice, and it isn't going to go away. You've got face up to it and do what you can to reduce the pain.

"One thing you can do is to have metrics in place well before you start so that you can really take your best shot at eliminating inefficiencies and redundancies. As you start teams, for instance, start doing a lot of surveys because you have to know what's working and what's not. Another is, be completely open about what you're doing and when and why. Both of these—metrics and openness—increase understanding."

CASE STUDY QUESTIONS

1. Why is the concept of a self-directed team frequently part of business process reengineering?
2. Why does the self-directed team concept affect reward systems and layers of management?
3. How does business process reengineering usually affect job content and the number of jobs in an organization?

Source: Adapted from Nell Margolis, "Voices of Experience," *Computerworld*, January 4, 1993, pp. 16–17. Used with permission.

SECTION II
Global Information Technology Management

The International Dimension

It's no secret that international dimensions are becoming more and more important in managing a business in the global economies and markets of the 1990s. Whether you become a manager in a large corporation or the owner of a small business, you will be affected by international business developments, and deal in some way with people, products, or services whose origin is not from your home country. For example:

> The global corporation may have a product that was designed in a European country, with components manufactured in Taiwan and Korea. It may be assembled in Canada and sold as a standard model in Brazil, and in the United States as a model fully loaded with options. Transfer pricing of the components and assembled product may be determined with an eye to minimizing tax liability. Freight and insurance may be contracted for relet through a Swiss subsidiary, which earns a profit subject only to cantonal taxes. The principal financing may be provided from the Eurodollar market based in London. Add the complexities of having the transactions in different countries, with foreign exchange hedge contract gains and losses that sometimes offset trading losses and gains, and one has a marvelously complex management control problem [28].

Thus, international issues in business management are vitally important today. This means that international issues in accounting, marketing, finance, production/operations, human resource management, and, of course, information systems and information technology are also very important to business success. Properly designed and managed information systems using appropriate information technologies are a key ingredient in international business. They provide vital information resources needed to support business activity in global markets.

Figure 11.14 illustrates the major dimensions of the job of managing global information technology that we will cover in this section. Notice that all global IT activities must be adjusted to take into account the cultural, political, and geoeconomic challenges that exist in the international business community. Developing appropriate business and IT strategies for the global marketplace should be the first step in global IT management. Once that is done, end user and IS managers can move on to developing (1) the *portfolio of applications* needed to support business/IT

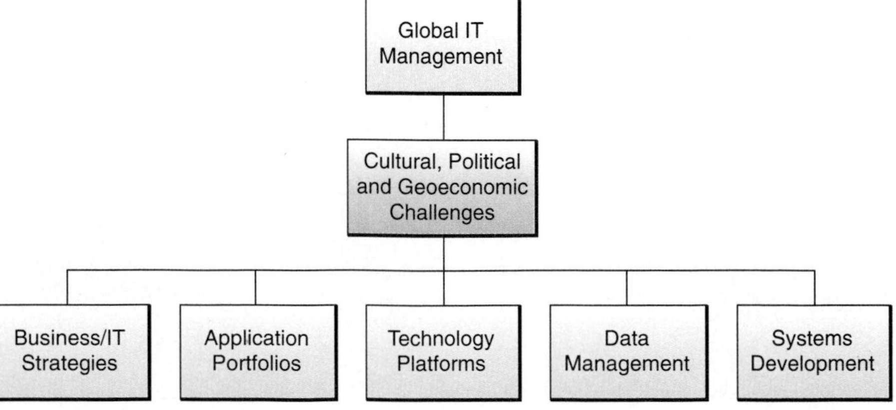

FIGURE 11.14
The major dimensions of global IT management.

strategies; (2) the hardware, software, and telecommunications *technology platforms* to support those applications; (3) the data management methods to provide necessary databases; and (4) the systems development projects that will produce the global information systems required.

Cultural, Political, and Geoeconomic Challenges

"Business as usual" is not good enough in global business operations. The same holds true for global IT management. Too many cultural, political, and geoeconomic (geographic and economic) realities must be confronted in order for a business to succeed in global markets. As we have just said, global IT management must focus on developing global business IT strategies and managing global application portfolios, technologies, platforms, databases, and systems development projects. But managers must also accomplish that from a perspective and through methods that take into account the cultural, political, and geographic differences that exist when doing business internationally.

For example, a major *political challenge* is that many countries have rules regulating or prohibiting transfer of data across their national boundaries (*transborder data flows*), especially personal information such as personnel records. Others severely restrict, tax, or prohibit imports of hardware and software. Still others have *local content* laws that specify the portion of the value of a product that must be added in that country if it is to be sold there. Other countries have *reciprocal trade agreements* that require a business to spend part of the revenue they earn in a country in that nation's economy [29].

Cultural challenges facing global business and IT managers include differences in languages, cultural interests, religions, customs, social attitudes, and political philosophies. Obviously, global IT managers must be trained and sensitized to such cultural differences before they are sent abroad or brought into a corporation's home country. Other cultural challenges include differences in work styles and business relationships. For example, should one take one's time to avoid mistakes, or hurry to get something done early? Should one go it alone or work cooperatively? Should the most experienced person lead, or should leadership be shared? The answers to such questions would depend on the culture you are in, and would spotlight cultural differences that might exist in the global workplace.

Geoeconomic challenges in global business and IT refer to the effects of geography on the economic realities of international business activities. The sheer physical distances involved are still a major problem, even in this day of electronic telecommunications and jet travel. For example, it may still take too long to fly in specialists when IT problems occur in a remote site. It is still difficult to communicate conveniently across the world's 24 time zones. It still is difficult to get good-quality telephone and telecommunications service in many countries. There still are problems finding the job skills required in some countries, or enticing specialists from other countries to live and work there. Finally, there are still problems (and opportunities) in the great differences in the cost of living and labor costs in various countries [22]. All of these geoeconomic challenges must be addressed when developing a company's global business and IT strategies. See Figure 11.15.

Global Business and IT Strategies

How much of a business need is there for **global information technology?** That is, do we need to use IT to support our company's international business operations? Figure 11.16 helps answer these questions by showing that many firms are moving toward **transnational** business strategies in which they integrate their global busi-

FIGURE 11.15
The global telecommunications command center of Electronic Data Systems in Plano, Texas. Global telecommunications networks are vital to doing business in global markets.

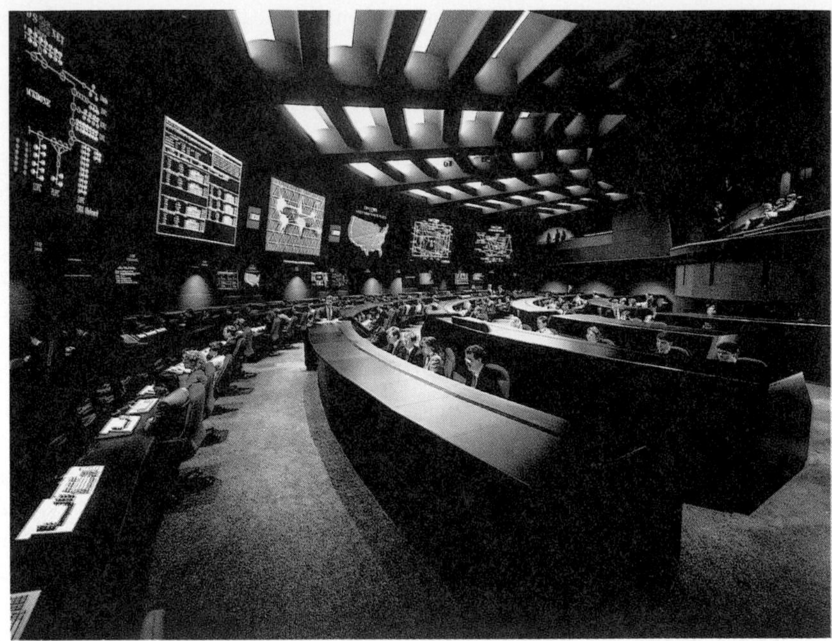

Courtesy of EDS Corporation.

FIGURE 11.16
Companies operating internationally are moving toward a transnational business strategy.

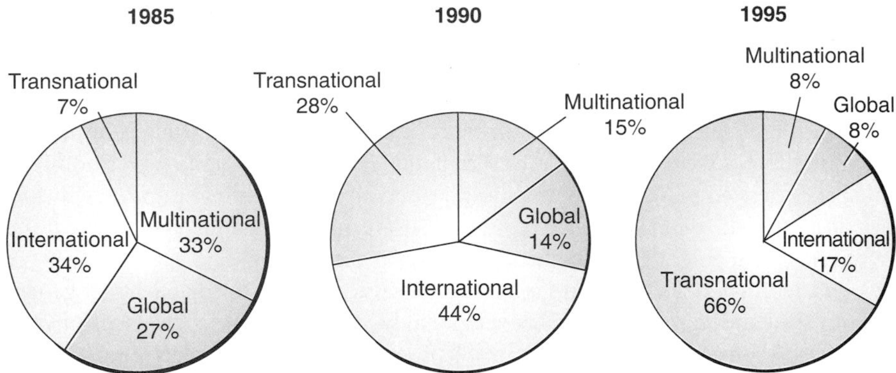

Source: Adapted from Blake Ives and Sirkka Jarvenpaa, "Wiring the Stateless Corporation: Empowering the Drivers and Overcoming the Barriers," *SIM Network*, September/October 1991, p. 48.

ness activities through close cooperation and interdependence among their international subsidiaries and their corporate headquarters. Businesses are moving away from (1) *multinational* strategies where foreign subsidiaries operate autonomously; (2) *international* strategies in which foreign subsidiaries are autonomous but are dependent on headquarters for new processes, products, and ideas; or (3) *global* strategies, where a company's worldwide operations are closely managed by corporate headquarters [1, 14].

In the transnational approach, a business depends heavily on its information systems and appropriate information technologies to help it integrate its global business activities. Instead of having independent IS units at its subsidiaries, or even a centralized IS operation directed from its headquarters, a transnational firm moves

FIGURE 11.17
Multinational versus transnational. Note some of the chief differences between multinational and transnational business and IT strategies.

	Business Strategies			IT Strategies		
	Structure	Priority	Coordination	Telecommunications	Transaction Processing	Systems Development
Multinational	Largely autonomous units, at level of country and/or region	Local response to national market demands and conditions	Mainly through the capital budget and reporting systems	Mainly individual business-unit and country/region networks; some shared networks, especially U.S. to Europe	Very limited needs for international systems; finance the exception, with worldwide cash management typical	Separate units matching country/region structure and key locations
Transnational	Selected key functions coordinated worldwide with equal emphasis on local autonomy and responsiveness	Entire business system optimized; operated as if there are no national boundaries	The main challenge: how to coordinate without intruding or overcontrolling	Integrated networks with substantial reach across international locations and range across key business functions	Transnational processing systems an essential part of business strategy	New cross-functional and cross-location planning mechanisms and collaborative teams

Source: Adapted from Peter Keen, *Shaping the Future: Business Design through Information Technology*, Boston: Harvard Business School Press, 1991, p. 72.

to integrate its IS operations. Thus, a transnational business tries to develop an integrated and cooperative worldwide hardware, software, and telecommunications architecture for its IT *platform*. Figure 11.17 outlines some of the chief differences between multinational and transnational business and IT strategies.

Global Business and IT Applications

The applications of information technology developed by global companies depend on their business and IT strategies and their expertise and experience in IT. However, their IT applications also depend on a variety of **business drivers**, that is, business requirements caused by the nature of the industry and its competitive or environmental forces. One example would be companies like airlines or hotel chains that have *global customers*, that is, customers who travel widely or have global operations. Such companies will need global IT capabilities for online transaction processing so they can provide fast, convenient customer service to their customers or face losing them to their competitors. The economies of scale provided by global business operations are another business driver that requires the support of global IT applications [14].

Companies whose products are available worldwide would be another example of how business needs can shape global IT. For example, Coca-Cola or Pepsi might use teleconferencing to make worldwide product announcements, and use computer-based marketing systems to coordinate global marketing campaigns. Other companies with global operations have used IT to move parts of their operations to lower-cost sites. For example, Citibank moved its credit card processing operations to Sioux Falls, South Dakota, American Airlines moved much of its data entry work to Barbados, while other firms have looked to Ireland and India as sources of low-cost software development [14, 22]. Figure 11.18 summarizes some of the business requirements that make global IT a competitive necessity.

Of course, many global IT applications, particularly finance, accounting, and office applications, have been in operation for many years. For example, most multinational companies had global financial budgeting and cash management systems, and more recently office automation applications such as fax and E-mail systems. However, as global operations expand and global competition heats up, there is increasing pressure for companies to install global transaction processing applications for their customers and suppliers. Examples include global point-of-sale systems for customers and global electronic data interchange systems for suppliers. Figure 11.19 illustrates the distribution of global IT applications that

FIGURE 11.18
Business drivers for global IT. These are some of the business reasons behind global IT applications.

Global customers. Customers are people who may travel anywhere or companies with global operations. Global IT can help provide fast, convenient service.

Global products. Products are the same throughout the world or are assembled by subsidiaries throughout the world. Global IT can help manage worldwide marketing and quality control.

Global operations. Parts of a production or assembly process are assigned to subsidiaries based on changing economic or other conditions. Only global IT can support such geographic flexibility.

Global resources. The use and cost of common equipment, facilities, and people are shared by subsidiaries of a global company. Global IT can keep track of such shared resources.

Global collaboration. The knowledge and expertise of colleagues in a global company can be quickly accessed, shared, and organized to support individual or group efforts. Only global IT can support such electronic collaboration.

Source: Adapted from Blake Ives and Sirkka Jarvenpaa, "Applications of Global Information Technology: Key Issues for Management," *MIS Quarterly*, March 1991, p. 40.

FIGURE 11.19
Types of global IT applications. Note the change expected from office and financial applications to those that support customers and suppliers.

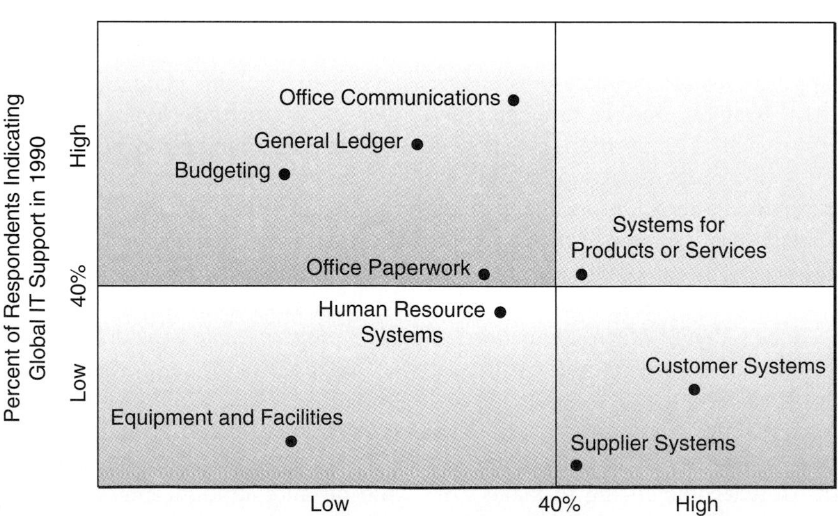

Source: Adapted from Blake Ives and Sirkka Jarvenpaa, "Wiring the Stateless Corporation: Empowering the Drivers and Overcoming the Barriers," *SIM Network*, September/October 1991, p. 4C.

existed in 1990 and are expected by 1995 by over 100 companies with international operations.

Global IT Platforms

The choice of *technology platforms* (also called the *technology infrastructure*) is another major dimension of global IT management. That is, what hardware, software, telecommunications networks, and computing facilities will be needed to support our global business operations? Answering this question is a major challenge of global IT management. The choice of a global IT platform is not only technically complex, but also has major political and cultural implications.

For example, hardware choices are difficult in some countries because of high prices, high tariffs, import restrictions, long lead times for government approvals, lack of local service or spare parts, and lack of documentation tailored to local conditions. Software choices can also present unique problems. Software packages developed in Europe may be incompatible with American or Asian versions, even when purchased from the same hardware vendor. Well-known U.S. software packages may be unavailable because there is no local distributor, or because the software publisher refuses to supply markets that disregard software licensing and copyright agreements [14].

Telecommunications network and computing facilities decisions also present major challenges in global IT management. In Chapter 5, we discussed some of the managerial challenges and business planning strategies posed by telecommunications network technologies. Obviously, global telecommunications networks which cross many international boundaries make such issues even more complex.

Figure 11.20 shows that companies with global business operations usually establish additional data centers (computer centers) in their subsidiaries in other countries. These data centers meet local and regional computing needs, and even help balance global computing work loads through communications satellite links.

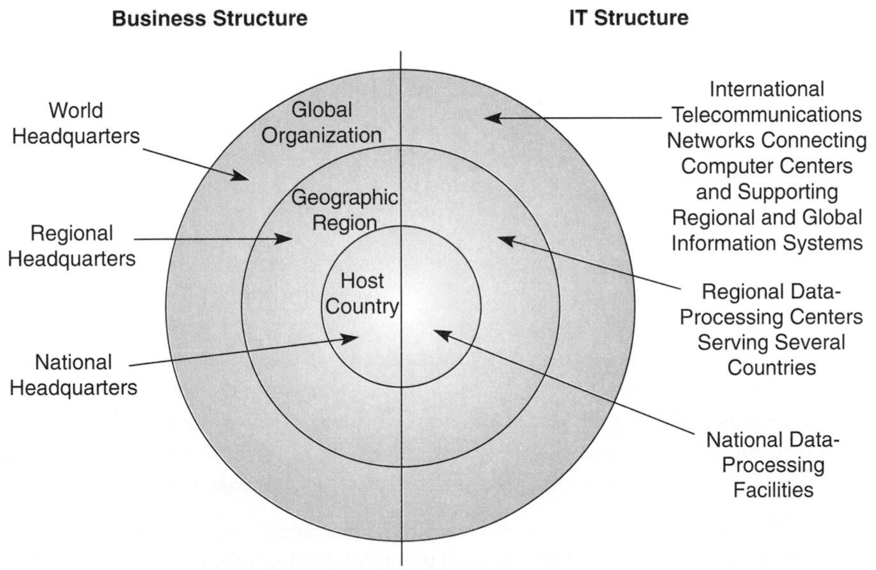

FIGURE 11.20
Global business and technology structures. Note how a global IT structure reflects a company's global business structure.

Source: Adapted from Edward Roche, *Managing Information Technology in Multinational Corporations* (New York: Macmillan, 1992), p. 50.

However, off-shore data centers can pose major management problems in headquarter's support, hardware and software acquisition, maintenance, and security:

> establishing locations for international data centers presents several challenges: overlapping working hours; local computing and labor regulations; potential theft; sabotage and terrorism; unreliable power sources; availability of completely redundant network backup capability; and the like [14].

Global Data Issues

Global data issues have been a subject of political controversy and technology barriers in global business operations for many years. A major example is the issue of **transborder data flows** (TDF), in which business data flows across international borders over the telecommunications networks of global information systems. Many countries view transborder data flows as violating their national sovereignty because it avoids customs duties and regulations for the import or export of goods and services. Other countries may view TDF as a violation of their privacy legislation since, in many cases, data about individuals is being moved out of the country without stringent privacy safeguards. Still others view transborder data flows as violating their laws to protect local IT industry from competition, or their labor regulations for protecting local jobs [6].

Figure 11.21 outlines some of the fears and responses of several countries to global data issues. Notice that this includes not only transborder data flows, but also regulation of files and databases stored in a host country. Recent research seems to indicate that data issues have not been as much of a problem for global business as had been feared. This is due primarily to difficulties in enforcing such laws, and to efforts by host countries to encourage foreign investment. However, the data issues that still seem politically sensitive are those that affect the movement of personal data in payroll and personnel applications [6, 14].

Other important global data issues are concerned with global data management and standardization of data. Common data definitions are necessary for sharing data among the parts of an international business. Differences in language, culture, and technology platforms can make global data standardization quite difficult. For example, a sale may be called "an 'order booked' in the United Kingdom, an 'order scheduled' in Germany, and an 'order produced' in France" [25]. However, businesses are moving ahead to standardize data definitions and structures. By involving their subsidiaries in data modeling and database design, they hope to develop a global data architecture that supports their global business objectives [14].

Global Systems Development

Just imagine the challenges of developing efficient, effective, and responsive applications for business end users domestically. Then multiply that by the number of countries and cultures that may use a global IT system. That's the challenge of managing global systems development. Naturally, there are conflicts over local versus global system requirements, and difficulties in agreeing on common system features such as multilingual user interfaces and flexible design standards. And all of this effort must take place in an environment that promotes involvement and "ownership" of a system by local end users. Thus, one IT manager estimates that

> it takes 5 to 10 times more time to reach an understanding and agreement on system requirements and deliverables when the users and developers are in different countries. This is partially explained by travel requirements and language and cultural differences, but technical limitations also contribute to the problem [14].

Country	Presumed Fear	Actual Response
Brazil	Information colonialism and a lack of development of a domestic information industry.	All companies must maintain copies of all databases physically within the country; offshore processing is prohibited.
Canada	Exportation of corporate information to headquarters in other countries (especially the U.S.). Abuses of the personal privacy of its citizens. Loss of cultural and national sovereignty.	1980 Banking Act prohibits processing data transactions outside of the country unless approved by the government. Limitations on the number of direct access links for international data transmission and limitations on satellite usage.
France	Basically the same as Canada.	Imposition of taxes on and duties on information and information transfers. Requires every database maintained in France to be registered with the government.
Germany	A lack of development of a domestic information industry. Abuses of personal privacy.	Regulations which favor the domestic information industry and control of private leased telecommunication lines which connect to public communications networks. Data records on German nationals must be kept in Germany.
Sweden	Abuses of privacy. Domestic economic data may not be accessible if stored abroad.	Has a data protection law and a commission to license and approve all data systems. Prohibits offshore processing and storage of data.
Taiwan	National and economic security.	Government monitoring of data transmissions.

Source: Adapted from William Carper, "Societal Impacts and Consequences of Transborder Data Flows," in Shailendra Palvia et al., *The Global Issues of Information Technology Management* (Harrisburg, Pa.: Idea Group Publishing, 1992), p. 443.

FIGURE 11.21
Global data issues. Note the fears and responses by some countries to the issues of transborder data flows and control of global databases.

Other systems development issues arise from disturbances caused by systems implementation and maintenance activities. For example: "An interruption during a third shift in New York City will present midday service interruptions in Tokyo." Another major development issue relates to the trade-offs between developing one system that can run on multiple computer and operating system platforms, or letting each local site customize the software for its own platform [14]. See Figure 11.22.

Several strategies can be used to solve some of the systems development problems that arise in global IT [14, 28]. First is transforming an application used by the home office into a global application. However, often the system used by a subsidiary that has the best version of an application will be chosen for global use. Another approach is setting up a *multinational development team* with key people from several subsidiaries to ensure that the system design meets the needs of local sites as well as corporate headquarters.

A third approach is called *parallel development*. That's because parts of the system are assigned to different subsidiaries and the home office to develop at the

FIGURE 11.22
Using the IEF CASE tool at NyKredit in Denmark. The global use of information technology depends on international systems development efforts.

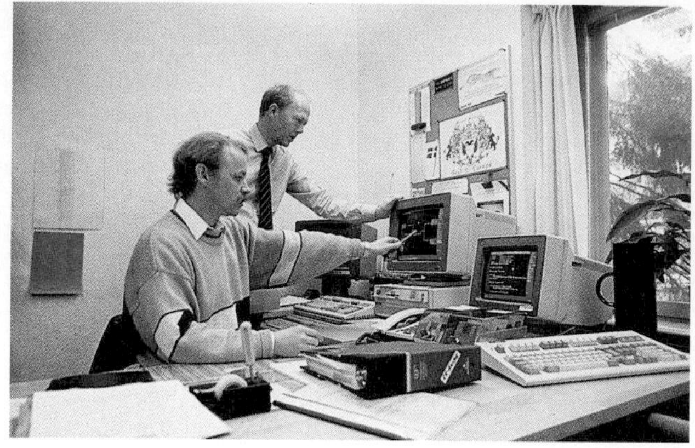

Courtesy of Texas Instruments.

same time, based on the expertise and experience at each site. Another approach is the concept of *centers of excellence*. In this approach, an entire system may be assigned for development to a particular subsidiary based on the subsidiary's expertise in the business or technical dimensions needed for successful development. Obviously, all of these approaches require managerial oversight and coordination to meet the global needs of a business.

You and Global IT Management

> Most companies fail to have in place a coherent information-*technology* strategy. Their IT infrastructure does not match or facilitate their emerging global *business* strategy. Few multinationals have discovered the potential of computer and communications technology to transform their operations on a global basis. A company may have a single product sold globally, but no globally rationalized product database. It may be fighting a battle for centralized control when the business strategy needs to be different for each national market. It most likely has many different national data centers when it could better serve strategy with regionalized data processing of selected applications and resources [28].

Now that we have covered the basic dimensions of global IT management, it is time to acknowledge that much work remains to be done to implement global IT strategies. As a future managerial end user or IS manager, the global business success of the company you work for will be in your hands. But now at least you know the dimensions of the problems and opportunities that arise from the use of information technology to support global business operations.

First, you must discover if your company has a global business strategy and a strategy for how information technology can support global business operations. If not, you can begin to play a role, however small, in developing such strategies. Then you must discover or help develop the IT applications to support your global business activities. This includes providing your ideas for the hardware, software, and telecommunications platform and databases you need to do business globally. This process can be a gradual one. For example, as a managerial end user, you can follow the steps used by the Digital Equipment Corporation for gradually applying telecommunications networks to business activities:

REAL WORLD CASE

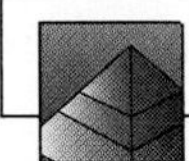

ABB Power Generation and Hypo Bank: Global IT Management

"I sense that sometimes there's less trust in technology [in Europe] and a strong urge to do things manually," says Patrick Carney, director of IS at ABB Power Generation, Inc. The Brunswick, New Jersey, firm is a division of ASEA Brown Boveri, a Swedish/Swiss-owned engineering conglomerate.

Even so, spunky IS managers are not only surviving in unknown territory, but in some cases also driving technology innovation and standardization for the entire company.

That's the case at ABB Power, which is helping to introduce downsizing, groupware, and Microsoft Windows to its Zurich-based corporation. Carney says the unit places a top priority on facilitating communications between its 100-plus U.S. divisions and the rest of its enterprise, and the unit is now 100 percent Windows-compliant.

But it's taken time for the parent to catch on, Carney says. He attributes this to the firm's centralized computing philosophy and a matrix management structure that he says can be confusing.

However, Zurich-based ASEA Brown has also proven to be open-minded: Downsizing successes for U.S. divisions have convinced the parent to standardize on several leading-edge technologies, including Lotus, CC:Mail, and Notes software. "They've seen the benefits we've attained," Carney adds, "so they 're starting to ramp up." The parent is also using its U.S. subsidiaries to test client/server computing.

However, while PC software in the United States is often a cheap commodity, Europeans sometimes pay up to three times for the same product, which must be customized and is then slapped with stiff tariffs. A copy of Microsoft Office, which costs about $470 in the United States, sells for more than $1,000 in Europe, Carney says.

Joe Michael Sanchez, assistant treasurer responsible for MIS at Hypo Bank in New York, knows the challenge well. As MIS chief at the first U.S. office of Munich, Germany-based Bayerische Hypotheken und Wechsel-Bank, Sanchez decided to use Fischer International Systems Watchdog PC security software. But when the bank's European subsidiaries decided to also use the $170 package, they discovered that the cost of buying through a middleman shot the price to $450 to $500 a copy.

Fortunately, Sanchez says, the parent firm was able to work out a better, more affordable deal with Fischer. "Now they're able to ship a European version from New York and bypass the middleman, who was trying to buy his new Mercedes from us," Sanchez jokes.

Purchasing problems aside, Sanchez says the language barrier can also be an issue. Many of his German managerial peers were taught to speak and understand an older, more formal brand of English, explains Sanchez, a seven-year Hypo Bank employee. That can make it tough to explain the intricacies of an IS project. Plus, Germans typically ask fewer questions than most American would, he says, and are proud. That sometimes tempts them to voice more understanding than actually exists, Sanchez adds.

Hypo Bank is also developing a global wide-area network. Although the bank's head office is in Germany, most systems testing is conducted in New York under Sanchez's supervision. He says the bank prefers to do most of its IS development in the United States because both technology and skilled technologists are more readily available than in Europe.

CASE STUDY QUESTIONS

1. What cultural, political, or geoeconomic challenges are faced by the U.S.-based IS managers of ABB Power and Hypo Bank?
2. How have global operations affected technology platforms at ABB Power and Hypo Bank?
3. How have global operations affected systems development issues at ABB Power and Hypo Bank?

Source: Adapted from Thomas Hoffman, "Here and There," *Computerworld*, April 12, 1993, pp. 81–82. Used with permission.

- **Link up.** Connect simple business functions like electronic mail, word processing, and spreadsheets across departments and sites.
- **Build up.** Add more critical business applications like ordering, pricing, forecasting, and customer and product data.
- **Join up.** Expand the links to other units, customers, and suppliers [28].

As a managerial end user, global IT management will be one of your many managerial responsibilities. Like other areas of global business management, it requires an added dimension of sensitivity to the cultural, political, and geoeconomic realities of doing business with people in other countries. But it also offers an exciting challenge of competing successfully in a dynamic global arena to bring your products or services to customers throughout the world.

Summary

- **Managers and IT.** Information technology is changing the distribution, relationships, resources, and responsibilities of managers. That is, IT is eliminating layers of management, enabling more collaborative forms of management, providing managers with significant information and computing resources, and confronting managers with a major information resource management challenge.
- **IS Performance.** Information systems are not being used effectively, efficiently, or economically by many organizations. The experiences of successful organizations reveal that the basic ingredient of high-quality information system performance is extensive and meaningful management and user involvement in the planning and control of information technology. Thus, managers may serve on executive steering committees and create an IS management function within their business units.
- **Organizations and IT.** The people, tasks, technology, culture, and structure of an organization affect how it will organize and use information technology. Thus, many variations exist, which reflect the attempts of organizations to tailor their organizational structures and applications to their particular business activities and management philosophy, as well as to the capabilities of centralized or distributed information systems.
- **Information Resource Management.** Managing the use of information technology in an organization has become a major managerial responsibility. End user managers should use an information resource management approach to manage the data and information, hardware and software, telecommunications networks, and people resources of their business units and work groups for the overall benefit of their organizations. The information systems function in an organization may be headed by a chief information officer who oversees the organization's strategic use of information technology (strategic management). IRM also involves managing data and IS personnel (resource management), telecommunications and advances in information technologies (technology management), and end user computing (distributed management). The activities of information services can be grouped into three basic functional categories: systems development, operations, and technical services (functional management).
- **Managing Global IT.** The international dimensions of managing global information technology include dealing with cultural, political, and geoeconomic challenges posed by various countries, developing appropriate business and IT strategies for the global marketplace, and developing a portfolio of global IT applications and a technology platform to support them. In addition, database management methods have to be developed and systems development projects managed to produce the global information systems that are required to compete successfully in the global marketplace.
- **Global Business and IT Strategies and Issues.** Many companies are moving toward transnational business strategies in which they integrate the global business activities of their subsidiaries and headquarters. This requires that they develop an integrated IT platform, that is, an integrated hardware, software, and telecommunications architecture to support global IT applications that meet their unique global business requirements. Global IT and end user managers must deal with restrictions on the availability of hardware and software, restrictions on transborder data flows and movement of personal data, and difficulties with developing common data definitions and system requirements.

Key Terms and Concepts

These are the key terms and concepts of this chapter. The page number of their first explanation is in parentheses.

1. Advanced Technology Management (423)
2. Centralization or decentralization (416)
   a. Information systems
   b. Operations and management
3. Chargeback systems (421)
4. Chief information officer (419)
5. Cultural, political, and geoeconomic challenges (427)
6. Data administration (422)
7. Data center (420)
8. Development center (420)
9. Downsizing (417)
10. End user services (424)
11. Global business drivers (429)
12. Global information technology (427)
13. Global IT management (426)
    a. applications (429)
    b. business/IT strategies (427)
    c. Data issues (432)
    d. IT platforms (431)
    e. systems development (432)
14. Impact of information technology (410)
    a. On management (410)
    b. On organizations (414)
15. Information center (424)
16. Information resource management (418)
    a. Five dimensions of IRM
17. Information services functions (422)
18. Information systems performance (412)
19. Management involvement (413)
20. Managing IS personnel (421)
21. Operations management (420)
22. Organizations as sociotechnical systems (414)
23. Outsourcing (417)
24. Reengineering of business processes (415)
25. System performance monitor (420)
26. Systems development management (419)
27. Technical services (419)
28. Telecommunications management (422)
29. Transborder data flows (432)
30. Transnational strategy (427)

Review Quiz

Match one of the key terms and concepts listed above with one of the brief examples and definitions listed below. Try to find the best fit for answers that seem to fit more than one term or concept. Defend your choices.

____ 1. Managers now have a lot of information, information processing power, and responsibility for information systems.

____ 2. Information technology affects the people, tasks, technology, culture, and structure of organizations.

____ 3. Information system resources can be distributed throughout an organization or consolidated in corporate data centers.

____ 4. Information systems can help management increase the number of regional and branch offices or consolidate operations.

____ 5. The management of data, information, hardware, software, and IS personnel as organizational resources.

____ 6. Managing information technology is a distributed, functional responsibility focusing on the strategic management of IS resources and technologies.

____ 7. Computers have not been used efficiently, effectively, and economically.

____ 8. A management steering committee is an example.

____ 9. End users need information centers or other forms of liaison, consulting, and training support.

____ 10. Includes the basic functions of systems development, operations, and technical services.

____ 11. An executive that oversees all information systems technology for an organization.

____ 12. Managing systems analysis and design, computer programming, and systems maintenance activities.

____ 13. Planning and controlling data center operations.

____ 14. Developing and enforcing data standards and doing strategic data planning.

____ 15. Corporate locations for computer system operations.

____ 16. A support group for an organization's professional programmers and systems analysts.

____ 17. A support group for an organization's end users.

____ 18. Rapidly changing technological developments must be anticipated, identified, and implemented.

____ 19. An IS function that includes user services, telecommunications management, and technology management.

_____ 20. Telecommunications networks and their hardware and software must be developed, administered, and maintained.

_____ 21. Software that helps monitor and control computer systems in a data center.

_____ 22. The cost of IS services may be allocated back to end users.

_____ 23. Recruiting and developing information services employees.

_____ 24. Many business firms are replacing their mainframe systems with networked microcomputers.

_____ 25. Using IT to support a company's international business operations.

_____ 26. Integrating global business activities through cooperation among international subsidiaries and corporate headquarters.

_____ 27. Differences in customs, governmental regulations, and the cost of living are examples.

_____ 28. Global customers, products, operations, resources, and collaboration.

_____ 29. Applying IT to global transaction processing systems is an example.

_____ 30. The goal of some organizations is to develop an integrated worldwide hardware, software, and telecommunications platform.

_____ 31. Transborder data flows and security of personnel databases is a top concern.

_____ 32. Standardizing computer systems, software packages, telecommunications networks, and computing facilities.

_____ 33. Agreement is needed on common user interfaces and other design features in global IT.

_____ 34. Global telecommunications networks move data across national boundaries.

Discussion Questions

1. What has been the impact of information technology on the work relationships, activities, and resources of managers?
2. What should end user managers do about the fact that "a large number of top business executives feel that IS spending is out of control and that their IS executives still fail to see technology in business terms"?
3. Refer to the Real World Case on Cigna Corporation. What role does information technology play in business process reengineering?
4. How is information technology affecting the modern organization? Will middle management wither away? What will take its place?
5. Should the IS function in a business be centralized or decentralized? What recent developments support your answer?
6. Refer to the Real World Case on ABB Power Generation and Hypo Bank. How might cultural, political, and geoeconomic issues affect application portfolios and data management issues in a global company?
7. What do you think are the most important cultural, political, or geoeconomic challenges facing managers of firms with global operations? Why?
8. What are several major dimensions of global IT management? How would cultural, political, or geoeconomic challenges affect each of them?
9. Why do you think firms with global business operations are moving away from multinational, global, and international strategies toward a transnational business strategy? How does this affect global IT management?
10. What important business "drivers" or requirements do you think are most responsible for a company's use of global IT? Give several examples to illustrate your answer.

Real World Problems

1. Thomas Giammo, U.S. Patent and Trademark Office: Mismanaging Systems Development

Thomas Giammo, assistant commissioner for information systems for the U.S. Patent and Trademark Office, is an ideal crusader for a better way of managing systems development. In more than 30 years as an IS professional, most of it in the federal government, he has seen more than a few systems development fiascos. One of the earliest was a U.S. Air Force logistics system that crashed and burned in the 1970s after the Air Force had spent a whopping half-billion dollars on it. "They realized they had to do a process redesign, and they put together a massive team to do it," Giammo recalls. "But it was so huge they couldn't think it through. They couldn't get it started." The first attempt to overhaul the systems at the Social Security Administration, which began in 1976, fared no better, Giammo says. "My first task when I came in 1979 was to kill the project. They had spent millions of dollars and produced nothing. They could never drive it down to a level of detail needed to go forward," he says.

In 1988, Giammo was tapped by the Deputy Secretary

of Commerce to rescue a $289-million effort to automate operations at the U.S. Patent and Trademark Office. "It was a genuine collapse of a very large project, a recognizable shambles," he says. "The problem was it was being managed in a linear fashion. We locked things in that shouldn't have been, and in lockstep we kept producing the wrong things. I began to see patterns in these projects," Giammo says. "I thought, "by and large these are not stupid or slothful people. There must be something stopping them from doing what is expected of them.'" The fundamental problem, Giammo concludes, was that these huge projects were being managed with techniques more appropriate to an earlier era in which discrete, relatively simple processes, such as payroll or personnel, were automated. "Now, we are moving up the org chart; we are integrating at higher and higher levels," Giammo says. "It is no longer possible to get that degree of certainty implicit in the traditional development methodologies."

So Giammo is the driving force behind an emerging body of principles and practices he calls Managed Evolutionary Development (MED). In the gospel according to MED, if you are embarking on a large development project, you need not, and indeed cannot, resolve all uncertainties and eliminate all risks up front. Rather, by explicitly recognizing and documenting the unknowns, it is possible to proceed safely with the project while the uncertainties get resolved in a carefully managed way.

a. What do you think are the basic causes for the systems development failures described in this case?
b. What do you think of Thomas Giammo's solution to such problems? Explain.

Source: Adapted from Gary Anthes, "Welcome to the Unknown Zone," *Computerworld*, February 9, 1993, pp. 55–56. Used with permission.

2. Pfizer, Inc.: Outsourcing PC Software Support

As part of a plan to focus information systems management on business issues rather than tactical support, Pfizer, Inc., in New York has outsourced PC software support in Corporate Software, Inc., in Canton, Massachusetts. Under terms of the contract, Corporate Software will provide day-to-day support for 1,400 PCs running Microsoft Windows and DOS and IBM's OS/2. "We have been spending far too much time on installing software and dealing with memory management issues on PCs," said Russ Baris, director of pharmaceutical systems at Pfizer. "The pact provides us with better use of the software on our systems and allows our staff to focus on the strategic parts of Pfizer business. It's crazy to pay someone $100,000 a year to be a systems analyst and have them spend their time answering questions about WordPerfect," says Esther Dyson, president of EDventure Holdings, Inc., in New York. "Supporting PC software users is critical to the mission getting done but not to designing the mission."

Pfizer is organized under a structure where IS personnel act as systems consultants to business units, Baris said. Outsourcing software support gives Pfizer clout when it comes to resolving technical problems, he added. "We've experienced tremendous frustration trying to get any one software vendor to accept responsibility for a problem. And every company we've talked to about client/server has expressed the same frustration," Baris said. Since making the switch, Baris said, user feedback has been positive, in part because Corporate Software has installed a help desk at its Canton facility. Pfizer intends to sign up for a CD-ROM software distribution service being created by Corporate Software. "Our service is designed to allow employees to focus on business problems, and we'll take care of the tactical issues," said Randy Burkhart, vice president and general manager of the services business unit at Corporate Software.

a. Why did Pfizer outsource PC software support?
b. Is this a good idea for other types of businesses? Explain.

Source: Adapted from Michael Vizard, "Pfizer Gains Support," *Computerworld*, March 8, 1993, p. 8. Used with permission.

3. Holiday Inns and Twentieth Century-Fox Film: Using Global Systems Integrators

"We're faced with having installations in quite a lot of different countries. If we try to source our hardware needs locally, it takes a lot of effort," said Ian Butterworth, regional vice president responsible for international information technology at Holiday Inns, Inc., in Brussels. Holiday Inns' primary data center is located in Atlanta, but the hotelier maintains IS operations in its management offices in Brussels and Hong Kong, as well as in each of the company's 200 international hotels. To better support these operations, Holiday Inns relies on International Computer Group (ICG), a Paris-based systems integrator. For example, Butterworth said Holiday Inns used ICG last year to install IBM's OfficeVision systems in its Hong Kong offices. ICG coordinated the effort from Paris by using a slew of computer equipment suppliers in the Pacific Rim. Butterworth said the arrangement suited him just fine. "For me, it makes the difference between dealing with one contact and five different hardware vendors. It's a hell of a lot easier to deal with one central contact, and it helps us focus on where our IT spending is going," Butterworth noted.

Twentieth Century-Fox Film Corp. takes a similar approach to global IS projects. The Los Angeles-based motion picture producer has 30 offices worldwide, with 15 of those requiring information systems. According to Jean-Pierre Salib, director of systems responsible for all foreign subsidiaries in MIS, Twentieth Century-Fox has used ICG as a single point of contact for hardware and services in France, England, Holland, Italy, Spain, and Germany. Using a central IS provider has helped the filmmaker in several key areas, Salib said. Because Twentieth Century-Fox works exclusively with ICG to provide equipment and services internationally, the vendor is aware of the user's standard hardware and software guidelines. Salib, who is based in Paris, said it is easier for him to deal with ICG in Paris than it is to deal with other vendors across different time zones. Plus, because Twentieth Century-Fox does not have an IS staff for its smaller offices in Europe, the company relies on ICG to provide services such as network administration.

a. What do systems integrators do?

b. Why do global companies link Holiday Inns and Twentieth Century-Fox use systems integrators?

Source: Adapted from Thomas Hoffman, "Bridging the IS Continental Divide," *Computerworld*, March 8, 1993, p. 87. Used with permission.

4. Citicorp: Managing Global Telecommunications Networks

One year after launching a global effort to consolidate more than 100 telecommunications networks, Citicorp has reduced costs by $60 million, some $10 million more than originally estimated, bank officials said. The bank said its better than expected savings were achieved by the following measures:

- Consolidating five worldwide telcom centers into one.
- Blending eight help desks into one.
- Standardizing on networking platforms and protocols.

The Citicorp Global Information Network (CGIN) initiative is a key component of Citicorp's cost-cutting endeavors, which include software and hardware asset management programs. CGIN is an effort by Citicorp to develop a single global backbone for all company networks based on the Open Systems Interconnect (OSI) standard so Citicorp's products and services can be accessed through any location on the network. Citicorp executives said the consolidations have resulted in minimal staff reductions. CGIN currently has 1,100 network and telecommunications staff members worldwide. The CGIN project is also meant to give Citicorp a competitive advantage as the $219.3 billion bankholding company further expands its telecommunications services to end users and customers.

a. Why is Citicorp consolidating its global telecommunications networks?

b. What benefits have resulted?

Source: Adapted from Thomas Hoffman, "Citicorp Reaps Net Benefits," *Computerworld*, March 15, 1993, p. 6. Used with permission.

Application Exercises

1. Acme Trucking Company

The Acme Trucking Company is planning to distribute a Christmas bonus to its divers. They want the bonuses they distribute to give an extra reward to drivers who have been with the firm for several years (since turnover has been a problem for Acme) and whose efficiency rating is particularly high. Thus a two-part bonus is planned, with a portion determined by years of service and a second component paid only to those drivers with a high efficiency rating.

The president of Acme has proposed the following criteria for bonuses:

Employees with less than five years of service	$500
Employees with more than five years of service	$900
Additional bonus for employees whose efficiency rating is 90 or above	$750

However, he wants to be able to see the effects of changes in any of the bonus parameters (years of service to earn the higher bonus, efficiency rating needed to earn the additional bonus, and the bonus dollar amounts) on the amount of bonus money paid. Then he will meet with the vice presidents of operations, finance, and human resource management to finalize plans for distributing the bonuses.

a. Prepare a spreadsheet, based on the data shown in Figure 11.23, that will give the amount of bonus paid to each driver and the total cost of the bonus plan using the president's initial estimates, and produce a printout of your results.

b. Change the parameters of your spreadsheet as follows:

Years of service required for the higher bonus	Seven years
Efficiency rating required for added bonus	95
Bonus levels	
Less than seven years	$500
Seven years or more	$1,100
Efficiency bonus	$1,000

Get a printout showing the results of these changes.

c. Write a short memo recommending a bonus plan for Acme, with an explanation of why you are recommending it.

d. Write a short critique of the bonus planning process at Acme, with recommendations on how it could be improved.

2. ABC Shipping Company

ABC Shipping Company has decided to implement a new inventory control system by purchasing a software package from a vendor and adapting it. A three-member committee was selected to evaluate the packages supplied by competing vendors and select the best package. This committee has identified four vendors whose software seems to meet their minimum requirements. It has developed a set of criteria, shown below, to be used in evaluating the alternative packages. The committee has also agreed on a set of weights to be used based on the relative importance of these criteria. For instance, flexibility is considered three times as important as

Driver's Name	Years of Service	Efficiency Rating
Barnes, Joseph	3	92
Coles, Joyce	6	97
Varney, Alex	9	82
Norris, Bill	5	90
Ferris, John	2	94
Lewis, Ann	4	88
Adams, Ansel	12	98
Yates, Billie	1	93
Mason, Berry	5	76
Davis, Jack	1	91
Evans, Alan	6	86
Macy, Doyle	16	89
Towns, Dawn	3	95
Smith, Dan	5	77

FIGURE 11.23
Drivers' years of service and efficiency ratings.

	Jones				Ellis				Flowers			
Category	A	B	C	D	A	B	C	D	A	B	C	D
Efficiency	7	8	5	9	6	9	7	8	5	7	6	9
Flexibility	8	6	8	7	9	7	8	8	7	7	9	8
Security	5	7	9	6	6	8	10	7	6	7	9	5
Language	8	9	7	8	8	10	7	10	7	8	7	9
Documentation	9	5	8	7	10	4	9	7	9	6	9	7
Hardware	9	7	9	5	9	6	9	6	10	6	8	5

FIGURE 11.24

	Ratings					
Category	Jones	Ellis	Flowers	Averate Rating	Weight	Weighted Score
Efficiency	7	6	5	6	.10	.60
Flexibility	8	9	7	8	.30	2.40
Security	5	6	6	5.67	.10	.57
Language	8	8	7	7.67	.15	1.15
Documentation	9	10	9	9.67	.20	1.93
Hardware	9	9	10	9.33	.15	1.40
				Total weighted score		8.05

FIGURE 11.25

efficiency for this system and thus is assigned 30 percent of the total evaluation, while efficiency counts for only 10 percent.

Criteria	Weight
Efficiency	10%
Flexibility	30
Security	10
Language	15
Documentation	20
Hardware	15

After demonstrations by vendors (A, B, C, D), of the three committee members (John Jones, Jean Ellis, Sandra Flowers) evaluated the performance of each of the alternative software packages in each of the evaluation categories, giving a score from 1 to 10. The ratings compiled by the committee members are shown in Figure 11.24.

An overall rating for each package is to be computed by averaging the three ratings for each category, multiplying that average by the weighting factor for that category, and finally adding these weighted scores for all categories to produce an overall score. For example, the overall rating for vendor A would be calculated as shown in Figure 11.25.

a. Create a spreadsheet to record these ratings and calculate the weighted score for each package. Your spreadsheet should have an output area that allows just the weighted scores, by category and total, to be printed. Get a printout of the entire spreadsheet and a separate printout showing just this output area.

b. Create a graph of your spreadsheet that will allow the weighted average scores for the packages on each evaluation category to be compared.

c. Briefly explain how the committee could use their weighted scores to select the best software package.

Review Quiz Answers

1. *14a*
2. *14b*
3. *2a*
4. *2b*
5. *16*
6. *16a*
7. *18*
8. *19*
9. *10*
10. *17*
11. *4*
12. *25*
13. *21*
14. *6*
15. *7*
16. *8*
17. *15*
18. *27*
19. *26*
20. *28*
21. *24*
22. *3*
23. *20*
24. *9*
25. *12*
26. *30*
27. *5*
28. *1*
29. *13a*
30. *13b*
31. *13c*
32. *13d*
33. *13e*
34. *29*

Selected References

1. Alavi, Maryam, and Gregory Young. "Information Technology in an International Enterprise: An Organizing Framework." In Palvia et al., *The Global Issues of Information Technology Management.* Harrisbury, Pa.: Idea Group Publishing, 1992.
2. Allen, Brandt, and Andrew Boynton. "Information Architecture: In Search of Effecient Flexibility." *MIS Quarterly*, December 1991.
3. Beath, Cynthia. "Supporting the Information Technology Champion." *MIS Quarterly*, September 1991.
4. Brittlestone, Robert. "Computerization: Out of Control?" *Computerworld*, March 12, 1990.
5. Carlyle, Ralph. "The Tomorrow Organization." *Datamation*, February 1, 1990.
6. Carper, William. "Societal Impacts and Consequences of Transborder Data Flows." In Palvia et al., *The Global Issues of Information Technology Management.* Harrisburg, Pa.: Idea Group Publishing, 1992.
7. Cash, James, Jr.; F. Warren McFarlan; James McKenney; and Lynda Applegate. *Corporate Information Systems Management: Text and Cases.* 3rd ed. Homewood, Ill.: Richard D. Irwin, 1992.
8. Clark, Thomas. "Corporate Systems Management: An Overview and Research Perspective." *Communications of the ACM*, February 1992.
9. Couger, J. Daniel. "New Challenges in Motivating MIS Personnel." In *Handbook of IS Management.* 3rd ed. Boston: Auerbach, 1991.
10. Drucker, Peter. "The Coming of the New Organization." *Harvard Business Review*, January/February 1988.
11. Frenzel, Carroll. *Management of Information Technology.* Boston: Boyd & Fraser, 1992.
12. Fried, Louis. "A Blueprint for Change." *Computerworld*, December 2, 1991.
13. Goodhue, Dale; Judith Quillard; and John Rockart. "Managing the Data Resource: A Contingency Perspective." *MIS Quarterly*, September 1988.
14. Ives, Blake, and Sirkka Jarvenpaa. "Applications of Global Information Technology: Key Issues for Management." *MIS Quarterly*, March 1991.
15. Keen, Peter. *Computing in Time: Using Telecommunications for Strategic Advantage.* New York: Ballinger, 1988.
16. Keen, Peter. *Shaping the Future: Business Design through Information Technology.* Boston: Harvard Business School, 1991.
17. King, William, and Vikram Sethi. "A Framework for Transnational Systems." In Palvia et al., *The Global Issues of Information Technology Management.* Harrisburg, Pa.: Idea Group Publishing, 1992.
18. King, William, and Vikram Sethi. "An Analysis of International Information Regimes." *International Information Systems*, January 1992.
19. Leavitt, H. J., and T. L. Whisler. "Management in the 1980s." *Harvard Business Review*, November/December 1958.
20. Manheim, Marvin. "Global Information Technology: Issues and Strategic Opportunities." *International Information Systems*, January 1992.
21. McFarlan, F. Warren. "The Expert's Opinion." *Information Resources Management Journal*, Fall 1991.
22. McFarlan, F. Warren. "Multinational CIO: Challenge for the 1990s." In Palvia et al., *The Global Issues of Information Technology Management.* Harrisburg, Pa.: Idea Group Publishing, 1992.
23. Morison, Robert. "The Shape of IS to Come." *Indications*, July/August 1990.

24. Moynihan, Tony. "What Chief Executives and Senior Managers Want from Their IT Departments." *MIS Quarterly*, March 1990.

25. Niederman, Fred; James Brancheau; and James Weatherbe. "Information Systems Management Issues for the 1990's." *MIS Quarterly*, December 1991.

26. O'Brien, James, and James Morgan. "A Multidimensional Model of Information Resource Management." *Information Resources Management Journal*, Spring 1991.

27. Palvia, Shailendra; Prashant Palvia; and Ronald Zigli, eds. *The Global Issues of Information Technology Management*. Harrisburg, Pa.: Idea Group Publishing, 1992.

28. Roche, Edward. *Managing Information Technology in Multinational Corporations*. New York: Macmillan, 1992.

29. Rochester, Jack, and David Douglass. "Building a Global IT Infrastructure." *I/S Analyzer*, June 1991.

30. Rockart, John, and James Short. "IT in the 1990s: Managing Organizational Interdependence." *Sloan Management Review*, Winter 1989.

31. Tom, Paul. *Managing Information as a Corporate Resource*. 2nd ed. New York: HarperCollins, 1991.

32. Wiseman, Charles. *Strategic Information Systems*. Homewood, Ill.: Richard D. Irwin, 1988.

Security and Ethical Challenges of Information Technology

CHAPTER OUTLINE

CHAPTER 12

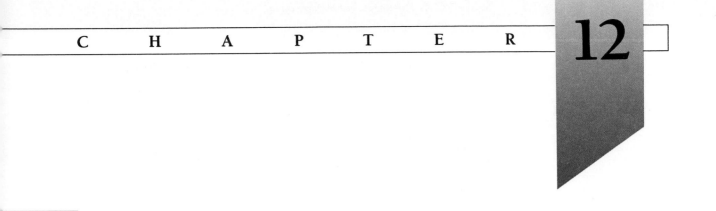

LEARNING OBJECTIVES

The purpose of this chapter is to give you an understanding of how managers should manage and control the use of information systems in an organization by analyzing (1) control methods for information system performance and security, and (2) ethical and societal challenges of information technology.

Section I discusses how the quality and security of information systems can be promoted by a variety of information system, procedural, and facility controls.

Section II discusses fundamental ethical concepts in business and information technology and how society is affected by IT in employment, individuality, working conditions, privacy, crime, health, and solutions to societal problems.

After reading and studying this chapter, you should be able to:

1. Outline several types of information system controls, procedural controls, and physical facility controls that can be used to ensure the quality and security of information systems.
2. Discuss ways to control the performance and security of end user computing systems.
3. Identify several ethical principles that affect the use and management of information technology.
4. Identify several ethical issues in how information technology affects employment, individuality, working conditions, privacy, crime, health and solutions to societal problems.
5. Identify what end users and IS managers can do to lessen the harmful effects and increase the beneficial effects of information technology.

SECTION
Information Systems Security and Control

Why Controls Are Needed

As a manager, you will be responsible for the control of the quality and performance of information systems in your business unit. Like any other vital business asset, the resources of information systems hardware, software, and data need to be protected by built-in controls to ensure their quality and security. That's why controls are needed. Computers have proven that they can process huge volumes of data and perform complex calculations more accurately than manual or mechanical information systems. However, we know that (1) errors do occur in computer-based systems, (2) computers have been used for fraudulent purposes, and (3) computer systems and their software and data resources have been accidentally or maliciously destroyed.

There is no question that computers have had some detrimental effect on the detection of errors and fraud. Manual and mechanical information processing systems use paper documents and other media that can be visually checked by information processing personnel. Several persons are usually involved in such systems and, therefore, cross-checking procedures are easily performed. These characteristics of manual and mechanical information processing systems facilitate the detection of errors and fraud.

Computer-based information systems, on the other hand, use machine-sensible media such as magnetic disks and tape. They accomplish processing manipulations within the electronic circuitry of a computer system. The ability to check visually the progress of information processing activities and the contents of databases is significantly reduced. In addition, a relatively small number of personnel may effectively control processing activities that are critical to the survival of the organization. Therefore, the ability to detect errors and fraud can be reduced by computerization. This makes the development of various control methods a vital consideration in the design of new or improved information systems.

Effective controls are needed to ensure **information system security**, that is, the accuracy, integrity, and safety of information system activities and resources. Controls can minimize errors, fraud, and destruction in an information services organization. Effective controls provide **quality assurance** for information systems. That is, they can make a computer-based information system more free of errors and fraud and able to provide information products of higher quality than manual types of information processing. This can help reduce the potential negative impact (and increase the positive impact) that information technology can have on business survival and success and the quality of life in society.

What Controls Are Needed

Three major types of controls must be developed to ensure the quality and security of information systems. These control categories, illustrated in Figure 12.1, are:

- Information system controls.
- Procedural controls.
- Physical facility controls.

Information System Controls

Information system controls are methods and devices that attempt to ensure the accuracy, validity, and propriety of information system activities. Controls must be developed to ensure proper data entry, processing techniques, storage methods, and information output. Thus, information system controls are designed to monitor and

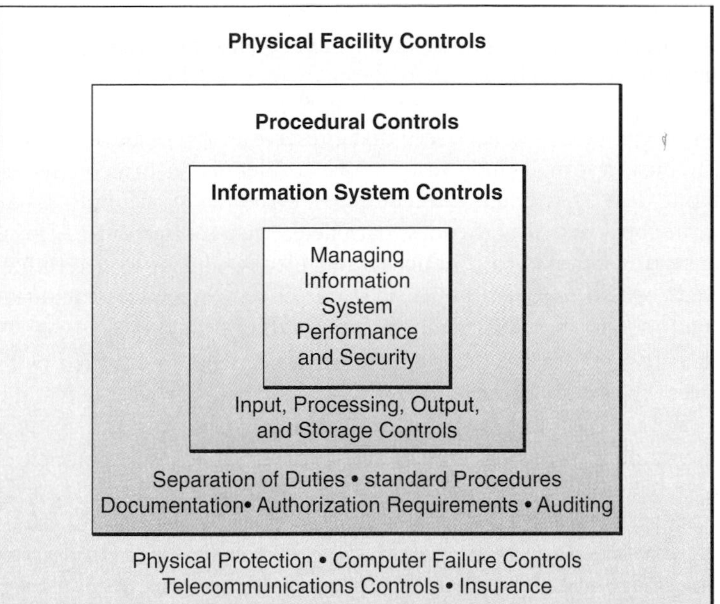

FIGURE 12.1
The controls needed for information system security. Specific types of controls can be grouped into three major categories: information systems, procedural, and physical facility controls.

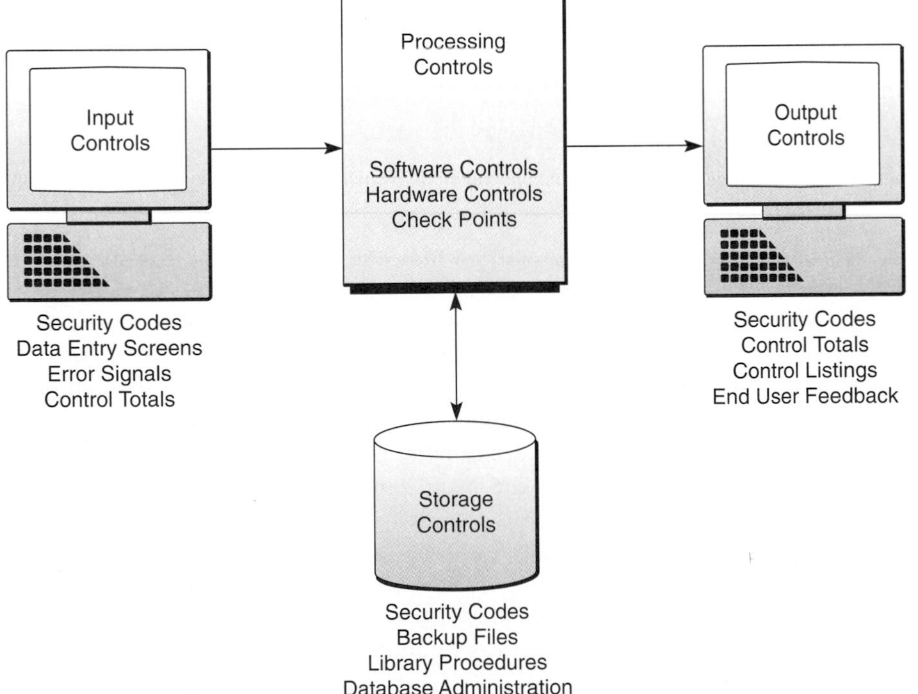

FIGURE 12.2
Examples of information system controls. Note that they are designed to monitor and maintain the quality and security of the input, processing, output, and storage activities of an information system.

maintain the quality and security of the input, processing, output, and storage activities of any information system. See Figure 12.2.

Input Controls

Have you heard the phrase "garbage in, garbage out (GIGO)"? That's why controls are needed for the proper entry of data into an information system. Examples include passwords and other security codes, formatted data entry screens, audible error signals, templates over the keys of key-driven input devices, and prerecorded and prenumbered forms. Input of source documents can also be controlled by registering them in a logbook when they are received by data entry personnel. Realtime systems that use direct access files frequently record all entries into the system on magnetic tape *control logs* that preserve evidence of all system inputs. Computer software can include instructions to identify incorrect, invalid, or improper input data as it enters the computer system. For example, a data entry program can check for invalid codes, data fields, and transactions. Also, the computer can be programmed to conduct reasonableness checks to determine if input data exceeds certain specified limits or is out of sequence. This includes the calculation and monitoring of selected **control totals**.

Data entry and other systems activities are frequently monitored by the use of control totals. For example, a record count is a control total that consists of counting the total number of source documents or other input records and comparing this total to the number of records counted at other stages of input preparation. If the totals do not match, a mistake has been made. Batch totals and hash totals are other forms of control totals. A *batch total* is the sum of a specific item of data within a batch of transactions, such as the sales amounts in a batch of sales transactions. *Hash totals* are the sum of data fields that are added together for control comparisons only. For example, employee social security numbers could be added to produce a control total in the input preparation of payroll documents.

Processing Controls

Once data is entered correctly into a computer system, it must be processed properly. Processing controls are developed to identify errors in arithmetic calculations and logical operations. They are also used to ensure that data are not lost or do not go unprocessed. Processing controls can include hardware controls and software controls.

Hardware Controls

Hardware controls are special checks built into the hardware to verify the accuracy of computer processing. Examples of hardware checks include:

- **Malfunction detection circuitry** within the computer that can monitor its operations. For example, *parity checks* are made to check for the loss of the correct number of bits in every byte of data processed. Another example is *echo checks*, which require that a signal be returned from a device or circuit to verify that it was properly activated. Other examples are redundant circuitry checks, arithmetic sign checks, and CPU timing and voltage checks.
- **Redundant components.** For example, multiple read-write heads on magnetic tape and disk devices check and promote the accuracy of reading and recording activities.
- **Switches and other devices.** For example, switches can be set that prohibit writing on magnetic tapes or disks. On magnetic tape reels, a removable plastic or metal ring can be removed to prevent writing on a tape. The write/protect notch on floppy disks has a similar function.
- **Special-purpose microprocessors and associated circuitry** that may be used to support *remote diagnostics* and maintenance. These allow off-site technicians to diagnose and correct some problems via a telecommunications link to the computer.

Software Controls

Some software controls are designed to ensure that the right data is being processed. For example, the operating system or other software checks the internal file labels at the beginning and end of magnetic tape and disk files. These labels contain information identifying the file as well as provide control totals for the data in the file. These internal file labels allow the computer to ensure that the proper storage file is being used and that the proper data in the file have been processed.

Another major software control is the establishment of checkpoints during the processing of a program. *Checkpoints* are intermediate points within a program being processed where intermediate totals, listings, or dumps of data are written on magnetic tape or disk or listed on a printer. Checkpoints minimize the effect of processing errors or failures, since processing can be restarted from the last checkpoint, rather than from the beginning of the program. They also help build an **audit trail**, which allows transactions being processed to be traced through all of the steps of processing.

Many input, processing, output, and storage controls may be provided by specialized system software packages known as **system security monitors.** System security monitors are programs that monitor the use of a computer system and protect its resources from unauthorized use, fraud, and destruction. Such programs provide the computer security needed to allow only authorized users to access the system. For example, identification codes and passwords are frequently used for this purpose. Security monitors also control the use of the hardware, software, and data resources of a computer system. For example, even authorized users may be restricted to the use of certain devices, programs, and data files. Finally, such programs monitor the use of the computer and collect statistics on any attempts at improper use. They produce reports to assist in maintaining the security of the system. See Figure 12.3.

Output Controls

How can we control the quality of the information products produced by an information system? Output controls are developed to ensure that information products are correct and complete and are transmitted to authorized users in a

Courtesy of Computer Associates.

FIGURE 12.3
Using a system security monitor: CA-Top Secret. Note how it records end user passwords and account activity.

timely manner. Several types of output controls are similar to input control methods. For example, output documents and reports are frequently logged, identified with route slips, and visually verified by input/output control personnel. Control totals on output are usually compared with control totals generated during the input and processing stages. Control listings can be produced that provide hard copy evidence of all output produced.

Prenumbered output forms can be used to control the loss of important output documents such as stock certificates or payroll check forms. Distribution lists help input-output control personnel ensure that only authorized users receive output. Access to the output of realtime processing systems is typically controlled by security codes that identify which users can receive output and the type of output they are authorized to receive. Finally, end users who receive output should be contacted for feedback on the quality of the output. This is an important function of systems maintenance and quality assurance activities.

Storage Controls

How can we protect our data resources? First, control responsibilities for files of computer programs and organizational databases may be assigned to a librarian or database administrator. These employees are responsible for maintaining and controlling access to the libraries and database of the organization. Second, many databases and files are protected from unauthorized or accidental use by security programs that require proper identification before they can be used. Typically, the operating system or security monitor protects the databases of realtime processing systems from unauthorized use or processing accidents. Account codes, passwords, and other **security codes** are frequently used to allow access to authorized users only. A catalog of authorized users enables the computer system to identify eligible users and determine which types of information they are authorized to receive.

Typically, a three-level password system is used. First, an end user logs on to the computer system by entering his or her unique identification code or user ID. The end user is then asked to enter a *password* in order to gain access into the system. Finally, to access an individual file, a unique *file name* must be entered. In some systems, the password to read the contents of a file is different from that required to write to a file (change its contents). This feature adds another level of protection to stored data resources.

Many firms also use *backup files,* which are duplicate files of data or programs. Such files may be stored off-premises, that is, in a location away from the computer center, sometimes in special storage vaults in remote locations. Many realtime processing systems use duplicate files that are updated by telecommunication links. Files are also protected by *file retention* measures, which involve storing copies of master files and transaction files from previous periods. If current files are destroyed, the files from previous periods are used to reconstruct new current files. Usually, several *generations* of files are kept for control purposes. Thus, master files from several recent periods of processing (known as *child, parent, grandparent* files, and so on) may be kept for backup purposes.

Procedural Controls

Procedural controls are methods that specify how the information services organization should be operated for maximum security. They facilitate the accuracy and integrity of computer operations and systems development activities.

Separation of Duties

Separation of duties is a basic principle of procedural control. It requires that the duties of systems development, computer operations, and control of data and program files be assigned to separate groups. For example, systems analysts and computer programmers may not be allowed to operate corporate mainframes or make changes to data or programs being processed. In addition, the responsibility for maintaining a library of data files and program files is assigned to a librarian or database administrator. Finally, a production control section may monitor the progress of information processing jobs, data entry activities, and the quality of input/output data. This is an important *quality assurance* function.

Standard Procedures and Documentation

Manuals of standard procedures for the operation of information systems are typically developed and maintained. Following standard procedures promotes uniformity and minimizes the chances of errors and fraud. It helps employees know what is expected of them in operating procedures and output quality. It is important that procedures be developed for both normal and unusual operating conditions. For example, procedures should tell employees what to do differently when their computers are not working. Finally, system, program, and operations documentation must be developed and kept up-to-date to ensure the correct processing of each application. Documentation is also invaluable in the maintenance of a system as needed improvements are made.

Authorization Requirements

Requests for systems development, program changes, or computer processing are frequently subjected to a formal review before authorization is given. For example, program changes generated by maintenance programmers should be approved by the manager of programming after consultation with the manager of computer operations and the manager of the affected end user department. Conversion to new hardware and software, installation of newly developed information systems, and changes to existing programs should be subjected to a formal notification and scheduling procedure. This minimizes their detrimental effects on the accuracy and integrity of ongoing computer operations.

Disaster Recovery

Natural and man-made disasters do happen. Hurricanes, earthquakes, fires, floods, criminal and terrorist acts, and human error can all severely damage an organization's computing resources, and thus the health of the organization itself. Many organizations, like airlines and banks, for example, are crippled by losing even a few hours of computing power. Many firms could survive only a few days without computing facilities. That's why organizations develop disaster recovery procedures and formalize them in a *disaster recovery plan.* It specifies which employees will participate in disaster recovery and what their duties will be, what hardware, software, and facilities will be used, and the priority of applications that will be processed. Arrangements with other companies for use of alternative facilities as a disaster recovery site and offsite storage of an organization's databases are also part of an effective disaster recovery effort.

Physical Facility Controls

Physical facility controls are methods that protect physical facilities and their contents from loss or destruction. Computer centers are subject to such hazards as accidents, natural disasters, sabotage, vandalism, unauthorized use, industrial espionage, destruction, and theft of resources. Therefore, physical safeguards and various control procedures are necessary to protect the hardware, software, and vital data resources of computer-using organizations. Figure 12.4 outlines major control strategies and specific control methods that are recommended to protect the information system resources of organizations and their end users.

Physical Protection Controls

Providing maximum security and disaster protection for a computer installation requires many types of controls. Only authorized personnel are allowed access to the

FIGURE 12.4
Recommended control strategies and methods to protect information system recources.

Control Strategy	Objective	Control Methods
Containment	Control access	Affect environment Reduce target attractiveness
	Isolate assets	Control access to target Plug holes in defense Remove target from threat
Deterrence	Deter motives	Advertise punishment Increase chances of being caught
	Prevent threats	Detect early Thwart attack
	Detect results	Detect all activity Review audit trails
Obfuscation	Conceal assets	Cryptography Hide physical assets Control proprietary information
	Disperse assets	Backup and recovery Alternative processing Multiple locations Isolation (barriers)
Recovery	Replace assets	Emergency procedures Backup and recovery Contingency planning
	Transfer loss	Insurance

Source: Adapted from Gerald Isaacson, "Physical Security Measures," in *The Handbook of MIS Management*, ed. Robert Umbaugh (Pennsauken, N.J.: Auerback Publishers, 1985), p. 610.

computer center through such techniques as identification badges for information services personnel, electronic door locks, burglar alarms, security police, closed-circuit TV, and other detection systems. The computer center should be protected from disaster by such safeguards as fire detection and extinguishing systems; fireproof storage vaults for the protection of files; emergency power systems; electromagnetic shielding; and temperature, humidity, and dust control.

Biometric Controls

Biometric controls are a fast-growing area of computer security. These are security measures provided by computer devices which measure physical traits that make each individual unique. This includes voice verification, fingerprints, hand geometry, signature dynamics, keystroke analysis, retina scanning, face recognition, and genetic pattern analysis. Biometric control devices use special-purpose sensors to measure and digitize a *biometric profile* of an individual's fingerprints, voice, or other physical trait. The digitized signal is processed and compared to a previously processed profile of the individual stored on magnetic disk. If the profiles match, the individual is allowed entry into a computer facility or given access to information system resources.

Telecommunications Controls

The telecommunications processors and control software described in Chapter 6 play a vital role in the control of data communications activity. In addition, data can be transmitted in scrambled form and unscrambled by the computer system for authorized users only. This process is called **encryption**. It transforms digital data into a scrambled code before it is transmitted and then decodes the data when it is received. Special hardware and software must be used for the encryption process. Other control methods are typically used, such as an automatic disconnect and callback system where the computer hangs up after you log on and calls you back to be sure you are at an authorized terminal.

Computer Failure Controls

"Sorry, the computer is down" is a well-known phrase to many end users. A variety of controls are needed to prevent such computer failure or minimize its effects. Computers fail for several reasons—power failure, electronic circuitry malfunctions, mechanical malfunctions of peripheral equipment, hidden programming errors, and computer operator errors. The information services department typically takes steps to prevent equipment failure and to minimize its detrimental effects. For example, computers with automatic and remote maintenance capabilities may be acquired. A program of preventive maintenance of hardware may be established. Adequate electrical supply, air conditioning, humidity control, and fire prevention standards must also be set. A backup computer system capability may be arranged with other computer-using organizations. Major hardware or software changes should be carefully scheduled and implemented to avoid problems. Finally, computer operators should have adequate training and supervision.

Many firms also use **fault tolerant** computer systems to ensure against computer failure. These systems have multiple central processors, peripherals, and system software. This may provide a *fail-safe* capability where the computer system continues to operate at the same level even if there is a major hardware or software failure. However, many fault tolerant computer systems offer a *fail-soft* capability where the computer system can continue to operate at a reduced but acceptable level in the event of a major system failure.

Controls for End User Computing

In Chapter 7, we outlined some of the risks of end user application development. We also discussed measures companies are taking to ensure the quality and security of end user applications. However, many firms are beginning to realize that, in many cases, end user–developed applications are performing extremely important business functions. Instead of merely being systems for personal productivity or decision support, these applications are supporting the accomplishment of important business activities that are critical to the success and survival of the firm. Thus, they can be called *company-critical* end user applications.

Figure 12.5 outlines what one major company defines as company-critical end user systems. It also summarizes the specific controls that must be observed or built in to all company-critical end user applications. What this firm and others are trying to do is protect themselves from the havoc that errors, fraud, destruction, and other hazards could cause to these critical applications and thus to the company itself. The controls involved are those that are standard practice in applications developed by professional IS departments. However, such controls were ignored in the rush to end user computing.

Figure 12.5 emphasizes a major point for managerial end users. Who is ultimately responsible for ensuring that proper controls are built in to company-critical applications? End user managers are! This emphasizes once again that managerial end users must accept the responsibility for managing the information system resources of their work groups, departments, and other business units.

Auditing Information Systems

An information services department should be periodically examined, or *audited,* by internal auditing personnel from the business firm. In addition, periodic audits by external auditors from professional accounting firms are a good business practice. Such audits should review and evaluate whether proper and adequate information

FIGURE 12.5
Criteria and controls for company-critical end user applications.

- A systems development approach that includes provisions for testing to determine whether the system is doing what it was designed to do and is consistent with company databases.
- Methods for notifying users when any changes in the system are planned and for testing the effect of those changes on live databases.
- Methods for validating compliance with formal work procedures.
- Documentation so that a system can survive the departure of its creator.
- Means for securing the physical system, data storage media, sign-on, file systems and printed information.
- Formal backup and recovery procedures.
- Training at least two people in the operation and maintenance of a system.
- A formal process for justifying and coordinating hardware and software acquisitions that includes a definition of the scope and purpose of the system, its business benefits, and a cost-benefit evaluation.

Source: Adapted from Jeff Moad, "The Second Wave," *Datamation*, February 1, 1989, p. 17.

system controls, procedural controls, physical facility controls, and other managerial controls have been developed and implemented. There are two basic approaches for auditing the information processing activities of computer-based information systems. They are known as (1) auditing around the computer and (2) auditing through the computer.

Auditing around a computer involves verifying the accuracy and propriety of computer input and output without evaluating the computer programs used to process the data. This is a simpler and easier method that does not require auditors with programming experience. However, this auditing method does not trace a transaction through all of its stages of processing and does not test the accuracy and integrity of computer programs. Therefore, it is recommended only as a supplement to other auditing methods.

Auditing through the computer involves verifying the accuracy and integrity of the computer programs that process the data, as well as the input and output of the computer system. Auditing through the computer requires a knowledge of computer operations and programming. Some firms employ special EDP auditors for this assignment. Special test data may be used to test processing accuracy and the control procedures built into the computer program. The auditors may develop special test programs or use audit software packages. See Figure 12.6.

EDP auditors use such programs to process their test data. Then they compare the results produced by their audit programs with the results generated by the computer user's own programs. One of the objectives of such testing is to detect the presence of unauthorized changes or patches to computer programs. Unauthorized program patches may be the cause of otherwise unexplainable errors or may be used for fraudulent purposes.

Auditing through the computer may be too costly for some computer applications. Therefore, a combination of both auditing approaches is usually employed. However, both auditing approaches must effectively contend with the changes caused by computer-based information systems to the *audit trail*.

An **audit trail** can be defined as the presence of documentation that allows a transaction to be traced through all stages of its information processing. This journey begins with a transaction's appearance on a source document and ends with its transformation into information on a final output document. The audit trail of

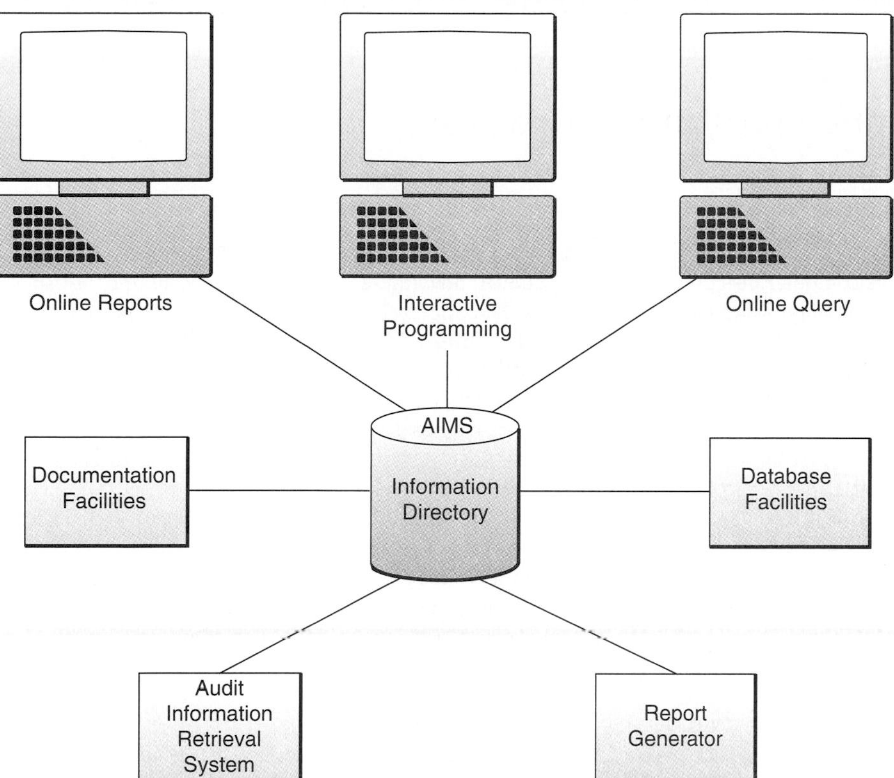

Source: Courtesy Computer Associates.

FIGURE 12.6
An example of the capabilities of an audit software package. This is Computer Associates' Audit Information Management System (AIMS).

manual information systems was quite visible and easy to trace. However, computer-based information systems have changed the form of the audit trail. Information formerly available to the auditor in the form of visual records is no longer available or is recorded on media that can be interpreted only by machines. For example, realtime transaction processing systems have increased the invisibility of the traditional audit trail. Paper documents and historical files are frequently eliminated when remote terminals and direct access files are used.

Such developments make the auditing of such systems a complex but vital assignment. Therefore, auditing personnel should be included on the project team of all major systems development projects and consulted before smaller critical systems projects are implemented. In addition, auditing personnel should be notified of changes to major computer programs caused by program maintenance activities. Such procedures give the auditor the opportunity to suggest methods of preserving the audit trail. The auditor can also ensure that adequate controls are designed into systems being developed or modified.

REAL WORLD CASE

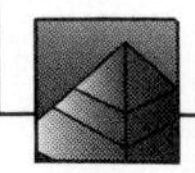

Virgin Atlantic and British Airways: Electronic Burglary

Settlement of a case in which Virgin Atlantic Airways accused British Airways of hacking its computer files to steal passenger lists underscores the vulnerability of supposedly confidential flight information. Airline analysts said the reservation systems of most major carriers are very open—and hence more vulnerable—because they are designed to share information in order to facilitate passenger travel. "All the airlines have access to each other's reservation system," said Tamir Rankow, chairman of the national automation committee of the American Society of Travel Agents in Washington, D.C. But, he cautioned, "that doesn't give them free access to the passenger name record. But I suppose a person just has to be at the right place at the right time to get anything they want."

Rankow added that the competitive battles now bloodying the airline industry could encourage the use of such espionage. "As they stumble over each other trying to get each other's first-class and business traffic, I suspect anything is possible," he said.

In the London lawsuit, the charges came as part of a bitter libel feud in which British Airways admitted making improper attempts to undermine its rival and agreed to pay Virgin Chairman Richard Branson and his company approximately $935,000 (610,000 pounds) in damages and more than $3 million in court costs. Had the libel case gone to trial, former British Airways employee Sadig Khalifa was prepared to testify to the illegal use of Virgin's counsel, Colin Howes of the London law firm Harbottle & Lewis.

According to Khalifa, he and other British Airways staff were shown how to tap into a segment of the British Airways Booking System computer that Virgin rented. Eventually, British Airways was allegedly able to obtain home telephone numbers of first-class passengers and other information on bookings and departure times. According to Virgin's lawyers, passengers were then called by British Airways staff who tried to get them to change their tickets to British Airways flights.

Security consultants said the type of corporate espionage British Airways was allegedly involved in is typical and quite simple. "This is a very, very easy procedure, requiring only a trip to Radio Shack to buy a couple hundred dollars worth of electronics," said Charles Cresson Wood, an independent security consultant in Sausalito, California. Wood added that such computer wiretap cases do not frequently come up on the news because "a lot of people don't know they're being wiretapped. These taps can go on for years before (or if) they are ever discovered."

CASE STUDY QUESTIONS

1. What is hacking? Is this case an example of hacking? Explain.
2. What IS security controls could have protected Virgin Atlantic? Explain.
3. What other types of business computing are vulnerable to hacking?

Source: Adapted from Elizabeth Heichler, "Airline Hacking Case Reveals CRS' Security Shortcomings," *Computerworld*, January 18, 1993, p. 2. Used with permission.

SECTION II

Ethical and Societal Challenges of Information Technology

The Ethical Dimension

Many see an ethical crisis in American business today. Activities such as fraud and consumer deception, kickbacks and bribery, insider trading, government contracting improprieties, conflicts of interest, questionable advertising claims, illegal disposal of hazardous materials, intentional violations of workplace safety regulations, and the laundering of drug-trafficking money by financial institutions are becoming all too commonplace. When such illegal activity is coupled with legal but unethical or questionable activities such as the "dumping" of pesticides banned in the U.S. in Third World countries; maintaining South African investments that directly support the practice of apartheid; engaging in less than honorable sales negotiations; using bluffing and deception to reach labor agreements; providing gratuities or sexual favors to prospective private buyers—it is no wonder that the public image of business and corporate life suffers [14].

Whether we are in an ethical crisis or not is a subject of debate. But what is not debatable is that we are in the midst of an **information revolution**, in which information technology has dramatically magnified our ability to acquire, manipulate, store, and communicate information. Thanks to information technology, we have electronic tools which let us retrieve and communicate information in seconds to practically any person, in any place, at any time of the day. Thanks to IT, we can now communicate easily, work cooperatively, share resources, and make decisions, all electronically. But also thanks to information technology, it has now become possible to engage in ethical or unethical business practices electronically anywhere in the world.

That's why it is important for you to understand the ethical dimensions of working in business and using information technology. As a future managerial end user, it will be your responsibility to make decisions about business activities and the use of IT which will always have an ethical dimension that must be considered.

For example, should you electronically monitor your employees' work activities and electronic mail? Should you let employees use their work computers for private business, or take home copies of software for their personal use? Should you electronically access your employees' personnel records or workstation files? Should you sell information about your customers, extracted from transaction processing systems, to other companies? These are a few examples of the types of decisions you will have to make which have a controversial ethical dimension. So let's take a closer look at ethical considerations in business and information technology.

Ethical Foundations

There are several *ethical philosophies* which you can use to help guide you in ethical decision making. Four basic ethical philosophies are egoism, natural law, utilitarianism, and respect for persons [9]. Briefly, these alternative ethical philosophies are:

Egoism. What is best for a given individual is right.

Natural law. Humans should promote their own health and life, propagate, pursue knowledge of the world and God, pursue close relationships with other people, and submit to legitimate authority.

Utilitarianism. Those actions are right that produce the greatest good for the greatest number of people.

Respect for persons. People should be treated as an end and not as a means to an end; and actions are right if everyone adopts the moral rule presupposed by the action.

There are many theories of how humans apply their chosen ethical philosophies to the decisions and choices they have to make daily in work and other areas of their lives. For example, one theory focuses on people's decision-making processes, and stresses how various factors or our perceptions of them affect our ethical decision-making process. Figure 12.7 illustrates this **ethical model.** Notice how individual attributes; personal, professional, and work environments; and government/legal and social environments may affect our decision processes and lead to ethical or unethical behavior.

Another example is a *behavioral stage* theory, which says that people go through several stages of *moral evolution* before they settle on one level of ethical reasoning. Figure 12.8 illustrates the stages in this model of ethical behavior. In this

FIGURE 12.7
A model of ethical decision making. Note the factors that may affect our ethical decision making process.

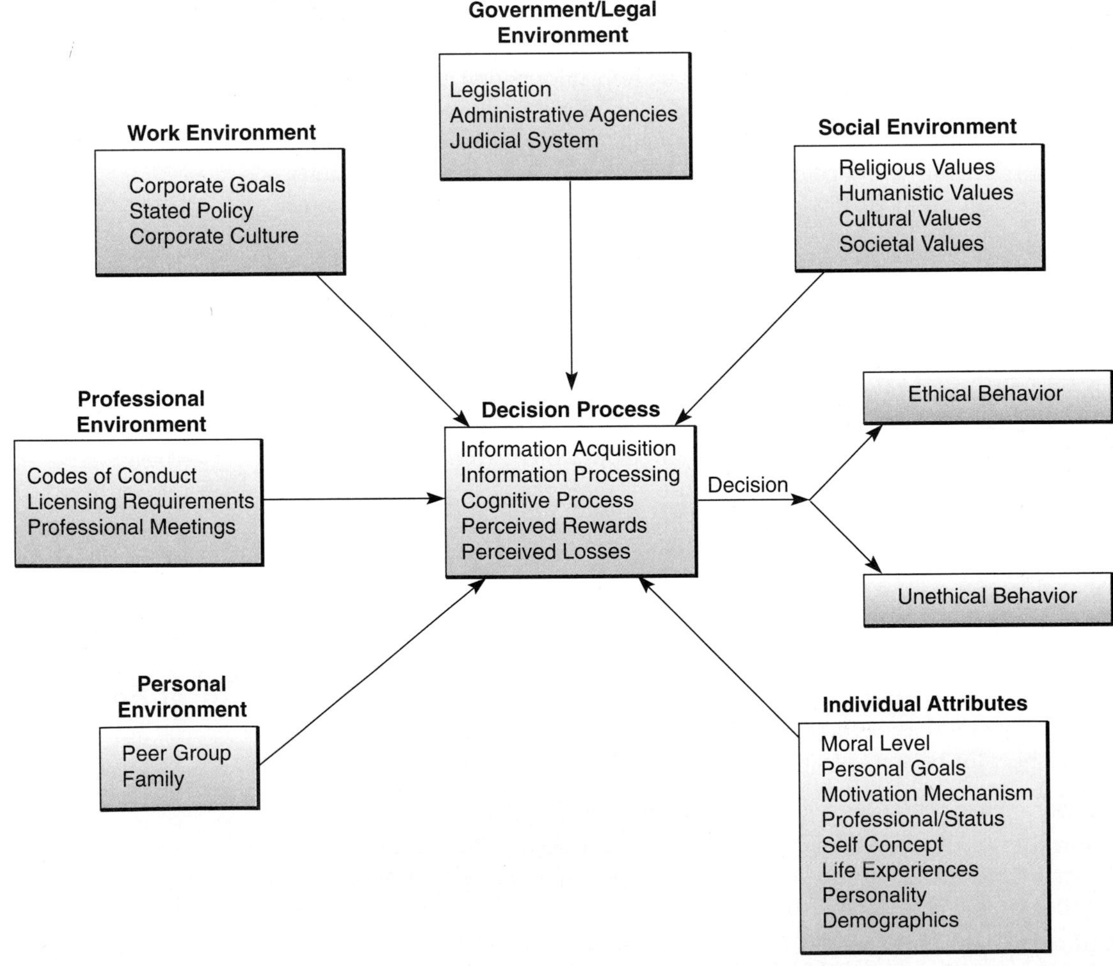

Source: Adapted from Michael Bommer et al., "A Behavioral Model of Ethical and Unethical Decision Making," in Roy Dejoie et al., *Ethical Issues in Information Systems* (Boston: Boyd & Fraser, 1991), p. 19.

model, if you reach the final stage of moral evolution, your actions are guided by self-chosen ethical principles, not by fear, guilt, social pressure, and so on.

Business Ethics

Business ethics is concerned with answering two basic questions:

- How do business professionals come to *know* what is right in carrying out business tasks?
- How can they then *do* what is right once they have recognized it?

In terms of its content, business ethics can be subdivided into two separate areas [14]. The first is sometimes called *managerial mischief*. It concerns the illegal, unethical, or questionable practices of managers or organizations, their causes, and their possible remedies. The second can be called *moral mazes in management*. It is concerned with the numerous ethical questions that managers must confront as part of their daily business decision making. For example, Figure 12.9 outlines some of the basic categories of ethical issues and specific business practices that have serious ethical consequences. Notice that the issues of employee privacy, security of company records, and workplace safety are highlighted because they have been major areas of ethical controversy in information technology.

Ethical and Societal Dimensions of IT

Figure 12.10 illustrates several important aspects of the ethical and societal dimensions of information technology. It emphasizes that the use of information technology in business has major impacts on society, and thus raises serious ethical considerations in areas such as privacy, crime, health, working conditions, individuality, employment, and the search for societal solutions through IT. However, you should realize that information technology can have a beneficial effect, as well as a negative effect, in each of these areas. For example, computerizing a production process may have the adverse effect of eliminating jobs, and the beneficial effect of

FIGURE 12.8
Stages of moral evolution. Note how people may evolve in their moral orientation through several levels of ethical reasoning.

Stages of Morality		Illustrative Behavior
Level I: Preconventional morality		
Stage 1	Punishment orientation	Obeys rules to avoid punishment
Stage 2	Reward orientation	Conforms to obtain rewards or to have favors returned
Level II: Conventional morality		
Stage 3	Good-boy/good-girl orientation	Conforms to avoid disapproval of others
Stage 4	Authority orientation	Upholds laws and social rules to avoid censure of authorities and guilt about not "doing one's duty"
Level III: Postconventional morality		
Stage 5	Social-contract orientation	Actions guided by principles commonly agreed on as essential to the public welfare—upheld to retain respect of peers and self-respect
Stage 6	Ethical principle orientation	Actions guided by self-chosen ethical principles (that usually value justice, dignity, and equality)—upheld to avoid self-condemnation

Source: Adapted from Gerald Baxter and Charles Rarick, "Education for the Moral Development of Managers: Kohberg's Stages of Moral Development and Integrative Education," in Roy Dejoie et al., *Ethical Issues in Information Systems* (Boston: Boyd & Fraser, 1991), p. 39.

FIGURE 12.9
Basic categories of ethical business issues. Information technology has caused ethical controversy in the areas of employee privacy, security of company records, and workplace safety.

Equity	Rights	Honesty	Exercise of Corporate Power
Executive Salaries Comparable Worth Product Pricing	Corporate Due Process Employee Health Screening *Employee Privacy* Sexual Harassment Affirmative Action Equal Employment Opportunity Shareholder Interests Employment at Will Whistle-blowing	Employee Conficts of Interest *Security of Company Records* Inappropriate Gifts Advertising Content Government Contract Issues Financial and Cash Management Procedures Questionable Business Practices in Foreign Countries	Political Action Committees *Workplace Safety* Product Safety Environmental Issues Disinvestment Corporate Contributions Social Issues Raised by Religious Organizations Plant/Facility Closures and Downsizing

Source: Adapted from The Conference Board, "Defining Corporate Ethics," in Peter Madsen and Jay Shafritz, *Essentials of Business Ethics* (New York: Meridian, 1990), p. 18.

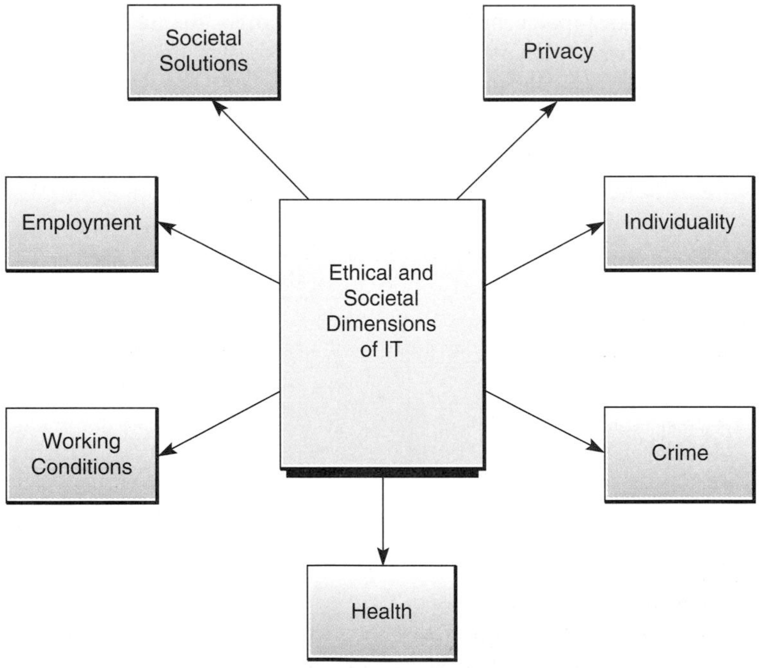

FIGURE 12.10
Major aspects of the ethical and societal dimensions of information technology. Remember that IT can have both a positive and a negative effect on society in each of the areas shown.

improving the working conditions and job satisfaction of employees that remain, while producing products of higher quality at less cost. So your job as a managerial end user should involve managing your work activities and those of others to try to minimize the negative effects of IT and maximize its beneficial effects. That would represent an ethically responsible use of information technology.

Ethics and Information Technology

To help you in making such ethical choices, it might be helpful to keep in mind four **ethical principles** that can serve as guidelines in the implementation of any form of technology [15].

- **Proportionality.** The good achieved by the technology must outweigh the harm or risk. Moreover, there must be no alternative that achieves the same or comparable benefits with less harm or risk.
- **Informed consent.** Those affected by the technology should understand and accept the risks.
- **Justice.** The benefits and burdens of the technology should be distributed fairly. Those who benefit should bear their fair share of the risks, and those who do not benefit should not suffer a significant increase in risk.
- **Minimized risk.** Even if judged acceptable by the other three guidelines, the technology must be implemented so as to avoid all unnecessary risk.

Another way to understand the ethical dimensions of IT is to consider the basic ethical issues that arise from its use. Richard Mason has posed four basic ethical issues, which deal with the vulnerability of people to information technology [8]. It is based on the concept that information forms the intellectual capital of individual human beings. However, information systems can rob people of their intellectual capital. For example, people can lose information without compensation and without their permission. People can also be denied access to information or be exposed to erroneous information. Mason summarizes these four ethical issues with the acronym PAPA—privacy, accuracy, property, and accessibility.

- **Privacy.** What information about one's self or one's associations must a person reveal to others, under what conditions, and with what safeguards? What things can people keep to themselves and not be forced to reveal to others?
- **Accuracy.** Who is responsible for the authenticity, fidelity, and accuracy of information? Similarly, who is to be held accountable for errors in information and how is the injured party to be made whole?
- **Property.** Who owns information? What are the just and fair prices for its exchange? Who owns the channels, especially the airways, through which information is transmitted? How should access to this scarce resource be allocated?
- **Accessibility.** What information does a person or an organization have a right or a privilege to obtain, under what conditions, and with what safeguards?

In answering these questions, Mason proposes the development of a new social contract, where information technology will help ensure everyone's right to fulfill his or her human potential. In this new social contract, information systems should be designed to ensure accuracy and not invade a person's privacy. Channels of information should be protected and information made accessible to avoid information illiteracy or deprivation. Finally, information systems should be designed to protect an individual's intellectual capital from unauthorized exposure, loss, or damage. Developing, protecting, and enforcing this social contract then becomes the responsibility of end users, managers, and IS professionals.

IT and Employment

The impact of information technology on **employment** is a major ethical concern and is directly related to the use of computers to achieve automation. There can be no doubt that the use of information technology has created new jobs and increased productivity, while also causing a significant reduction in some types of job opportunities. Computers used for office information processing or for the numerical control of machine tools are accomplishing tasks formerly performed by many clerks and machinists. Also, jobs created by information technology within a computer-using organization require different types of skills and education than do the jobs eliminated by computers. Therefore, individuals may become unemployed unless they can be retrained for new positions or new responsibilities.

However, there can be no doubt that information technology has created a host of new job opportunities for the manufacture, sale, and maintenance of computer hardware and software, and for other information system services. Many new jobs, such as systems analysts, computer programmers, and computer operators, have been created in computer-using organizations. New jobs have also been created in service industries that provide services to the computer industry and to computer-using firms. Additional jobs have been created because information technology makes possible the production of complex industrial and technical goods and services that would otherwise be impossible to produce. Thus, jobs have been created by activities that are heavily dependent on information technology, in such areas as space exploration, microelectronic technology, and scientific research.

IT and Individuality

A frequent criticism of information technology concerns its negative effect on the **individuality** of people. Computer-based systems are criticized as impersonal systems that dehumanize and depersonalize activities that have been computerized, since they eliminate the human relationships present in noncomputer systems. Although it is more efficient for an information system to deal with an individual as a number than as a name, many people feel a loss of identity when they seem to be just another number.

Another aspect of the loss of individuality is the regimentation of the individual that seems to be required by some computer-based systems. These systems do not seem to possess any flexibility. They demand strict adherence to detailed procedures if the system is to work. The negative impact of IT on individuality is reinforced by horror stories that describe how inflexible and uncaring computer-based systems are when it comes to rectifying their own mistakes. Many of us are familiar with instances where computerized customer billing and accounting systems continued to demand payment and send warning notices to a customer whose account has already been paid, despite repeated attempts by the customer to have the error corrected.

However, computer-based systems can be ergonomically engineered to accommodate **human factors** that minimize depersonalization and regimentation. Figure 12.11 outlines some of the human factors that are accommodated in the design of application software. People-oriented and user-friendly information systems can thus be developed. The computer hardware, software, graphical user interface, and other IT capabilities that make such systems possible are increasing rather than decreasing. For example, use of microcomputers has dramatically improved the development of people-oriented end user and work group information systems. Even everyday products and services have been improved through microprocessor-powered "smart" products.

IT and Working Conditions

Information technology has eliminated monotonous or obnoxious tasks in the office and the factory that formerly had to be performed by people. For example, word processing and desktop publishing make producing office documents a lot easier to do, while robots have taken over repetitive welding and spray painting jobs in the

Human Factor	End User Computer Knowledge	
	Novice	**Experienced**
1. Tone	Explanatory and polite	Short and to the point
2. Use of humor	Careful	None
3. Bypasses	None	Allow
4. Warnings	Many	Rarely
5. Screen format	Menu	Inquiry
6. Input verification	Always	Rarely
7. Highlighting	Some (judiciously)	Little
8. Defaults	With explanation	Without explanation
9. Screen discontinuation	Keyed response to prompt	Keyed response without prompt
10. Help function	Full, unsolicited	Upon request

Source: Adapted from Merle P. Martin, "Adaptive General Audience Modes: A Research Framework," in *Human Factors in Management Information Systems, ed. Jane M. Carey* (Norwood, N.J.: Ablex Publishing, 1988), p. 73.

FIGURE 12.11
Human factors can be accommodated in the design of applications software to support a range of end users.

automotive industry. In many instances, this allows people to concentrate on more challenging and interesting assignments, upgrades the skill level of the work to be performed, and creates challenging jobs requiring highly developed skills in the computer industry and within computer-using organizations. Thus, information technology can be said to upgrade the *quality of work* because it can upgrade the quality of working conditions and the content of work activities.

Of course, it must be remembered that some jobs created by information technology, data entry, for example, are quite repetitive and routine. Also, to the extent that computers are utilized in some types of automation, IT must take some responsibility for the criticism of assembly-line operations that require the continual repetition of elementary tasks, thus forcing a worker to work like a machine instead of like a skilled craftsperson. Many automated operations are also criticized for relegating people to a do-nothing standby role, where workers spend most of their time waiting for infrequent opportunities to "push some buttons." Such effects do have a detrimental effect on the quality of work, but they must be compared to the less burdensome and more creative jobs created by information technology.

Computer Monitoring

One of the most explosive ethical issues concerning the quality of work is **computer monitoring.** That is, computers are being used to monitor the productivity and behavior of millions of employees while they work. Supposedly, computer monitoring is done so employers can collect productivity data about their employees to increase the efficiency and quality of service. However, computer monitoring has been criticized as unethical because it monitors individuals, not just work, and is done continually, thus violating workers' privacy and personal freedom. For example, when you call to make a reservation, an airline reservation agent may be timed on the exact number of seconds he or she took per caller, the time between calls, and the number and length of breaks taken. In addition, your conversation may also be monitored [8, 10]. See Figure 12.12.

Computer monitoring has been criticized as an invasion of the privacy of employees because, in many cases, they do not know that they are being monitored or don't know how the information is being used. Critics also say that an employee's right of due process may be harmed by the improper use of collected data to make personnel decisions. Since computer monitoring increases the stress on employees

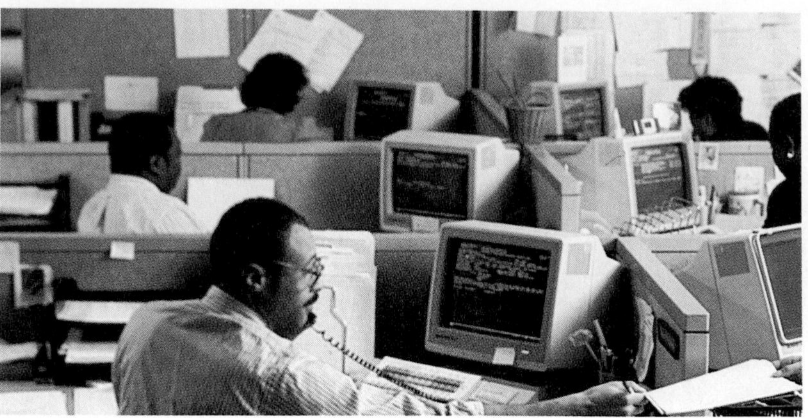

FIGURE 12.12
Computer monitoring can be used to record the productivity and behavior of people while they work.

Richard Palsey/Stock Boston.

who must work under constant electronic surveillance, it has also been blamed for causing health problems among monitored workers. Finally, computer monitoring has been blamed for robbing workers of the dignity of their work. In effect, computer monitoring creates an "electronic sweatshop," where workers are forced to work at a hectic pace under poor working conditions.

Political pressure is building to outlaw or regulate computer monitoring in the workplace. For example, the Privacy for Consumers and Workers Act is working its way through both houses of the U.S. Congress. This proposed law would regulate computer monitoring and protect the worker's right to know and right to privacy. Public advocacy groups, labor unions, and many legislators are pushing for action. In the meantime, lawsuits by monitored workers against employers are increasing rapidly. Jury awards to workers have been in the hundreds of thousands of dollars [8]. Thus, computer monitoring of workers is one ethical issue that won't go away.

Privacy Issues

Information technology makes it technically and economically feasible to collect, store, integrate, interchange, and retrieve data and information quickly and easily. This characteristic has an important beneficial effect on the efficiency and effectiveness of computer-based information systems. However, the power of information technology to store and retrieve information can have a negative effect on the **right to privacy** of every individual. Confidential information on individuals contained in centralized computer databases by credit bureaus, government agencies, and private business firms has been stolen or misused, resulting in the invasion of privacy, fraud, and other injustices. The unauthorized use of such information has seriously damaged the privacy of individuals. Errors in such databases could seriously hurt the credit standing or reputation of an individual.

Some of the important privacy issues being debated in business and government include the following [23]:

- Accessing individuals' private conversations and records (*violation of privacy*).
- Always knowing where a person is—especially as mobile and paging services become more closely associated with people rather than places (*computer monitoring*).
- Using customer information to market additional business services (*computer matching*).

- Collecting telephone numbers and other personal information to build individual customer profiles (*unauthorized personal files*).
- Using automated equipment either to originate calls or to collect caller information (*caller identification*).

Computer Matching

Unauthorized use or mistakes in the **computer matching** of personal data is another controversial threat to privacy. Individuals have been mistakenly arrested and jailed, and people have been denied credit because their physical profiles or social security numbers have been used to match them incorrectly or improperly with the wrong individuals. A newer threat is the unauthorized matching of computerized information about you extracted from the databases of sales transaction processing systems, and sold to *information brokers* or other companies. You are then subjected to a barrage of unsolicited promotional material and sales contacts [10].

Such developments were possible before the advent of computers. However, the speed and power of large computer systems networked to direct access databases and remote terminals greatly increases the potential for such injustices. The trend toward nationwide telecommunication networks with integrated databases by business firms and government agencies substantially increases the potential for the misuse of computer-stored information.

Privacy Laws

In the United States, the Federal Privacy Act strictly regulates the collection and use of personal data by governmental agencies (except for law enforcement investigative files, classified files, and civil service files). The law specifies that individuals have the right to inspect their personal records, make copies, and correct or remove erroneous or misleading information. It also specifies that federal agencies (1) must annually disclose the types of personal data files they maintain, (2) cannot disclose personal information on an individual to any other individual or agency except under certain strict conditions, (3) must inform individuals of the reasons for requesting personal information from them, (4) must retain personal data records only if it is "relevant and necessary to accomplish" an agency's legal purpose, and (5) must "establish appropriate administrative, technical, and physical safeguards to ensure the security and confidentiality of records" [8, 10, 20].

In 1986, the Electronic Communications Privacy Act and the Computer Fraud and Abuse Act were enacted by the U.S. Congress. These federal laws are a major attempt to enforce the privacy of computer-based files and communications. These laws prohibit intercepting data communications messages, stealing or destroying data, or trespassing in federal government–related computer systems [5]. In 1988, the Computer Matching and Privacy Act became law in the United States. It regulates the matching of data held in federal agency files to verify eligibility for federal programs. Such legislation should emphasize and accelerate the efforts of systems designers to use hardware, software, and procedural controls to maintain the accuracy and confidentiality of computerized databases.

Computer Crime

Computer crime is a growing threat caused by the criminal or irresponsible actions of a small minority of computer professionals and end users who are taking advantage of the widespread use of computers and information technology in our society. It thus presents a major challenge to the ethical use of IT. Computer crime also poses serious threats to the security of computer-based information systems and makes the development of effective control methods a top priority.

Computer Crime Laws

One way to understand computer crime is to see how current legislation defines it. A good example of this is the U.S. Computer Fraud and Abuse Act of 1986. In a nutshell, this law says that computer crime involves access of "federal interest" computers (used by the federal government), or operating in interstate or foreign commerce (1) with intent to defraud, (2) resulting in more than a $1,000 loss, or (3) to gain access to certain medical computer systems. Trafficking in computer access passwords is also prohibited. Penalties for violations of this law are severe. They include 1 to 5 years in prison for a first offense, 10 years for a second offense, and 20 years for three or more offenses. Fines could range up to $250,000 or twice the value of stolen data [8, 10].

The Data Processing Management Association (DPMA) defines computer crime more specifically. In its Model Computer Crime Act, the DPMA defines computer crime as including (1) the unauthorized use, access, modification, and destruction of hardware, software, or data resources, (2) the unauthorized release of information, (3) the unauthorized copying of software, (4) denying an end user access to his or her own hardware, software, or data resources, and (5) using or conspiring to use computer resources to illegally obtain information or tangible property.

Examples of Computer Crime

Another way to understand computer crime is to examine examples of major types of criminal activity involving computers. This typically involves the theft of money, services, software and data, destruction of data and software, especially by *computer viruses,* malicious access or *hacking,* violation of privacy, and violations of antitrust or international law [9, 20]. Figure 12.13 illustrates the results of a survey to identify computer crime.

Money Theft

Many computer crimes involve the theft of money. They almost always involve fraudulent alteration of computer files to cover the tracks of the thieves, or to swindle money from others based on falsified records. For example, in the famous Volkswagen AG case of 1987, a group of company executives altered computerized foreign exchange accounting files to hide their theft of almost $253 million. In the most famous computer swindle, The Equity Funding case of 1977, a group of con artists used a large insurance company's computers to generate thousands of falsified insurance policies with a face value of over $2 billion. The policies were then used as collateral to swindle investors out of more than $600 million for worthless stock in a fictitious company.

FIGURE 12.13
Types of computer crime. Note that theft of money and services are the most prevalent criminal acts.

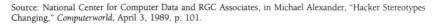

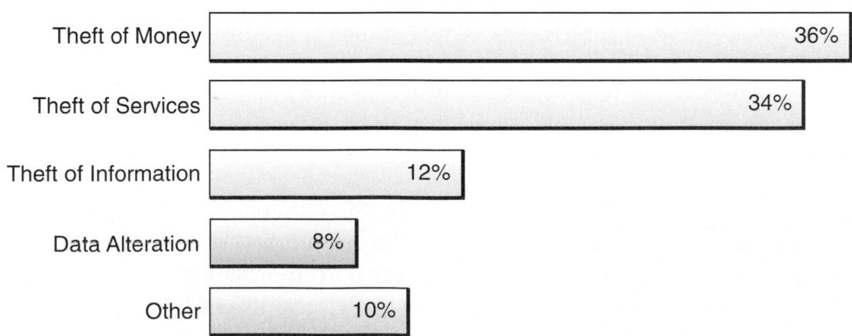

Source: National Center for Computer Data and RGC Associates, in Michael Alexander, "Hacker Stereotypes Changing," *Computerworld,* April 3, 1989, p. 101.

Service Theft

The unauthorized use of a computer system is called service theft. A common example is unauthorized use of company-owned microcomputers by employees. This may range from doing private consulting or personal finances to playing video games. If it's unauthorized use of someone else's computer, it's service theft. More serious cases are also more blatant. In one example, the manager of a university computer center in New York state and his assistant secretly used the school's computer to provide a variety of commercial computing services to their business clients.

Software Theft

Computer programs are valuable property and thus are the subject of theft from computer systems. However, unauthorized copying of software or **software piracy** is also a major form of software theft. Several major cases involving the unauthorized copying of software have been widely reported. These include lawsuits by the Software Publishers Association, an industry association of software developers, against major corporations that allowed unauthorized copying of their programs. Lotus Development Corporation and other software companies have also won lawsuits against competitors who marketed copies, or *clones* that had the "look and feel" of their popular software packages.

Unauthorized copying is illegal because software is intellectual property which is protected by copyright law and user licensing agreements. For example, in the United States, commercial software packages are protected by the Computer Software Piracy and Counterfeiting Amendment to the Federal Copyright Act. In most cases, the purchase of a commercial software package is really a payment to license its "fair use" by an individual end user. Therefore, many companies sign site licenses which allow them to legally make a certain number of copies for use by their employees at a particular location. Other legal copying alternatives are *shareware,* which allows you to make copies of software for others, and *public domain* software, which is not copyrighted.

Data Alteration or Theft

Making illegal changes to data is another form of computer crime. For example, an employee of the University of Southern California was convicted of taking payments from students for changing their grades. Other reported schemes involved changes in credit information, and changes in Department of Motor Vehicles records that facilitated the theft of the cars to which the records referred. More recently, employees of the U.S. Social Security Administration were indicted for selling confidential personal information to *information brokers*. Also indicted were Virginia state police and other officers who sold criminal histories from the National Crime Information Center database [3]. See Figure 12.14.

Computer Viruses: Destruction of Data and Software

One of the most destructive examples of computer crime involves the creation of **computer viruses** or *worms*. Virus is the more popular term but, technically, a virus is a program code that cannot work without being inserted into another program. A worm is a distinct program that can run unaided. In either case, these programs copy annoying or destructive routines into the networked computer systems of anyone who accesses computers infected with the virus or who uses copies of magnetic disks taken from infected computers. Thus, a computer virus or worm can spread destruction among many users. Though they sometimes display only humorous messages, they more often destroy the contents of memory, hard disks, and other storage devices. Copy routines in the virus or worm spread the virus and destroy the data and software of many computer users.

FIGURE 12.14
Computer crime: illegal sale of confidential personal information in government files.

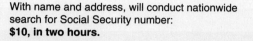

Dossiers for sale

A 1990 sales brochure from Nationwide Electronic Tracking in Tampa, Fla., provides the following price list for obtaining confidential information

With name and address, will conduct nationwide search for Social Security number: **$10, in two hours.**

With name and Social Security number, will obtain recent places of employment and subject's earnings (last 10 years): **$175, in three to five days.**

Subject's credit history: **$10, in one to two hours.**

Subject's criminal history: **$100, in one week.**

With subject's name and address, will obtain names, phone numbers and addresses of up to nine current neighbors: **$10, in one to two hours.**

Source: Mitch Betts, "Personal Data More Public Than You Think," *Computerworld*, March 9, 1992, p. 14.

A good example of the disruptive and destructive potential of computer viruses was the contamination of the Internet telecommunications network in November 1988. The computer virus was developed by Robert Morris, a graduate student at Cornell, who was convicted in 1990 of violating the Computer Fraud and Abuse Act. Its constant replication of itself overwhelmed the memory capacity of over 6,000 infected computers in the Internet network. Cost in computer time lost and cleanup efforts was estimated to exceed $100 million [9]. Figure 12.15 identifies a few of the hundreds of computer viruses that have been identified at infected computer sites.

Computer viruses typically enter a computer system through illegal or borrowed copies of software, or through network links to other computer systems. Copies of software downloaded from electronic bulletin boards can be another source of viruses. A virus usually copies itself into the files of a computer's operating system. Then the virus spreads to main memory and copies itself onto the computer's hard disk and any inserted floppy disks. The virus spreads to other computers through telecommunications links or floppy disks from infected computers. Thus, as a good end user computing practice, you should avoid using software from questionable sources without checking for viruses. You should also regularly use vaccine programs which can help diagnose and remove computer viruses from infected files on your hard disk or in a network. See Figure 12.16.

Malicious Access

Hacking, in computerese, is the obsessive use of computers, or the unauthorized access and use of computer systems. Illegal hackers may steal or damage data and programs. One of the issues in hacking is what to do about a hacker who commits only "electronic breaking and entering," that is, gets access to a computer system, reads some files, but neither steals nor damages anything. This situation is common in computer crime cases that are prosecuted. In California, a court found that the typical computer crime statute language prohibiting "malicious" access to a com-

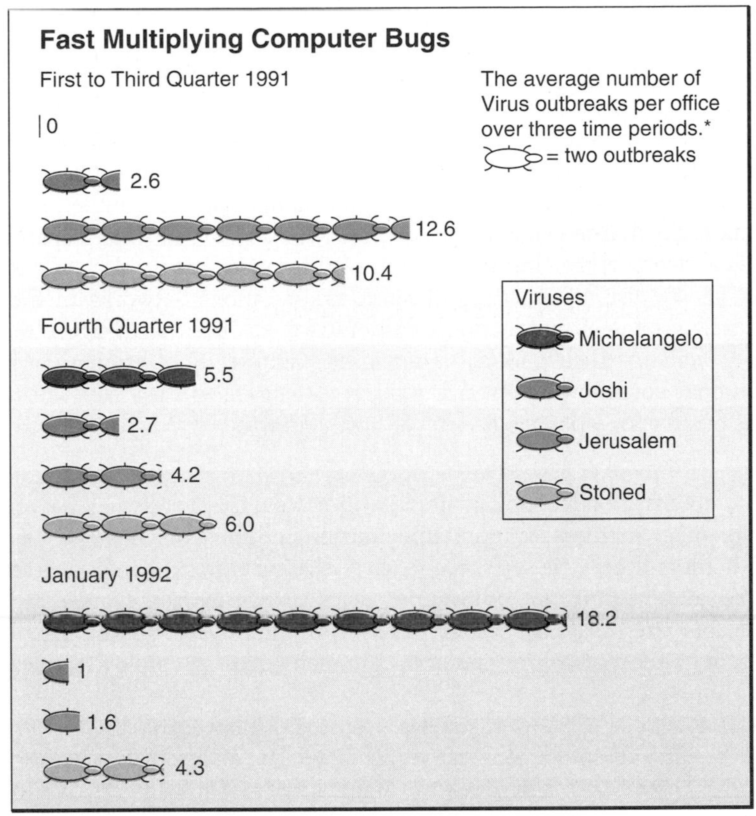

Source: Stephen Miller, "Sophisticated Virus-Fighters," *The New York Times,* March 8, 1992, p. 8, Business.

FIGURE 12.15
Examples of computer virus infections in business.

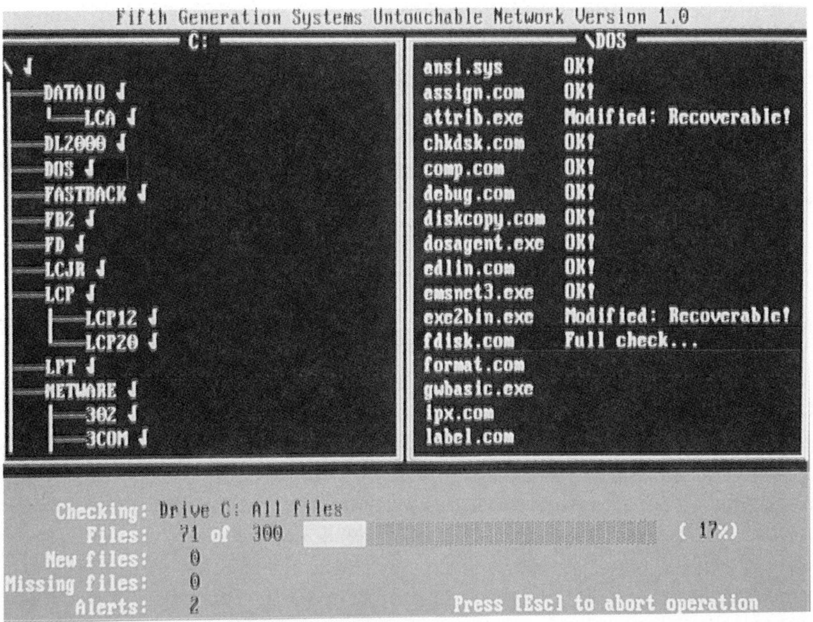

Courtesy of Texas Instruments.

FIGURE 12.16
An example of the display of a computer vaccine program to eliminate computer viruses.

puter system did apply to any users gaining unauthorized access to others' computer systems [9].

Violation of Antitrust or International Law

Computer-based information systems can violate antitrust or international laws and regulations. For example, some strategic information systems attempt to build business alliances that involve the sharing of telecommunications networks or other information system resources among organizations that are competitors in the marketplace. Such arrangements have been challenged by the U.S. Department of Justice as anticompetitive and in violation of the antitrust law. Also, as we saw in Chapter 11, the use of international telecommunications networks in the global information systems of multinational corporations has been challenged by several nations as violating their national sovereignty. Because such information systems cross national borders, they involve *transborder data flows* that may violate tariff, taxation, privacy, or labor regulations of host countries.

Health Issues

The use of information technology in the workplace raises a variety of health issues. Heavy use of computers is reportedly causing health problems like job stress, damaged arm and neck muscles, eye strain, radiation exposure, and even death by computer-caused accidents. For example, *computer monitoring* is blamed as a major cause of computer-related job stress. Workers, unions, and government officials criticize computer monitoring as putting so much stress on employees that it leads to health problems [8, 10].

People who sit at PC workstations or visual display terminals (VDTs) in fast-paced, repetitive-keystroke jobs can suffer a variety of health problems such as *cumulative trauma disorder* or *repetitive strain disorder*. Their fingers, wrists, arms, necks, and backs may become so weak and painful that they cannot work. Many times strained muscles, back pain, and nerve damage may result. Some computer workers also suffer from *carpal tunnel syndrome*, a painful, crippling ailment of the hand and wrist which typically requires surgery to cure [4].

Prolonged viewing of video displays causes eyestrain and other health problems in employees who must do this all day. Radiation caused by the *cathode ray tubes* (CRTs) that produce most video displays is another health concern. CRTs produce an electromagnetic field which may cause harmful radiation of employees who work too close for too long in front of video monitors. Some pregnant workers have reported miscarriages and fetal deformities due to prolonged exposure to CRTs at work. However, several studies have failed to find conclusive evidence concerning this problem. Still, several organizations recommend that female workers minimize their use of CRTs during pregnancy [19].

Ergonomics

Solutions to some of these health problems are based on the science of **ergonomics**, sometimes called *human factors engineering*. The goal of ergonomics is to design healthy work environments that are safe, comfortable, and pleasant for people to work in, thus increasing employee morale and productivity. Ergonomics stresses the healthy design of the workplace, workstations, computers and other machines, and even software packages. Other health issues may require ergonomic solutions emphasizing *job design*, rather than workplace design. For example, this may require policies providing for work breaks every few hours from heavy VDT use, while limiting the CRT exposure of pregnant workers. Ergonomic job design can also provide more variety in job tasks for those workers who spend most of their workday at computer workstations [2]. See Figure 12.17.

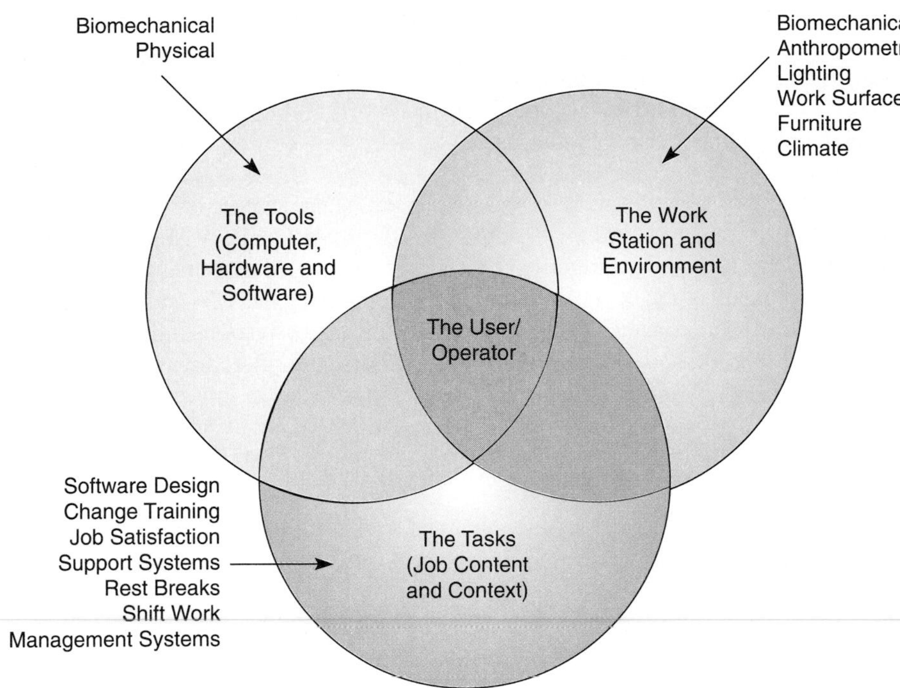

FIGURE 12.17
Ergonomic factors in the workplace. Note that good ergonomic design considers tools, tasks, the workstation, and environment.

Source: Adapted Courtesy of IBM Corporation.

Societal Solutions

Before we conclude this section, it would be good to emphasize that information technology can have many beneficial effects on society. Information technology can be used to solve human and social problems through societal applications such as medical diagnosis, computer-assisted instruction, governmental program planning, environmental quality control, and law enforcement. For example, computers can be used to help diagnose an illness, prescribe necessary treatment, and monitor the progress of hospital patients. Computer-assisted instruction (CAI) allows a computer to serve as "tutor," since it uses conversational computing to tailor instruction to the needs of a particular student. This is a tremendous benefit to students, especially those with learning disabilities.

Information technology can be used for crime control through various law enforcement applications. For example, computerized alarm systems allow police to identify and respond quickly to evidences of criminal activity. Computers have been used to monitor the level of pollution in the air and in bodies of water, to detect the sources of pollution, and to issue early warnings when dangerous levels are reached. Computers are also used for the program planning of many government agencies in such areas as urban planning, population density and land use studies, highway planning, and urban transit studies. Computers are being used in job placement systems to help match unemployed persons with available jobs. These and other applications illustrate that information technology can be used to help solve the problems of society.

You and Ethical Responsibility

As a business end user, you have a responsibility to do something about some of the abuses of information technology in the workplace. Whether you are a manager, end user, or IS professional, you should accept the ethical responsibilities that come with your work activities. That includes properly performing your role as a vital human resource in the computer-based information systems you help develop and use in your organization. In this section, we have outlined several ethical principles that can serve as the basis for ethical conduct by managers, end users, and IS professionals. But what more specific guidelines might help your ethical use of information technology?

One way to answer this question is to examine statements of responsibilities contained in codes of professional conduct for IS professionals. A good example is the code of professional conduct of the Data Processing Management Association (DPMA), an organization of professionals in the computing field. Its code of conduct outlines the ethical considerations inherent in the major responsibilities of an IS professional. Figure 12.18 is a portion of the DPMA code of conduct.

FIGURE 12.18
Part of the DPMA standards of professional conduct. This code can serve as a model for ethical conduct by end users as well as IS professionals.

DPMA Standards of Professional Conduct

In recognition of my obligation to my employer I shall:

- Make every effort to ensure that I have the most current knowledge and that the proper expertise is available when needed.
- Avoid conflicts of interest and ensure that my employer is aware of any potential conflicts.
- Present a fair, honest, and objective viewpoint.
- Protect the proper interests of my employer at all times.
- Protect the privacy and confidentiality of all information entrusted to me.
- Not misrepresent or withhold information that is germane to the situation.
- Not attempt to use the resources of my employer for personal gain or for any purpose without proper approval.
- Not exploit the weakness of a computer system for personal gain or personal satisfaction.

In recognition of my obligation to my profession I shall:

- Be honest in all my professional relationships.
- Take appropriate action in regard to any illegal or unethical practices that come to my attention. However, I will bring charges against any person only when I have reasonable basis for believing in the truth of the allegation and without regard to personal interest.
- Endeavor to share my special knowledge.
- Cooperate with others in achieving understanding and identifying problems.
- Not use or take credit for the work of others without specific acknowledgment and authorization.
- Not take advantage of the lack of knowledge or inexperience on the part of others for personal gain.

In recognition of my obligation to society I shall:

- Protect the privacy and confidentiality of all information entrusted to me.
- Use my skill and knowledge to inform the public in all areas of my expertise.
- To the best of my ability, ensure that the products of my work are used in a socially responsible way.
- Support, respect, and abide by the appropriate local, state, provincial, and Federal laws.
- Never misrepresent or withhold information that is germane to a problem or a situation of public concern nor will I allow any such known information to remain unchallenged.
- Not use knowledge of a confidential or personal nature in any unauthorized manner to achieve personal gain.

Source: Adapted from Bruce E. Spiro, "Ethics in the Information Age," *Information Executive*, Fall, 1989, p. 40.

REAL WORLD CASE

Cornell University: Computer Crime

An unofficial team of Apple Macintosh virus busters scored a victory last week by leading authorities to two virus authors and providing information that led to their arrests. This is one of the rare instances in which a virus author has been arrested for creating and disseminating a virus, said Eugene Spafford, a member of the Macintosh virus team. Spafford is also an assistant professor of computer science at Purdue University in West Lafayette, Indiana.

David S. Blumenthal and Mark A. Pilgram, both 19 and sophomores at Cornell University, were arraigned on Feb. 24 and charged with computer tampering in the second degree, a misdemeanor. Other charges will probably be filed after the investigation is completed, a Cornell public safety officer said. The Federal Bureau of Investigation is also probing the incident.

The students, who were arrested and released on bail, face a maximum penalty of one year in jail, the public safety officer said. They are accused of creating a Macintosh virus, known as MBDF-A, deliberately infecting two computer games with the virus, and using a third game as a Trojan horse to transport the virus. The students created all three games as well.

The virus infects the Macintosh's operating system software file and other applications by attaching itself to other programs. It was not designed to destroy data but could cause some infected programs to malfunction and perhaps cause system crashes, said Jeffrey Shulman, a team member and author of a shareware program called Virus-Detective.

The three games—Obnoxious Tetris, Tetricycle and Ten Tile Puzzle—were launched from a computer at Cornell via the Internet and deposited in several computerized archival systems around the world, including the Sumex-Aim at Stanford University.

"I'd say more than 200 people downloaded the games in a couple of days," said William Lipa, a team member who administers the Macintosh file section of the Sumex-Aim system at Stanford University.

A mathematics professor in Wales downloaded the games, discovered they were infected and sent copies of the virus for analysis to John Norstad, a team member. Norstad is the author of Disinfectant, an antivirus package, and a network analyst at the academic computing center at Northwestern University in Evanston, Illinois.

Norstad alerted Lipa, who determined that the games had been transmitted from Cornell. "It was very easy to see where they had purportedly been E-mailed from, which was an account at Cornell," Lipa said.

Other team members notified Cornell officials, who immediately began their own investigation. The logs of computer systems in a computer laboratory confirmed that the virus had been released at Cornell, a university spokeswoman said. "Both (students) were employed by the computer information lab, and it is believed that one of the computers in the lab, of which one of the guys was an operator, was used to launch this," the spokeswoman said. Following the discovery, the students were arrested, their rooms searched, and computer equipment and disks confiscated.

Cornell received national attention in November 1988 when Robert T. Morris, then a computer science graduate student, injected a worm program into the Internet international network and caused thousands of computers to crash.

CASE STUDY QUESTIONS

1. Why would two college students create and spread computer viruses?
2. Did David Blumenthal and Mark Pilgram commit a computer crime? If so, should they be punished?
3. What can be done to fight computer viruses?

Source: Adapted from Michael Alexander, "Mac Virus Busters Nab Two Suspects," *Computerworld*, March 2, 1992, p. 4. Used with permission.

The DPMA code provides guidelines for ethical conduct in the development and use of information technology. End users and IS professionals would live up to their ethical responsibilities by voluntarily following such guidelines. For example, you can be a **responsible end user** by (1) acting with integrity, (2) increasing your professional competence, (3) setting high standards of personal performance, (4) accepting responsibility for your work, and (5) advancing the health, privacy, and general welfare of the public. Then you would be demonstrating ethical conduct, avoiding computer crime, and increasing the security of any information system you develop or use.

As a business end user, you should insist that the ethical and societal dimensions of information technology be considered when computer-based information systems are being developed and used. For example, a major design objective should be to develop systems that can be easily and effectively used by people. The objectives of the system must also include protection of the privacy of the individuals and the defense of the system against computer crime. Control hardware, software, and procedures must be included in the systems design. The potential for misuse and malfunction of a proposed system must be analyzed and controlled with respect to all of an organization's present and potential stakeholders, individuals, and society as a whole.

It should be obvious to you that many of the detrimental effects of information technology are caused by individuals or organizations that are not accepting the ethical responsiblity for their actions. Like other powerful technologies, information technology possesses the potential for great harm or great good for all humankind. If managers, end users, and IS professionals accept their ethical responsibilities, then information technology can help make this world a better place for all of us.

Summary

- **IS Security and Control.** One of the most important responsibilities of the management of computer-using business firms is to assure the security and quality of its information services activities. Controls are needed that ensure the accuracy, integrity, and safety of the information system activities and resources of the organization and its end users. Such controls attempt to minimize errors, fraud, and destruction, and can be grouped into three major categories: (1) information system controls, (2) procedural controls, and (3) physical facility controls, as summarized in Figures 12.1 and 12.2.
- **The Ethical Foundations of IT.** Business and IT activities involve many ethical considerations. Various ethical philosophies and models of ethical behavior may be used by people in forming ethical judgments. These serve as a foundation for ethical principles and codes which can serve as guidelines for dealing with ethical business issues that may arise in the use of information technology.
- **Ethical and Societal Dimensions of IT.** Information technology raises serious ethical and societal issues in terms of the impact of IT on employment, individuality, working conditions, computer monitoring, privacy, computer matching, health, and computer crime. Managerial end users and IS professionals can help solve the problems of improper use of IT by assuming their ethical responsibilities for the ergonomic design, beneficial use, and enlightened management of information technology in our society.

Key Terms and Concepts

These are the key terms and concepts of this chapter. The page number of their first explanation is in parentheses.

1. Auditing information systems (453)
2. Audit trail (451)
3. Biometric controls (452)
4. Business ethics (459)
5. Computer crime (465)
   a. Examples (466)
   b. Laws (466)
6. Computer matching (465)
7. Computer monitoring (463)
8. Computer virus (467)
9. Control of end user computing (453)

10. Control totals (448)
11. Disaster recovery (451)
12. Encryption (452)
13. Ergonomics (470)
14. Ethical and societal dimensions of IT (459)
    a. Employment (461)
    b. Individuality (462)
    c. Health (470)
    d. Privacy (464)
    e. Societal solutions (471)
    f. Working conditions (462)
15. Ethical models (458)
16. Ethical philosophies (457)
17. Ethical principles (461)
18. Fault tolerant (453)
19. Hacking (468)
20. Human factors (462)
21. Information system controls (446)
22. Information system security (446)
23. Physical facility controls (451)
24. Privacy laws (465)
25. Procedural controls (450)
26. Quality assurance (446)
27. Responsible end user (471)
28. Security codes (450)
29. Software piracy (475)
30. System security monitor (449)

Review Quiz

Match one of the key terms and concepts listed above with one of the brief examples or definitions listed below. Try to find the best fit for answers that seem to fit more than one term or concept. Defend your choices.

____ 1. Ensuring the accuracy, integrity, and safety of information system activities and resources.

____ 2. A computer-based information system must be evaluated on the excellence of its information products and services.

____ 3. Control totals, error signals, and security codes are examples.

____ 4. The separation of the duties of computer programmers and computer operators is an example.

____ 5. Fire and access detection systems are examples.

____ 6. Software that can control access and use of a computer system.

____ 7. A computer system can continue to operate even after a major system failure if it has this capability.

____ 8. Periodically examine the accuracy and integrity of computer processing.

____ 9. The presence of documentation that allows a transaction to be traced through all stages of information processing.

____ 10. Managerial end users are responsible for information system controls in their business units.

____ 11. Using your voice or fingerprints to identify you electronically.

____ 12. A plan to continue IS operations during an emergency.

____ 13. The sum of subtotals must equal a grand total.

____ 14. Scrambling data during its transmission.

____ 15. Passwords, user IDs, and account codes are examples.

____ 16. Examples are egoism, natural law, utilitarianism, and respect for persons.

____ 17. Ethical choices may result from decision-making processes or behavioral stages.

____ 18. Managers must confront numerous ethical questions in their businesses.

____ 19. Ethical guidelines in the use of information and information technology.

____ 20. Employees may have to retrain or transfer.

____ 21. Computer-based systems may depersonalize human activities.

____ 22. Constant long-term use of computers at work may cause health problems.

____ 23. Personal information is in computer-accessible files.

____ 24. Computer-based monitoring of environmental quality is an example.

____ 25. Tedious jobs are decreased and jobs are made more challenging.

____ 26. Using computers to identify individuals that fit a certain profile.

____ 27. Regulate the collection, access, and use of personal data.

____ 28. Using computers to monitor the activities of workers.

____ 29. People have a variety of needs when operating computers.

____ 30. Using computers to steal money, services, software, or data.

____ 31. It is illegal to access a computer with intent to defraud.

____ 32. Unauthorized copying of software.

____ 33. Electronic breaking and entering into a computer system.

____ 34. A program makes copies of itself and destroys data and programs.

____ 35. Designing computer hardware, software, and workstations that are safe, comfortable, and easy to use.

____ 36. End users should act with integrity and competence in their use of information technology.

Discussion Questions

1. How do IS controls, procedural controls, and facility controls improve IS performance and security? Give several examples to illustrate your answer.
2. Refer to the Real World Case on Virgin Atlantic and British Airways in the chapter. Why is it so easy to break into networks like airline reservation systems? How can such systems be better protected?
3. What artificial intelligence techniques can a business use to improve computer security and fight computer crime?
4. What controls are needed for end user computing? Give an example of three controls that could be used at your school or work.
5. What is disaster recovery? How could it be implemented at your school or work?
6. Refer to the Real World Case on Cornell University in the chapter. How serious a threat are computer viruses and other types of computer crime to business and society?
7. Is there an ethical crisis in business today? What role does information technology play in unethical business practices?
8. What business decisions will you have to make as a manager that have both an ethical and IT dimension? Give several examples to illustrate your answer.
9. Refer to the Real World Case on Cornell University. What types of computer crime (such as software piracy and hacking) have you experienced or observed? How could these crimes have been avoided or curtailed?
10. What would be examples of one positive and one negative effect for each of the ethical and societal dimensions of IT illustrated in Figure 12.10? Give it a try.

Real World Problems

1. Rusty & Edie's: Electronic Bulletin Boards and Software Piracy

When Rusty & Edie's, the third-largest bulletin board in the United States, was shut down recently by the Federal Bureau of Investigation, electronic debates raged across CompuServe over whether Rusty and Edie's in fact allowed subscribers to pirate software, as the FBI alleges. The arguments may be moot, however, because while the FBI decides whether to press criminal charges against the bulletin board service, proprietors Russell and Edie Hardenburgh have been wiped out of business. At last month's raid on the 6-year-old bulletin board—run out of the Hardenburghs' home—the FBI seized Rusty & Edie's servers, PCs, and peripherals supporting 124 incoming nodes and 19G bytes of storage space. The equipment will sit idle in an Ohio warehouse until FBI and Software Publishers Association (SPA) officials comb through the bulletin board service's massive files and documentation to determine whether Rusty and Edie's supported or encouraged illegal downloading of copyrighted software by its 14,000 subscribers worldwide.

This is the first raid since Congress raised software piracy from a misdemeanor to a felony in October. Under the law, convicted pirates face up to five years' jail time and $250,000 in fines if they are found to have stolen more than 10 copies of a package with a value of more than $2,500. The law shows that "the government is now willing to put resources behind this crime," said Ilene Rosenthal, SPA's general counsel. SPA estimates put U.S. losses from software piracy in 1991 at $1.2 billion. The SPA contends that "several hundred thousand dollars" worth of copyrighted games and business applications had been downloaded by subscribers from Rusty and Edie's, including titles such as Broderbund Software, Inc.'s Printshop Graphics, Quarterdeck Office Systems' Q-Ram, Microsoft Corp.'s Flight Simulator and Adobe Systems, Inc.'s Illustrator.

a. How might electronic bulletin board systems contribute to software piracy?

b. Why are the penalties for software piracy so severe?

Source: Adapted from Kim Nash and Christopher Lundquist, "First Raid Tests Felony Law," *Computerworld,* March 15, 1993, p. 43. Used with permission.

2. John Alden Life Insurance: Disaster Recovery

A disaster recovery plan kept John Alden Life Insurance up and running after the wrath of Hurricane Andrew had shut down most of south Florida. "Our plan was activated according to the status of the hurricane," says Carlos Miro, vice president for technology services at the Miami-headquartered insurance firm. "When a hurricane watch was declared, we started contacting vendors and making other preparations. As soon as there was a hurricane warning, we started evacuating our operations to a Chicago recovery center. Without our disaster recovery plan, we could have been out of business in three days."

What did John Alden learn from its experience? "We learned three important things," Miro explains. "First, we realized that we had underestimated the effect such a disaster would have on our operations. Even though we've been testing the recovery plan twice a year since 1984, we missed some things and took others for granted. "Second," he continues, "we learned that we needed better management of communications within the company. During a crisis, we have to know who's doing what and what each person's responsibilities are. Finally, we realized that we should have communicated more effectively with other parts of our organization. We are a national company, and some offices in other parts of the country thought it was business as usual in our office."

a. How important is disaster recovery planning? Explain.

b. What lessons about disaster recovery did John Alden learn from Hurricane Andrew?

Source: Adapted with permission from *Beyond Computing*, January/February 1993.

3. Atlantic Richfield and Siemens Corporation: The Electronic Mail Trail

More and more organizations are finding that employee's electronic-mail messages can land them in very hot water. The latest example is Atlantic Richfield Co. (Arco), which must defend against a $146 million lawsuit triggered by its E-mail. In a February 26, lawsuit, electronics giant Siemens Corp. accused Arco of committing fraud in the 1990 sale of Arco's solar energy subsidiary to Siemens. The suit, filed in U.S. District Court, alleged that Arco knew its solar products would not be commercially viable and hid that information from the buyer. Siemens said its charges are supported by numerous E-mail messages that allegedly were exchanged among Arco employees prior to the sale.

One E-mail message, which was written about two weeks before the deal closed, said: "We will attempt to finesse past Siemens the fact that we have had a great amount of trouble in successfully transitioning technology from the laboratory to the manufacturing floor." Another presale message read: "As it appears that IFS [Arco's solar technology] is a pipe dream, let Siemens have the pipe." In a prepared statement, Arco said it rejects the contention that a sophisticated company such as Siemens was "hoodwinked" into buying the solar business unit and added that it will fight the lawsuit. Arco said it did not misrepresent the facts about its technology or business. The lawsuit did not say how Siemens got the E-mail, nor did it provide any technical details.

a. How can someone legally obtain access to private E-mail messages?

b. How should companies deal with the potential legal liability posed by E-mail?

Source: Adapted from Mitch Betts, "E-Mail Paves Road to Court," *Computerworld*, March 29, 1993, p. 65. Used with permission.

4. Microsoft Corporation: Software Counterfeiting

Microsoft Corp. and Northern California law enforcement officials recently raided the offices of several alleged software pirates, netting 18 tons of counterfeit manuals, disks, and components relating to Microsoft's DOS 5.0 operating system and Windows Version 3.1. The bootleg products were produced under the trade names of Spring Circle and BTI. Neither holds replication rights for Microsoft products, Microsoft officials said. The raids took place in late January and February, 1993, and were conducted by the San Jose and Concord, California, police departments and officers from the Federal Bureau of Investigation and the Internal Revenue Service. The raids occurred at more than six Bay Area locations, including JT Litho, a printing and production house in Concord, and the homes of at least two of the principals involved in the production of the counterfeits.

Jim Lowe, a Microsoft corporate attorney, said similar raids against bootleg production facilities are expected to continue as the software industry gets tough on software piracy. "During the next several months, we anticipate more raids, both here and abroad," he said. Lowe added that users should be on constant alert for counterfeit products, which can be defective or carry viruses. Because Microsoft does not license firms to distribute DOS or Windows without a computer system, consumers should be on the lookout for such products available on a stand-alone basis.

a. Why would anyone want to make or buy counterfeit copies of computer software?

b. Is software counterfeiting a form of software piracy? Explain.

Source: Adapted from James Daly, "Police Snag Microsoft Bandits," *Computerworld*, March 8, 1993, p. 24. Used with permission.

Application Exercises

1. Computer Ethics: A Quiz

What is ethical? Unethical? These were the questions behind a landmark study of computing ethics by SRI International in Menlo Park, California. Some 27 business and information systems professions, ethical philosophers, and lawyers were asked to respond to two dozen scenarios and decide if they were ethical. Their responses later formed the basis of a book entitled *Ethical Conflicts: In Information and Computer Science, Technology and Business* (published by QUED Information Sciences, Inc., 1990). Here are five typical scenarios:

Situation 1: The Silent Manager. A programming department manager discovers that one of his programmers and another from the inventory control department involved in a corporate plan to defraud company stockholders by inflating company assets. The programs in question passed his quality assurance testing because they were identified as simulation and test files. Eventually, the fraud was discovered and the perpetrators were prosecuted. The programming manager—who is responsible for all application programming throughout the company but who had told no one of the scheme—was identified as an unindicted conspirator.

Question: Was the manager unethical in not responding to evidence of wrongdoing?

Situation 2: The Bare-Bones System. A programming analyst at a large retailer is charged with project responsibility for building a customer billing and credit system. During the project, money runs out. The programming analyst had continually warned management about impending problems but was told to keep going and finish the development of a bare-bones system as quickly and cheaply as possible. To meet this directive, several key features—including safeguards, error detection, and correction—had to be left out until later versions. After a difficult and costly conversion to the new system, a great many unfixable problems arose, including wrong and unreadable billings and credit statements. Customers were outraged, fraud increased, company profits fell, and the project leader was blamed for it all.

Question: Was it ethical for the production manager to order the system into production prematurely?

Situation 3: The Nosy Security Manager. The information security manager at a large company also acted as administrator of a huge electronic mail network. During his regular monitoring of mail, the manager discovered personal messages about football bets, sexual encounters, and other nonbusiness matters. Printed listings of the messages were regularly given to the company's human resources director and corporate security director. In some cases, managers punished employees, using the messages as evidence. Employees became angry, charging their privacy rights on E-mail were the same as on the company's telephone or interoffice mail system.

Question: Was it ethical for the information security manager to monitor E-mail and inform management of personal use?

Situation 4: All Work, No Play. The manager of research at a computer company explicitly told workers that anyone found playing games on company computers would be subject to dismissal. On a random inspection, a computer game was discovered in the files of a programmer, who was then punished.

Question: Was it ethical for the manager to prohibit the use of computer games in employee files?

Situation 5: It's Not Our Job. A software professional was charged with developing control software for part of a large system. The job looked straightforward and trouble-free. To work, the software required input from other units in the system. The developer then read an article by a noted software specialist and was convinced that input from the other units could not be trusted. So he decided that neither the software he was designing nor the unit his company was providing would do the job they were supposed to. He showed his supervisor the article and explained his concerns, but was told only to worry about his group's part of the project.

Question: Was it ethical for the developer to continue working on the project?

Responses of the SRI panel:

Situation 1: unethical, 23; not unethical, 1; no ethics issue, 0.

Situation 2: unethical, 24; not unethical, 0; no ethics issue, 0.

Situation 3: unethical, 22; not unethical, 2; no ethics issue, 0.

Situation 4: unethical, 7; not unethical, 5; no ethics issue, 13.

Situation 5: unethical, 12; not unethical, 7; no ethics issue, 1.

Prepare an outline that evaluates the ethical dimensions of each of the preceding scenarios as follows:

a. Answer the ethical questions after each scenario.
b. Explain your ethical reasoning for each answer.
c. Explain why you think the SRI panel responded as it did to each question.

2. **Robotic Ethics: A Horror Story**

In 1940, a 20-year old science fiction fan from Brooklyn found that he was growing tired of stories that endlessly repeated the myths of Frankenstein and Faust: Robots were created and destroyed their creator, robots were created and destroyed their creator—ad nauseam. So he began writing robot stories of his own. "[They were] robots stories of a new variety," he recalled. "Never, never was one of my robots to turn stupidly on his creator for no purpose but to demonstrate, for one more weary time, the crime and punishment of Faust. Nonsense! My robots were machines designed by engineers, not pseudo-men created by blasphemers. My robots reacted along the rational lines that existed in their 'brains' from the moment of construction."

In particular, he imagined that each robot's artificial brain would be imprinted with three engineering safeguards, three Laws of Robotics:

1. A robot may not injure a human being or, through inaction, allow a human being to come to harm.
2. A robot must obey the orders given it by human beings except where such orders would conflict with the first law.
3. A robot must protect its own existence as long as such protection does not conflict with the first or second law.

The young writer's name, of course, was Isaac Asimov (1920–1992) and the robot stories he began writing that year have become classics of science fiction, the standards by which others are judged. Indeed, because of Asimov one almost never reads about robots turning mindlessly on their masters anymore.

But the legends of Frankenstein and Faust are subtle ones, and as the world knows too well, engineering rationality is not always the same thing as wisdom. This insight was never captured better than in another science fiction classic: the dark fantasy "With Folded Hands," published by Jack Williamson in 1978. The robots of this story are created by an idealistic young scientist whose world, the planet Wing IV, has just been devastated by a senseless war. Sickened by humankind's taste for viciousness and destruction, and thinking to save men from themselves, he programs his robots to follow an Asimovian Prime Directive—"To Serve and Obey, and Guard Men from Harm." He establishes factories where the robots can duplicate themselves in profusion. He sends them forth to bring order, rationality, and peace to humanity. And he succeeds all too well, as the citizens of his world and other worlds soon began to realize:

> "Our function is to serve and obey, and guard men from harm," it cooed softly. "It is no longer necessary for men to care for themselves, because we exist to insure their safety and happiness. . . .
>
> . . . We are aiding the police department temporarily," it said. "But driving is really much too dangerous for human beings, under the Prime Directive. As soon as our service is complete, every car will have a humanoid driver. As soon as every human being is completely supervised, there will be no need for any police force whatsoever."

At last, the scientist realizes what he has done:

> "I found something worse than war and crime and want and death." His low rumbling voice held a savage bitterness. "Utter futility. Men sat with idle hands because there was nothing left for them to do . . . Perhaps they tried to play, but there was nothing left worth playing for. Most active sports were declared too dangerous for men, under the Prime Directive. Science was forbidden, because laboratories can manufacture danger. Scholarship was needless, because the humanoids could answer any question. Art had degenerated into a grim reflection of futility. Purpose and hope were dead. No goal was left for existence. . . . No wonder men had tried to kill me!"

He attempts to destroy his robots by destroying the central electronic brain that controls them. The robots stop him; this is clearly a violation of the Prime Directive, for how can they serve humans if they themselves are hindered? He flees to another world and tries again. And again. And again. Each time he is thwarted, as the robots continue to spread from planet to planet faster than he can run from them. And in the end, the robots devise a simple brain operation to cure his "hallucinations": " 'We have learned to make all men happy, under the Prime Directive,' the mechanical promised him cheerfully. 'Our service is perfect at last.' "

Prepare a brief ethical evaluation of this story that answers the following questions:

a. What went wrong on planet Wing IV? What should the young scientist have done to stop the robots from taking over?

b. Are Asimov's three Laws of Robotics good ethical guidelines for robots? What about Williamson's Prime Directive? Explain your reasoning.

c. How does this example of robotic ethics apply to human ethics? How does it apply to the use of information technology by business end users and IS specialists? Give several examples to illustrate your answer.

Review Quiz Answers

1. 22
2. 26
3. 21
4. 25
5. 23
6. 30
7. 18
8. 1
9. 2
10. 9
11. 3
12. 11
13. 10
14. 12
15. 28
16. 16
17. 15
18. 4
19. 17
20. 14a
21. 14b
22. 14c
23. 14d
24. 14e
25. 14f
26. 6
27. 24
28. 7
29. 20
30. 5a
31. 5b
32. 29
33. 19
34. 8
35. 13
36. 27

Selected References

1. Alexander, Michael. "Password: User Awareness." *Computerworld,* October 7, 1991.
2. Attaran, Moshen, and John Haut. "Using Ergonomic Principles to Improve Worker Productivity." *Information Executive,* Summer 1989.
3. Betts, Mitch. "Personal Data More Public Than You Think." *Computerworld,* March 9, 1992.
4. Betts, Mitch. "Repetitive Stress Claims Soar." *Computerworld,* November 19, 1990.

5. Bozeman, Jean. "There's No Time for Downtime." *Computerworld,* April 13, 1992.

6. Carey, Jane, ed. *Human Factors in Information Systems: An Organizational Perspective.* Norwood, N.J.: Ablex, 1991.

7. Couger, J. Daniel. "Preparing IS Students to Deal with Ethical Issues." *MTS Quarterly,* June 1989.

8. Dejoie, Roy; George Fowler; and David Paradice, eds. *Ethical Issues in Information Systems.* Boston: Boyd & Fraser, 1991.

9. Denning, Peter, ed. *Computers under Attack: Intruders, Worms, and Viruses.* Reading, Mass.: Addison-Wesley Publishing, 1990.

10. Dunlop, Charles, and Rob Kling, eds. *Computerization and Controversy: Value Conflicts and Social Choices.* San Diego: Academic Press, 1991.

11. Gallegos, Frederick, and Martin Hellman, *Audit and Control of Information Systems,* Cincinnati: South-Western Publishing, 1987.

12. Harrington, Susan. "What Corporate America Is Teaching about Ethics." *Academy of Management Executive* 5, no. 1, (1991).

13. Ives, Blake, and Sirkka Jarvenpaa. "Wiring the Stateless Corporation: Empowering the Drivers and Overcoming the Barriers." *SIM Network,* September/October 1991.

14. Madsen, Peter, and Jay Shafritz, eds. *Essentials of Business Ethics.* New York: Meridian, 1990.

15. McFarland, Michael. "Ethics and the Safety of Computer Systems." *Computer,* February 1991.

16. Mykytyn, Kathleen; Peter Mykytyn; and Craig Slinkman. "Expert Systems: A Question of Liability?" *MIS Quarterly,* March 1990.

17. Ranier, Rex, Jr.; Charles Snyder; and Houston Carr. "Risk Analysis for Information Technology." *Journal of Management Information Systems,* Summer 1991.

18. Rifkin, Glen. "The Ethics Gap." *Computerworld,* October 14, 1991.

19. Savage, J. A. "VDT Liability Raises Questions." *Computerworld,* February 4, 1991.

20. Straub, Detmar, and Rosann Collins. "Key Information Liability Issues Facing Managers: Software Piracy, Proprietary Databases, and Individual Rights to Privacy." *MIS Quarterly,* June 1990.

22. Weber, Ron. *EDP Auditing: Conceptual Foundations and Practice.* 2nd ed. New York: McGraw-Hill, 1988.

23. Wolinsky, Carol, and James Sylvester. "From Washington: Privacy in the Telecom Age." *Communications of the ACM,* February 1992.

Continuing Real World Case

Omaha Vision Center—Part 4: Selection and Implementation

The Selection Process

The computer system selection process at the Omaha Vision Center involved analysis of several manufacturers and their systems. However, only the four proposals listed in Figure 2 of Part 2 displayed the minimum requirements for the practice. Because of the doctor's tenuous approval of the computer, Weber felt it imperative that he get the minimum capabilities at the lowest price. This immediately eliminated the Nielson system. It was a total package with tremendous expansion capability but was simply too expensive for the practice.

The Data Systems Corporation (DSC) system was not a networked system. The company was developing a network for its system that was due out before the practice was set to purchase. A new network would almost certainly have numerous kinks to work out. The doctor would be sensitive to any perceived faults. Weber could not risk the untried product. The DSC system was deleted from the list.

Advanced Software Company (ASC) made a strong presentation but was simply not able to provide the full medical support necessary. In addition, ASC was a small concern backed by a CPA firm. Weber wondered about the company's ability to stay afloat in this competitive market. He needed the assurance of a stronger organization.

Ivy Technologies seemed to meet all the requirements for the vision center. Ivy was developed by an ophthalmologist in St. Louis for his own practice. It was marketed nationwide by a very strong organization with a 10-year track record. The recommendations for the system were encouraging in all areas—software, hardware, training, and support. The system was able to meet the practice's needs and allow for expansion. Weber was further pleased with the component nature of the software. With Ivy, he would be able to purchase different modules as he required them. This would keep the initial outlay down to a reasonable—and palatable—level. See Figure 4.

Following a month of negotiation, the center purchased the Ivy system. The entire process had taken over four months and involved a great deal of the administrator's time. It was hoped that now the staff could be trained to get the system moving along successfully. The efficiency of the practice should begin to pick up.

FIGURE 4
A Summary of the Final Selection Evaluations

- *Nielson Computer Company*—most powerful, complete, expandable, and expensive networked system.
- *Data Systems Corporation*—an incomplete and untried networked system.
- *Advanced Software Company*—complete but nonexpandable with questionable support for a non-networked system.
- *Ivy Technologies*—best all-around networked system, a specialized, flexible, modular system from a strong vendor.

Implementation Problems

The search for the system had emphasized hardware and software acquisition. Little though had been devoted to integration of the information system and the practice. The simple placement of computer equipment onto the staff members' desks had been only the beginning of the struggle.

Carl still had to develop a plan for building an information system without disrupting the flow of the medical practice. The staff at the vision center had no previous experience with computers—not even home PCs. Weber was the only one with any background in this area.

In January 1991, the system was delivered to the office in boxes. A training technician was sent the following day to set up the system and train the office staff for two days. All went well in the installation and training. The system worked well from the start, and training, although only an overview of the major functions and operations, seemed to pique some interest from all in attendance. Weber felt that "things were going to be just fine."

What Next?

Shortly after the training technician returned to St. Louis, the system was fully operational, and Weber realized that there was a gap in his planning. Now that it was here, what would he really get from the computer? The questions started to flow. What reports should he have? What backup procedures should be followed? Who would be responsible for what operations? Weber had already spent far too much time in getting the system to this stage. He had neglected many other areas of the practice. Marketing was behind schedule. His dealings with Medicare had been delayed. Plans for developing satellite offices were waiting in the wings. And the doctor was asking, every day, why Carl spent so much time at the computer.

Weber had come to the practice from a much larger medical instrument distributor. He had supervised managers who implemented an IS plan. But now, with a much smaller staff with limited computer know-how, how was he to continue the implementation? He was not certain of the steps to follow in the small-office environment.

The other nagging problem was the direction of future development of the system. Which areas should be addressed and in what priority? Weber believed that, in order to really sell the system to the doctor and his staff, the system's full capabilities had to be demonstrated.

It was time to begin full implementation of IS at the Omaha Vision Center. But how?

Case Study Questions

1. What IS development and implementation problems do you recognize at the Omaha Vision Center?
2. Did Carl Weber use a good computer selection process? Explain.
3. Did Carl Weber make the right computer selection decision? Explain.
4. What would you have done differently to introduce computer systems to the Vision Center if you had been center administrator?

Glossary for Managerial End Users

Accounting Information Systems
Information systems that record and report business transactions, the flow of funds through an organization, and produce financial statements. This provides information for the planning and control of business operations, as well as for legal and historical record-keeping.

Active Data Dictionary
A data dictionary that automatically enforces standard data element definitions whenever end users and application programs use a DBMS to access an organization's databases.

Ada
A programming language named after Augusta Ada Byron, considered the world's first computer programmer. Developed for the U.S. Department of Defense as a standard high-order language.

Ad Hoc Inquiries
Unique, unscheduled, situation-specific information requests.

ALGOL: ALGOrithmic Language
An international procedure-oriented language that is widely used in Europe. Like FORTRAN, it was designed primarily for scientific-mathematical applications.

Algorithm
A set of well-defined rules or processes for the solution of a problem in a finite number of steps.

Analog Computer
A computer that operates on data by measuring changes in continuous physical variables such as voltage, resistance, and rotation. Contrast with *Digital computer*.

Analytical Modeling
Interactive use of computer-based mathematical models to explore decision alternatives using what-if analysis, sensitivity analysis, goal-seeking analysis, and optimization analysis.

APL: A Programming Language
A mathematically oriented language originated by Kenneth E. Iverson of IBM. Realtime and interactive versions of APL are used by many time-sharing systems.

Application Development
See *Systems development*.

Application Generator
A software package that supports the development of an application through an interactive terminal dialogue, where the programmer/analyst defines screens, reports, computations, and data structures.

Application Portfolio
A planning tool used to evaluate present and proposed information systems applications in terms of the amount of revenue or assets invested in information systems which support major business functions.

Application Software
Programs that specify the information processing activities required for the completion of specific tasks of computer users. Examples are electronic spreadsheet and word processing programs or inventory or payroll programs.

Application-Specific Programs
Application software packages that support specific applications of end users in business, science and engineering, and other areas.

Arithmetic-Logic Unit (ALU)
The unit of a computing system containing the circuits that perform arithmetic and logical operations.

Artificial Intelligence (AI)
A science and technology whose goal is to develop computers that can think, as well as see, hear, walk, talk, and feel. A major thrust is the development of computer functions normally associated with human intelligence, for example, reasoning, inference, learning, and problem solving. Major areas of AI research and development include cognitive science, computer science, robotics, and natural interface applications.

ASCII: American Standard Code for Information Interchange
A standard code used for information interchange among data processing systems, communication systems, and associated equipment

Assembler
A computer program that translates an assembler language into machine language

Assembler Language
A programming language that utilizes symbols to represent operation codes and storage locations.

Asynchronous
Involving a sequence of operations without a regular or predictable time relationship. Thus operations do not happen at regular timed intervals, but an operation will begin only after a previous operation is completed. In data transmission, involves the use of start and stop bits with each character to indicate the beginning and end of the character being transmitted.

Audio-Response Unit
An output device of a computer system whose output consists of the spoken word. Also called a voice synthesizer.

Audit Trail
The presence of media and procedures that allow a transaction to be traced through all stages of information processing, beginning with its appearance on a source document and ending with its transformation into information on a final output document.

Automatic Teller Machine (ATM)
A special-purpose transaction terminal used to provide remote banking services.

Automation
The automatic transfer and positioning of work by machines or the automatic operation and control of a work process by machines, that is, without significant human intervention or operation.

Auxiliary Storage
Storage that supplements the primary storage of the computer. Same as *Secondary storage.*

Back-End Processor
Typically a smaller general-purpose computer that is dedicated to database processing using a database management system (DBMS). Also called a database machine.

Background Processing
The automatic execution of lower-priority computer programs when higher-priority programs are not using the resources of the computer system. Contrast with *Foreground processing.*

Backward-Chaining
An inference process which justifies a proposed conclusion by determining if it will result when rules are applied to the facts in a given situation.

Bar Codes
Vertical marks or bars placed on merchandise tags, or packaging that can be sensed and read by optical character-reading devices. The width and combination of vertical lines are used to represent data.

Barriers to Entry
Technological, financial, or legal requirements which deter firms from entering an industry.

BASIC: Beginner's All-Purpose Symbolic Instruction Code
A programming language developed at Dartmouth College that is popular for microcomputer and time-sharing systems.

Batch Processing
A category of data processing in which data is accumulated into "batches" and processed periodically. Contrast with *Realtime processing.*

Baud
A unit of measurement used to specify data transmission speeds. It is a unit of signaling speed equal to the number of discrete conditions or signal events per second. In many data communications applications it represents one bit per second.

Binary
Pertaining to characteristic or property involving a selection, choice, or condition in which there are two possibilities, or pertaining to the number system that utilizes a base of two.

Biometric Controls
Computer-based security methods that measure physical traits and characteristics such as fingerprints, voice prints, retina scans, and so on.

Bit
A contraction of "binary digit." It can have the value of either 0 or 1.

Black Box Approach
Concentrating on defining the boundaries, interfaces, inputs, and outputs of a system instead of studying the technical details of the transformation processes of a system.

Block
A grouping of continguous data records or other data elements that are handled as a unit.

Bootstrap
A technique in which the first few instructions of a program are sufficient to bring the rest of itself into the computer from an input device.

Branch
A transfer of control from one instruction to another in a computer program that is not part of the normal sequential execution of the instructions of the program.

Buffer
Temporary storage used to compensate for a difference in rate of flow of data, or time of occurrence of events, when transmitting data from one device to another.

Bug
A mistake or malfunction.

Bulletin Board System (BBS)
A service of personal computer networks in which electronic messages, data files, or programs can be stored for other subscribers to read or copy.

Bundling
The inclusion of software, maintenance, training, and other products or services in the price of a computer system.

Bus
A set of conducting paths for movement of data and instructions that interconnects the various components of the CPU.

Business Ethics
An area of ethical philosophy concerned with developing ethical principles and promoting ethical behavior and practices in the accomplishment of business tasks and decision making.

Business Information System
Information systems within a business organization that support one of the traditional functions of business such as marketing, finance, or production. Business information systems can be either operations or management information systems.

Byte
A sequence of adjacent binary digits operated on as a unit and usually shorter than a computer word. In many computer systems, a byte is a grouping of eight bits that can represent one alphabetic or special character or can be "packed" with two decimal digits.

C
A low-level structured programming language developed by AT&T-Bell Laboratories. It resembles a machine-independent assembler language and is popular for software package development.

Cache Memory
A high-speed temporary storage area in the CPU for storing parts of a program or data during processing.

Capacity Management
The use of planning and control methods to forecast and control information processing job loads, hardware and software usage, and other computer system resource requirements.

Cathode Ray Tube (CRT)
An electronic vacuum tube (television picture tube) that displays the output of a computer system.

CD-ROM
An optical disk technology for microcomputers featuring compact disks with a storage capacity of over 500 megabytes.

Cellular Radio
A radio communications technology that divides a metropolitan area into a honeycomb of cells to greatly increase the number of frequencies and thus the

users that can take advantage of mobile phone service.

Central Processing Unit (CPU)
The unit of a computer system that includes the circuits that control the interpretation and execution of instructions. In many computer systems, the CPU includes the arithmetic-logic unit, the control unit, and primary storage unit.

Channel
A path along which signals can be sent. More specifically, a small special-purpose processor that controls the movement of data between the CPU and input/output devices.

Charge-Coupled Device (CCD)
A slower serial access form of semiconductor memory that uses a silicon crystal's own structure to store data.

Chargeback Systems
Methods of allocating costs to end user departments based on the information services rendered and information system resources utilized.

Check Bit
A binary check digit; for example, a parity bit.

Check Digit
A digit in a data field that is utilized to check for errors or loss of characters in the data field as a result of data transfer operations.

Check Point
A place in a program where a check or a recording of data for restart purposes is performed.

Chief Information Officer
A senior management position that oversees all information technology for a firm, concentrating on long-range information system planning and strategy.

Client/Server Network
A computing environment where end user workstations (clients) are connected to micro or mini LAN servers and possibly to mainframe *superservers*.

Clock
A device that generates periodic signals utilized to control the timing of a computer. Also, a register whose contents change at regular intervals in such a way as to measure time.

Coaxial Cable
A sturdy copper or aluminum wire wrapped with spacers to insulate and protect it. Groups of coaxial cables may also be bundled together in a bigger cable for ease of installation.

COBOL: COmmon Business Oriented Language
A widely used business data processing programming language.

CODASYL: COnference on DAta SYstems Languages
The group of representatives of users and computer manufacturers who developed and maintain the COBOL language.

Code
Computer instructions.

Cognitive Science
An area of artificial intelligence which focuses on researching how the human brain works and how humans think and learn, in order to apply such findings to the design of computer-based systems.

Cognitive Styles
Basic patterns in how people handle information and confront problems.

Cognitive Theory
Theories about how the human brain works and how humans think and learn.

Common Carrier
An organization that supplies communications services to other organizations and to the public as authorized by government agencies.

Communications Satellite
Earth satellites placed in stationary orbits above the equator that serve as relay stations for communications signals transmitted from earth stations.

Competitive Forces
A firm must confront (1) rivalry of competitors within its industry, (2) threats of new entrants, (3) threats of substitutes, (4) the bargaining power of customers, and (5) the bargaining power of suppliers.

Competitive Strategies
A firm can develop cost leadership, product differentiation, and business innovation strategies to confront its competitive forces.

Compiler
A program that translates a high-level programming language into a machine-language program.

Computer
A device that has the ability to accept data, internally store and execute a program of instructions, perform mathematical, logical, and manipulative operations on data, and report the results.

Computer-Aided Design (CAD)
The use of computers and advanced graphics hardware and software to provide interactive design assistance for engineering and architectural design.

Computer-Aided Engineering
The use of computers to simulate, analyze, and evaluate models of product designs and production processes developed using computer-aided design methods.

Computer-Aided Manufacturing (CAM)
The use of computers to automate the production process and operations of a manufacturing plant. Also called factory automation.

Computer-Aided Planning (CAP)
The use of software packages as tools to support the planning process.

Computer-Aided Software Engineering (CASE)
Same as computer-aided systems engineering, but emphasizing the importance of software development.

Computer-Aided Systems Engineering (CASE)
Using software packages to accomplish and automate many of the activities of information systems development, including software development or programming.

Computer Application
The use of a computer to solve a specific problem or to accomplish a particular job for an end user. For example, common business computer applications include sales order processing, inventory control, and payroll.

Computer-Assisted Instruction (CAI)
The use of computers to provide drills, practice exercises, and tutorial sequences to students.

Computer-Based Information System
An information system that uses computer hardware and software to perform its information processing activities.

Computer Crime
Criminal actions accomplished through the use of computer systems, especially with intent to defraud, destroy, or make unauthorized use of computer system resources.

Computer Ethics
A system of principles governing the legal, professional, social, and moral re-

sponsibilities of computer specialists and end users.

Computer Generations
Major stages in the historical development of computing.

Computer Graphics
Using computer-generated images to analyze and interpret data, present information, and do computer-aided design and art.

Computer Industry
The industry composed of firms that supply computer hardware, software, and services.

Computer-Integrated Manufacturing (CIM)
An overall concept that stresses that the goals of computer use in factory automation should be to simplify, automate, and integrate production processes and other aspects of manufacturing.

Computer Matching
Using computers to screen and match data about individual characteristics provided by a variety of computer-based information systems and databases in order to identify individuals for business, government, or other purposes.

Computer Monitoring
Using computers to monitor the behavior and productivity of workers on the job and in the workplace.

Computer Program
A series of instructions or statements, in a form acceptable to a computer, prepared in order to achieve a certain result.

Computer System
Computer hardware as a system of input, processing, output, storage, and control components. Thus a computer system consists of input and output devices, primary and secondary storage devices, the central processing unit, the control unit within the CPU, and other peripheral devices.

Computer Terminal
Any input/output device connected by telecommunications links to a computer.

Computer Virus or Worm
Program code that copies its destructive program routines into the computer systems of anyone who accesses computer systems which have used the program, or anyone who uses copies of data or programs taken from such computers. This spreads the destruction of data and programs among many computer users. Technically, a *virus* will not run unaided, but must be inserted into another program, while a *worm* is a distinct program that can run unaided.

Concentrator
A special-purpose computer that accepts information from many terminals using slow-speed lines and transmits data to a main computer system over a high-speed line.

Concurrent Processing
The generic term for the capability of computers to work on several tasks at the same time, that is, concurrently. This may involve specific capabilities such as overlapped processing. multiprocessing, multiprogramming, multitasking, parallel processing, and so on.

Connectivity
The degree to which hardware, software, and databases can be easily linked together in a telecommunications network.

Context Diagram
The highest level data flow diagram. It defines the boundaries of a system by showing a single major process and the data inputs and outputs and external entities involved.

Control
(1) The systems component that evaluates feedback to determine whether the system is moving toward the achievement of its goal and then makes any necessary adjustments to the input and processing components of the system to ensure that proper output is produced. (2) A management function that involves observing and measuring organizational performance and environmental activities and modifying the plans and activities of the organization when necessary.

Control Listing
A detailed report that describes each transaction occurring during a period.

Control Totals
Accumulating totals of data at multiple points in an information system to ensure correct information processing.

Control Unit
A subunit of the central processing unit that controls and directs the operations of the computer system. The control unit retrieves computer instructions in proper sequence, interprets each instruction, and then directs the other parts of the computer system in their implementation.

Conversion
The process in which the hardware, software, people, and data resources of an old information system must be converted to the requirements of a new information system. This usually involves a parallel, phased, pilot, or plunge conversion process from the old to the new system.

Cooperative Processing
Information processing which allows the computers in a distributed processing network to share the processing of parts of an end user's application.

Cost/Benefit Analysis
Identifying the advantages or benefits and the disadvantages or costs of a proposed solution.

Counter
A device such as a register or storage location used to represent the number of occurrences of an event.

Critical Success Factors
A small number of key factors that executives consider critical to the success of the enterprise. These are key areas where successful performance will assure the success of the organization and attainment of its goals.

Cross-Functional Information Systems
Information systems which are integrated combinations of business information systems, thus sharing information resources across the functional units of an organization.

Cryogenics
The study and use of devices utilizing the properties of materials at super cold temperatures. The superconductive nature of such materials provides ultra-high-speed computer logic and memory circuits.

Cursor
A movable point of light displayed on most video display screens to assist the user in the input of data.

Cybernetic System
A system that uses feedback and control components to achieve a self-monitoring and self-regulating capability.

Cylinder
An imaginary vertical cylinder consisting of the vertical alignment of data

tracks on each surface of magnetic disks, which are accessed simultaneously by the read/write heads of a disk device.

Data
Facts or observations about physical phenomena or business transactions. More specifically, data are objective measurements of the *attributes* (characteristics) of *entities* such as people, places, things, and events.

Data Administration
A data resource management function which involves the establishment and enforcement of policies and procedures for managing data as a strategic corporate resource.

Data Bank
A comprehensive collection of libraries of data.

Database
A collection of logically related records or files. A database consolidates many records previously stored in separate files so that a common pool of data records serves many applications.

Database Administration
A data resource management function which includes responsibility for developing and maintaining the organization's data dictionary, designing and monitoring the performance of databases, and enforcing standards for database use and security.

Database Administrator
A specialist responsible for maintaining standards for the development, maintenance, and security of an organization's databases.

Database Management Approach
An approach to the storage and processing of data in which independent files are consolidated into a common pool or database of records available to different application programs and end users for processing and data retrieval.

Database Management System (DBMS)
A set of computer programs that controls the creation, maintenance, and utilization of the databases of an organization.

Data Center
An organizational unit which uses centralized computing resources to perform information processing activities for an organization. Also known as a computer center.

Data Communications
See *Telecommunications.*

Data Design
The design of the logical structure of databases and files to be used by a proposed information system. This produces detailed descriptions of the entities, relationships, data elements, and integrity rules for system files and databases.

Data Dictionary
A software module and database containing descriptions and definitions concerning the structure, data elements, interrelationships, and other characteristics of an organization's databases.

Data Entry
The process of converting data into a form suitable for entry into a computer system. Also called data capture or input preparation.

Data Flow Diagram
A graphic diagramming tool which uses a few simple symbols to illustrate the flow of data among external entities, processing activities, and data storage elements.

Data Management
Control program functions that provide access to data sets, enforce data storage conventions, and regulate the use of input/output devices.

Data Model
A conceptual framework which defines the logical relationships among the data elements needed to support a basic business or other process.

Data Modeling
A process where the relationships between data elements are identified and defined to develop data models.

Data Planning
A corporate planning and analysis function that focuses on data resource management. It includes the responsibility for developing an overall information policy and data architecture for the firm's data resources.

Data Processing
The execution of a systematic sequence of operations performed upon data to transform it into information.

Data Resource Management
A managerial activity that applies information systems technology and management tools to the task of managing an organization's data resources. Its three major components are database administration, data administration, and data planning.

Debug
To detect, locate, and remove errors from a program or malfunctions from a computer.

Decision Making Process
A process of intelligence, design, and choice activities which result in the selection of a particular course of action.

Decision Support System (DSS)
An information system that utilizes decision models, a database, and a decision maker's own insights in an ad hoc, interactive analytical modeling process to reach a specific decision by a specific decision maker.

Demand Reports and Responses
Information provided whenever a manager or end user demands it.

Desktop Accessory Package
A software package which provides features such as a calculator, note page, alarm clock, phone directory, and appointment book that is available as a pop-up window on a computer display screen at the touch of a key.

Desktop Publishing
The use of microcomputers, laser printers, and page-makeup software to produce a variety of printed materials, formerly done only by professional printers.

Development Centers
Systems development consultant groups formed to serve as consultants to the professional programmers and systems analysts of an organization to improve their application development efforts.

Digital Computer
A computer that operates on digital data by performing arithmetic and logical operations on the data. Contrast with *Analog Computer.*

Digitizer
A device that is used to convert drawings and other graphic images on paper or other materials into digital data that is entered into a computer system.

Direct Access
A method of storage where each storage position has a unique address and can be individually accessed in approximately the same period of time without having to search through other storage positions.

Direct Access Storage Device (DASD)
A storage device that can directly access data to be stored or retrieved, for example, a magnetic disk unit.

Direct Data Organization
A method of data organization in which logical data elements are distributed randomly on or within the physical data medium. For example, logical data records distributed randomly on the surfaces of a magnetic disk file. Also called direct organization.

Direct Input/Out
Devices such as terminals that allow data to be input into a computer system or output from the computer system without the use of machine-readable media.

Direct Memory Access (DMA)
A type of computer architecture in which intelligent components other than the CPU (such as a channel) can directly access data in main memory.

Disaster Recovery
Methods for ensuring that an organization recovers from natural and human-caused disasters that affect its computer-based operations.

Disk Pack
A removable unit containing several magnetic disks that can be mounted on a magnetic disk storage unit.

Distributed Databases
The concept of distributing databases or portions of a database at remote sites where the data is most frequently referenced. Sharing of data is made possible through a network that interconnects the distributed databases.

Distributed Processing
A form of decentralization of information processing made possible by a network of computers dispensed throughout an organization. Processing of user applications is accomplished by several computers interconnected by a telecommunications network rather than relying on one large centralized computer facility or on the decentralized operation of several independent computers.

Document
(1) A medium on which data has been recorded for human use, such as a report or invoice. (2) In word processing, a generic term for text material such as letters, memos, reports, and so on.

Documentation
A collection of documents or information that describes a computer program, information system, or required data processing operations.

Downtime
The time interval during which a device is malfunctioning or inoperative.

DSS Generator
A software package for a decision support system which contains modules for database, model, and dialogue management.

Dump
To copy the contents of all or part of a storage device, usually from an internal device, onto an external storage device.

Duplex
In communications, pertaining to a simultaneous two-way independent transmission in both directions.

EBCDIC: Extended Binary Coded Decimal Interchange Code
An eight-bit code that is widely used by mainframe computers.

Echo Check
A method of checking the accuracy of transmission of data in which the received data are returned to the sending device for comparison with the original data.

Economic Feasibility
Whether expected costs savings, increased revenue, increased profits and reductions in required investment exceed the costs of developing and operating a proposed system.

EDI: Electronic Data Interchange
The electronic transmission of source documents between the computers of different organizations.

Edit
To modify the form or format of data, for example, to insert or delete characters such as page numbers or decimal points.

Edit Report
A report that describes errors detected during processing.

EFT: Electronic Funds Transfer
The development of banking and payment systems that transfer funds electronically instead of using cash or paper documents such as checks.

Electronic Data Processing (EDP)
The use of electronic computers to process data automatically.

Electronic Document Management
An image processing technology in which an electronic document may consist of digitized voice notes and electronic graphics images, as well as digitized images of traditional documents.

Electronic Mail
The transmission, storage, and distribution of text material in electronic form over communications networks.

Electronic Meeting Systems (EMS)
The use of video and audio communications to allow conferences and meetings to be held with participants who may be geographically dispersed or may be present in the same room. This may take the form of group decision support systems, teleconferencing, or other methods.

Electronic Spreadsheet Package
An application program used as a computerized tool for analysis, planning, and modeling that allows users to enter and manipulate data into an electronic worksheet of rows and columns.

Emulation
To imitate one system with another so that the imitating system accepts the same data, executes the same programs, and achieves the same results as the imitated system.

Encryption
To scramble data or convert it, prior to transmission, to a secret code that masks the meaning of the data to unauthorized recipients. Similar to enciphering.

End User
Anyone who uses an information system or the information it produces.

End User Computing Systems
Computer-based information systems that directly support both the operational and managerial applications of end users. Also, the direct, hands-on use of computers by end users.

Enterprise Analysis
A planning process that emphasizes how computerbased information systems will improve the performance and competitive position of a business enterprise. This includes planning how information systems can support the basic

business processes, functions, and organizational units of an organization.

Enterprise Model
A conceptual framework which defines the structures and relationships of business processes and data elements, as well as other planning structures, such as critical success factors, and organizational units.

Entropy
The tendency of a system to lose a relatively stable state of equilibrium.

Ergonomics
The science and technology emphasizing the safety, comfort, and ease of use of human-operated machines such as computers. The goal of ergonomics is to produce systems that are user friendly, that is, safe, comfortable, and easy to use. Ergonomics is also called human factors engineering.

Evaluation Criteria
Key areas in which a proposed solution will be evaluated.

Exception Reports
Reports produced only when exceptional conditions occur, or reports produced periodically which contain information only about exceptional conditions.

Executive Information Systems
An information system that provides strategic information tailored to the needs of top management.

Executive Support System
An executive information system with additional capabilities, including data analysis, decision support, electronic mail, and personal productivity tools.

Expert System
A computer-based information system that uses its knowledge about a specific complex application area to act as an expert consultant to users. The system consists of a knowledge base and software modules that perform inferences on the knowledge, and communicates answers to a user's questions.

Facilities Management
The use of an external service organization to operate and manage the information processing facilities of an organization.

Facsimile
The transmission of images and their reconstruction and duplication on some form of paper at a receiving station.

Fault-Tolerant Systems
Computers with multiple central processors, peripherals, and system software that are able to continue operations even if there is a major hardware or software failure.

Feasibility Study
A preliminary study that investigates the information needs of end users and the objectives, constraints, basic resource requirements, cost/benefits, and feasibility of proposed projects.

Feedback
(1) Data or information concerning the components and operations of a system. (2) The use of part of the output of a system as input to the system.

Fiber Optics
The technology that uses cables consisting of very thin filaments of glass fibers that can conduct the light generated by lasers at frequencies that approach the speed of light.

Field
A data element that consists of a grouping of characters that describe a particular attribute of an entity. For example, the name field or salary field of an employee.

Fifth-Generation
The next generation of computing, which will provide computers that will be able to see, hear, talk, and think. This would depend on major advances in parallel processing, user input/output methods, and artificial intelligence.

File
A collection of related data records treated as a unit. Sometimes called a data set.

File Maintenance
The activity of keeping a file up-to-date by adding, changing, or deleting data.

File Management
Controlling the creation, deletion, access, and use of files of data and programs.

File Processing
Utilizing a file for data processing activities such as file maintenance, information retrieval, or report generation.

Financial Information Systems
Information systems that support financial managers in the financing of a business and the allocation and control of financial resources. Includes cash and securities management, capital budgeting, financial forecasting, and financial planning.

Firmware
The use of microprogrammed read only memory circuits in place of "hardwired" logic circuitry. See also *Microprogramming*.

Flip-Flop
A circuit or device containing active elements, capable of assuming either one of two states at a given time. Synonymous with *toggle*.

Floating-Point
Pertaining to a number representation system in which each number is represented by two sets of digits. One set represents the significant digits or fixed-point "base" of the number, while the other set of digits represents the "exponent," which indicates the precision of the number.

Floppy Disk
A small plastic disk coated with iron oxide that resembles a small phonograph record enclosed in a protective envelope. It is a widely used form of magnetic disk media that provides a direct access storage capability for microcomputer systems.

Flowchart
A graphical representation in which symbols are used to represent operations, data, flow, logic, equipment, and so on. A program flowchart illustrates the structure and sequence of operations of a program, while a system flowchart illustrates the components and flows of information systems.

Foreground Processing
The automatic execution of the computer programs that have been designed to preempt the use of computing facilities. Contrast with *Background processing*.

Format
The arrangement of data on a medium.

FORTRAN: FORmula TRANslation
A high-level programming language widely utilized to develop computer programs that perform mathematical computations for scientific, engineering, and selected business applications.

Forward-Chaining
An inference strategy that reaches a conclusion by applying rules to facts to

determine if any facts satisfy a rule's conditions in a particular situation.

Fourth-Generation Languages (4GL)
Programming languages that are easier to use than high-level languages like BASIC, COBOL, or FORTRAN. They are also known as nonprocedural, natural, or very high-level languages.

Frame
A collection of knowledge about an entity or other concept consisting of a complex package of slots, that is, data values describing the characteristics or attributes of an entity.

Frame-Based Knowledge
Knowledge represented in the form of a hierarchy or network of frames.

Front-End Processor
Typically a smaller, general-purpose computer that is dedicated to handling data communications control functions in a communications network, thus relieving the host computer of these functions.

Fuzzy Logic Systems
Computer-based systems that can process data that are incomplete or only partially correct, i.e., fuzzy data. Such systems can solve unstructured problems with incomplete knowledge, as humans do.

General-Purpose Application Programs
Programs that can perform information processing jobs for users from all application areas. For example, word processing programs, electronic spreadsheet programs, and graphics programs can be used by individuals for home, education, business, scientific, and many other purposes.

General-Purpose Computer
A computer that is designed to handle a wide variety of problems. Contrast with *Special-purpose computer*.

Generate
To produce a machine-language program for performing a specific data processing task based on parameters supplied by a programmer or user.

Generator
A computer program that performs a generating function.

Gigabyte
One billion bytes. More accurately, 2 to the 30th power, or 1,073,741,824 in decimal notation.

GIGO
A contraction of "Garbage In, Garbage Out," which emphasizes that information systems will produce erroneous and invalid output when provided with erroneous and invalid input data or instructions.

Global Information Technology
The use of computer-based information systems and telecommunications networks using a variety of information technologies to support global business operations and management.

Goal Seeking Analysis
Making repeated changes to selected variables until a chosen variable reaches a target value.

Graphical User Interface
A software interface that relies on icons, bars, buttons, boxes, and other images to initiate computer-based tasks for users.

Graphics
Pertaining to symbolic input or output from a computer system, such as lines, curves, and geometric shapes, using video display units or graphics plotters and printers.

Graphics Pen and Tablet
A device that allows an end user to draw or write on a pressure sensitive tablet and have their handwriting or graphics digitized by the computer and accepted as input.

Graphics Software
A program that helps users generate graphics displays.

Group Decision Making
Decisions made by groups of people coming to an agreement on a particular issue.

Group Decision Support System (GDSS)
A decision support system which provides support for decision making by groups of people.

Groupware
Software packages which support work activities by members of a work group whose workstations are interconnected by a local area network.

Hacking
(1) Obsessive use of a computer. (2) The unauthorized access and use of computer systems.

Handshaking
Exchange of predetermined signals when a connection is established between two communications terminals.

Hard Copy
A data medium or data record that has a degree of permanence and that can be read by people or machines.

Hardware
(1) Machines and media. (2) Physical equipment, as opposed to computer programs or methods of use. (3) Mechanical, magnetic, electrical, electronic, or optical devices. Contrast with *Software*.

Hash Total
The sum of numbers in a data field that are not normally added, such as account numbers or other identification numbers. It is utilized as a control total, especially during input/output operations of batch processing systems.

Header Label
A machine-readable record at the beginning of a file containing data for file identification and control.

Heuristic
Pertaining to exploratory methods of problem solving in which solutions are discovered by evaluation of the progress made toward the final result. It is an exploratory trial-and-error approach guided by rules of thumb. Opposite of algorithmic.

Hexadecimal
Pertaining to the number system with a base of 16. Synonymous with sexadecimal.

Hierarchical Data Structure
A logical data structure in which the relationships between records form a hierarchy or tree structure. The relationships among records are one-to-many, since each data element is related only to one element above it.

High-Level Language
A programming language that utilizes macro instructions and statements that closely resemble human language or mathematical notation to describe the problem to be solved or the procedure to be used. Also called a compiler language.

HIPO Chart (Hierarchy + Input/Processing/Output)
Also known as an IPO chart. A design and documentation tool of structured programming utilized to record input/

processing/output details of hierarchical program modules.

Hollerith
Pertaining to a type of code or punched card utilizing 12 rows per column and usually 80 columns per card. Named after Herman Hollerith, who originated punched card data processing.

Homeostasis
A relatively stable state of equilibrium of a system.

Host Computer
Typically a larger central computer that performs the major data processing tasks in a computer network.

Human Factors
Hardware and software capabilities that can affect the comfort, safety, ease of use, and user customization of computer-based information systems.

Human Information Processing
A conceptual framework about the human cognitive process which uses an information processing context to explain how humans capture, process, and use information.

Human Resource Information Systems (HRIS)
Information systems that support human resource management activities such as recruitment, selection and hiring, job placement and performance appraisals, and training and development.

Hypermedia
Documents that contain multiple forms of media, including text, graphics, video, and sound, which can be interactively searched like hypertext.

Hypertext
A methodology for the construction and interactive use of text material, in which a body of text in electronic form is indexed in a variety of ways so it can be quickly searched by a reader.

Icon
A small figure on a video display that looks like a familiar office or other device such as a file folder (for storing a file), a wastebasket (for deleting a file), or a calculator (for switching to a calculator mode).

Image Processing
A computer-based technology which allows end users to electronically capture, store, process, and retrieve images that may include numeric data, text, handwriting, graphics, documents, and photographs. Image processing makes heavy use of optical scanning and optical disk technologies.

Impact Printers
Printers that form images on paper through the pressing of a printing element and an inked ribbon or roller against the face of a sheet of paper.

Index
An ordered reference list of the contents of a file or document together with keys or reference notations for identification or location of those contents.

Index Sequential
A method of data organization in which records are organized in sequential order and also referenced by an index. When utilized with direct access file devices, it is known as index sequential access method or ISAM.

Inference Engine
The software component of an expert system which processes the rules and facts related to a specific problem and makes associations and inferences resulting in recommended courses of action.

Information
Information is data placed in a meaningful and useful context for an end user.

Information Architecture
A conceptual framework that defines the basic structure, content, and relationships of the organizational databases that provide the data needed to support the basic business processes of an organization.

Information Center
A support facility for the end users of an organization. It allows users to learn to develop their own application programs and to accomplish their own information processing tasks. End users are provided with hardware support, software support, and people support (trained user consultants).

Information Float
The time when a document is in transit between the sender and receiver, and thus unavailable for any action or response.

Information Processing
A concept that covers both the traditional concept of processing numeric and alphabetic data, and the processing of text, images, and voices. It emphasizes that the production of information products for users should be the focus of processing activities.

Information Quality
The degree to which information has content, form, and time characteristics which give it value to specific end users.

Information Reporting System
A management information system which produces prespecified reports, displays, and responses on a periodic, exception, or demand basis.

Information Resource Management (IRM)
A management concept that views data, information, and computer resources (computer hardware, software, and personnel) as valuable organizational resources that should be efficiently, economically, and effectively managed for the benefit of the entire organization.

Information Retrieval
The methods and procedures for recovering specific information from stored data.

Information System
A set of people, procedures, and resources that collects, transforms, and disseminates information in an organization. Or, a system that accepts data resources as input and processes them into information products as output. Also, a system that uses the resources of hardware (machines and media), software (programs and procedures), and people (users and specialists) to perform input, processing, output, storage, and control activities that transform data resources into information products.

Information System Resources
People, hardware, software, and data are the resources of an information system.

Information System Specialist
A person whose occupation is related to the providing of information system services; for example, a systems analyst, programmer, or computer operator.

Information Systems Development
See *Systems Development*.

Information Systems Planning
A formal planning process which develops plans for developing and managing information systems that will support the goals of the organization. This includes strategic, tactical, and operational planning activities.

Information Technology (IT)
Hardware, software, telecommunications, database management, and other information processing technologies used in computer-based information systems.

Information Theory
The branch of learning concerned with the likelihood of accurate transmission or communication of messages subject to transmission failure, distortion, and noise.

Information Warehouse
A central source of data that has been extracted from various organizational databases and standardized and integrated for use throughout an organization.

Input
Pertaining to a device, process, or channel involved in the insertion of data into a data processing system. Opposite of *Output.*

Input/Out (I/O)
Pertaining to either input or output, or both.

Input/Output Interface Hardware
Devices such as I/O ports, I/O busses, buffers, channels, and input/output control units, which assist the CPU in its input/output assignments. These devices make it possible for modern computer systems to perform input, output, and processing functions simultaneously.

Inquiry Processing
Computer processing which supports the realtime interrogation of online files and databases by end users.

Instruction
A grouping of characters that specifies the computer operation to be performed.

Intangible Benefits and Costs
The nonquantifiable benefits and costs of a proposed solution or system.

Integrated Circuit
A complex microelectronic circuit consisting of interconnected circuit elements that cannot be disassembled because they are placed on or within a "continuous substrate" such as a silicon chip.

Integrated Packages
Software that combines the ability to do several general-purpose applications (such as word processing, electronic spread-sheet, and graphics) into one program.

Integrative Information Systems
Information systems that combine the capabilities of several types of information systems.

Intelligent Terminal
A terminal with the capabilities of a microcomputer, which can thus perform many data processing and other functions without accessing a larger computer.

Interactive Processing
A type of realtime processing in which users can interact with a computer on a realtime basis.

Interactive Video
Computer-based systems that integrate image processing with text, audio, and video processing technologies, which makes interactive multimedia presentations possible.

Interface
A shared boundary, such as the boundary between two systems. For example, the boundary between a computer and its peripheral devices.

Interorganizational Information Systems
Information systems that interconnect an organization with other organizations, such as a business and its customers and supplies.

Interpreter
A computer program that translates and executes each source language statement before translating and executing the next one.

Interrupt
A condition that causes an interruption in a processing operation during which another task is performed. At the conclusion of this new assignment, control may be transferred back to the point where the original processing operation was interrupted or to other tasks with a higher priority.

Inverted File
A file that references entities by their attributes.

Iterative
Pertaining to the repeated execution of a series of steps.

Job
A specified group of tasks prescribed as a unit of work for a computer.

Job Control Language (JCL)
A language for communicating with the operating system of a computer to identify a job and describe its requirements.

Joystick
A small lever set in a box used to move the cursor on the computer's display screen.

K
An abbreviation for the prefix "kilo," which is 1,000 in decimal notation. When referring to storage capacity it is equivalent to 2 to the 10th power, or 1,024 in decimal notation.

Key
One or more fields within a data record that are used to identify it or control its use.

Keyboarding
Using the keyboard of a microcomputer or computer terminal.

Key-to-Disk
Data entry using a keyboard device to record data directly onto a magnetic disk.

Knowledge Base
A computer-accessible collection of knowledge about a subject in a variety of forms, such as facts and rules of inference, frames, and objects.

Knowledge-Based Information System
An information system which adds a knowledge base to the database and other components found in other types of computer-based information systems.

Knowledge Engineer
A specialist who works with experts to capture the knowledge they possess in order to develop a knowledge base for expert systems and other knowledge-based systems.

Knowledge Workers
People whose primary work activities include creating, using, and distributing information.

Label
One or more characters used to identify a statement or an item of data in a computer program or the contents of the data file.

Language Translator Program
A program that converts the programming language instructions in a computer program into machine language code. Major types include assemblers, compilers, and interpreters.

Large-Scale Integration (LSI)
A method of constructing electronic cir-

cuits in which thousands of circuits can be placed on a single semiconductor chip.

Layout Forms and Screens
Tools used to construct the formats and generic content of input/output media and methods for the user interface, such as display screens and reports.

Light Pen
A photoelectronic device that allows data to be entered or altered on the face of a video display terminal.

Line Printer
A device that prints all characters of a line as a unit.

Liquid Crystal Displays (LCDs)
Electronic visual displays that form characters by applying an electrical charge to selected silicon crystals.

List Organization
A method of data organization that uses indexes and pointers to allow for nonsequential retrieval.

List Processing
A method of processing data in the form of lists.

Local Area Network (LAN)
A communications network that typically connects computers, terminals, and other computerized devices within a limited physical area such as an office, building, manufacturing plant, or other worksite.

Locking in Customers and Suppliers
Building valuable relationships with customers and suppliers which deter them from abandoning a firm for its competitors or intimidating it into accepting less profitable relationships.

Logical Data Elements
Data elements that are independent of the physical data media on which they are recorded.

Logical System Design
Developing general specifications for how basic information systems activities can meet end user requirements.

LOGO
An interactive graphical language used as a tool for learning a variety of concepts (color, direction, letters, words, sounds, etc.) as well as learning to program and use the computer. Forms and figures are used (sprites and turtles) that a child learns to move around on the screen to accomplish tasks.

Loop
A sequence of instructions in a computer program that is executed repeatedly until a terminal condition prevails.

Machine Cycle
The timing of a basic CPU operation as determined by a fixed number of electrical pulses emitted by the CPU's timing circuitry or internal clock.

Machine Language
A programming language where instructions are expressed in the binary code of the computer.

Macro Instruction
An instruction in a source language that is equivalent to a specified sequence of machine instructions.

Magnetic Bubble
An electromagnetic storage device that stores and moves data magnetically as tiny magnetic spots that look like bubbles under a microscope as they float on the surface of a special type of semiconductor chip.

Magnetic Core
Tiny rings composed of iron oxide and other materials strung on wires that provide electrical current that magnetizes the cores. Data is represented by the direction of the magnetic field of groups of cores. Widely used as the primary storage media in second- and third-generation computer systems.

Magnetic Disk
A flat circular plate with a magnetic surface on which data can be stored by selective magnetization of portions of the curved surface.

Magnetic Drum
A circular cylinder with a magnetic surface on which data can be stored by selective magnetization of portions of the curved surface.

Magnetic Ink
An ink that contains particles of iron oxide that can be magnetized and detected by magnetic sensors.

Magnetic Ink Character Recognition (MICR)
The machine recognition of characters printed with magnetic ink. Primarily used for check processing by the banking industry.

Magnetic Tape
A plastic tape with a magnetic surface on which data can be stored by selective magnetization of portions of the surface.

Mag Stripe Card
A plastic wallet-size card with a strip of magnetic tape on one surface; widely used for credit/debit cards.

Mainframe
A larger-size computer system, typically with a separate central processing unit, as distinguished from microcomputer and minicomputer systems.

Management Functions
Management as a process of planning, organizing, staffing, directing, and controlling activities.

Management Information System (MIS)
An information system that provides information to support managerial decision making. More specifically, an information reporting system, executive information system, or decision support system.

Management Levels
Management as the performance of planning and control activities at the strategic, tactical, and operational levels of an organization.

Managerial End User
A manager, entrepreneur, or managerial-level professional who personally uses information systems. Also, the manager of the department or other organizational unit that relies on information systems.

Managerial Roles
Management as the performance of a variety of interpersonal, information, and decision roles.

Manual Data Processing
(1) Data processing requiring continual human operation and intervention that utilizes simple data processing tools such as paper forms, pencils, and filing cabinets. (2) All data processing that is not automatic, even if it utilizes machines such as typewriters and calculators.

Manufacturing Information Systems
Information systems which support the planning, control, and accomplishment of manufacturing processes. This includes concepts such as computer integrated manufacturing (CIM) and technologies such as computer-aided manufacturing (CAM) or computer-aided design (CAD).

Marketing Information Systems
Information systems which support the planning, control, and transaction processing required for the accomplishment of marketing activities, such as sales management, advertising and promotion.

Mark-Sensing
The electrical sensing of manually recorded conductive marks on a nonconductive surface.

Mass Storage
Secondary storage devices with extra-large storage capacities such as magnetic or optical disks.

Master File
A data file containing relatively permanent information, which is utilized as an authoritative reference and is usually updated periodically. Contrast with *Transaction File*.

Mathematical Model
A mathematical representation of a process, device, or concept.

Media
All tangible objects on which data are recorded.

Megabyte
One million bytes. More accurately, 2 to the 20th power, or 1,048,576 in decimal notation.

Memory
Same as *Storage*.

Menu
A displayed list of items (usually the names of alternative applications, files, or activities) from which an end user makes a selection.

Menu Driven
A characteristic of interactive computing systems that provides menu displays and operator prompting to assist an end user in performing a particular job.

Meta-Data
Data about data, that is, data describing the structure, data elements, interrelationships, and other characteristics of a database.

Microcomputer
A very small computer, ranging in size from a "computer on a chip" to a small typewriter-size unit.

Micrographics
The use of microfilm, microfiche, and other microforms to record data in greatly reduced form.

Microprocessor
A microcomputer central processing unit (CPU) on a chip. Without input/output or primary storage capabilities in most types.

Microprogram
A small set of elementary control instructions called microinstructions or microcode.

Microprogramming
The use of special software (microprograms) to perform the functions of special hardware (electronic control circuitry). Microprograms stored in a read-only storage module of the control unit interpret the machine language instructions of a computer program and decode them into elementary microinstructions, which are then executed.

Microsecond
A millionth of a second.

Millisecond
A thousandth of a second.

Minicomputer
A small (for example, the size of a desk) electronic, digital, stored-program, general-purpose computer.

Model Base
An organized collection of conceptual, mathematical, and logical models that express business relationships, computational routines, or analytical techniques. Such models are stored in the form of programs and program subroutines, command files, and spreadsheets.

Modem
(MOdulator-DEModulator) A device that converts the digital signals from input/output devices into appropriate frequencies at a transmission terminal and converts them back into digital signals at a receiving terminal.

Monitor
Software or hardware that observes, supervises, controls, or verifies the operations of a system.

Mouse
A small device that is electronically connected to a computer and is moved by hand on a flat surface in order to move the cursor on a video screen in the same direction. Buttons on the mouse allow users to issue commands and make responses or selections.

Multimedia Presentations
Providing information using a variety of media, including text and graphics displays, voice and other audio, photographs, and video segments.

Multiplex
To interleave or simultaneously transmit two or more messages on a single channel.

Multiplexer
An electronic device that allows a single communications channel to carry simultaneous data transmission from many terminals.

Multiprocessing
Pertaining to the simultaneous execution of two or more instructions by a computer or computer network.

Multiprocessor Computer Systems
Computer systems that use a multiprocessor architecture in the design of their central processing units. This includes the use of support microprocessors and multiple instruction processors, including parallel processor designs.

Multiprogramming
Pertaining to the concurrent execution of two or more programs by a computer by interleaving their execution.

Multitasking
The concurrent use of the same computer to accomplish several different information processing tasks. Each task may require the use of a different program, or the concurrent use of the same copy of a program by several users.

Nanosecond
One billionth of a second.

Natural Language
A programming language that is very close to human language. Also called very high-level language.

Network
An interconnected system of computers, terminals, and communications channels and devices.

Network Architecture
A master plan designed to promote an open, simple, flexible, and efficient telecommunications environment through the use of standard protocols, standard communications hardware and software interfaces, and the design of a standard multilevel telecommunications interface between end users and computer systems.

Network Data Structure
A logical data structure which allows many-to-many relationships among data records. It allows entry into a database at multiple points, because any data element or record can be related to many other data elements.

Neural Networks
Computer processors or software whose architecture is based on the human brain's mesh-like neuron structure. Neural networks can process many

pieces of information simultaneously and can learn to recognize patterns and programs themselves to solve related problems on their own.

Node
A terminal point in a communications network.

Nonimpact Printers
Printers that use specially treated paper that form characters by laser, thermal (heat), electrostatic, or electrochemical processes.

Nonprocedural Languages
Programming languages that allow users and professional programmers to specify the results they want without specifying how to solve the problem.

Numerical Control
Automatic control of a machine process by a computer which makes use of numerical data, generally introduced as the operation is in process. Also called machine control.

Object
A data element that includes both data and the methods or processes that act on that data.

Object-Based Knowledge
Knowledge represented as a network of objects.

Objectives
Accomplishments a system is supposed to achieve.

Object-Oriented Language
An object-oriented programming (OOP) language used to develop programs which create and use objects to perform information processing tasks.

Object Program
A compiled or assembled program composed of executable machine instructions. Contrast with *Source Program.*

Octal
Pertaining to the number representation system with a radix of eight.

OEM: Original Equipment Manufacturer
A firm that manufactures and sells computers by assembling components produced by other hardware manufacturers.

Office Automation (OA)
The use of computer-based information systems that collect, process, store, and transmit electronic messages, documents, and other forms of office communications among individuals, work groups, and organizations.

Office Management Systems
Office automation systems which integrate a variety of computer-based support services, including desktop accessories, electronic mail, and electronic task management.

Offline
Pertaining to equipment or devices not under control of the central processing unit.

Online
Pertaining to equipment or devices under control of the central processing unit.

Online Transaction Processing (OLTP)
A realtime transaction processing system.

Operand
That which is operated upon. That part of a computer instruction that is identified by the address part of the instruction.

Operating Environment Package
Software packages or modules which add a graphics-based interface between end users, the operating system, and their application programs, and may also provide a multitasking capability.

Operating System
The main control program of a computer system. It is a system of programs that controls the execution of computer programs and may provide scheduling, debugging, input/output control, system accounting, compilation, storage assignment, data management, and related services.

Operation Code
A code that represents specific operations to be performed upon the operands in a computer instruction.

Operational Feasibility
The willingness and ability of management, employees, customers, and suppliers to operate, use, and support a proposed system.

Operations Information System
An information system that collects, processes, and stores data generated by the operations systems of an organization and produces data and information for input into a management information system or for the control of an operations system.

Operations System
A basic subsystem of the business firm that constitutes its input, processing, and output components. Also called a physical system.

Opportunity
A basic condition that presents the potential for desirable results in an organization or other system.

Optical Character Recognition (OCR)
The machine identification of printed characters through the use of light-sensitive devices.

Optical Disks
A secondary storage medium using laser technology to read tiny spots on a plastic disk. The disks are currently capable of storing billions of characters of information.

Optical Scanner
A device that optically scans characters or images and generates their digital representations.

Optimization Analysis
Finding an optimum value for selected variables in a mathematical model, given certain constraints.

Organizational Feasibility
How well a proposed information system supports the objectives of an organization's strategic plan for information systems.

Output
Pertaining to a device, process, or channel involved with the transfer of data or information out of an information processing system.

Overlapped Processing
Pertaining to the ability of a computer system to increase the utilization of its central processing unit by overlapping input/output and processing operations.

Packet
A group of data and control information in a specified format that is transmitted as an entity.

Packet Switching
A data tranmission process that transmits addressed packets such that a channel is occupied only for the duration of transmission of the packet.

Page
A segment of a program or data, usually of fixed length.

Paging
A process that automatically and continually transfers pages of programs and data between primary storage and direct access storage devices. It provides computers with multiprogramming and virtual memory capabilities.

Parallel Processing
Executing many instructions at the same time, that is, in parallel. Performed by advanced computers using many instruction processors organized in clusters or networks.

Parity Bit
A check bit appended to an array of binary digits to make the sum of all the binary digits, including the check bit, always odd or always even.

Pascal
A high-level, general-purpose, structured programming language named after Blaise Pascal. It was developed by Niklaus Wirth of Zurich in 1968.

Pattern Recognition
The identification of shapes, forms, or configurations by automatic means.

PCM: Plug Compatible Manufacturer
A firm that manufactures computer equipment that can be plugged into existing computer systems without requiring additional hardware or software interfaces.

Pen-Based Computers
Tablet-style microcomputers that recognize handwriting and hand drawing done by a pen-shaped device on their pressure-sensitive display screens.

Performance Monitor
A software package that monitors the processing of computer system jobs, helps develop a planned schedule of computer operations that can optimize computer system peformance, and produces detailed statistics that are used for computer system capacity planning and control.

Periodic Reports
Providing information to managers using a prespecified format designed to provide information on a regularly scheduled basis.

Peripheral Devices
In a computer system, any unit of equipment, distinct from the central processing unit, that provides the system with input, output, or storage capabilities.

Personal Information Manager (PIM)
A software package which helps end users store, organize, and retrieve text and numerical data in the form of notes, lists, memos, and a variety of other forms.

Physical System Design
Design of the user interface methods and products, database structures, and processing and control procedures for a proposed information system, including hardware, software, and personnel specifications.

Picosecond
One trillionth of a second.

PILOT: Programmed Inquiry, Learning Or Teaching
A special-purpose language designed to develop CAI (computer-aided instruction) programs.

PL/1: Programming Language 1
A procedure-oriented, high-level, general-purpose programming language designed to combine the features of COBOL, FORTRAN, and ALGOL.

Plasma Display
Output devices that generate a visual display with electrically charged particles of gas trapped between glass plates.

Plotter
A hard-copy output device that produces drawings and graphical displays on paper or other materials.

Pointer
A data element associated with an index, a record, or other set of data that contains the address of a related record.

Pointing Devices
Devices which allow end users to issue commands or make choices by moving a cursor on the display screen.

Point-of-Sale (POS) Terminal
A computer terminal used in retail stores that serves the function of a cash register as well as collecting sales data and performing other data processing functions.

Port
(1) Electronic circuitry that provides a connection point between the CPU and input/output devices. (2) A connection point for a communications line on a CPU or other front-end device.

Postimplementation Review
Monitoring and evaluating the results of an implemented solution or system.

Presentation Graphics
Using computer-generated graphics to enhance the information presented in reports and other types of presentations.

Prespecified Reports
Reports whose format is specified in advance to provide managers with information periodically, on an exception basis, or on demand.

Private Branch Exchange (PBX)
A switching device that serves as an interface between the many telephone lines within a work area and the local telephone company's main telephone lines or trunks. Computerized PBXs can handle the switching of both voice and data in the local area networks that are needed in such locations.

Problem
A basic condition that is causing undesirable results in an organization or other system.

Procedure-Oriented Language
A programming language designed for the convenient expression of procedures used in the solution of a wide class of problems.

Procedures
Sets of instructions used by people to complete a task.

Process Control
The use of a computer to control an ongoing physical process such as petrochemical production.

Process Design
The design of the programs and procedures needed by a proposed information system, including detailed program specifications and procedures.

Processor
A hardware device or software system capable of performing operations upon data.

Program
A set of instructions that cause a computer to perform a particular task.

Programmed Decision
A decision that can be automated by basing it on a decision rule that outlines the steps to take when confronted with the need for a specific decision.

Programmer
A person mainly involved in designing, writing, and testing computer programs.

Programming
The design, writing, and testing of a program.

Programming Language
A language used to develop the instructions in computer programs.

Programming Tools
Software packages or modules which

provide editing and diagnostic capabilities and other support facilities to assist the programming process.

Project Management
Managing the accomplishment of an information system development project according to a specific project plan, in order that a project is completed on time, within its budget, and meets its design objectives.

Prompt
Messages that assist a user in performing a particular job. This would include error messages, correction suggestions, questions, and other messages that guide an end user.

Protocol
A set of rules and procedures for the control of communications in a communications network.

Prototype
A working model. In particular, a working model of an information system which includes tentative versions of user input and output, databases and files, control methods, and processing routines.

Prototyping
The rapid development and testing of working models, or prototypes, of new information system applications in an interactive, iterative process involving both systems analysts and end users.

Pseudocode
An informal design language of structured programming that expresses the processing logic of a program module in ordinary human language phrases.

Public Information Networks
Network provided by various organizations and companies to personal computer users that offer a variety of computing and other information services.

Punched Card
A card punched with a pattern of holes to represent data.

Punched Tape
A tape on which a pattern of holes or cuts is used to represent data.

Quality Assurance
Methods for ensuring that information systems are free from errors and fraud and provide information products of high quality.

Query Language
A high-level, human-like language provided by a database management system that enables users to easily extract data and information from a database.

Queue
(1) A waiting line formed by items in a system waiting for service. (2) To arrange in or form a queue.

Random Access
Same as *Direct Access*.

Random Access Memory (RAM)
One of the basic types of semiconductor memory used for temporary storage of data or programs during processing. Each memory position can be directly sensed (read) or changed (write) in the same length of time, irrespective of its location on the storage medium.

Read Only Memory (ROM)
A basic type of semiconductor memory used for permanent storage. Can only be read, not "written," that is, changed. Variations are Programmable Read Only Memory (PROM) and Erasable Programmable Read Only Memory (EPROM).

Realtime
Pertaining to the performance of data processing during the actual time a business or physical process transpires, in order that results of the data processing can be used in supporting the completion of the process.

Realtime Processing
Data processing in which data is processed immediately rather than periodically. Also called online processing. Contrast with *Batch Processing*.

Record
A collection of related data fields treated as a unit.

Reduced Instruction Set Computer (RISC)
A CPU architecture which optimizes processing speed by the use of a smaller number of basic machine instructions than traditional CPU designs.

Redundancy
In information processing, the repetition of part or all of a message to increase the chance that the correct information will be understood by the recipient.

Register
A device capable of storing a specified amount of data such as one word.

Relational Data Structure
A logical data structure in which all data elements within the database are viewed as being stored in the form of simple tables. DBMS packages based on the relational model can link data elements from various tables as long as the tables share common data elements.

Remote Access
Pertaining to communication with the data processing facility by one or more stations that are distant from that facility.

Remote Job Entry (RJE)
Entering jobs into a batch processing system from a remote facility.

Report Generator
A feature of database management system packages which allows an end user to quickly specify a report format for the display of information retrieved from a database.

Reprographics
Copying and duplicating technology and methods.

Resource Management
An operating system function which controls the use of computer system resources such as primary storage, secondary storage, CPU processing time, and input/output devices by other system software and application software packages.

Robotics
The technology of building machines (robots) with computer intelligence and humanlike physical capabilities.

Routine
An ordered set of instructions that may have some general or frequent use.

RPG: Report Program Generator
A problem-oriented language that utilizes a generator to construct programs that produce reports and perform other data processing tasks.

Rule
Statements which typically take the form of a premise and a conclusion such as IF-THEN rules, i.e., IF (condition), THEN (conclusion).

Rule-Based Knowledge
Knowledge represented in the form of rules and statements of fact.

Schema
An overall conceptual or logical view of the relationships between the data in a database.

Scientific Method
An analytical methodology which involves (1) recognizing phenomena, (2) formulating a hypothesis about the causes or effects of the phenomena, (3)

testing the hypothesis through experimentation, (4) evaluating the results of such experiments, and (5) drawing conclusions about the hypothesis.

Secondary Storage
Storage that supplements the primary storage of a computer. Synonymous with *Auxiliary Storage*.

Sector
A subdivision of a track on a magnetic disk surface.

Security Codes
Passwords, identification codes, account codes, and other codes that limit the access and use of computer-based system resources to authorized users.

Security Monitor
A software package which monitors the use of a computer system and protects its resources from unauthorized use, fraud, and vandalism.

Semiconductor Memory
Microelectronic storage circuitry etched on tiny chips of silicon or other semiconducting material. The primary storage of most modern computers consists of microelectronic semiconductor storage chips for random access memory (RAM) and read only memory (ROM).

Semistructured Decisions
Decisions involving procedures which can be partially prespecified, but not enough to lead to a definite recommended decision.

Sensitivity Analysis
Observing how repeated changes to a single variable affects other variables in a mathematical model.

Sequential Access
A sequential method of storing and retrieving data from a file. Contrast with *Random Access*.

Sequential Data Organization
Organizing logical data elements according to a prescribed sequence.

Serial
Pertaining to the sequential or consecutive occurrence of two or more related activities in a single device or channel.

Server
A computer that supports telecommunications in a local area network, as well as the sharing of peripheral devices, software, and databases among the workstations in the network.

Service Bureau
A firm offering computer and data processing services. Also called a computer service center.

Smart Products
Industrial and consumer products, with "intelligence" provided by built-in microcomputers or microprocessors that significantly improve the performance and capabilities of such products.

Software
Computer programs and procedures concerned with the operation of an information system. Contrast with *Hardware*.

Software Package
A computer program supplied by computer manufacturers, independent software companies, or other computer users. Also known as canned programs, proprietary software, or packaged programs.

Software Piracy
Unauthorized copying of software.

Solid State
Pertaining to devices such as transistors and diodes whose operation depends on the control of electric or magnetic phenomena in solid materials.

Source Data Automation
The use of automated methods of data entry that attempt to reduce or eliminate many of the activities, people, and data media required by traditional data entry methods.

Source Document
A document that is the original formal record of a transaction, such as a purchase order or sales invoice.

Source Program
A computer program written in a language that is subject to a translation process. Contrast with *Object Program*.

Special-Purpose Computer
A computer that is designed to handle a restricted class of problems. Contrast with *General-Purpose Computer*.

Spooling
Simultaneous peripheral operation online. Storing input data from low-speed devices temporarily on high-speed secondary storage units, which can be quickly accessed by the CPU. Also, writing output data at high speeds onto magnetic tape or disk units from which it can be transferred to slow-speed devices such as a printer.

Stage Analysis
A planning process in which the information system needs of an organization are based on an analysis of its current stage in the growth cycle of the organization and its use of information systems technology.

Standards
Measures of performance developed to evaluate the progress of a system towards its objectives.

Storage
Pertaining to a device into which data can be entered, in which it can be held, and from which it can be retrieved at a later time.

Strategic Information Systems
Information systems that provide a firm with competitive products and services that give it a strategic advantage over its competitors in the marketplace. Also, information systems which promote business innovation, improve operational efficiency, and build strategic information resources for a firm.

Structure Chart
A design and documentation technique to show the purpose and relationships of the various modules in a program.

Structured Decisions
Decisions which are structured by the decision procedures or decision rules developed for them. They involve situations where the procedures to follow when a decision is needed can be specified in advance.

Structured Programming
A programming methodology that uses a top-down program design and a limited number of control structures in a program to create highly structured modules of program code.

Structured Query Language (SQL)
A query language that is becoming a standard for advanced database management system packages. A query's basic form is SELECT. . . . FROM . . . WHERE.

Structured Walk-Throughs
A structured programming methodology that requires a peer review by other programmers of program design and coding to minimize and reveal errors in the early stages of programming.

Subroutine
A routine that can be part of another program routine.

Subschema
A subset or transformation of the logical view of the database schema that is required by a particular user application program.

Subsystem
A system that is a component of a larger system.

Supercomputer
A special category of large computer

systems that are the most powerful available. They are designed to solve massive computational problems.

Superconductor
Materials which can conduct electricity with almost no resistance. This allows the development of extremely fast and small electronic circuits. Formerly only possible at super cold temperatures near absolute zero. Recent developments promise superconducting materials near room temperature.

Switch
(1) A device or programming technique for making a selection.
(2) A computer that controls message switching among the computers and terminals in a telecommunications network.

Switching Costs
The costs in time, money, effort, and inconvenience that it would take a customer or supplier to switch its business to a firm's competitors.

Synchronous
A characteristic in which each event, or the performance of any basic operation, is constrained to start on, and usually to keep in step with, signals from a timing clock. Contrast with *Asynchronous*.

System
(1) A group of interrelated or interacting elements forming a unified whole.
(2) A group of interrelated components working together toward a common goal by accepting inputs and producing outputs in an organized transformation process. (3) An assembly of methods, procedures, or techniques unified by regulated interaction to form an organized whole.
(4) An organized collection of people, machines, and methods required to accomplish a set of specific functions.

System Component Matrix
A matrix framework that documents the hardware, software, people, and data resources used, the system activities performed, and the information products produced by an information system.

System Design Standards
Standards that promote the design of common system features such as user interfaces, programming interfaces, and telecommunications support.

System Flowchart
A graphic diagramming tool used to show the flow of information processing activities as data are processed by people and devices.

System Requirements
The information system capabilities required to meet the information needs of end users. Also called functional requirements.

System Software
Programs that control and support operations of a computer system. System software includes a variety of programs such as operating systems, database management systems, communications control programs, service and utility programs, and programming language translators.

System Specifications
The product of the systems design stage. It consists of specifications for the hardware, software, facilities, personnel, databases, and the user interface of a proposed information system.

System Support Programs
Programs that support the operations, management, and users of a computer system by providing a variety of support services. Examples are system utilities and performance monitors.

Systems Analysis
(1) Analyzing in detail the components and requirements of a system. (2) Analyzing in detail the information needs of an organization, the characteristics and components of presently utilized information systems, and the functional requirements of proposed information systems.

Systems Approach
A systematic process of problem solving based on the scientific method, which defines problems and opportunities in a systems context. Data is gathered describing the problem or opportunity, and alternative solutions are identified and evaluated. Then the best solution is selected and implemented, and its success evaluated.

Systems Context
Recognizing systems, subsystems, and components of systems in a situation. Also called a systemic view.

Systems Design
Deciding how a proposed information system will meet the information needs of end users. Includes logical and physical design activities, and user interface, data, and process design activities which produce system specifications that satisfy the system requirements developed in the systems analysis stage.

Systems Development
(1) Conceiving, designing, and implementing a system. (2) Developing information systems by a process of investigation, analysis, design, implementation, and maintenance. Also called the systems development life cycle (SDLC), information systems development, or application development.

Systems Development Tools
Graphical, textual, and computer-aided tools and techniques which are used to help analyze, design, and document the development of an information system. They are typically used to represent (1) the components and flows of a system, (2) the user interface, (3) data attributes and relationships, and (4) detailed system processes.

Systems Implementation
The stage of systems development in which hardware and software are acquired, developed, and installed, the system is tested and documented, people are trained to operate and use the system, and an organization converts to the use of a newly developed system.

Systems Investigation
The screening, selection, and preliminary study of a proposed information system solution to a business problem.

Systems Maintenance
The monitoring, evaluating, and modifying of a system to make desirable or necessary improvements.

Tangible Benefits and Costs
The quantifiable benefits and costs of a proposed solution or system.

Task Management
A basic operating system function that manages the accomplishment of the computing tasks of users by a computer system.

Technical Feasibility
Whether reliable hardware and software capable of meeting the needs of a proposed system can be acquired or developed by an organization in the required time.

Technology Implementation
Methods for ensuring end user acceptance and productive use of newly installed information system technologies.

Technology Management
The establishment of organizational groups to identify, introduce, and monitor the assimilation of new information system technologies into organizations.

Telecommunications
Pertaining to the transmission of signals

over long distances, including not only data communications but also the transmission of images and voices using radio, television, and other communications technologies.

Telecommunications Channel
The part of a telecommunications network that connects the message source with the message receiver. It includes the physical equipment used to connect one location to another for the purpose of transmitting and receiving information.

Telecommunications Controller
A data communications interface device (frequently a special-purpose mini or microcomputer) that can control a telecommunications network containing many terminals.

Telecommunications Control Program
A computer program that controls and supports the communications between the computers and terminals in a telecommunications network.

Telecommunications Monitors
Computer programs that control and support the communications between the computers and terminals in a telecommunications network.

Telecommunications Processors
Multiplexers, concentrators, communications controllers, and cluster controllers that allow a communications channel to carry simultaneous data transmissions from many terminals. They may also perform error monitoring, diagnostics and correction, modulation-demodulation, data compression, data coding and decoding, message switching, port contention, buffer storage, and serving as an interface to satellite and other communications networks.

Telecommuting
The use of telecommunications to replace commuting to work from one's home.

Teleconferencing
The use of video communications to allow business conferences to be held with participants who are scattered across a country, continent, or the world.

Telephone Tag
The process that occurs when two people who wish to contact each other by telephone repeatedly miss each other's phone calls.

Teleprocessing
Using telecommunications for computer-based information processing.

Terabyte
One trillion bytes. More accurately, 2 to the 40th power, or 1,009,511,627,776 in decimal notation.

Text Data
Words, phrases, sentences, and paragraphs used in documents and other forms of communication.

Throughput
The total amount of useful work performed by a data processing system during a given period of time.

Time-Sharing
Providing computer services to many users simultaneously while providing rapid responses to each.

Top-Down Design
A methodology of structured programming in which a program is organized into functional modules, with the programmer designing the main module first and then the lower-level modules.

Touch-Sensitive Screen
An input device that accepts data input by the placement of a finger on or close to the CRT screen.

Track
The portion of a moving storage medium, such as a drum, tape, or disk, that is accessible to a given reading head position.

Trackball
A rollerball device set in a case used to move the cursor on a computer's display screen.

Transaction
An event that occurs as part of doing business, such as a sale, purchase, deposit, withdrawal, refund, transfer, payment, and so on.

Transaction Document
A document produced as part of a business transaction, e.g., a purchase order, paycheck, sales receipt, or customer invoice.

Transaction File
A data file containing relatively transient data to be processed in combination with a master file. Contrast with *Master file*.

Transaction Processing Cycle
A cycle of basic transaction processing activities including data entry, transaction processing, database maintenance, document and report generation, and inquiry processing.

Transaction Processing System
An information system that processes data arising from the occurrence of business transactions.

Transaction Terminal
Terminals used in banks, retail stores, factories, and other worksites that are used to capture transaction data at its point of origin. Examples are point-of-sale (POS) terminals and automated teller machines (ATMs).

Transborder Data Flows
The flow of business data over telecommunications networks across international borders.

Transform Algorithm
Performing an arithmetic computation on a record key and using the result of the calculation as an address for that record. Also known as key transformation or hashing.

Transnational Strategy
A management approach in which an organization integrates its global business activities through close cooperation and interdependence among its headquarters operations and international subsidiaries, and its use of appropriate global information technologies.

Turnaround Document
Output of a computer system (such as customer invoices and statements) that is designed to be returned to the organization as machine-readable input.

Turnaround Time
The elapsed time between submission of a job to a computing center and the return of the results.

Unbundling
The separate pricing of hardware, software, and other related services.

Universal Product Code (UPC)
A standard identification code using bar coding, printed on products which can be read by the optical supermarket scanners of the grocery industry.

Unstructured Decisions
Decisions which must be made in situations where it is not possible to specify in advance most of the decision procedures to follow.

User Friendly
A characteristic of human-operated equipment and systems that makes

them safe, comfortable, and easy to use.

User Interface
That part of an operating system or other program that allows users to communicate with it to load programs, access files, and accomplish other computing tasks.

User Interface Design
Designing the interactions between end users and computer systems, including input/output methods and the conversion of data between human-readable and machine-readable forms.

Utility Program
A standard set of routines that assists in the operation of a computer system by performing some frequently required process such as copying, sorting, or merging.

Value-Added Carriers
Third-party vendors who lease telecommunications lines from common carriers and offer a variety of telecommunications services to customers.

Value-Added Resellers (VARs)
Companies which provide industry-specific software for use with the computer systems of selected manufacturers.

Value Chain
Viewing a firm as a series or chain of basic activities that add value to its products and services and thus add a margin of value to the firm.

Videotex
An interactive information service provided over phone lines or cable TV channels.

Virtual Machine
Pertaining to the simulation of one type of computer system by another computer system.

Virtual Memory
The use of secondary storage devices as an extension of the primary storage of the computer, thus giving the appearance of a larger main memory than actually exists.

Virtual Reality
The use of multisensory human/computer interfaces that enables human users to experience computer-simulated objects, entities, spaces, and "worlds" as if they actually existed.

VLSI
Very Large-Scale Integration. Semiconductor chips containing hundreds of thousands of circuits.

Voice Mail
A variation of electronic mail where digitized voice messages rather than electronic text are accepted, stored, and transmitted.

Voice Recognition
Direct conversion of spoken data into electronic form suitable for entry into a computer system. Also called voice data entry.

Volatile Memory
Memory (such as electronic semiconductor memory) that loses its contents when electrical power is interrupted.

Wand
A handheld optical character recognition device used for data entry by many transaction terminals.

What-If Analysis
Observing how changes to selected variables affect other variables in a mathematical model.

Wide Area Network (WAN)
A data communications network covering a large geographic area.

Window
One section of a computer's multiple section display screen, each of which can have a different display.

Wireless LANs
Using radio or infrared transmissions to link devices in a local area network.

Word
(1) A string of characters considered as a unit. (2) An ordered set of bits (usually larger than a byte) handled as a unit by the central processing unit.

Word Processing
The automation of the transformation of ideas and information into a readable form of communication. It involves the use of computers to manipulate text data in order to produce office communications in the form of documents.

Work Group Computing
End user computing in a work group environment in which members of a work group may use a local area network to share hardware, software, and databases to accomplish group assignments.

Workstation
A computer terminal or micro or mini computer system designed to support the work of one person. Also, a high-powered computer to support the work of professionals in engineering, science, and other areas that require extensive computing power and graphics capabilities.

Name Index

Organization Index

Subject Index